# Vauxhall/Opel Corsa
# Owners Workshop Manual

## John S. Mead, A. K. Legg LAE MIMI and Peter T. Gill

**Models covered**

*(5577 – 416)*

Hatchback & Corsavan. Also covers most features of Combo Van

**Petrol:** 1.0 litre (973cc & 998cc) 3-cyl, 1.2 litre (1199cc & 1229cc) & 1.4 litre (1364cc & 1389cc) 4-cyl
**Turbo-diesel:** 1.3 litre (1248cc) CDTi & 1.7 litre (1686cc) DTi

*Does NOT cover models with 1.7 litre CDTi (Z17DTH) diesel engine introduced October 2003,
or 1.8 litre petrol engine, or dual fuel models*
*Does NOT cover new Corsa range introduced September 2006*

ABCDE
FGHIJ
KLMNO
PQRST

© Haynes Publishing 2013

A book in the **Haynes Owners Workshop Manual Series**

ISBN **978 0 85733 577 7**

**British Library Cataloguing in Publication Data**
A catalogue record for this book is available from the British Library.

Printed in the USA

**Haynes Publishing**
Sparkford, Yeovil, Somerset BA22 7JJ, England

**Haynes North America, Inc**
861 Lawrence Drive, Newbury Park, California 91320, USA

**Haynes Publishing Nordiska AB**
Box 1504, 751 45 UPPSALA, Sverige

# Contents

## LIVING WITH YOUR VAUXHALL CORSA

## Roadside Repairs

## Weekly Checks

## MAINTENANCE

### Routine maintenance and servicing

**Vauxhall Corsa petrol models**

**Vauxhall Corsa diesel models**

# Contents

The Vauxhall Corsa was first introduced to the European market in Spring 1993 and has had numerous mechanical revisions and three facelifts during the course of the production run. This manual covers versions from October 2000 up to August 2006 which includes both the second and third facelifts, and the accompanying mechanical revisions.

A variety of engines are available in the Corsa range: 1.0, 1.2 and 1.4 litre petrol engines, and 1.3 and 1.7 litre diesel engines. All except the 1.0 litre engine are of the 4-cylinder double-overhead camshaft (DOHC) in-line configuration; the 1.0 litre has 3 cylinders. The engines all have fuel injection, and are fitted with a range of emission control systems. A 1.8 litre petrol engine is also available, but is not covered by this manual.

The Corsa is available in 3- and 5-door Hatchback, Corsavan (3-door Van based on Hatchback) and Combo Van body styles, with a wide range of fittings and interior trim depending on the model specification.

Fully-independent front suspension is fitted; the rear suspension is semi-independent, with a beam axle and trailing arms.

The manual gearbox is of the five-speed all synchromesh type, and a four-speed electronically-controlled automatic transmission is available as an option on certain models. An 'Easytronic' manual/automatic transmission is also available.

A wide range of standard and optional equipment is available within the Corsa range to suit most tastes, including central locking, electric windows, electric sunroof, anti-lock braking system, electronic alarm system and supplemental restraint systems.

For the home mechanic, the Corsa is a relatively straightforward vehicle to maintain, and most of the items requiring frequent attention are easily accessible.

## Your Vauxhall Corsa Manual

The aim of this manual is to help you get the best value from your vehicle. It can do so in several ways. It can help you decide what work must be done (even should you choose to get it done by a garage), provide information on routine maintenance and servicing, and give a logical course of action and diagnosis when random faults occur. However, it is hoped that you will use the manual by tackling the work yourself. On simpler jobs it may even be quicker than booking the car into a garage and going there twice, to leave and collect it. Perhaps most important, a lot of money can be saved by avoiding the costs a garage must charge to cover its labour and overheads.

The manual has drawings and descriptions to show the function of the various components so that their layout can be understood. Tasks are described and photographed in a clear step-by-step sequence.

References to the 'left' and 'right' of the vehicle are in the sense of a person in the driver's seat facing forward.

## Acknowledgements

Thanks are due to Draper Tools Limited, who provided some of the workshop tools, and to all those people at Sparkford who helped in the production of this Manual.

**We take great pride in the accuracy of information given in this manual, but vehicle manufacturers make alterations and design changes during the production run of a particular vehicle of which they do not inform us. No liability can be accepted by the authors or publishers for loss, damage or injury caused by errors in, or omissions from, the information given.**

Working on your car can be dangerous. This page shows just some of the potential risks and hazards, with the aim of creating a safety-conscious attitude.

# General hazards

### Scalding

• Don't remove the radiator or expansion tank cap while the engine is hot.
• Engine oil, transmission fluid or power steering fluid may also be dangerously hot if the engine has recently been running.

### Burning

• Beware of burns from the exhaust system and from any part of the engine. Brake discs and drums can also be extremely hot immediately after use.

### Crushing

• When working under or near a raised vehicle, always supplement the jack with axle stands, or use drive-on ramps.
*Never venture under a car which is only supported by a jack.*
• Take care if loosening or tightening high- torque nuts when the vehicle is on stands. Initial loosening and final tightening should be done with the wheels on the ground.

### Fire

• Fuel is highly flammable; fuel vapour is explosive.
• Don't let fuel spill onto a hot engine.
• Do not smoke or allow naked lights (including pilot lights) anywhere near a vehicle being worked on. Also beware of creating sparks (electrically or by use of tools).
• Fuel vapour is heavier than air, so don't work on the fuel system with the vehicle over an inspection pit.
• Another cause of fire is an electrical overload or short-circuit. Take care when repairing or modifying the vehicle wiring.
• Keep a fire extinguisher handy, of a type suitable for use on fuel and electrical fires.

### Electric shock

• Ignition HT and Xenon headlight voltages can be dangerous, especially to people with heart problems or a pacemaker. Don't work on or near these systems with the engine running or the ignition switched on.

• Mains voltage is also dangerous. Make sure that any mains-operated equipment is correctly earthed. Mains power points should be protected by a residual current device (RCD) circuit breaker.

### Fume or gas intoxication

• Exhaust fumes are poisonous; they can contain carbon monoxide, which is rapidly fatal if inhaled. Never run the engine in a confined space such as a garage with the doors shut.
• Fuel vapour is also poisonous, as are the vapours from some cleaning solvents and paint thinners.

### Poisonous or irritant substances

• Avoid skin contact with battery acid and with any fuel, fluid or lubricant, especially antifreeze, brake hydraulic fluid and Diesel fuel. Don't syphon them by mouth. If such a substance is swallowed or gets into the eyes, seek medical advice.
• Prolonged contact with used engine oil can cause skin cancer. Wear gloves or use a barrier cream if necessary. Change out of oil-soaked clothes and do not keep oily rags in your pocket.
• Air conditioning refrigerant forms a poisonous gas if exposed to a naked flame (including a cigarette). It can also cause skin burns on contact.

### Asbestos

• Asbestos dust can cause cancer if inhaled or swallowed. Asbestos may be found in gaskets and in brake and clutch linings. When dealing with such components it is safest to assume that they contain asbestos.

# Special hazards

### Hydrofluoric acid

• This extremely corrosive acid is formed when certain types of synthetic rubber, found in some O-rings, oil seals, fuel hoses etc, are exposed to temperatures above 4000C. The rubber changes into a charred or sticky substance containing the acid. *Once formed, the acid remains dangerous for years. If it gets onto the skin, it may be necessary to amputate the limb concerned.*
• When dealing with a vehicle which has suffered a fire, or with components salvaged from such a vehicle, wear protective gloves and discard them after use.

### The battery

• Batteries contain sulphuric acid, which attacks clothing, eyes and skin. Take care when topping-up or carrying the battery.
• The hydrogen gas given off by the battery is highly explosive. Never cause a spark or allow a naked light nearby. Be careful when connecting and disconnecting battery chargers or jump leads.

### Air bags

• Air bags can cause injury if they go off accidentally. Take care when removing the steering wheel and trim panels. Special storage instructions may apply.

### Diesel injection equipment

• Diesel injection pumps supply fuel at very high pressure. Take care when working on the fuel injectors and fuel pipes.

⚠ *Warning: Never expose the hands, face or any other part of the body to injector spray; the fuel can penetrate the skin with potentially fatal results.*

# Remember...

### DO

• Do use eye protection when using power tools, and when working under the vehicle.

• Do wear gloves or use barrier cream to protect your hands when necessary.

• Do get someone to check periodically that all is well when working alone on the vehicle.

• Do keep loose clothing and long hair well out of the way of moving mechanical parts.

• Do remove rings, wristwatch etc, before working on the vehicle – especially the electrical system.

• Do ensure that any lifting or jacking equipment has a safe working load rating adequate for the job.

### DON'T

• Don't attempt to lift a heavy component which may be beyond your capability – get assistance.

• Don't rush to finish a job, or take unverified short cuts.

• Don't use ill-fitting tools which may slip and cause injury.

• Don't leave tools or parts lying around where someone can trip over them. Mop up oil and fuel spills at once.

• Don't allow children or pets to play in or near a vehicle being worked on.

The following pages are intended to help in dealing with common roadside emergencies and breakdowns. You will find more detailed fault finding information at the back of the manual, and repair information in the main chapters.

## If your car won't start and the starter motor doesn't turn

- ☐ If it's a model with automatic transmission, make sure the selector is in the P or N position.
- ☐ Open the bonnet and make sure that the battery terminals are clean and tight.
- ☐ Switch on the headlights and try to start the engine. If the headlights go very dim when you're trying to start, the battery is probably flat. Get out of trouble by jump starting (see next page) using a friend's car.

## If your car won't start even though the starter motor turns as normal

- ☐ Is there fuel in the tank?
- ☐ Is there moisture on electrical components under the bonnet? Switch off the ignition, then wipe off any obvious dampness with a dry cloth. Spray a water-repellent aerosol product (WD-40 or equivalent) on ignition and fuel system electrical connectors like those shown in the photos. (Note that diesel engines don't usually suffer from damp).

**1** On petrol engines, check that the wiring to the ignition module is connected firmly.

**2** Check that the air mass meter wiring is connected securely.

**3** Check the security and condition of the battery connections.

Check that electrical connections are secure (with the ignition switched off) and spray them with a water-dispersant spray like WD-40 if you suspect a problem due to damp

**4** Check all multiplugs and wiring connectors for security.

**5** Check that all fuses are still in good condition and none have blown.

# Jump starting

When jump-starting a car, observe the following precautions:

✓ Before connecting the booster battery, make sure that the ignition is switched off.

*Caution: Remove the key in case the central locking engages when the jump leads are connected*

✓ Ensure that all electrical equipment (lights, heater, wipers, etc) is switched off.

✓ Take note of any special precautions printed on the battery case.

✓ Make sure that the booster battery is the same voltage as the discharged one in the vehicle.

✓ If the battery is being jump-started from the battery in another vehicle, the two vehicles MUST NOT TOUCH each other.

✓ Make sure that the transmission is in neutral (or PARK, in the case of automatic transmission).

 *Budget jump leads can be a false economy, as they often do not pass enough current to start large capacity or diesel engines. They can also get hot.*

 *Jump starting will get you out of trouble, but you must correct whatever made the battery go flat in the first place. There are three possibilities:*

*1 The battery has been drained by repeated attempts to start, or by leaving the lights on.*

*2 The charging system is not working properly (alternator drivebelt slack or broken, alternator wiring fault or alternator itself faulty).*

*3 The battery itself is at fault (electrolyte low, or battery worn out).*

**1** Connect one end of the red jump lead to the positive (+) terminal of the flat battery

**2** Connect the other end of the red lead to the positive (+) terminal of the booster battery.

**3** Connect one end of the black jump lead to the negative (-) terminal of the booster battery

**4** Connect the other end of the black jump lead to a bolt or bracket on the engine block, well away from the battery, on the vehicle to be started.

**5** Make sure that the jump leads will not come into contact with the fan, drive-belts or other moving parts of the engine.

**6** Start the engine using the booster battery and run it at idle speed. Switch on the lights, rear window demister and heater blower motor, then disconnect the jump leads in the reverse order of connection. Turn off the lights etc.

# Wheel changing

 **Warning: Do not change a wheel in a situation where you risk being hit by other traffic. On busy roads, try to stop in a lay-by or a gateway. Be wary of passing traffic while changing the wheel – it is easy to become distracted by the job in hand.**

**Note:** *Later models may be equipped with a puncture repair kit instead of a spare wheel. The kit is stored in the spare wheel location and consists of a bottle of sealant and an electric compressor. Follow the instructions supplied with the kit, or contained in the vehicle handbook when using the puncture repair kit.*

## Preparation

☐ When a puncture occurs, stop as soon as it is safe to do so.
☐ Park on firm level ground, if possible, and well out of the way of other traffic.
☐ Use hazard warning lights if necessary.

☐ If you have one, use a warning triangle to alert other drivers of your presence.
☐ Apply the handbrake and engage first or reverse gear (or Park on models with automatic transmission).

☐ Chock the wheel diagonally opposite the one being removed – a couple of large stones will do for this.
☐ If the ground is soft, use a flat piece of wood to spread the load under the jack.

## Changing the wheel

**1** Lift the floor covering and unscrew the spare wheel clamp nut. Lift out the spare wheel.

**2** Remove the tools from the toolbag stored beneath the spare wheel. Use the special clip to pull off the wheel trim.

**3** Slacken each wheel bolt by half a turn.

**4** Make sure the jack is located on firm ground, and engage the jack head correctly with the sill. Raise the jack until the wheel is clear of the ground.

**5** Unscrew the wheel bolts and remove the wheel. Fit the spare wheel and screw in the bolts. Lightly tighten the bolts with the wheelbrace then lower the car to the ground.

**6** Securely tighten the wheel bolts in a diagonal sequence then refit the wheel trim. Stow the punctured wheel and tools back in the luggage compartment.

## Finally . . .

☐ Check the tyre pressure on the wheel just fitted. If it is low, or if you don't have a pressure gauge with you, drive slowly to the next garage and inflate the tyre to the correct pressure.
☐ The wheel bolts should be slackened and retightened to the specified torque at the earliest possible opportunity.
☐ Have the damaged tyre or wheel repaired as soon as possible, or another puncture will leave you stranded.

# Identifying leaks

Puddles on the garage floor or drive, or obvious wetness under the bonnet or underneath the car, suggest a leak that needs investigating. It can sometimes be difficult to decide where the leak is coming from, especially if an engine undershield is fitted. Leaking oil or fluid can also be blown rearwards by the passage of air under the car, giving a false impression of where the problem lies.

 **Warning: Most automotive oils and fluids are poisonous. Wash them off skin, and change out of contaminated clothing, without delay.**

 *The smell of a fluid leaking from the car may provide a clue to what's leaking. Some fluids are distinctively coloured. It may help to remove the engine undershield, clean the car carefully and to park it over some clean paper overnight as an aid to locating the source of the leak.*
*Remember that some leaks may only occur while the engine is running.*

### Sump oil

Engine oil may leak from the drain plug...

### Oil from filter

...or from the base of the oil filter.

### Gearbox oil

Gearbox oil can leak from the seals at the inboard ends of the driveshafts.

### Antifreeze

Leaking antifreeze often leaves a crystalline deposit like this.

### Brake fluid

A leak occurring at a wheel is almost certainly brake fluid.

### Power steering fluid

Power steering fluid may leak from the pipe connectors on the steering rack.

# Towing

When all else fails, you may find yourself having to get a tow home – or of course you may be helping somebody else. Long-distance recovery should only be done by a garage or breakdown service. For shorter distances, DIY towing using another car is easy enough, but observe the following points:

☐ Use a proper tow-rope – they are not expensive. The vehicle being towed must display an ON TOW sign in its rear window.
☐ Always turn the ignition key to the 'On' position when the vehicle is being towed, so that the steering lock is released, and the direction indicator and brake lights work.

☐ The towing eye is supplied in the vehicle toolkit which is stored in the luggage compartment with the spare wheel (see *Wheel changing*). To fit the eye, unclip the access cover from the relevant bumper and screw the eye firmly into position. Note that the eye has an **anti-clockwise** thread. The wheelbrace can be used to tighten the eye.
☐ Before being towed, release the handbrake and select neutral on the transmission.
*Caution: On models with automatic transmission, do not tow the car at speeds in excess of 50 mph or for a distance greater than 60 miles. If towing speeds/ distances are to exceed these limits, then*

*the car must be towed with its front wheels off the ground.*
☐ Note that greater-than-usual pedal pressure will be required to operate the brakes, since the vacuum servo unit is only operational with the engine running.
☐ The driver of the car being towed must keep the tow-rope taut at all times to avoid snatching.
☐ Make sure that both drivers know the route before setting off.
☐ Only drive at moderate speeds and keep the distance towed to a minimum. Drive smoothly and allow plenty of time for slowing down at junctions.

## Introduction

There are some very simple checks which need only take a few minutes to carry out, but which could save you a lot of inconvenience and expense.

These *Weekly checks* require no great skill or special tools, and the small amount of time they take to perform could prove to be very well spent, for example:

☐ Keeping an eye on tyre condition and pressures, will not only help to stop them wearing out prematurely, but could also save your life.

☐ Many breakdowns are caused by electrical problems. Battery-related faults are particularly common, and a quick check on a regular basis will often prevent the majority of these.

☐ If your car develops a brake fluid leak, the first time you might know about it is when your brakes don't work properly. Checking the level regularly will give advance warning of this kind of problem.

☐ If the oil or coolant levels run low, the cost of repairing any engine damage will be far greater than fixing the leak, for example.

## Underbonnet check points

### ◄ 1.2 litre petrol

**1** *Engine oil level dipstick*

**2** *Engine oil filler cap*

**3** *Coolant expansion tank cap*

**4** *Brake (and clutch) fluid reservoir*

**5** *Screen washer fluid reservoir*

**6** *Battery*

### ◄ 1.3 litre diesel

**1** *Engine oil level dipstick*

**2** *Engine oil filler cap*

**3** *Coolant expansion tank cap*

**4** *Brake (and clutch) fluid reservoir*

**5** *Screen washer fluid reservoir*

**6** *Battery*

# Engine oil level

## Before you start

✔ Make sure that the car is on level ground.
✔ The oil level must be checked with the engine at normal operating temperature, however, wait at least 5 minutes after the engine has been switched off

**HAYNES HINT** *If the oil is checked immediately after driving the vehicle, some of the oil will remain in the upper engine components, resulting in an inaccurate reading on the dipstick.*

## The correct oil

Modern engines place great demands on their oil. It is very important that the correct oil for your car is used (see *Lubricants and fluids*).

## Car care

● If you have to add oil frequently, you should check whether you have any oil leaks. Place some clean paper under the car overnight, and check for stains in the morning. If there are no leaks, then the engine may be burning oil.
● Always maintain the level between the upper and lower dipstick marks (see photo 3). If the level is too low, severe engine damage may occur. Oil seal failure may result if the engine is overfilled by adding too much oil.

**1** The dipstick is brightly coloured for easy identification (see *Underbonnet check points* for exact location). Withdraw the dipstick.

**3** Note the level on the end of the dipstick, which should be between the upper (MAX) mark and lower (MIN) mark.

**2** Using a clean rag or paper towel remove all oil from the dipstick. Insert the clean dipstick into the tube as far as it will go, then withdraw it again.

**4** Oil is added through the filler cap. Unscrew the cap and top-up the level. A funnel may help to reduce spillage. Add the oil slowly, checking the level on the dipstick frequently. Avoid overfilling (see *Car care*).

---

# Coolant level

⚠ *Warning: Do not attempt to remove the expansion tank pressure cap when the engine is hot, as there is a very great risk of scalding. Do not leave open containers of coolant about, as it is poisonous.*

## Car Care

● Adding coolant should not be necessary on a regular basis. If frequent topping-up is required, it is likely there is a leak. Check the radiator, all hoses and joint faces for signs of staining or wetness, and rectify as necessary.

● It is important that antifreeze is used in the cooling system all year round, not just during the winter months. Don't top up with water alone, as the antifreeze will become too diluted.

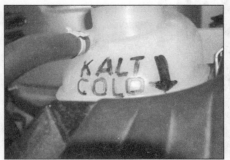
**1** The coolant level varies with the temperature of the engine. When the engine is cold, the coolant level should be near the COLD (or KALT) mark.

**2** If topping-up is necessary, **wait until the engine is cold**. Slowly unscrew the cap to release any pressure present in the cooling system and remove it.

**3** Add a mixture of water and antifreeze to the expansion tank until the coolant level is up to the Cold/Kalt mark.

# Brake and clutch fluid level

⚠️ **Warning:**
• *Brake fluid can harm your eyes and damage painted surfaces, so use extreme caution when handling and pouring it.*
• *Do not use fluid that has been standing open for some time, as it absorbs moisture from the air, which can cause a dangerous loss of braking effectiveness.*
• *The fluid level in the reservoir will drop slightly as the brake pads and shoes wear down, but the fluid level must never be allowed to drop below the MIN mark.*

## Before you start

✔ Make sure that the car is on level ground.

✔ Cleanliness is of great importance when dealing with the braking system, so take care to clean around the reservoir cap before topping-up. Use only clean brake fluid.

## Safety first!

● If the reservoir requires repeated topping-up, this is an indication of a fluid leak somewhere in the system, which should be investigated immediately.

● If a leak is suspected, the car should not be driven until the braking system has been checked. Never take any risks where brakes are concerned.

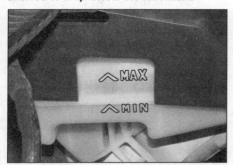

**1** The MIN and MAX marks are indicated on the reservoir. The fluid level must be kept between the marks at all times.

**2** If topping-up is necessary, first lift the plastic cover then wipe clean the area around the filler cap to prevent dirt entering the hydraulic system. Unscrew the reservoir cap.

**3** Carefully add fluid, taking care not to spill it onto the surrounding components. Use only the specified fluid; mixing different types can cause damage to the system. Then securely refit the cap and wipe off any spilt fluid.

# Washer fluid level

● Screenwash additives not only keep the windscreen clean during bad weather, they also prevent the washer system freezing in cold weather – which is when you are likely to need it most. Don't top-up using plain water, as the screenwash will become diluted, and will freeze in cold weather.

⚠️ **Warning: On no account use engine coolant antifreeze in the screen washer system – this may damage the paintwork.**

**1** The screenwasher fluid reservoir is located at the rear right-hand corner of the engine compartment.

**2** When topping-up the reservoir, a screenwash additive should be added in the quantities recommended on the bottle.

# Tyre condition and pressure

It is very important that tyres are in good condition, and at the correct pressure - having a tyre failure at any speed is highly dangerous. Tyre wear is influenced by driving style - harsh braking and acceleration, or fast cornering, will all produce more rapid tyre wear. As a general rule, the front tyres wear out faster than the rears. Interchanging the tyres from front to rear ("rotating" the tyres) may result in more even wear. However, if this is completely effective, you may have the expense of replacing all four tyres at once! Remove any nails or stones embedded in the tread before they penetrate the tyre to cause deflation. If removal of a nail does reveal that the tyre has been punctured, refit the nail so that its point of penetration is marked. Then immediately change the wheel, and have the tyre repaired by a tyre dealer.

Regularly check the tyres for damage in the form of cuts or bulges, especially in the sidewalls. Periodically remove the wheels, and clean any dirt or mud from the inside and outside surfaces. Examine the wheel rims for signs of rusting, corrosion or other damage. Light alloy wheels are easily damaged by "kerbing" whilst parking; steel wheels may also become dented or buckled. A new wheel is very often the only way to overcome severe damage.

New tyres should be balanced when they are fitted, but it may become necessary to re-balance them as they wear, or if the balance weights fitted to the wheel rim should fall off. Unbalanced tyres will wear more quickly, as will the steering and suspension components. Wheel imbalance is normally signified by vibration, particularly at a certain speed (typically around 50 mph). If this vibration is felt only through the steering, then it is likely that just the front wheels need balancing. If, however, the vibration is felt through the whole car, the rear wheels could be out of balance. Wheel balancing should be carried out by a tyre dealer or garage.

## 1 Tread Depth - visual check

The original tyres have tread wear safety bands (B), which will appear when the tread depth reaches approximately 1.6 mm. The band positions are indicated by a triangular mark on the tyre sidewall (A).

## 2 Tread Depth - manual check

Alternatively, tread wear can be monitored with a simple, inexpensive device known as a tread depth indicator gauge.

## 3 Tyre Pressure Check

Check the tyre pressures regularly with the tyres cold. Do not adjust the tyre pressures immediately after the vehicle has been used, or an inaccurate setting will result.

# Tyre tread wear patterns

### Shoulder Wear

**Underinflation (wear on both sides)**
Under-inflation will cause overheating of the tyre, because the tyre will flex too much, and the tread will not sit correctly on the road surface. This will cause a loss of grip and excessive wear, not to mention the danger of sudden tyre failure due to heat build-up.
*Check and adjust pressures*
**Incorrect wheel camber (wear on one side)**
*Repair or renew suspension parts*
**Hard cornering**
*Reduce speed!*

### Centre Wear

**Overinflation**
Over-inflation will cause rapid wear of the centre part of the tyre tread, coupled with reduced grip, harsher ride, and the danger of shock damage occurring in the tyre casing.
*Check and adjust pressures*

*If you sometimes have to inflate your car's tyres to the higher pressures specified for maximum load or sustained high speed, don't forget to reduce the pressures to normal afterwards.*

### Uneven Wear

Front tyres may wear unevenly as a result of wheel misalignment. Most tyre dealers and garages can check and adjust the wheel alignment (or "tracking") for a modest charge.
**Incorrect camber or castor**
*Repair or renew suspension parts*
**Malfunctioning suspension**
*Repair or renew suspension parts*
**Unbalanced wheel**
*Balance tyres*
**Incorrect toe setting**
*Adjust front wheel alignment*
**Note:** *The feathered edge of the tread which typifies toe wear is best checked by feel.*

# Wiper blades

**1** Check the condition of the wiper blades; if they are cracked or show any signs of deterioration, or if the glass swept area is smeared, renew them. Wiper blades should be renewed annually.

**2** To remove a windscreen wiper blade, pull the arm fully away from the screen until it locks. Swivel the blade through 90°, press the locking tab with your fingers and slide the blade out of the arm's hooked end.

**3** Don't forget to check the tailgate wiper blade as well. To remove the blade, depress the retaining tab and slide the blade out of the hooked end of the arm.

# Battery

*Caution: Before carrying out any work on the vehicle battery, read the precautions given in 'Safety first!' at the start of this manual.*

✔ Make sure that the battery tray is in good condition, and that the clamp is tight. Corrosion on the tray, retaining clamp and the battery itself can be removed with a solution of water and baking soda. Thoroughly rinse all cleaned areas with water. Any metal parts damaged by corrosion should be covered with a zinc-based primer, then painted.

✔ Periodically (approximately every three months), check the charge condition of the battery as described in Chapter 5A.

✔ If the battery is flat, and you need to jump start your vehicle, see *Roadside Repairs*.

**1** The battery is located at the rear left-hand side of the engine compartment. The exterior of the battery should be inspected periodically for damage such as a cracked case or cover.

**2** Check the tightness of the battery cable clamps to ensure good electrical connections. You should not be able to move them. Also check each cable for cracks and frayed conductors.

*Battery corrosion can be kept to a minimum by applying a layer of petroleum jelly to the clamps and terminals after they are reconnected.*

**3** If corrosion (white, fluffy deposits) is evident, remove the cables from the battery terminals, clean them with a small wire brush, then refit them. Automotive stores sell a tool for cleaning the battery post . . .

**4** . . . as well as the battery cable clamps.

# Electrical systems

✔ Check all external lights and the horn. Refer to the appropriate Sections of Chapter 12 for details if any of the circuits are found to be inoperative.

✔ Visually check all accessible wiring connectors, harnesses and retaining clips for security, and for signs of chafing or damage.

 *If you need to check your brake lights and indicators unaided, back up to a wall or garage door and operate the lights. The reflected light should show if they are working properly.*

**1** If a single indicator light, brake stop-light or headlight has failed, it is likely that a bulb has blown and will need to be renewed. Refer to Chapter 12 for details. If both stop-lights have failed, it is possible that the switch has failed (see Chapter 9).

**2** If more than one indicator light or tail light has failed it is likely that either a fuse has blown or that there is a fault in the circuit (see Chapter 12). The main fuses are located in the fuse/relay box situated at the left-hand front corner of the engine compartment.

**3** To renew a blown fuse, remove it, where applicable, using the plastic tool provided. Fit a new fuse of the same rating, available from car accessory shops. It is important that you find the reason that the fuse blew (see *Electrical fault finding* in Chapter 12).

# Lubricants and fluids

**Engine***

Petrol . . . . . . . . . . . . . . . . . . . . . . . . . . . . . . . . . . . . . . . . . . .   Multigrade engine oil, viscosity SAE 0W/30, 0W/40, 5W/30 or
5W/40 to specification ACEA A3, ACEA A3/B3, ACEA A3/B3/B4
or higher

Diesel . . . . . . . . . . . . . . . . . . . . . . . . . . . . . . . . . . . . . . . . . .   Multigrade engine oil, viscosity SAE 0W/30, 0W/40, 5W/30 or
5W/40 to specification ACEA B3, ACEA A3/B3, ACEA A3/B3/B4
or higher

**Manual gearbox** . . . . . . . . . . . . . . . . . . . . . . . . . . . . . . .   Vauxhall/Opel gear oil (09 120 541)

**Easytronic transmission** . . . . . . . . . . . . . . . . . . . . . . . .   Vauxhall/Opel gear oil (09 120 541)

**Automatic transmission**. . . . . . . . . . . . . . . . . . . . . . . . .   Vauxhall/Opel A/T fluid (09 117 946)

**Cooling system**

Models up to September 2003 . . . . . . . . . . . . . . . . . . . .   Vauxhall/Opel antifreeze (19 40 650/09 194 431)

Models from October 2003 . . . . . . . . . . . . . . . . . . . . . . .   Vauxhall/Opel silicate-free coolant (93 170 402)

**Brake/clutch fluid reservoir** . . . . . . . . . . . . . . . . . . . . .   Hydraulic fluid to DOT 4

**\* Note:** *The engine oil specification shown is for vehicles operating under the normal maintenance intervals given at the start of Chapters 1A and 1B.
If the vehicle is operating under the extended ECOService-Flex maintenance intervals, long-life oil (Vauxhall specification GM-LL-A-025 for petrol
engines, or GM-LL-B-025 for diesel engines)* **must** *be used at all times. Refer to Chapter 1A or 1B for further information.*

# Tyre pressures (cold)

**Note:** *Pressures are quoted for standard tyre fitments (see Chapter 10); consult a dealer or tyre specialist for alternative or revised
recommendations.*

| Corsa and Corsavan | Front | Rear |
|---|---|---|
| **Normal load (up to 3 passengers)** | | |
| 1.0 litre petrol except ECO models . . . . . . . . . . . . . . . . . . . . | 2.2 bars (32 psi) | 1.8 bars (26 psi) |
| 1.0 litre petrol ECO models: | | |
|   175/65 R 14 (for minimum fuel consumption). . . . . . . . . . . . | 2.7 bars (39 psi) | 2.5 bars (36 psi) |
|   175/65 R 14 (for improving driving comfort). . . . . . . . . . . . | 2.4 bars (35 psi) | 2.4 bars (35 psi) |
| 1.2 litre petrol models. . . . . . . . . . . . . . . . . . . . . . . . . . . . . . . | 2.2 bars (32 psi) | 1.8 bars (26 psi) |
| 1.4 litre petrol models: | | |
|   175/65 R 14 and 185/55 R 15. . . . . . . . . . . . . . . . . . . . . . . | 2.3 bars (33 psi) | 2.1 bars (30 psi) |
|   195/45 R 16 . . . . . . . . . . . . . . . . . . . . . . . . . . . . . . . . . . . . . | 2.4 bars (35 psi) | 2.2 bars (32 psi) |
| 1.3 and 1.7 litre diesel models: | | |
|   175/65 R 14 and 185/55 R 15 . . . . . . . . . . . . . . . . . . . . . . | 2.3 bars (33 psi) | 2.1 bars (30 psi) |
|   195/45 R 16 . . . . . . . . . . . . . . . . . . . . . . . . . . . . . . . . . . . . . | 2.4 bars (35 psi) | 2.2 bars (32 psi) |
| **Fully laden** | | |
| 1.0 litre petrol except ECO models . . . . . . . . . . . . . . . . . . . | 2.4 bars (35 psi) | 2.8 bars (41 psi) |
| 1.0 litre petrol ECO models . . . . . . . . . . . . . . . . . . . . . . . . . | 2.7 bars (39 psi) | 3.0 bars (44 psi) |
| 1.2 litre petrol models. . . . . . . . . . . . . . . . . . . . . . . . . . . . . . . | 2.4 bars (35 psi) | 2.8 bars (41 psi) |
| 1.4 litre petrol models: | | |
|   All except SRi models. . . . . . . . . . . . . . . . . . . . . . . . . . . . . | 2.4 bars (35 psi) | 2.8 bars (41 psi) |
|   SRi models . . . . . . . . . . . . . . . . . . . . . . . . . . . . . . . . . . . . . | 2.6 bars (38 psi) | 3.0 bars (44 psi) |
| 1.3 and 1.7 litre diesel models: | | |
|   All except 195/45 R 16 . . . . . . . . . . . . . . . . . . . . . . . . . . . . | 2.4 bars (35 psi) | 2.8 bars (41 psi) |
|   195/45 R 16 . . . . . . . . . . . . . . . . . . . . . . . . . . . . . . . . . . . . . | 2.6 bars (38 psi) | 3.0 bars (44 psi) |

| Combo Van | | |
|---|---|---|
| **Normal load (up to 2 persons and 100 kg load)** | | |
| All tyre sizes . . . . . . . . . . . . . . . . . . . . . . . . . . . . . . . . . . . . . | 2.4 bars (35 psi) | 2.4 bars (35 psi) |
| **Fully laden** | | |
| All tyre sizes . . . . . . . . . . . . . . . . . . . . . . . . . . . . . . . . . . . . . | 2.4 bars (35 psi) | 3.5 bars (51 psi) |

# Chapter 1 Part A:
# Routine maintenance and servicing – petrol models

## Contents

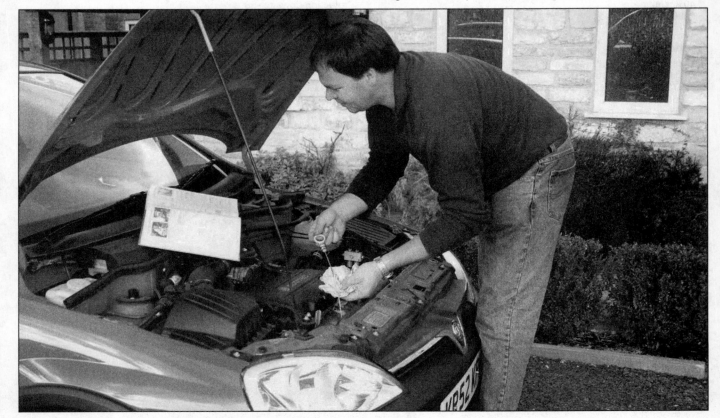

## Degrees of difficulty

| | | | | |
|---|---|---|---|---|
| **Easy,** suitable for novice with little experience  | **Fairly easy,** suitable for beginner with some experience | **Fairly difficult,** suitable for competent DIY mechanic | **Difficult,** suitable for experienced DIY mechanic | **Very difficult,** suitable for expert DIY or professional 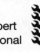 |

**Lubricants and fluids**................................ Refer to *Weekly checks* on page 0•17

## Capacities

### Engine oil
Oil change, including filter:
| | |
|---|---|
| 1.0 litre engines ......................................... | 3.0 litres |
| 1.2 litre engines ......................................... | 3.5 litres |
| 1.4 litre engines ......................................... | 3.5 litres |
Difference between MAX and MIN dipstick marks................ 1.0 litre

### Cooling system
Manual transmission models ............................... 4.9 litres
Automatic transmission models:
| | |
|---|---|
| Without air conditioning .................................. | 6.5 litres |
| With air conditioning..................................... | 6.7 litres |

**Fuel tank** ..................................................... 45.0 litres

**Manual gearbox** ........................................ 1.6 litres

**Easytronic transmission** ............................... 1.6 litres

**Automatic transmission**................................. 4.0 litres (approximately)

## Cooling system
Antifreeze mixture:
| | |
|---|---|
| 40% antifreeze ......................................... | Protection down to -28°C |
| 50% antifreeze ......................................... | Protection down to -40°C |

## Ignition system

| Spark plugs: | Type | Electrode gap |
|---|---|---|
| 1.0 litre 12-valve petrol engine: | | |
|    973 cc, Z10XE and Z10XE-ECO......................... | FLR 8 LDCU | 1.0 mm |
|    998 cc, Z10XEP ...................................... | FQR 8 LEU2 | 0.9 mm |
| 1.2 litre 16-valve petrol engine: | | |
|    1199 cc, Z12XE ...................................... | FLR 8 LDCU | 1.0 mm |
|    1229 cc, Z12XEP ..................................... | FQR 8 LEU2 | 0.9 mm |
| 1.4 litre 16-valve petrol engine: | | |
|    1364 cc, Z14XEP ..................................... | FQR 8 LEU2 | 0.9 mm |
|    1389 cc, Z14XE ...................................... | FLR 8 LDCU | 1.0 mm |

## Suspension and steering
Tyre pressures ............................................. Refer to end of *Weekly checks* on page 0•17

## Torque wrench settings

| | Nm | lbf ft |
|---|---|---|
| Automatic transmission fluid drain plug........................ | 40 | 30 |
| Oil filter housing cap to filter housing (paper element filter)........... | 10 | 7 |
| Roadwheel bolts.............................................. | 110 | 81 |
| Spark plugs ................................................. | 25 | 18 |
| Sump drain plug: | | |
|   All engines except 1.4 litre Z14XE ......................... | 10 | 7 |
|   1.4 litre Z14XE engines: | | |
|     Hexagon bolt with metal seal ring ......................... | 45 | 33 |
|     Torx bolt with rubber seal ring ........................... | 14 | 10 |

The maintenance intervals in this manual are provided with the assumption that you, not the dealer, will be carrying out the work. These are the minimum maintenance intervals based on the standard service schedule recommended by the manufacturer for vehicles driven daily. If you wish to keep your vehicle in peak condition at all times, you may wish to perform some of these procedures more often. We encourage frequent maintenance, because it enhances the efficiency, performance and resale value of your vehicle.

If the vehicle is driven in dusty areas, used to tow a trailer, or driven frequently at slow speeds (idling in traffic) or on short journeys, more frequent maintenance intervals are recommended.

When the vehicle is new, it should be serviced by a dealer service department (or other workshop recognised by the vehicle manufacturer as providing the same standard of service) in order to preserve the warranty. The vehicle manufacturer may reject warranty claims if you are unable to prove that servicing has been carried out as and when specified, using only original equipment parts or parts certified to be of equivalent quality.

### Flexible maintenance intervals

Later Corsa models covered by this manual are also capable of operating under the flexible maintenance interval plan known as Vauxhall ECOService-Flex. Under this flexible maintenance plan, a maximum service interval of 2 years or 25 000 miles can be achieved under ideal conditions. Information on a number of variables such as distance driven, driving cycles, engine operating conditions, coolant temperature and oil temperature are obtained and stored in the engine management ECU. Based on this information, the ECU calculates the remaining distance until the next service is due and displays this distance on the service interval indicator.

The ECOService-Flex plan is entirely dependent on the exclusive use of specially developed 'long-life' engine oils meeting Vauxhall specification GM-LL-A-025. If any other type of oil is used (such as engine oils meeting the conventional ACEA specifications) then the shorter maintenance intervals shown in the following schedule must be adhered to.

As stated earlier, it is our philosophy that frequent maintenance is always the preferred option, however it is up to the individual owner as to the course of action to be adopted.

## Every 250 miles or weekly
- [ ] Refer to Weekly checks

## Every 10 000 miles or 6 months – whichever comes first
- [ ] Renew the engine oil and filter (Section 3)

**Note:** *Vauxhall recommend that the engine oil and filter are changed every 20 000 miles or 12 months if the vehicle is being operated under the standard service schedule. However, oil and filter changes are good for the engine and we recommend that the oil and filter are renewed more frequently, especially if the vehicle is used on a lot of short journeys.*

## Every 20 000 miles or 12 months – whichever comes first
- [ ] Check all underbonnet and underbody components, pipes and hoses for leaks (Section 4)
- [ ] Check the auxiliary drivebelt and tensioner (Section 5)
- [ ] Check the operation of the horn, all lights, and the wipers and washers (Section 6)
- [ ] Check the tightness of the roadwheel bolts (Section 7)
- [ ] Check the condition of the brake pads (renew if necessary), the calipers and discs (Section 8)
- [ ] Check the operation of the handbrake and adjust if necessary (Section 9)
- [ ] Check the headlight beam alignment (Section 10)
- [ ] Check the condition of all brake fluid pipes and hoses (Section 11)
- [ ] Check the Easytronic clutch hydraulic fluid level (Section 12)
- [ ] Check the bodywork and underbody for damage and corrosion, and check the condition of the underbody corrosion protection (Section 13)
- [ ] Check the condition of the exhaust system components (Section 14)
- [ ] Lubricate all door, bonnet and tailgate hinges and locks (Section 15)

## Every 20 000 miles or 12 months – whichever comes first (continued)
- [ ] Check the condition of the front suspension and steering components, particularly the rubber gaiters and seals (Section 16)
- [ ] Check the condition of the rear suspension components (Section 17)
- [ ] Check the condition of the driveshaft joint gaiters and the driveshaft joints (Section 18)
- [ ] Carry out a road test (Section 19)
- [ ] Reset the service interval indicator (Section 20)

## Every 20 000 miles or 2 years – whichever comes first
- [ ] Renew the pollen filter (Section 21)

## Every 40 000 miles or 2 years – whichever comes first
- [ ] Renew the battery for the remote control handset (Section 22)
- [ ] Renew the brake and clutch fluid (Section 23)
- [ ] Renew the coolant (Section 24)

## Every 40 000 miles or 4 years – whichever comes first
- [ ] Renew the air cleaner filter element (Section 25)
- [ ] Renew the spark plugs (Section 26)
- [ ] Renew the timing belt (1.4 litre Z14XE engines) (Section 27)*
- [ ] Renew the fuel filter (Section 28)
- [ ] Renew the automatic transmission fluid (Section 29)
- [ ] Check the condition of the rear brake shoes (renew if necessary), drums and wheel cylinders (Section 30)

**\* Note:** *The normal interval for timing belt renewal is 60 000 miles or 6 years, however, it is strongly recommended that the interval used is 40 000 miles on vehicles which are subjected to intensive use, ie, mainly short journeys or a lot of stop-start driving. The actual belt renewal interval is therefore very much up to the individual owner, but bear in mind that severe engine damage will result if the belt breaks.*

## Underbonnet view of a 1.2 litre Z12XEP engine model

1  Engine oil level dipstick
2  Engine oil filler cap
3  Engine mounting
4  Air cleaner assembly
5  Front suspension strut
   upper mounting
6  Screen washer fluid
   reservoir
7  Air mass meter
8  Brake (and clutch) fluid
   reservoir
9  Throttle body
10 Ignition module
11 Coolant expansion tank
12 Battery
13 Fuse/relay box
14 ABS hydraulic modulator
15 Oil filter

## Front underbody view of a 1.2 litre model

1  Exhaust front pipe
2  Steering track rods
3  Front suspension lower
   arms
4  Front brake calipers
5  Steering gear
6  Alternator
7  Engine mounting rear
   torque link
8  Right-hand driveshaft
9  Final drive cover plate
10 Manual transmission
11 Engine oil drain plug
12 Air conditioning
   compressor
13 Electric cooling fan
14 Front subframe

## Rear underbody view of a 1.2 litre model

1  Handbrake cable
2  Rear suspension coil
   springs
3  Exhaust tailpipe and
   silencer
4  Exhaust heat shield
5  Rear anti-roll bar
6  Rear suspension trailing
   arms and rear axle
7  Fuel filter
8  Fuel tank

# Maintenance procedures

## 1  General information

1 This Chapter is designed to help the home mechanic maintain his/her vehicle for safety, economy, long life and peak performance.
2 The Chapter contains a master maintenance schedule, followed by sections dealing specifically with each task on the schedule. Visual checks, adjustments, component renewal and other helpful items are included. Refer to the accompanying illustrations of the engine compartment and the underside of the vehicle for the locations of the various components.
3 Servicing of your vehicle in accordance with the mileage/time maintenance schedule and the following sections will provide a planned maintenance programme, which should result in a long and reliable service life. This is a comprehensive plan, so maintaining some items but not others at the specified service intervals will not produce the same results.
4 As you service your vehicle, you will discover that many of the procedures can – and should – be grouped together, because of the particular procedure being performed, or because of the close proximity of two otherwise-unrelated components to one another. For example, if the vehicle is raised for any reason, the exhaust can be inspected at the same time as the suspension and steering components.

5 The first step in this maintenance programme is to prepare yourself before the actual work begins. Read through all the sections relevant to the work to be carried out, then make a list and gather together all the parts and tools required. If a problem is encountered, seek advice from a parts specialist, or a dealer service department.

## 2  Regular maintenance

1 If, from the time the vehicle is new, the routine maintenance schedule is followed closely, and frequent checks are made of fluid levels and high-wear items, as suggested throughout this manual, the engine will be kept in relatively good running condition, and the need for additional work will be minimised.
2 It is possible that there will be times when the engine is running poorly due to the lack of regular maintenance. This is even more likely if a used vehicle, which has not received regular and frequent maintenance checks, is purchased. In such cases, additional work may need to be carried out, outside of the regular maintenance intervals.
3 If engine wear is suspected, a compression test (Chapter 2A or 2B) will provide valuable information regarding the overall performance of the main internal components. Such a test can be used as a basis to decide on the extent of the work to be carried out. If for example

a compression test indicates serious internal engine wear, conventional maintenance as described in this Chapter will not greatly improve the performance of the engine, and may prove a waste of time and money, unless extensive overhaul work (Chapter 2E) is carried out first.
4 The following series of operations are those most often required to improve the performance of a generally poor-running engine:

### Primary operations

a) Clean, inspect and test the battery ('Weekly checks').
b) Check all the engine-related fluids ('Weekly checks').
c) Check the condition and tension of the auxiliary drivebelt (Section 5).
d) Renew the spark plugs (Section 26).
e) Renew the fuel filter (Section 28).
f) Check the condition of the air cleaner filter element, and renew if necessary (Section 25).
g) Check the condition of all hoses, and check for fluid leaks (Section 4).

5 If the above operations do not prove fully effective, carry out the following secondary operations:

### Secondary operations

All items listed under Primary operations, plus the following:
a) Check the ignition system (Chapter 5B).
b) Check the charging system (Chapter 5A).
c) Check the fuel system (Chapter 4A or 4B).

# Every 10 000 miles or 6 months

### 3 Engine oil and filter renewal

 *Frequent oil and filter changes are the most important preventative maintenance procedures which can be undertaken by the DIY owner. As engine oil ages, it becomes diluted and contaminated, which leads to premature engine wear.*

**1** Before starting this procedure, gather together all the necessary tools and materials. Also make sure that you have plenty of clean rags and newspapers handy, to mop-up any

**3.3 Removing the oil filler cap**

**HAYNES HINT**

*As the drain plug threads release, move it sharply away so the stream of oil issuing from the sump runs into the container, not up your sleeve.*

**3.13b . . . then clip the new oil filter element to the cap**

spills. Ideally, the engine oil should be warm, as it will drain more easily, and more built-up sludge will be removed with it. Take care not to touch the exhaust or any other hot parts of the engine when working under the vehicle. To avoid any possibility of scalding, and to protect yourself from possible skin irritants and other harmful contaminants in used engine oils, it is advisable to wear gloves when carrying out this work.

**2** Access to the underside of the vehicle will be greatly improved if it can be raised on a lift, driven onto ramps, or jacked up and supported on axle stands (see *Jacking and vehicle support*). Whichever method is chosen, make sure that the vehicle remains level, or if it is at an angle, that the drain plug is at the lowest point. The drain plug is located at the rear of the sump.

**3** Remove the oil filler cap from the camshaft cover (twist it through a quarter-turn anti-clockwise and withdraw it) **(see illustration)**.

**4** Using a spanner, or preferably a suitable socket and bar, slacken the drain plug about half a turn. Position the draining container under the drain plug, then remove the plug completely **(see Haynes Hint)**.

**5** Allow some time for the oil to drain, noting that it may be necessary to reposition the container as the oil flow slows to a trickle.

**6** Two different types of oil filter will be encountered on engines covered by this manual. On 1.0, 1.2 and 1.4 litre Z14XEP engines, the oil filter is of the paper element

**3.7 Oil filter (arrowed) on 1.0, 1.2 and 1.4 litre X14XEP engines**

**3.14a Fit the cap and filter element assembly to the oil filter housing . . .**

type, which is removed from the oil filter housing and then a new element is fitted to the housing. On early 1.4 litre Z14XE engines, the filter is of the metal container type, which is unscrewed and removed as a unit from the engine, and then a new container is screwed into position. On later versions of this 1.4 litre Z14XE engine, a paper element type filter is used. Proceed as described under the following sub-Sections, according to filter type.

### Paper element type filter

**7** The oil filter housing is located at the front left-hand side of the engine **(see illustration)**.

**8** Move the container into position under the oil filter housing. Note, on some models it may be necessary to undo the retaining bolts and remove the engine undertray.

**9** Unscrew the oil filter housing cap and withdraw the cap together with the filter from the oil filter housing.

**10** Withdraw the filter from the oil filter housing cap.

**11** Use clean rags to remove all remaining oil, dirt and sludge from the oil filter housing.

**12** Remove the sealing O-ring from the oil filter housing cap.

**13** Fit a new sealing O-ring to the oil filter housing cap then clip the new oil filter element to the cap **(see illustrations)**.

**14** Fit the cap and filter element assembly to the oil filter housing and screw the cap into position. Finally, tighten the cap to the specified torque **(see illustrations)**.

**3.13a Fit a new sealing O-ring to the oil filter housing cap . . .**

**3.14b . . . screw the assembly into place and tighten the cap to the specified torque**

## Metal container type filter

**15** The oil filter is located at the front left-hand side of the engine. Note that access is most easily obtained from underneath the front of the vehicle.

**16** Move the container into position under the oil filter.

**17** Using an oil filter removal tool if necessary, slacken the filter initially, then unscrew it by hand the rest of the way (see illustration). Empty the oil in the old filter into the container. To ensure that the old filter is completely empty before disposal, puncture the filter dome in at least two places and allow any remaining oil to drain through the punctures and into the container.

**18** Use a clean rag to remove all oil, dirt and sludge from the filter sealing area on the engine. Check the old filter to make sure that the rubber sealing ring has not stuck to the engine. If it has, carefully remove it.

**19** Apply a light coating of clean engine oil to the sealing ring on the new filter, then screw the filter into position on the engine. Tighten the filter firmly by hand only – **do not** use any tools.

## All engines

**20** After all the oil has drained, wipe the drain plug and the sealing washer/O-ring with a clean rag. Examine the condition of the sealing washer/O-ring, and renew it if it shows signs of damage which may prevent an oil-tight seal. Clean the area around the drain plug opening, and refit the plug complete with the washer/O-ring. Tighten the plug to the specified torque, using a torque wrench.

**21** Fill the engine through the filler hole in the camshaft cover, using the correct grade and type of oil (refer to *Weekly checks* for details of topping-up). Pour in half the specified quantity of oil first, then wait a few minutes for the oil to drain into the sump. Continue to add oil, a small quantity at a time, until the level is up to the lower mark on the dipstick. Adding a further 1.0 litre will bring the level up to the upper mark on the dipstick.

**22** Start the engine and run it until it reaches normal operating temperature. While the engine is warming-up, check for leaks around the oil filter and the sump drain plug.

**23** Stop the engine, and wait at least five minutes for the oil to settle in the sump once

**3.17 Using an oil filter removal tool to slacken the filter on early 1.4 litre Z14XE engines**

more. With the new oil circulated and the filter now completely full, recheck the level on the dipstick, and add more oil as necessary.

**24** Dispose of the used engine oil and filter safely, with reference to *General repair procedures* in the Reference Chapter of this manual. Do not discard the old filter with domestic household waste. The facility for waste oil disposal provided by many local council refuse tips generally has a filter receptacle alongside.

# Every 20 000 miles or 12 months

## 4 Hose and fluid leak check

**1** Visually inspect the engine joint faces, gaskets and seals for any signs of water or oil leaks. Pay particular attention to the areas around the camshaft cover, cylinder head, oil filter and sump joint faces. Similarly, check the transmission and (where applicable) the air conditioning compressor for oil leakage. Bear in mind that, over a period of time, some very slight seepage from these areas is to be expected; what you are really looking for is any indication of a serious leak. Should a leak be found, renew the offending gasket or oil seal by referring to the appropriate Chapters in this manual.

**2** Also check the security and condition of all the engine-related pipes and hoses. Ensure that all cable ties or securing clips are in place, and in good condition. Clips which are broken or missing can lead to chafing of the hoses pipes or wiring, which could cause more serious problems in the future.

**3** Carefully check the radiator hoses and heater hoses along their entire length. Renew any hose which is cracked, swollen or deteriorated. Cracks will show up better if the hose is squeezed. Pay close attention to the hose clips that secure the hoses to the cooling system components. Hose clips can pinch and puncture hoses, resulting in cooling system leaks. If wire-type hose clips are used, it may be a good idea to update them with screw-type clips.

**4** Inspect all the cooling system components (hoses, joint faces, etc) for leaks. Where any problems of this nature are found on system components, renew the component or gasket with reference to Chapter 3 (see Haynes Hint).

**5** Where applicable, inspect the automatic transmission fluid cooler hoses for leaks or deterioration.

**6** With the vehicle raised, inspect the petrol tank and filler neck for punctures, cracks and other damage. The connection between the filler neck and tank is especially critical. Sometimes, a rubber filler neck or connecting hose will leak due to loose retaining clamps or deteriorated rubber.

**7** Carefully check all rubber hoses and metal fuel lines leading away from the petrol tank. Check for loose connections, deteriorated hoses, crimped lines and other damage. Pay particular attention to the vent pipes and hoses, which often loop up around the filler neck and can become blocked or crimped. Follow the lines to the front of the vehicle, carefully inspecting them all the way. Renew damaged sections as necessary. Similarly, whilst the vehicle is raised, take the opportunity to inspect all underbody brake fluid pipes and hoses.

**8** From within the engine compartment, check the security of all fuel hose attachments and pipe unions, and inspect the fuel hoses and vacuum hoses for kinks, chafing and deterioration.

**9** Where applicable, check the condition of the automatic transmission fluid pipes.

## 5 Auxiliary drivebelt check and renewal

**Note:** *The manufacturers recommend that the tensioner roller is checked and if necessary renewed at the same time as the drivebelt.*

### Checking

**1** The ribbed type auxiliary drivebelt drives the alternator, coolant pump (except 1.4 litre Z14XE engines) and the air conditioning compressor where applicable. An automatic drivebelt tensioner is fitted, and there is no requirement to check the drivebelt tension.

*A leak in the cooling system will usually show up as white- or antifreeze-coloured deposits on the area adjoining the leak.*

**5.7a Auxiliary drivebelt tensioner on the 1.0, 1.2 and 1.4 litre Z14XEP engines**

| 1 | Tensioner body | 2 | Locking pin/bolt |

**2** The belt should be inspected along its entire length, and if it is found to be worn, frayed or cracked, it should be renewed as a precaution against breakage in service.

### Renewal

**3** Apply the handbrake, then jack up the front of the vehicle and support it on axle stands (see *Jacking and vehicle support*). Remove the right-hand front roadwheel and the wheel arch liner cover for access to the right-hand side of the engine.
**4** With reference to the appropriate part of Chapter 4, remove the air cleaner housing for additional working clearance.
**5** If the drivebelt is to be re-used, mark it to indicate its normal running direction.
**6** On 1.0, 1.2 and 1.4 litre Z14XEP engines,

**5.7b Auxiliary drivebelt tensioner on the 1.4 litre Z14XE engine**

1 *Locking pin/bolt*
2 *Turn the tensioner as indicated to release the tension*

support the engine and remove the right-hand engine mounting with reference to Chapter 2A. **Note:** *On these engines, the engine mounting locates within the auxiliary drivebelt.*
**7** Note the routing of the drivebelt, then, using a Torx key or spanner (as applicable) on the pulley centre bolt, turn the tensioner clockwise (1.0, 1.2 and 1.4 litre Z14XEP engines) or anti-clockwise (1.4 litre Z14XE engines) against the spring tension. Hold the tensioner in this position by inserting a suitable locking pin/bolt through the special hole provided **(see illustrations)**.
**8** Slip the auxiliary drivebelt off of the pulleys.
**9** Locate the auxiliary drivebelt onto the pulleys in the correct routing. If the drivebelt is being re-used, make sure it is fitted the correct way around.
**10** Turn back the tensioner and remove the locking bolt, then release it, making sure that the drivebelt ribs locate correctly on each of the pulley grooves.
**11** On 1.0, 1.2 and 1.4 litre Z14XEP engines, refit the right-hand engine mounting with reference to Chapter 2A.
**12** Refit the air cleaner housing, then refit the wheel arch liner and roadwheel, and lower the vehicle to the ground.

### 6 Electrical system check

**1** Check the operation of all the electrical equipment, ie, lights, direction indicators, horn, etc. Refer to the appropriate sections of Chapter 12 for details if any of the circuits are found to be inoperative.
**2** Note that the stop-light switch is described in Chapter 9.
**3** Check all accessible wiring connectors, harnesses and retaining clips for security, and for signs of chafing or damage. Rectify any faults found.

### 7 Roadwheel bolt tightness check

**1** Where applicable, remove the wheel trims from the wheels.
**2** Using a torque wrench on each wheel bolt in turn, ensure that the bolts are tightened to the specified torque.
**3** Where applicable, refit the wheel trims on completion, making sure they are fitted correctly.

### 8 Brake pad and disc check

**1** With the vehicle on level ground, chock the rear wheels, apply the handbrake, then jack up the front of the vehicle and support securely on axle stands; remove the roadwheels (see *Jacking and vehicle support*).
**2** Check the thickness of the friction material on each brake pad.

> **HAYNES HiNT** *For a quick check, the thickness can be measured through the aperture in the caliper body.*

**3** If any pad is worn to the specified minimum thickness or less, all four pads must be renewed (see Chapter 9).
**4** The view through the caliper inspection hole gives a rough indication of the state of the brake pads. For a comprehensive check, the brake pads should be removed and cleaned. This will allow the operation of the caliper to be checked, and the condition of the brake disc itself to be fully examined on both sides. Chapter 9 contains a detailed description of how the brake disc should be checked for wear and/or damage.
**5** On completion, refit the roadwheels and lower the vehicle to the ground.

### 9 Handbrake operation and adjustment check

**1** With the vehicle on a slight slope, apply the handbrake lever by up to 7 clicks of the ratchet, and check that it holds the vehicle stationary, then release the lever and check that there is no resistance to movement of the vehicle.
**2** If necessary, adjust the handbrake lever as described in Chapter 9.

### 10 Headlight beam alignment check

**1** Accurate adjustment of the headlight beam is only possible using optical beam-setting equipment, and this work should therefore be carried out by a Vauxhall dealer or service station with the necessary facilities.

## 11 Brake fluid pipe and hose check

1 The brake hydraulic system includes a number of metal pipes, which run from the master cylinder to the front and rear brake assemblies, and the hydraulic modulator on models with an anti-lock braking system (ABS). Flexible hoses are fitted between the pipes and the front and rear brake assemblies, to allow for steering and suspension movement.
2 When checking the system, first look for signs of leakage at the pipe or hose unions, then examine the flexible hoses for signs of cracking, chafing or deterioration of the rubber. Bend the hoses sharply between the fingers (but do not actually bend them double, or the casing may be damaged) and check that this does not reveal previously-hidden cracks, cuts or splits. Check that the pipes and hoses are securely fastened in their clips.
3 Carefully working along the length of the metal pipes, look for dents, kinks, damage of any sort, or corrosion. Light corrosion can be polished off, but if the depth of pitting is significant, the pipe must be renewed.

## 12 Clutch hydraulic fluid level check (Easytronic models)

1 The clutch hydraulic fluid level markings are on the side of the fluid reservoir located on the front of the transmission. The use of a mirror will be helpful.
2 Check that the level of the fluid is at or near the MAX marking on the side of the reservoir **(see illustration)**.
3 If topping-up is required, unscrew the filler cap and pour in fresh fluid until the level is at the MAX marking. Retighten the cap on completion.

## 13 Bodywork and underbody condition check

**Note:** *This work should be carried out by a Vauxhall dealer in order to validate the vehicle warranty. The work includes a thorough inspection of the vehicle paintwork and underbody for damage and corrosion.*

### Bodywork damage/corrosion

1 Once the car has been washed, and all tar spots and other surface blemishes have been cleaned off, carefully check all paintwork, looking closely for chips or scratches. Pay particular attention to vulnerable areas such as the front panels (bonnet and spoiler), and

**12.2 Clutch fluid reservoir (1) on Easytronic models**

around the wheel arches. Any damage to the paintwork must be rectified as soon as possible, to comply with the terms of the manufacturer's anti-corrosion warranties; check with a Vauxhall dealer for details.
2 If a chip or light scratch is found which is recent and still free from rust, it can be touched-up using the appropriate touch-up stick which can be obtained from Vauxhall dealers. Any more serious damage, or rusted stone chips, can be repaired as described in Chapter 11, but if damage or corrosion is so severe that a panel must be renewed, seek professional advice as soon as possible.
3 Always check that the door and ventilation opening drain holes and pipes are completely clear, so that water can drain out.

### Corrosion protection

4 The wax-based underbody protective coating should be inspected annually, preferably just prior to Winter, when the underbody should be washed down as thoroughly as possible without disturbing the protective coating. Any damage to the coating should be repaired using a suitable wax-based sealer. If any of the body panels are disturbed for repair or renewal, do not forget to re-apply the coating. Wax should be injected into door cavities, sills and box sections, to maintain

**14.3 Exhaust mountings**

the level of protection provided by the vehicle manufacturer – seek the advice of a Vauxhall dealer.

## 14 Exhaust system check

1 With the engine cold (at least an hour after the vehicle has been driven), check the complete exhaust system from the engine to the end of the tailpipe. The exhaust system is most easily checked with the vehicle raised on a hoist, or suitably-supported on axle stands, so that the exhaust components are readily visible and accessible (see *Jacking and vehicle support*).
2 Check the exhaust pipes and connections for evidence of leaks, severe corrosion and damage. Make sure that all brackets and mountings are in good condition, and that all relevant nuts and bolts are tight. Leakage at any of the joints or in other parts of the system will usually show up as a black sooty stain in the vicinity of the leak.
3 Rattles and other noises can often be traced to the exhaust system, especially the brackets and mountings **(see illustration)**. Try to move the pipes and silencers. If the components are able to come into contact with the body or suspension parts, secure the system with new mountings. Otherwise separate the joints (if possible) and twist the pipes as necessary to provide additional clearance.

## 15 Hinge and lock lubrication

1 Work around the vehicle and lubricate the hinges of the bonnet, doors and tailgate with a light machine oil.
2 Lightly lubricate the bonnet release mechanism and exposed section of inner cable with a smear of grease.
3 Check the security and operation of all hinges, latches and locks, adjusting them where required (see Chapter 11). Check the operation of the central locking system.
4 Check the condition and operation of the tailgate struts, renewing them both if either is leaking or no longer able to support the tailgate securely when raised.

## 16 Front suspension and steering check

1 Apply the handbrake, then raise the front of the vehicle and securely support it on axle stands (see *Jacking and vehicle support*).
2 Inspect the balljoint dust covers and the steering gear gaiters for splits, chafing or deterioration.
3 Any wear of these components will cause loss of lubricant, and may allow water to

**16.4 Check for wear in the hub hearings by grasping the wheel and trying to rock it**

enter the components, resulting in rapid deterioration of the balljoints or steering gear.

4 Grasp each roadwheel at the 12 o'clock and 6 o'clock positions, and try to rock it **(see illustration)**. Very slight free play may be felt, but if the movement is appreciable, further investigation is necessary to determine the source. Continue rocking the wheel while an assistant depresses the footbrake. If the movement is now eliminated or significantly reduced, it is likely that the hub bearings are at fault. If the free play is still evident with the footbrake depressed, then there is wear in the suspension joints or mountings.

5 Now grasp each wheel at the 9 o'clock and 3 o'clock positions, and try to rock it as before. Any movement felt now may again be caused by wear in the hub bearings or the steering track rod end balljoints. If the track rod end balljoint is worn, the visual movement will be obvious.

6 Using a large screwdriver or flat bar, check for wear in the suspension mounting bushes by levering between the relevant suspension component and its attachment point. Some movement is to be expected, as the mountings are made of rubber, but excessive wear should be obvious. Also check the condition of any visible rubber bushes, looking for splits, cracks or contamination of the rubber.

7 Check for any signs of fluid leakage around the suspension strut/shock absorber bodies, or from the rubber gaiters around the piston rods. Should any fluid be noticed, the suspension strut/shock absorber is defective

**18.1 Check the condition of the driveshaft gaiters (1) and retaining clips (2)**

internally, and should be renewed. **Note:** *Suspension struts/shock absorbers should always be renewed in pairs on the same axle.*

8 With the vehicle standing on its wheels, have an assistant turn the steering wheel back-and-forth about an eighth of a turn each way. There should be very little, if any, lost movement between the steering wheel and roadwheels. If this is not the case, closely observe the joints and mountings previously described, but in addition check the steering column rubber coupling for wear, and also check the steering gear itself.

9 The efficiency of each suspension strut/shock absorber may be checked by bouncing the vehicle at each corner. Generally speaking, the body will return to its normal position and stop after being depressed. If it rises and returns on a rebound, the suspension strut/shock absorber is probably suspect. Also examine the suspension strut/shock absorber upper and lower mountings for any signs of wear.

## 17 Rear suspension check

1 Chock the front wheels, then jack up the rear of the vehicle and support securely on axle stands (see *Jacking and vehicle support*).
2 Inspect the rear suspension components for any signs of obvious wear or damage. Pay particular attention to the rubber mounting bushes, and renew if necessary (see Chapter 10).
3 Grasp each roadwheel at the 12 o'clock and 6 o'clock positions **(see illustration 16.4)**, and try to rock it. Any excess movement indicates incorrect adjustment or wear in the wheel bearings. Wear may also be accompanied by a rumbling sound when the wheel is spun, or a noticeable roughness if the wheel is turned slowly. The wheel bearing can be renewed as described in Chapter 10.
4 Check the rear shock absorbers in a similar manner to that described in Section 16 for the front shock absorbers.

## 18 Driveshaft check

1 With the vehicle raised and securely supported on stands, turn the steering onto full-lock, then slowly rotate each front roadwheel. Inspect the condition of the outer constant velocity (CV) joint rubber gaiters **(see illustration)**, while squeezing the gaiters to open out the folds. Check for signs of cracking, splits or deterioration of the rubber, which may allow the grease to escape and lead to water and grit entering the joint. Also check the security and condition of the retaining clips. Repeat these checks on the inner CV joints. If any damage or deterioration

is found, the gaiters should be renewed as described in Chapter 8.
2 At the same time, check the general condition of the CV joints themselves by first holding the driveshaft and attempting to rotate the wheel. Repeat this check by holding the inner joint and attempting to rotate the driveshaft. Any appreciable movement indicates wear in the joints, wear in the driveshaft splines, or a loose front hub nut.

## 19 Road test

### Instruments and electrical equipment

1 Check the operation of all instruments and electrical equipment.
2 Make sure that all instruments read correctly, and switch on all electrical equipment in turn, to check that it functions properly.

### Steering and suspension

3 Check for any abnormalities in the steering, suspension, handling or road 'feel'.
4 Drive the vehicle, and check that there are no unusual vibrations or noises.
5 Check that the steering feels positive, with no excessive 'sloppiness', or roughness, and check for any suspension noises when cornering and driving over bumps.

### Drivetrain

6 Check the performance of the engine, clutch (where applicable), gearbox/transmission and driveshafts.
7 Listen for any unusual noises from the engine, clutch and gearbox/transmission.
8 Make sure that the engine runs smoothly when idling, and that there is no hesitation when accelerating.
9 Check that, where applicable, the clutch action is smooth and progressive, that the drive is taken up smoothly, and that the pedal travel is not excessive. Also listen for any noises when the clutch pedal is depressed.
10 On manual gearbox models, check that all gears can be engaged smoothly without noise, and that the gear lever action is smooth and not abnormally vague or 'notchy'.
11 On automatic transmission models, make sure that all gearchanges occur smoothly, without snatching, and without an increase in engine speed between changes. Check that all the gear positions can be selected with the vehicle at rest. If any problems are found, they should be referred to a Vauxhall dealer.
12 Listen for a metallic clicking sound from the front of the vehicle, as the vehicle is driven slowly in a circle with the steering on full-lock. Carry out this check in both directions. If a clicking noise is heard, this indicates wear in a driveshaft joint, in which case renew the joint if necessary (see Chapter 8).

## Braking system

**13** Make sure that the vehicle does not pull to one side when braking, and that the wheels do not lock when braking hard.

**14** Check that there is no vibration through the steering when braking.

**15** Check that the handbrake operates correctly without excessive movement of the lever, and that it holds the vehicle stationary on a slope.

**16** Test the operation of the brake servo unit as follows. With the engine off, depress the footbrake four or five times to exhaust the vacuum. Hold the brake pedal depressed, then start the engine. As the engine starts, there should be a noticeable 'give' in the brake pedal as vacuum builds-up. Allow the engine to run for at least two minutes, and then switch it off. If the brake pedal is depressed now, it should be possible to detect a hiss from the servo as the pedal is depressed. After about four or five applications, no further hissing should be heard, and the pedal should feel considerably harder.

### 20 Service interval indicator reset

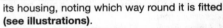

### Models up to September 2003

**1** With the ignition switched off, depress and hold the reset button located on the instrument panel.

**2** Switch on the ignition and press and hold the reset button for two more seconds at least. The InSP indicator should flash for two seconds, after which the text '____' should appear before releasing the reset button. When the button is released, the odometer or clock will appear again.

### Models from October 2003

**3** With the ignition switched off, depress and hold the reset button located on the instrument panel. After approximately 3 seconds the message 'InSP 0' will appear. Keep the reset button depressed and also depress the brake pedal.

**4** Switch on the ignition, with the reset button and brake pedal still depressed, and 'InSP - - - -' will appear, flashing, in the display. Keep the reset button and brake pedal depressed until the display changes.

**5** After approximately 10 seconds the display will change to show the maximum mileage before the next required service. Release the reset button and the brake pedal. When the button and brake pedal are released, the odometer or clock will appear again.

**6** This procedure resets the service interval indicator back to the ECOService-Flex, 2 years or 25 000 miles flexible maintenance interval. If the standard maintenance schedule described in this Chapter is being used, then the interval until the next service, which will be shown on the display, is irrelevant. If it is wished to have the service interval indicator altered to show the standard maintenance intervals described in this Chapter, it will be necessary to have the system reprogrammed using dedicated Vauxhall diagnostic equipment.

# Every 20 000 miles or 2 years

### 21 Pollen filter renewal

**1** Peel the bonnet seal off the engine compartment bulkhead, and remove it from the vehicle **(see illustration)**.

**2** Lift the brake fluid reservoir cover, and remove the battery wiring harness cover from the water deflector **(see illustration)**.

**3** Undo the retaining screw, then unclip the battery wiring harness from the water deflector **(see illustrations)**.

**4** Lift the water deflector, then release the two retaining clips and lift the pollen filter out from its housing, noting which way round it is fitted **(see illustrations)**.

**5** Wipe clean the filter housing and install the new filter, making sure it is the correct way up. Ensure that the filter is correctly seated, and secure it in position with the retaining clips.

**6** Refitting is the reverse of the removal procedure.

**21.1 Peel the bonnet seal off the engine compartment bulkhead**

**21.2 Remove the battery wiring harness cover from the water deflector**

**21.3a Undo the retaining screw . . .**

**21.3b . . . then unclip the battery wiring harness from the water deflector**

**21.4a Release the two retaining clips . . .**

**21.4b . . . and lift the pollen filter from its housing**

**22.1a Prise the key section away . . .**

**22.1b . . . from the remote control . . .**

**22.1c . . . and open the battery cover**

# Every 40 000 miles or 2 years

## 22 Remote control battery renewal

**Note:** *The following procedure must be performed within 3 minutes, otherwise the remote control unit will have to be reprogrammed.*

**1** Using a screwdriver, prise the key section from the remote control unit. Then prise the battery cover from the remote control unit **(see illustrations)**.

**2** Note how the battery is fitted, then carefully remove it from the contacts.

**3** Fit the new battery and refit the cover making sure that it clips fully onto the base. Refit the key section.

## 23 Brake and clutch fluid renewal

**Note:** *It is not possible for the home mechanic to bleed the clutch hydraulic system on Easytronic models.*

⚠️ **Warning: Hydraulic fluid can harm your eyes and damage painted surfaces, so use extreme caution when handling and pouring it. Do not use fluid that has been standing open for some time, as it absorbs moisture from the air. Excess moisture can cause a dangerous loss of braking effectiveness.**

**1** The procedure is similar to that for the bleeding of the hydraulic system as described in Chapters 9 (brake) and 6 (clutch).

**2** Working as described in Chapter 9, open the first bleed screw in the sequence, and pump the brake pedal gently until nearly all the old fluid has been emptied from the master cylinder reservoir. Top-up to the MAX level with new fluid, and continue pumping until only the new fluid remains in the reservoir, and new fluid can be seen emerging from the bleed screw. Tighten the screw, and top up the reservoir level up to the MAX level line.

**HAYNES HiNT** *Old hydraulic fluid is invariably much darker in colour than the new, making it easy to distinguish the two.*

**3** Work through all the remaining bleed screws in the sequence until new fluid can be seen at all of them. Be careful to keep the master cylinder reservoir topped-up to above the MIN level at all times, or air may enter the system and greatly increase the length of the task.

**4** When the operation is complete, check that all bleed screws are securely tightened, and that their dust caps are refitted. Wash off all traces of spilt fluid, and recheck the master cylinder reservoir fluid level.

**5** Check the operation of the brakes before taking the car on the road.

**6** Similarly, bleed the clutch hydraulic system with reference to Chapter 6.

## 24 Coolant renewal

**Note:** *Vauxhall do not specify renewal intervals for the antifreeze mixture, as the mixture used to fill the system when the vehicle is new is designed to last the lifetime of the vehicle. However, it is strongly recommended that the coolant is renewed at the intervals specified in the 'Maintenance schedule', as a precaution against possible engine corrosion problems. This is particularly advisable if the coolant has been renewed using an antifreeze other than that specified by Vauxhall. With many antifreeze types, the corrosion inhibitors become progressively less effective with age. It is up to the individual owner whether or not to follow this advice.*

⚠️ **Warning: Wait until the engine is cold before starting this procedure. Do not allow antifreeze to come in contact with your skin, or with the painted surfaces of the vehicle. Rinse off spills immediately with plenty of water. Never leave antifreeze lying around in** an open container, or in a puddle on the driveway or garage floor. Children and pets are attracted by its sweet smell, but antifreeze is fatal if ingested.

### Cooling system draining

**1** To drain the cooling system, first cover the expansion tank cap with a wad of rag, and slowly turn the cap anti-clockwise to relieve the pressure in the cooling system (a hissing sound will normally be heard). Wait until any pressure remaining in the system is released, then continue to turn the cap until it can be removed.

**2** Where necessary, remove the splash guard from under the radiator and engine.

**3** The coolant drain plug is located at the bottom of the radiator right-hand end tank. Position a container beneath the radiator then unscrew the drain plug and allow the coolant to drain.

**4** As no cylinder block drain plug is fitted, it is not possible to drain all of the coolant. Due consideration must be made for this when refilling the system, in order to maintain the correct concentration of antifreeze.

**5** If the coolant has been drained for a reason other than renewal, then provided it is clean and less than two years old, it can be re-used.

### Cooling system flushing

**6** If coolant renewal has been neglected, or if the antifreeze mixture has become diluted, then in time the cooling system may gradually lose efficiency, as the coolant passages become restricted due to rust, scale deposits, and other sediment. The cooling system efficiency can be restored by flushing the system clean.

**7** The radiator should be flushed independently of the engine, to avoid unnecessary contamination.

**8** To flush the radiator, disconnect the top and bottom hoses at the radiator, then insert a garden hose into the radiator top inlet. Direct a flow of clean water through the radiator, and continue flushing until clean water emerges from the radiator bottom outlet. If after a reasonable period, the water still does not run clear, the radiator can be flushed with a good proprietary cleaning agent. It is important that the cleaning agent manufacturer's instructions are followed carefully. If the contamination is particularly bad, insert the hose in the radiator bottom outlet, and flush the radiator in the reverse direction ('reverse-flushing').

**9** To flush the engine block, the thermostat must be removed, because it will be shut, and would otherwise prevent the flow of water around the engine. The thermostat can be removed as described in Chapter 3. Take care not to introduce dirt or debris into the system if this approach is used.

**10** With the radiator top and bottom hoses disconnected from the radiator, insert a hose into the top hose. Direct a clean flow of water through the engine, and continue flushing until clean water emerges from the radiator bottom hose.

**11** On completion of flushing, refit the thermostat with reference to Chapter 3, and reconnect the hoses.

### Cooling system filling

**12** Before attempting to fill the cooling system, make sure that all hoses and clips are in good condition, and that the clips are tight. Note that an antifreeze mixture must be used all year round, to prevent corrosion of the alloy engine components.

**13** Remove the expansion tank cap, and fill the system by slowly pouring the coolant into the expansion tank to prevent airlocks from forming.

**14** If the coolant is being renewed, begin by pouring in a couple of litres of water, followed by the correct quantity of undiluted antifreeze, then top-up with more water.

**15** Top-up the coolant level to the KALT (or COLD) mark on the expansion tank, then refit the expansion tank cap.

**16** Start the engine and run it until it reaches normal operating temperature, then stop the engine and allow it to cool.

**17** Check for leaks, particularly around disturbed components. Check the coolant level in the expansion tank, and top-up if necessary. Note that the system must be cold before an accurate level is indicated in the expansion tank. If the expansion tank cap is removed while the engine is still warm, cover the cap with a thick cloth, and unscrew the cap slowly to gradually relieve the system pressure (a hissing sound will normally be heard). Wait until any pressure remaining in the system is released, then continue to turn the cap until it can be removed.

### Antifreeze mixture

**18** Always use an ethylene-glycol based antifreeze which is suitable for use in mixed-metal cooling systems. The quantity of antifreeze and levels of protection are indicated in the Specifications.

**19** Before adding antifreeze, the cooling system should be completely drained, preferably flushed, and all hoses and clips checked for condition and security.

**20** After filling with antifreeze, a label should be attached to the radiator or expansion tank, stating the type and concentration of antifreeze used, and the date installed. Any subsequent topping-up should be made with the same type and concentration of antifreeze.

*Caution: Do not use engine antifreeze in the windscreen/tailgate washer system, as it will cause damage to the vehicle paintwork. A screenwash should be added to the washer system in the quantities recommended on the bottle.*

# Every 40 000 miles or 4 years

### 25 Air cleaner filter element renewal

**1** Disconnect the wiring plug from the air mass meter, then slacken the clamp and withdraw the air mass meter from the air cleaner cover **(see illustration)**.
**2** Unclip the purge valve from the side of the air cleaner cover **(see illustration)**.
**3** Undo the screws, lift off the air cleaner cover **(see illustrations)**.
**4** Lift out the air cleaner element **(see illustration)**.
**5** Wipe out the casing and the cover.

**6** Fit the new filter, noting that the rubber locating flange should be uppermost, and secure the cover with the screws.

**7** Reconnect the air mass meter to the cover and tighten the clamp, then reconnect the wiring.

25.1 **Disconnect the wiring plug from the air mass meter . . .**

25.2 **. . . unclip the purge valve . . .**

25.3a **. . . then undo the screws . . .**

25.3b **. . . remove the cover . . .**

25.4 **. . . and lift out the air cleaner element**

**26.4a Unscrew the spark plugs . . .**

**26.4b . . . and remove them**

### 26 Spark plug check and renewal

1 The correct functioning of the spark plugs is vital for the correct running and efficiency of the engine. It is essential that the plugs fitted are appropriate for the engine, the suitable type being specified at the beginning of this Chapter.

2 If the correct type of plug is used and the engine is in good condition, the spark plugs should not need attention between scheduled renewal intervals, except for adjustment of their gaps. Spark plug cleaning is rarely necessary, and should not be attempted unless specialised equipment is available, as damage can easily be caused to the firing ends.

3 To gain access to the spark plugs, remove

**26.9a Measuring a spark plug electrode gap using a feeler blade**

**26.9b Measuring a spark plug electrode gap using a wire gauge**

the ignition module as described in Chapter 5B.

4 Unscrew the plugs using a spark plug spanner, a suitable box spanner, or a deep socket and extension bar **(see illustrations)**. Keep the socket in alignment with the spark plugs, otherwise if it is forcibly moved to either side, the porcelain top of the spark plug may be broken off. As each plug is removed, examine it as follows.

5 Examination of the spark plugs will give a good indication of the condition of the engine. If the insulator nose of the spark plug is clean and white, with no deposits, this is indicative of a weak mixture or too hot a plug (a hot plug transfers heat away from the electrode slowly, while a cold plug transfers heat away quickly).

6 If the tip and insulator nose are covered with hard black-looking deposits, then this is indicative that the idle mixture is too rich. Should the plug be black and oily, then it is likely that the engine is fairly worn, as well as the mixture being too rich.

7 If the insulator nose is covered with light-tan to greyish-brown deposits, then the mixture is correct and it is likely that the engine is in good condition.

8 The spark plug gap is of considerable

**HAYNES HiNT**

*It's often difficult to insert spark plugs into their holes without cross-threading them. To avoid this possibility, fit a short piece of rubber hose over the end of the spark plug. The flexible hose acts as a universal joint, to help align the plug with the plug hole. Should the plug begin to cross-thread, the hose will slip on the spark plug, preventing thread damage.*

importance as, if it is too large or too small, the size of the spark and its efficiency will be seriously impaired. For the best results, the spark plug gap should be set in accordance with the Specifications at the beginning of this Chapter.

9 To set the spark plug gap, measure the gap between the electrodes with a feeler blade, and then bend open, or close, the outer plug electrode until the correct gap is achieved **(see illustrations)**. The centre electrode should never be bent, as this may crack the insulation and cause plug failure, if nothing worse.

10 Special spark plug electrode gap adjusting tools are available from most motor accessory shops.

11 Before fitting the new spark plugs, check that the threaded connector sleeves on the top of the plug are tight, and that the plug exterior surfaces and threads are clean.

12 Screw in the spark plugs by hand where possible, then tighten them to the specified torque. Take extra care to enter the plug threads correctly, as the cylinder head is of light alloy construction **(see Haynes Hint)**.

13 On completion, refit the ignition module as described in Chapter 5B.

### 27 Timing belt renewal (1.4 litre Z14XE engines)

Renew the timing belt and tensioner with reference to Chapter 2B.

### 28 Fuel filter renewal

1 The fuel filter is located under the rear of the vehicle **(see illustration)**.

2 Depressurise the fuel system as described in Chapter 4A or 4B.

3 Chock the front wheels, then jack up the rear of the vehicle, and support securely on axle stands (see *Jacking and vehicle support*). On ECO models, unbolt the air guide plates and stone protectors from the underbody.

4 Position a suitable container below the fuel filter, to catch spilt fuel.

5 Disconnect the quick-release fittings and

**28.1 Fuel filter location**

remove the fuel hoses from the fuel filter, noting their locations to ensure correct refitting. A Vauxhall special tool is available to disconnect the hose connectors, but provided care is taken, the connections can be released using a pair of long-nosed pliers, or a similar tool, to depress the retaining tangs. Be prepared for fuel spillage, and take adequate precautions. Vauxhall recommend that the connecting clips of the quick-release connectors are renewed whenever removed.

**6** Lift the retaining tab and push the filter forwards, out of the mounting bracket. Note the orientation of the fuel flow direction arrow.

**7** Fitting the new filter is a reversal of removal, bearing in mind the following points.

  a) *Ensure that the filter is fitted with the flow direction arrow on the filter body pointing in the direction of fuel flow (see illustration).*

  b) *Ensure that the hoses are reconnected to their correct locations, as noted before removal.*

  c) *Before lowering the vehicle to the ground (and refitting the air guide plates on ECO models), run the engine and check for leaks. If leakage is evident, stop the engine immediately and rectify the problem without delay.*

## 29 Automatic transmission fluid renewal

### Draining

**1** This operation is much quicker and more efficient if the vehicle is first taken on a journey of sufficient length to warm the engine/transmission up to normal operating temperature.

**2** Apply the handbrake, then jack up the front of the vehicle and support it on axle stands (see *Jacking and vehicle support*).

**3** Place a suitable container under the drain plug located at the lower right-hand side of the transmission housing.

**4** Wipe clean the area around the drain plug, then unscrew the plug and allow the fluid to drain into the container.

**5** After all the fluid has drained, wipe the drain plug and the sealing washer with a clean rag. Examine the condition of the sealing washer, and renew it if it shows signs of scoring or

**28.7 Ensure that the flow direction arrow points in the direction of the fuel flow**

other damage which may prevent a perfect seal. Clean the area around the drain plug opening, and refit the plug complete with the washer. Tighten the plug to the specified torque and lower the car to the ground.

### Refilling

**6** Refill the transmission through the dipstick tube with the correct quantity and type of fluid, then check the level as follows.

**7** Lower the vehicle to the ground. Note that the vehicle must be parked on level ground for an accurate level check.

**8** If the transmission fluid is cold (ie, if the engine is cold), the level check must be completed with the engine idling, within one minute of the engine being started.

**9** With the engine idling, fully depress the brake pedal, and move the gear selector lever smoothly through all positions, finishing in position P.

**10** With the engine still idling, withdraw the transmission fluid level dipstick (located at the left-hand side of the engine compartment, next to the engine oil level dipstick). Pull up the lever on the top of the dipstick to release it from the tube. Wipe the dipstick clean with a lint-free rag, re-insert it and withdraw it again.

**11** If the transmission fluid was cold at the beginning of the procedure, the fluid level should be on the MIN mark on the side of the dipstick marked +20°C. Note that 0.4 litres of fluid is required to raise the level from the MIN to the MAX mark **(see illustration)**.

**12** If the transmission fluid was at operating temperature at the beginning of the procedure (ie, if the vehicle had been driven for at least 12 miles), the fluid level should be between

**29.11 Automatic transmission fluid level dipstick markings**

*A Markings for fluid at operating temperature*
*B Markings for cold fluid*

the MIN and MAX marks on the side of the dipstick marked +80°C. Note that 0.2 litres of fluid is required to raise the level from the MIN to the MAX mark.

**13** If topping-up is necessary, stop the engine, and top-up with the specified type of fluid through the transmission dipstick tube.

**14** Recheck the level, and refit the dipstick on completion.

## 30 Rear brake shoe, drum and wheel cylinder check

**1** Chock the front wheels, then jack up the rear of the vehicle, and support it securely on axle stands (see *Jacking and vehicle support*).

**2** For a quick check, the thickness of friction material remaining on one of the brake shoes can be observed through the hole in the brake backplate which is exposed by prising out the sealing grommet. If a rod of the same diameter as the specified minimum friction material thickness is placed against the shoe friction material, the amount of wear can be assessed. An electric torch or inspection light will probably be required. If the friction material on any shoe is worn down to the specified minimum thickness or less, all four shoes must be renewed as a set (see Chapter 9).

**3** For a comprehensive check, the brake drum should be removed and cleaned. This will allow the wheel cylinders to be checked, and the condition of the brake drum itself to be fully examined (see Chapter 9).

# Chapter 1  Part B:
# Routine maintenance and servicing – diesel models

## Contents

## Degrees of difficulty

| Easy, suitable for novice with little experience | Fairly easy, suitable for beginner with some experience | Fairly difficult, suitable for competent DIY mechanic | Difficult, suitable for experienced DIY mechanic | Very difficult, suitable for expert DIY or professional |

**Lubricants and fluids**. . . . . . . . . . . . . . . . . . . . . . . . . . . . . . . . . .  Refer to *Weekly checks* on page 0•17

## Capacities

### 1.3 litre models

Engine oil:
  Oil change, including filter . . . . . . . . . . . . . . . . . . . . . . . . . . . . . . .  3.2 litres
  Difference between MAX and MIN dipstick marks. . . . . . . . . . . . . .  1.0 litres
Cooling system. . . . . . . . . . . . . . . . . . . . . . . . . . . . . . . . . . . . . . . .  6.1 litres
Fuel tank . . . . . . . . . . . . . . . . . . . . . . . . . . . . . . . . . . . . . . . . . . . . .  45.0 litres
Manual gearbox . . . . . . . . . . . . . . . . . . . . . . . . . . . . . . . . . . . . . . . .  1.6 litres
Easytronic transmission . . . . . . . . . . . . . . . . . . . . . . . . . . . . . . . . .  1.6 litres

### 1.7 litre models

Engine oil:
  Oil change, including filter . . . . . . . . . . . . . . . . . . . . . . . . . . . . . . .  4.5 litres
  Difference between MAX and MIN dipstick marks. . . . . . . . . . . . . .  1.0 litres
Cooling system. . . . . . . . . . . . . . . . . . . . . . . . . . . . . . . . . . . . . . . .  7.1 litres
Fuel tank:
  Hatchback and Corsavan. . . . . . . . . . . . . . . . . . . . . . . . . . . . . . . .  44.0 litres
  Combo Van. . . . . . . . . . . . . . . . . . . . . . . . . . . . . . . . . . . . . . . . . . .  52.0 litres
Manual gearbox . . . . . . . . . . . . . . . . . . . . . . . . . . . . . . . . . . . . . . . .  1.6 litres

## Cooling system

Antifreeze mixture:
  40% antifreeze . . . . . . . . . . . . . . . . . . . . . . . . . . . . . . . . . . . . . . . . .  Protection down to -28°C
  50% antifreeze . . . . . . . . . . . . . . . . . . . . . . . . . . . . . . . . . . . . . . . . .  Protection down to -40°C

## Suspension and steering

Tyre pressures . . . . . . . . . . . . . . . . . . . . . . . . . . . . . . . . . . . . . . . . .  Refer to end of *Weekly checks* on page 0•17

## Torque wrench settings

| | Nm | lbf ft |
|---|---|---|
| **1.3 litre models** | | |
| Fuel filter housing cover retaining ring | 30 | 22 |
| Oil filter housing cover | 25 | 18 |
| Roadwheel bolts | 110 | 81 |
| Sump drain plug | 20 | 15 |
| **1.7 litre models** | | |
| Balance weight to driveshaft | 10 | 7 |
| Fuel filter housing cover centre bolt | 8 | 6 |
| Oil filter housing cover | 25 | 18 |
| Reversing light switch | 20 | 15 |
| Roadwheel bolts | 110 | 81 |
| Sump drain plug | 78 | 58 |

# Maintenance schedule – diesel models

The maintenance intervals in this manual are provided with the assumption that you, not the dealer, will be carrying out the work. These are the minimum maintenance intervals based on the standard service schedule recommended by the manufacturer for vehicles driven daily. If you wish to keep your vehicle in peak condition at all times, you may wish to perform some of these procedures more often. We encourage frequent maintenance, because it enhances the efficiency, performance and resale value of your vehicle.

If the vehicle is driven in dusty areas, used to tow a trailer, or driven frequently at slow speeds (idling in traffic) or on short journeys, more frequent maintenance intervals are recommended.

When the vehicle is new, it should be serviced by a dealer service department (or other workshop recognised by the vehicle manufacturer as providing the same standard of service) in order to preserve the warranty. The vehicle manufacturer may reject warranty claims if you are unable to prove that servicing has been carried out as and when specified, using only original equipment parts or parts certified to be of equivalent quality.

### Flexible maintenance intervals

Later Corsa models covered by this manual are also capable of operating under the flexible maintenance interval plan known as

Vauxhall ECOService-Flex. Under this flexible maintenance plan, a maximum service interval of 2 years or 30 000 miles can be achieved under ideal conditions. Information on a number of variables such as distance driven, driving cycles, engine operating conditions, coolant temperature and oil temperature are obtained and stored in the engine management ECU. Based on this information, the ECU calculates the remaining distance until the next service is due and displays this distance on the service interval indicator.

The ECOService-Flex plan is entirely dependent on the exclusive use of specially developed 'long-life' engine oils meeting Vauxhall specification GM-LL-B-025. If any other type of oil is used (such as engine oils meeting the conventional ACEA specifications) then the shorter maintenance intervals shown in the following schedule must be adhered to.

As stated earlier, it is our philosophy that frequent maintenance is always the preferred option, however it is up to the individual owner as to the course of action to be adopted.

## Every 250 miles or weekly

☐ Refer to *Weekly checks*

## Every 10 000 miles or 6 months – whichever comes first

☐ Renew the engine oil and filter (Section 3)

**Note:** *Vauxhall recommend that the engine oil and filter are changed every 20 000 miles or 12 months if the vehicle is being operated under the standard service schedule. However, oil and filter changes are good for the engine and we recommend that the oil and filter are renewed more frequently, especially if the vehicle is used on a lot of short journeys.*

## Every 20 000 miles or 12 months – whichever comes first

☐ Check all underbonnet and underbody components, pipes and hoses for leaks (Section 4)
☐ Check the auxiliary drivebelt and tensioner (Section 5)
☐ Check the operation of the horn, all lights, and the wipers and washers (Section 6)
☐ Check the tightness of the roadwheel bolts (Section 7)
☐ Check the condition of the brake pads (renew if necessary), the calipers and discs (Section 8)
☐ Check the operation of the handbrake and adjust if necessary (Section 9)
☐ Check the headlight beam alignment (Section 10)
☐ Check the condition of all brake fluid pipes and hoses (Section 11)
☐ Check the bodywork and underbody for damage and corrosion, and check the condition of the underbody corrosion protection (Section 12)
☐ Check the condition of the exhaust system components (Section 13)
☐ Drain water from the fuel filter (Section 14)

## Every 20 000 miles or 12 months – whichever comes first (continued)

☐ Lubricate all door, bonnet and tailgate hinges and locks (Section 15)
☐ Check the condition of the front suspension and steering components, particularly the rubber gaiters and seals (Section 16)
☐ Check the condition of the rear suspension components (Section 17)
☐ Check the condition of the driveshaft joint gaiters and the driveshaft joints (Section 18)
☐ Carry out a road test (Section 19)
☐ Reset the service interval indicator (Section 20)

## Every 20 000 miles or 2 years – whichever comes first

☐ Renew the fuel filter (Section 21)
☐ Renew the pollen filter (Section 22)

## Every 40 000 miles or 2 years – whichever comes first

☐ Renew the battery for the remote control handset (Section 23)
☐ Renew the brake (and clutch) fluid (Section 24)
☐ Renew the coolant (Section 25)

## Every 40 000 miles or 4 years – whichever comes first

☐ Renew the air cleaner filter element (Section 26)
☐ Check the condition of the rear brake shoes (renew if necessary), the drums and wheel cylinders (Section 27)

## Every 60 000 miles or 6 years – whichever comes first

☐ Renew the timing belt and tensioner – 1.7 litre engines (Section 28)
**Note:** *The normal interval for timing belt renewal, as recommended by Vauxhall, is 100 000 miles or 10 years, however, it is strongly recommended that the interval is reduced to 60 000 miles or 6 years on vehicles which are subject to intensive use, ie, mainly short journeys or a lot of stop-start driving. The actual belt renewal interval is therefore very much up to the individual owner, but bear in mind that severe engine damage will result if the belt breaks.*

## Every 100 000 miles or 10 years – whichever comes first

☐ Check and adjust the valve clearances – 1.7 litre engines (Section 29)

## Underbonnet view of a 1.3 litre model

1 Engine oil filter
2 Engine oil filler cap
3 Air cleaner assembly
4 Hot film mass airflow meter
5 Front suspension strut upper mounting
6 Screen washer fluid reservoir
7 Brake fluid reservoir
8 Engine oil dipstick
9 Fuel filter
10 Battery
11 Coolant expansion tank
12 Fuse/relay box
13 Engine management electronic control unit (ECU)
14 Additional relay box
15 ABS hydraulic modulator

## Front underbody view of a 1.3 litre model

1 Exhaust front pipe
2 Steering track rods
3 Front suspension lower arms
4 Front brake calipers
5 Engine mounting rear torque link
6 Right-hand driveshaft
7 Engine oil drain plug
8 Final drive cover plate
9 Air conditioning compressor
10 Catalytic converter
11 Engine mounting front torque link
12 Front subframe

## Underbonnet view of a 1.7 litre Y17DTL model

1  Engine oil level dipstick
2  Engine oil filler cap
3  Air cleaner assembly
4  Hot film mass airflow
   meter
5  Front suspension strut
   upper mountings
6  Washer fluid reservoir
7  Brake fluid reservoir
8  Engine electronic control
   unit (ECU)
9  Air inlet duct
10 Coolant hoses on heater
   matrix
11 Fuel filter
12 Battery
13 Coolant expansion tank
14 Engine compartment fuse
   and relay box
15 Turbocharger

## Front underbody view of a 1.7 litre Y17DTL model

1  Exhaust front pipe
2  Steering track rods
3  Front suspension lower
   arms
4  Steering gear
5  Engine mounting rear
   torque link
6  Right-hand driveshaft
7  Final drive cover plate
8  Front brake calipers
9  Engine oil drain plug
10 Manual transmission
11 Air conditioning
   compressor
12 Engine mounting front
   torque link
13 Front suspension
   subframe
14 Electric cooling fan

## Rear underbody view

1  Handbrake cable
2  Rear suspension coil springs
3  Exhaust tailpipe and silencer
4  Exhaust heat shield
5  Rear anti-roll bar
6  Rear suspension trailing arms and rear axle
7  Fuel tank

# Maintenance procedures

## 1  General information

1  This Chapter is designed to help the home mechanic maintain his/her vehicle for safety, economy, long life and peak performance.

2  The Chapter contains a master maintenance schedule, followed by sections dealing specifically with each task on the schedule. Visual checks, adjustments, component renewal and other helpful items are included. Refer to the accompanying illustrations of the engine compartment and the underside of the vehicle for the locations of the various components.

3  Servicing of your vehicle in accordance with the mileage/time maintenance schedule and the following sections will provide a planned maintenance programme, which should result in a long and reliable service life. This is a comprehensive plan, so maintaining some items but not others at the specified service intervals will not produce the same results.

4  As you service your vehicle, you will discover that many of the procedures can – and should – be grouped together, because of the particular procedure being performed, or because of the close proximity of two otherwise-unrelated components to one another. For example, if the vehicle is raised for any reason, the exhaust can be inspected at the same time as the suspension and steering components.

5  The first step in this maintenance programme is to prepare yourself before the actual work begins. Read through all the sections relevant to the work to be carried out, then make a list and gather together all the parts and tools required. If a problem is encountered, seek advice from a parts specialist, or a dealer service department.

## 2  Regular maintenance

1  If, from the time the vehicle is new, the routine maintenance schedule is followed closely, and frequent checks are made of fluid levels and high-wear items, as suggested throughout this manual, the engine will be kept in relatively good running condition, and the need for additional work will be minimised.

2  It is possible that there will be times when the engine is running poorly due to the lack of regular maintenance. This is even more likely if a used vehicle, which has not received regular and frequent maintenance checks, is purchased. In such cases, additional work may need to be carried out, outside of the regular maintenance intervals.

3  If engine wear is suspected, a compression test, or leakdown test (refer to Chapter 2C) will provide valuable information regarding the overall performance of the main internal components. Such a test can be used as a basis to decide on the extent of the work to

be carried out. If, for example, a compression test indicates serious internal engine wear, conventional maintenance as described in this Chapter will not greatly improve the performance of the engine, and may prove a waste of time and money, unless extensive overhaul work (Chapter 2D) is carried out first.

4  The following series of operations are those most often required to improve the performance of a generally poor-running engine:

### Primary operations

a) Clean, inspect and test the battery ('Weekly checks').
b) Check all the engine-related fluids ('Weekly checks').
c) Check the condition and tension of the auxiliary drivebelt (Section 5).
d) Check the condition of the air filter, and renew if necessary (Section 26).
e) Renew the fuel filter (Section 21).
f) Check the condition of all hoses, and check for fluid leaks (Section 4).

5  If the above operations do not prove fully effective, carry out the following secondary operations:

### Secondary operations

All items listed under Primary operations, plus the following:
a) Check the charging system (Chapter 5A).
b) Check the preheating system (Chapter 5C).
c) Check the fuel system (Chapter 4D)

3.3 Remove the oil filler cap (arrowed) from the filler tube

3.4 Sump drain plug (arrowed)

# Every 10 000 miles or 6 months

## 3 Engine oil and filter renewal

### 1.3 litre engines

**1** Before starting this procedure, gather together all the necessary tools and materials. Also make sure that you have plenty of clean rags and newspapers handy, to mop-up any spills. Ideally, the engine oil should be warm, as it will drain more easily, and more built-up sludge will be removed with it. Take care not to touch the exhaust or any other hot parts of the engine

 *Frequent oil and filter changes are the most important preventative maintenance procedures which can be undertaken by the DIY owner. As engine oil ages, it becomes diluted and contaminated, which leads to premature engine wear.*

when working under the vehicle. To avoid any possibility of scalding, and to protect yourself from possible skin irritants and other harmful contaminants in used engine oils, it is advisable to wear gloves when carrying out this work.
**2** Firmly apply the handbrake then jack up the front of the vehicle and support it on axle stands (see *Jacking and vehicle support*).
**3** Remove the oil filler cap from the filler tube at the front of the engine **(see illustration)**.
**4** Using a suitable socket and bar, slacken the drain plug about half a turn **(see illustration)**.
**5** Position the draining container under the drain plug, then remove the plug completely. If possible, try to keep the plug pressed into the sump while unscrewing it by hand the last couple of turns **(see Haynes Hint)**.
**6** Allow some time for the oil to drain, noting that it may be necessary to reposition the container as the oil flow slows to a trickle.
**7** Make sure there is a container below the position of the oil filter, which is located on the front, right-hand side of the cylinder block.

*As the drain plug threads release, move it sharply away so the stream of oil issuing from the sump runs into the container, not up your sleeve.*

**8** Undo the nut and two screws and remove the metal heat shield located over the filter housing **(see illustration)**.
**9** Using a large socket, unscrew the cover and remove it from the top of the oil filter housing **(see illustration)**. Lift out the old filter element.
**10** Wipe clean the oil filter cover and the filter housing.

3.8 Undo the nut two screws (arrowed) and remove the metal heat shield located over the filter housing

3.9 Unscrew the cover and remove it from the top of the oil filter housing

3.11a Lubricate the sealing rings of the new filter . . .

3.11b . . . then insert the filter into the housing

3.12a Renew the sealing ring on the oil filter cover . . .

3.12b . . . and lubricate the new sealing ring

3.13 Wipe the drain plug clean and renew the sealing ring

**11** Lubricate the sealing rings of the new filter with clean engine oil, then insert the filter into the housing **(see illustrations)**.

**12** Renew the sealing ring on the oil filter cover, and lubricate the new sealing ring with clean engine oil **(see illustrations)**. Refit the oil filter cover and tighten it to the specified torque. Refit the heat shield over the filter housing.

**13** After all the oil has drained, wipe the drain plug clean and renew the sealing O-ring **(see illustration)**. Clean the area around the drain plug opening, refit the plug and tighten it to the specified torque.

**14** Remove the old oil and all tools from under the vehicle then lower the vehicle to the ground.

**15** Fill the engine through the filler tube, using the correct grade and type of oil (refer to *Weekly Checks* for details of topping-up). Pour in half the specified quantity of oil first, then wait a few minutes for the oil to drain into the sump.

Continue to add oil, a small quantity at a time, until the level is up to the lower mark on the dipstick. Adding approximately a further 1.0 litre will bring the level up to the upper mark on the dipstick.

**16** Start the engine and run it until it reaches normal operating temperature. While the engine is warming-up, check for leaks around the oil filter and the sump drain plug.

**17** Stop the engine, and wait at least five minutes for the oil to settle in the sump once more. With the new oil circulated and the filter now completely full, recheck the level on the dipstick, and add more oil as necessary.

**18** Dispose of the used engine oil and the old filter safely with reference to *General repair procedures* in the Reference Chapter of this manual. Do not discard the old filter with domestic household waste. The facility for waste oil disposal provided by many local council refuse tips generally has a filter receptacle alongside.

### 1.7 litre engines

**19** Before starting this procedure, gather together all the necessary tools and materials. Also make sure that you have plenty of clean rags and newspapers handy, to mop up any spills. Ideally, the engine oil should be warm, as it will drain more easily, and more built-up sludge will be removed with it. Take care not to touch the exhaust or any other hot parts of the engine when working under the vehicle. To avoid any possibility of scalding, and to protect yourself from possible skin irritants and other harmful contaminants in used engine oils, it is advisable to wear gloves when carrying out this work.

**20** Firmly apply the handbrake then jack up the front of the vehicle and support it on axle stands (see *Jacking and vehicle support*). Remove the undertray from under the engine compartment.

**21** Remove the oil filler cap **(see illustration)**.

**22** Using a spanner, or preferably a suitable socket and bar, slacken the drain plug about half a turn **(see illustration)**.

**23** Position the draining container under the drain plug, then remove the plug completely. If possible, try to keep the plug pressed into the sump while unscrewing it by hand the last couple of turns **(see Haynes Hint on previous page)**.

**24** Allow some time for the oil to drain, noting that it may be necessary to reposition the container as the oil flow slows to a trickle.

**25** Make sure there is a container below the position of the oil filter, which is located on the rear, left-hand side of the cylinder block **(see illustration)**.

**26** Using a large socket, unscrew the cover and remove it from the top of the oil filter

3.21 Removing the oil filler cap

3.22 Sump drain plug

3.25 The oil filter is located on the rear of the cylinder block

housing **(see illustrations)**. Lift out the old filter element.

**27** Fit the new filter element to the housing or cover **(see illustration)**.

**28** Renew the sealing rings then refit the oil filter cover and tighten it to the specified torque **(see illustration)**.

**29** After all the oil has drained, wipe the drain plug and the sealing washer with a clean rag. Examine the condition of the sealing washer, and renew it if it shows signs of scoring or other damage which may prevent an oil-tight seal. Clean the area around the drain plug opening, and refit the plug complete with the washer and tighten it to the specified torque.

**30** Remove the old oil and all tools from under the vehicle then lower the vehicle to the ground.

**31** Fill the engine through the filler hole, using the correct grade and type of oil (refer to *Weekly Checks* for details of topping-up). Pour in half the specified quantity of oil first, then wait a few minutes for the oil to drain into the sump. Continue to add oil, a small quantity at a time, until the level is up to the lower mark on the dipstick. Adding approximately a further 1.0 litre will bring the level up to the upper mark on the dipstick.

**32** Start the engine and run it for a few minutes, while checking for leaks around the oil filter seal and the sump drain plug. Note that there may be a delay of a few seconds before the low oil pressure warning light goes out when the engine is first started, as the

**3.26a Unscrew the cover . . .**

**3.26b . . . and remove the filter element**

**3.27 Fitting the element to the cover**

**3.28 Sealing rings on the cover and pin**

oil circulates through the new oil filter and the engine oil galleries before the pressure buildsup.

**33** Stop the engine, and wait a few minutes for the oil to settle in the sump once more.

With the new oil circulated and the filter now completely full, recheck the level on the dipstick, and add more oil as necessary.

**34** Dispose of the used engine oil safely with reference to *General repair procedures*.

# Every 20 000 miles or 12 months

## 4  Hose and fluid leak check

**1** Visually inspect the engine joint faces, gaskets and seals for any signs of water or oil leaks. Pay particular attention to the areas around the camshaft cover, cylinder head, oil filter and sump joint faces. Similarly, check the transmission and (where applicable) the air conditioning compressor for oil leakage. Bear in mind that, over a period of time, some very slight seepage from these areas is to be expected; what you are really looking for is any indication of a serious leak. Should a leak be found, renew the offending gasket or oil seal by referring to the appropriate Chapters in this manual.

**2** Also check the security and condition of all the engine-related pipes and hoses. Ensure that all cable ties or securing clips are in place, and in good condition. Clips which are broken or missing can lead to chafing of the hoses pipes or wiring, which could cause more serious problems in the future.

**3** Carefully check the radiator hoses and heater hoses along their entire length. Renew any hose which is cracked, swollen or deteriorated. Cracks will show up better if the hose is squeezed. Pay close attention to the hose clips that secure the hoses to the

cooling system components. Hose clips can pinch and puncture hoses, resulting in cooling system leaks. If wire-type hose clips are used, it may be a good idea to update them with screw-type clips.

**4** Inspect all the cooling system components (hoses, joint faces, etc) for leaks **(see Haynes Hint)**. Where any problems of this nature are found on system components, renew the component or gasket with reference to Chapter 3.

**5** With the vehicle raised, inspect the petrol tank and filler neck for punctures, cracks and other damage. The connection between the filler neck and tank is especially critical. Sometimes, a rubber filler neck or connecting hose will leak due to loose retaining clamps or deteriorated rubber.

**6** Carefully check all rubber hoses and metal fuel lines leading away from the petrol tank. Check for loose connections, deteriorated hoses, crimped lines and other damage. Pay particular attention to the vent pipes and hoses, which often loop up around the filler neck and can become blocked or crimped. Follow the lines to the front of the vehicle, carefully inspecting them all the way. Renew damaged sections as necessary. Similarly, whilst the vehicle is raised, take the opportunity to inspect all underbody brake fluid pipes and hoses.

**7** From within the engine compartment, check the security of all fuel hose attachments and pipe

unions, and inspect the fuel hoses and vacuum hoses for kinks, chafing and deterioration.

## 5  Auxiliary drivebelt check and renewal

**Note:** *The manufacturers recommend that the tensioner roller is checked and if necessary renewed at the same time as the drivebelt.*

### Checking

**1** The ribbed type auxiliary drivebelt drives the alternator, coolant pump and the air conditioning

*A leak in the cooling system will usually show up as white- or antifreeze-coloured deposits on the area adjoining the leak.*

compressor where applicable. An automatic drivebelt tensioner is fitted, and there is no requirement to check the drivebelt tension.

2 The belt should be inspected along its entire length, and if it is found to be worn, frayed or cracked, it should be renewed as a precaution against breakage in service.

### Renewal

3 Apply the handbrake, then jack up the front of the vehicle and support it on axle stands (see *Jacking and vehicle support*). Remove the right-hand front roadwheel and the wheel arch liner cover for access to the right-hand side of the engine.

4 If the drivebelt is to be re-used, mark it to indicate its normal running direction. Note the run of the drivebelt around the pulleys.

5 Using a spanner on the pulley centre bolt, turn the tensioner clockwise against the spring tension. Hold the tensioner in this position by inserting a suitable locking pin or drill bit through the special hole provided **(see illustration)**.

6 Slip the drivebelt from the pulleys.

7 Locate the new drivebelt on the pulleys in the correct routing. If the drivebelt is being re-used, make sure it is fitted the correct way around.

8 Turn back the tensioner and remove the locking pin/drill bit, then release it, making sure that the drivebelt ribs locate correctly on each of the pulley grooves.

9 Refit the wheel arch liner and roadwheel, and lower the vehicle to the ground.

### 6 Electrical system check

1 Check the operation of all the electrical equipment, ie, lights, direction indicators, horn, etc. Refer to the appropriate sections of Chapter 12 for details if any of the circuits are found to be inoperative.

2 Note that the stop-light switch is described in Chapter 9.

3 Check all accessible wiring connectors, harnesses and retaining clips for security, and for signs of chafing or damage. Rectify any faults found.

### 7 Roadwheel bolt tightness check

1 Where applicable, remove the wheel trims from the wheels.

2 Using a torque wrench on each wheel bolt in turn, ensure that the bolts are tightened to the specified torque.

3 Where applicable, refit the wheel trims on completion, making sure they are fitted correctly.

### 8 Brake pad and disc check

1 With the vehicle on level ground, chock the rear wheels, apply the handbrake, then jack up

**5.5 Lock the tensioner in the released position by inserting a drill bit or similar through the hole provided**

the front of the vehicle and support securely on axle stands; remove the roadwheels (see *Jacking and vehicle support*).

2 Check the thickness of the friction material on each brake pad.

 **HAYNES HINT** *For a quick check, the thickness can be measured through the aperture in the caliper body.*

3 If any pad is worn to the specified minimum thickness or less, all four pads must be renewed (see Chapter 9).

4 The view through the caliper inspection hole gives a rough indication of the state of the brake pads. For a comprehensive check, the brake pads should be removed and cleaned. This will allow the operation of the caliper to be checked, and the condition of the brake disc itself to be fully examined on both sides. Chapter 9 contains a detailed description of how the brake disc should be checked for wear and/or damage.

5 On completion, refit the roadwheels and lower the vehicle to the ground.

### 9 Handbrake operation and adjustment check

1 With the vehicle on a slight slope, apply the handbrake lever by up to 7 clicks of the ratchet, and check that it holds the vehicle stationary, then release the lever and check that there is no resistance to movement of the vehicle.

2 If necessary, adjust the handbrake lever as described in Chapter 9.

### 10 Headlight beam alignment check

1 Accurate adjustment of the headlight beam is only possible using optical beam-setting equipment, and this work should therefore be carried out by a Vauxhall dealer or service station with the necessary facilities.

### 11 Brake fluid pipe and hose check

1 The brake hydraulic system includes a number of metal pipes, which run from the master cylinder to the front and rear brake assemblies, and the hydraulic modulator on models with an anti-lock braking system (ABS). Flexible hoses are fitted between the pipes and the front and rear brake assemblies, to allow for steering and suspension movement.

2 When checking the system, first look for signs of leakage at the pipe or hose unions, then examine the flexible hoses for signs of cracking, chafing or deterioration of the rubber. Bend the hoses sharply between the fingers (but do not actually bend them double, or the casing may be damaged) and check that this does not reveal previously-hidden cracks, cuts or splits. Check that the pipes and hoses are securely fastened in their clips.

3 Carefully working along the length of the metal pipes, look for dents, kinks, damage of any sort, or corrosion. Light corrosion can be polished off, but if the depth of pitting is significant, the pipe must be renewed.

### 12 Bodywork and underbody condition check

**Note:** *This work should be carried out by a Vauxhall dealer in order to validate the vehicle warranty. The work includes a thorough inspection of the vehicle paintwork and underbody for damage and corrosion.*

### Bodywork damage/corrosion

1 Once the car has been washed, and all tar spots and other surface blemishes have been cleaned off, carefully check all paintwork, looking closely for chips or scratches. Pay particular attention to vulnerable areas such as the front panels (bonnet and spoiler), and around the wheel arches. Any damage to the paintwork must be rectified as soon as possible, to comply with the terms of the manufacturer's anti-corrosion warranties; check with a Vauxhall dealer for details.

2 If a chip or light scratch is found which is recent and still free from rust, it can be touched-up using the appropriate touch-up stick which can be obtained from Vauxhall dealers. Any more serious damage, or rusted stone chips, can be repaired as described in Chapter 11, but if damage or corrosion is so severe that a panel must be renewed, seek professional advice as soon as possible.

3 Always check that the door and ventilation opening drain holes and pipes are completely clear, so that water can drain out.

### Corrosion protection

4 The wax-based underbody protective

**13.3 Exhaust mountings**

**14.1 Disconnect the wiring connector (arrowed) from the fuel filter**

**14.4 Fuel filter drain screw (arrowed)**

coating should be inspected annually, preferably just prior to Winter, when the underbody should be washed down as thoroughly as possible without disturbing the protective coating. Any damage to the coating should be repaired using a suitable wax-based sealer. If any of the body panels are disturbed for repair or renewal, do not forget to re-apply the coating. Wax should be injected into door cavities, sills and box sections, to maintain the level of protection provided by the vehicle manufacturer – seek the advice of a Vauxhall dealer.

## 13 Exhaust system check

**1** With the engine cold (at least an hour after the vehicle has been driven), check the complete exhaust system from the engine to the end of the tailpipe. The exhaust system is most easily checked with the vehicle raised on a hoist, or suitably-supported on axle stands, so that the exhaust components are readily visible and accessible (see *Jacking and vehicle support*).
**2** Check the exhaust pipes and connections for evidence of leaks, severe corrosion and damage. Make sure that all brackets and mountings are in good condition, and that all relevant nuts and bolts are tight. Leakage at any of the joints or in other parts of the system will usually show up as a black sooty stain in the vicinity of the leak.
**3** Rattles and other noises can often be traced to the exhaust system, especially the brackets and mountings **(see illustration)**. Try to move the pipes and silencers. If the components are able to come into contact with the body or suspension parts, secure the system with new mountings. Otherwise separate the joints (if possible) and twist the pipes as necessary to provide additional clearance.

## 14 Fuel filter water draining

**Caution: Before starting any work on the fuel filter, wipe clean the filter assembly**

*and the area around it; it is essential that no dirt or other foreign matter is allowed into the system. Obtain a suitable container into which the filter can be drained and place rags or similar material under the filter assembly to catch any spillages. Do not allow diesel fuel to contaminate components such as the starter motor, the coolant hoses and engine mountings, and any wiring.*

**1** The fuel filter is located on the left-hand side of the bulkhead at the rear of the engine compartment, next to the coolant expansion tank. First, disconnect the wiring from the fuel filter cover **(see illustration)**.
**2** Using a screwdriver inserted from the right-hand side, depress the retaining clip and lift the filter from the crash box
**3** In addition to taking the precautions noted above to catch any fuel spillages, connect a tube to the drain screw on the base of the fuel filter. Place the other end of the tube in a clean jar or can.
**4** Loosen the drain screw approximately one complete turn and allow the filter to drain until clean fuel, free of dirt or water, emerges from the tube (approximately 100 cc is usually sufficient) **(see illustration)**.
**5** Tighten the drain screw securely and remove the drain tube.
**6** Insert the filter in the crash box making sure that the retaining clip engages.
**7** Reconnect the wiring.
**8** On completion, dispose of the drained fuel safely. Check all disturbed components to ensure that there are no leaks (of air or fuel) when the engine is restarted.

## 15 Hinge and lock lubrication

**1** Work around the vehicle and lubricate the hinges of the bonnet, doors and tailgate with a light machine oil.
**2** Lightly lubricate the bonnet release mechanism and exposed section of inner cable with a smear of grease.
**3** Check the security and operation of all hinges, latches and locks, adjusting them where required (see Chapter 11). Check the operation of the central locking system.

**4** Check the condition and operation of the tailgate struts, renewing them both if either is leaking or no longer able to support the tailgate securely when raised.

## 16 Front suspension and steering check

**1** Apply the handbrake, then raise the front of the vehicle and securely support it on axle stands (see *Jacking and vehicle support*).
**2** Inspect the balljoint dust covers and the steering gear gaiters for splits, chafing or deterioration.
**3** Any wear of these components will cause loss of lubricant, and may allow water to enter the components, resulting in rapid deterioration of the balljoints or steering gear.
**4** Grasp each roadwheel at the 12 o'clock and 6 o'clock positions, and try to rock it **(see illustration)**. Very slight free play may be felt, but if the movement is appreciable, further investigation is necessary to determine the source. Continue rocking the wheel while an assistant depresses the footbrake. If the movement is now eliminated or significantly reduced, it is likely that the hub bearings are at fault. If the free play is still evident with the footbrake depressed, then there is wear in the suspension joints or mountings.
**5** Now grasp each wheel at the 9 o'clock and 3 o'clock positions, and try to rock it as before. Any movement felt now may again be caused by wear in the hub bearings or the steering track rod end balljoints. If the track

**16.4 Check for wear in the hub bearings by grasping the wheel and trying to rock it**

**18.1 Check the condition of the driveshaft gaiters (1) and retaining clips (2)**

rod end balljoint is worn, the visual movement will be obvious.

6 Using a large screwdriver or flat bar, check for wear in the suspension mounting bushes by levering between the relevant suspension component and its attachment point. Some movement is to be expected, as the mountings are made of rubber, but excessive wear should be obvious. Also check the condition of any visible rubber bushes, looking for splits, cracks or contamination of the rubber.

7 Check for any signs of fluid leakage around the suspension strut/shock absorber bodies, or from the rubber gaiters around the piston rods. Should any fluid be noticed, the suspension strut/shock absorber is defective internally, and should be renewed. **Note:** *Suspension struts/shock absorbers should always be renewed in pairs on the same axle.*

8 With the vehicle standing on its wheels, have an assistant turn the steering wheel back-and-forth about an eighth of a turn each way. There should be very little, if any, lost movement between the steering wheel and roadwheels. If this is not the case, closely observe the joints and mountings previously described, but in addition check the steering column rubber coupling for wear, and also check the steering gear itself.

9 The efficiency of each suspension strut/shock absorber may be checked by bouncing the vehicle at each corner. Generally speaking, the body will return to its normal position and stop after being depressed. If it rises and returns on a rebound, the suspension strut/shock absorber is probably suspect. Also examine the suspension strut/shock absorber upper and lower mountings for any signs of wear.

## 17 Rear suspension check

1 Chock the front wheels, then jack up the rear of the vehicle and support securely on axle stands (see *Jacking and vehicle support*).
2 Inspect the rear suspension components for any signs of obvious wear or damage. Pay particular attention to the rubber mounting bushes, and renew if necessary (see Chapter 10).

3 Grasp each roadwheel at the 12 o'clock and 6 o'clock positions **(see illustration 16.4)**, and try to rock it. Any excess movement indicates incorrect adjustment or wear in the wheel bearings. Wear may also be accompanied by a rumbling sound when the wheel is spun, or a noticeable roughness if the wheel is turned slowly. The wheel bearing can be renewed as described in Chapter 10.
4 Check the rear shock absorbers in a similar manner to that described in Section 16 for the front shock absorbers.

## 18 Driveshaft check

1 With the vehicle raised and securely supported on stands, turn the steering onto full-lock, then slowly rotate each front roadwheel. Inspect the condition of the outer constant velocity (CV) joint rubber gaiters **(see illustration)**, while squeezing the gaiters to open out the folds. Check for signs of cracking, splits or deterioration of the rubber, which may allow the grease to escape and lead to water and grit entering the joint. Also check the security and condition of the retaining clips. Repeat these checks on the inner CV joints. If any damage or deterioration is found, the gaiters should be renewed as described in Chapter 8.
2 At the same time, check the general condition of the CV joints themselves by first holding the driveshaft and attempting to rotate the wheel. Repeat this check by holding the inner joint and attempting to rotate the driveshaft. Any appreciable movement indicates wear in the joints, wear in the driveshaft splines, or a loose front hub nut.

## 19 Road test

### Instruments and electrical equipment

1 Check the operation of all instruments and electrical equipment.
2 Make sure that all instruments read correctly, and switch on all electrical equipment in turn, to check that it functions properly.

### Steering and suspension

3 Check for any abnormalities in the steering, suspension, handling or road 'feel'.
4 Drive the vehicle, and check that there are no unusual vibrations or noises.
5 Check that the steering feels positive, with no excessive 'sloppiness', or roughness, and check for any suspension noises when cornering and driving over bumps.

### Drivetrain

6 Check the performance of the engine, clutch (where applicable), gearbox and driveshafts.

7 Listen for any unusual noises from the engine, clutch and gearbox.
8 Make sure that the engine runs smoothly when idling, and that there is no hesitation when accelerating.
9 Check that the clutch action is smooth and progressive, that the drive is taken up smoothly, and that the pedal travel is not excessive. Also listen for any noises when the clutch pedal is depressed.
10 Check that all gears can be engaged smoothly without noise, and that the gear lever action is smooth and not abnormally vague or 'notchy'.
11 Listen for a metallic clicking sound from the front of the vehicle, as the vehicle is driven slowly in a circle with the steering on full-lock. Carry out this check in both directions. If a clicking noise is heard, this indicates wear in a driveshaft joint, in which case renew the joint if necessary (see Chapter 8).

### Braking system

12 Make sure that the vehicle does not pull to one side when braking, and that the wheels do not lock when braking hard.
13 Check that there is no vibration through the steering when braking.
14 Check that the handbrake operates correctly without excessive movement of the lever, and that it holds the vehicle stationary on a slope.
15 Test the operation of the brake servo unit as follows. With the engine off, depress the footbrake four or five times to exhaust the vacuum. Hold the brake pedal depressed, then start the engine. As the engine starts, there should be a noticeable 'give' in the brake pedal as vacuum builds-up. Allow the engine to run for at least two minutes, and then switch it off. If the brake pedal is depressed now, it should be possible to detect a hiss from the servo as the pedal is depressed. After about four or five applications, no further hissing should be heard, and the pedal should feel considerably harder.

## 20 Service interval indicator reset

### Models up to September 2003

1 With the ignition switched off, depress and hold the reset button located on the instrument panel.
2 Switch on the ignition and press and hold the reset button for two more seconds at least. The InSP indicator should flash for two seconds, after which the text '____' should appear before releasing the reset button. When the button is released, the odometer or clock will appear again.

### Models from October 2003

3 With the ignition switched off, depress and hold the reset button located on the instrument

panel. After approximately 3 seconds the message 'InSP 0' will appear. Keep the reset button depressed and also depress the brake pedal.

**4** Switch on the ignition, with the reset button and brake pedal still depressed, and 'InSP - - - -' will appear, flashing, in the display. Keep the reset button and brake pedal depressed until the display changes.

**5** After approximately 10 seconds the display will change to show the maximum mileage before the next required service. Release the reset button and the brake pedal. When the button and brake pedal are released, the odometer or clock will appear again.

**6** This procedure resets the service interval indicator back to the ECOService-Flex, 2 years or 30 000 miles flexible maintenance interval. If the standard maintenance schedule described in this Chapter is being used, then the interval until the next service, which will be shown on the display, is irrelevant. If it is wished to have the service interval indicator altered to show the standard maintenance intervals described in this Chapter, it will be necessary to have the system reprogrammed using dedicated Vauxhall diagnostic equipment.

# Every 20 000 miles or 2 years

## 21 Fuel filter renewal

### 1.3 litre engines

*Caution: Before starting any work on the fuel filter, wipe clean the filter assembly and the area around it; it is essential that no dirt or other foreign matter is allowed into the system. Obtain a suitable container into which the filter can be drained and place rags or similar material under the filter assembly to catch any spillages. Do not allow diesel fuel to contaminate* *components such as the starter motor, the coolant hoses and engine mountings, and any wiring.*

**Note:** *Vauxhall special tool EN-46784-010, or a suitable alternative will be required to unscrew the filter housing cover retaining ring.*

**1** Disconnect the battery negative terminal (refer to *Disconnecting the battery* in the Reference Chapter).

**2** Disconnect the wiring connector from the fuel filter cover **(see illustration 14.1)**.

**3** Detach the three fuel hose quick-release connectors and remove the hoses from the fuel filter housing and cover. A Vauxhall special tool (KM-796-A) is available to disconnect the hose connectors, but provided care is taken, the connections can be released using two screwdrivers, a pair of long-nosed pliers, or similar, to depress the retaining tangs **(see illustrations)**. Suitably cover or plug the open hose connections to prevent dirt entry.

**4** Using a screwdriver inserted from the right-hand side, depress the retaining clip and lift the filter housing from the crash box **(see illustration)**.

**5** Unclip the expansion tank coolant hose and the wiring harness from the fuel filter crash box, and disconnect the harness connector **(see illustrations)**.

**6** Release the retaining clip, lift the coolant expansion tank from its location and place it to one side **(see illustration)**.

**7** Unscrew the outer retaining nut, slacken the

**21.3a Depress the retaining tangs of the quick-release fittings . . .**

**21.3b . . . and remove the three hoses from the fuel filter housing and cover**

**21.4 Depress the retaining clip and lift the filter housing from the crash box**

**21.5a Unclip the expansion tank coolant hose and the wiring harness from the crash box . . .**

**21.5b . . . and disconnect the harness connector**

**21.6 Release the retaining clip and lift the expansion tank from its location**

**21.7a Unscrew the outer retaining nut (arrowed) and slacken the inner nut . . .**

**21.7b . . . then remove the crash box from the bulkhead**

**21.9a Using a home-made tool to slacken the filter housing cover retaining ring**

**21.9b Once the retaining ring has been slackened, unscrew it from the filter housing**

**21.10a Lift the cover together with the filter element from the housing . . .**

**21.10b . . . and recover the O-ring seal**

inner nut and remove the crash box from the bulkhead **(see illustrations)**.

**8** Position the crash box in a vice and tighten the vice just sufficiently to prevent the crash box from rotating.

**9** Refit the fuel filter housing to the crash

**21.11 Turn the filter element anti-clockwise to release it from the cover**

box, then unscrew the filter housing cover retaining ring using the Vauxhall special tool or a suitable alternative **(see illustrations)**.

**10** Lift the cover together with the filter element from the housing and recover the O-ring seal **(see illustrations)**.

**21.13a Align the arrow stamped on the new filter element . . .**

**11** Turn the filter element approximately 50° anti-clockwise to release it from the cover **(see illustration)**.

**12** Empty the fuel from the filter housing, then thoroughly clean the housing and cover with a lint-free cloth.

**13** Align the arrow on the new filter element with the corresponding arrow on the cover then push the filter onto the cover until it locks in position **(see illustrations)**.

**14** Locate a new O-ring seal on the filter housing, then fit the element and cover to the housing **(see illustrations)**.

**15** Lubricate the threads of the retaining ring then screw the ring onto the housing. Tighten the retaining ring to the specified torque using the special tool or alternative.

**16** Remove the filter assembly from the crash box and remove the crash box from the vice.

**17** Refit the crash box to the car and clip the expansion tank back into position.

**21.13b . . . with the corresponding arrow stamped on the cover then push the filter onto the cover**

**21.14a Locate a new O-ring seal on the filter housing . . .**

**21.14b . . . then fit the element and cover to the housing**

**18** Reconnect the wiring connector, then secure the harness and coolant hose in position on the crash box.

**19** Insert the filter assembly in the crash box, making sure that the retaining clip engages. Reconnect the fuel hoses and the wiring connector.

**20** On completion, dispose of the drained fuel safely. Check all disturbed components to ensure that there are no leaks (of air or fuel) when the engine is restarted.

**21** Reconnect the battery, then start the engine and bleed the fuel system as described in Chapter 4C.

### 1.7 litre engines

**22** Completely drain the fuel filter with reference to Section 14.

**23** With the filter body upright in a suitable container, undo the centre screw, and remove the lid from the filter body **(see illustration)**. Note the position of the cover in relation to the body to ensure correct refitting.

**24** Remove the upper seal, filter element, spring and lower seal **(see illustrations)**. Discard the seals as a new ones must be fitted.

**25** Empty the fuel from the filter body and dispose of it safely.

**26** Wipe clean the filter body and lid.

**27** Fit the lower seal and spring inside the housing.

**28** Insert the new filter element, then if possible fill the filter body with fresh fuel in order to assist the self-purging process. Ideally the fuel level should be just below the rim of the body.

**29** Refit the cover to the housing together with a new upper seal, then refit the centre

**21.23  Remove the cover . . .**

bolt and tighten it to the specified torque. **Do not** overtighten the cover screw.

**30** Refit the fuel filter with reference to Section 14.

**31** Start the engine and bleed the fuel system as described in Chapter 4D.

### 22  Pollen filter renewal

**1** Peel the bonnet seal off the engine compartment bulkhead, and remove it from the vehicle **(see illustration)**.

**2** Lift the brake fluid reservoir cover, and remove the battery wiring harness cover from the water deflector **(see illustration)**.

**3** Undo the retaining screw, then unclip the battery wiring harness from the water deflector **(see illustrations)**.

**4** Lift the water deflector, then release the two retaining clips and lift the pollen filter out from

**21.24a . . . upper seal . . .**

**21.24b . . . and filter element**

its housing, noting which way round it is fitted **(see illustrations)**.

**5** Wipe clean the filter housing and install the new filter, making sure it is the correct way up. Ensure that the filter is correctly seated, and secure it in position with the retaining clips.

**6** Refitting is the reverse of the removal procedure.

**22.1  Peel the bonnet seal off the engine compartment bulkhead**

**22.2  Remove the battery wiring harness cover from the water deflector**

**22.3a  Undo the retaining screw . . .**

**22.3b . . . then unclip the battery wiring harness from the water deflector**

**22.4a  Release the two retaining clips . . .**

**22.4b . . . and lift the pollen filter from its housing**

**23.1a Prise the key section away . . .**

**23.1b . . . from the remote control . . .**

**23.1c . . . and open the battery cover**

# Every 40 000 miles or 2 years

## 23 Remote control battery renewal

**Note:** *The following procedure must be performed within 3 minutes, otherwise the remote control unit will have to be reprogrammed.*

**1** Using a screwdriver, prise the key section from the remote control unit. Then prise the battery cover from the remote control unit **(see illustrations)**.

**2** Note how the battery is fitted, then carefully remove it from the contacts.

**3** Fit the new battery and refit the cover making sure that it clips fully onto the base. Refit the key section.

## 24 Brake and clutch fluid renewal

**Note:** *It is not possible for the home mechanic to bleed the clutch hydraulic system on Easytronic models.*

⚠️ *Warning: Hydraulic fluid can harm your eyes and damage painted surfaces, so use extreme caution when handling and pouring it. Do not use fluid that has been standing open for some time, as it absorbs moisture from the air. Excess moisture can cause a dangerous loss of braking effectiveness.*

**1** The procedure is similar to that for the bleeding of the hydraulic system as described in Chapters 9 (brake) and 6 (clutch).

**2** Working as described in Chapter 9, open the first bleed screw in the sequence, and pump the brake pedal gently until nearly all the old fluid has been emptied from the master cylinder reservoir. Top-up to the MAX level with new fluid, and continue pumping until only the new fluid remains in the reservoir, and new fluid can be seen emerging from the bleed screw. Tighten the screw, and top the reservoir level up to the MAX level line.

**HAYNES HINT** *Old hydraulic fluid is invariably much darker in colour than new fluid, making it easy to distinguish the two.*

**3** Work through all the remaining bleed screws in the sequence until new fluid can be seen at all of them. Be careful to keep the master cylinder reservoir topped-up to above the MIN level at all times, or air may enter the system and greatly increase the length of the task.

**4** When the operation is complete, check that all bleed screws are securely tightened, and that their dust caps are refitted. Wash off all traces of spilt fluid, and recheck the master cylinder reservoir fluid level.

**5** Check the operation of the brakes before taking the car on the road.

**6** Similarly, bleed the clutch hydraulic system with reference to Chapter 6.

## 25 Coolant renewal

**Note:** *Vauxhall do not specify renewal intervals for the antifreeze mixture, as the mixture used to fill the system when the vehicle is new is designed to last the lifetime of the vehicle. However, it is strongly recommended that the coolant is renewed at the intervals specified in the 'Maintenance schedule', as a precaution against possible engine corrosion problems. This is particularly advisable if the coolant has been renewed using an antifreeze other than that specified by Vauxhall. With many antifreeze types, the corrosion inhibitors become progressively less effective with age. It is up to the individual owner whether or not to follow this advice.*

⚠️ *Warning: Wait until the engine is cold before starting this procedure. Do not allow antifreeze to come in contact with your skin, or with the painted surfaces of the vehicle. Rinse off spills immediately with plenty of water.*

*Never leave antifreeze lying around in an open container, or in a puddle on the driveway or garage floor. Children and pets are attracted by its sweet smell, but antifreeze is fatal if ingested.*

### Cooling system draining

**1** To drain the cooling system, first cover the expansion tank cap with a wad of rag, and slowly turn the cap anti-clockwise to relieve the pressure in the cooling system (a hissing sound will normally be heard). Wait until any pressure remaining in the system is released, then continue to turn the cap until it can be removed.

**2** Where necessary, remove the splash guard from under the radiator and engine.

**3** The coolant drain plug is located at the bottom of the radiator end tank. Position a container beneath the radiator then unscrew the drain plug and allow the coolant to drain.

**4** As no cylinder block drain plug is fitted, it is not possible to drain all of the coolant. Due consideration must be made for this when refilling the system, in order to maintain the correct concentration of antifreeze.

**5** If the coolant has been drained for a reason other than renewal, then provided it is clean and less than two years old, it can be re-used.

### Cooling system flushing

**6** If coolant renewal has been neglected, or if the antifreeze mixture has become diluted, then in time, the cooling system may gradually lose efficiency, as the coolant passages become restricted due to rust, scale deposits, and other sediment. The cooling system efficiency can be restored by flushing the system clean.

**7** The radiator should be flushed independently of the engine, to avoid unnecessary contamination.

**8** To flush the radiator, disconnect the top and bottom hoses at the radiator, then insert a garden hose into the radiator top inlet. Direct a flow of clean water through the radiator, and continue flushing until clean water emerges from the radiator bottom outlet. If after a reasonable period the water still does not run clear, the radiator can be flushed with a good proprietary cleaning agent. It is important that the cleaning agent manufacturer's instructions are followed carefully. If the contamination is particularly bad, insert the hose in the radiator bottom outlet, and flush the radiator in the reverse direction ('reverse-flushing').

9 To flush the engine block, the thermostat must be removed, because it will be shut, and would otherwise prevent the flow of water around the engine. The thermostat can be removed as described in Chapter 3. Take care not to introduce dirt or debris into the system if this approach is used.

10 With the radiator top and bottom hoses disconnected from the radiator, insert a hose into the top hose. Direct a clean flow of water through the engine, and continue flushing until clean water emerges from the radiator bottom hose.

11 On completion of flushing, refit the thermostat with reference to Chapter 3, and reconnect the hoses.

### Cooling system filling

12 Before attempting to fill the cooling system, make sure that all hoses and clips are in good condition, and that the clips are tight. Note that an antifreeze mixture must be used all year round, to prevent corrosion of the alloy engine components.

13 Remove the expansion tank cap, and fill the system by slowly pouring the coolant into the expansion tank to prevent airlocks from forming.

14 If the coolant is being renewed, begin by pouring in a couple of litres of water, followed by the correct quantity of undiluted antifreeze, then top-up with more water.

15 Top-up the coolant level to the KALT (or COLD) mark on the expansion tank, then refit the expansion tank cap.

16 Start the engine and run it until it reaches normal operating temperature, then stop the engine and allow it to cool.

17 Check for leaks, particularly around disturbed components. Check the coolant level in the expansion tank, and top-up if necessary. Note that the system must be cold before an accurate level is indicated in the expansion tank. If the expansion tank cap is removed while the engine is still warm, cover the cap with a thick cloth, and unscrew the cap slowly to gradually relieve the system pressure (a hissing sound will normally be heard). Wait until any pressure remaining in the system is released, then continue to turn the cap until it can be removed.

### Antifreeze mixture

18 Always use an ethylene-glycol based antifreeze which is suitable for use in mixed-metal cooling systems. The quantity of antifreeze and levels of protection are indicated in the Specifications.

19 Before adding antifreeze, the cooling system should be completely drained, preferably flushed, and all hoses and clips checked for condition and security.

20 After filling with antifreeze, a label should be attached to the radiator or expansion tank, stating the type and concentration of antifreeze used, and the date installed. Any subsequent topping-up should be made with the same type and concentration of antifreeze.

*Caution: Do not use engine antifreeze in the windscreen/tailgate washer system, as it will cause damage to the vehicle paintwork. A screenwash should be added to the washer system in the quantities recommended on the bottle.*

# Every 40 000 miles or 4 years

### 26 Air cleaner filter element renewal

1 The air cleaner is located in the front right-hand corner of the engine compartment.

2 Disconnect the wiring connector, then loosen the clip and detach the hot film mass airflow meter from the air cleaner cover **(see illustration)**.

3 Undo the screws and lift the cover from the air cleaner **(see illustrations)**.

4 Lift out the element **(see illustration)**.

5 Wipe out the casing and the cover.

6 Fit the new filter, noting that the rubber locating flange should be uppermost, and secure the cover with the screws.

7 Refit the hot film mass airflow meter to the cover and tighten the clip. Reconnect the wiring connector.

### 27 Rear brake shoe, drum and wheel cylinder check

1 Chock the front wheels, then jack up the rear of the vehicle, and support it securely on axle stands (see *Jacking and vehicle support*).

2 For a quick check, the thickness of friction

26.2 Detach the hot film mass airflow meter . . .

26.3a . . . then undo the screws . . .

26.3b . . . lift off the cover . . .

26.4 . . . and lift out the element

material remaining on one of the brake shoes can be observed through the hole in the brake backplate which is exposed by prising out the sealing grommet. If a rod of the same diameter as the specified minimum friction material thickness is placed against the shoe friction material, the amount of wear can be assessed. An electric torch or inspection light will probably be required. If the friction material on any shoe is worn down to the specified minimum thickness or less, all four shoes must be renewed as a set (see Chapter 9).

3 For a comprehensive check, the brake drum should be removed and cleaned. This will allow the wheel cylinders to be checked, and the condition of the brake drum itself to be fully examined (see Chapter 9).

## 28 Timing belt and tensioner renewal (1.7 litre engines)

Refer to Chapter 2D.

## 29 Valve clearance check and adjustment (1.7 litre engines)

Refer to Chapter 2D.

# Chapter 2  Part A:
# 1.0, 1.2 and 1.4 litre (Z14XEP) petrol engine in-car repair procedures

## Contents

## Degrees of difficulty

| Easy, suitable for novice with little experience | Fairly easy, suitable for beginner with some experience | Fairly difficult, suitable for competent DIY mechanic | Difficult, suitable for experienced DIY mechanic | Very difficult, suitable for expert DIY or professional |
|---|---|---|---|---|

## Specifications

### General

Engine type:

| | |
|---|---|
| 1.0 litre engine | Three-cylinder, in-line, water-cooled. Double overhead camshafts, chain-driven, acting on rocker arms and hydraulic valve lifters |
| 1.2 and 1.4 litre engines | Four-cylinder, in-line, water-cooled. Double overhead camshafts, chain-driven, acting on rocker arms and hydraulic valve lifters |

Manufacturer's engine codes*:

| | |
|---|---|
| 1.0 litre engine | Z10XE, Z10XE-ECO and Z10XEP |
| 1.2 litre engine | Z12XE and Z12XEP |
| 1.4 litre engine | Z14XEP |

Bore:

| | |
|---|---|
| Z10XEP, Z12XEP and Z14XEP engines | 73.40 mm |
| Z10XE, Z10XE-ECO and Z12XE engines | 72.5 mm |

Stroke:

| | |
|---|---|
| Z10XE, Z10XE-ECO and Z10XP engines | 78.60 mm |
| Z12XE and Z12XEP engines. | 72.60 mm |
| Z14XEP engine | 80.60 mm |

Capacity:

| | |
|---|---|
| Z10XE and Z10XE-ECO engines | 973 cc |
| Z10XEP engine | 998 cc |
| Z12XE engine | 1199 cc |
| Z12XEP engine | 1229 cc |
| Z14XEP engine | 1364 cc |

Firing order:

| | |
|---|---|
| Z10XE, Z10XE-ECO and Z10XEP engines | 1-2-3 (No 1 cylinder at timing chain end of engine) |
| All other engines | 1-3-4-2 (No 1 cylinder at timing chain end of engine) |
| Direction of crankshaft rotation | Clockwise (viewed from timing chain end of engine) |

Compression ratio:

| | |
|---|---|
| Z10XE, Z10XE-ECO and Z12XE engines | 10.1:1 |
| All other engines | 10.5:1 |

\* For details of engine code location, see 'Vehicle identification' in the Reference Chapter.

### Lubrication system

| | |
|---|---|
| Minimum oil pressure at 80°C | 1.5 bars at idle speed |
| Oil pump type | Gear-type, driven directly from crankshaft |
| Gear-to-housing clearance (endfloat) | 0.020 to 0.065 mm |

## Flywheel

Maximum permissible lateral run-out of starter ring gear . . . . . . . . . .   0.50 mm
Refinishing limit (maximum depth of material which may be
  removed from clutch friction surface). . . . . . . . . . . . . . . . . . . . . .   0.30 mm

## Torque wrench settings

| | Nm | lbf ft |
|---|---|---|
| Air conditioning compressor to cylinder block. . . . . . . . . . . . . . . . . . | 20 | 15 |
| Auxiliary drivebelt tensioner to cylinder block: | | |
|   M8 bolt . . . . . . . . . . . . . . . . . . . . . . . . . . . . . . . . . . . . . . . . | 20 | 15 |
|   M10 bolt . . . . . . . . . . . . . . . . . . . . . . . . . . . . . . . . . . . . . . . | 55 | 41 |
| Big-end bearing cap bolts*: | | |
|   M6 bolts: | | |
|     Stage 1 . . . . . . . . . . . . . . . . . . . . . . . . . . . . . . . . . . . . . | 10 | 7 |
|     Stage 2 . . . . . . . . . . . . . . . . . . . . . . . . . . . . . . . . . . . . . | Angle-tighten a further 60° | |
|     Stage 3 . . . . . . . . . . . . . . . . . . . . . . . . . . . . . . . . . . . . . | Angle-tighten a further 15° | |
|   M6.5 bolts (marked RIBE from engine number 19P13554): | | |
|     Stage 1 . . . . . . . . . . . . . . . . . . . . . . . . . . . . . . . . . . . . . | 13 | 10 |
|     Stage 2 . . . . . . . . . . . . . . . . . . . . . . . . . . . . . . . . . . . . . | Angle-tighten a further 60° | |
|     Stage 3 . . . . . . . . . . . . . . . . . . . . . . . . . . . . . . . . . . . . . | Angle-tighten a further 15° | |
| Camshaft bearing cap bolts. . . . . . . . . . . . . . . . . . . . . . . . . . . . | 8 | 6 |
| Camshaft sprocket bolt*: | | |
|   Stage 1 . . . . . . . . . . . . . . . . . . . . . . . . . . . . . . . . . . . . . . . | 50 | 37 |
|   Stage 2 . . . . . . . . . . . . . . . . . . . . . . . . . . . . . . . . . . . . . . . | Angle-tighten a further 60° | |
| Catalytic converter support bracket bolts . . . . . . . . . . . . . . . . . . . | 20 | 15 |
| Catalytic converter-to-exhaust manifold nuts . . . . . . . . . . . . . . . . . | 35 | 26 |
| Coolant pump blanking plug . . . . . . . . . . . . . . . . . . . . . . . . . . . . | 15 | 11 |
| Coolant pump bolts: | | |
|   Petrol engines. . . . . . . . . . . . . . . . . . . . . . . . . . . . . . . . . . . | 8 | 6 |
| Coolant pump cover bolts . . . . . . . . . . . . . . . . . . . . . . . . . . . . . | 8 | 6 |
| Coolant pump pulley bolts . . . . . . . . . . . . . . . . . . . . . . . . . . . . . | 20 | 15 |
| Crankshaft pulley hub-to-crankshaft bolt*: | | |
|   Stage 1 . . . . . . . . . . . . . . . . . . . . . . . . . . . . . . . . . . . . . . . | 150 | 111 |
|   Stage 2 . . . . . . . . . . . . . . . . . . . . . . . . . . . . . . . . . . . . . . . | Angle-tighten a further 45° | |
| Cylinder block baseplate to cylinder block*: | | |
|   M6 bolts: | | |
|     Stage 1 . . . . . . . . . . . . . . . . . . . . . . . . . . . . . . . . . . . . . | 10 | 7 |
|     Stage 2 . . . . . . . . . . . . . . . . . . . . . . . . . . . . . . . . . . . . . | Angle-tighten a further 60° | |
|   M8 bolts: | | |
|     Stage 1 . . . . . . . . . . . . . . . . . . . . . . . . . . . . . . . . . . . . . | 25 | 18 |
|     Stage 2 . . . . . . . . . . . . . . . . . . . . . . . . . . . . . . . . . . . . . | Angle-tighten a further 60° | |
| Cylinder block closure bolt (for TDC setting tool) . . . . . . . . . . . . . . | 60 | 44 |
| Cylinder head bolts*: | | |
|   Stage 1 . . . . . . . . . . . . . . . . . . . . . . . . . . . . . . . . . . . . . . . | 25 | 18 |
|   Stage 2 . . . . . . . . . . . . . . . . . . . . . . . . . . . . . . . . . . . . . . . | Angle-tighten a further 60° | |
|   Stage 3 . . . . . . . . . . . . . . . . . . . . . . . . . . . . . . . . . . . . . . . | Angle-tighten a further 60° | |
|   Stage 4 . . . . . . . . . . . . . . . . . . . . . . . . . . . . . . . . . . . . . . . | Angle-tighten a further 60° | |
| Engine mountings: | | |
|   Left-hand: | | |
|     Mounting-to-body bolts . . . . . . . . . . . . . . . . . . . . . . . . . . . | 25 | 18 |
|     Mounting bracket-to-transmission bracket . . . . . . . . . . . . . . . | 80 | 59 |
|     Rubber mounting through-bolt: | | |
|       Stage 1 . . . . . . . . . . . . . . . . . . . . . . . . . . . . . . . . . . | 80 | 59 |
|       Stage 2 . . . . . . . . . . . . . . . . . . . . . . . . . . . . . . . . . . | Angle-tighten a further 45° | |
|       Stage 3 . . . . . . . . . . . . . . . . . . . . . . . . . . . . . . . . . . | Angle-tighten a further 15° | |
|     Transmission bracket-to-transmission . . . . . . . . . . . . . . . . . . | 60 | 44 |
|   Rear mounting/torque link . . . . . . . . . . . . . . . . . . . . . . . . . . | 80 | 59 |
|   Rear mounting/torque link bracket to transmission*: | | |
|     Stage 1 . . . . . . . . . . . . . . . . . . . . . . . . . . . . . . . . . . . . . | 80 | 59 |
|     Stage 2 . . . . . . . . . . . . . . . . . . . . . . . . . . . . . . . . . . . . . | Angle-tighten a further 45° | |
|   Right-hand: | | |
|     Engine bracket-to-engine bolts . . . . . . . . . . . . . . . . . . . . . . | 60 | 44 |
|     Mounting-to-body bolts . . . . . . . . . . . . . . . . . . . . . . . . . . . | 40 | 30 |
|     Mounting-to-engine bracket bolts: | | |
|       Stage 1 . . . . . . . . . . . . . . . . . . . . . . . . . . . . . . . . . . | 60 | 44 |
|       Stage 2 . . . . . . . . . . . . . . . . . . . . . . . . . . . . . . . . . . | Angle-tighten a further 30° | |
|       Stage 3 . . . . . . . . . . . . . . . . . . . . . . . . . . . . . . . . . . | Angle-tighten a further 15° | |
| Engine-to-transmission bolts. . . . . . . . . . . . . . . . . . . . . . . . . . . . | 60 | 44 |

## Torque wrench settings (continued)

| | Nm | lbf ft |
|---|---|---|
| Exhaust manifold securing nuts*: | | |
| 1.0 and 1.2 litre Z12XEP engines . . . . . . . . . . . . . . . . . . . . . . . . . . . | 20 | 15 |
| 1.2 litre Z12XE and 1.4 litre engines. . . . . . . . . . . . . . . . . . . . . . | 15 | 11 |
| Flywheel bolts*: | | |
| Stage 1 . . . . . . . . . . . . . . . . . . . . . . . . . . . . . . . . . . . . . . . . . . | 35 | 26 |
| Stage 2 . . . . . . . . . . . . . . . . . . . . . . . . . . . . . . . . . . . . . . . . . . | Angle-tighten a further 30° | |
| Front subframe*: | | |
| Stage 1 . . . . . . . . . . . . . . . . . . . . . . . . . . . . . . . . . . . . . . . . . . | 90 | 66 |
| Stage 2 . . . . . . . . . . . . . . . . . . . . . . . . . . . . . . . . . . . . . . . . . . | Angle-tighten a further 45° | |
| Stage 3 . . . . . . . . . . . . . . . . . . . . . . . . . . . . . . . . . . . . . . . . . . | Angle-tighten a further 15° | |
| Fuel feed and return hose unions. . . . . . . . . . . . . . . . . . . . . . . . | 15 | 11 |
| Inlet manifold support bracket to cylinder block . . . . . . . . . . . . . | 20 | 15 |
| Oil filter housing cap to filter housing. . . . . . . . . . . . . . . . . . . . . | 10 | 7 |
| Oil filter housing to cylinder block . . . . . . . . . . . . . . . . . . . . . . . | 20 | 15 |
| Roadwheel bolts. . . . . . . . . . . . . . . . . . . . . . . . . . . . . . . . . . . . | 110 | 81 |
| Sump to cylinder block baseplate/timing cover. . . . . . . . . . . . . . | 10 | 7 |
| Sump to transmission . . . . . . . . . . . . . . . . . . . . . . . . . . . . . . . . | 40 | 30 |
| Timing chain tension rail pivot bolt. . . . . . . . . . . . . . . . . . . . . . . | 20 | 15 |
| Timing chain tensioner closure bolt (for locking pin access) . . . . . . . . | 50 | 37 |
| Timing cover bolts: | | |
| M10. . . . . . . . . . . . . . . . . . . . . . . . . . . . . . . . . . . . . . . . . . . . . | 35 | 26 |
| M6. . . . . . . . . . . . . . . . . . . . . . . . . . . . . . . . . . . . . . . . . . . . . . | 8 | 6 |
| Timing cover oil fill channel closure plug . . . . . . . . . . . . . . . . . . . | 50 | 37 |

*Use new fasteners.

## 1  General information

### How to use this Chapter

This Part of Chapter 2 describes the repair procedures which can reasonably be carried out on the engine while it remains in the vehicle. If the engine has been removed from the vehicle and is being dismantled as described in Chapter 2E, any preliminary dismantling procedures can be ignored.

Note that, while it may be possible physically to overhaul items such as the piston/connecting rod assemblies while the engine is in the vehicle, such tasks are not usually carried out as separate operations, and usually require the execution of several additional procedures (not to mention the cleaning of components and of oilways); for this reason, all such tasks are classed as major overhaul procedures, and are described in Chapter 2E.

Chapter 2E describes the removal of the engine/transmission unit from the vehicle, and the full overhaul procedures which can then be carried out.

### Engine description

The engine is of three-cylinder (1.0 litre) or four-cylinder (1.2 and 1.4 litre) in-line type, with double overhead camshafts (DOHC). The engine is mounted transversely at the front of the vehicle. Apart from the obvious difference in the number of cylinders, the engines are all virtually identical in their internal construction.

The XEP units are termed 'Twinport' engines due to the design of the inlet manifold and cylinder head combustion chambers. Vacuum-operated flap valves located in the inlet manifold are opened or closed according to engine operating conditions, to create a variable venturi manifold arrangement. This system has significant advantages in terms of engine power, fuel economy and reduced exhaust emissions. The XE engine utilises a conventional single tract inlet manifold without the twinport system.

The crankshaft runs in four (1.0 litre) or five (1.2 and 1.4 litre) shell-type main bearings with crankshaft endfloat being controlled by thrustwashers which are an integral part of No 3 main bearing shells (1.0 litre engines), or No 4 main bearing shells (1.2 and 1.4 litre engines).

The connecting rods are attached to the crankshaft by horizontally-split shell-type big-end bearings. The pistons are attached to the connecting rods by gudgeon pins, which are an interference fit in the connecting rod small-end bores. The aluminium-alloy pistons are fitted with three piston rings – two compression rings and an oil control ring.

The camshafts are driven from the crankshaft by a hydraulically-tensioned timing chain. Each cylinder has four valves (two inlet and two exhaust), operated via rocker arms which are supported at their pivot ends by hydraulic self-adjusting valve lifters (tappets). One camshaft operates the inlet valves, and the other operates the exhaust valves.

The inlet and exhaust valves are each closed by a single valve spring, and operate in guides pressed into the cylinder head.

A rotor-type oil pump is located in the timing cover attached to the cylinder block, and is driven directly from the crankshaft.

The coolant pump is located externally on the timing cover, and is driven by the auxiliary drivebelt.

### Operations with engine in place

The following operations can be carried out without having to remove the engine from the vehicle.

a) Removal and refitting of the cylinder head.
b) Removal and refitting of the timing cover.
c) Removal and refitting of the timing chain, tensioner and sprockets.
d) Removal and refitting of the camshafts.
e) Removal and refitting of the sump.
f) Removal and refitting of the big-end bearings, connecting rods, and pistons*.
g) Removal and refitting of the oil pump.
h) Renewal of the crankshaft oil seals.
i) Renewal of the engine mountings.
j) Removal and refitting of the flywheel.

* Although the operation marked with an asterisk can be carried out with the engine in the vehicle (after removal of the sump), it is preferable for the engine to be removed, in the interests of cleanliness and improved access. For this reason, the procedure is described in Chapter 2E.

## 2  Compression test – description and interpretation

**Note:** A suitable compression gauge will be required to carry out this test.

1 When engine performance is down, or if misfiring occurs which cannot be attributed to the ignition or fuel systems, a compression test can provide diagnostic clues as to the engine's condition. If the test is performed regularly, it can give warning of trouble before any other symptoms become apparent.

2 The engine must be fully warmed-up to normal operating temperature, and the battery must be fully-charged. The aid of an assistant will also be required.

**3** Remove the ignition module from the top of the camshaft cover as described in Chapter 5B. Ensure that the ignition is switched off then disconnect the two wiring plugs from the engine management electronic control unit located on the left-hand side of the inlet manifold.

**4** Remove all of the spark plugs from the engine (see Chapter 1A).

**5** Fit a compression tester to the No 1 spark plug hole (No 1 cylinder is nearest the timing chain end of the engine) – the type of tester which screws into the plug thread is to be preferred.

**6** Have an assistant hold the accelerator pedal fully depressed, at the same time cranking the engine over for approximately four seconds on the starter motor. After one or two revolutions, the compression pressure reading on the gauge should build-up to a maximum figure and then stabilise. Record the highest reading obtained.

**7** Repeat the test on the remaining cylinders, recording the pressure in each.

**8** All cylinders should produce very similar pressures. Note that the compression should build-up quickly in a healthy engine; low compression on the first stroke, followed by gradually-increasing pressure on successive strokes, indicates worn piston rings. A low compression reading on the first stroke, which does not build-up during successive strokes, indicates leaking valves or a blown head gasket (a cracked head could also be the cause). Deposits on the undersides of the valve heads can also cause low compression.

**9** If the pressure in any cylinder is significantly lower than that in the remaining cylinders, carry out the following test to isolate the cause. Introduce a teaspoonful of clean engine oil into the relevant cylinder through its spark plug hole, and repeat the test.

**10** If the addition of oil temporarily improves the compression pressure, this indicates that bore or piston wear is responsible for the pressure loss. No improvement suggests that leaking or burnt valves, or a blown head gasket may be to blame.

**11** A low reading from two adjacent cylinders is almost certainly due to the head gasket having blown between them; the presence of coolant in the engine oil will confirm this.

**12** If one cylinder is about 20 percent lower than the others, and the engine has a slightly rough idle, a worn camshaft lobe could be the cause.

**13** If the compression reading is unusually high, the combustion chambers are probably coated with carbon deposits. If this is the case, the cylinder head should be removed and decarbonised (see Chapter 2E).

**14** On completion of the test, refit the spark plugs, reconnect the electronic control unit wiring plugs (ensure that the ignition is switched off), and refit the ignition module.

### 3 Camshaft cover – removal and refitting

**Note:** *A new camshaft cover rubber seal will be required for refitting, and a suitable silicone sealant will be required to seal the timing cover-to-cylinder head upper joint.*

### Removal

**1** Disconnect the battery negative terminal (refer to *Disconnecting the battery* in the Reference Chapter).

**2** Disconnect the wiring connectors at the air mass meter, coolant temperature sensor, camshaft position sensor and oil pressure switch **(see illustrations)**.

**3** Lift the wiring harness trough from the camshaft cover and move it to one side **(see illustration)**.

**4** Disconnect the two breather hoses at the rear of the camshaft cover **(see illustration)**.

**5** Remove the ignition module from the centre of the camshaft cover as described in Chapter 5B.

**6** Progressively slacken the camshaft cover retaining bolts until they are all fully unscrewed. Note that the bolts are captive and will remain in place in the cover as it is removed.

**7** Lift the camshaft cover up and off the cylinder head **(see illustration)**.

### Refitting

**8** Remove the old seal from the camshaft cover, then examine the inside of the cover for a build-up of oil sludge or any other contamination, and if necessary clean the cover with paraffin, or a water-soluble solvent. Dry the cover thoroughly before refitting.

**9** Check the condition of the rubber seals on the camshaft cover retaining bolts. If the seals are in any way damaged or deformed, carefully tap the bolts out of the camshaft cover using a

3.2a Disconnect the wiring connectors at the air mass meter . . .

3.2b . . . coolant temperature sensor (A) and camshaft position sensor (B) . . .

3.2c . . . and at the oil pressure switch

3.3 Lift the wiring harness trough from the camshaft cover and move it to one side

3.4 Breather hoses on the rear of the camshaft cover

3.7 Lift the camshaft cover up and off the cylinder head

**3.9a If necessary, tap the bolts out of the camshaft cover . . .**

**3.9b . . . and fit new seals to the bolts**

**3.10 Fit a new rubber seal to the camshaft cover ensuring that it is correctly located in the cover groove**

soft-faced mallet and fit new seals to the bolts **(see illustrations)**.

**10** Fit a new rubber seal to the cover ensuring that it is correctly located in the camshaft cover groove **(see illustration)**.

**11** Inspect the joint between the timing cover and cylinder head, and cut off any projecting timing cover gasket using a sharp knife **(see illustration)**.

**12** Thoroughly clean the mating faces of the camshaft cover and cylinder head.

**13** Apply a 2 mm diameter bead of silicone sealant to the joint between the timing cover and cylinder head on each side **(see illustration)**.

**14** Locate the camshaft cover on the cylinder head and screw in the retaining bolts. Progressively and evenly tighten the retaining bolts securely.

**15** Refit the ignition module from the centre of the camshaft cover as described in Chapter 5B.

**16** Reconnect the two breather hoses to the right-hand rear of the camshaft cover.

**17** Locate the wiring harness trough in the camshaft cover slots then reconnect the air mass meter, coolant temperature sensor, camshaft position sensor and oil pressure switch wiring connectors.

**18** Reconnect the battery negative terminal on completion.

## 4 Valve timing – checking and adjustment

*Note: Certain special tools will be required for this operation. Read through the entire procedure to familiarise yourself with the work involved, then either obtain the manufacturer's special tools, or use the alternatives described. New gaskets and sealing rings will also be required for all disturbed components.*

### Checking

**1** Disconnect the battery negative terminal (refer to *Disconnecting the battery* in the Reference Chapter).

**2** Remove the air cleaner assembly as described in Chapter 4A.

**3** Remove the camshaft cover as described in Section 3.

**3.11 Cut off any projecting timing cover gasket using a sharp knife**

**4** Firmly apply the handbrake, then jack up the front of the car and support it securely on axle stands (see *Jacking and vehicle support*). Remove the right-hand front roadwheel and the wheel arch liner for access to the crankshaft pulley.

**5** On models with air conditioning, release the tension on the auxiliary drivebelt and lock the tensioner in the released position as described in the auxiliary drivebelt renewal procedure in Chapter 1A. Note that it is not necessary to completely remove the drivebelt, as this would entail removal of the right-hand engine mounting bracket. With the drivebelt tension released, slip the belt off the compressor pulley. Unbolt the compressor from the cylinder block, release the refrigerant lines from their brackets and support the compressor clear of the engine. **Do not** disconnect the refrigerant lines from the compressor.

**6** Using a socket or spanner on the crankshaft

**4.6 Turn the crankshaft until the TDC notch (A) on the pulley is located just before the cast lug (B) on the timing cover**

**3.13 Apply a bead of silicone sealant to the joint between the timing cover and cylinder head on each side**

pulley hub bolt, turn the crankshaft in the normal direction of rotation (clockwise as viewed from the right-hand side of the car) until the TDC notch on the crankshaft pulley is located just before the cast lug on the timing cover **(see illustration)**.

**7** Check that No 1 piston is on the compression stroke by observing No 1 cylinder camshaft lobes. All four lobes should be pointing outwards (away from the engine) **(see illustration)**. If they are not, No 1 piston is on the exhaust stroke and the crankshaft should be turned through a further full turn, stopping once again just before the TDC notch aligns with the lug on the timing cover.

**8** Undo the closure bolt from the crankshaft TDC position setting hole. The plug is located on the front facing side of the cylinder block baseplate, adjacent to the timing cover joint. Note that a new closure bolt sealing ring will be required for refitting.

**4.7 With No 1 piston on the compression stroke, the camshaft lobes for No 1 cylinder should be pointing outwards**

Tool Tip 1: A commercially-available clutch aligning tool can be used as a TDC positioning tool.

4.10a The end of the tool must engage with the slot in the crankshaft web (arrowed) – shown with engine partially dismantled

4.10b Clutch aligning tool in position in the TDC setting hole

4.12 Camshaft setting tool (arrowed) made from steel strip and inserted into the camshaft slots

4.15a Vauxhall/Opel camshaft sensor phase disc positioning tool (KM-954)

4.15b Home-made cardboard alternative camshaft sensor phase disc positioning tool in place

**9** If the Vauxhall TDC positioning pin KM-952 is available, insert the tool into the TDC position setting hole. Slowly turn the crankshaft in the normal direction of rotation until the tool engages with the TDC slot in the crankshaft, and moves fully in, up to its stop.

**10** In the absence of the Vauxhall tool, a typical commercially-available clutch aligning tool of the type having interchangeable cones and collars of various diameters can be used as an alternative (see Tool Tip 1). Assemble the tool so that the end collar (the part that

normally engages with the crankshaft spigot bearing) is of 12 mm diameter, and the sliding cone (the part that normally engages with the clutch disc hub) is of 17.5 mm diameter. Insert the tool into the TDC position setting hole, and slowly turn the crankshaft in the normal direction of rotation until the end collar engages with the TDC slot in the crankshaft web. Push the cone fully into the setting hole as far as it will go, and the crankshaft should now be locked in the TDC position (see illustrations).

**11** If the Vauxhall camshaft setting tool KM-953 is available, insert the tool into the slots in the left-hand end of the camshafts. Ensure that the tool is inserted fully, up to its stop, to lock both camshafts.

**12** In the absence of the Vauxhall tool, a camshaft setting tool can be made out of 5 mm thick flat steel strip, approximately 20 mm wide and long enough to engage both camshaft slots. Insert the setting tool into the camshaft slots to lock the camshafts in the TDC position (see illustration). Note that a ready-made equivalent is available from tool stockists.

**13** If it is not possible to insert the camshaft setting tool, then the valve timing must be adjusted as described in paragraphs 17 to 35 below.

**14** If all is satisfactory so far, the position of the camshaft position sensor phase disc on the inlet camshaft should be checked. This check entails the use of Vauxhall camshaft sensor phase disc positioning tool KM-954. If this tool is not available, an alternative can be fabricated as follows.

**15** The Vauxhall positioning tool (KM-954) is a relatively substantial die-casting, the purpose of which is to check the position of the phase disc, and also to hold the phase disc in the correct position on the camshaft sprocket if adjustment is required. During the workshop procedures undertaken for the preparation of this manual, we discovered that a tool made from stiff cardboard (such that used for the cover of a Haynes manual) worked just as well as the factory tool (see illustrations and Tool Tip 2).

ALL DIMENSIONS IN MM

27·5
60°
84°
32·5
8
2
63
127
H32566

Tool Tip 2: A home-made camshaft sensor phase disc positioning tool can be fabricated using the dimensions shown.

**16** Using the Vauxhall positioning tool, or the home-made alternative, check to see if the tool will engage with the phase disc on the camshaft, and also seat squarely on the timing cover surface. If it does, proceed to paragraph 31. If adjustment is required, proceed as follows.

### Adjustment

**Note:** *New camshaft sprocket retaining bolts will be required for this operation.*

**17** Remove the camshaft sensor phase disc positioning tool, and the tool used to lock the camshafts in position.

**18** Unscrew the timing chain tensioner closure plug from the timing cover, located just below the heater hose union on the coolant pump. Note that a new closure bolt sealing ring will be required for refitting **(see illustration)**.

**19** Using a suitable spanner engaged with the flats provided on the inlet camshaft, apply tension in a clockwise direction (as viewed from the right-hand side of the car) to the camshaft, to take up any slack in the timing chain **(see illustration)**. This will push the timing chain tensioner plunger fully into its bore.

**20** Hold the camshaft in this position and retain the tensioner plunger in the released position by inserting a 2 mm diameter roll-pin, approximately 30 mm long, through the closure plug aperture and into the hole on the tensioner body **(see illustrations)**.

**21** Slacken and remove the sprocket retaining bolts for both camshafts, using a spanner to counterhold each camshaft as the bolts are slackened.

**22** Fit the new bolts to both camshaft sprockets and tighten them finger tight only at this stage. Check that the phase disc on the inlet camshaft can still be turned.

**23** Again, using the spanner on the camshaft flats, turn the camshafts slightly, as necessary, until the camshaft setting tool can be reinserted into the slots in the ends of the camshafts.

**24** Remove the roll-pin used to hold the timing chain tensioner plunger in the retracted position.

**25** Turn the camshaft sensor phase disc slightly, as necessary, and locate the Vauxhall positioning tool (KM-954), or the home-made alternative over the disc and in contact with the timing cover. If the Vauxhall tool is being used, bolt it into position on the timing cover.

**26** Tighten the camshaft sprocket retaining bolts to 10 Nm (7 lbf ft). The inlet camshaft sprocket bolts should be tightened first. Note that this is just an initial torque loading to hold the sprockets and the phase disc in position when the setting tools are removed.

**27** Remove the crankshaft, camshaft and phase disc setting tools, then tighten the camshaft sprocket retaining bolts to the specified torque in the stages given in the Specifications. The inlet camshaft sprocket bolts should be tightened first. Counterhold the camshafts using the spanner on the camshaft flats as the sprocket bolts are tightened.

**4.18  Unscrew the timing chain tensioner closure plug from the timing cover**

**28** Turn the crankshaft through two complete revolutions, stopping just before the TDC notch on the crankshaft pulley aligns with the cast lug on the timing cover **(see illustration 4.6)**. Check that all four lobes for No 1 cylinder are pointing outwards (away from the engine).

**29** Slowly turn the crankshaft further until the TDC position setting tool can once again be inserted to lock the crankshaft.

**30** It should now be possible to re-insert the camshaft setting tool into the slots in the camshafts, and to fit the camshaft sensor phase disc setting tool over the disc. If this is not possible repeat the entire adjustment procedure.

**31** If all is satisfactory, remove all the setting/aligning tools and refit the timing chain tensioner and cylinder block closure bolts using new sealing rings. Tighten both closure bolts to the specified torque.

**32** On models with air conditioning, refit the compressor to the cylinder block and tighten the mounting bolts to the specified torque. Refit the refrigerant lines to their relevant clips or brackets, then refit the auxiliary drivebelt as described in Chapter 1A.

**33** Refit the wheel arch liner and the roadwheel. Tighten the roadwheel bolts to the specified torque, then lower the vehicle to the ground.

**34** Refit the camshaft cover as described in Section 3.

**35** Refit the air cleaner assembly as described in Chapter 4A, then reconnect the battery negative terminal.

**4.20a  Insert a 2 mm diameter roll-pin, approximately 30 mm long, through the closure plug aperture . . .**

**4.19  Use a spanner on the flats of the inlet camshaft to take up any slack in the timing chain**

## 5  Crankshaft pulley – removal and refitting

### Removal

**1** Firmly apply the handbrake, then jack up the front of the car and support it securely on axle stands (see *Jacking and vehicle support*). Remove the right-hand roadwheel and the wheel arch liner. Where necessary remove the engine undertray.

**2** Release the tension on the auxiliary drivebelt and lock the tensioner in the released position as described in the auxiliary drivebelt renewal procedure in Chapter 1A. Note that it is not necessary to completely remove the drivebelt, as this would entail removal of the right-hand engine mounting bracket.

**3** With the drivebelt tension released, slip the belt off the crankshaft pulley.

**4** Using quick-drying paint, or similar, make an alignment mark between the crankshaft pulley and the pulley hub. It should only be possible to refit the pulley in one position, but it is advisable to make an alignment mark anyway.

**5** Unscrew the six crankshaft pulley retaining bolts and remove the pulley from the hub **(see illustration)**. If necessary, prevent the crankshaft from turning as the pulley bolts are slackened using a spanner or socket on the pulley hub bolt.

**4.20b  . . . and into the hole on the tensioner body (arrowed)**

**5.5 Undo the six bolts and remove the crankshaft pulley from the pulley hub**

### Refitting

6 Align the marks made on removal and locate the pulley on the hub.

7 Refit the six retaining bolts and progressively tighten them securely.

8 Refit the auxiliary drivebelt over the crankshaft pulley and ensure that it is correctly seated in the other pulleys.

9 Unlock the auxiliary drivebelt tensioner as described in Chapter 1A to retension the drivebelt.

10 Refit the wheel arch liner and the roadwheel and tighten the wheel bolts to the specified torque.

11 Lower the car to the ground.

## 6 Timing cover and chain
– removal and refitting

**Note:** *The special tools described in Section 4 will also be required for this operation. Read through the entire procedure and also the procedures contained in Section 4 to familiarise yourself with the work involved, then either obtain the manufacturer's special tools, or use the alternatives described. New gaskets and sealing rings will also be required for all disturbed components, together with new camshaft sprocket retaining bolts. A tube of silicone sealant will be needed to seal the joint between the cylinder block and cylinder head.*

### Removal

1 Disconnect the battery negative terminal

**6.9 Radiator lower hose on the coolant pump**

(refer to *Disconnecting the battery* in the Reference Chapter).

2 Apply the handbrake, then jack up the front of the vehicle and support it on axle stands (see *Jacking and vehicle support*). Remove the right-hand roadwheel. On ECO models, remove the engine undertray sections.

3 Drain the cooling system as described in Chapter 1A. Tighten the drain plug after draining the system.

4 Remove the air cleaner assembly as described in Chapter 4A.

5 At the right-hand end of the engine, loosen the clip and disconnect the throttle body preheater hose from the thermostat housing.

6 Loosen the clip and disconnect the heater feed hose from the coolant pump.

7 Disconnect the wiring from the oil pressure switch, coolant temperature sensor and camshaft position sensor, then unclip the wiring conduit and move it to one side.

8 Loosen the clips and disconnect the radiator upper hose from the radiator and thermostat housing.

9 Loosen the clip and disconnect the radiator lower hose from the coolant pump **(see illustration)**.

10 Remove the ignition module as described in Chapter 5B.

11 Disconnect the crankcase ventilation hose from the camshaft cover.

12 Progressively slacken the camshaft cover retaining bolts until they are all fully unscrewed. Note that the bolts are captive and will remain in place in the cover as it is removed. Lift the camshaft cover up and off the cylinder head.

13 Remove the auxiliary drivebelt cover from under the right-hand wheel arch.

14 Position a container beneath the engine sump, then unscrew the drain plug and drain the engine oil. Clean, refit and tighten the drain plug on completion.

15 Refer to Chapter 4A, and disconnect the wiring from the oxygen sensor on the catalytic converter, then unbolt the exhaust front pipe from the exhaust manifold, taking care to support the flexible section. **Note:** *Angular movement in excess of 10° can cause permanent damage to the flexible section.*

16 Release the mounting rubbers and support the front of the exhaust pipe to one side.

**6.17 The coolant pump pulley retaining bolts**

17 Slacken, but do not remove, the three coolant pump pulley retaining bolts **(see illustration)**.

18 On models without air conditioning, turn the auxiliary drivebelt tensioner pulley bolt clockwise then insert a suitable pin through the spring centre shaft to lock the spring in its compressed state. Note the routing of the drivebelt, then remove it from the pulleys – mark the drivebelt for fitted direction. **Note:** *The drivebelt cannot be removed completely until the right-hand engine mounting has been removed.* Unscrew the auxiliary drivebelt tensioner lower mounting bolt and the tensioner roller upper pivot bolt. Remove the tensioner from the timing cover.

19 On models with air conditioning, turn the auxiliary drivebelt tensioner pulley bolt clockwise to tension the spring, then insert a suitable pin through the hole in the tensioner body and into the hole in the timing cover to lock the spring. Note the routing of the drivebelt, then remove it from the pulleys – mark the drivebelt for fitted direction. **Note:** *The drivebelt cannot be removed completely until the right-hand engine mounting has been removed.* Turn the tensioner pulley bolt clockwise again and remove the locking pin, then gradually release the tensioner until it is fully released. Unbolt the tensioner from the timing cover.

20 Remove the alternator as described in Chapter 5A.

21 Remove the sump as described in Section 11.

22 The engine must now be supported while the right-hand engine mounting is removed. To do this, use a hoist attached to the top of the engine, or make up a wooden frame to locate on the crankcase and use a trolley jack.

23 Remove the right-hand engine mounting bracket with reference to Section 15, then remove the auxiliary drivebelt.

24 Fully unscrew the bolts and remove the coolant pump pulley from its drive flange.

25 On models with air conditioning, unbolt the compressor from the cylinder block, release the refrigerant lines from their brackets and support the compressor clear of the engine. **Do not** disconnect the refrigerant lines from the compressor.

26 Undo the three bolts securing the thermostat housing cover to the coolant pump. Remove the sealing ring from the housing cover noting that a new one will be required for refitting.

27 Using a socket or spanner on the crankshaft pulley hub bolt, turn the crankshaft in the normal direction of rotation (clockwise as viewed from the right-hand side of the car) until the TDC notch on the crankshaft pulley is located just before the cast lug on the timing cover **(see illustration 4.6)**.

28 Check that No 1 piston is on the compression stroke by observing No 1 cylinder camshaft lobes. All four lobes should be pointing outwards (away from the engine). If they are not, No 1 piston is on the exhaust

**6.31 Slacken the crankshaft pulley hub retaining bolt (arrowed)**

**6.42 Push back the timing chain tensioner plunger and secure it in the released position with a 2 mm diameter roll-pin**

**6.43 Undo the two bolts (arrowed) and remove the timing chain sliding rail from the cylinder head**

stroke and the crankshaft should be turned through a further full turn, stopping once again just before the TDC notch aligns with the lug on the timing cover.

**29** Using quick-drying paint, or similar, make an alignment mark between the crankshaft pulley and the pulley hub. It should only be possible to refit the pulley in one position, but it is advisable to make an alignment mark anyway.

**30** Unscrew the six crankshaft pulley retaining bolts and remove the pulley from the hub. If necessary, prevent the crankshaft from turning as the pulley bolts are slackened, using a spanner or socket on the pulley hub bolt.

**31** Using a suitable socket, initially slacken (but do not remove) the crankshaft pulley hub retaining bolt **(see illustration)**. The crankshaft can be prevented from turning as the bolt is slackened using Vauxhall special tool KM-956 or a similar tool which will engage with the flats on each side of the pulley hub. Alternatively, remove the starter motor, and lock the flywheel ring gear teeth using a suitable hooked tool bolted to the bellhousing.

**32** Undo the closure bolt from the crankshaft TDC position setting hole. The plug is located on the front facing side of the cylinder block baseplate, adjacent to the timing cover joint. Note that a new closure bolt sealing ring will be required for refitting.

**33** Temporarily place the crankshaft pulley back on the hub and check that the TDC notch is still positioned just before the lug on the timing cover.

**34** Slowly turn the crankshaft in the normal direction of rotation until the TDC positioning pin (or suitable alternative) described in Section 4, engages with the TDC slot in the crankshaft.

**35** Remove the crankshaft pulley, if still in place, and check that the punch mark on the pulley hub is in the 11 o'clock position.

**36** Insert the camshaft setting tool described in Section 4 into the slots in the ends of the camshafts.

**37** Unscrew the coolant pump retaining bolts, noting the locations of the three short bolts. The short bolts secure the pump to the timing cover, and the long bolts secure the pump

**6.44 Undo the two bolts (arrowed) and remove the timing chain guide rail from the cylinder block**

and the timing cover to the cylinder block and cylinder head.

**38** Withdraw the coolant pump from the timing cover, noting that it may be necessary to tap the pump lightly with a soft-faced mallet to free it from the locating dowels.

**39** Recover the pump sealing ring/gasket noting that a new one must be used for refitting.

**40** Unscrew the previously-slackened crankshaft pulley hub retaining bolt and remove the hub from the crankshaft. Note that a new bolt will be required for refitting.

**41** Undo the timing cover retaining bolts and remove the timing cover from the engine. The cover will be initially tight as it is located on dowels and secured by sealant. If necessary, gently tap it off using a soft-faced mallet.

**42** Fully push back the timing chain tensioner plunger and secure it in the released position

**6.46a Lift the timing chain off the sprockets and remove the chain . . .**

**6.45 Undo the lower pivot bolt and remove the timing chain tension rail from the cylinder block**

by inserting a 2 mm diameter roll-pin, approximately 30 mm long, in the hole on the tensioner body **(see illustration)**.

**43** Undo the two bolts and remove the timing chain sliding rail from the top of the cylinder head **(see illustration)**.

**44** Undo the two bolts and remove the timing chain (front) guide rail from the cylinder block **(see illustration)**.

**45** Undo the lower pivot bolt and remove the timing chain (rear) tension rail from the cylinder block **(see illustration)**.

**46** Lift the timing chain off the sprockets and remove the chain, then remove the drive sprocket from the crankshaft **(see illustrations)**.

**47** Remove the composite gasket from the cylinder block baseplate, cylinder block, and cylinder head, using a plastic spatula if necessary to release the sealant **(see**

**6.46b . . . then remove the drive sprocket from the crankshaft**

**6.47 Remove the timing cover composite gasket from the cylinder block baseplate, cylinder block, and cylinder head**

**6.55 Apply a 2 mm diameter bead of silicone sealant to the joint between the cylinder block and cylinder head on each side**

**6.57 Slide the timing chain drive sprocket onto the crankshaft with the markings facing outwards**

**illustration)**. Note that if the cylinder head has ever been previously removed, the gasket will be a two-piece type, with a split at the cylinder head-to cylinder block joint. A new gasket will be required for refitting.

**48** Thoroughly clean the timing cover and remove all traces of gasket and sealant from all the mating surfaces. Similarly clean the cylinder block baseplate, cylinder block and cylinder head mating surfaces. Ensure that all traces of old sealant are removed, particularly from the area of the cylinder head-to-cylinder block joint.

**49** Inspect the timing chain, sprockets, sliding rail, guide rail and tension rail for any sign of wear or deformation, and renew any suspect components as necessary. Renew the crankshaft timing chain end oil seal in the timing cover as a matter of course using the procedures described in Section 13.

**50** It is advisable to check the condition of the timing chain tensioner at this stage, as described in Section 7.

**51** Obtain all new gaskets and components as necessary ready for refitting.

### Refitting

**52** Commence refitting by inserting a new coolant pump gasket or rubber seal into the timing cover.

**53** Check that the locating dowels are in place, and that the mating surfaces are clean and dry, then locate the pump in position on the timing cover.

**54** Refit the three coolant pump short retaining bolts, ensuring that the bolts are fitted to their correct locations (refer to Chapter 3 if necessary). Tighten the bolts to the specified torque.

**55** Apply a 2 mm diameter bead of silicone

sealant to the joint between the cylinder block and cylinder head on each side **(see illustration)**. The bead should be long enough to fill the joint in the area covered by the timing cover gasket. Similarly, apply silicone sealant to the joint between the cylinder block and baseplate.

**56** Ensure that the locating dowels are in position, then locate the new timing cover gasket in place on the cylinder head, cylinder block and baseplate.

**57** Slide the timing chain drive sprocket onto the crankshaft with the markings facing outwards **(see illustration)**.

**58** Engage the timing chain with the drive sprocket then, keeping it tight on the exhaust camshaft side, feed the chain up and over the camshaft sprockets **(see illustration)**.

**59** Place the timing chain tension rail in position, refit the lower pivot bolt and tighten the bolt to the specified torque.

**60** Attach the timing chain guide rail to the cylinder block and secure with the two bolts tightened securely.

**61** Refit the timing chain sliding rail to the cylinder head and secure with the two bolts tightened securely.

**62** Remove the roll-pin used to secure the timing chain tensioner plunger in the released position.

**63** Locate the timing cover in position and refit all the retaining bolts, finger tight only at this stage. Now tighten all the bolts to the specified torque, starting with the bolts around the coolant pump first, followed by the bolts around the periphery of the cover.

**64** Refit the sump as described in Section 11.

**65** Remove the position setting tools used to lock the crankshaft and camshafts in the TDC position.

**66** Lubricate the crankshaft pulley hub with engine oil, then refit the hub to the crankshaft, ensuring that the punch mark on the hub is in the 11 o'clock position **(see illustration)**.

**67** Screw in the new pulley hub retaining bolt and tighten it to the specified torque, in the stages given in the Specifications **(see illustrations)**. Prevent crankshaft rotation as the bolt is tightened, using the method employed for removal.

**68** Refit the crankshaft pulley to the pulley

**6.58 Keeping the timing chain tight on the exhaust camshaft side, locate the chain over the sprockets**

**6.66 Lubricate the crankshaft pulley hub, then refit the hub to the crankshaft**

**6.67a Screw in the new pulley hub retaining bolt . . .**

**6.67b . . . tighten it to the specified torque . . .**

**6.67c ... then through the specified angle in the stages given in the Specifications**

hub, with the marks made on removal aligned, and tighten the six bolts securely.

69 Turn the crankshaft through two complete revolutions, stopping just before the TDC notch on the crankshaft pulley aligns with the cast lug on the timing cover. Check that all four lobes for No 1 cylinder are pointing outwards (away from the engine).

70 Slowly turn the crankshaft further until the TDC position setting tool can once again be inserted to lock the crankshaft.

71 It should now be possible to re-insert the camshaft setting tool into the slots in the camshafts. If the setting tool cannot be inserted, carry out the valve timing adjustment procedures contained in Section 4.

72 If all is satisfactory, remove all the setting/aligning tools and refit the closure bolt to the cylinder block using a new sealing ring. Tighten the closure bolt to the specified torque.

73 Refit the coolant pump pulley and tighten the three bolts to the specified torque. To prevent the pulley turning as the bolts are tightened, hold the pulley using a screwdriver engaged with one of the bolts and the pump centre spindle. Alternatively, wait until the auxiliary drivebelt has been refitted and tighten the bolts then.

74 Ensure that the mating surfaces are clean, then fit a new sealing ring to the thermostat housing cover. Refit the cover to the coolant pump and tighten the bolts securely.

75 On models with air conditioning, refit the compressor to the cylinder block and tighten the mounting bolts to the specified torque. Refit the refrigerant lines to their relevant clips or brackets.

76 Refit the alternator as described in Chapter 5A.

77 Refit the auxiliary drivebelt tensioner and tighten the mounting bolts to the specified torque.

78 Rotate the tensioner pulley bolt clockwise as for removal, refit the auxiliary drivebelt as previously noted and release the tensioner.

79 Refit the right-hand engine mounting bracket with reference to Section 15.

80 Refit the exhaust front pipe and oxygen sensor with reference to Chapter 4A.

81 Refill the engine with fresh oil with reference to Chapter 1A.

82 Refit the auxiliary drivebelt cover.

83 Refit the camshaft cover and reconnect the crankcase ventilation hose as described in Section 3.

84 Refit the ignition module and cover.

85 Reconnect the radiator top and bottom hoses and heater hose to their respective connections.

86 Reconnect the wiring to the oil pressure switch, coolant temperature sensor and camshaft position sensor, then clip the wiring conduit in position.

87 Reconnect the throttle body preheater hose and tighten the clip.

88 Refit the air cleaner assembly as described in Chapter 4A.

89 Refill the cooling system as described in Chapter 1A, then reconnect the battery negative terminal.

90 Refit the engine undertray as necessary, then refit the roadwheel and lower the vehicle to the ground.

## 7 Timing chain tensioner – removal, inspection and refitting

### Removal

1 Remove the timing cover as described in Section 6.

2 Undo the two tensioner retaining bolts and remove the tensioner from the cylinder head **(see illustration)**.

3 Extract the roll-pin used to retain the tensioner plunger in the retracted position and

**7.2 Undo the two retaining bolts and remove the timing chain tensioner from the cylinder head**

**7.3b ... and withdraw the tensioner plunger and spring**

withdraw the tensioner plunger and spring **(see illustrations)**.

### Inspection

4 Examine the components for any sign of wear, deformation or damage and, if evident, renew the complete tensioner assembly.

### Refitting

5 Lubricate the tensioner spring and plunger, then insert the spring, followed by the plunger into the tensioner body.

6 Fully compress the tensioner plunger and reinsert the retaining roll-pin **(see illustration)**.

7 Refit the tensioner assembly to the cylinder head and tighten the retaining bolts securely.

## 8 Camshaft sprockets – removal and refitting

**Note:** *The special tools described in Section 4 will also be required for this operation. Read through the entire procedure and also the procedures contained in Section 4 to familiarise yourself with the work involved, then either obtain the manufacturer's special tools, or use the alternatives described. New gaskets and sealing rings will also be required for all disturbed components, together with new camshaft sprocket retaining bolts.*

### Removal

1 Disconnect the battery negative terminal (refer to *Disconnecting the battery* in the Reference Chapter).

**7.3a Extract the roll-pin used to retain the tensioner plunger in the retracted position ...**

**7.6 Timing chain tensioner plunger fully retracted and locked with the roll-pin**

**2** Remove the air cleaner assembly as described in Chapter 4A.

**3** Disconnect the wiring from the oil pressure switch, coolant temperature sensor and camshaft position sensor, then unclip the wiring conduit and move it to one side.

**4** Remove the ignition module as described in Chapter 5B.

**5** Disconnect the crankcase ventilation hose from the camshaft cover.

**6** Progressively slacken the camshaft cover retaining bolts until they are all fully unscrewed. Note that the bolts are captive and will remain in place in the cover as it is removed. Lift the camshaft cover up and off the cylinder head.

**7** Firmly apply the handbrake, then jack up the front of the car and support it securely on axle stands (see *Jacking and vehicle support*). Remove the right-hand front roadwheel and the wheel arch liner for access to the crankshaft pulley.

**8** On models with air conditioning, release the tension on the auxiliary drivebelt and lock the tensioner in the released position as described in the auxiliary drivebelt renewal procedure in Chapter 1A. Note that it is not necessary to completely remove the drivebelt, as this entails removal of the right-hand engine mounting bracket. With the drivebelt tension released, slip the belt off the compressor pulley. Unbolt the compressor from the cylinder block, release the refrigerant lines from their brackets and support the compressor clear of the engine. **Do not** disconnect the refrigerant lines from the compressor.

**9** Using a socket or spanner on the crankshaft pulley hub bolt, turn the crankshaft in the normal direction of rotation (clockwise as viewed from the right-hand side of the car) until the TDC notch on the crankshaft pulley is located just before the cast lug on the timing cover **(see illustration 4.6)**.

**10** Check that No 1 piston is on the compression stroke by observing No 1 cylinder camshaft lobes. All four lobes should be pointing outwards (away from the engine). If they are not, No 1 piston is on the exhaust stroke and the crankshaft should be turned through a further full turn, stopping once again just before the TDC notch aligns with the lug on the timing cover.

**11** Unscrew the timing chain tensioner closure bolt from the front of the timing cover, below the heater hose union on the coolant pump. Note that a new closure bolt sealing ring will be required for refitting.

**12** Obtain a suitable roll-pin or similar of 2 mm diameter and approximately 30 mm long to use as a timing chain tensioner locking tool.

**13** Using a suitable spanner engaged with the flats provided on the inlet camshaft, apply tension in a clockwise direction (as viewed from the right-hand side of the car) to the camshaft, to take up any slack in the timing chain. This will push the timing chain tensioner plunger fully into its bore.

**14** Hold the camshaft in this position and retain the tensioner plunger in the released position by inserting the roll-pin through the closure plug aperture and into the hole on the tensioner body.

**15** Undo the two bolts and remove the timing chain sliding rail from the top of the cylinder head.

**16** Slacken the sprocket retaining bolts for both camshafts, using the spanner to counterhold each camshaft as the bolts are slackened **(see illustration)**. Remove the bolt for the sprocket(s) being removed together with the camshaft position sensor phase disc, if removing the inlet camshaft. Withdraw the relevant sprocket(s) from the camshaft(s), disengage the timing chain and remove the sprocket(s) from the engine.

### Refitting

**17** Engage the sprocket(s) with the timing chain and locate the sprocket(s) on the camshaft(s). Fit the new retaining bolt(s) together with the phase disc, if working on the inlet camshaft. Note that new retaining bolts must be fitted to **both** sprockets, even if only one sprocket was removed. Tighten the bolts finger tight only at this stage and check that the phase disc on the inlet camshaft can still be turned.

**18** Refit the timing chain sliding rail to the top of the cylinder head and secure with the two bolts tightened securely.

**19** Using the spanner on the camshaft flats, turn the camshafts slightly, as necessary, until the camshaft setting tool described in Section 4 can be inserted into the slots in the ends of the camshafts.

**20** Turn the camshaft sensor phase disc as necessary until the phase disc positioning tool (or suitable alternative) described in Section 4 can be located over the phase disc. If the Vauxhall tool is being used, bolt it to the top of the timing cover. If the alternative tool described is being used, ensure that its base is in contact with the timing cover.

**21** Remove the roll-pin used to hold the timing chain tensioner plunger in the retracted position.

**22** Undo the closure bolt from the crankshaft TDC position setting hole. The plug is located on the front facing side of the cylinder block baseplate, adjacent to the timing cover joint. Note that a new closure bolt sealing ring will be required for refitting.

**23** Slowly turn the crankshaft in the normal direction of rotation until the TDC positioning pin (or suitable alternative), described in Section 4, engages with the TDC slot in the crankshaft.

**24** Tighten the camshaft sprocket retaining bolts to 10 Nm (7 lbf ft). Note that this is just an initial torque loading to hold the sprockets and the phase disc in position when the setting tools are removed.

**25** Remove the crankshaft, camshaft and phase disc setting tools, then tighten the camshaft sprocket retaining bolts to the specified torque in the stages given in the Specifications. Counterhold the camshafts using the spanner on the camshaft flats as the sprocket bolts are tightened.

**26** Turn the crankshaft through two complete revolutions, stopping just before the TDC notch on the crankshaft pulley aligns with the cast lug on the timing cover. Check that all four lobes for No 1 cylinder are pointing outwards (away from the engine).

**27** Slowly turn the crankshaft further until the TDC position setting tool can once again be inserted to lock the crankshaft.

**28** It should now be possible to re-insert the camshaft setting tool into the slots in the camshafts, and to fit the camshaft sensor phase disc setting tool over the disc. If this is not possible carry out the valve timing adjustment procedure contained in Section 4.

**29** If all is satisfactory, remove all the setting/aligning tools and refit the timing chain tensioner and cylinder block closure bolts using new sealing rings. Tighten both closure bolts to the specified torque.

**30** On models with air conditioning, refit the compressor to the cylinder block and tighten the mounting bolts to the specified torque. Refit the refrigerant lines to their relevant clips or brackets, then refit the auxiliary drivebelt as described in Chapter 1A.

**31** Refit the wheel arch liner and the roadwheel. Tighten the roadwheel bolts to the specified torque, then lower the vehicle to the ground.

**32** Refit the camshaft cover as described in Section 3.

**33** Refit the ignition module and cover, and reconnect the wiring.

**34** Reconnect the wiring to the oil pressure switch, coolant temperature sensor and camshaft position sensor, then clip the wiring conduit into position.

**35** Refit the air cleaner assembly as described in Chapter 4A, then reconnect the battery negative terminal.

**8.16 Slacken the camshaft sprocket retaining bolts using a spanner to counterhold each camshaft as the bolts are slackened**

## 9  Camshafts, hydraulic tappets and rocker arms – removal and refitting

### Removal

**1** Remove the camshaft sprocket(s) as described in Section 8.

**9.2  Camshaft bearing cap identification numbers (arrowed)**

**9.4  Lift off the camshaft bearing caps, keeping them in order – shown with cylinder head removed**

**9.5  Lift the camshafts from their locations in the cylinder head – shown with cylinder head removed**

**2** Observe the identification numbers and markings on the camshaft bearing caps **(see illustration)**. On the project car used during the compilation of this manual, the bearing caps with odd numbers were fitted to the exhaust camshaft, and the caps with the even numbers were fitted to the inlet camshaft. However, this may not be the case on other engines. Also, as it is possible to fit the caps either way round, it will be necessary to mark the caps with quick-drying paint, or identify them in some way, so that they can be refitted in exactly the same position. On the project car, all the numbers could be read the correct way up, when viewed from the exhaust camshaft side of the engine. Again, this may not always be the case.

**3** With the bearing caps correctly identified, and working in a spiral pattern from the outside to the inside, initially slacken the bearing cap bolts, one at a time, by half a turn. When all the bolts have been initially slackened, repeat the procedure, slackening the bolts by a further half a turn. Continue until all the bolts have been fully-slackened. The camshaft will rise up under the action of the valve springs as the bolts are slackened. Ensure that the camshaft rises uniformly and does not jam in its bearings.

**4** When all the bolts have been slackened, remove the bolts and lift off the bearing caps, keeping them in order according to the identification method decided on **(see illustration)**.

**5** Note the installed position of the camshafts before removal – the cam lobes for No 1 cylinder should be pointing outwards (ie, away from the centre). Carefully lift the camshafts from their locations in the cylinder head. If both camshafts are removed, identify them as exhaust and inlet **(see illustration)**.

**6** Obtain sixteen small, clean plastic containers, and number them inlet 1 to 8 and exhaust 1 to 8; alternatively, divide a larger container into sixteen compartments and number each compartment accordingly. Withdraw each rocker arm and hydraulic tappet in turn, and place them in their respective container **(see illustrations)**. Do not interchange the rocker arms and tappets, or the rate of wear will be much increased.

## Inspection

**7** Examine the camshaft bearing surfaces and cam lobes for signs of wear ridges and scoring. Renew the camshaft if any of these conditions are apparent. Examine the condition of the bearing surfaces, both on the camshaft journals and in the cylinder head/bearing caps. If the head bearing surfaces are worn excessively, the cylinder head will need to be renewed.

**8** Examine the rocker arm and hydraulic tappet bearing surfaces for wear ridges and scoring. Renew any rocker arm or tappet on which these conditions are apparent.

**9** If either camshaft is being renewed, it will be necessary to renew all the rocker arms and tappets for that particular camshaft also.

## Refitting

**10** Before refitting, thoroughly clean all the components and the cylinder head and bearing cap journals.

**11** Liberally oil the cylinder head hydraulic tappet bores and the tappets. Carefully refit the tappets to the cylinder head, ensuring that each tappet is refitted to its original bore.

**12** Lay each rocker arm in position over its respective tappet.

**13** Liberally oil the camshaft bearings in the cylinder head and the camshaft lobes, then place the camshafts in the cylinder head. Turn the camshafts so that the cam lobes for No 1 cylinder are pointing outwards as noted during removal.

**14** Refit all the bearing caps to their respective

locations ensuring they are fitted the correct way round as noted during removal.

**15** Working in a spiral pattern from the inside to the outside, initially tighten the bearing cap bolts, one at a time, by half a turn. When all the bolts have been initially tightened, repeat the procedure, tightening the bolts by a further half a turn. Continue until all the bearing caps are in contact with the cylinder head and the bolts are very lightly tightened.

**16** Again, working in a spiral pattern from inside to outside, tighten all the bolts to the specified torque.

**17** Refit the camshaft sprockets as described in Section 8.

**10  Cylinder head –**
  removal and refitting

**Note 1:** *The engine must be cold when removing the cylinder head. A new cylinder head gasket, timing cover gasket, cylinder head bolts, camshaft sprocket bolts, together with seals and sealing rings, will be required for refitting. A suitable sealant will also be needed to seal the timing cover-to-cylinder block joint.*
**Note 2:** *The special tools described in Section 4 will also be required for this operation. Read through the entire procedure and also the procedures contained in Section 4 to familiarise yourself with the work involved, then either obtain the manufacturer's special tools, or use the alternatives described.*

**9.6a  Withdraw each rocker arm . . .**

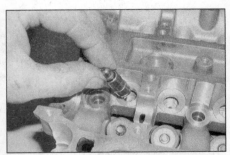

**9.6b  . . . and hydraulic tappet in turn, and place them in their respective containers – shown with cylinder head removed**

**10.10 Undo the bolt (arrowed) securing the support bracket to the base of the inlet manifold**

## Removal

1 Apply the handbrake, then jack up the front of the vehicle and support it on axle stands (see *Jacking and vehicle support*). Remove the right-hand roadwheel. On ECO models, remove the engine undertray sections.

2 Disconnect the battery negative terminal (refer to *Disconnecting the battery* in the Reference Chapter), then remove the battery and battery tray as described in Chapter 5A.

3 Drain the cooling system as described in Chapter 1A.

4 On 1.2 and 1.4 litre models, remove the front bumper as described in Chapter 11.

5 Remove the air cleaner assembly as described in Chapter 4A. Also remove the air inlet duct from the front of the engine compartment by unscrewing the single bolt.

6 Remove the throttle body as described in Chapter 4A, Section 10.

7 Disconnect the heater feed hose from the coolant pump and position it to one side.

8 Disconnect the brake servo vacuum line from the inlet manifold. Where applicable, also disconnect the evaporative system hose from the manifold.

9 Where applicable, undo the two bolts and remove the cover over the fuel rail. Similarly, undo the two bolts and release the wiring harness support bracket from the rear of the inlet manifold.

10 From under the car, undo the bolt securing the support bracket to the base of the inlet manifold. Slacken the bolt securing the bracket to the cylinder block and twist the bracket to one side **(see illustration)**.

11 On 1.0 litre engines, detach the additional lower wiring harness bracket from the inlet manifold.

12 Disconnect the heater return hose from the EGR coolant flange, and unclip the wiring harness.

13 Depressurise the fuel system as described in Chapter 4A, then disconnect the fuel feed and return hoses from the fuel rail, noting their locations to aid refitting. Be prepared for fuel spillage, and take adequate precautions. Clamp or plug the open ends of the hoses, to minimise further fuel loss.

14 Disconnect the wiring from the following components:
   a) *Oil pressure switch.*
   b) *Coolant temperature sensor.*
   c) *Camshaft position sensor.*
   d) *Fuel injectors.*
   e) *Throttle valve adjuster.*
   f) *Engine electronic control unit (LH end of engine).*
   g) *Wiring combination plug (LH end of engine).*
   h) *EGR valve.*

15 Release the ignition module cover from the centre of the camshaft cover and remove it toward the transmission end of the engine. Disconnect the wiring plug from the left-hand end of the module.

16 Disconnect the earth cables from the electronic control unit bracket.

17 Undo the two bolts, one at each end, securing the plastic fuel injector wiring trough to the top of the fuel rail. Note that these bolts also secure the fuel rail to the inlet manifold. With the injector wiring disconnected, lift the wiring trough up and off the injectors. Place the trough to one side.

18 Remove the auxiliary drivebelt cover from under the right-hand wheel arch.

19 Refer to Chapter 4A, Section 10, and disconnect the wiring from the oxygen sensor on the catalytic converter, then unbolt the exhaust front pipe/catalytic converter from the exhaust manifold, taking care to support the flexible section. **Note:** *Angular movement in excess of 10° can cause permanent damage to the flexible section.*

20 Release the mounting rubbers and support the front of the exhaust pipe to one side.

21 Slacken, but do not remove, the three coolant pump pulley retaining bolts.

22 Unscrew the nuts and disconnect the wiring from the starter motor. Also, release the cable ties.

23 Unbolt the two wiring harness brackets from the inlet manifold.

24 On models without air conditioning, turn the auxiliary drivebelt tensioner pulley bolt clockwise then insert a suitable pin through the spring centre shaft to lock the spring in its compressed state. Note the routing of the drivebelt, then remove it from the pulleys – mark the drivebelt for fitted direction. **Note:** *The drivebelt cannot be removed completely until the right-hand engine mounting has been removed.* Unscrew the auxiliary drivebelt tensioner lower mounting bolt and the tensioner roller upper pivot bolt. Remove the tensioner from the timing cover.

25 On models with air conditioning, turn the auxiliary drivebelt tensioner pulley bolt clockwise to tension the spring, then insert a suitable pin through the hole in the tensioner body and into the hole in the timing cover to lock the spring. Note the routing of the drivebelt, then remove it from the pulleys – mark the drivebelt for fitted direction. **Note:** *The drivebelt cannot be removed completely until the right-hand engine mounting has been removed.* Turn the tensioner pulley bolt clockwise again and remove the locking pin, then gradually release the tensioner until it is fully released. Unbolt the tensioner from the timing cover.

26 Undo the bolt securing the oil dipstick guide tube to the exhaust manifold and withdraw the dipstick and guide tube from the cylinder block baseplate. To do this, turn the guide tube forward. Suitably cover or plug the guide tube aperture in the cylinder block baseplate to prevent dirt ingress.

27 Disconnect the wiring from the oxygen sensor on the exhaust manifold at the left-hand front of the engine, then unscrew the sensor from the head. Refer to Chapter 4A, Section 10, if necessary.

28 Unbolt the left-hand engine lifting eye from the cylinder head, complete with attached wiring harness.

29 On models with air conditioning, unbolt the compressor from the cylinder block, release the refrigerant lines from their brackets and support the compressor clear of the engine. **Do not** disconnect the refrigerant lines from the compressor.

30 Unbolt the exhaust manifold heat shield **(see illustration)**, then unscrew the mounting nuts and withdraw the exhaust manifold from the cylinder head. Recover the gasket.

31 Remove the oil filter from the filter housing as described in Chapter 1A. Remove as much of the oil remaining in the filter housing as possible using clean rags.

32 Undo the three bolts and remove the oil filter housing from the cylinder block **(see illustration)**. Place absorbent rags below the housing as it is removed to catch any remaining oil. Recover the filter housing seal noting that a new seal will be required for refitting.

**10.30 Undo the two bolts (arrowed) and remove the exhaust manifold heat shield**

**10.32 Undo the three bolts and remove the oil filter housing from the cylinder block**

**33** Loosen the clips and disconnect the radiator upper hose from the radiator and thermostat housing.

**34** The engine must now be supported while the right-hand engine mounting is removed. To do this, use a hoist attached to the top of the engine, or make up a wooden frame to locate beneath the sump and use a trolley jack.

**35** Remove the right-hand engine mounting bracket with reference to Section 15, then remove the auxiliary drivebelt.

**36** Fully unscrew the bolts and remove the coolant pump pulley from its drive flange.

**37** Undo the three bolts securing the thermostat housing cover to the coolant pump. Remove the sealing ring from the housing cover noting that a new one will be required for refitting.

**38** Undo the bolts securing the coolant pump and timing cover to the cylinder head **(see illustration)**. Note that it is not necessary to remove all the coolant pump bolts as three are shorter than the rest, and only secure the pump to the timing cover.

**39** Remove the camshaft cover as described in Section 3.

**40** Using a socket or spanner on the crankshaft pulley hub bolt, turn the crankshaft in the normal direction of rotation (clockwise as viewed from the right-hand side of the car) until the TDC notch on the crankshaft pulley is located just before the cast lug on the timing cover (see Section 4).

**41** Check that No 1 piston is on the compression stroke by observing No 1 cylinder camshaft lobes. All four lobes should be pointing outwards (away from the engine). If they are not, No 1 piston is on the exhaust stroke and the crankshaft should be turned through a further full turn, stopping once again just before the TDC notch aligns with the lug on the timing cover.

**42** Undo the closure bolt from the crankshaft TDC position setting hole. The plug is located on the front facing side of the cylinder block baseplate, adjacent to the timing cover joint. Note that a new closure bolt sealing ring will be required for refitting.

**43** Slowly turn the crankshaft in the normal direction of rotation until the TDC positioning pin (or suitable alternative), described in Section 4, engages with the TDC slot in the crankshaft.

**44** Obtain a suitable roll-pin, or similar, of 2 mm diameter and approximately 30 mm long, to use as a timing chain tensioner locking tool.

**45** Using a suitable spanner engaged with the flats provided on the inlet camshaft, apply tension in a clockwise direction (as viewed from the right-hand side of the car) to the camshaft, to take up any slack in the timing chain. This will push the timing chain tensioner plunger fully into its bore.

**46** Hold the camshaft in this position and retain the tensioner plunger in the released position by inserting the roll-pin through the closure plug aperture and into the hole on the tensioner body.

**10.38  Undo the bolts (1) securing the coolant pump, and the bolts (arrowed) securing the timing cover, to the cylinder head**

**47** Undo the two bolts and remove the timing chain sliding rail from the top of the cylinder head.

**48** Slacken the sprocket retaining bolts for both camshafts, using the spanner to counterhold each camshaft as the bolts are slackened. Remove both sprocket bolts together with the camshaft position sensor phase disc from the inlet camshaft. Ease the sprockets and chain off the camshafts and rest the sprockets on the top of the timing cover.

**49** Undo the retaining bolt and remove the camshaft position sensor from the front of the timing cover.

**50** Working in the specified sequence, progressively slacken the cylinder head retaining bolts half a turn at a time until all the bolts are loose **(see illustrations)**. Remove the bolts from their locations noting that new bolts will be required for refitting.

**51** Slightly raise the cylinder head so it just clears the cylinder block face and move the head toward the transmission end of the engine. The head will be initially tight due to the sealant on the timing cover gasket and head gasket. Note that the locating dowel holes on the cylinder head are elongated to allow the head to move sideways slightly.

**52** As soon as sufficient clearance exists, lift the cylinder head up and off the cylinder block. At the same time, release the timing chain guide rail from the peg on the cylinder head, and guide the chain tensioner clear of the tensioning rail. Check that the tensioner locking pin is not dislodged as the cylinder head is lifted up. Place the cylinder head on wooden blocks after removal to avoid damage to the valves. Recover the cylinder head gasket.

**10.50a  Cylinder head bolt slackening sequence – 1.0 litre engines**

**10.50b  Cylinder head bolt slackening sequence – 1.2 and 1.4 litre engines**

**10.57 Before refitting the cylinder head, insert the camshaft setting tool (arrowed) into the slots in the ends of the camshafts**

## Preparation for refitting

**53** The mating faces of the cylinder head and cylinder block must be perfectly clean before refitting the head. Scouring agents are available for this purpose, but acceptable results can be achieved by using a hard plastic or wood scraper to remove all traces of gasket and carbon. The same method can be used to clean the piston crowns. Take particular care to avoid scoring or gouging the cylinder head mating surfaces during the cleaning operations, as aluminium alloy is easily damaged. Make sure that the carbon is not allowed to enter the oil and water passages – this is particularly important for the lubrication system, as carbon could block the oil supply to the engine's components. Using adhesive tape and paper, seal the water, oil and bolt holes in the cylinder block. To prevent carbon entering the gap between the pistons and bores, smear a little grease in the gap. After cleaning each piston, use a small brush to remove all traces of grease and carbon from the gap, then wipe away the remainder with a clean rag.

**54** Check the mating surfaces of the cylinder block and the cylinder head for nicks, deep scratches and other damage. If slight, they may be removed carefully with a file, but if excessive, machining may be the only alternative to renewal. If warpage of the cylinder head gasket surface is suspected, use a straight-edge to check it for distortion. Refer to Part E of this Chapter if necessary.

**55** Thoroughly clean the threads of the cylinder head bolt holes in the cylinder block.

**10.67a Tighten the cylinder head bolts to the Stage 1 torque setting using a torque wrench**

**10.60 Position the cylinder head gasket on the block with the words OBEN/TOP uppermost**

Ensure that the bolts run freely in their threads, and that all traces of oil and water are removed from each bolt hole.

**56** Using a sharp knife, partially cut through the timing cover gasket flush with the top of the cylinder block. Release the gasket from the timing cover and bend it in half to break it off at the cut line. Remove the upper part of the gasket, and thoroughly clean the mating surface, paying particular attention to the cylinder block edge where it contacts the timing cover.

**57** Before refitting the cylinder head, using the spanner on the camshaft flats, turn the camshafts slightly, as necessary, until the camshaft setting tool described in Section 4 can be inserted into the slots in the ends of the camshafts **(see illustration)**. With the tool in position, the camshaft lobes for No 1 cylinder should be pointing outward.

## Refitting

**58** Prior to locating the cylinder head gasket on the cylinder block, cut off the two protruding tabs at the timing cover end of the gasket, flush with the gasket edge.

**59** Apply a 2 mm diameter bead of silicone sealant to the joint between the cylinder block and the timing cover on each side.

**60** Check that the locating dowels are in position in the cylinder block, then lay the new gasket on the block face, with the words OBEN/TOP uppermost **(see illustration)**. Push the gasket hard up against the timing cover so that it engages with the sealant.

**61** Position the new timing cover gasket

**10.67b Tighten the cylinder head bolts through the Stage two, three and four angles using an angle tightening gauge**

upper part on the timing cover, so that its lower ends engage with the sealant. Temporarily insert the left- and right-hand upper timing cover mounting bolts to locate the gasket in the correct position.

**62** Apply a further 2 mm diameter bead of silicone sealant to the joint between the cylinder block and the timing cover on each side.

**63** Carefully lower the cylinder head into position on the gasket, guiding the chain tensioner past the tensioning rail and guiding the tensioner locking pin into the timing cover access hole. Check also that the timing chain guide rail engages with cylinder head peg.

**64** Once the head is seated on its dowels, tap it towards the timing cover with a rubber mallet.

**65** Refit the three lower timing cover retaining bolts (one at each side, and one below the coolant pump). Tighten the three bolts to the specified torque.

**66** Remove the camshaft setting tool from the camshaft slots.

**67** Fit the new cylinder head retaining bolts and screw in the bolts until they contact the cylinder head. Working in the **reverse** order to the loosening sequence shown earlier in this Section, tighten the cylinder head bolts to the Stage one torque setting given in the Specifications, using a torque wrench. Again working in the correct order, tighten all the bolts through the Stage two angle using an angle measuring gauge **(see illustrations)**. Repeat for Stage three and Stage four.

**68** Slacken the three previously-fitted bolts securing the timing cover to the cylinder head.

**69** Refit the bolts around the coolant pump and tighten them securely.

**70** Refit the remaining timing cover retaining bolts and tighten them to the specified torque.

**71** Using the spanner on the camshaft flats, turn the camshafts slightly, as necessary, until the camshaft setting tool can once again be inserted into the camshaft slots.

**72** Engage the camshaft sprockets with their respective camshafts, and fit the new retaining bolts together with the phase disc on the inlet camshaft. Tighten the bolts finger tight only at this stage and check that the phase disc on the inlet camshaft can still be turned.

**73** Refit the timing chain sliding rail to the top of the cylinder head and secure with the two bolts tightened securely.

**74** Remove the roll-pin used to hold the timing chain tensioner plunger in the retracted position.

**75** Turn the camshaft sensor phase disc as necessary until the phase disc positioning tool (or suitable alternative), described in Section 4, can be located over the phase disc. If the Vauxhall tool is being used, bolt it to the top of the timing cover. If the alternative tool described is being used, ensure that its base is in contact with the timing cover.

**76** Tighten the camshaft sprocket retaining bolts to 10 Nm (7 lbf ft). Note that this is just an initial torque loading to hold the sprockets and the phase disc in position when the setting tools are removed. Tighten the inlet camshaft sprocket bolt first, followed by the exhaust camshaft sprocket bolt.

**77** Remove the crankshaft, camshaft and phase disc setting tools, then tighten the camshaft sprocket retaining bolts to the specified torque in the stages given in the Specifications. Counterhold the camshafts using the spanner on the camshaft flats as the sprocket bolts are tightened.

**78** Turn the crankshaft through two complete revolutions, stopping just before the TDC notch on the crankshaft pulley aligns with the cast lug on the timing cover. Check that all four lobes for No 1 cylinder are pointing outwards (away from the engine).

**79** Slowly turn the crankshaft further until the TDC position setting tool can once again be inserted to lock the crankshaft.

**80** It should now be possible to re-insert the camshaft setting tool into the slots in the camshafts, and to fit the camshaft sensor phase disc setting tool over the disc. If this is not possible carry out the valve timing adjustment procedure contained in Section 4.

**81** If all is satisfactory, remove all the setting/ aligning tools and refit the timing chain tensioner and cylinder block closure bolts using new sealing rings. Tighten both closure bolts to the specified torque.

**82** Refit the camshaft position sensor using a new sealing ring and tighten the retaining bolt securely.

**83** On models with air conditioning, refit the compressor to the cylinder block and tighten the mounting bolts to the specified torque. Refit the refrigerant lines to their relevant clips or brackets.

**84** Refit the camshaft cover as described in Section 3.

**85** Ensure that the mating surfaces are clean, then fit a new sealing ring to the thermostat housing cover. Refit the cover to the coolant pump and tighten the bolts securely.

**86** Refit the coolant pump pulley and tighten the three bolts to the specified torque. To prevent the pulley turning as the bolts are tightened, hold the pulley using a screwdriver engaged with one of the bolts and the pump centre spindle. Alternatively, wait until the auxiliary drivebelt has been refitted and tighten the bolts then.

**87** Refit the right-hand engine mounting bracket together with the auxiliary drivebelt with reference to Section 15. Remove the hoist or trolley jack supporting the engine.

**88** Reconnect the radiator top hose and tighten the clips.

**89** Thoroughly clean the mating surfaces of the oil filter housing and cylinder block, and refit the housing using a new seal. Refit and tighten the retaining bolts to the specified torque.

**90** Fit a new sealing O-ring to the oil filter

housing cap, then clip the new oil filter element to the cap.

**91** Fit the cap and filter element assembly to the oil filter housing and screw the cap into position. Finally, tighten the cap to the specified torque.

**92** Refit the exhaust manifold, together with a new gasket, and tighten the mounting nuts to the specified torque. Refit the exhaust manifold heat shield.

**93** Refit the left-hand engine lifting eye to the cylinder head and tighten the bolts securely. Attach the wiring harness.

**94** Refer to Chapter 4A and refit the oxygen sensor to the exhaust manifold. Reconnect the wiring.

**95** Renew the oil dipstick guide tube O-rings and lubricate the O-rings with petroleum jelly. Insert the guide tube into the cylinder block baseplate then secure the tube to the exhaust manifold with the retaining bolt.

**96** Refit the auxiliary drivebelt tensioner and tighten the mounting bolts to the specified torque.

**97** Rotate the tensioner pulley bolt clockwise as for removal, refit the auxiliary drivebelt as previously noted and release the tensioner.

**98** Refit the wiring harness brackets to the inlet manifold.

**99** Reconnect the wiring to the starter motor and tighten the nuts. Secure the cable with ties.

**100** Reconnect the catalytic converter to the exhaust manifold using a new flange gasket. Tighten the converter-to-manifold nuts to the specified torque first, followed by the support bracket bolts. Refit the mounting rubbers, then refit the oxygen sensor with reference to Chapter 4A. Reconnect the wiring.

**101** Refit the auxiliary drivebelt cover under the right-hand wheel arch.

**102** Refit the injector wiring and trough to the top of the fuel rail.

**103** Reconnect the earth cables to the electronic control unit bracket.

**104** Refit the ignition module with reference to Chapter 5B, and reconnect the wiring.

**105** Reconnect the wiring to the following components:
 a) Oil pressure switch.
 b) Coolant temperature sensor.
 c) Camshaft position sensor.
 d) Fuel injectors.
 e) Throttle valve adjuster.
 f) Engine electronic control unit (LH end of engine).
 g) Wiring combination plug (LH end of engine).
 h) EGR valve.

**106** Reconnect the fuel feed and return hoses to the fuel rail.

**107** Disconnect the heater return hose to the EGR coolant flange, and secure the wiring harness.

**108** On 1.0 litre engines, attach the lower wiring harness bracket to the inlet manifold.

**109** Refit and tighten the bolt securing the

support bracket to the base of the inlet manifold.

**110** Refit the wiring harness support bracket to the rear of the inlet manifold.

**111** Reconnect the brake servo vacuum line to the inlet manifold.

**112** Where applicable, refit the cover over the fuel rail.

**113** Reconnect the heater feed hose to the coolant pump and tighten the clip.

**114** Refit the throttle body as described in Chapter 4A.

**115** Refit the air cleaner assembly with reference to Chapter 4A. Also refit the air inlet duct to the front of the engine compartment.

**116** Refit or reconnect the battery as applicable.

**117** Refill the cooling system and top-up the engine oil with reference to Chapter 1A.

**118** Refit the roadwheel then lower the vehicle to the ground.

## 11 Sump and oil pick-up pipe – removal and refitting

**Note:** *A new sump gasket must be used on refitting. If the oil pick-up pipe is removed, a new O-ring should be used on refitting.*

### Removal

**1** Firmly apply the handbrake, then jack up the front of the car and support it securely on axle stands (see *Jacking and vehicle support*). Remove the right-hand roadwheel. On ECO models, remove the engine undertray sections.

**2** Drain the engine oil, with reference to Chapter 1A, then refit and tighten the sump drain plug.

**3** Refer to Chapter 4A, Section 10, and disconnect the wiring from the oxygen sensor on the catalytic converter, then unbolt the exhaust front pipe from the exhaust manifold, taking care to support the flexible section. **Note:** *Angular movement in excess of 10° can cause permanent damage to the flexible section.* Release the mounting rubbers and support the front of the exhaust pipe to one side to allow removal of the sump.

**4** Remove the auxiliary drivebelt cover from under the right-hand wheel arch.

**5** Undo the bolts securing the sump to the cylinder block baseplate, timing cover and transmission bellhousing, then withdraw the sump. If necessary, tap the sump with a soft-faced mallet to free it from its location – do not lever between the sump and cylinder block baseplate mating faces. Recover the gasket.

**6** To remove the oil baffle plate, undo the retaining bolts and remove the baffle plate from the cylinder block baseplate.

**7** If desired, the oil pick-up pipe can be removed from the sump by unscrewing the two support bracket retaining bolts and the two bolts securing the flange to the end face of the sump. Lift out the pick-up pipe

11.7a  Undo the bolts (arrowed) . . .

11.7b  . . . remove the oil pick-up pipe . . .

11.7c  . . . and recover the O-ring from the flange

11.11a  Apply a 2 mm diameter bead of silicone sealant to the joint between the timing cover and cylinder block on each side . . .

11.11b  . . . then place a new gasket on the sump and locate the sump on the cylinder block baseplate – shown with engine removed

11.12  If the engine has been separated from the transmission, use a straight-edge to check the transmission mating face alignment when refitting the sump

and recover the O-ring from the flange **(see illustrations)**. Note that a new O-ring will be required for refitting.

### Refitting

**8** Thoroughly clean the inside and outside of the sump ensuring that all traces of old gasket are removed from the mating face. Also clean the cylinder block baseplate mating face to remove all traces of old gasket.

**9** If the oil pick-up pipe has been removed, fit a new O-ring to the flange, then refit the pipe to the sump. Refit the flange bolts and support bracket bolts, then tighten the flange bolts securely. Tighten the support bracket bolts securely.

**10** If removed, refit the oil baffle plate and secure with the retaining bolts tightened securely.

**11** Apply a 2 mm diameter bead of silicone

sealant to the joint between the timing cover and cylinder block, on each side. Place a new gasket on the sump, then locate the sump on the cylinder block baseplate **(see illustrations)**. Refit the securing bolts and tighten them finger tight at this stage.

**12** If the engine has been removed from the car and separated from the transmission, use a straight-edge to check that the transmission mating face is aligned with the cylinder block baseplate mating face **(see illustration)**.

**13** Tighten the bolts securing the sump to the cylinder block baseplate and timing cover progressively and securely. Now tighten the bolts securing the sump to the transmission bellhousing to the specified torque.

**14** Refit the auxiliary drivebelt cover under the right-hand wheel arch.

**15** Reconnect the exhaust system front pipe/catalytic converter to the manifold as

described in Chapter 4A. Also, reconnect the wiring to the oxygen sensor.

**16** Refit the roadwheel, and where necessary the engine undertray sections, then lower the car to the ground and refill the engine with oil as described in Chapter 1A.

### 12 Oil pump –
removal, inspection and refitting

**Note:** *A new pressure relief valve cap sealing ring and new oil fill channel closure plug sealing ring will be required for refitting.*

### Removal

**1** Remove the timing cover and chain as described in Section 6.

**2** Remove the securing screws/bolts and withdraw the oil pump cover from the rear of the timing cover **(see illustration)**.

**3** Remove the inner and outer rotor from the timing cover and wipe them clean. Also clean the rotor location in the timing cover.

**4** The oil pressure relief valve components can also be removed from the timing cover by unscrewing the cap. Withdraw the cap and sealing ring, the spring and plastic pin, and the plunger **(see illustrations)**.

### Inspection

**5** Locate the inner and outer rotor back in the timing cover, noting that the chamfer on the outer rotor outside diameter must face the timing cover.

12.2  Remove the securing screws and withdraw the oil pump cover from the rear of the timing cover

12.4a  Unscrew the oil pressure relief valve cap and sealing ring . . .

**12.4b ... then withdraw the spring and plastic pin ...**

**12.4c ... and the plunger**

**12.6 Check the oil pump gear endfloat using a straight-edge and feeler gauge**

**6** Check the clearance between the end faces of the gears and the housing (endfloat) using a straight-edge and a feeler gauge **(see illustration)**.

**7** If the clearance is outside the specified limits, renew the components as necessary.

**8** Examine the pressure relief valve spring and plunger, and renew if any sign of damage or wear is evident.

**9** Ensure that the rotor location in the interior of the timing cover is scrupulously clean before commencing reassembly.

### Refitting

**10** Thoroughly clean the pressure relief valve components, and lubricate them with clean engine oil before refitting. Insert the plunger, the spring and plastic pin, then refit the cap using a new sealing ring. Tighten the cap securely.

**11** Ensure that the gears are clean, then lubricate them with clean engine oil, and refit them to the pump body. Ensure that the chamfer on the outer rotor outside diameter faces the timing cover.

**12** Ensure that the mating faces of the rear cover and the pump housing are clean, then refit the rear cover. Refit and tighten the securing screws securely.

**13** Fit a new crankshaft oil seal to the timing cover as described in Section 13.

**14** Refit the timing chain and cover to the engine as described in Section 6.

**15** After refitting the timing cover, unscrew the oil fill channel closure bolt from the lower front facing side of the timing cover. Using a pump type oil can filled with clean engine oil, insert the oil can spout into the oil channel, so that the spout pushes back the internal ball valve. Prime the pump by filling it with oil until the oil runs out of the fill channel. Refit the closure plug using a new sealing ring and tighten it to the specified torque.

### 13 Crankshaft oil seals – renewal

### Timing chain end oil seal

**Note:** A new crankshaft pulley hub retaining bolt will be required for refitting.

**1** Disconnect the battery negative terminal (refer to *Disconnecting the battery* in the Reference Chapter).

**2** Remove the air cleaner assembly as described in Chapter 4A.

**3** Firmly apply the handbrake, then jack up the front of the car and support it securely on axle stands (see *Jacking and vehicle support*). Remove the right-hand front roadwheel and the wheel arch liner for access to the crankshaft pulley.

**4** Release the tension on the auxiliary drivebelt and lock the tensioner in the released position as described in the auxiliary drivebelt renewal procedure in Chapter 1A. Note that it is not necessary to completely remove the drivebelt, as this would entail removal of the right-hand engine mounting bracket. With the drivebelt tension released, slip the belt off the crankshaft pulley.

**5** Using a socket or spanner on the crankshaft pulley hub bolt, turn the crankshaft in the normal direction of rotation (clockwise as viewed from the right-hand side of the car) until the TDC notch on the crankshaft pulley is located just before the cast lug on the timing cover **(see illustration 4.6)**.

**6** Using quick-drying paint, or similar, make an alignment mark between the crankshaft pulley and the pulley hub. It should only be possible to refit the pulley in one position, but it is advisable to make an alignment mark anyway.

**7** Unscrew the six crankshaft pulley retaining bolts and remove the pulley from the hub. If necessary, prevent the crankshaft from turning

**13.10 Carefully prise out the crankshaft oil seal from the timing cover – shown with timing cover removed**

as the pulley bolts are slackened, using a spanner or socket on the pulley hub bolt.

**8** Using a suitable socket, slacken the crankshaft pulley hub retaining bolt. The crankshaft can be prevented from turning as the bolt is slackened, using Vauxhall special tool KM-956 or a similar tool which will engage with the flats on each side of the pulley hub. Alternatively, remove the starter motor, and lock the flywheel ring gear teeth using a suitable hooked tool bolted to the bellhousing.

**9** Unscrew the slackened crankshaft pulley hub retaining bolt and remove the hub from the crankshaft. Note that a new bolt will be required for refitting.

**10** The seal can now be carefully prised out with a screwdriver or similar hooked tool **(see illustration)**.

**11** Clean the oil seal seat with a wooden or plastic scraper.

**12** Grease the lips of the new seal, and tap it into position until it is flush with the outer face of the timing cover, using a suitable socket or tube, or a wooden block **(see illustration)**.

**13** Refit the crankshaft pulley hub to the crankshaft, ensuring that the punch mark on the pulley hub is in the 11 o'clock position.

**14** Screw in the new pulley hub retaining bolt and tighten it to the specified torque, in the stages given in the Specifications. Prevent crankshaft rotation as the bolt is tightened, using the method employed for removal.

**15** Refit the crankshaft pulley to the pulley hub, with the marks made on removal aligned, and tighten the six bolts securely.

**13.12 Tap the new seal into position until it is flush with the outer face of the timing cover – shown with timing cover removed**

**13.23  Locate the seal over the crankshaft and into the recess – shown with engine removed**

**16** Refit the auxiliary drivebelt as described in Chapter 1A.

**17** Refit the air cleaner assembly as described in Chapter 4A.

**18** Refit the wheel arch liner and roadwheel, tightening the wheel bolts to the specified torque.

**19** Lower the car to the ground, then reconnect the battery negative terminal.

### Transmission end oil seal

**20** Remove the flywheel as described in Section 14.

**21** Carefully prise out the old seal from its location using a screwdriver or similar hooked tool.

**22** Clean the oil seal seat with a wooden or plastic scraper.

**14.4  If the engine is removed, lock the flywheel with a suitable tool**

**14.12a  Tighten the flywheel bolts to the specified torque using a torque wrench . . .**

**13.24  Tap the seal into position until it is flush – shown with engine removed**

**23** Grease the lips of the new seal, then carefully locate the seal over the crankshaft and into the recess in the cylinder block and baseplate **(see illustration)**.

**24** Tap the seal into position using a suitable socket or tube, or a wooden block, until it is flush with the outer faces of the cylinder block and baseplate **(see illustration)**.

**25** Refit the flywheel as described in Section 14.

---

**14 Flywheel –**
removal, inspection
and refitting

**Note:** *New flywheel securing bolts must be used on refitting.*

**14.5  Unscrew the securing bolts, and remove the flywheel – shown with engine removed**

**14.12b  . . . then through the specified angle using an angle tightening gauge**

### Removal

**1** Remove the transmission as described in Chapter 7A or 7C, as applicable.

**2** Remove the clutch assembly as described in Chapter 6.

**3** Although the flywheel bolt holes are offset so that the flywheel can only be fitted in one position, it will make refitting easier if alignment marks are made between the flywheel and the end of the crankshaft.

**4** Prevent the flywheel from turning by jamming the ring gear teeth using a suitable tool **(see illustration)**.

**5** Unscrew the securing bolts, and remove the flywheel **(see illustration)**.

*Caution: Take care, as the flywheel is heavy.*

### Inspection

**6** If the teeth on the flywheel starter ring are badly worn, or if some are missing, then it will be necessary to remove the ring and fit a new one.

**7** The old ring can be split with a cold chisel, after drilling a shallow hole between two gear teeth. Take great care not to damage the flywheel during this operation, and wear eye protection at all times. Once the ring has been split, it will spread apart, and can be lifted from the flywheel.

**8** The new ring gear must be heated evenly to between 180 and 230°C. Unless facilities for heating by oven or flame are available, leave the fitting to a Vauxhall dealer or engineering works. The new ring gear must not be overheated during this work, or the temper of the metal will be affected.

**9** The ring should be tapped gently down onto its register, and left to cool naturally – the contraction of the metal on cooling will ensure that it is a secure and permanent fit.

*Caution: Make sure that the ring is fitted the correct way round, so that the starter motor pinion teeth will engage the tooth 'lead-in' bevel machined on one side of the flywheel teeth.*

**10** If the clutch friction disc contact surface of the flywheel is scored, or on close inspection shows signs of small hair cracks (caused by overheating), it may be possible to have the flywheel surface-ground, provided the overall thickness of the flywheel is not reduced too much. Consult a Vauxhall dealer or a specialist engine repairer and, if grinding is not possible, renew the flywheel complete.

### Refitting

**11** Offer the flywheel to the end of the crankshaft, and align the previously-made marks on the flywheel and crankshaft.

**12** Coat the threads of the new flywheel bolts with thread-locking compound (note that new bolts may be supplied ready-coated), then fit the bolts and tighten them to the specified torque, whilst preventing the flywheel from turning as during removal **(see illustrations)**.

**13** Refit the clutch as described in Chapter 6, then refit the transmission as described in Chapter 7A or 7C, as applicable.

**15.8 Right-hand engine mounting-to-engine bracket bolts (A) and mounting-to-body bolts (B)**

**15.13 Left-hand engine mounting bracket-to-transmission bracket bolts (arrowed)**

**15.25 Undo the nut and bolt (arrowed) securing the torque link to the mounting on the transmission bracket**

## 15 Engine/transmission mountings – inspection and renewal

### Inspection

**1** To improve access, firmly apply the handbrake, then jack up the front of the vehicle and support it on axle stands (see *Jacking and vehicle support*).

**2** Check the mounting blocks (rubbers) to see if they are cracked, hardened or separated from the metal at any point. Renew the mounting block if any such damage or deterioration is evident.

**3** Check that all the mounting securing nuts and bolts are securely tightened, using a torque wrench to check if possible.

**4** Using a large screwdriver, or a similar tool, check for wear in the mounting blocks by carefully levering against them to check for free play. Where this is not possible, enlist the aid of an assistant to move the engine/transmission unit back-and-forth, and from side-to-side, while you observe the mountings. While some free play is to be expected, even from new components, excessive wear should be obvious. If excessive free play is found, check first to see that the securing nuts and bolts are correctly tightened, then renew any worn components as described in the following paragraphs.

### Renewal

**Note:** *Before slackening any of the engine mounting bolts/nuts, the relative positions of the mountings to their various brackets should be marked to ensure correct alignment upon refitting.*

### Right-hand mounting

**5** Apply the handbrake, then jack up the front of the vehicle and support it on axle stands

(see *Jacking and vehicle support*). Remove the right-hand roadwheel and the wheel arch liner for access to the crankshaft pulley.

**6** Remove the air cleaner as described in Chapter 4A.

**7** Attach a suitable hoist and lifting tackle to the engine lifting brackets on the cylinder head, and support the weight of the engine.

**8** Unscrew the four mounting bolts and remove the right-hand mounting from the engine mounting bracket and body **(see illustration)**. If necessary, the engine mounting bracket may be unbolted from the cylinder block.

**9** If necessary, refit the engine mounting bracket and tighten the bolts to the specified torque, then locate the new mounting block on the body and engine bracket, and tighten the bolts to the specified torque.

**10** Remove the hoist, then refit the air cleaner.

**11** Refit the wheel arch liner and right-hand roadwheel, then lower the vehicle to the ground.

### Left-hand mounting

**12** Attach a suitable hoist and lifting tackle to the engine lifting brackets on the cylinder head, and support the weight of the engine.

**13** Using a Torx socket, unscrew the two bolts securing the mounting bracket to the transmission bracket **(see illustration)**.

**14** Undo the four bolts securing the mounting to the body and the three bolts securing the transmission bracket to the transmission.

**15** Slightly lower the engine, then unclip the clutch hydraulic line from the mounting bracket. Remove the mounting assembly from the car.

**16** If necessary, undo the through-bolt and separate the rubber mounting from the mounting bracket.

**17** If removed, refit the rubber mounting to the mounting bracket and tighten the through-bolt to the specified torque.

**18** Locate the mounting brackets in position and, where necessary, clip the clutch hydraulic line onto the bracket.

**19** Raise the engine and insert the bolts, then tighten them to the specified torque.

**20** Disconnect the hoist and lifting tackle.

### Rear mounting/torque link

**21** Apply the handbrake, then jack up the front of the vehicle and support it on axle stands (see *Jacking and vehicle support*).

**22** Attach a suitable hoist and lifting tackle to the engine lifting brackets on the cylinder head, and support the weight of the engine.

**23** Refer to Chapter 4A, Section 10, and disconnect the wiring from the oxygen sensor on the catalytic converter, then unbolt the exhaust front pipe from the exhaust manifold, taking care to support the flexible section. **Note:** *Angular movement in excess of 10° can cause permanent damage to the flexible section.*

**24** Release the mounting rubbers and support the front of the exhaust pipe to one side.

**25** Working under the vehicle, remove the nut and bolt securing the torque link to the mounting on the transmission bracket **(see illustration)**.

**26** Remove the bolt securing the torque link to the subframe, and remove the link.

**27** Undo the bolts securing the torque link rubber mounting bracket to the transmission and remove the bracket and mounting.

**28** Locate the new mounting bracket in position. Insert the bolts and tighten to the specified torque.

**29** Refit the torque link to the subframe and mounting, insert the bolts/nuts and tighten to the specified torque.

**30** Refit the exhaust front pipe with reference to Chapter 4A.

**31** Remove the hoist and lower the vehicle to the ground.

# Chapter 2 Part B:
# 1.4 litre (Z14XE) petrol engine in-car repair procedures

## Contents

## Degrees of difficulty

| **Easy,** suitable for novice with little experience 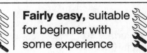 | **Fairly easy,** suitable for beginner with some experience | **Fairly difficult,** suitable for competent DIY mechanic | **Difficult,** suitable for experienced DIY mechanic | **Very difficult,** suitable for expert DIY or professional  |
|---|---|---|---|---|

## Specifications

### General

| | |
|---|---|
| Engine type | Four-cylinder, in-line, water-cooled. Double overhead camshafts, belt-driven, acting on hydraulic valve lifters |
| Manufacturer's engine code* | Z14XE |
| Bore | 77.60 mm |
| Stroke | 73.40 mm |
| Capacity | 1389 cc |
| Firing order | 1-3-4-2 (No 1 cylinder at timing belt end) |
| Direction of crankshaft rotation | Clockwise (viewed from timing belt end of engine) |
| Compression ratio | 10.5:1 |

* For details of engine code location, see 'Vehicle identification' in the Reference Chapter.

### Camshaft

| | |
|---|---|
| Endfloat | 0.040 to 0.144 mm |
| Camshaft bearing journal diameter | 27.939 to 27.960 mm |
| Maximum permissible radial run-out | 0.040 mm |

### Lubrication system

| | |
|---|---|
| Minimum oil pressure at 80°C | 1.5 bars at idle speed |
| Oil pump type | Gear-type, driven directly from crankshaft |
| Oil pump clearances: | |
|    Inner-to-outer gear clearance (backlash) | 0.10 to 0.20 mm |
|    Gear-to-housing clearance (endfloat) | 0.03 to 0.10 mm |

## Torque wrench settings

| | Nm | lbf ft |
|---|---|---|
| Big-end bearing cap bolts*: | | |
| Stage 1 . . . . . . . . . . . . . . . . . . . . . . . . . . . . . . . . . . . . . . . . . | 25 | 18 |
| Stage 2 . . . . . . . . . . . . . . . . . . . . . . . . . . . . . . . . . . . . . . . . . | Angle-tighten a further 30° | |
| Camshaft bearing cap bolts . . . . . . . . . . . . . . . . . . . . . . . . . . . . . | 8 | 6 |
| Camshaft sprocket bolt*: | | |
| Stage 1 . . . . . . . . . . . . . . . . . . . . . . . . . . . . . . . . . . . . . . . . . | 50 | 37 |
| Stage 2 . . . . . . . . . . . . . . . . . . . . . . . . . . . . . . . . . . . . . . . . . | Angle-tighten a further 60° | |
| Stage 3 . . . . . . . . . . . . . . . . . . . . . . . . . . . . . . . . . . . . . . . . . | Angle-tighten a further 15° | |
| Crankshaft pulley bolt*: | | |
| Stage 1 . . . . . . . . . . . . . . . . . . . . . . . . . . . . . . . . . . . . . . . . . | 95 | 70 |
| Stage 2 . . . . . . . . . . . . . . . . . . . . . . . . . . . . . . . . . . . . . . . . . | Angle-tighten a further 30° | |
| Stage 3 . . . . . . . . . . . . . . . . . . . . . . . . . . . . . . . . . . . . . . . . . | Angle-tighten a further 15° | |
| Cylinder head bolts*: | | |
| Stage 1 . . . . . . . . . . . . . . . . . . . . . . . . . . . . . . . . . . . . . . . . . | 25 | 18 |
| Stage 2 . . . . . . . . . . . . . . . . . . . . . . . . . . . . . . . . . . . . . . . . . | Angle-tighten a further 90° | |
| Stage 3 . . . . . . . . . . . . . . . . . . . . . . . . . . . . . . . . . . . . . . . . . | Angle-tighten a further 90° | |
| Stage 4 . . . . . . . . . . . . . . . . . . . . . . . . . . . . . . . . . . . . . . . . . | Angle-tighten a further 90° | |
| Stage 5 . . . . . . . . . . . . . . . . . . . . . . . . . . . . . . . . . . . . . . . . . | Angle-tighten a further 45° | |
| Driveplate bolts* . . . . . . . . . . . . . . . . . . . . . . . . . . . . . . . . . . . | 60 | 44 |
| Engine mountings: | | |
| Left-hand: | | |
| Mounting-to-body bolts . . . . . . . . . . . . . . . . . . . . . . . . . . . . | 25 | 18 |
| Mounting bracket to transmission bracket . . . . . . . . . . . . . . . . . | 80 | 59 |
| Rubber mounting through-bolt: | | |
| Stage 1 . . . . . . . . . . . . . . . . . . . . . . . . . . . . . . . . . . . . . | 80 | 59 |
| Stage 2 . . . . . . . . . . . . . . . . . . . . . . . . . . . . . . . . . . . . . | Angle-tighten a further 45° | |
| Stage 3 . . . . . . . . . . . . . . . . . . . . . . . . . . . . . . . . . . . . . | Angle-tighten a further 15° | |
| Transmission bracket to transmission . . . . . . . . . . . . . . . . . . . . | 60 | 44 |
| Rear: | | |
| Rear mounting/torque link . . . . . . . . . . . . . . . . . . . . . . . . . . . | 80 | 59 |
| Rear mounting/torque link bracket to transmission*: | | |
| Stage 1 . . . . . . . . . . . . . . . . . . . . . . . . . . . . . . . . . . . . . | 80 | 59 |
| Stage 2 . . . . . . . . . . . . . . . . . . . . . . . . . . . . . . . . . . . . . | Angle-tighten a further 45° | |
| Right-hand: | | |
| Engine bracket-to-engine bolts . . . . . . . . . . . . . . . . . . . . . . . . | 60 | 44 |
| Mounting-to-body bolts . . . . . . . . . . . . . . . . . . . . . . . . . . . . | 40 | 30 |
| Mounting-to-engine bracket bolts: | | |
| Stage 1 . . . . . . . . . . . . . . . . . . . . . . . . . . . . . . . . . . . . . | 60 | 44 |
| Stage 2 . . . . . . . . . . . . . . . . . . . . . . . . . . . . . . . . . . . . . | Angle-tighten a further 30° | |
| Stage 3 . . . . . . . . . . . . . . . . . . . . . . . . . . . . . . . . . . . . . | Angle-tighten a further 15° | |
| Engine-to-transmission bolts . . . . . . . . . . . . . . . . . . . . . . . . . . . . | 60 | 44 |
| Exhaust front pipe to manifold* . . . . . . . . . . . . . . . . . . . . . . . . . . | 25 | 18 |
| Exhaust manifold to cylinder head* . . . . . . . . . . . . . . . . . . . . . . . . | 22 | 16 |
| Front subframe*: | | |
| Stage 1 . . . . . . . . . . . . . . . . . . . . . . . . . . . . . . . . . . . . . . . . . | 90 | 66 |
| Stage 2 . . . . . . . . . . . . . . . . . . . . . . . . . . . . . . . . . . . . . . . . . | Angle-tighten a further 45° | |
| Stage 3 . . . . . . . . . . . . . . . . . . . . . . . . . . . . . . . . . . . . . . . . . | Angle-tighten a further 15° | |
| Inlet manifold support: | | |
| To cylinder block . . . . . . . . . . . . . . . . . . . . . . . . . . . . . . . . . . . | 35 | 26 |
| To manifold . . . . . . . . . . . . . . . . . . . . . . . . . . . . . . . . . . . . . . | 20 | 15 |
| Inlet manifold to cylinder head . . . . . . . . . . . . . . . . . . . . . . . . . . . | 20 | 15 |
| Main bearing cap bolts*: | | |
| Stage 1 . . . . . . . . . . . . . . . . . . . . . . . . . . . . . . . . . . . . . . . . . | 50 | 37 |
| Stage 2 . . . . . . . . . . . . . . . . . . . . . . . . . . . . . . . . . . . . . . . . . | Angle-tighten a further 45° | |
| Stage 3 . . . . . . . . . . . . . . . . . . . . . . . . . . . . . . . . . . . . . . . . . | Angle-tighten a further 15° | |
| Oil pressure relief valve plug to oil pump . . . . . . . . . . . . . . . . . . . . | 50 | 37 |
| Roadwheel bolts . . . . . . . . . . . . . . . . . . . . . . . . . . . . . . . . . . . . | 110 | 81 |
| Sump-to-cylinder block bolts . . . . . . . . . . . . . . . . . . . . . . . . . . . . | 10 | 7 |
| Sump-to-transmission bolts . . . . . . . . . . . . . . . . . . . . . . . . . . . . . | 40 | 30 |
| Thermostat housing to cylinder head . . . . . . . . . . . . . . . . . . . . . . . | 20 | 15 |
| Timing belt idler roller bolts . . . . . . . . . . . . . . . . . . . . . . . . . . . . . | 25 | 18 |
| Timing belt tensioner bolt . . . . . . . . . . . . . . . . . . . . . . . . . . . . . . | 20 | 15 |

* Use new bolts.

## 1 General information

### How to use this Chapter

**1** This Part of Chapter 2 describes the repair procedures which can reasonably be carried out on the engine while it remains in the vehicle. If the engine has been removed from the vehicle and is being dismantled as described in Chapter 2E, any preliminary dismantling procedures can be ignored.

**2** Note that, while it may be possible physically to overhaul items such as the piston/connecting rod assemblies while the engine is in the vehicle, such tasks are not generally carried out as separate operations, and usually require the execution of several additional procedures (not to mention the cleaning of components and of oilways); for this reason, all such tasks are classed as major overhaul procedures, and are described in Chapter 2E.

**3** Chapter 2E describes the removal of the engine/transmission unit from the vehicle, and the full overhaul procedures which can then be carried out.

### Engine description

**4** The engine is of the in-line four-cylinder, double overhead camshaft (DOHC) type, mounted transversely at the front of the car, with the transmission attached to its left-hand end **(see illustration)**.

**5** The crankshaft runs in five shell-type bearings, and the centre bearing incorporates thrust bearing shells to control crankshaft endfloat.

**6** The connecting rods are attached to the crankshaft by horizontally-split shell-type big-end bearings. The pistons are attached to the connecting rods by gudgeon pins, which are an interference fit in the connecting rod small-end bores. The aluminium-alloy pistons are fitted with three piston rings – two compression rings and an oil control ring.

**7** Both camshafts are driven from the crankshaft by a toothed composite-rubber timing belt. Each cylinder has four valves (two inlet and two exhaust), operated directly from the camshafts via hydraulic self-adjusting valve lifters (tappets). One camshaft operates the inlet valves, and the other operates the exhaust valves. The inlet and exhaust valves are each closed by a single valve spring, and operate in guides pressed into the cylinder head.

**8** A gear-type oil pump is located in a housing attached to the front of the cylinder block, and is driven directly from the crankshaft.

**9** The coolant pump is located at the front of the cylinder block, and is driven by the timing belt.

### Operations with engine in place

**10** The following operations can be carried out without having to remove the engine from the vehicle.

a) Removal and refitting of the cylinder head.
b) Removal and refitting of the timing belt and sprockets.
c) Removal and refitting of the camshafts.
d) Removal and refitting of the sump.
e) Removal and refitting of the big-end bearings, connecting rods, and pistons*.
f) Removal and refitting of the oil pump.
g) Renewal of the engine mountings.
h) Removal and refitting of the driveplate.

* Although the operation marked with an asterisk can be carried out with the engine in the vehicle (after removal of the sump), it is preferable for the engine to be removed, in the interests of cleanliness and improved access. For this reason, the procedure is described in Chapter 2E.

## 2 Compression test – description and interpretation

**Note:** A suitable compression gauge will be required to carry out this test.

**1** When engine performance is down, or if misfiring occurs which cannot be attributed

**1.4 Front sectional view of engine**

to the ignition or fuel systems, a compression test can provide diagnostic clues as to the engine's condition. If the test is performed regularly, it can give warning of trouble before any other symptoms become apparent.

**2** The engine must be fully warmed-up to normal operating temperature, and the battery must be fully-charged. The aid of an assistant will also be required.

**3** Remove the ignition module from the top of the camshaft cover as described in Chapter 5B. Ensure that the ignition is switched off then disconnect the two wiring plugs from

the engine management electronic control unit located on the left-hand side of the inlet manifold.

**4** Remove all of the spark plugs from the engine (see Chapter 1A).

**5** Fit a compression tester to the No 1 spark plug hole (No 1 cylinder is nearest the timing belt end of the engine) – the type of tester which screws into the plug thread is to be preferred.

**6** Have an assistant hold the accelerator pedal fully-depressed, at the same time cranking the engine over for approximately four seconds on

the starter motor. After one or two revolutions, the compression pressure reading on the gauge should build-up to a maximum figure and then stabilise. Record the highest reading obtained.

**7** Repeat the test on the remaining cylinders, recording the pressure in each.

**8** All cylinders should produce very similar pressures; a difference of more than 1 bar between any two cylinders indicates a fault. Note that the compression should build-up quickly in a healthy engine; low compression on the first stroke, followed by gradually-increasing pressure on successive strokes, indicates worn piston rings. A low compression reading on the first stroke, which does not build-up during successive strokes, indicates leaking valves or a blown head gasket (a cracked head could also be the cause). Deposits on the undersides of the valve heads can also cause low compression.

**9** If the pressure in any cylinder is significantly lower than that in the remaining cylinders, carry out the following test to isolate the cause. Introduce a teaspoonful of clean engine oil into the relevant cylinder through its spark plug hole, and repeat the test.

**10** If the addition of oil temporarily improves the compression pressure, this indicates that bore or piston wear is responsible for the pressure loss. No improvement suggests that leaking or burnt valves, or a blown head gasket may be to blame.

**11** A low reading from two adjacent cylinders is almost certainly due to the head gasket having blown between them; the presence of coolant in the engine oil will confirm this.

**12** If one cylinder is about 20 percent lower than the others, and the engine has a slightly rough idle, a worn camshaft lobe could be the cause.

**13** If the compression reading is unusually high, the combustion chambers are probably coated with carbon deposits. If this is the case, the cylinder head should be removed and decarbonised (see Chapter 2D).

**14** On completion of the test, refit the spark plugs, reconnect the electronic control unit wiring plugs (ensure that the ignition is switched off), and refit the ignition module.

**3.6a Timing mark positions with No 1 piston at TDC**

*1 Camshaft sprocket timing marks aligned with top edge of cylinder head*
*2 TDC sensor wheel timing mark aligned with mark on timing belt cover*
*3 Crankshaft sprocket timing mark aligned with mark on timing belt cover*
*4 Timing belt tensioner bolt*
*5 Coolant pump mark aligned with mark on cylinder block*

### 3 Top dead centre (TDC) for No 1 piston – locating

**1** Top dead centre (TDC) is the highest point in the cylinder that a piston reaches as the crankshaft turns. Each piston reaches TDC at the end of the compression stroke, and again at the end of the exhaust stroke. For the purpose of timing the engine, TDC refers to the position of No 1 piston at the end of its compression stroke. No 1 piston and cylinder are at the timing belt end of the engine.

**2** Disconnect the battery negative terminal (refer to *Disconnecting the battery* in the Reference Chapter).

**3.6b  Camshaft sprocket timing marks (A) aligned with top edge of cylinder head (B)**

**3.6c  Crankshaft sprocket timing mark (A) aligned with mark (B) on timing belt cover**

**3**  Remove the upper outer timing belt cover as described in Section 6.

**4**  Apply the handbrake, then jack up the front of the vehicle and support it on axle stands (see *Jacking and vehicle support*). Remove the right-hand front roadwheel, then remove the wheel arch inner cover for access to the crankshaft pulley.

**5**  Using a suitable spanner or socket on the crankshaft pulley bolt, rotate the crankshaft to bring No 1 piston to TDC. Note that turning the engine will be made much easier if the spark plugs are removed first (see Chapter 1A).

**6**  The timing marks must be aligned as follows **(see illustrations)**.

   *a) The timing marks on the camshaft sprockets must be directly opposite each other, and aligned with the top edge of the cylinder head.*

   *b) The timing mark on the crankshaft speed/ position sensor wheel must be aligned with the pointer (raised line) on the timing belt cover. Note that if the crankshaft pulley and lower outer timing belt cover have been removed, the timing mark on the crankshaft sprocket can be used instead of the mark on the pulley. The mark on the crankshaft sprocket must align with the corresponding mark on the rear timing belt cover (there may be two marks on the sprocket, in which case ignore the mark with a cross stamped across it).*

**4  Camshaft cover –**
   removal and refitting

### Removal

**1**  Disconnect the battery negative terminal (refer to *Disconnecting the battery* in the Reference Chapter).

**2**  Unscrew the oil filler cap, then undo the bolts and remove the engine top cover. Refit the cap.

**3**  Remove the air cleaner assembly as described in Chapter 4B.

**4**  Remove the ignition module from the spark plugs with reference to Chapter 5B.

**5**  Disconnect the throttle valve module preheater hose from the thermostat housing.

**6**  Disconnect the two crankcase ventilation breather hoses from the camshaft cover.

**7**  Disconnect the oxygen sensor wiring and unclip it from the support.

**8**  Progressively loosen the camshaft cover securing bolts (preferably working from the ends of the cover towards the centre, in a spiral pattern), then withdraw the bolts.

**9**  Lift the camshaft cover from the cylinder head, and recover the gasket.

### Refitting

**10**  Clean the mating surfaces of the camshaft cover and cylinder head.

**11**  Apply sealant to the two semi-circular cut-outs at the transmission end of the cylinder head, and to each side of the camshaft bearing caps at the timing belt end of the cylinder head **(see illustration)**.

**12**  Ensure that the gasket is located correctly on the camshaft cover (if necessary, smear it with light grease to hold it in place).

**13**  Fit the cover to the cylinder head, then

**4.11  Apply sealant to the semi-circular cut-outs indicated (1)**

refit the securing bolts. Progressively tighten the bolts securely, working from the centre to the ends of the cover, in a spiral pattern.

**14**  Reconnect the oxygen sensor wiring and clip it in the support.

**15**  Reconnect the crankcase ventilation breather hoses to the camshaft cover.

**16**  Reconnect the throttle valve module preheater hose to the thermostat housing.

**17**  Refit the ignition module to the spark plugs with reference to Chapter 5B.

**18**  Refit the air cleaner assembly as described in Chapter 4B.

**19**  Refit the engine top cover, then reconnect the battery negative lead.

**5  Crankshaft pulley –**
   removal and refitting

**Note:** *A new crankshaft pulley bolt will be required for refitting.*

### Removal

**1**  Apply the handbrake, then jack up the front of the vehicle and support it on axle stands (see *Jacking and vehicle support*). Remove the right-hand front roadwheel, then remove the wheel arch inner cover for access to the crankshaft pulley.

**2**  Remove the auxiliary drivebelt as described in Chapter 1A.

**3**  To prevent the crankshaft from turning as the pulley bolt is unscrewed, remove the starter motor, and lock the driveplate ring gear teeth using a suitable tool.

**4**  Unscrew the pulley bolt and recover the washer fitted behind it, then remove the pulley.

### Refitting

**5**  On refitting, ensure that the notch in the pulley fits over the locating lug on the crankshaft sprocket.

**6**  Prevent the crankshaft from turning as during removal, then fit the new pulley

**6.2 Removing the upper outer timing belt cover**

**6.7a Lower outer timing belt cover upper securing bolt (arrowed) . . .**

**6.7b . . . and lower (arrowed) securing bolt**

**6.13 Rear timing belt cover securing bolts – arrowed (seen with timing belt and sprockets still fitted)**

securing bolt, ensuring that the washer is in place under the bolt head.

7 Tighten the bolt to the specified torque, in the stages given in the Specifications.

8 Refit and tension the auxiliary drivebelt, as described in Chapter 1A.

## 6 Timing belt covers – removal and refitting

### *Upper outer cover*

#### Removal

1 Remove the air cleaner assembly as described in Chapter 4B.

2 Unscrew the three securing bolts, and unclip the cover **(see illustration)**.

**7.13 Withdraw the camshaft position sensor**

#### Refitting

3 Refitting is a reversal of removal.

### *Lower outer cover*

#### Removal

4 Apply the handbrake, then jack up the front of the vehicle and support it on axle stands (see *Jacking and vehicle support*). Remove the right-hand front roadwheel, then remove the wheel arch inner cover for access to the crankshaft pulley.

5 Remove the upper outer timing belt cover, as described previously in this Section.

6 Remove the crankshaft pulley, as described in Section 5.

7 Remove the two securing bolts, then release the four clips, and withdraw the lower outer cover **(see illustrations)**.

#### Refitting

8 Refitting is a reversal of removal, but fit the crankshaft pulley with reference to Section 5.

### *Rear cover*

#### Removal

9 Remove the upper and lower outer covers as described previously in this Section.

10 Remove the timing belt, sprockets and inlet-side idler roller, as described in Sections 7 and 8.

11 Unscrew the securing bolt and remove the timing belt tensioner.

12 Unbolt the right-hand engine mounting bracket from the cylinder block.

13 Unscrew the two upper and two lower

securing screws, and withdraw the rear cover from the engine **(see illustration)**.

#### Refitting

14 Refitting is a reversal of removal, bearing in mind the following points:
   a) *Tighten the right-hand engine mounting bolts to the specified torque.*
   b) *Refit the timing belt sprockets as described in Section 8.*
   c) *Refit and tension the timing belt as described in Section 7.*
   d) *Refit the outer timing belt covers as described previously in this Section.*

## 7 Timing belt – removal, refitting and adjustment

### *Removal*

1 Apply the handbrake, then jack up the front of the vehicle and support it on axle stands (see *Jacking and vehicle support*). Remove the right-hand front roadwheel, then remove the wheel arch inner cover for access to the crankshaft pulley.

2 Disconnect the battery negative terminal (refer to *Disconnecting the battery* in the Reference Chapter).

3 Unscrew the oil filler cap, then undo the bolts and remove the engine top cover. Refit the cap.

4 Remove the air cleaner assembly and air duct as described in Chapter 4B.

5 Remove the auxiliary drivebelt as described in Chapter 1A. This involves locking the tensioner before removing the drivebelt.

6 With the auxiliary drivebelt removed, remove the locking pin then unscrew the bolt and remove the tensioner from the engine.

7 Turn the crankshaft to bring No 1 piston to top dead centre, as described in Section 3. If necessary, the spark plugs may be removed to enable the engine to be turned more easily (refer to Chapter 1A).

8 Remove the crankshaft pulley with reference to Section 5. To enable the crankshaft to be turned, temporarily refit the crankshaft pulley retaining bolt.

9 Unscrew the bolt and unclip the lower timing belt cover.

10 Attach a suitable hoist and lifting tackle to the engine lifting brackets, and support the weight of the engine. Alternatively, support the engine with a trolley jack and block of wood positioned beneath the sump.

11 Unbolt and remove the right-hand engine mounting. There are two bolts on the engine and two bolts on the body panel.

12 Unscrew the bolts and unclip the upper timing belt cover.

13 Unscrew the two bolts securing the camshaft position sensor mounting bracket to the cylinder head, and move the sensor/bracket assembly to one side **(see illustration)**. If necessary, disconnect the wiring.

**14** Check that the timing marks are still aligned, then loosen the belt tensioner securing bolt sufficiently to completely relieve the tension in the belt. If necessary, turn the tensioner clockwise to relieve the tension, using a suitable hexagon bit or Allen key engaged with the hole provided in the tensioner front plate **(see illustration)**.

**15** Slide the timing belt from the sprockets, and withdraw it from the engine **(see illustration)**. Take note of any arrows marked on the belt to indicate the direction of rotation (if necessary, mark the belt to aid correct refitting).

### Refitting

**16** Ensure that No 1 piston is still positioned at top dead centre, as described in Section 3.

**17** If the coolant pump has been disturbed, check the position of the pump. Carefully ease away the rear timing belt cover and check that the edge of the pump flange is aligned with mark on the cylinder block. If necessary, loosen the securing bolts, and turn the pump as required to align the marks, then tighten the bolts securely.

**18** Refit the timing belt around the sprockets, starting at the crankshaft sprocket, and working in sequence **(see illustration)**. **Note:** *When fitting the belt over the inlet camshaft sprocket, ensure that the belt does not jump a tooth on the sprocket, and make sure that the timing marks on both camshaft sprockets stay positioned directly opposite each other, and aligned with the top edge of the cylinder head. If the original timing belt is being refitted, make sure its direction of rotation is as noted before removal.*

### Adjustment

**Note:** *The engine must be cold when checking and adjusting the timing belt tension.*

**19** Check that the front section of the timing belt between the crankshaft pulley and exhaust camshaft sprocket is taut. This will ensure the slack is on the tensioner section of the belt.

**20** With the tensioner securing bolt loosened, engage a suitable hexagon bit or Allen key with the hole provided in the tensioner front plate, and turn the tensioner anti-clockwise until the tension indicator pointer is positioned just before the left stop of the adjustment plate. Tighten the tensioner securing bolt in this position.

**21** Using a suitable socket or spanner on the crankshaft pulley bolt, turn the crankshaft clockwise through two complete revolutions, until No 1 piston is again positioned at top dead centre. Check that the timing marks are correctly aligned as described in Section 3.

**22** Engage the hexagon bit or Allen key with the hole in the tensioner adjustment plate, then slacken the tensioner securing bolt, and carefully turn the plate clockwise to slacken the belt. If a new timing belt has been fitted, the tension indicator pointer should be positioned on the NEW mark **(see illustration)**. If a 'run-in' belt has been fitted (one that has been

**7.14 Timing belt tensioner securing bolt (1) and hexagon hole (2) in front plate**

**7.15 Sliding the timing belt from the sprockets**

H.28121

**7.18 Fit the timing belt around the sprockets in the order shown**

| | | |
|---|---|---|
| 1 Crankshaft sprocket | 4 Exhaust-side idler roller | 6 Inlet camshaft sprocket |
| 2 Timing belt tensioner | 5 Exhaust camshaft sprocket | 7 Inlet-side idler roller |
| 3 Coolant pump sprocket | | |

**7.22  Align the pointer (1) with the relevant mark on the tensioner roller (2)**

used for more than a few hours), the tension indicator pointer should be positioned on the USED mark. Tighten the tensioner securing bolt to the specified torque.

**23** Turn the crankshaft clockwise through two complete revolutions, as described previously,

**8.2a  Using a Torx bit engaged with the rear timing belt cover bolt hole to counterhold the inlet camshaft sprocket**

**8.3  Removing the inlet camshaft sprocket**

and check that the tension indicator pointer is still positioned correctly – if not, repeat the procedure.

**24** Where removed, refit the spark plugs with reference to Chapter 1A.

**25** Refit the camshaft position sensor and mounting bracket. Clean the threads of the mounting bolts and apply locking fluid to them before inserting them and tightening them securely. Reconnect the wiring.

**26** Refit the upper and lower timing belt covers.

**27** Refit the right-hand engine mounting and tighten the bolts to the specified torque.

**28** Remove the engine hoist or support jack.

**29** Refit the crankshaft pulley with reference to Section 5.

**30** Refit the auxiliary drivebelt tensioner and tighten the bolts, then refit the drivebelt with reference to Chapter 1A.

**31** Refit the engine top cover, and reconnect the battery negative lead.

**32** Refit the wheel arch inner cover, then refit the roadwheel and lower the vehicle to the ground.

---

**8   Timing belt sprockets, tensioner and idler rollers – removal and refitting**

### *Camshaft sprockets*

#### Removal

**1** Remove the timing belt as described in Section 7.

**8.2b  Counterholding the inlet camshaft using a spanner on the flats in front of No 1 cam lobe**

**8.11  Refit the crankshaft sprocket with the locating flange and pulley locating lug outermost**

**2** The camshaft sprocket bolt must be prevented from turning as the sprocket bolt is unscrewed, and this can be achieved in one of three ways as follows **(see illustrations)**.

a) *Pass a suitable Torx bit and extension bar through one of the holes in the camshaft sprocket, to engage with the rear timing belt cover bolt. Use the Torx bit and extension bar to counterhold the sprocket as the bolt is loosened.*

b) *With the camshaft cover removed as described in Section 4, prevent the camshaft from turning by holding it with a suitable spanner on the flats provided in front of No 1 cam lobe.*

c) *Make up a forked tool and use it to hold the sprocket stationary by means of the holes in the sprocket face.*

**3** Unscrew and remove the camshaft sprocket bolts, noting the washers under each bolt head **(see illustration)**.

**4** Withdraw the sprockets from the end of the camshaft, keeping them identified for location.

**Note:** *The exhaust camshaft sprocket is fitted with lugs which activate the camshaft position sensor.*

#### Refitting

**5** Commence refitting by offering the camshaft sprockets to their respective camshafts. Each sprocket must be fitted so that the timing mark is visible on the outer face.

**6** Refit the sprocket securing bolts, ensuring that the washers are in place, and tighten the bolts to the specified torque, preventing the camshaft from turning as during removal.

**7** Where applicable, refit the camshaft cover as described in Section 4.

**8** Refit and tension the timing belt as described in Section 7.

### *Crankshaft sprocket*

**Note:** *A new crankshaft pulley retaining bolt will be required for refitting.*

#### Removal

**9** Remove the timing belt as described in Section 7.

**10** Remove the sprocket from the end of the crankshaft.

#### Refitting

**11** Refit the crankshaft sprocket with the locating flange and locating lug for the crankshaft pulley outermost **(see illustration)**.

**12** Refit and tension the timing belt as described in Section 7.

### *Tensioner*

#### Removal

**13** Remove the timing belt as described in Section 7.

**14** Unscrew the central securing bolt, and withdraw the tensioner.

#### Refitting

**15** Refit the tensioner, ensuring that the lug on the tensioner backplate engages with the corresponding hole in the oil pump.

**16** Refit the tensioner securing bolt, but do not tighten the bolt fully until the timing belt has been tensioned.

**17** Refit and tension the timing belt, as described in Section 7.

### Idler rollers

#### Removal

**18** Remove the timing belt as described in Section 7.

**19** Unscrew the securing bolt, and remove the relevant idler roller.

#### Refitting

**20** If both idler rollers have been removed, note that the larger-diameter roller fits on the inlet side of the engine **(see illustration)**.

**21** Refit the relevant idler roller, and tighten the securing bolt to the specified torque.

**22** Refit the timing belt as described in Section 7.

---

## 9  Camshaft oil seals – renewal

**1** Remove the relevant camshaft sprocket as described in Section 8.

**2** Punch or drill a small hole in the centre of the now-exposed oil seal.

**3** Screw in a self-tapping screw, and pull on the screw with pliers to extract the seal.

**4** Clean the oil seal seat with a wooden or plastic scraper.

**5** Wind a thin band of tape around the end of the camshaft, to protect the lips of the new oil seal as it is fitted.

**6** Grease the lips of the new seal, then fit it to the housing. Ideally, the seal should be drawn into position using a suitable socket or tube and washer, and a bolt **(see illustration)**. Alternatively, the seal can be tapped into position. The seal should be fitted with its outer face flush with the housing. Take care not to damage the seal lips during fitting.

**7** Carefully remove the tape from the end of the camshaft.

**8** Refit the camshaft sprocket as described in Section 8.

---

## 10  Camshafts and hydraulic tappets – removal, inspection and refitting

**Note:** *New timing belt end oil seals and a tube of suitable sealant will be required when refitting.*

### Removal

**1** Remove the camshaft cover as described in Section 4.

**2** Remove the camshaft sprockets as described in Section 8.

**3** Unbolt the timing belt rear cover from the cylinder head and block.

**4** Check the camshaft bearing caps for

**8.20  Timing belt idler rollers (arrowed)**

**10.4a  Camshaft bearing cap numbering sequence (No 1 at timing belt end)**

identification marks, and if none are present, make corresponding marks on the bearing caps and the top surface of the cylinder head using a centre-punch (take care not to damage the cylinder head or bearing caps). Note the orientation of the bearing caps before removal, as they must be refitted in exactly the same positions from which they are removed. The inlet (rear) camshaft caps are usually numbered 1 to 5, and the exhaust (front) camshaft caps 6 to 10, with corresponding numbers cast into the cylinder head **(see illustrations)**.

**5** Before removing the camshaft, check the endfloat using a dial gauge or a feeler gauge. If the endfloat is outside the specified limits, the camshaft must be renewed.

**10.6  Camshaft bearing cap bolt loosening sequence**

**9.6  Fitting a new camshaft oil seal using a socket and bolt**

**10.4b  Camshaft bearing cap numbers (exhaust camshaft shown)**

**6** Working on one camshaft at a time, progressively loosen the bearing cap bolts, a half or one turn at a time, in the inward spiral sequence shown **(see illustration)**. This is necessary to progressively relieve the tension in the valve springs, and prevent undue stress on the camshaft.

**7** With all of the bolts removed, withdraw the bearing caps from the cylinder head, then lift out the camshafts, keeping them identified for location **(see illustrations)**.

**8** Remove the hydraulic valve lifters (tappets) from their bores, using a rubber suction plunger tool. Keep the valve lifters upright at all times, with the oil groove at the bottom **(see illustration)**. Immerse them, in order of removal, in a container of clean engine oil until they are to be refitted.

### Inspection

**9** With the camshafts removed, examine

**10.7a  Removing a camshaft bearing cap**

10.7b  Lifting the exhaust camshaft from the cylinder head

10.8  Remove the valve lifters from the cylinder head, and store with the oil groove (arrowed) at the bottom

10.12  Lubricate the contact faces of the valve lifters, camshaft lobes and bearings with molybdenum disulphide paste

10.13  Coat the timing belt end bearing cap mating faces of the cylinder head (arrowed) with sealing compound

10.16  Camshaft bearing cap bolt tightening sequence (exhaust camshaft shown)

the bearing surfaces in the cylinder head for signs of obvious wear or pitting. If evident, the cylinder head and all the bearing caps must be renewed as a matched set, as it is not possible to renew the bearings individually. The camshafts should show no marks or scoring on the journal or cam lobe surfaces. If evident, renew them.

10  It is advisable to renew the oil seals as a matter of course. Prise the old seals from the camshafts and discard them.

### Refitting

11  Commence refitting by turning the crankshaft anti-clockwise by 60°. This will position Nos 1 and 4 pistons a third of the way down the bore, and prevent any chance of the valves touching the piston crowns as the camshafts are being fitted. This could happen if any of the hydraulic valve lifters have excessive oil in them before the pressure of the valve springs forces it out.

12  Lubricate the cylinder head hydraulic tappet bores, tappets, camshaft lobes, and bearing surfaces (see illustration). Carefully refit the tappets to the cylinder head, ensuring that each tappet is refitted to its original bore.

13  Coat the timing belt end bearing cap mating faces on the cylinder head with sealant (see illustration).

14  Place the camshafts in their original positions on the cylinder head, temporarily refit the camshaft sprockets, and check that the timing marks are still aligned with No 1 piston at TDC, as described in Section 3. Remove the sprockets.

15  Loosely refit the bearing caps in their original positions as noted during removal, then insert the bolts and finger-tighten them.

16  Working on one camshaft at a time, progressively tighten the bearing cap bolts to the specified torque, one turn at a time, in the outward spiral sequence shown (see illustration).

17  Wipe away any excess sealant from the timing belt end bearing caps.

18  Lubricate the lips of the new camshaft oil seals with a little grease, and fit them as described in Section 9.

19  Refit the timing belt rear cover and tighten the bolts.

20  Refit the camshaft sprockets as described in Section 8.

21  Refit the camshaft cover as described in Section 4.

## 11  Cylinder head – removal and refitting

Note: The engine must be cold when removing the cylinder head. A new cylinder head gasket and new cylinder head bolts must be used on refitting.

### Removal

1  Apply the handbrake, then jack up the front of the vehicle and support it on axle stands (see Jacking and vehicle support). Remove the right-hand front roadwheel, then remove the wheel arch inner cover for access to the crankshaft pulley.

2  Depressurise the fuel system as described in Chapter 4B.

3  Disconnect the battery negative terminal (refer to Disconnecting the battery in the Reference Chapter).

4  Drain the cooling system as described in Chapter 1A.

5  Remove the camshaft cover as described in Section 4.

6  Disconnect the wiring from the coolant temperature sensor on the thermostat housing on the right-hand front of the cylinder head (see illustration).

7  Remove the camshaft sprockets, timing belt tensioner, and the timing belt idler rollers, as described in Section 8.

8  Remove the rear timing belt cover with reference to Section 6.

9  Refer to Chapter 4B and unbolt the exhaust front pipe from the exhaust manifold, taking

**11.6 Disconnect the wiring from the coolant temperature sensor (1) and the temperature gauge sender (2)**

**11.11 Disconnect the wiring from the crankshaft speed/position sensor**

**11.14 Disconnecting the fuel return hose from the fuel pressure regulator**

care to support the flexible section. **Note:** *Angular movement in excess of 10° can cause permanent damage to the flexible section.* Release the mounting rubbers and support the front of the exhaust pipe to one side.

**10** Unscrew the upper bolt securing the support bracket to the inlet manifold, and loosen only the bottom bolt.

**11** Unscrew the bolt and remove the earth cable, then disconnect the engine management wiring loom from the following, noting its routing:

  a) *Throttle body.*
  b) *Knock sensor.*
  c) *Inlet manifold absolute pressure sensor.*
  d) *EGR valve.*
  e) *Engine control unit (throttle body).*
  f) *Combination plug.*
  g) *Crankshaft speed/position sensor (see illustration).*
  h) *Oil pressure switch.*

**12** Release the cable ties and place the wiring loom to one side.

**13** Unscrew the three securing bolts, and remove the upper alternator mounting bracket. Pivot the alternator rearwards away from the manifold as far as it will go.

**14** Unscrew the union nut, and disconnect the return hose from the fuel pressure regulator **(see illustration).** Be prepared for fuel spillage, and clamp or plug the hose to reduce fuel loss and to prevent dirt ingress. Similarly, disconnect the fuel supply hose from the fuel rail.

**15** Disconnect the wiring from the injectors **(see illustration),** then unscrew the bolts and remove the fuel rail.

**16** Refer to Chapter 4B, Section 10, and remove the throttle body and the manifold absolute pressure sensor.

**17** Remove the inlet manifold with reference to Chapter 4B.

**18** Loosen the clips and remove the upper hose from the radiator and thermostat housing **(see illustration).**

**19** Loosen the clips and disconnect the two heater hoses from the left-hand end of the cylinder head.

**20** Remove the engine vent flange from the engine control unit bracket.

**21** Remove the exhaust manifold with reference to Chapter 4B. Recover the gasket.

**11.15 Disconnect the wiring connectors for the fuel injectors**

**22** Make a final check to ensure that all relevant hoses, pipes and wires have been disconnected.

**23** Working in a spiral pattern from the outside inwards, progressively loosen the cylinder

**11.18 Disconnect the coolant hose from the thermostat housing**

head bolts. First loosen all the bolts by quarter of a turn, then loosen all the bolts by half a turn, then finally slacken all the bolts fully and withdraw them from the cylinder head. Recover the washers **(see illustrations).**

**11.23a Cylinder head bolt loosening sequence**

**11.23b Remove the cylinder head bolts and washers**

**11.24 Lifting the cylinder head from the cylinder block**

**11.28 Cylinder head gasket OBEN/TOP marking should be at timing belt end of engine**

**24** Lift the cylinder head from the cylinder block **(see illustration)**. If necessary, tap the cylinder head gently with a soft-faced mallet to free it from the block, but **do not** lever at the mating faces. Note that the cylinder head is located on dowels.

**25** Recover the cylinder head gasket, and discard it.

### Refitting

**26** Clean the cylinder head and block mating faces by careful scraping. Take care not to damage the cylinder head, which is made of light alloy, and is easily scored. Cover the coolant passages and other openings with masking tape or rag, to prevent dirt and carbon falling in. Mop out all the oil from the bolt holes; if oil is left in the holes, hydraulic pressure could crack the block when the bolts are refitted.

**27** Turn the crankshaft so that all the pistons are positioned approximately half-way down their bores. This will prevent the possibility of the valves contacting the pistons as the cylinder head is refitted.

**28** Commence refitting by locating a new cylinder head gasket on the block, so that the word OBEN or TOP is uppermost at the timing belt end of the engine **(see illustration)**.

**29** With the mating faces scrupulously clean, locate the cylinder head on the block so that the positioning dowels engage in their holes.

**30** Fit the **new** cylinder head bolts, ensuring that (where fitted) the washers are in place under their heads, and screw in the bolts *by hand* as far as possible.

**31** Tighten the bolts in sequence and in the five stages given in the Specifications – ie, tighten all bolts to the Stage 1 torque using a torque wrench, then tighten all bolts to Stage 2,

and so on using an angle tightening gauge **(see illustrations)**.

**32** Refit the exhaust manifold together with a new gasket with reference to Chapter 4B.

**33** Refit the engine vent flange to the engine control unit bracket.

**34** Reconnect the two heater hoses to the left-hand end of the cylinder head and tighten the clips.

**35** Refit the upper hose to the radiator and thermostat housing and tighten the clips.

**36** Refit the inlet manifold with reference to Chapter 4B.

**37** Refer to Chapter 4B, and refit the throttle body and the manifold absolute pressure sensor.

**38** Refit the fuel rail and tighten the mounting bolts, then reconnect the wiring to the injectors.

**39** Reconnect the supply hose to the fuel rail, and the return hose to the fuel pressure regulator.

**40** Refit the alternator upper mounting bracket and tighten the bolts.

**41** Reconnect the wiring to the components listed in paragraph 11, then secure the wiring with cable ties.

**42** Refit the inlet manifold support bracket and tighten the bolts.

**43** Refer to Chapter 4B and refit the exhaust front pipe to the exhaust manifold. Refit the mounting rubbers.

**44** Refit the rear timing belt cover with reference to Section 6.

**45** Refit the camshaft sprockets, timing belt tensioner, and the timing belt idler rollers, with reference to Section 8.

H28796

**11.31a Cylinder head bolt tightening sequence**

**11.31b Tightening a cylinder head bolt using an angle gauge**

**46** Reconnect the wiring to the coolant temperature sensor on the thermostat housing.

**47** Refit the camshaft cover with reference to Section 4.

**48** Refit the wheel arch inner cover and front roadwheel, then lower the vehicle to the ground.

**49** Reconnect the battery negative lead.

**50** Check that all relevant hoses, pipes and wires, etc, have been reconnected. Check the security of the fuel hose connections.

**51** Refill and bleed the cooling system with reference to Chapter 1A.

**52** When the engine is started, check for signs of oil or coolant leakage.

## 12 Sump and oil pick-up pipe – removal and refitting

### Removal

**1** Apply the handbrake, then jack up the front of the vehicle and support it on axle stands (see *Jacking and vehicle support*). Remove the right-hand front roadwheel, then remove the wheel arch inner cover for access to the crankshaft pulley end of the engine.

**2** Disconnect the battery negative terminal (refer to *Disconnecting the battery* in the Reference Chapter).

**3** Drain the engine oil as described in Chapter 1A, then clean the drain plug, renew the sealing ring, refit the plug and tighten it securely.

**4** Disconnect the wiring from the oxygen sensor and release it from the support bracket.

**5** Refer to Chapter 4B and unbolt the exhaust front pipe from the exhaust manifold, taking care to support the flexible section. **Note:** *Angular movement in excess of 10° can cause permanent damage to the flexible section.* Release the mounting rubbers and support the front of the exhaust pipe to one side.

**6** Prise out the closure plug from the transmission end of the sump.

**7** Unscrew and remove the bolts securing the sump to the transmission.

**8** Unscrew and remove the bolts securing the sump to the oil pump housing.

**9** Unscrew the securing bolts, and withdraw the sump. If necessary, tap the sump with a soft-faced mallet to free it from the cylinder block – **do not** lever between the sump and cylinder block mating faces.

**10** If desired, the oil pick-up pipe can be removed by unscrewing the single bolt securing the support bracket to the cylinder block and the two bolts securing the pipe flange to the oil pump. Recover the O-ring.

### Refitting

**11** Clean all traces of the old gasket from the mating faces of the cylinder block and sump. Also clean the threads of the sump securing bolts.

**12** If the oil pick-up pipe has been removed, refit it together with a new O-ring, and tighten the mounting bolts securely.

**13** Apply an even bead of sealing compound to the sump mating face **(see illustration)**. **Note:** *For the sealant we used, refitting must be completed within 10 minutes.*

**14** Refit the sump to the cylinder block, insert the bolts, and tighten them progressively to the specified torque, noting that the transmission bolts are tightened to a higher torque than the remaining bolts.

**15** Refit the closure plug.

**16** Refer to Chapter 4B and refit the exhaust front pipe to the exhaust manifold. Refit the mounting rubbers.

**17** Reconnect the wiring to the oxygen sensor and clip it onto the support bracket.

**18** Reconnect the battery negative lead.

**19** Refit the wheel arch inner cover and roadwheel, then lower the vehicle to the ground.

**20** Refill the engine with oil as described in Chapter 1A.

## 13 Oil pump – removal, inspection and refitting

**Note:** *A new oil pump gasket and a new crankshaft oil seal must be used on refitting.*

### Removal

**1** Remove the rear timing belt cover as described in Section 6.

**2** Remove the sump and oil pick-up pipe as described in Section 12.

**3** Disconnect the wiring from the oil pressure switch mounted in the oil pump.

**12.13 Apply an even bead of sealing compound to the sump mating face**

**4** Where necessary, unbolt the crankshaft speed/position sensor bracket from the oil pump. Move the sensor/bracket assembly to one side, taking care not to damage the sensor.

**5** Remove the securing bolts, and withdraw the oil pump from the cylinder block **(see illustration)**. Recover the gasket.

**13.5 Oil pump securing bolts (arrowed)**

**13.7 Removing an oil pump rear cover securing screw**

**13.8 Oil pressure relief valve components**

1 *Plunger*  3 *Sealing ring*
2 *Spring*   4 *Plug*

**13.10 Check the clearance between the inner and outer gear teeth . . .**

**13.11 . . . and between the end faces of the gears and the housing**

**13.16 Gear outer face identification mark (arrowed)**

**13.18 Fitting a new crankshaft oil seal to the oil pump**

## Inspection

**Note:** *A new pressure relief valve sealing ring should be used on reassembly, and sealing compound will be required to coat the pump housing mating face.*

**6** With the oil pump removed, proceed as follows.

**7** Remove the securing screws and withdraw the rear cover **(see illustration)**. The screws may be very tight, in which case it may be necessary to use an impact driver to remove them.

**8** The oil pressure relief valve components can be removed from the pump by unscrewing the cap. Withdraw the cap, sealing ring, spring and plunger **(see illustration)**.

**13.21 Refitting the oil pump (shown with engine removed from vehicle and inverted)**

1 *Tape wound around crankshaft*
2 *Flats on crankshaft engage with inner oil pump gear*

**9** Prise the oil seal from the pump using a screwdriver.

**10** Check the clearance between the inner and outer gear teeth (backlash) using a feeler gauge **(see illustration)**.

**11** Check the clearance between the end faces of the gears and the housing (endfloat) using a straight-edge and a feeler gauge **(see illustration)**.

**12** If any of the clearances are outside the specified limits, renew the components as necessary.

**13** Examine the pressure relief valve spring and plunger, and renew if any sign of damage or wear is evident.

**14** Ensure that the interior of the pump body is scrupulously clean before commencing reassembly.

**15** Discard the old pressure relief valve sealing ring, then thoroughly clean the pressure relief valve components, and lubricate them with clean engine oil before refitting. Use a new sealing ring.

**16** Ensure that the gears are clean, then lubricate them with clean engine oil, and refit them to the pump body, noting that the outer gear is marked with a punch dot to indicate its outer face (ie, the face nearest the pump cover) **(see illustration)**.

**17** Ensure that the mating faces of the rear cover and the pump housing are clean, then coat the pump housing mating face with suitable sealing compound, and refit the rear cover. Refit and tighten the securing screws.

**18** Fit a new crankshaft oil seal to the recess

in the pump body, using a suitable socket or tube, so that the seal is flush with the outer face of the housing **(see illustration)**.

### Refitting

**19** Thoroughly clean the mating faces of the oil pump and cylinder block, then locate a new gasket on the block.

**20** Wind a thin layer of tape around the end of the crankshaft, to prevent damage to the oil seal lips as the pump is refitted.

**21** With the new oil seal fitted, grease the oil seal lips, then refit the pump, ensuring that the inner gear engages with the flats on the crankshaft **(see illustration)**.

**22** Tighten the securing bolts securely, then carefully remove the tape from the crankshaft.

**23** Where necessary, refit the crankshaft speed/position sensor and its securing bracket, and tighten the securing bolt.

**24** Reconnect the wiring to the oil pressure switch.

**25** Refit the oil pick-up pipe and sump, as described in Section 12.

**26** Refit the rear timing belt cover as described in Section 6.

## 14 Crankshaft oil seals – renewal

### Timing belt end oil seal

**1** Remove the crankshaft sprocket as described in Section 8.

**2** Punch or drill a small hole in the centre of the now-exposed oil seal.

**3** Screw in a self-tapping screw, and pull on the screw with pliers to extract the seal **(see illustration)**. Several attempts may be necessary. Be careful not to damage the sealing face of the crankshaft.

**4** Clean the oil seal seat with a wooden or plastic scraper.

**5** Wind a thin band of tape around the end of the crankshaft, to protect the lips of the new oil seal as it is fitted.

**6** Grease the lips of the new seal, and tap it into position until it is flush with the outer face of the oil pump body, using a suitable socket or tube **(see illustration)**. Take care not to damage the seal lips during fitting.

**7** Carefully remove the tape from the end of the crankshaft.

**8** Refit the crankshaft sprocket, as described in Section 8.

### Driveplate end oil seal

**9** Remove the driveplate as described in Section 15.

**10** Proceed as described in paragraphs 2 to 4 inclusive of this Section.

**11** Grease the lips of the new seal, then tap the seal into position using a suitable tube, until flush with the outer faces of the cylinder block and main bearing cap.

**HAYNES HINT** *Wind a length of tape around the end of the crankshaft to reduce the possibility of damage to the lips of the oil seal as the seal is fitted.*

**12** Refit the driveplate as described in Section 15.

### 15 Driveplate –
removal and refitting

**Note:** *New driveplate securing bolts must be used on refitting.*

### Removal

**1** Remove the automatic transmission as described in Chapter 7B.

**2** Although the driveplate bolt holes are offset so that the driveplate can only be fitted in one position, it will make refitting easier if alignment marks are made between the driveplate and the end of the crankshaft.

**3** Prevent the driveplate from turning by locking the ring gear teeth using a suitable tool.

**4** Unscrew the securing bolts, and remove the driveplate.

### Refitting

**5** Offer the driveplate to the end of the crankshaft, and align with the previously-made mark on the crankshaft.

**14.3 Using a self-tapping screw and a pair of pliers to extract the crankshaft oil seal**

**6** Coat the threads of the new bolts with thread-locking compound (note that new bolts may be supplied ready-coated), then fit the bolts and tighten them as given in the Specifications, whilst preventing the driveplate from turning as during removal.

**7** Refit the automatic transmission as described in Chapter 7B.

### 16 Engine/transmission
mountings –
inspection and renewal

### Inspection

**1** To improve access, firmly apply the handbrake, then jack up the front of the vehicle and support it on axle stands (see *Jacking and vehicle support*).

**2** Check the mounting blocks (rubbers) to see if they are cracked, hardened or separated from the metal at any point. Renew the mounting block if any such damage or deterioration is evident.

**3** Check that all the mounting securing nuts and bolts are securely tightened, using a torque wrench to check if possible.

**4** Using a large screwdriver, or a similar tool, check for wear in the mounting blocks by carefully levering against them to check for free play. Where this is not possible, enlist the aid of an assistant to move the engine/transmission unit back-and-forth, and from side-to-side, while you observe the mountings. While some free play is to be expected, even from new components, excessive wear should be obvious. If excessive free play is found, check first to see that the securing nuts and bolts are correctly tightened, then renew any worn components as described in the following paragraphs.

### Renewal

**Note:** *Before slackening any of the engine mounting bolts/nuts, the relative positions of the mountings to their various brackets should be marked to ensure correct alignment upon refitting.*

### Right-hand mounting

**5** Apply the handbrake, then jack up the front of the vehicle and support it on axle stands

**14.6 Tapping a new crankshaft oil seal into position**

(see *Jacking and vehicle support*). Remove the right-hand roadwheel and the wheel arch liner for access to the crankshaft pulley.

**6** Remove the air cleaner as described in Chapter 4B.

**7** Attach a suitable hoist and lifting tackle to the engine lifting brackets on the cylinder head, and support the weight of the engine.

**8** Unscrew the four mounting bolts and remove the right-hand mounting from the engine mounting bracket and body. **Note:** *The engine mounting bracket can only be unbolted from the cylinder block after removal of the timing belt.*

**9** If necessary, refit the engine mounting bracket and tighten the bolts to the specified torque, then locate the new mounting block on the body and engine bracket, and tighten the bolts to the specified torque.

**10** Remove the hoist, then refit the air cleaner.

**11** Refit the wheel arch liner and right-hand roadwheel, then lower the vehicle to the ground.

### Left-hand mounting

**12** Attach a suitable hoist and lifting tackle to the engine lifting brackets on the cylinder head, and support the weight of the engine.

**13** Using a Torx socket, unscrew the two bolts securing the mounting bracket to the transmission bracket.

**14** Undo the four bolts securing the mounting to the body and the three bolts securing the transmission bracket to the transmission.

**15** Slightly lower the engine, then remove the mounting assembly from the car.

**16** If necessary, undo the through-bolt and separate the rubber mounting from the mounting bracket.

**17** If removed, refit the rubber mounting to the mounting bracket and tighten the through-bolt to the specified torque.

**18** Locate the mounting brackets in position.

**19** Raise the engine and insert the bolts, then tighten them to the specified torque.

**20** Disconnect the hoist and lifting tackle.

### Rear mounting/torque link

**21** Apply the handbrake, then jack up the front of the vehicle and support it on axle stands (see *Jacking and vehicle support*).

**22** Attach a suitable hoist and lifting tackle

to the engine lifting brackets on the cylinder head, and support the weight of the engine.

**23** Refer to Chapter 4B, Section 10, and disconnect the wiring from the oxygen sensor on the catalytic converter, then unbolt the exhaust front pipe from the exhaust manifold, taking care to support the flexible section. **Note:** *Angular movement in excess of 10° can cause permanent damage to the flexible section.*

**24** Release the mounting rubbers and support the front of the exhaust pipe to one side.

**25** Working under the vehicle, remove the nut and bolt securing the torque link to the mounting on the transmission bracket.

**26** Remove the bolt securing the torque link to the subframe, and remove the link.

**27** Undo the bolts securing the torque link rubber mounting bracket to the transmission and remove the bracket and mounting.

**28** Locate the new mounting bracket in position. Insert the bolts and tighten to the specified torque.

**29** Refit the torque link to the subframe and mounting, insert the bolts/nuts and tighten to the specified torque.

**30** Refit the exhaust front pipe with reference to Chapter 4B.

**31** Remove the hoist and lower the vehicle to the ground.

# Chapter 2 Part C:
# 1.3 litre diesel engine in-car repair procedures

## Contents

## Degrees of difficulty

| Easy, suitable for novice with little experience | Fairly easy, suitable for beginner with some experience | Fairly difficult, suitable for competent DIY mechanic | Difficult, suitable for experienced DIY mechanic | Very difficult, suitable for expert DIY or professional |
|---|---|---|---|---|

## Specifications

### General

| | |
|---|---|
| Engine type........................................... | Four-cylinder, in-line, water-cooled. Chain-driven double overhead camshafts, 16 valves |
| Manufacturer's engine code*............................ | Z13DT or Y13DT |
| Bore ................................................ | 69.6 mm |
| Stroke............................................... | 82.0 mm |
| Capacity............................................. | 1248 cc |
| Firing order .......................................... | 1-3-4-2 (No 1 cylinder at timing chain end) |
| Direction of crankshaft rotation ......................... | Clockwise (viewed from timing chain end of engine) |
| Compression ratio .................................... | 18.0:1 |

* For details of engine code location, see 'Vehicle identification' in the Reference Chapter.

### Compression pressures

| | |
|---|---|
| Maximum difference between any two cylinders.................. | 1.5 bar |

### Lubrication system

| | |
|---|---|
| Oil pump type.......................................... | Gear-type, driven directly from crankshaft |
| Oil pressure at 80°C (approximate) ....................... | 1.4 bars at idle speed |
| Oil pump clearances: ................................... | |
|    Outer rotor-to-body clearance ..................... | 0.10 to 0.23 mm |
|    Rotor endfloat.................................... | 0.050 to 0.075 mm |

## Torque wrench settings

| | Nm | lbf ft |
|---|---|---|
| Auxiliary drivebelt tensioner to cylinder block . . . . . . . . . . . . . . . . . . . . | 50 | 37 |
| Big-end bearing cap nuts*: | | |
|     Stage 1 . . . . . . . . . . . . . . . . . . . . . . . . . . . . . . . . . . . . . . . . . . . . | 20 | 15 |
|     Stage 2 . . . . . . . . . . . . . . . . . . . . . . . . . . . . . . . . . . . . . . . . . . . . | Angle-tighten a further 40° | |
| Camshaft drive gear bolts . . . . . . . . . . . . . . . . . . . . . . . . . . . . . . . . . . | 150 | 111 |
| Camshaft housing closure bolts . . . . . . . . . . . . . . . . . . . . . . . . . . . . . . | 15 | 11 |
| Camshaft housing to cylinder head: | | |
|     M8 stud bolts . . . . . . . . . . . . . . . . . . . . . . . . . . . . . . . . . . . . . . . | 25 | 18 |
|     M7 bolts . . . . . . . . . . . . . . . . . . . . . . . . . . . . . . . . . . . . . . . . . . | 18 | 13 |
| Camshaft position sensor retaining bolt . . . . . . . . . . . . . . . . . . . . . . . . | 7 | 5 |
| Camshaft sprocket bolt . . . . . . . . . . . . . . . . . . . . . . . . . . . . . . . . . . . . | 150 | 111 |
| Catalytic converter support bracket to sump reinforcement bracket . . | 25 | 18 |
| Catalytic converter-to-turbocharger nuts . . . . . . . . . . . . . . . . . . . . . . . | 25 | 18 |
| Coolant pipe-to-heat exchanger bolts . . . . . . . . . . . . . . . . . . . . . . . . . | 9 | 7 |
| Coolant pump nuts . . . . . . . . . . . . . . . . . . . . . . . . . . . . . . . . . . . . . . . | 9 | 7 |
| Crankshaft pulley hub to crankshaft** . . . . . . . . . . . . . . . . . . . . . . . . . | 230 | 170 |
| Crankshaft pulley to pulley hub . . . . . . . . . . . . . . . . . . . . . . . . . . . . . . | 25 | 18 |
| Cylinder block baseplate bolts*: | | |
|     M10 bolts: | | |
|         Stage 1 . . . . . . . . . . . . . . . . . . . . . . . . . . . . . . . . . . . . . . . | 20 | 15 |
|         Stage 2 . . . . . . . . . . . . . . . . . . . . . . . . . . . . . . . . . . . . . . . | Angle-tighten a further 90° | |
|     M8 bolts . . . . . . . . . . . . . . . . . . . . . . . . . . . . . . . . . . . . . . . . . . | 30 | 22 |
| Cylinder head bolts*: | | |
|     Stage 1 . . . . . . . . . . . . . . . . . . . . . . . . . . . . . . . . . . . . . . . . . . . . | 40 | 30 |
|     Stage 2 . . . . . . . . . . . . . . . . . . . . . . . . . . . . . . . . . . . . . . . . . . . . | Angle-tighten a further 90° | |
|     Stage 3 . . . . . . . . . . . . . . . . . . . . . . . . . . . . . . . . . . . . . . . . . . . . | Angle-tighten a further 90° | |
| Engine mountings: | | |
|     Front mounting/torque link . . . . . . . . . . . . . . . . . . . . . . . . . . . . . . . | 60 | 44 |
|     Front mounting/torque link bracket to transmission . . . . . . . . . . . . . | 95 | 70 |
|     Left-hand: | | |
|         Mounting-to-body bolts . . . . . . . . . . . . . . . . . . . . . . . . . . . . . . . | 25 | 18 |
|         Mounting bracket to transmission bracket*: | | |
|             Stage 1 . . . . . . . . . . . . . . . . . . . . . . . . . . . . . . . . . . . . . . | 80 | 59 |
|             Stage 2 . . . . . . . . . . . . . . . . . . . . . . . . . . . . . . . . . . . . . . | Angle-tighten a further 60° | |
|         Rubber mounting through-bolt: | | |
|             Stage 1 . . . . . . . . . . . . . . . . . . . . . . . . . . . . . . . . . . . . . . | 80 | 59 |
|             Stage 2 . . . . . . . . . . . . . . . . . . . . . . . . . . . . . . . . . . . . . . | Angle-tighten a further 45° | |
|             Stage 3 . . . . . . . . . . . . . . . . . . . . . . . . . . . . . . . . . . . . . . | Angle-tighten a further 15° | |
|         Transmission bracket to transmission . . . . . . . . . . . . . . . . . . . . . | 60 | 44 |
|     Rear mounting/torque link . . . . . . . . . . . . . . . . . . . . . . . . . . . . . . . | 80 | 59 |
|     Rear mounting/torque link bracket to transmission*: | | |
|         Stage 1 . . . . . . . . . . . . . . . . . . . . . . . . . . . . . . . . . . . . . . . | 80 | 59 |
|         Stage 2 . . . . . . . . . . . . . . . . . . . . . . . . . . . . . . . . . . . . . . . | Angle-tighten a further 45° | |
|     Right-hand: | | |
|         Engine bracket-to-engine bolts . . . . . . . . . . . . . . . . . . . . . . . . . . | 60 | 44 |
|         Mounting-to-body bolts . . . . . . . . . . . . . . . . . . . . . . . . . . . . . . . | 40 | 30 |
|         Mounting-to-engine bracket bolts*: | | |
|             Stage 1 . . . . . . . . . . . . . . . . . . . . . . . . . . . . . . . . . . . . . . | 60 | 44 |
|             Stage 2 . . . . . . . . . . . . . . . . . . . . . . . . . . . . . . . . . . . . . . | Angle-tighten a further 30° | |
| Engine-to-transmission bolts . . . . . . . . . . . . . . . . . . . . . . . . . . . . . . . | 60 | 44 |
| Flywheel bolts*: | | |
|     Stage 1 . . . . . . . . . . . . . . . . . . . . . . . . . . . . . . . . . . . . . . . . . . . . | 30 | 22 |
|     Stage 2 . . . . . . . . . . . . . . . . . . . . . . . . . . . . . . . . . . . . . . . . . . . . | Angle-tighten a further 60° | |
|     Stage 3 . . . . . . . . . . . . . . . . . . . . . . . . . . . . . . . . . . . . . . . . . . . . | Angle-tighten a further 15° | |
| Fuel rail mounting bracket to camshaft housing . . . . . . . . . . . . . . . . . . | 25 | 18 |
| Fuel rail-to-mounting bracket bolts . . . . . . . . . . . . . . . . . . . . . . . . . . . | 25 | 18 |
| Oil cooler/heat exchanger to oil filter housing . . . . . . . . . . . . . . . . . . . | 9 | 7 |
| Oil filter housing cover . . . . . . . . . . . . . . . . . . . . . . . . . . . . . . . . . . . . | 25 | 18 |
| Oil filter housing to cylinder block . . . . . . . . . . . . . . . . . . . . . . . . . . . . | 9 | 7 |
| Sump drain plug . . . . . . . . . . . . . . . . . . . . . . . . . . . . . . . . . . . . . . . . . | 20 | 15 |
| Sump reinforcement bracket bolts . . . . . . . . . . . . . . . . . . . . . . . . . . . . | 30 | 22 |
| Sump to cylinder block baseplate . . . . . . . . . . . . . . . . . . . . . . . . . . . . | 9 | 7 |
| Timing chain guide rail bolts . . . . . . . . . . . . . . . . . . . . . . . . . . . . . . . . | 9 | 7 |
| Timing chain tensioner bolts . . . . . . . . . . . . . . . . . . . . . . . . . . . . . . . . | 9 | 7 |
| Timing chain tensioner rail pivot bolt . . . . . . . . . . . . . . . . . . . . . . . . . . | 9 | 7 |
| Timing cover retaining nuts/bolts . . . . . . . . . . . . . . . . . . . . . . . . . . . . . | 9 | 7 |
| Turbocharger oil supply pipe banjo union bolts . . . . . . . . . . . . . . . . . . | 12 | 9 |

* Use new fasteners
** Left-hand thread

## 1  General information

### How to use this Chapter

This Part of Chapter 2 describes the repair procedures which can reasonably be carried out on the engine while it remains in the vehicle. If the engine has been removed from the vehicle and is being dismantled as described in Chapter 2E, any preliminary dismantling procedures can be ignored.

Note that, while it may be possible physically to overhaul items such as the piston/connecting rod assemblies while the engine is in the vehicle, such tasks are not usually carried out as separate operations, and usually require the execution of several additional procedures (not to mention the cleaning of components and of oilways); for this reason, all such tasks are classed as major overhaul procedures, and are described in Chapter 2E.

Chapter 2E describes the removal of the engine/transmission unit from the vehicle, and the full overhaul procedures which can then be carried out.

### Engine description

The 1.3 litre common-rail diesel engine is of sixteen-valve, in-line four-cylinder, double overhead camshaft (DOHC) type, mounted transversely at the front of the car with the transmission attached to its left-hand end.

The crankshaft runs in five main bearings. Thrustwashers are fitted to No 3 main bearing shell (upper half) to control crankshaft endfloat.

The cylinder block is made of cast iron and the cylinder bores are an integral part of the block. On this type of engine the cylinder bores are sometimes referred to as having dry liners. An aluminium baseplate is bolted to the cylinder block and forms the lower half of the crankcase.

The connecting rods rotate on horizontally-split bearing shells at their big-ends. The pistons are attached to the connecting rods by gudgeon pins, which are a sliding fit in the connecting rod small-end eyes and retained by circlips. The aluminium-alloy pistons are fitted with three piston rings – two compression rings and an oil control ring.

The camshafts are situated in a separate housing bolted to the top of the cylinder head. The exhaust camshaft is driven by the crankshaft by a hydraulically-tensioned timing chain and drives the inlet camshaft via a spur gear. Each cylinder has four valves (two inlet and two exhaust), operated via rocker arms which are supported at their pivot ends by hydraulic self-adjusting valve lifters (tappets). One camshaft operates the inlet valves, and the other operates the exhaust valves.

The inlet and exhaust valves are each closed by a single valve spring, and operate in guides pressed into the cylinder head.

A rotor-type oil pump is located in the timing cover attached to the cylinder block, and is driven directly from the crankshaft. An oil cooler (heat exchanger) is fitted to keep the oil temperature stable under arduous operating conditions.

The coolant pump is located externally on the timing cover, and is driven by the auxiliary drivebelt.

### Operations with engine in place

The following operations can be carried out without having to remove the engine from the vehicle.

a) Removal and refitting of the cylinder head.
b) Removal and refitting of the timing cover.
c) Removal and refitting of the timing chain, tensioner, sprockets and guide rails.
d) Removal and refitting of the camshaft housing.
e) Removal and refitting of the hydraulic tappets and rocker arms.
f) Removal and refitting of the camshafts.
g) Removal and refitting of the sump.
h) Removal and refitting of the big-end bearings, connecting rods, and pistons*.
i) Removal and refitting of the oil pump.
j) Removal and refitting of the oil cooler/ heat exchanger.
k) Renewal of the crankshaft oil seals.
l) Renewal of the engine mountings.
m) Removal and refitting of the flywheel.

* Although the operation marked with an asterisk can be carried out with the engine in the vehicle (after removal of the sump), it is preferable for the engine to be removed, in the interests of cleanliness and improved access. For this reason, the procedure is described in Chapter 2E.

## 2  Compression and leakdown test – description and interpretation

### Compression test

**Note:** *A compression tester specifically designed for diesel engines must be used for this test.*

**1** When engine performance is down, or if misfiring occurs which cannot be attributed to the fuel system, a compression test can provide diagnostic clues as to the engine's condition. If the test is performed regularly, it can give warning of trouble before any other symptoms become apparent.

**2** A compression tester specifically intended for diesel engines must be used, because of the higher pressures involved. The tester is connected to an adapter which screws into the glow plug or injector hole. On these models, an adapter suitable for use in the glow plug holes will be required, due to the design of the injectors. It is unlikely to be worthwhile buying such a tester for occasional use, but it may be possible to borrow or hire one – if not, have the test performed by a garage.

**3** Unless specific instructions to the contrary are supplied with the tester, observe the following points:

a) The battery must be in a good state of charge, the air filter must be clean, and the engine should be at normal operating temperature.
b) All the glow plugs should be removed before starting the test (see Chapter 5C).
c) Disconnect the wiring connector from the engine management electronic control unit (see Chapter 4C) to prevent the engine from running or fuel from being discharged.

**4** There is no need to hold the accelerator pedal down during the test, because the diesel engine air inlet is not throttled.

**5** Crank the engine on the starter motor; after one or two revolutions, the compression pressure should build-up to a maximum figure, and then stabilise. Record the highest reading obtained.

**6** Repeat the test on the remaining cylinders, recording the pressure in each.

**7** All cylinders should produce very similar pressures; any difference greater than that specified indicates the existence of a fault. Note that the compression should build-up quickly in a healthy engine; low compression on the first stroke, followed by gradually-increasing pressure on successive strokes, indicates worn piston rings. A low compression reading on the first stroke, which does not build-up during successive strokes, indicates leaking valves or a blown head gasket (a cracked head could also be the cause). **Note:** *The cause of poor compression is less easy to establish on a diesel engine than on a petrol one. The effect of introducing oil into the cylinders ('wet' testing) is not conclusive, because there is a risk that the oil will sit in the recess on the piston crown instead of passing to the rings.*

**8** On completion of the test, reconnect the electronic control unit wiring connector then refit the glow plugs as described in Chapter 5C.

### Leakdown test

**9** A leakdown test measures the rate at which compressed air fed into the cylinder is lost. It is an alternative to a compression test, and in many ways it is better, since the escaping air provides easy identification of where pressure loss is occurring (piston rings, valves or head gasket).

**10** The equipment needed for leakdown testing is unlikely to be available to the home mechanic. If poor compression is suspected, have the test performed by a dealership.

## 3  Engine assembly/ valve timing holes – general information and usage

**Note:** *Do not attempt to rotate the engine whilst the camshafts are locked in position. If the engine is to be left in this state for a long period of time, it is a good idea to place suitable warning notices inside the car, and in the engine compartment. This will reduce the possibility of the engine being accidentally*

**3.2  Camshaft timing slot (arrowed) for use with the camshaft locking tools**

**3.3a  Inserting the Vauxhall crankshaft locking tool through the timing hole in the bellhousing**

**3.3b  Using a drill bit (arrowed) to lock the crankshaft through the additional timing hole provided in the flywheel**

*cranked on the starter motor, which is likely to cause damage with the locking tools in place.*

**1** To accurately set the valve timing for all operations requiring removal and refitting of the timing chain, timing slots are machined in the camshafts and corresponding holes are drilled in the camshaft housing. Timing holes are also drilled in the flywheel, and transmission bellhousing. The holes are used in conjunction with camshaft and crankshaft locking tools to lock the camshafts and crankshaft when all the pistons are positioned at the mid-point of their stroke. This arrangement prevents the possibility of the valves contacting the pistons when refitting the cylinder head or timing chain, and also ensures that the correct valve timing can be obtained. The design of the engine is such that there are no conventional timing marks on the crankshaft or camshaft sprockets to indicate the normal TDC position. Therefore, for any work on the timing chain, camshafts or cylinder head, the locking tools must be used.

**2** The Vauxhall special tool for locking the camshafts consists a spring loaded plunger which is free to slide in the bore of the tool body. The tool body is screwed into the camshaft housing timing hole (after removal of a closure plug) so that the sliding plunger contacts the exhaust camshaft. The plunger is retained in contact with the camshaft by the spring. The crankshaft is then rotated by means of the crankshaft pulley bolt until a machined slot in the camshaft aligns with the tool plunger **(see illustration)**. The spring then forces the plunger into engagement with the slot, locking the camshaft in the timing position. To accurately check the valve timing,

or for any work that entails removal of the camshafts or their drive gears, two of these tools will be required, one for each camshaft.

**3** The Vauxhall special tool for locking the crankshaft is simply a 6 mm diameter pin which is inserted through a hole in the bellhousing to engage with a corresponding hole in the rim of the flywheel. An additional hole is provided in the inner face of the flywheel with a corresponding hole in the cylinder block, for use when the transmission has been removed **(see illustrations)**.

**4** The Vauxhall tool numbers are as follows:
*Camshaft locking tool: EN-46781*
*Crankshaft locking tool (bellhousing into flywheel): EN-46785*
*Crankshaft locking tool (flywheel into cylinder block): EN-46778*

**5** Although the Vauxhall camshaft locking tools (or aftermarket equivalents) are relatively inexpensive and should be readily available, it is possible to fabricate suitable alternatives, with the help of a local machine shop, as described below. Once the tools have been made up, their usage is described in the relevant Sections of this Chapter where the tools are required.

### Camshaft locking tool

**6** Lift off the plastic cover over the top of the engine.

**7** Unscrew the three bolts securing the plastic wiring harness guide to the top of the camshaft housing.

**8** Release the locking catches securing the wiring connectors to the four injectors, then disconnect the injector wiring, while at the

same time moving the wiring harness guide forward **(see illustration)**.

**9** Unscrew the closure bolt from the valve timing checking hole on the front face of the camshaft housing. The bolt is located above, and just between, Nos 2 and 3 glow plugs.

**10** Using the closure bolt as a pattern, obtain a length of threaded dowel rod, or suitable bolt to screw into the closure bolt hole. With the help of a machine shop or engineering works, make up the camshaft locking tool by having the dowel rod or bolt machined **(see illustrations)**. Note that for some of the procedures described in this Chapter, two locking tools will be needed, one for each camshaft.

**11** To refit the closure bolt, thoroughly clean the bolt threads and apply suitable thread-locking compound. Screw the bolt into the camshaft housing and tighten to the specified torque.

**12** Securely reconnect the injector wiring connectors, then refit and tighten the three wiring harness guide retaining bolts. Refit the engine cover on completion.

### Crankshaft locking tools

**13** Suitable drill bits or dowel rods can be used as alternatives for the Vauxhall special tools described previously. Their respective diameters are as follows:
*Crankshaft locking tool (bellhousing into flywheel): 6.0 mm diameter*
*Crankshaft locking tool (flywheel into cylinder block): 9.0 mm diameter*

**3.8  Disconnect the injector wiring then move the wiring harness guide forward**

**3.10a  To make an alternative camshaft locking tool . . .**

**3.10b  . . . have suitable dowel rods or bolts machined to the dimensions shown**

**4.8 Undo the three bolts and remove the engine lifting bracket and fuel rail mounting bracket from the camshaft housing**

 **4  Valve timing –**
checking and adjustment

**Note:** *Certain special tools will be required for this operation. Read through the entire procedure to familiarise yourself with the work involved, then either obtain the manufacturer's special tools, or use the alternatives described. New gaskets and sealing rings will also be required for all disturbed components.*

### Checking

**1** Disconnect the battery negative terminal (refer to *Disconnecting the battery* in the Reference Chapter).
**2** Remove the turbocharger charge air pipe as described in Chapter 4C, Section 3.
**3** Disconnect the wiring connector at the camshaft position sensor on the top of the camshaft housing.
**4** Disconnect the wiring connectors at the four glow plugs.
**5** Unscrew the three bolts securing the plastic wiring harness guide to the top of the camshaft housing.
**6** Release the locking catches securing the wiring connectors to the four injectors, then disconnect the injector wiring, while at the same time moving the wiring harness guide forward **(see illustration 3.8)**.
**7** Undo the two retaining bolts securing the fuel rail to the mounting bracket.
**8** Undo the three bolts and remove the engine lifting bracket and fuel rail mounting bracket from the camshaft housing **(see illustration)**. After removal of the mounting bracket, take care not to apply any force to the fuel rail otherwise damage could be caused to the high-pressure fuel pipes.
**9** Unscrew the closure bolt from the valve timing checking hole on each side of the camshaft housing **(see illustration)**.
**10** The camshafts must now be set to the timing position, to enable a camshaft locking tool to be inserted (see Section 3).
**11** If the Vauxhall camshaft locking tools or similar alternatives are available, screw one of the tools into each of the valve timing checking holes. Ensure that the mark on the tool plunger is facing upwards **(see**

**4.9 Unscrew the closure bolt from the valve timing checking hole on each side of the camshaft housing**

**illustration)**. Using a socket or spanner on the crankshaft pulley hub bolt, turn the crankshaft in the normal direction of rotation (clockwise as viewed from the right-hand side of the car) until the spring-loaded plungers of the locking tools slide into engagement with the slot on each camshaft. There will be an audible click from each tool when this happens and the plungers will be seen to move in, towards the camshafts.
**12** If the home-made locking tools described in Section 3 are being used, insert a screwdriver through the valve timing checking hole on the front of the camshaft housing, and into contact with the exhaust camshaft. Using a socket or spanner on the crankshaft pulley hub bolt, turn the crankshaft in the normal direction of rotation (clockwise as viewed from the right-hand side of the car) until the screwdriver can be felt to engage with the slot in the camshaft. Screw the tool into the camshaft housing until resistance is felt, then turn the crankshaft slightly until the camshaft

**4.12a If the home-made tools are being used, screw one of the tools (arrowed) into each timing hole in the camshaft housing . . .**

**4.11 If the Vauxhall camshaft locking tools (1) are being used, screw the tools into the valve timing checking holes. Ensure that the mark on the tool plunger (arrowed) is facing upwards**

slot is correctly aligned, and the tool can be screwed fully in **(see illustrations)**. Repeat this procedure for the inlet camshaft.
**13** Firmly apply the handbrake, then jack up the front of the car and support it securely on axle stands (see *Jacking and vehicle support*).
**14** Insert the Vauxhall crankshaft locking tool or suitable alternative (see Section 3) into the timing hole at the base of the transmission bellhousing and into engagement with the flywheel **(see illustrations)**. It may be

**4.12b . . . so the end of the tool engages with the slot in the camshaft (shown with camshaft removed)**

**4.14a Insert the camshaft locking tool through the bellhousing into engagement with the flywheel. Hold the tool in place with the spring**

necessary to turn the crankshaft very slightly one way or the other (within the limits of any slack afforded by the timing chain/tensioner) to allow the tool to fully engage.

15  If the crankshaft locking tool has engaged fully, then the valve timing is correct. Refit the disturbed components as described in the following paragraphs. If it is not possible to fully insert the crankshaft locking tool, then it will be necessary to adjust the valve timing as described in paragraphs 24 to 33.

16  Remove the camshaft locking tools from both sides of the camshaft housing.

17  Thoroughly clean the closure bolt threads and apply suitable thread-locking compound. Screw the bolts into the camshaft housing and tighten to the specified torque.

18  Place the engine lifting bracket and fuel rail mounting bracket in position on the camshaft housing. Refit the three retaining bolts and tighten to the specified torque.

19  Locate the fuel rail on the mounting bracket, insert the two bolts and tighten to the specified torque.

20  Reconnect the fuel injector wiring connectors and secure with the locking catches.

21  Refit the three bolts securing the plastic wiring harness guide to the top of the camshaft housing.

22  Reconnect the wiring connectors at the four glow plugs and at the camshaft position sensor.

23  Refit the turbocharger charge air pipe as described in Chapter 4C, Section 3, then

**4.14b  Alternatively, use a suitable drill bit . . .**

reconnect the battery and lower the car to the ground.

### Adjustment

24  Remove the crankshaft pulley as described in Section 5.

25  It will now be necessary to hold the crankshaft pulley hub to enable the retaining bolt to be removed. Vauxhall special tool KM-662-C is available for this purpose, however, a home-made tool can easily be fabricated **(see Tool Tip)**.

26  Using the Vauxhall tool or the home-made alternative, hold the pulley hub stationary and unscrew the retaining bolt. **Note:** *The pulley hub retaining bolt has a **left-hand thread** and is unscrewed by turning it clockwise.*

27  Withdraw the pulley hub from the crankshaft and refit the retaining bolt sufficiently tight to allow the crankshaft to be turned.

28  Using a socket or spanner on the crankshaft pulley hub bolt, turn the crankshaft as necessary, until it is possible to fully insert the crankshaft locking tool into engagement with the flywheel.

29  Undo the bolt, refit the crankshaft pulley hub, and refit the bolt.

30  Hold the pulley hub using the holding tool and tighten the bolt to the specified torque.

31  Remove the crankshaft locking tool.

32  Refit the crankshaft pulley as described in Section 5.

33  Refit the disturbed components as described in paragraphs 16 to 23.

### 5  Crankshaft pulley – removal and refitting

### Removal

1  Apply the handbrake, then jack up the front of the vehicle and support it on axle stands (see *Jacking and vehicle support*). Remove the right-hand front roadwheel and the inner wheel arch liner for access to the crankshaft pulley.

2  Remove the auxiliary drivebelt as described in Chapter 1B. Prior to removal, mark the direction of rotation on the belt to ensure the belt is refitted the same way around.

**4.14c  . . . and hold it in place with an elastic band**

3  Slacken and remove the four retaining bolts securing the pulley to the pulley hub. If necessary, prevent the crankshaft from turning by holding the pulley hub retaining bolt with a socket.

### Refitting

4  Refit the crankshaft pulley to the pulley hub. Refit the pulley retaining bolts, tightening them to the specified torque.

5  Refit the auxiliary drivebelt as described in Chapter 1B using the mark made prior to removal to ensure the belt is fitted the correct way around.

6  Refit the wheel arch liner and roadwheel, then lower the car to the ground and tighten the wheel bolts to the specified torque.

### 6  Timing cover – removal and refitting

**Note:** *The special tools described in Section 3, together with additional tools, will be required for this operation. Read through the entire procedure and also the procedures contained in Section 3 to familiarise yourself with the work involved, then either obtain the manufacturer's special tools, or use the alternatives described, where applicable. New gaskets and sealing rings will be needed for all disturbed components, together with a tube of suitable gasket sealant.*

### Removal

1  Disconnect the battery negative terminal (refer to *Disconnecting the battery* in the Reference Chapter).

2  Referring to the procedures contained in Chapter 1B, drain the engine oil and the

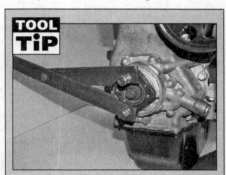

*To make a sprocket holding tool, obtain two lengths of steel strip about 6 mm thick by about 30 mm wide or similar, one 600 mm long, the other 200 mm long (all dimensions are approximate). Bolt the two strips together to form a forked end, leaving the bolt slack so that the shorter strip can pivot freely. At the other end of each 'prong' of the fork, drill a suitable hole and fit a nut and bolt to allow the tool to be bolted to the crankshaft pulley hub.*

**6.13 Undo nut and two bolts (arrowed) and remove the oil filter heat shield**

**6.14 Undo the two bolts (arrowed) securing the coolant pipe to the heat exchanger**

**6.15 Unscrew the turbocharger oil supply pipe banjo union bolt (arrowed) from the oil filter housing**

cooling system. Refit the drain plug, using a new seal, when the oil has drained. Close the cooling system when the coolant has drained.

**3** Remove the crankshaft pulley as described in Section 5.

**4** Remove the air cleaner assembly and the turbocharger charge air pipe and charge air hose as described in Chapter 4C, Section 3.

**5** Disconnect the wiring connector at the camshaft position sensor on the top of the camshaft housing.

**6** Disconnect the wiring connectors at the four glow plugs.

**7** Unscrew the three bolts securing the plastic wiring harness guide to the top of the camshaft housing.

**8** Release the locking catches securing the wiring connectors to the four injectors, then disconnect the injector wiring, while at the same time moving the wiring harness guide forward **(see illustration 3.8)**.

**9** Unscrew the closure bolt from the valve timing checking hole on the exhaust camshaft side of the camshaft housing **(see illustration 4.9)**.

**10** If the Vauxhall camshaft locking tool or similar alternative is available (see Section 3), screw the tool into the valve timing checking hole. Ensure that the mark on the tool plunger is facing upwards. Using a socket or spanner on the crankshaft pulley hub bolt, turn the crankshaft in the normal direction of rotation (clockwise as viewed from the right-hand side of the car) until the spring-loaded plunger of the locking tool slides into engagement with the slot on the camshaft. There will be an audible click from the tool when this happens,

and the plunger will be seen to move in towards the camshaft.

**11** If the home-made locking tool described in Section 3 is being used, insert a screwdriver through the valve timing checking hole on the front of the camshaft housing, and into contact with the exhaust camshaft. Using a socket or spanner on the crankshaft pulley hub bolt, turn the crankshaft in the normal direction of rotation (clockwise as viewed from the right-hand side of the car) until the screwdriver can be felt to engage with the slot in the camshaft. Screw the tool into the camshaft housing until resistance is felt, then turn the crankshaft slightly until the camshaft slot is correctly aligned, and the tool can be screwed fully in **(see illustrations 4.12a and 4.12b)**.

**12** Referring to the procedures contained in Chapter 4C, Section 19, separate the exhaust system front section from the catalytic converter.

**13** Undo the upper nut and two lower bolts and remove the oil filter heat shield **(see illustration)**.

**14** Undo the two bolts securing the coolant pipe to the heat exchanger on the oil filter housing **(see illustration)**. Release the retaining clip securing the other end of the pipe to the hose on the thermostat housing. Undo the pipe support bracket bolt, release the wiring harness from the retaining clip and remove the coolant pipe from the engine. Recover the gasket noting that a new one will be required for refitting.

**15** Unscrew the banjo union bolt and release the turbocharger oil supply pipe from the oil filter housing **(see illustration)**. Recover the

two copper washers from the banjo union, and suitably cover the end of the pipe to prevent dirt entry. Note that new copper washers will be required for refitting.

**16** Slacken the retaining clip and disconnect the radiator bottom hose from the outlet at the base of the oil filter housing.

**17** Undo the three bolts securing the heat shield support bracket to the heat exchanger on the oil filter housing **(see illustration)**.

**18** Undo the remaining bolt and remove the oil filter housing and heat exchanger assembly from the cylinder block. Recover the rubber seal from the rear of the housing. Note that a new seal will be required for refitting.

**19** From under the car, undo the bolt securing the catalytic converter support bracket to the sump reinforcement bracket.

**20** Suitably support the weight of the catalytic converter on blocks or on a jack. Bend back the locking plate tabs and unscrew the three bolts securing the catalytic converter flange to the turbocharger **(see illustration)**. Remove the bolts and locking plate, noting that a new locking plate will be required for refitting.

**21** Separate the catalytic converter from the turbocharger and recover the gasket **(see illustration)**. Carefully lower the converter and remove it from under the car. Note that a new gasket will be required for refitting.

**22** It will now be necessary to hold the crankshaft pulley hub to enable the retaining bolt to be removed. Vauxhall special tool KM-662-C is available for this purpose, however, a home-made tool can easily be fabricated. Refer to the Tool Tip in Section 4.

**23** Using the Vauxhall tool or the home-made

**6.17 Undo the three bolts (arrowed) securing the heat shield support bracket to the heat exchanger**

**6.20 Unscrew the three bolts (arrowed) securing the catalytic converter to the turbocharger**

**6.21 Separate the catalytic converter from the turbocharger and recover the gasket**

**6.26  Remove the sump reinforcement bracket from the cylinder block baseplate and transmission bellhousing**

**6.27  Disconnect the oil level sensor wiring connector**

**6.30  Right-hand engine mounting retaining bolts (arrowed)**

**6.31  Undo the four bolts (arrowed) and remove the engine bracket**

**6.33  Release the wiring harness from the timing cover support clips**

**6.34  Undo the retaining bolt and detach the crankcase ventilation hose attachment**

alternative, hold the pulley hub stationary and unscrew the retaining bolt. **Note:** *The pulley hub retaining bolt has a **left-hand thread** and is unscrewed by turning it clockwise.*

**24**  Withdraw the pulley hub from the crankshaft and refit the retaining bolt sufficiently tight to allow the crankshaft to be turned.

**25**  Insert the Vauxhall crankshaft locking tool or suitable alternative (see Section 3) into the timing hole at the base of the transmission bellhousing and into engagement with the flywheel **(see illustrations 4.14a, 4.14b and 4.14c)**. It may be necessary to turn the crankshaft very slightly one way or the other, by means of the pulley retaining bolt, to allow the tool to fully engage.

**26**  Undo the five bolts securing the sump reinforcement bracket to the cylinder block baseplate and transmission bellhousing and remove the bracket **(see illustration)**. Note

the locations of the different length bolts to aid refitting.

**27**  Disconnect the oil level sensor wiring connector at the rear of the sump **(see illustration)**.

**28**  Undo the thirteen bolts and two nuts securing the sump to the cylinder block baseplate and timing cover. Using a wide-bladed scraper or similar tool inserted between the sump and baseplate, carefully break the joint, then remove the sump from under the car.

**29**  Connect a suitable hoist and lifting tackle to the right-hand end of the engine and support its weight. If available, the type of support bar which locates in the engine compartment side channels is to be preferred. Alternatively, support the engine on a jack with a block of wood positioned between the jack head and cylinder block baseplate.

**30**  Mark the bolt positions for correct refitting, then undo the two bolts securing the right-hand engine mounting to the body and the two bolts securing the mounting to the engine bracket **(see illustration)**. Remove the mounting.

**31**  Undo the four bolts securing the engine bracket to the cylinder block and cylinder head and remove the engine bracket **(see illustration)**.

**32**  Undo the centre retaining bolt and remove the auxiliary drivebelt tensioner from the timing cover.

**33**  Release the wiring harness from the support clips on the timing cover and move the harness to one side **(see illustration)**.

**34**  Undo the retaining bolt and detach the crankcase ventilation hose attachment at the timing cover **(see illustration)**.

**35**  Working through the apertures in the pulley, unscrew and remove the four coolant pump retaining nuts **(see illustration)**.

**36**  Withdraw the coolant pump from the cylinder block studs. **Note:** *Coolant which is trapped in the cylinder block will leak out when the pump is removed.*

**37**  Recover the pump sealing ring, and discard it; a new one must be used on refitting.

**38**  Undo the retaining bolt and remove the wiring harness support clip bracket from the top of the timing cover **(see illustration)**.

**39**  Undo the fourteen bolts and three nuts securing the timing cover to the cylinder block, cylinder block baseplate, cylinder head and camshaft housing. Using a flat-bladed screwdriver inserted behind the lugs on the

**6.35  Working through the pulley apertures, unscrew and remove the coolant pump retaining nuts**

**6.38  Undo the retaining bolt (arrowed) and remove the wiring harness support clip bracket**

**6.39a Using a flat-bladed screwdriver inserted behind the lugs on the edge of the timing cover . . .**

**6.39b . . . carefully prise the cover free and remove it from the engine**

**6.43 Apply a bead of sealant across the housing joints**

edge of the timing cover, carefully prise the cover free and remove it from the engine **(see illustrations)**. Recover the timing cover gasket, a new gasket will be required for refitting.

**40** Thoroughly clean the timing cover and remove all traces of gasket and sealant from all the mating surfaces. Similarly clean the cylinder block baseplate, cylinder block, cylinder head and camshaft housing mating surfaces. Ensure that all traces of old sealant are removed, particularly from the joint areas between these components.

**6.45 Timing cover tightening sequence. Arrows indicate the location of the three nuts**

**41** Obtain all new gaskets and components as necessary ready for refitting. In addition, a new crankshaft oil seal will be required together with a tube of Loctite 5900 sealant, or equivalent. Vauxhall special tool EN-46775, or a suitable alternative, will be required to centralise the timing cover during refitting.

### Refitting

**42** Prior to refitting the timing cover, ensure that the face of the timing chain sprocket on the crankshaft is free from oil or grease.

**43** Apply a 2 mm bead of Loctite 5900 across the camshaft housing-to-cylinder head joint, the cylinder head-to-cylinder block joint and the cylinder block-to-baseplate joint **(see illustration)**.

**44** Place the new gasket in position on the engine then locate the timing cover over the gasket. Insert the Vauxhall tool (EN-46775) or a suitable equivalent, over the crankshaft and into engagement with the timing cover.

**45** Refit the fourteen bolts and three nuts securing the timing cover to the engine, and tighten them to the specified torque, in sequence **(see illustration)**.

**46** Remove the centering tool and carefully prise out the old crankshaft oil seal with a screwdriver or similar hooked tool. Clean the oil seal seat with a wooden or plastic scraper.

**47** Lubricate the lips of the new seal, with clean engine oil and tap it into position until it is flush with the outer face of the timing cover, using a suitable socket or tube, or a wooden block.

**48** Refit the wiring harness support clip bracket to the top of the timing cover.

**49** Ensure that the coolant pump and cylinder block mating surfaces are clean and dry. Fit a new sealing ring to the pump, and install the pump in the cylinder block.

**50** Refit the pump retaining nuts, tightening them to the specified torque.

**51** Insert the crankcase ventilation hose attachment to the timing cover and secure with the retaining bolt.

**52** Refit the wiring harness to the support clips on the timing cover.

**53** Thoroughly clean the crankshaft pulley hub, ensuring that the timing chain sprocket contact face is free from oil or grease.

**54** Refit the pulley hub to the crankshaft, then refit the retaining bolt. Using the method

employed on removal to hold the pulley hub stationary, tighten the retaining bolt to the specified torque.

**55** Refit the auxiliary drivebelt tensioner, ensuring that the lug on the tensioner body engages with the hole in the cylinder block **(see illustration)**. Refit the retaining bolt and tighten the bolt to the specified torque.

**56** Locate the engine bracket in position, refit the four retaining bolts and tighten to the specified torque.

**57** Refit the right-hand engine mounting and secure the mounting to the body and engine bracket with the four retaining bolts. Tighten the bolts to the specified torque. Remove the hoist or jack used to support the engine.

**58** Thoroughly clean the inside and outside of the sump ensuring that all traces of old sealant are removed from the mating face. Also clean the cylinder block baseplate mating face to remove all traces of old sealant.

**59** Apply a 2 mm bead of Loctite 5900 to the sump mating face, ensuring the sealant bead runs around the inside of the bolt holes **(see illustration)**. Position the sump on the cylinder block baseplate, then refit the thirteen bolts and two nuts. Progressively tighten the bolts/nuts to the specified torque. Reconnect the oil level sensor wiring connector.

**60** Refit the sump reinforcement bracket to the cylinder block baseplate and transmission bellhousing and secure with the five bolts, tightened to the specified torque.

**61** Using a new gasket, position the catalytic converter on the turbocharger. Insert the three retaining bolts, with a new locking plate and

**6.55 Refit the auxiliary drivebelt tensioner ensuring that the lug (arrowed) engages with the hole in the cylinder block**

**6.59 Apply a bead of sealant to the sump mating face, ensuring the bead runs around the inside of the bolt holes**

tighten the bolts to the specified torque. Bent over the tabs of the locking plate to retain the bolts.

**62** From under the car, refit the bolt securing the catalytic converter support bracket to the sump reinforcement bracket and tighten the bolt to the specified torque.

**63** Place a new rubber seal on the oil filter housing, ensuring the seal is fully engaged with the housing grooves **(see illustration)**.

**64** Position the oil filter housing on the cylinder block and fit the lower left retaining bolt finger tight. Place the heat shield support bracket in position and fit the remaining three retaining bolts. Tighten the four bolts to the specified torque.

**65** Connect the radiator bottom hose to the outlet at the base of the oil filter housing and secure with the retaining clip.

**66** Using a new copper washer on each side of the banjo union, refit the turbocharger oil supply pipe and screw in the banjo union bolt. Tighten the bolt to the specified torque.

**6.63 Place a new rubber seal on the oil filter housing, ensuring it fully engages with the housing grooves**

**67** Locate a new gasket over the heat exchanger coolant pipe and bend over the tabs of the gasket to retain it on the flange **(see illustration)**.

**68** Engage the coolant pipe with the hose on the thermostat housing, then position the pipe flange on the heat exchanger. Refit the two bolts and tighten them to the specified torque. At the other end of the pipe, tighten the hose retaining clip, refit and tighten the pipe support bracket bolt and secure the wiring harness with the retaining clip.

**69** Place the heat shield over the oil filter, refit the two lower bolts and tighten them finger tight. Refit the two upper nuts securing the heat shield(s), then tighten the engine lifting bracket bolt, the manifold heat shield upper nuts and the oil filter heat shield lower bolts securely.

**70** Refit the exhaust system components with reference to Chapter 4C, Section 19.

**71** Refit the crankshaft pulley as described in Section 5.

**72** Remove the camshaft and crankshaft locking tools. Turn the engine through two complete revolutions, then check that the locking tools can be reinserted. Remove the locking tools.

**73** Thoroughly clean the threads of the closure bolt and apply suitable thread-locking compound. Screw the bolt into the camshaft housing and tighten to the specified torque.

**74** Reconnect the fuel injector wiring connectors and secure with the locking catches.

**75** Refit the three bolts securing the plastic

**6.67 Locate a new gasket over the heat exchanger coolant pipe and bend over the tabs to retain it on the flange**

wiring harness guide to the top of the camshaft housing.

**76** Reconnect the camshaft position sensor wiring connector.

**77** Reconnect the glow plug wiring connectors.

**78** Refit the air cleaner assembly and the turbocharger charge air pipe and charge air hose as described in Chapter 4C, Section 3.

**79** Refill the engine with fresh oil with reference to Chapter 1B.

**80** Refill the cooling system as described in Chapter 1B, then reconnect the battery negative terminal.

**81** Refit the wheel arch liner and roadwheel, then lower the car to the ground and tighten the wheel bolts to the specified torque.

## 7 Timing chain, sprockets, tensioner and guide rails – removal and refitting

### Removal

**1** Remove the timing cover as described in Section 6.

**2** Push the timing chain tensioner plunger back into its bore and insert a suitable drill bit or similar tool to retain it in the released position **(see illustration)**.

**3** Undo the two retaining bolts and remove the tensioner from the cylinder head **(see illustration)**.

**4** Undo the lower pivot bolt and remove the chain tensioner rail **(see illustrations)**.

**7.2 Push the timing chain tensioner plunger back into its bore and retain it using a suitable drill bit (arrowed)**

**7.3 Undo the two bolts and remove the tensioner from the cylinder head**

**7.4a Undo the lower pivot bolt . . .**

**7.4b ... and remove the chain tensioner rail**

**5** Slide the crankshaft sprocket off the end of the crankshaft. Slip the chain off the camshaft sprocket and remove it, together with the crankshaft sprocket **(see illustration)**.

**6** It will now be necessary to hold the camshaft sprocket to enable the retaining bolt to be removed. Vauxhall special tools KM-956-1 and KM-6347 are available for this purpose, however, a home-made tool can easily be fabricated **(see Tool Tip)**.

**7** Using the holding tool to prevent rotation of the camshaft, slacken the sprocket retaining bolt. Remove the holding tool, unscrew the retaining bolt and remove the sprocket **(see illustrations)**.

**8** Undo the two retaining bolts and remove the timing chain guide rail **(see illustration)**.

**9** Inspect the timing chain, sprockets, tensioner rail and guide rail for any sign of wear or deformation, and renew any suspect components as necessary.

**10** Push the timing chain tensioner plunger into the tensioner body and remove the locking drill bit. Check that the tensioner plunger is free to move in out of the tensioner body with no trace of binding. If any binding or sticking of the plunger is felt, renew the tensioner assembly. On completion of the check, or if a new tensioner is being fitted, Compress the plunger and refit the locking drill bit.

### Refitting

**11** Locate the timing chain guide rail in position, refit the two retaining bolts and tighten the bolts to the specified torque.

**12** Fit the sprocket to the camshaft and screw in the retaining bolt. Using the method

**7.7a Using the holding tool to prevent rotation, slacken the camshaft sprocket retaining bolt ...**

**7.5 Slip the chain off the camshaft sprocket and remove it together with the crankshaft sprocket**

employed on removal to hold the sprocket, tighten the retaining bolt to the specified torque.

**13** Thoroughly clean the crankshaft and crankshaft sprocket, ensuring that there is no oil or grease on the contact faces.

**14** Place the sprocket in the timing chain, then engage the chain over the camshaft sprocket. Slide the crankshaft sprocket over the end of the crankshaft.

**15** Refit the timing chain tensioner rail, screw in the lower pivot bolt and tighten the bolt to the specified torque.

**16** Refit the timing chain tensioner and tighten the two retaining bolts to the specified torque. Depress the tensioner plunger, withdraw the locking drill bit and release the plunger.

**17** Refit the timing cover as described in Section 6.

**8   Camshaft housing –**
      removal and refitting

### Removal

**1** Remove the high-pressure fuel pump as described in Chapter 4C, Section 10.

**2** Remove the fuel rail as described in Chapter 4C, Section 11.

**3** Remove the fuel injectors as described in Chapter 4C, Section 12.

**4** Disconnect the engine wiring harness at the following connectors, if not already done:
   a) Crankshaft speed/position sensor.
   b) Manifold pressure sensor.

**7.7b ... then unscrew the bolt and remove the sprocket**

*To make a sprocket holding tool, obtain two lengths of steel strip about 6 mm thick by about 30 mm wide or similar, one 600 mm long, the other 200 mm long (all dimensions are approximate). Bolt the two strips together to form a forked end, leaving the bolt slack so that the shorter strip can pivot freely. At the other end of each 'prong' of the fork, drill a suitable hole and fit a nut and bolt. The bolts can be engaged with the holes in the sprocket to hold the sprocket stationary.*

   c) EGR valve.
   d) Starter/alternator.

**5** Move the disconnected wiring harness to one side.

**6** Remove the timing cover as described in Section 6.

**7** Remove the timing chain, sprockets and tensioner as described in Section 7.

**8** Undo the three bolts and remove the engine lifting bracket and fuel rail mounting bracket from the camshaft housing.

**9** Undo the sixteen bolts, and two stud bolts, securing the camshaft housing to the cylinder head.

**10** Lift the camshaft housing off the cylinder head and recover the gasket.

**11** Thoroughly clean the mating faces of the cylinder head and camshaft housing and obtain a new gasket for refitting.

### Refitting

**12** Check that all the hydraulic tappets and rocker arms are correctly positioned in the cylinder head and none have been disturbed.

**7.8 Undo the two retaining bolts (arrowed) and remove the timing chain guide rail**

**8.13a  Place a new gasket on the cylinder head . . .**

**8.13b  . . . locate the camshaft housing in position . . .**

**8.13c  . . . then refit the two stud bolts to align the assembly**

13 Place a new gasket on the cylinder head, then locate the camshaft housing in position. Refit the two stud bolts to align the assembly but only tighten them finger tight at this stage **(see illustrations)**.

14 Using a straight-edge, align the front face of the camshaft housing with the front face of the cylinder head. Lightly tighten the two stud bolts to retain the housing and maintain the alignment.

15 Refit the sixteen camshaft housing retaining bolts, noting that the longer bolt is fitted at the flywheel end of the housing between the high-pressure fuel pump and vacuum pump locations. Progressively screw in the retaining bolts to gradually draw the housing down and into contact with the cylinder head.

16 Using the straight-edge, check the alignment of the camshaft housing and cylinder head once more and correct if necessary.

**8.17  Camshaft housing retaining bolt tightening sequence**

17 Working in sequence, tighten the camshaft housing retaining bolts to the specified torque **(see illustration)**. Note that the torque setting for the two stud bolts is different from the other bolts.

18 Refit the engine lifting bracket and fuel rail mounting bracket to the camshaft housing. Refit the three retaining bolts and tighten to the specified torque.

19 Refit the timing chain, sprockets and tensioner as described in Section 7.

20 Refit the timing cover as described in Section 6.

21 Reconnect the engine wiring harness to the connectors listed in paragraph 4.

22 Refit the fuel injectors as described in Chapter 4C, Section 12.

23 Refit the fuel rail as described in Chapter 4C, Section 11.

24 Refit the high-pressure fuel pump as described in Chapter 4C, Section 10.

## 9  Camshafts – removal, inspection and refitting

**Note:** *An additional camshaft locking tool (two in total) will be required for this operation (see Section 3).*

### Removal

1 Carry out the operations described in Section 8, paragraphs 1 to 8.

2 Before removing the camshaft housing completely, the retaining bolts for the camshaft drive gears and sprocket should be slackened as follows.

3 It will be necessary to hold the camshaft sprocket to enable the drive gear and sprocket retaining bolts to be slackened. Vauxhall special tools KM-956-1 and KM-6347 are available for this purpose, however, a home-made tool can easily be fabricated **(see Tool Tip in Section 7)**.

4 Working through the vacuum pump aperture, and using the holding tool to prevent rotation of the camshaft, slacken the inlet camshaft drive gear retaining bolt. Working through the high-pressure fuel pump aperture, slacken the exhaust camshaft drive gear retaining bolt in the same way.

5 Again, using the holding tool, slacken the camshaft sprocket retaining bolt.

6 Continue with the camshaft housing removal procedure as described in Section 8, paragraphs 9 to 11.

7 With the camshaft housing removed, unscrew the retaining bolt and withdraw the camshaft position sensor from the top of the housing.

8 Turn the housing over and remove the camshaft locking tool.

9 Unscrew the previously-slackened retaining bolt, lift off the drive gear and carefully withdraw the inlet camshaft from the camshaft housing **(see illustrations)**. Using quick-drying paint, correction fluid or a label, suitably mark the sprocket and camshaft to identify them as the inlet components.

10 At the exhaust camshaft, unscrew the previously-slackened retaining bolt and lift off the camshaft sprocket. Unscrew the retaining bolt, lift off the drive gear and carefully

**9.9a  Unscrew the previously slackened retaining bolt . . .**

**9.9b  . . . lift off the drive gear . . .**

**9.9c  . . . and carefully withdraw the inlet camshaft from the camshaft housing**

withdraw the exhaust camshaft from the camshaft housing (see illustrations). Using quick-drying paint, correction fluid or a label, suitably mark the sprocket and camshaft to identify them as the exhaust components.

## Inspection

**11** Examine the camshaft bearing surfaces and cam lobes for signs of wear ridges and scoring. Renew the camshaft if any of these conditions are apparent. Examine the condition of the bearing surfaces in the camshaft housing. If the any wear or scoring is evident, the camshaft housing will need to be renewed.

**12** If either camshaft is being renewed, it will be necessary to renew all the rocker arms and tappets for that particular camshaft also (see Section 10).

**13** Check the condition of the camshaft drive gears and sprocket for chipped or damaged teeth, wear ridges and scoring. Renew any components as necessary.

## Refitting

**14** Prior to refitting, thoroughly clean all components and dry with a lint-free cloth. Ensure that all traces of oil and grease are removed from the contact faces of the drive gears, sprocket and camshafts.

**15** Lubricate the exhaust camshaft bearing journals in the camshaft housing and carefully insert the exhaust camshaft. Ensuring that the contact faces are clean and dry, refit the drive gear to the camshaft and insert the retaining bolt. Screw in the bolt two or three turns at this stage.

**16** Locate the sprocket on the exhaust camshaft with the writing on the sprocket facing away from the camshaft housing. Insert the retaining bolt and screw in the bolt two or three turns at this stage.

**17** Lubricate the inlet camshaft bearing journals in the camshaft housing and carefully insert the inlet camshaft. Ensuring that the contact faces are clean and dry, refit the drive gear to the camshaft and insert the retaining bolt. Screw in the bolt two or three turns at this stage.

**18** Turn each camshaft to align the timing slot with the valve timing checking hole in the camshaft housing. Insert the camshaft locking tools (either the Vauxhall tool or the home-made equivalent described in Section 3)

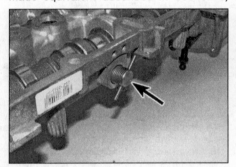

**9.18 Insert the locking tools (arrowed) to lock the camshafts in the timing position**

**9.10a Unscrew the previously-slackened retaining bolt and lift off the exhaust camshaft sprocket**

**9.10c . . . lift off the drive gear . . .**

ensuring that the tools fully engage with the camshaft slots (see illustration).

**19** With the camshafts locked in the timing position, tighten the drive gear retaining bolts and the sprocket retaining bolt to 20 Nm (15 lbf ft). Note that this is only an initial setting to retain the components. Final tightening is carried out after the camshaft housing has been refitted to the cylinder head.

**20** Refit the camshaft position sensor to the camshaft housing and tighten the retaining bolt securely.

**21** Refit the camshaft housing to the cylinder head as described in Section 8, paragraphs 12 to 17.

**22** With the camshaft housing installed, final tightening of the drive gear and sprocket retaining bolts can be carried out.

**23** Using the method employed on removal to hold the sprocket, tighten the sprocket retaining bolt to the specified torque (see illustration).

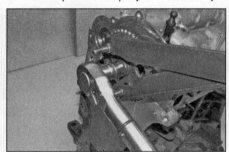

**9.23 Hold the sprocket with the tool and tighten the retaining bolt to the specified torque**

**9.10b Unscrew the retaining bolt . . .**

**9.10d . . . and carefully withdraw the exhaust camshaft from the camshaft housing**

**24** While still holding the sprocket with the tool, tighten the exhaust camshaft drive gear retaining bolt to the specified torque followed by the inlet camshaft drive gear retaining bolt (see illustration).

**25** Remove the locking tool from the inlet camshaft, but leave the exhaust camshaft locking tool in place.

**26** Continue with the camshaft housing refitting procedure as described in Section 8, paragraphs 18 to 24.

## 10 Hydraulic tappets and rocker arms – removal, inspection and refitting

## Removal

**1** Remove the camshaft housing as described in Section 8.

**9.24 While still holding the sprocket with the tool, tighten the drive gear retaining bolt on each camshaft**

**10.3a Withdraw each rocker arm and hydraulic tappet in turn . . .**

**10.3b . . . then unclip the rocker arm from the tappet**

**2** Obtain sixteen small, oil-tight clean plastic containers, and number them inlet 1 to 8 and exhaust 1 to 8; alternatively, divide a larger container into sixteen compartments and number each compartment accordingly.
**3** Withdraw each rocker arm and hydraulic tappet in turn, unclip the rocker arm from the tappet, and place them in their respective container **(see illustrations)**. Do not interchange the rocker arms and tappets, or the rate of wear will be much increased. Fill each container with clean engine oil and ensure that the tappet is submerged.

### Inspection

**4** Examine the rocker arm and hydraulic tappet bearing surfaces for wear ridges and scoring. Renew any rocker arm or tappet on which these conditions are apparent.
**5** If any new hydraulic tappets are obtained, they should be immersed in a container of clean engine oil prior to refitting.

### Refitting

**6** Liberally oil the cylinder head hydraulic tappet bores and the tappets. Working on one assembly at a time, clip the rocker arm back onto the tappet, then refit the tappet to the cylinder head, ensuring that it is refitted to its original bore. Lay the rocker arm over its respective valve.
**7** Refit the remaining tappets and rocker arms in the same way.
**8** With all the tappets and rocker arms in place, refit the camshaft housing as described in Section 8.

**11.6 Undo the two bolts (arrowed) and free the oil separator from the inlet manifold**

---

**11 Cylinder head –**
  removal and refitting

**Note:** *New cylinder head retaining bolts will be required for refitting.*

### Removal

**1** Remove the camshaft housing as described in Section 8, and the hydraulic tappets and rocker arms as described in Section 10.
**2** Remove the turbocharger charge air pipe as described in Chapter 4C, Section 3.
**3** Remove the exhaust gas recirculation (EGR) valve as described in Chapter 4E.
**4** Withdraw the engine oil dipstick, then undo the retaining bolt securing the dipstick guide tube to the inlet manifold.
**5** Using a small screwdriver, lift up the locking catch and disconnect the manifold pressure sensor wiring connector.
**6** Undo the two bolts and free the crankcase ventilation system oil separator from the inlet manifold **(see illustration)**.
**7** Working in the **reverse** of the tightening sequence **(see illustration 11.27b)**, progressively slacken the cylinder head bolts by half a turn at a time, until all bolts can be unscrewed by hand. Note that an M12 RIBE socket bit will be required to unscrew the bolts. Remove the cylinder head bolts and recover the washers.
**8** Engage the help of an assistant and lift the cylinder head from the cylinder block. Take care as it is a bulky and heavy assembly.

**11.16 Cylinder head gasket thickness identification hole (arrowed)**

**9** Remove the gasket and keep it for identification purposes (see paragraph 16).
**10** If the cylinder head is to be dismantled for overhaul, then refer to Part D of this Chapter.

### Preparation for refitting

**11** The mating faces of the cylinder head and cylinder block/crankcase must be perfectly clean before refitting the head. Use a hard plastic or wood scraper to remove all traces of gasket and carbon; also clean the piston crowns. Take particular care, as the surfaces are damaged easily. Also, make sure that the carbon is not allowed to enter the oil and water passages – this is particularly important for the lubrication system, as carbon could block the oil supply to any of the engine's components. Using adhesive tape and paper, seal the water, oil and bolt holes in the cylinder block/crankcase. To prevent carbon entering the gap between the pistons and bores, smear a little grease in the gap. After cleaning each piston, use a small brush to remove all traces of grease and carbon from the gap, then wipe away the remainder with a clean rag. Clean all the pistons in the same way.
**12** Check the mating surfaces of the cylinder block/crankcase and the cylinder head for nicks, deep scratches and other damage. If slight, they may be removed carefully with a file, but if excessive, machining may be the only alternative to renewal.
**13** Ensure that the cylinder head bolt holes in the crankcase are clean and free of oil. Syringe or soak up any oil left in the bolt holes. This is most important in order that the correct bolt tightening torque can be applied and to prevent the possibility of the block being cracked by hydraulic pressure when the bolts are tightened.
**14** The cylinder head bolts must be discarded and renewed, regardless of their apparent condition.
**15** If warpage of the cylinder head gasket surface is suspected, use a straight-edge to check it for distortion. Refer to Part D of this Chapter if necessary.
**16** On this engine, the cylinder head-to-piston clearance is controlled by fitting different thickness head gaskets. The gasket thickness can be determined by looking at the left-hand front corner of the gasket and checking on the number of holes **(see illustration)**.

| Holes in gasket | Gasket thickness |
| --- | --- |
| No holes | 0.67 to 0.77 mm |
| One hole | 0.77 to 0.87 mm |
| Two holes | 0.87 to 0.97 mm |

The correct thickness of gasket required is selected by measuring the piston protrusions as follows.
**17** Remove the crankshaft locking tool from the base of the bellhousing and temporarily refit the crankshaft pulley retaining bolt to enable the crankshaft to be turned.
**18** Mount a dial test indicator securely on the block so that its pointer can be easily pivoted between the piston crown and block mating surface. Turn the crankshaft to bring No 1

piston roughly to the TDC position. Move the dial test indicator probe over and in contact with No 1 piston. Turn the crankshaft back-and-forth slightly until the highest reading is shown on the gauge, indicating that the piston is at TDC.

**19** Zero the dial test indicator on the gasket surface of the cylinder block then carefully move the indicator over No 1 piston. Measure its protrusion at the highest point between the valve cut-outs, and then again at its highest point between the valve cut-outs at 90° to the first measurement **(see illustration)**. Repeat this procedure with No 4 piston.

**20** Rotate the crankshaft half a turn (180°) to bring No 2 and 3 pistons to TDC. Ensure the crankshaft is accurately positioned then measure the protrusions of No 2 and 3 pistons at the specified points. Once all pistons have been measured, rotate the crankshaft to position all the pistons at their mid-stroke and refit the crankshaft locking tool. If the tool will not engage the hole in the flywheel, turn the crankshaft one complete turn and try again.

**21** Select the correct thickness of head gasket required by determining the largest amount of piston protrusion, and using the following table.

| Piston protrusion measurement | Gasket thickness required |
|---|---|
| 0.028 to 0.127 mm | 0.67 to 0.77 mm (no holes) |
| 0.128 to 0.227 mm | 0.77 to 0.87 mm (one hole) |
| 0.228 to 0.327 mm | 0.87 to 0.97 mm (two holes) |

### Refitting

**22** Wipe clean the mating surfaces of the cylinder head and cylinder block/crankcase. Place the new gasket in position with the words ALTO/TOP uppermost.

**23** If not already done, rotate the crankshaft to position all the pistons at their mid-stroke and refit the crankshaft locking tool. If the

tool will not engage the hole in the flywheel, turn the crankshaft one complete turn and try again. Once the tool is in place, remove the crankshaft pulley hub retaining bolt.

**24** With the aid of an assistant, carefully refit the cylinder head assembly to the block, aligning it with the locating dowels.

**25** Apply a thin film of engine oil to the bolt threads and the underside of the bolt heads. Carefully enter each new cylinder head bolt into its relevant hole (*do not drop them in*). Screw all bolts in, by hand only, until finger-tight.

**26** Using a straight-edge, align the front face of the cylinder head with the front face of the cylinder block **(see illustration)**. Lightly tighten the cylinder head bolts to retain the head and maintain the alignment.

**27** Working progressively in sequence, tighten the cylinder head bolts to their Stage 1 torque setting, using a torque wrench and suitable socket **(see illustrations)**.

**28** Once all bolts have been tightened to the Stage 1 torque, working again in the same sequence, go around and tighten all bolts through the specified Stage 2 angle, then through the specified Stage 3 angle using an angle-measuring gauge **(see illustration)**.

**29** Refit the crankcase ventilation system oil

**11.19 Using a dial test indicator to measure piston protrusion**

separator to the inlet manifold and secure with the two bolts

**30** Reconnect the manifold pressure sensor wiring connector.

**31** Refit the dipstick guide tube to the inlet manifold, refit and tighten the retaining bolt, then insert the dipstick.

**32** Refit the exhaust gas recirculation (EGR) valve as described in Chapter 4D.

**33** Refit the turbocharger charge air pipe as described in Chapter 4C, Section 3.

**34** Refit the hydraulic tappets and rocker arms as described in Section 10 and the camshaft housing as described in Section 8.

**11.26 Using a straight-edge, align the front face of the cylinder head with the front face of the cylinder block**

**11.27a Working in sequence, tighten the cylinder head bolts to their Stage 1 torque, using a torque wrench**

**11.27b Cylinder head bolt tightening sequence**

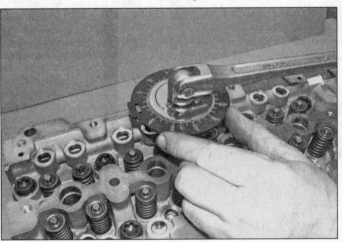

**11.28 Tighten the bolts through the Stage 2 and Stage 3 angle using an angle-measuring gauge**

**13.2a  Remove the oil pick-up pipe from the oil pump cover . . .**

**13.2b  . . . then remove the rubber seal from the pick-up pipe**

**13.3  Remove the screws and withdraw the oil pump cover from the rear of the timing cover**

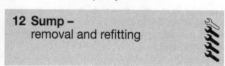

## 12 Sump –
### removal and refitting

### Removal

**1** Disconnect the battery negative terminal (refer to *Disconnecting the battery* in the Reference Chapter).
**2** Apply the handbrake, then jack up the front of the vehicle and support it on axle stands (see *Jacking and vehicle support*).
**3** Drain the engine oil as described in Chapter 1B, then fit a new sealing ring and refit the drain plug, tightening it to the specified torque. It is also recommended that the oil filter is renewed at the same time.
**4** Referring to the relevant procedures contained in Chapter 4C, Section 16, remove the catalytic converter from the turbocharger.

**13.4a  Remove the oil pump inner rotor . . .**

**13.5a  Unscrew the oil pressure relief valve cap . . .**

**5** Undo the five bolts securing the sump reinforcement bracket to the cylinder block baseplate and transmission bellhousing and remove the bracket **(see illustration 6.26)**. Note the locations of the different length bolts to aid refitting.
**6** Disconnect the oil level sensor wiring connector at the rear of the sump **(see illustration 6.27)**.
**7** Undo the thirteen bolts and two nuts securing the sump to the cylinder block baseplate and timing cover. Using a wide-bladed scraper or similar tool inserted between the sump and baseplate, carefully break the joint, then remove the sump from under the car.

### Refitting

**8** Thoroughly clean the inside and outside of the sump ensuring that all traces of old sealant are removed from the mating face. Also clean

**13.4b  . . . and outer rotor from the timing cover**

**13.5b  . . . then withdraw the spring . . .**

the cylinder block baseplate mating face to remove all traces of old sealant.
**9** Apply a 2 mm bead of Loctite 5900 to the sump mating face, ensuring the sealant bead runs around the inside of the bolt holes **(see illustration 6.59)**. Position the sump on the cylinder block baseplate, then refit the thirteen bolts and two nuts. Progressively tighten the bolts/nuts to the specified torque. Reconnect the oil level sensor wiring connector.
**10** Refit the sump reinforcement bracket to the cylinder block baseplate and transmission bellhousing and secure with the five bolts, tightened to the specified torque.
**11** Refit the catalytic converter to the turbocharger as described in the relevant procedures contained in Chapter 4C, Section 16.
**12** Lower the vehicle to the ground then fill the engine with fresh oil, with reference to Chapter 1B.
**13** Refill the cooling system as described in Chapter 1B, then reconnect the battery terminal.

## 13 Oil pump –
### removal, inspection and refitting

### Removal

**1** Remove the timing cover as described in Section 6.
**2** Undo the two retaining bolts and remove the oil pick-up pipe from the oil pump cover on the rear of the timing cover. Remove the rubber seal from the pick-up pipe, noting that a new seal will be required for refitting **(see illustrations)**.
**3** Remove the securing screws and withdraw the oil pump cover from the rear of the timing cover **(see illustration)**.
**4** Remove the inner and outer rotor from the timing cover and wipe them clean. Also clean the rotor location in the timing cover **(see illustrations)**.
**5** The oil pressure relief valve components can also be removed from the timing cover by unscrewing the cap. Withdraw the cap, the spring and the plunger **(see illustrations)**.

### Inspection

**6** Check for any signs of scoring, pitting,

scuffing or general wear on the rotors or their location in the timing cover. Renew any components as necessary. If the pump components are satisfactory, check the rotor clearances as follows.

7 Locate the inner and outer rotor back in the timing cover. Check the clearance between the end faces of the gears and the housing (endfloat) using a straight-edge and a feeler gauge **(see illustration)**.

8 Check the outer rotor-to-body clearance using a feeler gauge **(see illustration)**.

9 If the clearances are outside the specified limits, renew the components as necessary.

10 Examine the pressure relief valve spring and plunger, and renew if any sign of damage or wear is evident.

11 Ensure that the rotor location in the interior of the timing cover is scrupulously clean before commencing reassembly.

### Refitting

12 Thoroughly clean the pressure relief valve components, and lubricate them with clean engine oil before refitting. Insert the plunger and spring, then apply thread-locking compound to the cap threads and refit the cap. Tighten the cap securely.

13 Ensure that the rotors are clean, then lubricate them with clean engine oil. Locate the inner and outer rotor back in the timing cover, with the dot marks aligned and facing away from the timing cover **(see illustration)**.

14 Ensure that the mating faces of the rear cover and the pump housing are clean, then refit the rear cover. Refit and tighten the securing screws securely.

15 Fit a new rubber seal to the oil pick-up pipe and locate the pipe on the oil pump cover. Refit the two retaining bolts and tighten securely.

16 Refit the timing cover as described in Section 6.

## 14 Crankshaft oil seals
### – renewal

### Timing cover oil seal

**Note:** *The design of the engine is such, that once the crankshaft pulley hub bolt is undone the valve timing will be lost unless suitable locking tools are used to retain the camshafts and crankshaft in the timing position. Refer to the information contained in Section 3 for further details and obtain the tools described.*

1 Remove the crankshaft pulley as described in Section 5.

2 Disconnect the wiring connector at the camshaft position sensor on the top of the camshaft housing.

3 Disconnect the wiring connectors at the four glow plugs.

4 Unscrew the three bolts securing the plastic wiring harness guide to the top of the camshaft housing.

**13.5c . . . and the plunger**

**13.8 Checking the oil pump outer rotor-to-body clearance**

5 Release the locking catches securing the wiring connectors to the four injectors, then disconnect the injector wiring, while at the same time moving the wiring harness guide forward **(see illustration 3.8)**.

6 Unscrew the closure bolt from the valve timing checking hole on the exhaust camshaft side of the camshaft housing **(see illustration 4.9)**.

7 If the Vauxhall camshaft locking tool or similar alternative is available (see Section 3), screw the tool into the valve timing checking hole. Ensure that the mark on the tool plunger is facing upwards. Using a socket or spanner on the crankshaft pulley hub bolt, turn the crankshaft in the normal direction of rotation (clockwise as viewed from the right-hand side of the car) until the spring-loaded plunger of the locking tool slides into engagement with the slot on the camshaft. There will be an audible click from the tool when this happens, and the plunger will be seen to move in, towards the camshaft.

8 If the home-made locking tool described in Section 3 is being used, insert a screwdriver through the valve timing checking hole on the front of the camshaft housing, and into contact with the exhaust camshaft. Using a socket or spanner on the crankshaft pulley hub bolt, turn the crankshaft in the normal direction of rotation (clockwise as viewed from the right-hand side of the car) until the screwdriver can be felt to engage with the slot in the camshaft. Screw the tool into the camshaft housing until resistance is felt, then turn the crankshaft slightly until the camshaft slot is correctly aligned, and the tool can be screwed fully in **(see illustrations 4.12a and 4.12b)**.

**13.7 Checking the oil pump rotor endfloat**

**13.13 Locate the rotors in the timing cover with the dot marks (arrowed) aligned and facing away from the timing cover**

9 Once the camshaft is locked in position, insert the Vauxhall crankshaft locking tool or suitable alternative (see Section 3) into the timing hole at the base of the transmission bellhousing and into engagement with the flywheel **(see illustrations 4.14a, 4.14b and 4.14c)**. It may be necessary to turn the crankshaft very slightly one way or the other (within the limits of any slack afforded by the timing chain/tensioner) to allow the tool to fully engage.

10 It will now be necessary to hold the crankshaft pulley hub to enable the retaining bolt to be removed. Vauxhall special tool KM-662-C is available for this purpose, however, a home-made tool can easily be fabricated **(see Tool Tip in Section 4)**.

11 Using the Vauxhall tool or the home-made alternative, hold the pulley hub stationary and unscrew the retaining bolt. **Note:** *The pulley hub retaining bolt has a **left-hand thread** and is unscrewed by turning it clockwise.*

12 Withdraw the pulley hub from the crankshaft.

13 Carefully prise out the old crankshaft oil seal with a screwdriver or similar hooked tool. Clean the oil seal seat with a wooden or plastic scraper.

14 Lubricate the lips of the new seal, with clean engine oil and tap it into position until it is flush with the outer face of the timing cover, using a suitable socket or tube, or a wooden block.

15 Thoroughly clean the crankshaft pulley hub, ensuring that the timing chain sprocket contact face is free from oil or grease.

16 Refit the pulley hub to the crankshaft,

**14.29  Lubricate the lips of the new crankshaft oil seal with white silicone grease**

**14.30  Fit the oil seal to the fitting tool, so that the seal lip is spread open toward the crankshaft side**

**14.31a  Position the seal, together with the fitting tool over the end of the crankshaft . . .**

**32** Once the seal is in position, remove the fitting tool (see illustration).
**33** Refit the flywheel as described in Section 16.

**14.31b  . . . then tap the seal into position using a suitable wooden block or similar**

then refit the retaining bolt. Using the method employed on removal to hold the pulley hub stationary, tighten the retaining bolt to the specified torque.
**17** Refit the crankshaft pulley to the pulley hub. Refit the pulley retaining bolts, tightening them to the specified torque.
**18** Remove the camshaft and crankshaft locking tools.
**19** Thoroughly clean the threads of the closure bolt and apply suitable thread-locking compound. Screw the bolt into the camshaft housing and tighten to the specified torque.
**20** Reconnect the fuel injector wiring connectors and secure with the locking catches.
**21** Reconnect the wiring connector at the camshaft position sensor.
**22** Reconnect the wiring connectors at the four glow plugs.
**23** Refit the three bolts securing the plastic

**15.11  Undo the three bolts (arrowed) and withdraw the heat exchanger from the oil filter housing**

**14.32  Once the seal is in position, remove the fitting tool**

wiring harness guide to the top of the camshaft housing.
**24** Refit the auxiliary drivebelt as described in Chapter 1B using the mark made prior to removal to ensure the belt is fitted the correct way around.
**25** Refit the wheel arch liner and roadwheel, then lower the car to the ground and tighten the wheel bolts to the specified torque.

### Transmission end oil seal

**Note:** *Vauxhall special tools EN-4677-10 and EN-4677-20 or a suitable equivalent oil seal fitting tool will be required for this operation. A tube of white silicone grease (available from Vauxhall dealers) will also be needed.*
**26** Remove the flywheel as described in Section 16.
**27** Carefully prise out the old seal from its location using a screwdriver or similar hooked tool.
**28** Clean the oil seal seat with a wooden or plastic scraper.
**29** Liberally lubricate the lips of the new oil seal with white silicone grease (see illustration).
**30** Fit the seal to the Vauxhall tool, or equivalent fitting tool, so that the seal lip is spread open toward the crankshaft side (see illustration).
**31** Position the seal, together with the fitting tool over the end of the crankshaft, then tap the seal into position using a suitable socket or tube, or a wooden block, until it is flush with the outer faces of the cylinder block and baseplate (see illustrations).

### 15 Oil cooler/heat exchanger – removal and refitting

### Removal

**1** Disconnect the battery negative terminal (refer to *Disconnecting the battery* in the Reference Chapter).
**2** Referring to the procedures contained in Chapter 4C, Section 19, separate the exhaust system front section from the catalytic converter.
**3** Drain the cooling system as described in Chapter 1B.
**4** Remove the turbocharger charge air hose as described in Chapter 4C, Section 3.
**5** Undo the upper nut and two lower bolts and remove the oil filter heat shield (see illustration 6.13).
**6** Undo the two bolts securing the coolant pipe to the oil filter housing (see illustration 6.14). Recover the gasket, noting that a new one will be required for refitting.
**7** Unscrew the banjo union bolt and release the turbocharger oil supply pipe from the oil filter housing (see illustration 6.15). Recover the two copper washers from the banjo union, and suitable cover the end of the pipe to prevent dirt entry. Note that new copper washers will be required for refitting.
**8** Slacken the retaining clip and disconnect the radiator bottom hose from the outlet at the base of the oil filter housing.
**9** Undo the three bolts securing the heat shield support bracket to the heat exchanger on the oil filter housing (see illustration 6.17).
**10** Undo the remaining bolt and remove the oil filter housing and heat exchanger assembly from the cylinder block. Recover the rubber seal from the rear of the housing. Note that a new seal will be required for refitting.
**11** Undo the three retaining bolts and withdraw the heat exchanger from the oil filter housing (see illustration). Recover the four sealing rings, noting that new sealing rings will be required for refitting.

## Refitting

**12** Thoroughly clean the heat exchanger and oil filter housing, then fit the four new sealing rings to the filter housing.

**13** Place the heat exchanger in position and secure with the three retaining bolts, securely tightened.

**14** Place a new rubber seal on the oil filter housing, ensuring the seal is fully engaged with the housing grooves **(see illustration 6.63)**.

**15** Position the oil filter housing on the cylinder block and fit the lower left retaining bolt finger tight. Place the heat shield support bracket in position and fit the remaining three retaining bolts. Tighten the four bolts to the specified torque.

**16** Connect the radiator bottom hose to the outlet at the base of the oil filter housing and secure with the retaining clip.

**17** Using a new copper washer on each side of the banjo union, refit the turbocharger oil supply pipe and screw in the banjo union bolt. Tighten the bolt to the specified torque.

**18** Locate a new gasket over the coolant pipe and bend over the tabs of the gasket to retain it on the flange.

**19** Position the pipe flange on the oil filter housing. Refit the two bolts and tighten them to the specified torque.

**20** Place the heat shield over the oil filter and secure with the two lower bolts and upper nut.

**21** Refit the turbocharger charge air hose as described in Chapter 4C, Section 3.

**22** Refit the exhaust system components with reference to Chapter 4C, Section 19.

**23** Lower the vehicle to the ground, then reconnect the battery negative terminal.

**24** Refill the cooling system as described in Chapter 1B.

## 16 Flywheel –
removal, inspection and refitting

**Note:** *New flywheel retaining bolts will be required on refitting.*

## Removal

**1** Remove the transmission as described in Chapter 7A then remove the clutch assembly as described in Chapter 6.

**2** Prevent the flywheel from turning by inserting one of the bellhousing-to-engine retaining bolts. Rest a large screwdriver against the bolt with its end in contact with the flywheel ring gear teeth.

**3** Slacken and remove the retaining bolts and remove the flywheel **(see illustration)**. Do not drop it, as it is very heavy.

## Inspection

**4** Examine the flywheel for wear or chipping of the ring gear teeth. Renewal of the ring gear is possible but is not a task for the home mechanic; renewal requires the new ring gear to be heated (up to 180° to 230ºC) to allow it to be fitted.

**16.3  Flywheel retaining bolts (arrowed)**

**5** Examine the flywheel for scoring of the clutch face. If the clutch face is scored, the flywheel may be surface-ground, but renewal is preferable.

**6** If there is any doubt about the condition of the flywheel, seek the advice of a Vauxhall dealer or engine reconditioning specialist. They will be able to advise if it is possible to recondition it or whether renewal is necessary.

## Refitting

**7** Clean the mating surfaces of the flywheel and crankshaft.

**8** Apply a drop of locking compound to the threads of each of the new flywheel retaining bolts (unless they are already precoated) then refit the flywheel and install the new bolts.

**9** Lock the flywheel using the method employed on removal then, working in a diagonal sequence, evenly and progressively tighten the retaining bolts to the specified torque setting.

**10** Refit the clutch as described in Chapter 6, then refit the transmission as described in Chapter 7A.

## 17 Engine/transmission mountings –
inspection and renewal

## Inspection

**1** To improve access, firmly apply the handbrake, then jack up the front of the vehicle

**17.8a  Right-hand engine mounting retaining bolts (arrowed)**

and support it on axle stands (see *Jacking and vehicle support*).

**2** Check the mounting blocks (rubbers) to see if they are cracked, hardened or separated from the metal at any point. Renew the mounting block if any such damage or deterioration is evident.

**3** Check that all the mounting securing nuts and bolts are securely tightened, using a torque wrench to check if possible.

**4** Using a large screwdriver, or a similar tool, check for wear in the mounting blocks by carefully levering against them to check for free play. Where this is not possible, enlist the aid of an assistant to move the engine/gearbox unit back-and-forth, and from side-to-side, while you observe the mountings. While some free play is to be expected, even from new components, excessive wear should be obvious. If excessive free play is found, check first to see that the securing nuts and bolts are correctly tightened, then renew any worn components as described in the following paragraphs.

## Renewal

**Note:** *Before slackening any of the engine mounting bolts/nuts, the relative positions of the mountings to their various brackets should be marked to ensure correct alignment upon refitting.*

### Right-hand mounting

**5** Apply the handbrake, then jack up the front of the vehicle and support it on axle stands (see *Jacking and vehicle support*).

**6** Remove the air cleaner as described in Chapter 4C.

**7** Attach a suitable hoist and lifting tackle to the engine lifting brackets on the cylinder head, and support the weight of the engine.

**8** Mark the position of the four mounting bracket bolts, then undo the two bolts securing the mounting to the body and the two bolts securing the mounting to the engine bracket **(see illustrations)**. Remove the mounting.

**9** If necessary, undo the four bolts securing the engine bracket to the cylinder block and cylinder head and remove the engine bracket **(see illustration 6.31)**.

**10** If removed, refit the engine mounting bracket and tighten the bolts to the specified torque

**17.8b  Mark the position of the bolts before unscrewing them**

**17.16  Front mounting/torque link**

**17.23  Left-hand engine mounting**

**17.34  Rear mounting/torque link**

11  Place the engine mounting in position and refit the four retaining bolts. Align the mounting in its original position, then tighten the bolts to the specified torque.

12  Remove the hoist, then refit the air cleaner as described in Chapter 4C.

13  On completion, lower the vehicle to the ground.

### Front mounting/torque link

14  Apply the handbrake, then jack up the front of the vehicle and support it on axle stands (see *Jacking and vehicle support*). Remove the right-hand roadwheel and the wheel arch liner for access to the crankshaft pulley.

15  Attach a suitable hoist and lifting tackle to the engine lifting brackets on the cylinder head, and support the weight of the engine.

16  Slacken and remove the nut and washer securing the mounting to the subframe bracket. Withdraw the bolt **(see illustration)**.

17  Undo the bolts securing the mounting bracket to the transmission, then manoeuvre the mounting and bracket out of position.

18  Check all components for signs of wear or damage, and renew as necessary.

19  On reassembly, refit the mounting bracket (aligning the previously-made marks) and tighten its bolts to the specified torque.

20  Locate the mounting in the subframe, ensuring it is fitted the correct way up, and manoeuvre the engine/transmission into position. Refit the mounting bolts and new nuts. Tighten them to the specified torque.

21  Lower the vehicle to the ground.

### Left-hand mounting

22  Attach a suitable hoist and lifting tackle to the engine lifting brackets on the cylinder head, and support the weight of the engine.

23  Using a Torx socket, unscrew the two bolts securing the mounting bracket to the transmission bracket **(see illustration)**.

24  Undo the four bolts securing the mounting to the body and the three bolts securing the transmission bracket to the transmission.

25  Slightly lower the engine, then unclip the clutch hydraulic line from the mounting bracket. Remove the mounting assembly from the car.

26  If necessary, undo the through bolt and separate the rubber mounting from the mounting bracket.

27  If removed, refit the rubber mounting to the mounting bracket and tighten the through-bolt to the specified torque.

28  Locate the mounting brackets in position

and, where necessary, clip the clutch hydraulic line onto the bracket.

29  Raise the engine and insert the bolts, then tighten them to the specified torque.

30  Disconnect the hoist and lifting tackle.

### Rear mounting/torque link

31  Apply the handbrake, then jack up the front of the vehicle and support it on axle stands (see *Jacking and vehicle support*).

32  Attach a suitable hoist and lifting tackle to the engine lifting brackets on the cylinder head, and support the weight of the engine.

33  Working under the vehicle, remove the nut and bolt securing the mounting to the transmission bracket.

34  Remove the bolt securing the mounting to the subframe, and withdraw the mounting/torque link **(see illustration)**.

35  If necessary, unbolt the bracket from the transmission. **Note:** *The bracket bolts and link bolts are of different lengths.*

36  Refit the bracket to the transmission and tighten the bolts to the specified torque.

37  Locate the new mounting/link in position. Insert the bolts and tighten to the specified torque.

38  Remove the hoist and lower the vehicle to the ground.

# Chapter 2 Part D:
# 1.7 litre diesel engine in-car repair procedures

## Contents

## Degrees of difficulty

| Easy, suitable for novice with little experience  | Fairly easy, suitable for beginner with some experience | Fairly difficult, suitable for competent DIY mechanic  | Difficult, suitable for experienced DIY mechanic | Very difficult, suitable for expert DIY or professional  |
|---|---|---|---|---|

## Specifications

**Note:** *Where specifications are given as N/A, no information was available at the time of writing. Refer to your Vauxhall dealer for the latest information available.*

### General

| | |
|---|---|
| Engine type. . . . . . . . . . . . . . . . . . . . . . . . . . . . . . . . . . . . . . . . . . . | Four-cylinder, in-line, water-cooled. Belt-driven double overhead camshaft, 16 valves |
| Manufacturer's engine code: | |
| With intercooler . . . . . . . . . . . . . . . . . . . . . . . . . . . . . . . . . . . . . . | Y17DT |
| Without intercooler . . . . . . . . . . . . . . . . . . . . . . . . . . . . . . . . . . . | Y17DTL |
| Bore . . . . . . . . . . . . . . . . . . . . . . . . . . . . . . . . . . . . . . . . . . . . . . . . | 79.0 mm |
| Stroke . . . . . . . . . . . . . . . . . . . . . . . . . . . . . . . . . . . . . . . . . . . . . . . | 86.0 mm |
| Capacity . . . . . . . . . . . . . . . . . . . . . . . . . . . . . . . . . . . . . . . . . . . . . | 1686 cc |
| Firing order . . . . . . . . . . . . . . . . . . . . . . . . . . . . . . . . . . . . . . . . . . . | 1-3-4-2 (No 1 cylinder at timing belt end) |
| Direction of crankshaft rotation . . . . . . . . . . . . . . . . . . . . . . . . . . . | Clockwise (viewed from timing belt end of engine) |
| Compression ratio . . . . . . . . . . . . . . . . . . . . . . . . . . . . . . . . . . . . . | 18.4:1 |
| Maximum power: | |
| Y17DT . . . . . . . . . . . . . . . . . . . . . . . . . . . . . . . . . . . . . . . . . . . . . | 55 kW at 4400 rpm |
| Y17DTL . . . . . . . . . . . . . . . . . . . . . . . . . . . . . . . . . . . . . . . . . . . . | 48 kW at 4400 rpm |
| Maximum torque: | |
| Y17DT . . . . . . . . . . . . . . . . . . . . . . . . . . . . . . . . . . . . . . . . . . . . . | 165 Nm at 1800 to 3000 rpm |
| Y17DTL . . . . . . . . . . . . . . . . . . . . . . . . . . . . . . . . . . . . . . . . . . . . | 130 Nm at 2000 to 3000 rpm |

### Compression pressures

| | |
|---|---|
| Standard. . . . . . . . . . . . . . . . . . . . . . . . . . . . . . . . . . . . . . . . . . . . . | 26.0 to 30.0 bar |
| Maximum difference between any two cylinders. . . . . . . . . . . . . . . | 1.5 bar |

### Valve clearances

| | |
|---|---|
| Engine cold: | |
| Inlet and exhaust . . . . . . . . . . . . . . . . . . . . . . . . . . . . . . . . . . . . . | 0.40 ± 0.05 mm |

## Camshaft

Endfloat . . . . . . . . . . . . . . . . . . . . . . . . . . . . . . . . . . . . . . . . . . . . . . .  N/A
Maximum permissible radial run-out . . . . . . . . . . . . . . . . . . . . . . . . .  0.05 mm
Camshaft lift:
   Inlet valve . . . . . . . . . . . . . . . . . . . . . . . . . . . . . . . . . . . . . . . . . .  7.8 to 7.68 mm
   Exhaust valve . . . . . . . . . . . . . . . . . . . . . . . . . . . . . . . . . . . . . . . .  7.95 to 7.77 mm
Bearing running clearance:
   Standard . . . . . . . . . . . . . . . . . . . . . . . . . . . . . . . . . . . . . . . . . . . .  N/A
   Service limit . . . . . . . . . . . . . . . . . . . . . . . . . . . . . . . . . . . . . . . . .  N/A

## Lubrication system

Oil pump type. . . . . . . . . . . . . . . . . . . . . . . . . . . . . . . . . . . . . . . . . .  Rotor-type, driven by timing belt
Minimum permissible oil pressure at idle speed, with engine
   at operating temperature (oil temperature of at least 80°C) . . . . . . .  1.27 bar (18 psi)

| Oil pump clearances: | Standard | Service limit |
|---|---|---|
| Outer rotor-to-body clearance . . . . . . . . . . . . . . . . . . . . . . . . . . . . . | 0.24 to 0.36 mm | 0.40 mm |
| Inner-to-outer rotor clearance . . . . . . . . . . . . . . . . . . . . . . . . . . . . . | 0.13 to 0.15 mm | 0.20 mm |
| Rotor endfloat. . . . . . . . . . . . . . . . . . . . . . . . . . . . . . . . . . . . . . . . . . | 0.035 to 0.100 mm | 0.150 mm |

## Torque wrench settings

| | Nm | lbf ft |
|---|---|---|
| Alternator support bracket to block: | | |
|   M10 bolt . . . . . . . . . . . . . . . . . . . . . . . . . . . . . . . . . . . . . . . . . . . | 48 | 35 |
|   M14 bolt . . . . . . . . . . . . . . . . . . . . . . . . . . . . . . . . . . . . . . . . . . . | 68 | 50 |
| Alternator to support bracket: | | |
|   M8 bolt . . . . . . . . . . . . . . . . . . . . . . . . . . . . . . . . . . . . . . . . . . . . | 19 | 14 |
|   M10 bolt . . . . . . . . . . . . . . . . . . . . . . . . . . . . . . . . . . . . . . . . . . . | 46 | 34 |
| Auxiliary belt guide roller to alternator support . . . . . . . . . . . . . . . . . | 38 | 28 |
| Auxiliary belt tensioner to alternator support. . . . . . . . . . . . . . . . . . . | 50 | 37 |
| Baffle plate-to-cylinder block bolts . . . . . . . . . . . . . . . . . . . . . . . . . | 19 | 14 |
| Big-end bearing cap nuts*: | | |
|   Stage 1 . . . . . . . . . . . . . . . . . . . . . . . . . . . . . . . . . . . . . . . . . . . . | 24 | 18 |
|   Stage 2 . . . . . . . . . . . . . . . . . . . . . . . . . . . . . . . . . . . . . . . . . . . . | Angle-tighten a further 100° | |
|   Stage 3 . . . . . . . . . . . . . . . . . . . . . . . . . . . . . . . . . . . . . . . . . . . . | Angle-tighten a further 15° | |
| Camshaft bearing cap nuts: | | |
|   M8 nuts. . . . . . . . . . . . . . . . . . . . . . . . . . . . . . . . . . . . . . . . . . . | 22 | 16 |
|   M10 nuts. . . . . . . . . . . . . . . . . . . . . . . . . . . . . . . . . . . . . . . . . . | 43 | 32 |
| Camshaft housing bolts . . . . . . . . . . . . . . . . . . . . . . . . . . . . . . . . . | 22 | 16 |
| Camshaft sprocket bolt . . . . . . . . . . . . . . . . . . . . . . . . . . . . . . . . . . | 64 | 47 |
| Camshaft thrust plate. . . . . . . . . . . . . . . . . . . . . . . . . . . . . . . . . . . . | 8 | 6 |
| Coolant pipe to cylinder block . . . . . . . . . . . . . . . . . . . . . . . . . . . . . | 95 | 70 |
| Coolant pump: | | |
|   Pulley retaining bolts . . . . . . . . . . . . . . . . . . . . . . . . . . . . . . . . . | 10 | 7 |
|   Pump retaining bolts . . . . . . . . . . . . . . . . . . . . . . . . . . . . . . . . . | 24 | 18 |
| Crankshaft pulley/vibration damper to sprocket . . . . . . . . . . . . . . . . | 20 | 15 |
| Crankshaft sprocket bolt . . . . . . . . . . . . . . . . . . . . . . . . . . . . . . . . . | 196 | 145 |
| Cylinder head bolts*: | | |
|   Stage 1 . . . . . . . . . . . . . . . . . . . . . . . . . . . . . . . . . . . . . . . . . . . . | 39 | 29 |
|   Stage 2 . . . . . . . . . . . . . . . . . . . . . . . . . . . . . . . . . . . . . . . . . . . . | Angle-tighten a further 60° | |
|   Stage 3 . . . . . . . . . . . . . . . . . . . . . . . . . . . . . . . . . . . . . . . . . . . . | Angle-tighten a further 13° | |
|   Stage 4 . . . . . . . . . . . . . . . . . . . . . . . . . . . . . . . . . . . . . . . . . . . . | Angle-tighten a further 60° | |
|   Stage 5 . . . . . . . . . . . . . . . . . . . . . . . . . . . . . . . . . . . . . . . . . . . . | Angle-tighten a further 13° | |
| Engine control unit bracket to camshaft housing: | | |
|   Bolt. . . . . . . . . . . . . . . . . . . . . . . . . . . . . . . . . . . . . . . . . . . . . . | 25 | 18 |
|   Nut . . . . . . . . . . . . . . . . . . . . . . . . . . . . . . . . . . . . . . . . . . . . . . | 10 | 7 |
| Engine mountings: | | |
|  Front torque link: | | |
|   Mounting-to-transmission bolts . . . . . . . . . . . . . . . . . . . . . . . . . | 60 | 44 |
|   Mounting to subframe . . . . . . . . . . . . . . . . . . . . . . . . . . . . . . . . | 55 | 41 |
|  Left-hand: | | |
|   Mounting to body . . . . . . . . . . . . . . . . . . . . . . . . . . . . . . . . . . . | 25 | 18 |
|   Mounting adaptor block: | | |
|    Stage 1 . . . . . . . . . . . . . . . . . . . . . . . . . . . . . . . . . . . . . . . . . | 80 | 59 |
|    Stage 2 . . . . . . . . . . . . . . . . . . . . . . . . . . . . . . . . . . . . . . . . . | Angle-tighten a further 45° | |
|    Stage 3 . . . . . . . . . . . . . . . . . . . . . . . . . . . . . . . . . . . . . . . . . | Angle-tighten a further 15° | |
|   Mounting to transmission: | | |
|    Stage 1 . . . . . . . . . . . . . . . . . . . . . . . . . . . . . . . . . . . . . . . . . | 80 | 59 |
|    Stage 2 . . . . . . . . . . . . . . . . . . . . . . . . . . . . . . . . . . . . . . . . . | Angle-tighten a further 60° | |
|    Stage 3 . . . . . . . . . . . . . . . . . . . . . . . . . . . . . . . . . . . . . . . . . | Angle-tighten a further 15° | |

## Torque wrench settings (continued)

| | Nm | lbf ft |
|---|---|---|
| **Engine mountings (continued):** | | |
| Rear torque link: | | |
|   Torque link to subframe and transmission bracket............. | 80 | 59 |
|   Torque link bracket to transmission: | | |
|     Stage 1 ............................................. | 80 | 59 |
|     Stage 2 ............................................. | Angle-tighten a further 45° | |
|     Stage 3 ............................................. | Angle-tighten a further 15° | |
| Right-hand: | | |
|   Mounting to body ..................................... | 40 | 30 |
|   Mounting to engine bracket: | | |
|     Stage 1 ............................................. | 60 | 44 |
|     Stage 2 ............................................. | Angle-tighten a further 30° | |
|     Stage 3 ............................................. | Angle-tighten a further 15° | |
|   Lower mounting bracket to engine block............... | 40 | 30 |
| Engine-to-transmission unit bolts: | | |
|   M10 bolts ............................................ | 40 | 30 |
|   M12 bolts ............................................ | 60 | 44 |
| Engine transport shackles ................................. | 20 | 15 |
| Exhaust manifold .......................................... | 24 | 18 |
| Front suspension subframe*: | | |
|   Stage 1 ............................................... | 90 | 66 |
|   Stage 2 ............................................... | Angle-tighten a further 45° | |
|   Stage 3 ............................................... | Angle-tighten a further 15° | |
| Flywheel bolts*: | | |
|   Stage 1 ............................................... | 30 | 22 |
|   Stage 2 ............................................... | Angle-tighten a further 60° | |
|   Stage 3 ............................................... | Angle-tighten a further 15° | |
| Injection pump sprocket nut ............................... | 69 | 51 |
| Injector pipe unions ...................................... | 23 | 17 |
| Inlet manifold ............................................ | 25 | 18 |
| Main bearing cap bolts.................................... | 88 | 65 |
| Oil drain plug ............................................ | 78 | 58 |
| Oil filter housing cover ................................... | 25 | 18 |
| Oil filter housing to cylinder block ....................... | 25 | 18 |
| Oil pressure relief valve bolt ............................. | 30 | 22 |
| Oil pressure switch....................................... | 21 | 15 |
| Oil pump pick-up/strainer bolts........................... | 19 | 14 |
| Oil pump sprocket to pump ............................... | 44 | 32 |
| Sump bolts: | | |
|   Sump pan-to-upper housing bolts..................... | 10 | 7 |
|   Upper housing-to-block bolts ........................ | 10 | 7 |
|   Upper housing to transmission ....................... | 40 | 30 |
| Thermostat housing cover ................................. | 24 | 18 |
| Thermostat housing to cylinder head...................... | 24 | 18 |
| Timing belt idler pulley bolt .............................. | 80 | 59 |
| Timing belt tensioner pulley to cylinder block ............. | 38 | 28 |

*Use new fasteners

## 1 General information

This Part of Chapter 2 describes those repair procedures that can reasonably be carried out on the 1.7 litre DOHC diesel engine while it remains in the car. If the engine has been removed from the car and is being dismantled as described in Part E, any preliminary dismantling procedures can be ignored.

Note that, while it may be possible physically to overhaul items such as the piston/connecting rod assemblies while the engine is in the car, such tasks are not normally carried out as separate operations.

Usually, several additional procedures (not to mention the cleaning of components and of oil ways) have to be carried out. For this reason, all such tasks are classed as major overhaul procedures, and are described in Part E of this Chapter.

Part E describes the removal of the engine/transmission unit from the vehicle, and the full overhaul procedures that can then be carried out.

### Engine description

The 1.7 litre (1686 cc) direct injection diesel engine is of sixteen-valve, in-line four-cylinder, double overhead camshaft (DOHC) type, mounted transversely at the front of the car with the transmission attached to its left-hand end.

The crankshaft runs in five main bearings.

Thrustwashers are fitted to No 2 main bearing shell (upper half) to control crankshaft endfloat.

The connecting rods rotate on horizontally-split bearing shells at their big-ends. The pistons are attached to the connecting rods by gudgeon pins, which are a sliding fit in the connecting rod small-end eyes and retained by circlips. The aluminium-alloy pistons are fitted with three piston rings – two compression rings and an oil control ring.

The cylinder block is made of cast iron and the cylinder bores are an integral part of the block. On this type of engine the cylinder bores are sometimes referred to as having dry liners.

The inlet and exhaust valves are each closed by coil springs, and operate in guides pressed into the cylinder head.

The inlet camshaft is driven by the crankshaft by a timing belt and rotates directly in the camshaft housing. The exhaust camshaft is driven by the inlet camshaft via a spur gear. The camshafts operate the valves via followers, which are situated directly below the camshafts. Valve clearances are adjusted using shims which are fitted between the camshafts and followers.

Lubrication is by means of an oil pump, which is driven by the timing belt. It draws oil through a strainer located in the sump, and then forces it through an externally-mounted filter into galleries in the cylinder block/crankcase. From there, the oil is distributed to the crankshaft (main bearings) and camshaft. The big-end bearings are supplied with oil via internal drillings in the crankshaft, while the camshaft bearings also receive a pressurised supply. The camshaft lobes and valves are lubricated by splash, as are all other engine components. An oil cooler is fitted to keep the oil temperature stable under arduous operating conditions.

### Operations with engine in place

The following work can be carried out with the engine in the car:

a) Compression pressure testing.
b) Camshaft cover – removal and refitting.
c) Timing belt cover – removal and refitting.
d) Timing belt – removal and refitting.
e) Timing belt tensioner and sprockets – removal and refitting.
f) Valve clearances – checking and adjustment.
g) Camshafts and followers – removal, inspection and refitting.
h) Cylinder head – removal and refitting.
i) Connecting rods and pistons – removal and refitting*.
j) Sump – removal and refitting.
k) Oil pump – removal, overhaul and refitting.
l) Oil cooler – removal and refitting.
m) Crankshaft oil seals – renewal.
n) Engine/transmission mountings – inspection and renewal.
o) Flywheel – removal, inspection and refitting.
p) Camshaft housing – removal and refitting.

**3.5 Align the timing mark on the crankshaft pulley with the pointer on the oil pump cover to bring No 1 piston to TDC**

* Although the operation marked with an asterisk can be carried out with the engine in the car after removal of the sump, it is better for the engine to be removed, in the interests of cleanliness and improved access. For this reason, the procedure is described in Chapter 2D.

### 2  Compression test – description and interpretation

#### Compression test

**Note:** A compression tester specifically designed for diesel engines must be used for this test.

1 When engine performance is down, or if misfiring occurs which cannot be attributed to the fuel system, a compression test can provide diagnostic clues as to the engine's condition. If the test is performed regularly, it can give warning of trouble before any other symptoms become apparent.

2 A compression tester specifically intended for diesel engines must be used, because of the higher pressures involved. The tester is connected to an adapter which screws into the glow plug or injector hole. On these models, an adapter suitable for use in the glow plug holes will be required, due to the design of the injectors. It is unlikely to be worthwhile buying such a tester for occasional use, but it may be possible to borrow or hire one – if not, have the test performed by a garage.

3 Unless specific instructions to the contrary are supplied with the tester, observe the following points:

a) The battery must be in a good state of charge, the air filter must be clean, and the engine should be at normal operating temperature.
b) All the glow plugs should be removed before starting the test (see Chapter 5C).
c) Release the retaining clip and disconnect the wiring connector from the fuel injection pump control unit (see Chapter 4C) to prevent the engine from running or fuel from being discharged.

4 There is no need to hold the accelerator pedal down during the test, because the diesel engine air inlet is not throttled.

5 Crank the engine on the starter motor; after one or two revolutions, the compression pressure should build-up to a maximum figure, and then stabilise. Record the highest reading obtained.

6 Repeat the test on the remaining cylinders, recording the pressure in each.

7 All cylinders should produce very similar pressures; any difference greater than that specified indicates the existence of a fault. Note that the compression should build-up quickly in a healthy engine; low compression on the first stroke, followed by gradually-increasing pressure on successive strokes,

indicates worn piston rings. A low compression reading on the first stroke, which does not build-up during successive strokes, indicates leaking valves or a blown head gasket (a cracked head could also be the cause). **Note:** *The cause of poor compression is less easy to establish on a diesel engine than on a petrol one. The effect of introducing oil into the cylinders ('wet' testing) is not conclusive, because there is a risk that the oil will sit in the recess on the piston crown instead of passing to the rings.*

8 On completion of the test, reconnect the injection pump wiring connector then refit the glow plugs as described in Chapter 5C.

#### Leakdown test

9 A leakdown test measures the rate at which compressed air fed into the cylinder is lost. It is an alternative to a compression test, and in many ways it is better, since the escaping air provides easy identification of where pressure loss is occurring (piston rings, valves or head gasket).

10 The equipment needed for leakdown testing is unlikely to be available to the home mechanic. If poor compression is suspected, have the test performed by a dealership.

### 3  Top dead centre (TDC) for No 1 piston – locating

**Note:** *If the engine is to be locked in position with No 1 piston at TDC on its compression stroke then a M6 and M8 bolt will be required.*

1 In its travel up and down its cylinder bore, Top Dead Centre (TDC) is the highest point that each piston reaches as the crankshaft rotates. While each piston reaches TDC both at the top of the compression stroke and again at the top of the exhaust stroke, for the purpose of timing the engine, TDC refers to the No 1 piston position at the top of its compression stroke.

2 Number 1 piston (and cylinder) is at the right-hand (timing belt) end of the engine, and its TDC position is located as follows. Note that the crankshaft rotates clockwise when viewed from the right-hand side of the car.

3 Firmly apply the handbrake, then jack up the front of the car and support it securely on axle stands (see *Jacking and vehicle support*). Remove the right-hand front roadwheel and the inner wheel arch liner for access to the crankshaft pulley. Where necessary, remove the engine compartment undertray.

4 Remove the timing belt upper cover as described in Section 6.

5 Using a socket and extension bar on the crankshaft sprocket bolt, rotate the crankshaft until the notch on the crankshaft pulley rim is aligned with the pointer on the base of the oil pump cover **(see illustration)**. Once the mark

3.7a  The camshaft sprocket can be locked using a M6 bolt . . .

3.7b  . . . and the injection pump sprocket by an M8 bolt

is correctly aligned, No 1 and 4 pistons are at TDC.

6  To determine which piston is at TDC on its compression stroke, check the position of the timing holes in the camshaft and injection pump sprockets. When No 1 piston is at TDC on its compression stroke, both sprocket holes will be aligned with the threaded holes in the cylinder head/block, and both exhaust camshaft lobes for cylinder No 1 will be pointing upwards if viewed through the oil filler hole. If the timing holes are 180° out of alignment then No 4 cylinder is at TDC on its compression stroke; rotate the crankshaft through a further complete turn (360°) to bring No 1 cylinder to TDC on its compression stroke.

7  With No 1 piston at TDC on its compression stroke, if necessary, the camshaft and fuel injection pump sprockets can be locked in position. Secure the camshaft sprocket in position by screwing a M6 bolt into the hole in the cylinder head and lock the injection pump sprocket in position by screwing a M8 bolt into the cylinder block **(see illustrations)**.

## 4  Camshaft cover – removal and refitting

### Removal

1  With reference to Chapter 4C, remove the air cleaner housing and air intake trunking complete with the hot film air mass meter.

2  On the Y17DT engine, unscrew the intercooler-to-turbocharger air inlet pipe mounting bolts, then release the crankcase ventilation hose from the camshaft cover. Move the air inlet pipe to one side.

3  Remove the engine control unit and bracket from the camshaft cover, as described in Chapter 4D, Section 8.

4  Unclip the wiring loom cable tie, undo the retaining screws/nut and remove the engine control unit bracket.

5  Undo the bolt, release the wiring loom retaining clip, and remove the engine transport shackle from the right-hand rear of the cylinder

head. Slacken the bolt securing the left-hand rear shackle.

6  Slacken the fuel injector pipe unions located at the fuel injection pump **(see illustration)**. Access to the unions on the pump is limited. We found it necessary to remove the oil cooler/filter housing retaining bolt, and prise the foam filling from between the injection pump and filter housing.

7  Undo the injector pipe unions at the injectors **(see illustration)**.

8  Remove the retaining bolts, and lift away the injector outer seals.

9  Unscrew the nuts and bolt and remove the oil dipstick tube bracket. Also, where necessary, unbolt the engine lifting eyes.

10  Note the locations of the 7 bolts and 3 studs securing the cover to the camshaft housing, then unscrew and remove them.

11  While an assistant carefully pushes the injection line to the rear, lift away the camshaft cover, complete with seal.

12  Examine the cover seal and O-rings for signs of damage or deterioration and renew if necessary **(see illustration)**.

4.6  Slacken the fuel injector pipe unions

4.7  Injector pipe unions at the injectors

4.12  Check the seal and O-ring on the underside of the cover

**4.14b Ensure the borehole is not covered in sealant**

**4.17 The injector seals are marked 'upper' and 'outside'**

**4.14a Apply sealant to areas (1) and (2)**

## Refitting

**13** Ensure the cover and camshaft housing surfaces are clean and dry then fit the seal to the cover groove.

**14** Apply sealant to the areas shown **(see illustrations)**. Ensure that the oil borehole at the right-hand end of the exhaust camshaft is not covered in sealant or by the gasket.

**15** While the assistant pushes the injection line to the rear, carefully lower the cover into position, ensuring the seal remains correctly seated. Insert the retaining bolts and studs in their correct locations, and tighten them securely.

**16** Refit the oil dipstick tube bracket and

tighten the nuts and bolt securely. Also refit the engine lifting eyes.

**17** Refit the injector outer seals and tighten the bolts. The injector outer seals are marked 'upper' and 'outer'. Fit the seals and make sure that the centre of the seal is pushed over the injector taper **(see illustration)**.

**18** Refit the injector pipe unions and tighten them to the specified torque. Where necessary, refit the foam filling and tighten the oil cooler/filter housing retaining bolt.

**19** Refit the engine transport shackles and the wiring loom retaining clip.

**20** Refit the engine control unit and bracket with reference to Chapter 4C.

**21** On the Y17DT engine, refit the turbocharger air inlet pipe and crankcase ventilation hose.

**22** Refit the air cleaner housing, trunking and hot film air mass meter with reference to Chapter 4C.

## 5 Crankshaft pulley – removal and refitting

### Removal

**1** Apply the handbrake, then jack up the front of the vehicle and support it on axle stands (see *Jacking and vehicle support*). Remove the right-hand front roadwheel and the inner wheel arch liner for access to the crankshaft pulley. Where necessary, remove the engine compartment undertray.

**2** Remove the auxiliary drivebelt as described in Chapter 1B **(see illustration)**. Prior to removal, mark the direction of rotation on the belt to ensure the belt is refitted the same way around.

**3** Slacken and remove the small retaining bolts securing the pulley to the crankshaft sprocket and remove the pulley from the engine **(see illustration)**. If necessary, prevent the crankshaft from turning by holding the sprocket retaining bolt with a socket.

### Refitting

**4** Refit the pulley to the crankshaft sprocket, aligning the pulley hole with the sprocket locating pin. Refit the pulley retaining bolts, tightening them to the specified torque.

**5** Refit the auxiliary drivebelt as described

**5.2 Removing the auxiliary drivebelt**

**5.3 Removing the crankshaft pulley**

**5.5 Refitting the auxiliary drivebelt**

**6.4 Undo the bolts and remove the right-hand engine mounting lower bracket**

**6.6 Undo the Torx bolt and release the wiring tray retaining clips (arrowed)**

in Chapter 1B using the mark made prior to removal to ensure the belt is fitted the correct way around **(see illustration)**.

**6** Refit the engine undertray, wheel arch liner and roadwheel, then lower the car to the ground and tighten the wheel bolts to the specified torque.

**6 Timing belt covers –**
removal and refitting

## *Removal*

### Upper cover

**1** Disconnect the battery negative lead (see *Disconnecting the battery* at the end of this manual).
**2** Remove the air cleaner assembly and ducting as described in Chapter 4C.

**3** Support the weight of the engine using a trolley jack with a block of wood placed on its head.
**4** Unbolt and remove the right-hand engine mounting and lower bracket with reference to Section 20 **(see illustration)**.
**5** With reference to Chapter 5A if necessary, disconnect the wiring plug and connection from the alternator.
**6** Unclip the brake servo and EGR vacuum lines then unscrew the bolt and remove the wiring harness trough from over the upper timing belt cover **(see illustration)**.
**7** Unscrew the eight upper cover retaining bolts, noting they are of different lengths **(see illustrations)**. Remove the upper cover.

### Lower cover

**8** Apply the handbrake, then jack up the front of the vehicle and support it on axle stands (see *Jacking and vehicle support*). Remove

the right-hand front roadwheel and the inner wheel arch liner for access to the crankshaft pulley. Where necessary, remove the engine compartment undertray.
**9** Remove the upper cover as described in paragraphs 1 to 7.
**10** Loosen only the bolts securing the pulley to the coolant pump **(see illustration)**.
**11** With reference to Chapter 1B, remove the auxiliary drivebelt. Prior to removal, mark the direction of rotation on the belt to ensure the belt is refitted the same way around.
**12** Remove the crankshaft pulley with reference to Section 5.
**13** Unscrew the bolts and remove the pulley from the coolant pump.
**14** Undo the three retaining bolts, and remove the lower cover from the oil pump housing **(see illustrations)**.
**15** Temporarily refit the bolt retaining the timing belt tensioner pulley bracket **(see illustration)**.

**6.7a Unscrew the eight retaining bolts . . .**

**6.7b . . . and remove the upper timing belt cover**

**6.10 Bolts securing the pulley to the water pump**

**6.14a Lower cover retaining bolts**

**6.14b Removing the lower cover**

**6.15 Temporarily refit the timing belt tensioner lower retaining bolt (arrowed)**

**6.19 Rear timing belt cover bolts**

**7.2a Camshaft sprocket locked in the TDC position with a bolt**

**7.2b Injection pump sprocket locked in the TDC position with a bolt**

### Rear cover

**16** Remove the timing belt as described in Section 7.

**17** Remove the timing belt tension and guide rollers, camshaft sprocket and injection pump sprocket with reference to Section 8.

**18** Detach the tensioner spring retainer.

**19** Undo the four retaining bolts, and remove the rear timing belt cover **(see illustration)**.

### *Refitting*

**20** Refitting is the reverse of removal, ensuring all retaining bolts are tightened securely.

---

### 7 Timing belt –
removal and refitting

**Note:** *The timing belt must be removed and refitted with the engine cold.*

### *Removal*

**1** Disconnect the battery negative lead (refer to *Disconnecting the battery* at the end of this manual).

**2** Position No 1 cylinder at TDC on its compression stroke as described in Section 3. Lock the camshaft and injection pump sprockets in position by screwing the bolts into the threaded holes in the cylinder head/block **(see illustrations)**.

**3** Remove the crankshaft pulley as described in Section 5, then unbolt and remove the water pump pulley **(see illustration)**.

**4** Unbolt and remove the timing belt upper and lower covers with reference to Section 6.

**5** Slacken the timing belt tensioner retaining bolt and, on early models, carefully unhook the tensioner spring from its locating pins. Note that on later models, the tensioner spring has been modified and is now attached to the bolt located above the tensioner – on

these models, loosen the centre bolt then use an Allen key to turn the tensioner anti-clockwise to release the tension. Hold the tensioner in this position and tighten the bolt **(see illustrations)**.

**6** Slide the timing belt off its sprockets and remove it from the engine **(see illustration)**. If the belt is to be re-used, use white paint or similar to mark the direction of rotation on the belt. **Do not** rotate the crankshaft until the timing belt has been refitted.

**7** Check the timing belt carefully for any signs of uneven wear, splitting or oil contamination, and renew it if there is the slightest doubt about its condition. If the engine is undergoing an overhaul and is approaching the specified interval for belt renewal (see Chapter 1B) renew the belt as a matter of course, regardless of its apparent condition. If signs of oil contamination are found, trace the source of the oil leak and rectify it, then wash down the engine timing belt area and all related components to remove all traces of oil.

### *Refitting*

**8** On reassembly, thoroughly clean the timing belt sprockets and ensure the camshaft and injection pump sprockets are locked correctly in position. Temporarily refit the crankshaft pulley to the sprocket and check that the pulley cut-out is still aligned with the pointer on the oil pump cover; the mark on the crankshaft sprocket should also be aligned with the mark on the oil pump cover **(see illustration)**.

**7.3 Removing the crankshaft pulley**

**7.5a Unhooking the tensioner spring on early models**

**7.5b Using an Allen key to release the tensioner on later models**

**7.6 Removing the timing belt**

**7.8 Align the notch on the crankshaft sprocket with the pointer on the oil pump cover (arrowed)**

**9** Remove the pulley and fit the timing belt over the crankshaft, oil pump, injection pump and camshaft sprockets, ensuring that the belt rear run is taut (ie, all slack is on the tensioner pulley side of the belt). Do not twist the belt sharply while refitting it. Ensure that the belt teeth are correctly seated centrally in the sprockets, and that the timing marks remain in alignment. If a used belt is being refitted, ensure that the arrow mark made on removal points in the normal direction of rotation, as before **(see illustration)**.

**10** On early models, tension the belt by refitting the tensioner pulley spring, ensuring it is correctly located on its pins. On later models, loosen the tensioner centre bolt to allow it to tension the timing belt, then tighten the bolt to hold the tensioner in this position.

**11** Check that the crankshaft sprocket timing mark is still correctly positioned then unscrew the locking bolts from the injection pump and camshaft sprockets.

**12** Slacken the tensioner pulley retaining bolt then rotate the crankshaft pulley approximately 60° backwards (anti-clockwise) to automatically adjust the timing belt tension. Hold the crankshaft pulley stationary and securely tighten the tensioner pulley retaining bolt.

**13** Rotate the crankshaft smoothly through two complete turns (720°) in the normal direction of rotation to settle the timing belt in position. Realign the crankshaft sprocket timing mark and check that the camshaft and injection pump sprocket locking bolts can be refitted.

**14** Refit the timing belt covers, crankshaft pulley and water pump pulley as described in Sections 5 and 6.

**15** Reconnect the battery negative lead (refer to *Disconnecting the battery* at the end of this manual).

| **8** | **Timing belt tensioner and sprockets –** removal and refitting |

## *Camshaft sprocket*

### Removal

**1** Remove the timing belt as described in Section 7. Prior to attempting to unscrew the sprocket retaining bolt, turn the crankshaft 60° **backwards** (anti-clockwise) to prevent any accidental piston-to-valve contact.

**2** With the locking bolt removed, hold the camshaft sprocket stationary using a tool engaged with the holes in the sprocket (see paragraph 8 of this Section).

**3** Slacken and remove the retaining bolt, then remove the sprocket from the end of the camshaft, noting which way around it is fitted **(see illustration)**. If the sprocket locating pin is a loose fit, remove it from the camshaft end and store it with the sprocket for safe-keeping.

**7.9  Timing belt routing**

### Refitting

**4** Ensure the locating pin is in position then refit the sprocket to the camshaft end, aligning its locating hole with the pin.

**5** Refit the sprocket retaining bolt, and tighten it to the specified torque while holding the sprocket stationary with the special tool. Rotate the crankshaft 60° forwards (clockwise) until the groove in the crankshaft timing belt sprocket is at 12 o'clock and aligns with the cast-in mark on the oil pump cover.

**6** Refit the timing belt as described in Section 7.

## *Injection pump sprocket*

### Removal

**7** Remove the timing belt as described in Section 7.

**8** With the sprocket locking bolt removed, hold the injection pump sprocket stationary

**8.3  Remove the camshaft sprocket**

**8.10  Using a puller to remove the injection pump sprocket**

using a tool engaged with the holes in the sprocket. The tool can be made using two lengths of steel strip (one long, the other short), and three nuts and bolts; one nut and bolt forms the pivot of a forked tool, with the remaining two nuts and bolts at the tips of the 'forks' to engage with the sprocket spokes **(see illustration)**.

**9** Slacken and remove the sprocket retaining nut.

**10** Using a suitable puller, remove the sprocket from the injection pump shaft, noting which way around it is fitted. If the Woodruff key is a loose fit in the pump shaft, remove it and store it with the sprocket for safe-keeping **(see illustration)**. **Note:** *The sprocket is a tapered-fit on the injection pump shaft.*

### Refitting

**11** Ensure the Woodruff key is correctly fitted to the pump shaft then refit the sprocket, aligning the sprocket groove with the key **(see illustration)**.

**12** Refit the retaining nut and tighten it to the specified torque whilst using the holding tool to prevent rotation.

**13** If not already done, align the sprocket timing hole with the threaded hole in the cylinder block and screw in the locking bolt.

**14** Refit the timing belt as described in Section 7.

## *Crankshaft sprocket*

### Removal

**15** Remove the timing belt as described in Section 7.

**8.8  Using a sprocket holding tool to prevent rotation as the injection pump sprocket nut is slackened**

**8.11  Align the keyway in the sprocket with the Woodruff key in the shaft**

**8.17 Slide the sprocket from the shaft**

**8.19 Fit the flanged spacer with the convex side away from the oil pump cover**

**8.21 Refit the sprocket retaining bolt and washer**

**16** Slacken the crankshaft sprocket retaining bolt. To prevent crankshaft rotation, have an assistant select 4th gear and apply the brakes firmly. If the engine is removed from the vehicle it will be necessary to lock the flywheel (see Section 18).
**17** Unscrew the retaining bolt and washer and remove the crankshaft sprocket from the end of the crankshaft. If the sprocket is a tight fit, draw it off of the crankshaft using a suitable puller **(see illustration)**. If the Woodruff key is a loose fit in the crankshaft, remove it and store it with the sprocket for safe-keeping.
**18** Slide the flanged spacer off of the crankshaft, noting which way around it is fitted.

### Refitting

**19** Refit the flanged spacer to the crankshaft with its convex surface facing away from the oil pump housing **(see illustration)**.
**20** Ensure the Woodruff key is correctly fitted

then slide on the crankshaft sprocket aligning its groove with the key.
**21** Refit the retaining bolt and washer then lock the crankshaft by the method used on removal, and tighten the sprocket retaining bolt to the specified torque setting **(see illustration)**.
**22** Refit the timing belt as described in Section 7.

## Oil pump sprocket

### Removal

**23** Remove the timing belt as described in Section 7.
**24** Prevent the oil pump sprocket from rotating using a socket and extension bar fitted to one of the oil pump cover bolts then slacken and remove the sprocket retaining nut.
**25** Remove the sprocket from the oil pump shaft, noting which way around it is fitted.

### Refitting

**26** Refit the sprocket, aligning it with the flat on the pump shaft, and fit the retaining nut. Tighten the sprocket retaining nut to the specified torque, using the socket and extension bar to prevent rotation **(see illustration)**.
**27** Refit the timing belt as described in Section 7.

## Tensioner assembly

### Removal

**28** Remove the timing belt as described in Section 7.
**29** On early models, carefully unhook the tensioner spring, unscrew the retaining bolts and remove the tensioner assembly from the engine. On later models, unscrew the tensioner centre bolt, then unhook the spring from the stud, and remove the tensioner **(see illustrations)**.

### Refitting

**30** Fit the tensioner assembly to the engine, tightening its retaining bolts by hand only. Refit the tensioner spring on early models. Make sure that the spring is located correctly on the bolt on later models.
**31** Refit the timing belt as described in Section 7.

## Idler pulley

### Removal

**32** Remove the timing belt as described in Section 7.
**33** Slacken and remove the retaining bolt and remove the idler pulley from the engine **(see illustration)**.

**8.26 Use a socket and extension bar on one of the oil pump cover bolts to prevent the sprocket from turning**

**8.29a Timing belt tensioner spring on early models**

**8.29b Unhook the spring to remove the tensioner on later models**

**8.29c The later tensioner removed from the engine**

**8.33 Timing belt idler pulley retaining bolt**

**Refitting**

**34** Refit the idler pulley and tighten the retaining bolt to the specified torque.

**35** Refit the timing belt as described in Section 7.

### 9 Camshaft oil seal – renewal

**1** Remove the camshaft sprocket as described in Section 8.

**2** Carefully punch or drill a small hole in the oil seal. Screw in a self-tapping screw, and pull on the screw with pliers to extract the seal (**see illustration**).

**3** Clean the seal housing, and polish off any burrs or raised edges which may have caused the seal to fail in the first place.

**4** Lubricate the lips of the new seal with clean engine oil, and press it into position using a suitable tubular drift (such as a socket) which bears only on the hard outer edge of the seal. Take care not to damage the seal lips during fitting; note that the seal lips should face inwards (**see illustration**).

**5** Refit the camshaft sprocket as described in Section 8.

### 10 Valve clearances – checking and adjustment

**Checking**

**1** The importance of having the valve clearances correctly adjusted cannot be overstressed, as they vitally affect the performance of the engine. The engine must be cold for the check to be accurate. The clearances are checked as follows.

**2** Apply the handbrake, then jack up the front of the vehicle and support it on axle stands (see *Jacking and vehicle support*). Remove the right-hand front roadwheel and the inner wheel arch liner for access to the crankshaft pulley. Where necessary, remove the engine compartment undertray.

**3** Remove the camshaft cover as described in Section 4, then remove the fuel injectors with reference to Chapter 4D.

**4** Using a socket and extension on the crankshaft sprocket bolt, rotate the crankshaft in the normal direction of rotation (clockwise when viewed from the right-hand end of the engine) until the notch on the crankshaft pulley is correctly aligned with the pointer on the base of the oil pump cover.

**5** Now rotate the crankshaft in the normal direction (clockwise) until the inlet camshaft lobes for No 1 cylinder (nearest the timing belt end of the engine) and the exhaust camshaft lobes for No 3 cylinder are pointing away from the followers. This indicates that these valves are completely closed, and the clearances can be checked.

**9.2 Pull the screw to extract the seal**

**6** On a piece of paper, draw the outline of the engine with the cylinders numbered from the timing belt end. Show the position of each valve, together with the specified valve clearance. Note that the clearance for both the inlet and exhaust valves is the same.

**7** With the cam lobes positioned as described in paragraph 5, using feeler blades, measure the clearance between the base of both No 1 cylinder inlet cam lobes and No 3 cylinder exhaust cam lobes and their followers. Record the clearances on the paper (**see illustration**).

**8** Rotate the crankshaft pulley through a half a turn (180°) to position No 3 cylinder inlet camshaft lobes and No 4 cylinder exhaust camshaft lobes pointing away from their followers. Measure the clearance between the base of the camshaft lobes and their followers and record the clearances on the paper.

**9** Rotate the crankshaft pulley through a half a turn (180°) to position No 2 cylinder exhaust camshaft lobes and No 4 cylinder inlet camshaft lobes pointing away from their followers. Measure the clearance between the base of the camshaft lobes and their followers and record the clearances on the paper.

**10** Rotate the crankshaft pulley through a half a turn (180°) to position No 1 cylinder exhaust camshaft lobes and No 2 cylinder inlet camshaft lobes pointing away from their followers. Measure the clearance between the base of the camshaft lobes and their followers and record the clearances on the paper.

**11** If all the clearances are correct, refit the cylinder head cover (see Section 4), and

**10.7 With the camshaft lobe pointing away from the follower measure the clearance**

**9.4 Press the oil seal into position using a tubular drift such as a socket**

injectors (see Chapter 4C), then refit the roadwheel and lower the vehicle to the ground and tighten the wheel bolts to the specified torque. If any clearance measured is not correct, adjustment must be carried out as described in the following paragraphs.

**Adjustment**

**12** Rotate the crankshaft clockwise until the inlet camshaft lobes for No 1 cylinder (nearest the timing belt end of the engine) and the exhaust camshaft lobes for No 3 cylinder are pointing away from the followers. With the crankshaft in this position, inlet valve No 1 and exhaust valve No 3 can be adjusted as follows.

**13** Rotate the follower until the groove on its upper edge is facing towards the front of the engine (exhaust followers), or rear of engine (inlet followers).

**14** In the absence of the special Vauxhall tool (KM-6090), position a large flat-bladed screwdriver between the edge of the follower and the base of the camshaft. Use the screwdriver to carefully depress the follower until there is enough clearance to allow the shim to be slid out from between the follower and camshaft (a magnetic tool is particularly useful for this task) (**see illustration**).

**15** Clean the shim, and measure its thickness with a micrometer. The shims carry thickness markings, but wear may have reduced the original thickness, so be sure to double-check (**see illustration**).

**16** Add the measured clearance of the valve to the thickness of the original shim then subtract the specified valve clearance from

**10.14 Carefully depress the follower and slide the shim out**

**10.15 The thickness of each shim should be stamped on one of its surfaces**

this figure. This will give you the thickness of the shim required. For example:

| | |
|---|---|
| Measured valve clearance | 0.45 mm |
| Plus thickness of the original shim | 2.70 mm |
| Equals | 3.15 mm |
| Minus clearance required | 0.40 mm |
| Thickness of shim required | 2.75 mm |

**17** Obtain the correct thickness of shim required and lubricate it with clean engine oil. Carefully depress the follower and slide the shim into position, with the thickness number downwards, ensuring it is correctly located. Check that the valve clearance is within limits.

> **HAYNES HINT**
> *It may be possible to correct the clearances by moving the shims around between the valves, but don't rotate the crankshaft with any shims missing. Keep a note of all the shim thicknesses to assist valve clearance adjustment when they need to be done again.*

**18** Rotate the crankshaft through half a turn (180°) to position No 3 cylinder inlet camshaft lobes and No 4 cylinder exhaust camshaft lobes pointing away from their followers. Adjust No 3 inlet and No 4 exhaust valve clearances as described in paragraphs 13 to 17.

**19** Rotate the crankshaft pulley through a half a turn (180°) to position No 2 cylinder exhaust camshaft lobes and No 4 cylinder inlet camshaft lobes pointing away from their followers. Adjust No 2 exhaust and No 4 inlet valve clearances as described in para-graphs 13 to 17.

**11.6 Insert a screw through the fixed gear and into the backlash compensating gear (arrowed)**

**20** Rotate the crankshaft pulley through a half a turn (180°) to position No 1 cylinder exhaust camshaft lobes and No 2 cylinder inlet camshaft lobes pointing away from their followers. Adjust No 1 exhaust and No 2 inlet valve clearances as described in paragraphs 13 to 17.

**21** Refit the camshaft cover (see Section 4) and the fuel injectors (Chapter 4D).

**22** Refit the engine undertray, inner wheel arch liner and roadwheel, and lower the car to the ground.

## 11 Camshafts and followers – removal, inspection and refitting

### Removal

**1** Apply the handbrake, then jack up the front of the vehicle and support it on axle stands (see *Jacking and vehicle support*). Remove the right-hand front roadwheel and the inner wheel arch liner for access to the crankshaft pulley. Where necessary, remove the engine compartment undertray.

**2** Remove the camshaft cover as described in Section 4.

**3** Drain the cooling system as described in Chapter 1B. **Note:** *This is recommended by the manufacturers as a precaution against coolant entering the combustion chambers when the injectors are removed. The injector heat sleeves may become displaced, causing coolant to leak into the cylinders.*

**4** Remove the fuel injectors with reference to Chapter 4D.

**5** Remove the timing belt and camshaft sprocket as described in Sections 7 and 8.

**6** The exhaust camshaft gear incorporates a backlash compensating gear. This must now be locked to the fixed exhaust camshaft gear by inserting a suitably-sized bolt/rod through the hole. This prevents the spring preload of the compensating gear being lost when either camshaft is removed. The Vauxhall tool (KM-955-2) is inserted from the compensating gear side, however, if preferred, a longer bolt may be inserted from the inner side of the camshaft gear after unscrewing the nuts and bolt, and removing the No 5 bearing cap from

**11.10 Lift out the cam followers and shims**

the left-hand (gearbox) end of the camshafts **(see illustration)**.

**7** Working opposite to the tightening sequence given in paragraph 19, slacken the camshaft bearing cap retaining nuts by one turn at a time, to relieve the pressure of the valve springs on the bearing caps gradually and evenly. Once the valve spring pressure has been relieved, the nuts can be fully unscrewed and removed.

*Caution: If the bearing cap nuts are carelessly slackened, the bearing caps may break. If any bearing cap breaks then the complete housing must be renewed, as the bearing caps are matched to the housing and are not available separately.*

**8** Remove the bearing caps, noting each caps correct fitted location. The bearing caps are numbered 1 to 5 and the arrow on each cap points towards the timing belt end of the engine.

**9** Lift the camshafts out of the cylinder head, and recover the oil seal from the inlet camshaft.

**10** Obtain sixteen small, clean plastic containers, and label them for identification. Alternatively, divide a larger container into compartments. Lift the followers and shims out from the top of the cylinder head and store each one in its respective fitted position. Make sure the followers and shims are not mixed up, to ensure the valve clearances remain correct on refitting **(see illustration)**.

### Inspection

**11** Examine the camshaft bearing surfaces and camshaft lobes for signs of wear ridges and scoring. Renew the camshaft if any of these conditions are apparent. Examine the condition of the bearing surfaces both on the camshaft journals and in the camshaft housing. If the housing bearing surfaces are worn excessively, the housing will need to be renewed.

**12** Support the camshaft end journals on V-blocks, and measure the run-out at the centre journal using a dial gauge. If the run-out exceeds the specified limit, the camshaft should be renewed.

**13** Examine the followers and their bores in the cylinder head for signs of wear or damage. If any follower is visibly worn it should be renewed.

### Refitting

**14** Where removed, lubricate the followers with clean engine oil and carefully insert each one into its original location in the cylinder head. Ensure each shim is correctly located in the top of its relevant follower **(see illustration)**.

**15** Rotate the crankshaft approximately 60° backwards (anti-clockwise) as a precaution against accidental piston-to-valve contact. Lubricate the camshaft followers with clean engine oil then lay the camshafts in position. Check that the exhaust camshaft backlash compensating gear is still locked to the fixed

**11.14 Ensure each shim is correctly located**

**11.15 Align the camshaft gear marks (arrowed)**

**11.17 Apply a smear of sealant to the No 1 camshaft-bearing cap**

gear. Ensure that the mark on the outer face exhaust camshaft gear lies between the two marks on the outer face of the inlet camshaft gear, and that the marks are approximately level with the upper edge of the camshaft housing **(see illustration)**. **Note:** *If the exhaust camshaft is being renewed, it will be necessary to obtain Vauxhall tool No KM 6092, and pretension the backlash compensating gear prior to installation.*

**16** Ensure the mating surfaces of the bearing caps and camshaft housing are clean and dry and lubricate the camshaft journals and lobes with clean engine oil.

**17** Apply a smear of suitable sealant (available from Vauxhall dealers) to the areas of the camshaft housing No 1 bearing cap mating surface **(see illustration)**.

**18** Refit the camshaft bearing caps in their original locations on the cylinder head and tighten the nuts by hand only at this stage. The caps are numbered 1 to 5 (No 1 cap being at the timing belt end of the engine) and the arrow cast onto the top of each cap should point towards the timing belt end of the engine **(see illustration)**. Remove the locking bolt/rod from No 5 bearing cap (if the bolt/rod was fitted from the inside, refit bearing caps 1 to 4

first, then remove the bolt/rod before refitting bearing cap 5.

**19** Working in the specified sequence, tighten the nuts by one turn at a time to gradually impose the pressure of the valve springs evenly on the bearing caps **(see illustration)**. Repeat this sequence until all bearing caps are in contact with the cylinder head then go around in the specified sequence and tighten them to the specified torque.

*Caution: If the bearing cap nuts are carelessly tightened, the bearing caps may break. If any bearing cap breaks then the complete housing must be renewed, as the bearing caps are matched to the housing and are not available separately.*

**20** Fit a new inlet camshaft oil seal as described in Section 9.

**21** Refit the camshaft sprocket and timing belt as described in Sections 7 and 8.

**22** Check the valve clearances as described in Section 10.

**23** Refit the fuel injectors as described in Chapter 4D, and the camshaft cover as described in Section 4.

**24** Refill the cooling system with reference to Chapter 1B.

**11.18 The arrows on the camshaft bearing caps should point towards the timing belt end of the engine**

## 12 Camshaft housing – removal, inspection and refitting

### Removal

**1** Remove the camshafts and followers as described in Section 11.

**2** Remove the two bolts securing the rear timing belt cover to the camshaft housing **(see illustration)**.

**11.19 Camshaft bearing cap tightening sequence**

**12.2 Remove the two bolts securing the rear timing belt cover to the camshaft housing**

12.3a Undo the charge air pipe bolts (arrowed)

12.3b Recover the EGR pipe gasket

**3** Where applicable, remove the bolts securing the charge air pipe and bracket to the left-hand end of the camshaft housing and inlet manifold. Undo the retaining clips and release the pipe from the inlet trunking. Undo the bolts securing the EGR (exhaust gas recirculation) pipe to the exhaust manifold and the left-hand end of the camshaft housing. Undo the large union at the EGR valve, and remove the pipe **(see illustrations)**. It should now be possible to remove the left-hand rear transport eye from the camshaft housing.
**4** Detach the hose from the leak-back

pipe, and disconnect the heater plug wiring connectors **(see illustration)**.
**5** On models with air conditioning, release the refrigerant hoses from the retaining clip on the right-hand side inner wing. Without undoing the refrigerant pipes, disconnect the wiring plug, unbolt the air conditioning compressor from its support bracket (3 bolts), and position it clear of the engine. Use a cable tie or similar to tie the compressor to the bonnet slam panel out of the way. Undo the three bolts and remove the air conditioning support bracket **(see illustrations)**.

**6** Slacken the camshaft housing-to-head retaining bolts 1/2 turn at a time, in the **reverse** sequence to that given in paragraph 12.
**7** Undo the bolts completely and remove the camshaft housing. Remove and discard the gasket **(see illustration)**.
**8** Unscrew the oil leak line banjo bolt and mounting bolt, and remove the line. Recover the sealing rings.

### Inspection

**9** Using a straight-edge, check the surface of the camshaft housing for distortion. It should be no more than that given for the cylinder head in Chapter 2E.

### Refitting

**10** Refit the oil leak line and tighten the banjo bolt and mounting bolt securely.
**11** Ensure all mating surfaces are clean and free from any gasket or sealant residue.
**12** With a new gasket in place, position the camshaft housing onto the cylinder head, and progressively tighten the housing bolts to the specified torque, in the sequence shown **(see illustration)**.
**13** Where applicable, refit the air conditioning compressor and bracket, reconnect the wiring plug, and support the refrigerant hoses in the clips.

12.3c Undo the large EGR union nut

12.4 Disconnect the fuel leak-back pipe

12.5a Tie the compressor to the slam panel . . .

12.5b . . . and remove the compressor mounting bracket

12.7 Remove the gasket

**14** Reconnect the heater plug wiring connectors and the leak-back pipe hose.
**15** Refit the transport eye, EGR valve and charge air pipe.
**16** Refit and tighten the two bolts securing the rear timing belt cover.
**17** Refit the camshafts and followers, and check the valve clearances, with reference to Sections 10 and 11.

## 13 Cylinder head – removal and refitting

**Caution: Be careful not to allow dirt into the fuel injection pump or injector pipes during this procedure.**
**Note:** *New cylinder head bolts will be required on refitting.*

### Removal

**1** Disconnect the battery negative lead (refer to *Disconnecting the battery* at the end of this manual).
**2** Drain the cooling system as described in Chapter 1B.
**3** Remove the camshaft housing and followers as described in Section 12 **(see illustration)**.
**4** On models with air conditioning, release the refrigerant hoses from the retaining clip on the right-hand side inner wing. Without undoing the refrigerant pipes, disconnect the wiring plug, unbolt the air conditioning compressor from its support bracket (3 bolts), and position it clear of the engine. Use a cable tie or similar to tie the compressor to the bonnet slam panel out of the way. Undo the three bolts and remove the air conditioning support bracket.
**5** Refer to Chapter 4D and unbolt the exhaust front pipe from the exhaust manifold/turbocharger, taking care to support the flexible section. **Note:** *Angular movement in excess of 10° can cause permanent damage to the flexible section.* Release the mounting rubbers and support the front of the exhaust pipe to one side.
**6** Unbolt and remove the oil dipstick tube and bracket. Also, release the vacuum hoses from the clips.
**7** Release the clips and disconnect the

**12.12 Camshaft housing bolts tightening sequence**

turbocharger oil return hose from the turbocharger and drain tube.
**8** Unscrew the nut while counterholding the threaded adapter, and remove the turbocharger oil feed line from the block.
**9** Unscrew the turbocharger bracket mounting bolt.
**10** Disconnect the vacuum hose from the turbocharger waste gate unit.
**11** Release the clamp then disconnect the air intake pipe from the turbocharger.
**12** Unbolt and remove the exhaust manifold heat shield.
**13** Unscrew the bolts securing the EGR (exhaust gas recirculation) pipe to the exhaust manifold and remove the gasket.
**14** Unscrew the bolt and remove the oil feed line banjo from the turbocharger. Recover the sealing rings.

**15** Unscrew the nuts and bolts securing the exhaust manifold to the cylinder head, and recover the washers. Withdraw the manifold and recover the gasket.
**16** Unscrew the nut and detach the brake servo vacuum line from the vacuum pump.
**17** Slacken and remove the bolts securing the timing belt rear cover to the end of the cylinder head/camshaft housing.
**18** Disconnect the wiring from the EGR solenoid valve and charge pressure sensor **(see illustrations)**.
**19** Unscrew the nut and remove the starter/alternator wiring harness bracket from the EGR valve.
**20** Disconnect the vacuum hose, unscrew the studs and bolts, and remove the EGR valve and gasket **(see illustration)**.
**21** Place a container beneath the oil filter,

**13.3 Store the followers the correct way up**

**13.18a Detach the EGR solenoid valve vacuum hose and wiring plug**

**13.18b Unplug the charge pressure sensor**

**13.20  Remove the EGR valve**

**13.23  Disconnect the coolant pipe from the cylinder head**

**13.25a  Coolant temperature sensor**

then unscrew the filter cover and detach the return hose from the housing.

**22** Remove the heater glow plugs with reference to Chapter 5C.

**23** Loosen the clips and disconnect the coolant hoses from the thermostat housing. Also disconnect the hose from the left-hand rear of the cylinder head **(see illustration)**.

**24** Unscrew the bolt and remove the wastegate unit vacuum hose bracket.

**25** Disconnect the wiring from the coolant temperature sensor, unscrew the retaining bolts and pull the thermostat housing and wastegate vacuum pipe bracket away from the left-hand end of the cylinder head **(see illustrations)**.

**26** Working in the **reverse** of the tightening sequence given in paragraph 43, progressively slacken the cylinder head bolts by half a turn at a time, until all bolts can be

unscrewed by hand. Remove the cylinder head bolts and recover the washers.

**27** Lift the cylinder head away; seek assistance if possible, as it is a heavy assembly **(see illustration)**. Remove the gasket, noting the two locating dowels fitted to the top of the cylinder block. If they are a loose fit, remove the locating dowels and store them with the head for safe-keeping. Keep the head gasket for identification purposes (see paragraph 34).

**28** If the cylinder head is to be dismantled for overhaul, then refer to Part E of this Chapter.

### Preparation for refitting

**29** The mating faces of the cylinder head and cylinder block/crankcase must be perfectly clean before refitting the head. Use a hard plastic or wood scraper to remove all traces of gasket and carbon; also clean the piston

crowns. Take particular care, as the surfaces are damaged easily. Also, make sure that the carbon is not allowed to enter the oil and water passages – this is particularly important for the lubrication system, as carbon could block the oil supply to any of the engine's components. Using adhesive tape and paper, seal the water, oil and bolt holes in the cylinder block/crankcase. To prevent carbon entering the gap between the pistons and bores, smear a little grease in the gap. After cleaning each piston, use a small brush to remove all traces of grease and carbon from the gap, then wipe away the remainder with a clean rag. Clean all the pistons in the same way.

**30** Check the mating surfaces of the cylinder block/crankcase and the cylinder head for nicks, deep scratches and other damage. If slight, they may be removed carefully with a file, but if excessive, machining may be the only alternative to renewal.

**31** Ensure that the cylinder head bolt holes in the crankcase are clean and free of oil. Syringe or soak up any oil left in the bolt holes. This is most important in order that the correct bolt tightening torque can be applied and to prevent the possibility of the block being cracked by hydraulic pressure when the bolts are tightened.

**32** The cylinder head bolts must be discarded and renewed, regardless of their apparent condition.

**33** If warpage of the cylinder head gasket surface is suspected, use a straight-edge to check it for distortion. Refer to Part E of this Chapter if necessary.

**34** On this engine, the cylinder head-to-piston clearance is controlled by fitting different thickness head gaskets. The gasket thickness can be determined by looking at the left-hand front corner of the gasket and checking on the number of holes **(see illustration)**.

| Holes in gasket | Gasket thickness |
| --- | --- |
| No holes | 1.45 mm |
| One hole | 1.50 mm |
| Two hole | 1.55 mm |

**The correct thickness of gasket required is selected by measuring the piston protrusions as follows.**

**35** Ensure that the crankshaft is still correctly

**13.25b  Remove the thermostat housing . . .**

**13.25c  . . . and wastegate vacuum pipe bracket**

**13.27  Lift the cylinder head away**

**13.34  Cylinder head gasket identification hole (arrowed)**

positioned in the TDC position. Mount a dial test indicator securely on the block so that its pointer can be easily pivoted between the piston crown and block mating surface. Zero the dial test indicator on the gasket surface of the cylinder block then carefully move the indicator over No 1 piston and measure the its protrusion at its highest point between the valve cut-outs, and then again at its highest point between the valve cut-outs at 90° to the first measurement **(see illustration)**. Repeat this procedure with No 4 piston.

**36** Rotate the crankshaft half a turn (180°) to bring No 2 and 3 pistons to TDC. Ensure the crankshaft is accurately positioned then measure the protrusions of No 2 and 3 pistons at the specified points. Once both pistons have been measured, rotate the crankshaft through a further one and a half turns (540°) to bring No 1 and 4 pistons back to TDC.

**37** Select the correct thickness of head gasket required by determining the largest amount of piston protrusion, and using the following table.

| Piston protrusion measurement | Gasket thickness required |
|---|---|
| 0.630 to 0.696 mm | 1.45 mm (no holes) |
| 0.697 to 0.763 mm | 1.50 mm (one hole) |
| 0.764 to 0.830 mm | 1.55 mm (two holes) |

### Refitting

**38** Wipe clean the mating surfaces of the cylinder head and cylinder block/crankcase.

**39** Check that the two locating dowels are in position then fit a new gasket to the cylinder block **(see illustration)**.

**40** If not already positioned at TDC, rotate the crankshaft so that No 1 piston is at its highest point in the cylinder. Now turn the crankshaft 60° backwards (anti-clockwise). This is to ensure that whilst the cylinder head and camshafts are being refitted, there is little chance of accidental piston-to-valve contact.

**41** With the aid of an assistant, carefully refit the cylinder head assembly to the block, aligning it with the locating dowels.

**42** Carefully enter each new cylinder head bolt into its relevant hole (do not drop them in). Screw all bolts in, by hand only, until finger-tight.

**43** Working progressively in a spiral sequence from the centre outwards, tighten the cylinder head bolts to their Stage 1 torque setting, using a torque wrench and suitable socket **(see illustration)**.

**44** Once all bolts have been tightened to the Stage 1 torque, working again in the same sequence, go around and tighten all bolts through the specified Stage 2, 3, 4 and 5 angles. It is recommended that an angle-measuring gauge is used to ensure accuracy **(see illustration)**. If a gauge is not available, use white paint to make alignment marks prior to tightening; the marks can then be used to check that the bolt has been rotated through the correct angle.

**45** The remaining procedure is a reversal

**13.35 Measure the piston projection at the highest points between the valve cut-outs**

J44608

**13.43 Tighten the bolts to the Stage 1 setting . . .**

of removal, but check the valve clearances as described in Section 10, and top up the coolant as described in Chapter 1B.

### 14 Sump – removal and refitting

#### Removal

**1** Disconnect the battery negative lead (refer to *Disconnecting the battery* at the end of this manual).

**2** Apply the handbrake, then jack up the front of the vehicle and support it on axle stands (see *Jacking and vehicle support*). Remove the right-hand front roadwheel and the inner wheel arch liner for access to the right-hand side of the engine. Where necessary, undo the retaining screws and remove the engine undertray.

**3** Drain the engine oil as described in Chapter 1B, then fit a new sealing washer and refit the drain plug, tightening it to the specified torque. It is also recommended that the oil filter is renewed at the same time.

**4** Remove the front section of the exhaust system with reference to Chapter 4D.

**5** Slacken and remove the bolts securing the sump lower pan to the upper housing then remove the sump pan from underneath the vehicle **(see illustration)**.

**6** Unscrew the bolts and remove the oil dipstick guide tube from the sump upper housing.

**7** Progressively slacken and remove the nuts

**13.39 Check the locating dowels are in place**

**13.44 . . . then to the Stage 2 setting**

and bolts securing the upper housing to the base of the cylinder block/oil pump cover and transmission. Break the joint by striking the housing with the palm of the hand, or using a wide plastic spatula carefully inserted in the joint between the housing and cylinder block. Lower the housing away from the engine and withdraw it from underneath the vehicle.

**8** While the sump is removed, take the opportunity to check the oil pump pick-up/strainer for signs of clogging or splitting. If necessary, unbolt the pick-up/strainer and remove it from the engine along with its sealing ring **(see illustration)**. The strainer can then be cleaned easily in solvent or renewed.

#### Refitting

**9** Remove all traces of dirt, oil and sealant from the mating surfaces of the sump upper housing and pan, the cylinder block and (where removed) the pick-up/strainer.

**14.5 If the lower pan is stuck to the main casting, carefully ease it away using a wide-bladed scraper**

**14.8  Remove the oil pick-up pipe and strainer**

**14.10  Fit a new oil pick-up pipe sealing ring**

**14.12  Position a new oil dipstick guide tube sealing ring**

**14.13  Refit the sump upper housing**

**14.16  Apply a bead of sealant and refit the pan to the sump upper housing**

**10** Where necessary, fit a new sealing ring to the oil pump pick-up/strainer and fit the strainer to the base of the cylinder block **(see illustration)**. Refit the strainer retaining bolt and tighten it to the specified torque.

**11** Ensure the upper housing and cylinder block mating surfaces are clean and dry, and apply a coat of suitable sealant (available from Vauxhall dealers) to the upper mating surface of the housing.

**12** Position a new dipstick guide tube rubber seal on the main casting **(see illustration)**.

**13** Offer up the upper housing and loosely refit all the retaining nuts and bolts **(see illustration)**. Note that the four long bolts correspond with the bolts holes at the rear of the housing. If the sump is being fitted with the engine removed from the vehicle and separated from the transmission, ensure that the rear face of the housing is flush with the transmission mounting face of the cylinder

block. Working out from the centre in a diagonal sequence, progressively tighten the upper housing retaining bolts to the specified torque setting.

**14** Refit the bolts securing the upper housing to the transmission housing and tighten them to the specified torque.

**15** Ensure that the oil dipstick guide tube is correctly positioned, refit the retaining bolts, and tighten securely.

**16** Ensure the upper housing and sump pan mating surfaces are clean and dry and apply a coat of suitable sealant (available from Vauxhall dealers) to the upper mating surface of the pan. Refit the pan to the base of the upper housing and tighten its retaining bolts to the specified torque **(see illustration)**.

**17** Refit the front section of the exhaust system with reference to Chapter 4D.

**18** Where removed, refit the engine undertray, lower the vehicle to the ground then fill

the engine with fresh oil, with reference to Chapter 1B.

**19** Reconnect the battery negative lead (refer to *Disconnecting the battery* at the end of this manual).

**15  Oil pump –**
removal, inspection and refitting

**Note:** *The oil pressure relief valve is screwed into the cylinder block and cannot be removed without disturbing the fuel injection pump (see paragraph 7).*

### Removal

**1** Remove the timing belt as described in Section 7.

**2** Remove the oil pump and crankshaft timing belt sprockets as described in Section 8.

**3** Remove the sump upper as housing described in Section 14.

**4** Slacken and remove the retaining bolts then slide the oil pump cover off of the end of the crankshaft, taking great care not to lose the locating dowels. Remove the sealing ring, which is fitted around the oil pump housing section of the cover, and discard it.

**5** Using a suitable marker pen, mark the surface of the pump outer rotor; the mark can then be used to ensure the rotor is refitted the correct way around.

**6** Remove the oil pump inner and outer rotors from the cylinder block **(see illustrations)**.

**7** If necessary, remove the fuel injection pump as described in Chapter 4C, and unscrew the oil pressure relief valve assembly from the rear of the cylinder block, where it is located on the right-hand side of the injection pump lower mounting bracket. Remove the sealing ring.

### Inspection

**8** Clean the components, and carefully examine the rotors, pump housing and cover for any signs of scoring or wear. Renew any component which shows signs of wear or damage. If the pump housing in the cylinder block is marked then seek the advice of a Vauxhall dealer on the best course of action.

**15.6a  Remove the oil pump inner rotor . . .**

**15.6b  . . . and outer rotor**

**15.9 Measure the inner rotor tip-to-outer rotor clearance**

**15.13 The seal fits flush with the housing**

**15.15 Fit a new seal to the oil pump cover**

**9** If the components appear serviceable, fit the rotors into the housing and measure the clearance between the outer rotor and pump housing, and the inner rotor tip-to-outer rotor clearance using feeler blades **(see illustration)**. Also measure the rotor endfloat, and check the flatness of the end cover. If the clearances exceed the specified tolerances, renew the worn components.

**10** If the relief valve has been removed, check that the valve piston is free to move easily and return smoothly under spring pressure. If not renew the valve assembly.

### Refitting

**11** Where removed, fit a new sealing ring to the oil pressure relief valve then refit the valve assembly to the cylinder block and tighten it to the specified torque setting. Refit the fuel injection pump with reference to Chapter 4D.

**12** Lubricate the pump rotors with clean engine oil and refit them to the pump housing, using the mark made prior to removal to ensure the outer rotor is fitted the correct way around.

**13** Prior to refitting, carefully lever out the crankshaft and oil pump oil seals using a flat-bladed screwdriver. Fit the new oil seals, ensuring that each seals sealing lip is facing inwards, and press them squarely into the housing using a tubular drift which bears only on the hard outer edge of the seal. Press each seal into position so that it is flush with the housing then lubricate the oil seal lips with clean engine oil **(see illustration)**.

**14** Ensure the mating surfaces of the oil pump and cylinder block are clean and dry and the locating dowels are in position. Remove all traces of sealant from the threads of the pump cover bolts.

**15** Fit a new seal into the groove around the oil pump housing section of the cover, and apply a bead of suitable sealant (available from Vauxhall dealers) to the pump cover mating surface **(see illustration)**.

**16** Carefully manoeuvre the oil pump cover into position, taking great care not to damage the oil seal lips on the crankshaft and inner rotor shaft. Locate the cover on the dowels making sure the pump sealing ring remains correctly positioned.

**17** Apply a smear of sealant to the threads of each cover retaining bolt then refit all bolts and tighten them securely. Note that the longer bolt corresponds to the lower left-hand bolt hole in the cover.

**18** Refit the timing belt sprockets and belt as described in Sections 7 and 8 then refit the sump as described in Section 14.

**19** On completion refill the engine with clean oil as described in Chapter 1B.

### 16 Oil pump seal – renewal

**1** Remove the oil pump sprocket as described in Section 8.

**2** Carefully punch or drill a small hole in the oil seal. Screw a self-tapping screw into the seal, and pull on the screw with pliers to extract the seal **(see illustration)**.

*Caution: Great care must be taken to avoid damage to the oil pump.*

**3** Clean the seal housing, and polish off any burrs or raised edges which may have caused the seal to fail in the first place.

**4** Lubricate the lips of the new seal with clean engine oil, and press it into position using a suitable tubular drift (such as a socket) which bears only on the hard outer edge of the seal. Take care not to damage the seal lips during fitting; note that the seal lips should face inwards.

**5** Refit the oil pump sprocket as described in Section 8.

**16.2 Pull the screw to extract the seal**

### 17 Oil cooler – removal and refitting

### Removal

**1** Apply the handbrake, then jack up the front of the vehicle and support it on axle stands (see *Jacking and vehicle support*). Where necessary, undo the retaining screws and remove the undertray to gain access to the oil cooler which is situated on the rear left-hand of the cylinder block.

**2** Disconnect the battery negative lead (refer to *Disconnecting the battery* at the end of this manual).

**3** Drain the cooling system as described in Chapter 1B. Alternatively, clamp the oil cooler coolant hoses directly above the cooler **(see illustration)**, and be prepared for some coolant loss as the hoses are disconnected. To improve access to the coolant hoses, remove the charge air pipe/hose.

**4** With reference to Chapter 4D, remove the air cleaner housing and air intake trunking complete with the hot film air mass meter.

**5** Disconnect the wiring from the engine control unit located over the inlet manifold, and release it from the support clip.

**6** On the Y17DT engine, unscrew the intercooler-to-turbocharger air inlet pipe mounting bolts, then release the crankcase ventilation hose from the camshaft cover. Move the air inlet pipe to one side.

**17.3 Coolant hoses on the oil cooler**

**17.15  Fit a new sealing ring to the recess in the housing**

**7** Disconnect the engine management wiring and unbolt the support bracket.

**8** Unscrew the nuts and remove the starter/alternator wiring harness bracket from the exhaust gas recirculation valve.

**9** Remove the turbocharger centre air supply pipe, and recover the gasket.

**10** Position a suitable container beneath the oil filter, then unscrew the filter cover. Undo the oil cooler return hose union, release the retaining clip and disconnect the return hose.

**11** Release the clips and disconnect the coolant hoses from the oil cooler, and release the wiring loom retaining clip.

**12** Remove the single bolt securing the oil filter housing to the cylinder block. Discard the sealing rings and obtain new ones.

**13** Unscrew the mounting bolts and remove the oil cooler from the oil filter housing. Discard the sealing rings and obtain new ones.

### Refitting

**14** Refit the oil cooler to the oil filter housing, together with new sealing rings, and tighten the bolts securely.

**15** Fit a new sealing ring to the recess in the rear of the oil filter housing, then locate the housing on the cylinder block. Insert the bolt and sealing washer, and tighten to the specified torque **(see illustration)**.

**16** Reconnect the coolant hoses and tighten the clips. Clip the wiring in place.

**17** Refit the oil filter return hose, and tighten the clips, then screw on the filter cover and tighten to the specified torque.

**18** Refit the turbocharger centre air supply pipe, together with a new gasket.

**18.2  Fabricate a locking tool to retain the flywheel**

**19** Remove the starter/alternator wiring harness bracket and tighten the nuts.

**20** Refit the engine management wiring bracket and reconnect the wiring.

**21** On the Y17DT engine, refit the air inlet pipe and tighten the bolts.

**22** Reconnect the wiring to the engine control unit, and attach it to the support clip.

**23** Refit the air cleaner housing and air intake trunking, complete with the hot film air mass meter, with reference to Chapter 4D.

**24** Reconnect the battery negative lead (refer to *Disconnecting the battery* at the end of this manual).

**25** Lower the vehicle to the ground. Top-up the engine oil level as described in *Weekly checks*.

**26** Refill or top-up the cooling system as described in *Weekly checks* or Chapter 1B (as applicable). Start the engine, and check the oil cooler for signs of leakage.

**18  Flywheel –**
removal, inspection
and refitting

**Note:** *New flywheel retaining bolts will be required on refitting.*

### Removal

**1** Remove the transmission as described in Chapter 7A then remove the clutch assembly as described in Chapter 6.

**2** Prevent the flywheel from turning by locking the ring gear teeth **(see illustration)**. Alternatively, bolt a strap between the flywheel and the cylinder block/crankcase. As an aid to refitting, make alignment marks between the flywheel and crankshaft using paint or a suitable marker pen. Note, however, that the flywheel will only fit in one position, as the bolts are slightly offset.

**3** Slacken and remove the retaining bolts and plate, then remove the flywheel **(see illustration)**. Do not drop it, as it is very heavy.

### Inspection

**4** Examine the flywheel for wear or chipping of the ring gear teeth. Renewal of the ring gear is possible but is not a task for the home

**18.3  Remove the flywheel bolts and recover the plate**

mechanic; renewal requires the new ring gear to be heated (up to 180° to 230°C) to allow it to be fitted.

**5** Examine the flywheel for scoring of the clutch face. If the clutch face is scored, the flywheel may be surface-ground, but renewal is preferable.

**6** If there is any doubt about the condition of the flywheel, seek the advice of a Vauxhall dealer or engine reconditioning specialist. They will be able to advise if it is possible to recondition it or whether renewal is necessary.

### Refitting

**7** Clean the mating surfaces of the flywheel and crankshaft.

**8** Apply a drop of locking compound to the threads of each of the new flywheel retaining bolts then refit the flywheel and retaining plate and install the new bolts. If the original is being refitted align the marks made prior to removal.

**9** Lock the flywheel using the method employed on dismantling then, working in a diagonal sequence, evenly and progressively tighten the retaining bolts to the specified Stage 1 torque setting.

**10** Once all bolts have been tightened to the Stage 1 torque, go around and tighten all bolts through the specified Stage 2 and Stage 3 angles. It is recommended that an angle-measuring gauge is used to ensure accuracy. If a gauge is not available, use white paint to make alignment marks prior to tightening. The marks can then be used to check that the bolt has been rotated through the correct angle.

**11** Refit the clutch as described in Chapter 6 then remove the locking tool and refit the transmission as described in Chapter 7A.

**19  Crankshaft oil seals –**
renewal

### Timing belt end oil seal

**1** Remove the crankshaft sprocket as described in Section 8.

**2** Carefully punch or drill two small holes opposite each other in the oil seal. Screw a self-tapping screw into each and pull on the screws with pliers to extract the seal.

**3** Clean the seal housing and polish off any burrs or raised edges which may have caused the seal to fail in the first place.

**4** Lubricate the lips of the new seal with clean engine oil and ease it into position on the end of the shaft. Press the seal squarely into position until it is flush with the housing. If necessary, a suitable tubular drift which bears only on the hard outer edge of the seal can be used to tap the seal into position. Take great care not to damage the seal lips during fitting and ensure that the seal lips face inwards.

**5** Wash off any traces of oil, then refit the crankshaft sprocket as described in Section 8.

## Flywheel end oil seal

**6** Remove the flywheel as described in Section 18.

**7** Renew the seal as described in paragraphs 2 to 4 **(see illustration)**.

**8** Refit the flywheel as described in Section 18.

---

**20 Engine/transmission mountings –** inspection and renewal

### Inspection

**1** To improve access, firmly apply the handbrake, then jack up the front of the vehicle and support it on axle stands (see *Jacking and vehicle support*).

**2** Check the mounting blocks (rubbers) to see if they are cracked, hardened or separated from the metal at any point. Renew the mounting block if any such damage or deterioration is evident.

**3** Check that all the mounting securing nuts and bolts are securely tightened, using a torque wrench to check if possible.

**4** Using a large screwdriver, or a similar tool, check for wear in the mounting blocks by carefully levering against them to check for free play. Where this is not possible, enlist the aid of an assistant to move the engine/gearbox unit back-and-forth, and from side-to-side, while you observe the mountings. While some free play is to be expected, even from new components, excessive wear should be obvious. If excessive free play is found, check first to see that the securing nuts and bolts are correctly tightened, then renew any worn components as described in the following paragraphs.

### Renewal

**Note:** *Before slackening any of the engine mounting bolts/nuts, the relative positions of the mountings to their various brackets should be marked to ensure correct alignment upon refitting.*

### Right-hand mounting

**5** Apply the handbrake, then jack up the front of the vehicle and support it on axle stands (see *Jacking and vehicle support*). Remove

**19.7 The seal fits flush with the housing**

the right-hand roadwheel and the wheel arch liner for access to the crankshaft pulley.

**6** Remove the air cleaner as described in Chapter 4D.

**7** Attach a suitable hoist and lifting tackle to the engine lifting brackets on the cylinder head, and support the weight of the engine.

**8** Mark the position of the mounting brackets and bolts, then unscrew the bolts and remove the right-hand mounting from the engine mounting bracket and body. If necessary, the lower mounting bracket may also be unbolted from the cylinder block **(see illustrations)**. **Note:** *Take great care not to place any excess stress on the exhaust system when raising or lowering the engine. If necessary, disconnect the front pipe from the manifold (see Chapter 4D).*

**9** If removed, refit the lower mounting bracket and tighten the bolts to the specified torque, then locate the new mounting block on the

body and engine mounting bracket, and tighten the bolts to the specified torque.

**10** Remove the hoist, then refit the air cleaner.

**11** Refit the wheel arch liner and right-hand roadwheel, then lower the vehicle to the ground.

### Front mounting/torque link

**12** Apply the handbrake, then jack up the front of the vehicle and support it on axle stands (see *Jacking and vehicle support*). Remove the right-hand roadwheel and the wheel arch liner for access to the crankshaft pulley.

**13** Attach a suitable hoist and lifting tackle to the engine lifting brackets on the cylinder head, and support the weight of the engine.

**14** Slacken and remove the nut and washer securing the mounting to the subframe bracket. Withdraw the bolt **(see illustration)**

**15** Undo the bolts securing the mounting bracket to the transmission, then manoeuvre the mounting and bracket out of position. **Note:** *Take great care not to place any excess stress on the exhaust system when raising or lowering the engine. If necessary, disconnect the front pipe from the manifold (see Chapter 4D).*

**16** Check all components for signs of wear or damage, and renew as necessary.

**17** On reassembly, refit the mounting bracket (aligning the previously made marks) and tighten its bolts to the specified torque.

**18** Locate the mounting in the subframe, ensuring it is fitted the correct way up, and manoeuvre the engine/transmission into position. Refit the mounting bolts and new nuts. Tighten them to the specified torque.

**20.8a Right-hand engine mounting**

**20.8b Mark the position of the bolts before unscrewing them**

**20.8c Bolts securing the lower mounting bracket to the cylinder block**

**20.8d Removing the lower mounting bracket**

**20.14 Front engine-to-subframe torque link**

**20.35 Rear engine-to-subframe torque link**

**19** Lower the vehicle to the ground.

### Left-hand mounting

**20** Release the clips and position the coolant expansion tank to one side.

**21** Attach a suitable hoist and lifting tackle to the engine lifting brackets on the cylinder head, and support the weight of the engine.

**22** Using a Torx socket, unscrew the two bolts securing the engine mounting bracket to the body mounting bracket.

**23** Unbolt the mounting brackets from the engine and body. Slightly lower the engine, then unclip the clutch hydraulic line from the mounting bracket. **Note:** *Take great care not to place any excess stress on the exhaust system when raising or lowering the engine. If necessary, disconnect the front pipe from the manifold (see Chapter 4D).*

**24** Unscrew the bolt and separate the adaptor block.

**25** Fit the new adaptor block and tighten the bolt to the specified torque.

**26** Locate the new mounting brackets in position and, where necessary, clip the clutch hydraulic line onto the bracket.

**27** Raise the engine and insert the bolts, then tighten them to the specified torque.

**28** Disconnect the hoist and lifting tackle.

**29** Refit the coolant expansion tank and attach the clips.

### Rear mounting/torque link

**30** Apply the handbrake, then jack up the front of the vehicle and support it on axle stands (see *Jacking and vehicle support*).

**31** Attach a suitable hoist and lifting tackle to the engine lifting brackets on the cylinder head, and support the weight of the engine.

**32** Refer to Chapter 4C and unbolt the exhaust front pipe from the exhaust manifold, taking care to support the flexible section. **Note:** *Angular movement in excess of 10° can cause permanent damage to the flexible section.*

**33** Release the mounting rubbers and support the front of the exhaust pipe to one side.

**34** Working under the vehicle, remove the nut and bolt securing the mounting to the transmission bracket.

**35** Remove the bolt securing the mounting to the subframe, and withdraw the mounting/torque link **(see illustration)**.

**36** If necessary, unbolt the bracket from the transmission. **Note:** *The bracket bolts and link bolts are of different lengths.*

**37** Refit the bracket to the transmission and tighten the bolts to the specified torque.

**38** Locate the new mounting/link in position. Insert the bolts and tighten to the specified torque.

**39** Refit the exhaust front pipe with reference to Chapter 4D.

**40** Remove the hoist and lower the vehicle to the ground.

# Chapter 2 Part E:
# Engine removal and overhaul procedures

## Contents

## Degrees of difficulty

| | | | | |
|---|---|---|---|---|
| **Easy,** suitable for novice with little experience  | **Fairly easy,** suitable for beginner with some experience | **Fairly difficult,** suitable for competent DIY mechanic | **Difficult,** suitable for experienced DIY mechanic | **Very difficult,** suitable for expert DIY or professional  |

## Specifications

### Engine identification

| Engine type | Manufacturer's engine code* |
|---|---|
| 1.0 litre 12-valve petrol engine: | |
| 973 cc | Z10XE and Z10XE-ECO |
| 998 cc | Z10XEP |
| 1.2 litre 16-valve petrol engine: | |
| 1199 cc | Z12XE |
| 1229 cc | Z12XEP |
| 1.4 litre 16-valve petrol engine: | |
| 1364 cc | Z14XEP |
| 1389 cc | Z14XE |
| 1.3 litre 16-valve diesel engine (1248 cc) | Y13DT and Z13DT |
| 1.7 litre 16-valve diesel engine (1686 cc) | Y17DT and Y17DTL |

*For details of engine code location, see 'Vehicle identification' in the Reference Chapter.*

## 1.0, 1.2 and 1.4 litre Z14XEP petrol engines

### Cylinder block

| | |
|---|---|
| Material. . . . . . . . . . . . . . . . . . . . . . . . . . . . . . . . . . . . . . . . . . . . . . | Cast iron |
| Cylinder bore diameter: | |
| All except Z10XE, Z10XE-ECO and Z12XE engines. . . . . . . . . . . . | 73.385 to 73.415 mm |
| Z10XE, Z10XE-ECO and Z12XE engines . . . . . . . . . . . . . . . . . . . | 72.485 to 72.515 mm |

### Pistons

| | |
|---|---|
| Piston diameter: | |
| All except Z10XE, Z10XE-ECO and Z12XE engines. . . . . . . . . . . . | 73.345 to 73.375 mm |
| Z10XE, Z10XE-ECO and Z12XE engines . . . . . . . . . . . . . . . . . . . | 72.465 to 72.495 mm |

### Piston rings

| | |
|---|---|
| Number of rings (per piston). . . . . . . . . . . . . . . . . . . . . . . . . . . . . | 2 compression, 1 oil control |
| Ring end gap: | |
| All except Z10XE, Z10XE-ECO and Z12XE engines: | |
| Compression. . . . . . . . . . . . . . . . . . . . . . . . . . . . . . . . . . . . . . | 0.30 to 0.45 mm |
| Oil control . . . . . . . . . . . . . . . . . . . . . . . . . . . . . . . . . . . . . . . . | 0.25 to 0.75 mm |
| Z10XE, Z10XE-ECO and Z12XE engines: | |
| Compression. . . . . . . . . . . . . . . . . . . . . . . . . . . . . . . . . . . . . . | 0.15 to 0.45 mm |
| Oil control . . . . . . . . . . . . . . . . . . . . . . . . . . . . . . . . . . . . . . . . | 0.25 to 0.75 mm |

### Cylinder head

| | |
|---|---|
| Material. . . . . . . . . . . . . . . . . . . . . . . . . . . . . . . . . . . . . . . . . . . . . . | Light alloy |
| Maximum permissible distortion of sealing face . . . . . . . . . . . . . . . | 0.025 mm |
| Overall height of cylinder head (sealing surface-to-sealing surface) . . . | 126.0 mm |
| Valve seat width: | |
| Inlet. . . . . . . . . . . . . . . . . . . . . . . . . . . . . . . . . . . . . . . . . . . . . . | 1.00 to 1.40 mm |
| Exhaust. . . . . . . . . . . . . . . . . . . . . . . . . . . . . . . . . . . . . . . . . . . | 1.40 to 1.80 mm |
| Valve seat angle . . . . . . . . . . . . . . . . . . . . . . . . . . . . . . . . . . . . . . | 45° |

### Crankshaft and bearings

| | |
|---|---|
| Number of main bearings: | |
| 1.0 litre engines . . . . . . . . . . . . . . . . . . . . . . . . . . . . . . . . . . . . | 4 |
| 1.2 and 1.4 litre engines . . . . . . . . . . . . . . . . . . . . . . . . . . . . . . | 5 |
| Main bearing journal diameter: | |
| Standard size . . . . . . . . . . . . . . . . . . . . . . . . . . . . . . . . . . . . . . | 50.004 to 50.017 mm (nominal) |
| Big-end bearing journal diameter: | |
| Standard size . . . . . . . . . . . . . . . . . . . . . . . . . . . . . . . . . . . . . . | 42.971 to 42.987 mm (nominal) |
| Crankshaft endfloat . . . . . . . . . . . . . . . . . . . . . . . . . . . . . . . . . . . | 0.100 to 0.200 mm |

### Valves and guides

| | |
|---|---|
| Stem diameter: | |
| Inlet valve: | |
| Standard . . . . . . . . . . . . . . . . . . . . . . . . . . . . . . . . . . . . . . . | 4.955 to 4.970 mm |
| Exhaust valve: | |
| Standard . . . . . . . . . . . . . . . . . . . . . . . . . . . . . . . . . . . . . . . | 4.945 to 4.960 mm |
| Valve head diameter: | |
| Inlet valve . . . . . . . . . . . . . . . . . . . . . . . . . . . . . . . . . . . . . . . . | 27.900 to 28.100 mm. |
| Exhaust valve . . . . . . . . . . . . . . . . . . . . . . . . . . . . . . . . . . . . . | 24.900 to 25.100 mm. |
| Maximum permissible valve stem play in guide: | |
| Inlet. . . . . . . . . . . . . . . . . . . . . . . . . . . . . . . . . . . . . . . . . . . . . . | 0.018 to 0.052 mm. |
| Exhaust. . . . . . . . . . . . . . . . . . . . . . . . . . . . . . . . . . . . . . . . . . . | 0.028 to 0.062 mm. |
| Valve clearances. . . . . . . . . . . . . . . . . . . . . . . . . . . . . . . . . . . . . | Automatic adjustment by hydraulic valve lifters |

## 1.4 litre Z14XE petrol engine

### Cylinder block

| | |
|---|---|
| Material. . . . . . . . . . . . . . . . . . . . . . . . . . . . . . . . . . . . . . . . . . . . . . | Cast iron |
| Cylinder bore diameter. . . . . . . . . . . . . . . . . . . . . . . . . . . . . . . . . . | 77.575 to 77.785 mm (nominal) |

### Pistons

| | |
|---|---|
| Piston diameter . . . . . . . . . . . . . . . . . . . . . . . . . . . . . . . . . . . . . . . | 77.555 to 77.605 mm (nominal) |

### Piston rings

| | |
|---|---|
| Number of rings (per piston). . . . . . . . . . . . . . . . . . . . . . . . . . . . . | 2 compression, 1 oil control |
| Ring end gap: | |
| Compression . . . . . . . . . . . . . . . . . . . . . . . . . . . . . . . . . . . . . . . | 0.300 to 0.500 mm |
| Oil control . . . . . . . . . . . . . . . . . . . . . . . . . . . . . . . . . . . . . . . . . . | 0.400 to 1.400 mm |

## 1.4 litre Z14XE petrol engine (continued)

### Cylinder head

| | |
|---|---|
| Material. | Light alloy |
| Maximum permissible distortion of sealing face | 0.025 mm |
| Overall height of cylinder head (sealing surface-to-sealing surface) | 134.90 to 135.10 mm |
| Valve seat width: | |
| Inlet. | 1.00 to 1.40 mm |
| Exhaust. | 1.40 to 1.80 mm |
| Valve seat angle | 45° |

### Crankshaft and bearings

| | |
|---|---|
| Number of main bearings. | 5 |
| Main bearing journal diameter: | |
| Standard. | 54.980 to 54.997 mm (nominal) |
| Big-end bearing journal diameter: | |
| Standard. | 42.971 to 42.987 mm (nominal) |
| Crankshaft endfloat | 0.100 to 0.202 mm |

### Valves and guides

| | |
|---|---|
| Stem diameter: | |
| Inlet valve: | |
| Standard. | 5.955 to 5.970 mm |
| Exhaust valve: | |
| Standard. | 5.935 to 5.950 mm |
| Valve head diameter: | |
| Inlet valve | 30.900 to 31.100 mm |
| Exhaust valve | 27.400 to 27.600 mm |
| Maximum permissible valve stem play in guide: | |
| Inlet. | 0.030 to 0.057 mm |
| Exhaust. | 0.050 to 0.077 mm |
| Valve clearances. | Automatic adjustment by hydraulic valve lifters |

## 1.3 litre diesel engine

### Cylinder block

| | |
|---|---|
| Material. | Cast iron |
| Cylinder bore diameters. | 69.600 to 69.630 mm (nominal) |

### Pistons

| | |
|---|---|
| Piston diameter | 69.520 to 69.550 mm (nominal) |

### Piston rings

| | |
|---|---|
| Number of rings (per piston). | 2 compression, 1 oil control |
| Ring end gap: | |
| Top compression ring. | 0.20 to 0.30 mm |
| Second compression ring. | 1.00 to 1.50 mm |
| Oil control ring | 0.25 to 0.50 mm |

### Cylinder head

| | |
|---|---|
| Material. | Light alloy |
| Maximum permissible distortion of sealing face | 0.1 mm |
| Overall height of cylinder head (sealing surface-to-sealing surface) | 105.45 to 105.55 mm |
| Valve seat width | 1.5 to 1.7 mm |
| Valve seat angle | 45° |

### Crankshaft and bearings

| | |
|---|---|
| Number of main bearings. | 5 |
| Main bearing journal diameter | 50.855 to 51.000 mm (nominal) |
| Big-end bearing journal (crankpin) diameter | 42.455 to 42.600 mm (nominal) |
| Endfloat | 0.055 to 0.265 mm |

### Valves and guides

| | |
|---|---|
| Valve stem diameter. | 5.90 to 5.94 mm |
| Valve head diameter. | 22.0 mm |
| Maximum permissible valve stem play in guide. | 0.028 to 0.064 mm |
| Valve clearances. | Automatic adjustment by hydraulic valve lifters |

## 1.7 litre diesel engine

### Cylinder block

| | |
|---|---|
| Material . . . . . . . . . . . . . . . . . . . . . . . . . . . . . . . . . . . . . . . . . . . . . . . . . | Cast iron |
| Cylinder bore diameters. . . . . . . . . . . . . . . . . . . . . . . . . . . . . . . . . . . . | 79.00 to 79.03 mm (nominal) |

### Pistons

| | |
|---|---|
| Piston-to-bore clearance . . . . . . . . . . . . . . . . . . . . . . . . . . . . . . . . . . . | 0.061 to 0.08 mm |
| Piston projection . . . . . . . . . . . . . . . . . . . . . . . . . . . . . . . . . . . . . . . . . . | 0.63 to 0.83 mm |

### Piston rings

| | |
|---|---|
| Number of rings (per piston). . . . . . . . . . . . . . . . . . . . . . . . . . . . . . . . . | 2 compression, 1 oil control |
| Ring end gap: | |
|    Top compression ring. . . . . . . . . . . . . . . . . . . . . . . . . . . . . . . . . . | 0.25 to 0.35 mm |
|    Second compression ring. . . . . . . . . . . . . . . . . . . . . . . . . . . . . . | 0.20 to 0.30 mm |
|    Oil control ring . . . . . . . . . . . . . . . . . . . . . . . . . . . . . . . . . . . . . . | 0.20 to 0.40 mm |

### Cylinder head

| | |
|---|---|
| Material . . . . . . . . . . . . . . . . . . . . . . . . . . . . . . . . . . . . . . . . . . . . . . . . . | Light alloy |
| Maximum gasket face distortion . . . . . . . . . . . . . . . . . . . . . . . . . . . . . | 0.1 mm |
| Cylinder head height . . . . . . . . . . . . . . . . . . . . . . . . . . . . . . . . . . . . . . | 94.95 to 95.05 mm |
| Valve seat width . . . . . . . . . . . . . . . . . . . . . . . . . . . . . . . . . . . . . . . . . . | 1.5 to 1.7 mm |
| Valve head depth below gasket face . . . . . . . . . . . . . . . . . . . . . . . . . | N/A |
| Valve seat angle . . . . . . . . . . . . . . . . . . . . . . . . . . . . . . . . . . . . . . . . . . | 90° |

### Crankshaft and bearings

| | |
|---|---|
| Endfloat . . . . . . . . . . . . . . . . . . . . . . . . . . . . . . . . . . . . . . . . . . . . . . . . . | 0.03 to 0.15 mm |
| Main bearing journal diameter . . . . . . . . . . . . . . . . . . . . . . . . . . . . . . | 51.928 to 51.938 mm (nominal) |
| Big-end bearing journal (crankpin) diameter . . . . . . . . . . . . . . . . . . | N/A |

### Valves and guides

| | Inlet | Exhaust |
|---|---|---|
| Valve stem diameter: | | |
|    Inlet . . . . . . . . . . . . . . . . . . . . . . . . . . . . . . . . . . . . . . . . . . . . . . | 6.00 mm | |
|    Exhaust. . . . . . . . . . . . . . . . . . . . . . . . . . . . . . . . . . . . . . . . . . . . | 6.00 mm | |
| Valve guide bore diameter . . . . . . . . . . . . . . . . . . . . . . . . . . . . . . . . . | 7.000 to 7.015 mm | |
| Valve guide length . . . . . . . . . . . . . . . . . . . . . . . . . . . . . . . . . . . . . . . | 41.75 to 42.25 mm | |
| Stem-to-guide clearance:. . . . . . . . . . . . . . . . . . . . . . . . . . . . . . . . . . | Inlet | Exhaust |
|    Standard. . . . . . . . . . . . . . . . . . . . . . . . . . . . . . . . . . . . . . . . . . . | 0.019 mm | 0.0215 mm |
|    Service limit . . . . . . . . . . . . . . . . . . . . . . . . . . . . . . . . . . . . . . . | N/A | N/A |
| Valve length . . . . . . . . . . . . . . . . . . . . . . . . . . . . . . . . . . . . . . . . . . . . | 98.45 mm | 98.10 mm |
| Valve head diameter. . . . . . . . . . . . . . . . . . . . . . . . . . . . . . . . . . . . . . | 27.5 mm | 26.5 mm |
| Valve seat angle at valve head . . . . . . . . . . . . . . . . . . . . . . . . . . . . . | 89° | 89° |

### Connecting rod

| | |
|---|---|
| Big-end side clearance. . . . . . . . . . . . . . . . . . . . . . . . . . . . . . . . . . . . | 0.25 to 0.58 mm |
| Maximum permissible weight difference between connecting rods . . . | 4 grams |

## Torque wrench settings

| | |
|---|---|
| **1.0, and 1.2 and 1.4 litre Z14XEP petrol engine**. . . . . . . . . . . . . . . . | Refer to Chapter 2A Specifications |
| **1.4 litre Z14XE petrol engine**. . . . . . . . . . . . . . . . . . . . . . . . . . . . . . . | Refer to Chapter 2B Specifications |
| **1.3 litre diesel engine**. . . . . . . . . . . . . . . . . . . . . . . . . . . . . . . . . . . . | Refer to Chapter 2C Specifications |
| **1.7 litre diesel engine**. . . . . . . . . . . . . . . . . . . . . . . . . . . . . . . . . . . . | Refer to Chapter 2D Specifications |

## 1  General information

Included in this Part of Chapter 2 are details of removing the engine/transmission from the car and general overhaul procedures for the cylinder head, cylinder block/crankcase and all other engine internal components.

The information given ranges from advice concerning preparation for an overhaul and the purchase of parts, to detailed step-by-step procedures covering removal, inspection, renovation and refitting of engine internal components.

After Section 6, all instructions are based on the assumption that the engine has been removed from the car. For information concerning in-car engine repair, as well as the removal and refitting of those external components necessary for full overhaul, refer to Part A, B, C or D of this Chapter (as applicable) and to Section 6. Ignore any preliminary dismantling operations described in Part A, B, C or D that are no longer relevant once the engine has been removed from the car.

Apart from torque wrench settings, which are given at the beginning of Part A, B, C or D (as applicable), all specifications relating to engine overhaul are at the beginning of this Part of Chapter 2.

## 2  Engine overhaul – general information

It is not always easy to determine when, or if, an engine should be completely overhauled, as a number of factors must be considered.

High mileage is not necessarily an indication that an overhaul is needed, while low mileage does not preclude the need for an overhaul. Frequency of servicing is probably the most important consideration. An engine which has had regular and frequent oil and filter changes, as well as other required maintenance, should give many thousands of miles of reliable service. Conversely, a neglected engine may require an overhaul very early in its life.

Excessive oil consumption is an indication that piston rings, valve seals and/or valve guides are in need of attention. Make sure that oil leaks are not responsible before deciding that the rings and/or guides are worn. Perform a compression test, as described in Part A or B (petrol engines) or C OR D (diesel engine) of this Chapter, to determine the likely cause of the problem.

Check the oil pressure with a gauge fitted in place of the oil pressure switch, and compare it with that specified. If it is extremely low, the main and big-end bearings, and/or the oil pump, are probably worn out.

Loss of power, rough running, knocking or metallic engine noises, excessive valve gear noise, and high fuel consumption may also point to the need for an overhaul, especially if they are all present at the same time. If a complete service does not cure the situation, major mechanical work is the only solution.

A full engine overhaul involves restoring all internal parts to the specification of a new engine. During a complete overhaul, the pistons and the piston rings are renewed, and the cylinder bores are reconditioned. New main and big-end bearings are generally fitted; if necessary, the crankshaft may be reground, to compensate for wear in the journals. The valves are also serviced as well, since they are usually in less-than-perfect condition at this point. Always pay careful attention to the condition of the oil pump when overhauling the engine, and renew it if there is any doubt as to its serviceability. The end result should be an as-new engine that will give many trouble-free miles.

Critical cooling system components such as the hoses, thermostat and coolant pump should be renewed when an engine is overhauled. The radiator should also be checked carefully, to ensure that it is not clogged or leaking.

Before beginning the engine overhaul, read through the entire procedure, to familiarise yourself with the scope and requirements of the job. Check on the availability of parts and make sure that any necessary special tools and equipment are obtained in advance. Most work can be done with typical hand tools, although a number of precision measuring tools are required for inspecting parts to determine if they must be renewed.

The services provided by an engineering machine shop or engine reconditioning specialist will almost certainly be required, particularly if major repairs such as crankshaft regrinding or cylinder reboring are necessary. Apart from carrying out machining operations, these establishments will normally handle the inspection of parts, offer advice concerning reconditioning or renewal and supply new components such as pistons, piston rings and bearing shells. It is recommended that the establishment used is a member of the Federation of Engine Re-Manufacturers, or a similar society.

Always wait until the engine has been completely dismantled, and until all components (especially the cylinder block/crankcase and the crankshaft) have been inspected, before deciding what service and repair operations must be performed by an engineering works. The condition of these components will be the major factor to consider when determining whether to overhaul the original engine, or to buy a reconditioned unit. Do not, therefore, purchase parts or have overhaul work done on other components until they have been thoroughly inspected. As a general rule, time is the primary cost of an overhaul, so it does not pay to fit worn or sub-standard parts.

As a final note, to ensure maximum life and minimum trouble from a reconditioned engine, everything must be assembled with care, in a spotlessly-clean environment.

## 3  Engine removal – methods and precautions

If you have decided that the engine must be removed for overhaul or major repair work, several preliminary steps should be taken.

Locating a suitable place to work is extremely important. Adequate work space, along with storage space for the car, will be needed. If a workshop or garage is not available, at the very least, a flat, level, clean work surface is required.

Cleaning the engine compartment and engine/transmission before beginning the removal procedure will help keep tools clean and organised.

An engine hoist will also be necessary. Make sure the equipment is rated in excess of the combined weight of the engine and transmission. Safety is of primary importance, considering the potential hazards involved in removing the engine/transmission from the car.

The help of an assistant is essential. Apart from the safety aspects involved, there are many instances when one person cannot simultaneously perform all of the operations required during engine/transmission removal.

Plan the operation ahead of time. Before starting work, arrange for the hire of or obtain all of the tools and equipment you will need. Some of the equipment necessary to perform engine/transmission removal and installation safely (in addition to an engine hoist) is as follows: a heavy duty trolley jack, complete sets of spanners and sockets as described in the rear of this manual, wooden blocks, and plenty of rags and cleaning solvent for mopping-up spilled oil, coolant and fuel. If the hoist must be hired, make sure that you arrange for it in advance, and perform all of the operations possible without it beforehand. This will save you money and time.

Plan for the car to be out of use for quite a while. An engineering machine shop or engine reconditioning specialist will be required to perform some of the work which cannot be accomplished without special equipment. These places often have a busy schedule, so it would be a good idea to consult them before removing the engine, in order to accurately estimate the amount of time required to rebuild or repair components that may need work.

During the engine/transmission removal procedure, it is advisable to make notes of the locations of all brackets, cable ties, earthing points, etc, as well as how the wiring harnesses, hoses and electrical connections are attached and routed around the engine and engine compartment. An effective way of doing this is to take a series of photographs of the various components before they are disconnected or removed; the resulting photographs will prove invaluable when the engine/transmission is refitted.

**4.6 Removing the bolt securing the column intermediate shaft to the steering gear pinion shaft**

Always be extremely careful when removing and refitting the engine/transmission. Serious injury can result from careless actions. Plan ahead and take your time, and a job of this nature, although major, can be accomplished successfully.

On all Corsa models, the engine must be removed complete with the transmission as an assembly. There is insufficient clearance in the engine compartment to remove the engine leaving the transmission in the vehicle. The assembly is removed by raising the front of the vehicle, and lowering the assembly from the engine compartment.

## 4 Petrol engine and transmission unit – removal, separation and refitting

**Note 1:** *The engine can be removed from the car only as a complete unit with the transmission; the two are then separated for overhaul. The engine/transmission unit is lowered out of position, and withdrawn from under the vehicle. Bearing this in mind, ensure the vehicle is raised sufficiently so that there is enough clearance between the front of the vehicle and the floor to allow the engine/transmission unit to be slid out once it has been lowered out of position.*

**Note 2:** *Such is the complexity of the power unit arrangement on these vehicles, and the variations that may be encountered according to model and optional equipment fitted, that the following should be regarded as a guide to the work involved, rather than a step-by-step procedure. Where differences are encountered, or additional component disconnection or removal is necessary, make notes of the work involved as an aid to refitting.*

### Removal

**1** Position the steering with the front roadwheels straight-ahead, and lock the steering by removing the ignition key.
**2** Apply the handbrake, then jack up the front of the vehicle and support it on axle stands (see *Jacking and vehicle support*). Remove both front roadwheels, and the right-hand inner wheel arch liner for access to the crankshaft pulley. Where necessary, remove the engine compartment undertray and the

**4.15a Disconnect the wiring from the alternator . . .**

engine top cover. Note that the vehicle must be raised sufficiently high (approximately 650 mm) to enable the engine/transmission assembly to be withdrawn from under the front of the vehicle.
**3** To improve access, remove the bonnet as described in Chapter 11.
**4** Disconnect the battery negative terminal (refer to *Disconnecting the battery* in the Reference Chapter).
**5** If necessary, drain the engine oil as described in Chapter 1A.
**6** Working in the driver's footwell, unscrew the nut and remove the bolt securing the column intermediate shaft to the steering gear pinion shaft. Separate the intermediate shaft from the pinion shaft by pulling the intermediate shaft upwards **(see illustration)**.
*Caution: To prevent damage to the airbag wiring contact unit, the steering lock must remain locked until the intermediate shaft is re-attached to the pinion shaft.*
**7** Remove the front bumper as described in Chapter 11.
**8** Drain the cooling system as described in Chapter 1A, then refit and tighten the drain plug.
**9** Remove the air cleaner assembly as described in Chapter 4A or 4B (as applicable).
**10** Release the clip and disconnect the upper preheater hose from the throttle body.
**11** On the bulkhead at the rear of the engine compartment, release the clips and disconnect the two hoses from the heater matrix.
**12** Depressurise the fuel system with reference to Chapter 4A or 4B (as applicable), then disconnect the fuel line from the throttle body. Be prepared for fuel spillage, and take adequate precautions. Clamp or plug the open ends of the hoses, to minimise further fuel loss.
**13** Disconnect the brake vacuum servo hose, and fuel evaporation purge hose.
**14** Loosen the clips and remove the upper and lower radiator hoses.
**15** Note the locations of the wiring to the various engine and transmission components, then disconnect them and move the wiring harness to one side **(see illustrations)**. At the same time, disconnect the battery positive lead and release the rubber seal from the engine compartment rear panel. Also disconnect wiring harness combination plug located near the battery.

**4.15b . . . and from the starter motor solenoid**

**16** On standard manual transmission models (not Easytronic), remove the filler cap from the brake/clutch fluid reservoir on the bulkhead, then tighten it onto a piece of polythene. This will reduce the loss of fluid when the clutch hydraulic hose is disconnected. Alternatively, fit a hose clamp to the flexible hose next to the clutch hydraulic connection on the transmission housing.
**17** Place some cloth rags beneath the hose, then prise out the retaining clip securing the clutch hydraulic pipe/hose end fitting to the top of the transmission bellhousing and detach the end fitting from the transmission **(see illustration)**. Gently squeeze the two legs of the retaining clip together and re-insert the retaining clip back into position in the end fitting. Discard the sealing ring from the pipe end; a new sealing ring must be used on refitting. Plug/cover both the union and pipe ends to minimise fluid loss and prevent the entry of dirt into the hydraulic system. **Note:** *Whilst the hose/pipe is disconnected, do not depress the clutch pedal.*
**18** On automatic transmission models, at the top of the transmission, unclip the selector lever cable, then unbolt the cable bracket. Release the wiring plug and selector lever position switch from the bracket, then disconnect and separate them.
**19** Remove both driveshafts as described in Chapter 8.
**20** On models with air conditioning, remove the auxiliary drivebelt (Chapter 1A), then unbolt the compressor from the engine **without disconnecting the refrigerant lines** and support the compressor to one side.

**4.17 Prise out the clip to disconnect the clutch hydraulic hose from the release cylinder pipe**

**21** On automatic transmission models, place a suitable container beneath the transmission quick-release fluid cooler hose connections at the transmission. Clamp the transmission fluid cooler hoses, then lever off the retaining clamps and disconnect them from the transmission, noting their locations. Be prepared for fluid spillage, and plug the open ends of the hoses and transmission, to minimise fluid loss and prevent dirt ingress. Tie the lines to one side.

**22** Attach a suitable hoist and lifting tackle to the engine lifting brackets on the cylinder head, and support the weight of the engine/transmission.

**23** Remove the front subframe as described in Chapter 10.

**24** Unscrew the two bolts securing the right-hand engine mounting to the engine lower mounting bracket. **Note:** *There is no need to remove the mounting, since the engine/transmission is lowered from the engine compartment.*

**25** Unscrew the two bolts securing the left-hand engine mounting to the transmission.

**26** Make a final check to ensure that all relevant pipes, hoses, wires, etc, have been disconnected, and that they are positioned clear of the engine and transmission.

**27** With the help of an assistant, carefully lower the engine/transmission assembly to the ground. Make sure that the surrounding components in the engine compartment are not damaged. Ideally, the assembly should be lowered onto a trolley jack or low platform with castors, so that it can easily be withdrawn from under the car.

**28** Ensure that the assembly is adequately supported, then disconnect the engine hoist and lifting tackle, and withdraw the engine/transmission assembly from under the front of the vehicle.

**29** Clean away any external dirt using paraffin or a water-soluble solvent and a stiff brush.

**30** With reference to Chapter 7A, 7B or 7C, unbolt the transmission from the engine. Carefully withdraw the transmission from the engine. On manual transmission models, ensure that its weight is not allowed to hang on the input shaft while engaged with the clutch friction disc. On automatic transmission models, ensure that the torque converter is removed together with the transmission so that it remains engaged with the oil pump. Note that the transmission locates on dowels positioned in the rear of the cylinder block.

### Refitting

**31** With reference to Chapter 7A, 7B or 7C, refit the transmission to the engine and tighten the bolts to the specified torque.

**32** With the front of the vehicle raised and supported on axle stands, move the engine/transmission assembly under the vehicle, ensuring that the assembly is adequately supported.

**33** Reconnect the hoist and lifting tackle to the engine lifting brackets, and carefully raise the engine/transmission assembly up into the engine compartment with the help of an assistant.

**34** Reconnect the right- and left-hand engine/transmission mountings and tighten the bolts to the specified torque given in Chapters 2A or 2B.

**35** Refit the front subframe as described in Chapter 10.

**36** Disconnect the hoist and lifting tackle from the engine lifting brackets.

**37** Refit the driveshafts as described in Chapter 8.

**38** On automatic transmission models, reconnect the quick-release fluid cooler hoses together with new O-ring seals to the transmission.

**39** On models with air conditioning, refit the compressor with reference to Chapter 3, then refit the auxiliary drivebelt with reference to Chapter 1A.

**40** On standard manual transmission models (not Easytronic), reconnect and bleed the clutch hydraulic connection at the transmission with reference to Chapter 6.

**41** On automatic transmission models, refit the selector lever position switch and selector lever cable with bracket.

**42** Reconnect the wiring to the various components as previously noted.

**43** Reconnect the upper and lower radiator hoses and tighten the clips.

**44** Reconnect the brake vacuum servo hose, and fuel evaporation purge hose.

**45** Reconnect the fuel line to the throttle body.

**46** Reconnect the heater matrix hoses and tighten the clips.

**47** Reconnect the upper preheater hose to the throttle body and tighten the clips.

**48** Refit the air cleaner assembly with reference to Chapter 4A or 4B (as applicable).

**49** Refit the front bumper with reference to Chapter 11.

**50** Reconnect the steering column intermediate shaft to the steering gear pinion shaft and tighten the bolt and nut with reference to Chapter 10.

**51** Check and if necessary top-up the transmission oil level as described in Chapter 7A or 7C, as appropriate.

**52** Make a final check to ensure that all relevant hoses, pipes and wires have been correctly reconnected.

**53** Reconnect the battery negative terminal.

**54** Refit the right-hand inner wheel arch liner, front roadwheels, and engine compartment undertray (where fitted), then lower the vehicle to the ground.

**55** Refill the engine with oil with reference to Chapter 1A.

**56** Refill and bleed the cooling system with reference to Chapter 1A.

**57** On automatic transmission models, check and top-up the fluid level with reference to Chapter 1A.

**58** Refit the bonnet as described in Chapter 11.

## 5 Diesel engine and transmission unit – removal, separation and refitting

**Note 1:** *The engine can be removed from the car only as a complete unit with the transmission; the two are then separated for overhaul. The engine/transmission unit is lowered out of position, and withdrawn from under the vehicle. Bearing this in mind, ensure the vehicle is raised sufficiently so that there is enough clearance between the front of the vehicle and the floor to allow the engine/transmission unit to be slid out once it has been lowered out of position.*

**Note 2:** *Such is the complexity of the power unit arrangement on these vehicles, and the variations that may be encountered according to model and optional equipment fitted, that the following should be regarded as a guide to the work involved, rather than a step-by-step procedure. Where differences are encountered, or additional component disconnection or removal is necessary, make notes of the work involved as an aid to refitting.*

### Removal

**1** Position the steering with the front roadwheels straight-ahead, and lock the steering by removing the ignition key.

**2** Apply the handbrake, then jack up the front of the vehicle and support it on axle stands (see *Jacking and vehicle support*). Remove both front roadwheels, and the right-hand inner wheel arch liner for access to the crankshaft pulley. Where necessary, remove the engine compartment undertray and the engine top cover. Note that the vehicle must be raised sufficiently high (approximately 650 mm) to enable the engine/transmission assembly to be withdrawn from under the front of the vehicle.

**3** To improve access, remove the bonnet as described in Chapter 11.

**4** Disconnect the battery negative terminal (refer to *Disconnecting the battery* in the Reference Chapter).

**5** If necessary, drain the engine oil as described in Chapter 1B.

**6** Working in the driver's footwell, unscrew the nut and remove the bolt securing the column intermediate shaft to the steering gear pinion shaft **(see illustration 4.6)**. Separate the intermediate shaft from the pinion shaft by pulling the intermediate shaft upwards.

***Caution: To prevent damage to the airbag wiring contact unit, the steering lock must remain locked until the intermediate shaft is re-attached to the pinion shaft.***

**7** Remove the front bumper as described in Chapter 11.

**8** Drain the cooling system as described in Chapter 1B, then refit and tighten the drain plug.

**9** Remove the air cleaner assembly and intake ducts as described in Chapter 4C.

**10** Remove the fuel filter as described in Chapter 1B.

**5.11a Unclip the expansion tank coolant hose and the wiring harness from the crash box . . .**

**5.11b . . . and disconnect the harness connector**

**5.12 Release the retaining clip and lift the expansion tank from its location**

11 Unclip the expansion tank coolant hose and the wiring harness from the fuel filter crash box, and disconnect the harness connector **(see illustrations)**.

12 Release the retaining clip, lift the coolant expansion tank from its location and place it to one side **(see illustration)**.

13 Unscrew the outer retaining nut, slacken the inner nut and remove the crash box from the bulkhead **(see illustrations)**.

14 Disconnect the vacuum hose at the quick-release fitting on the pump.

15 At the front left-hand side of the engine compartment, lift off the cover on the additional relay box and disconnect the two wiring connectors **(see illustration)**.

16 Using a screwdriver, release the retaining lug and lift the additional relay box out of its mounting bracket. Place the box to one side.

17 Undo the bolt and detach the earth lead located just to the left of the ABS hydraulic modulator.

18 Withdraw the locking plates, lift the locking levers and disconnect the two wiring connectors from the engine management ECU **(see illustrations)**.

19 On the bulkhead at the rear of the engine compartment, pull out the special locking spring clips and disconnect the quick-release connections for two hoses from the heater matrix **(see illustration)**.

20 Note the locations of the wiring to the relevant engine and transmission components, then disconnect them and move the wiring harness to one side. To do this, first disconnect the battery leads, release the rubber seal and plastic panel from the rear of the engine compartment, disconnect the wiring from the washer fluid reservoir warning switch, release the harness from the bulkhead and position it

on the engine. Where necessary, disconnect the wiring harness combination plug located near the battery. Depending on the reason for removing the engine/transmission, some wiring may remain connected.

21 Loosen the clips and remove the upper and lower radiator hoses.

22 Remove the filler cap from the brake/clutch fluid reservoir on the bulkhead, then tighten it onto a piece of polythene. This will reduce the loss of fluid when the clutch hydraulic hose is disconnected. Alternatively, fit a hose clamp to the flexible hose next to the clutch hydraulic connection on the transmission housing.

23 Place some cloth rags beneath the hose, then prise out the retaining clip securing the clutch hydraulic pipe/hose end fitting to the top of the transmission bellhousing and detach the end fitting from the transmission **(see illustration 4.17)**. Gently squeeze the

**5.13a Unscrew the outer retaining nut (arrowed) and slacken the inner nut . . .**

**5.13b . . . then remove the crash box from the bulkhead**

**5.15 Disconnect the wiring connectors (arrowed) in the relay box**

**5.18a Withdraw the locking plates . . .**

**5.18b . . . then lift the locking levers and disconnect the ECU wiring connectors**

**5.19 Disconnect the quick-release connections for the two heater matrix hoses**

two legs of the retaining clip together and re-insert the retaining clip back into position in the end fitting. Discard the sealing ring from the pipe end; a new sealing ring must be used on refitting. Plug/cover both the union and pipe ends to minimise fluid loss and prevent the entry of dirt into the hydraulic system. **Note:** *Whilst the hose/pipe is disconnected, do not depress the clutch pedal.*

**24** Remove both driveshafts as described in Chapter 8.

**25** On models with air conditioning, remove the auxiliary drivebelt (Chapter 1B), then unbolt the compressor from the engine **without disconnecting the refrigerant lines** and support the compressor to one side.

**26** Attach a suitable hoist and lifting tackle to the engine lifting brackets on the cylinder head, and support the weight of the engine/transmission.

**27** Remove the front subframe as described in Chapter 10.

**28** Mark the position of the right-hand engine mounting, then unscrew the two bolts securing the upper mounting to the engine bracket. **Note:** *There is no need to remove the mounting, since the engine/transmission is lowered from the engine compartment.*

**29** Unscrew the two bolts securing the left-hand engine mounting to the transmission.

**30** Make a final check to ensure that all relevant pipes, hoses, wires, etc, have been disconnected, and that they are positioned clear of the engine and transmission.

**31** With the help of an assistant, carefully lower to the ground the engine/transmission assembly. Make sure that the surrounding components in the engine compartment are not damaged. Ideally, the assembly should be lowered onto a trolley jack or low platform with castors, so that it can easily be withdrawn from under the car.

**32** Ensure that the assembly is adequately supported, then disconnect the engine hoist and lifting tackle, and withdraw the engine/transmission assembly from under the front of the vehicle.

**33** With the engine/transmission assembly removed, support the assembly on suitable blocks of wood, on a workbench (or failing that, on a clean area of the workshop floor).

**34** Clean away any external dirt using paraffin or a water-soluble solvent and a stiff brush.

**35** With reference to Chapter 5A, remove the starter motor.

**36** With reference to Chapter 7A or 7C, unbolt the transmission from the engine. Carefully withdraw the transmission and adapter plate from the engine, ensuring that its weight is not allowed to hang on the input shaft while engaged with the clutch friction disc.

**37** Note that the transmission locates on dowels positioned in the rear of the cylinder block. If they are loose, remove them and keep them in a safe place.

### Refitting

**38** Ensure the locating dowels are correctly positioned then locate the adapter plate on the engine. Carefully offer the transmission to the engine, until the locating dowels are engaged. Ensure that the weight of the transmission is not allowed to hang on the input shaft as it engages the clutch friction disc. With reference to Chapter 7A or 7C, complete the transmission refitting procedure and tighten the bolts to the specified torque.

**39** Refit the starter motor with reference to Chapter 5A.

**40** With the front of the vehicle raised and supported on axle stands, move the engine/transmission assembly under the vehicle, ensuring that the assembly is adequately supported.

**41** Reconnect the hoist and lifting tackle to the engine lifting brackets, and carefully raise the engine/transmission assembly up into the engine compartment with the help of an assistant.

**42** Reconnect the right- and left-hand engine/transmission mountings, making sure that the previously-made positional marks are complied with, and tighten the bolts to the specified torque given in Chapter 2C or 2D.

**43** Refit the front subframe as described in Chapter 10.

**44** Disconnect the hoist and lifting tackle from the engine lifting brackets.

**45** Refit both driveshafts as described in Chapter 8.

**46** On models with air conditioning, refit the compressor with reference to Chapter 3, then refit the auxiliary drivebelt with reference to Chapter 1B.

**47** Reconnect and bleed the clutch hydraulic connection at the transmission with reference to Chapter 6.

**48** Reconnect the upper and lower radiator hoses.

**49** Reconnect the wiring to the various components as previously noted.

**50** Reconnect the heater matrix hoses and tighten the clips.

**51** Reconnect the vacuum hose to the pump outlet.

**52** Refit the fuel filter crash box and the expansion tank.

**53** Reconnect the wiring connector, then secure the harness and coolant hose in position on the crash box.

**54** Refit the fuel filter as described in Chapter 1B.

**55** Refit the air cleaner assembly and intake ducts with reference to Chapter 4C or 4D.

**56** Refit the front bumper with reference to Chapter 11.

**57** Reconnect the steering column intermediate shaft to the steering gear pinion shaft and tighten the bolt and nut with reference to Chapter 10.

**58** Check and if necessary top-up the transmission oil level as described in Chapter 7A or 7C.

**59** Make a final check to ensure that all relevant hoses, pipes and wires have been correctly reconnected.

**60** Reconnect the battery negative terminal.

**61** Refit the right-hand inner wheel arch liner, front roadwheels, and engine compartment undertray (where fitted), then lower the vehicle to the ground.

**62** Refill the engine with oil with reference to Chapter 1B.

**63** Refill and bleed the cooling system with reference to Chapter 1B.

**64** Refit the bonnet as described in Chapter 11.

## 6 Engine overhaul – dismantling sequence

**1** It is much easier to dismantle and work on the engine if it is mounted on a portable engine stand. These stands can often be hired from a tool hire shop. Before the engine is mounted on a stand, the flywheel/driveplate should be removed, so that the stand bolts can be tightened into the end of the cylinder block/crankcase.

**2** If a stand is not available, it is possible to dismantle the engine with it blocked up on a sturdy workbench, or on the floor. Be extra careful not to tip or drop the engine when working without a stand.

**3** If you are going to obtain a reconditioned engine, all the external components must be removed first, to be transferred to the new engine (just as they will if you are doing a complete engine overhaul yourself). These components include the following:

a) *Engine wiring harness and supports.*
b) *Alternator and air conditioning compressor mounting brackets (as applicable).*
c) *Coolant pump (where applicable) and inlet/outlet housings.*
d) *Dipstick tube.*
e) *Fuel system components.*
f) *All electrical switches and sensors.*
g) *Inlet and exhaust manifolds and, where fitted, the turbocharger.*
h) *Oil filter and oil cooler/heat exchanger.*
i) *Flywheel/driveplate.*

**Note:** *When removing the external components from the engine, pay close attention to details that may be helpful or important during refitting. Note the fitted position of gaskets, seals, spacers, pins, washers, bolts, and other small items.*

**4** If you are obtaining a 'short' engine (which consists of the engine cylinder block/crankcase, crankshaft, pistons and connecting rods all assembled), then the cylinder head, sump, oil pump, and timing belt/chains (as applicable) will have to be removed also.

**5** If you are planning a complete overhaul, the engine can be dismantled, and the internal components removed, in the order given below.

### Petrol engines

a) *Inlet and exhaust manifolds (see Chapter 4A or 4B).*

b) *Timing belt, sprockets and tensioner (see Chapter 2B).*
c) *Coolant pump (see Chapter 3).*
d) *Cylinder head (see Chapter 2A or 2B).*
e) *Flywheel/driveplate (see Chapter 2A or 2B).*
f) *Sump (see Chapter 2A or 2B).*
g) *Oil pump (see Chapter 2A or 2B).*
h) *Timing chain and sprockets (see Chapter 2A).*
i) *Pistons/connecting rod assemblies (see Section 10).*
j) *Crankshaft (see Section 11).*

### Diesel engines

a) *Sump (see Chapter 2C or 2D).*
b) *Coolant pump (see Chapter 3).*
c) *Timing chain or belt and sprockets (see Chapter 2C or 2D).*
d) *Oil pump (see Chapter 2C or 2D).*
e) *Camshaft housing (see Chapter 2C or 2D).*
f) *Cylinder head (see Chapter 2C or 2D).*
g) *Inlet and exhaust manifolds (see Chapter 4C or 4D).*
h) *Flywheel (see Chapter 2C or 2D).*
i) *Pistons/connecting rod assemblies (see Section 10).*
j) *Crankshaft (see Section 11).*

**6** Before beginning the dismantling and overhaul procedures, make sure that you have all of the correct tools necessary. See *Tools and working facilities* for further information.

## 7 Cylinder head – dismantling

**Note:** *New and reconditioned cylinder heads are available from the manufacturer, and from engine overhaul specialists. Due to the fact that some specialist tools are required for the dismantling and inspection procedures, and new components may not be readily available, it may be more practical and economical for the home mechanic to purchase a reconditioned head rather than to dismantle, inspect and recondition the original head. A valve spring compressor tool will be required for this operation.*

**1** With the cylinder head removed as described in Chapter 2A, 2B, 2C or 2D, clean away all external dirt, and remove the following components as applicable, if not already done:

**7.5c** . . . **then withdraw the valve through the combustion chamber**

**7.2 Fit a valve spring compressor tool, ensuring that the arms of the compressor are securely positioned**

a) *Manifolds (see Chapter 4A, 4B, 4C or 4D).*
b) *Spark plugs (petrol engines – see Chapter 1A).*
c) *Glow plugs (diesel engines – see Chapter 5C).*
d) *Camshafts and hydraulic tappets (petrol engines – see Chapter 2A or 2B).*
e) *Hydraulic tappets and rocker arms (diesel engines – see Chapter 2C or 2D).*
f) *Engine lifting brackets.*

**2** To remove a valve, fit a valve spring compressor tool. Ensure that the arms of the compressor tool are securely positioned on the head of the valve and the spring cap **(see illustration)**. The valves are deeply-recessed on petrol engines, and a suitable extension piece may be required for the spring compressor.

**3** Compress the valve spring to relieve the pressure of the spring cap acting on the collets.

**7.5a Remove the valve spring cap** . . .

**7.5d Remove the valve stem oil seal** . . .

**7.4 Extract the two split collets by hooking them out using a small screwdriver**

**HAYNES HiNT** *If the spring cap sticks to the valve stem, support the compressor tool, and give the end a light tap with a soft-faced mallet to help free the spring cap.*

**4** Extract the two split collets by hooking them out using a small screwdriver, then slowly release the compressor tool **(see illustration)**.
**5** Remove the valve spring cap and the spring, then withdraw the valve through the combustion chamber. Remove the valve stem oil seal (using long-nosed pliers if necessary), and the spring seat **(see illustrations)**.
**6** Repeat the procedure for the remaining valves, keeping all components in strict order so that they can be refitted in their original positions, unless all the components are to be renewed. If the components are to be kept

**7.5b** . . . **and the spring** . . .

**7.5e** . . . **and the spring seat**

**7.6 Place each valve assembly in a labelled polythene bag or similar container**

and used again, place each valve assembly in a labelled polythene bag or a similar small container **(see illustration)**. Note that as with cylinder numbering, the valves are normally numbered from the timing chain (or timing belt) end of the engine. Make sure that the valve components are identified as inlet and exhaust, as well as numbered.

## 8 Cylinder head and valve components – cleaning and inspection

1 Thorough cleaning of the cylinder head and valve components, followed by a detailed inspection, will enable a decision to be made on whether further work is necessary before reassembling the components.

### Cleaning

2 Scrape away all traces of old gasket material and sealing compound from the cylinder head surfaces. Take care not to damage the cylinder head surfaces, as the head is made of light alloy.
3 Scrape away the carbon from the combustion chambers and ports, then wash the cylinder head thoroughly with paraffin or a suitable solvent.
4 Scrape off any heavy carbon deposits that may have formed on the valves, then use a power-operated wire brush to remove deposits from the valve heads and stems.

### Inspection

**Note:** *Be sure to perform all the following*

*inspection procedures before concluding that the services of a machine shop or engine overhaul specialist are required. Make a list of all items that require attention.*

### Cylinder head

5 Inspect the head very carefully for cracks, evidence of coolant leakage, and other damage. If cracks are found, a new cylinder head should be obtained.
6 Use a straight-edge and feeler blade to check that the cylinder head surface is not distorted **(see illustration)**. If the specified distortion limit is exceeded on 1.0 and 1.2 litre petrol engines, the cylinder head must be renewed, as machining is not possible, however, on the 1.4 litre petrol and diesel engines it may be possible to have the cylinder head resurfaced, provided that the overall height of the head is not reduced to less than the specified minimum.
7 Examine the valve seats in each of the combustion chambers. If the seats are severely pitted, cracked or burned, then they will need to be recut or renewed by an engine overhaul specialist. If only slight pitting is evident, this can be removed by grinding the valve heads and seats together with coarse, then fine, grinding paste, as described later in this Section.
8 If the valve guides are worn, indicated by a side-to-side motion of the valve, oversize valve guides are available, and valves with oversize stems can be fitted. This work is best carried out by an engine overhaul specialist. A dial gauge may be used to determine whether the amount of side play of a valve exceeds the specified maximum.
9 Check the tappet bores in the cylinder head for wear. If excessive wear is evident, the cylinder head must be renewed. Also check the tappet oil holes in the cylinder head for obstructions.

### Valves

10 Examine the head of each valve for pitting, burning, cracks and general wear, and check the valve stem for scoring and wear ridges. Rotate the valve, and check for any obvious indication that it is bent. Look for pitting and excessive wear on the end of each valve stem. If the valve appears satisfactory at this stage, measure the valve

stem diameter at several points using a micrometer **(see illustration)**. Any significant difference in the readings obtained indicates wear of the valve stem. Should any of these conditions be apparent, the valve(s) must be renewed. If the valves are in satisfactory condition, they should be ground (lapped) onto their respective seats to ensure a smooth gas-tight seal.
11 Valve grinding is carried out as follows. Place the cylinder head upside-down on a bench, with a block of wood at each end to give clearance for the valve stems.

 **HAYNES HINT** *A light spring placed under the valve head will greatly ease the grinding operation.*

12 Smear a trace of coarse carborundum paste on the seat face in the cylinder head, and press a suction grinding tool onto the relevant valve head. With a semi-rotary action, grind the valve head to its seat, lifting the valve occasionally to redistribute the grinding paste **(see illustration)**. When a dull, matt, even surface is produced on the faces of both the valve seat and the valve, wipe off the paste and repeat the process with fine carborundum paste. When a smooth unbroken ring of light grey matt finish is produced on both the valve and seat faces, the grinding operation is complete. Carefully clean away every trace of grinding paste, taking great care to leave none in the ports or in the valve guides. Clean the valves and valve seats with a paraffin-soaked rag, then with a clean rag, and finally, if an airline is available, blow the valves, valve guides and cylinder head ports clean.

### Valve springs

13 Check that all the valve springs are intact. If any one is broken, all should be renewed.
14 If possible, check the free height of the springs against new ones, then stand each spring on a flat surface and check it for squareness **(see illustration)**. If a spring is found to be too short, or damaged in any way, renew all the springs as a set. Springs suffer from fatigue, and it is a good idea to renew them even if they look serviceable.

**8.6 Checking the cylinder head surface for distortion**

**8.10 Measuring a valve stem diameter**

**8.12 Grinding-in a valve**

**8.14 Check each valve spring for squareness**

**9.5a Fit the new valve stem oil seal . . .**

**9.5b . . . and push it down using a suitable tube or socket, until the seal is fully engaged with the spring seat**

### Rocker arm components (all except 1.4 litre Z14XE engines)

**15** Check the rocker arm thrust faces (the areas that contact the tappets and valve stems) for pits, wear, score-marks or any indication that the surface-hardening has worn through. Check the rocker arm camshaft roller in the same manner. Renew any rocker arms which appear suspect.

### Hydraulic tappets (all except 1.7 litre diesel engines)

**16** Inspect the tappets for obvious signs of wear on the contact faces, and check the oil holes for obstructions, particularly for oil sludge. If excessive wear is evident, or if any tappet has been noisy in operation, all the tappets must be renewed as a set.

## 9 Cylinder head – reassembly

*Note: New valve stem oil seals should be used on reassembly. A valve spring compressor tool will be required for this operation.*

**1** With all the components cleaned, starting at one end of the cylinder head, fit the valve components as follows.

**2** Insert the appropriate valve into its guide (if new valves are being fitted, insert each valve into the location to which it has been ground), ensuring that the valve stem is well-lubricated with clean engine oil. If the original components are being refitted, all components must be refitted in their original positions.

**3** Fit the spring seat.

**4** New valve stem oil seals may be supplied with a fitting sleeve, which fits over the collet groove in the valve stem, to prevent damage to the oil seal as it is slid down the valve stem. If no sleeve is supplied, wind a short length of tape round the top of the valve stem to cover the collet groove.

**5** Lubricate the valve stem oil seal with clean engine oil, then push the oil seal down the valve stem using a suitable tube or socket, until the seal is fully engaged with the valve guide (see illustrations). Remove the fitting sleeve or the tape, as applicable, from the valve stem.

**6** Fit the valve spring and the spring cap.

**7** Fit the spring compressor tool, and

compress the valve spring until the spring cap passes beyond the collet groove in the valve stem.

**8** Refit the split collets to the groove in the valve stem, with the narrow ends nearest the spring.

**HAYNES HiNT** *Apply a little grease to the split collets, then fit the split collets into the groove. The grease should hold the collets in the groove.*

**9** Slowly release the compressor tool, ensuring that the collets are not dislodged from the groove. When the compressor is fully released, give the top of the valve assembly a tap with a soft-faced mallet to settle the components.

**10** Repeat the procedure for the remaining valves, ensuring that if the original components are being used, they are all refitted in their original positions.

**11** Refit the components removed in Section 7, paragraph 1.

## 10 Piston/connecting rod assemblies – removal

*Note: The mating faces of the connecting rods and the big-end bearing caps are 'rough' (not machined), which ensures perfect mating of each individual rod and bearing cap. When the components have been removed from the*

**10.3 Undo the bolts and remove the oil baffle plate from the cylinder block baseplate (petrol engines except Z14XE)**

*engine, extreme care should be taken not to damage the mating surfaces – eg, do not rest the bearing caps on the mating faces. Ensure that each bearing cap is kept together with its respective rod, to prevent any possibility of the components being refitted incorrectly.*

*Note: New big-end cap bolts will be required for reassembly.*

### 1.0, 1.2 and 1.4 litre Z14XEP engines

**1** Remove the cylinder head as described in Chapter 2A.

**2** Remove the sump and oil pick-up pipe, as described in Chapter 2A.

**3** Undo the retaining bolts and remove the oil baffle plate from the cylinder block baseplate (see illustration).

**4** If the connecting rods and big-end caps are not marked to indicate their positions in the cylinder block (ie, marked with cylinder numbers), suitably mark both the rod and cap with quick-drying paint or similar. Note which side of the engine the marks face and accurately record this also. There may not be any other way of identifying which way round the cap fits on the rod when refitting.

**5** Unscrew the big-end cap bolts from the first connecting rod, and remove the cap (see illustration). If the bearing shells are to be re-used, tape the cap and the shell together.

**6** Check the top of the cylinder bore for a wear ridge. If evident, carefully scrape it away with a ridge reamer tool, otherwise the piston rings may jam against the ridge as the piston is pushed out of the block.

**10.5 Unscrew the big-end cap bolts from the first connecting rod, and remove the cap (petrol engines except Z14XE)**

**10.7 Push the piston/rod assembly up and out of the top of the cylinder bore (petrol engines except Z14XE)**

**10.11 Big-end cap centre-punched identification marks. Note that lug on bearing cap faces the flywheel end of engine (Z14XE petrol engines)**

**10.18 The connecting rods and big-end caps should be marked to indicate their positions in the cylinder block (diesel engines)**

7 Place the wooden handle of a hammer against the bottom of the connecting rod, and push the piston/rod assembly up and out of the cylinder bore **(see illustration)**. Recover the bearing shell, and tape it to the connecting rod if it is to be re-used.

8 Remove the remaining assemblies in a similar way. Rotate the crankshaft as necessary to bring the big-end bolts to the most accessible position.

### 1.4 litre Z14XE engines

9 Remove the cylinder head as described in Chapter 2B.

10 Remove the sump and oil pick-up pipe, as described in Chapter 2B.

11 If the connecting rods and big-end caps are not marked to indicate their positions in the cylinder block (ie, marked with cylinder numbers), centre-punch them at adjacent points either side of the cap/rod joint. Note to which side of the engine the marks face **(see illustration)**.

12 Unscrew the big-end cap bolts from the first connecting rod, and remove the cap. If the bearing shells are to be re-used, tape the cap and the shell together.

13 Check the top of the cylinder bore for a wear ridge. If evident, carefully scrape it away with a ridge reamer tool, otherwise the piston rings may jam against the ridge as the piston is pushed out of the block.

14 Place the wooden handle of a hammer against the bottom of the connecting rod, and push the piston/rod assembly up and out of

the cylinder bore. Recover the bearing shell, and tape it to the connecting rod if it is to be re-used.

15 Remove the remaining three assemblies in a similar way. Rotate the crankshaft as necessary to bring the big-end bolts to the most accessible position.

### Diesel engines

16 Referring to Chapter 2C or 2D, remove the following components:
  a) *Timing cover (which includes the sump removal procedure).*
  b) *Timing chain or belt, sprockets and tensioner.*
  c) *Camshaft housing.*
  d) *Cylinder head.*

17 Undo the retaining bolts and remove the oil baffle plate from the cylinder block baseplate.

18 If the connecting rods and big-end caps are not marked to indicate their positions in the cylinder block (ie, marked with cylinder numbers), suitably mark both the rod and cap with quick-drying paint or similar **(see illustration)**. Note which side of the engine the marks face and accurately record this also. There may not be any other way of identifying which way round the cap fits on the rod, when refitting.

19 If there is a pronounced wear ridge at the top of any bore, it may be necessary to remove it with a scraper or ridge reamer to avoid piston damage during removal. Such a ridge indicates excessive wear of the cylinder bore.

20 Turn the crankshaft to bring pistons 1 and 4 to BDC (bottom dead centre).

21 Unscrew the bolts from No 1 piston big-end bearing cap. Take off the cap and recover the bottom half bearing shell. If the bearing shells are to be re-used, tape the cap and the shell together **(see illustration)**.

22 Using a hammer handle, push the piston up through the bore, and remove it from the top of the cylinder block. Recover the bearing shell, and tape it to the connecting rod for safe-keeping.

23 Loosely refit the big-end cap to the connecting rod, and secure with the bolts – this will help to keep the components in their correct order.

24 Remove No 4 piston assembly in the same way.

25 Turn the crankshaft through 180° to bring pistons 2 and 3 to BDC (bottom dead centre), and remove them in the same way.

### 11 Crankshaft – removal

1 Remove the flywheel/driveplate as described in Chapter 2A, 2B, 2C or 2D.

2 Remove the pistons and connecting rods, as described in Section 10. **Note:** *It may only be necessary to push the pistons part-way up the bores, rather than removing them completely. In this case the cylinder head can remain in place.*

3 Invert the engine so that the crankshaft is uppermost.

4 Before removing the crankshaft, check the endfloat using a dial gauge in contact with the end of the crankshaft. Push the crankshaft fully one way, and then zero the gauge. Push the crankshaft fully the other way, and check the endfloat **(see illustration)**. The result should be compared with the specified limit, and will give an indication as to the size of the main bearing shell thrust journal width which will be required for reassembly.

5 If a dial gauge is not available, a feeler gauge can be used to measure crankshaft endfloat. Push the crankshaft fully towards one end of the crankcase, and insert a feeler

**10.21 Take off the big-end bearing cap and recover the bottom half bearing shell (diesel engines)**

**11.4 Using a dial gauge to check the crankshaft endfloat**

**11.5 Checking the crankshaft endfloat with a feeler gauge**

**11.8 Lift the cylinder block baseplate off the cylinder block (petrol engines except Z14XE)**

**11.13 Main bearing cap identification marks (Z14XE petrol engines)**

gauge between the thrust flange of the main bearing shell and the machined surface of the crankshaft web **(see illustration)**. Before measuring, ensure that the crankshaft is fully forced towards one end of the crankcase, to give the widest possible gap at the measuring location. **Note:** *Measure at the bearing with the thrustwasher (see Section 18).*

### 1.0, 1.2 and 1.4 litre Z14XEP engines

**Note:** *New cylinder block baseplate retaining bolts will be required for refitting.*

**6** Working in a diagonal sequence, progressively slacken the outer (M6) bolts securing the cylinder block baseplate to the cylinder block.

**7** When all the outer bolts have been slackened, repeat the procedure on the inner (M8) retaining bolts.

**8** Remove all the bolts and lift the cylinder block baseplate off the cylinder block **(see illustration)**. If the baseplate is initially tight to remove, carefully tap it free using a soft-faced mallet.

**9** As the baseplate is withdrawn check that the lower main bearing shells come away with the baseplate. If they remain on the crankshaft journals, lift them off and refit them to their respective locations in the baseplate.

**10** Lift the crankshaft from the cylinder block and remove the crankshaft oil seal.

**11** Extract the upper bearing shells, and identify them for position if they are to be re-used.

### 1.4 litre Z14XE engines

**Note:** *New crankshaft main bearing bolts will be required for reassembly.*

**12** Remove the oil pump as described in Chapter 2B.

**13** The main bearing caps are normally numbered 1 to 4 from the timing belt end of the engine. The flywheel end cap is not marked. The numbers are read from the coolant pump side of the engine **(see illustration)**. If the bearing caps are not marked, centre-punch them to indicate their locations, and note to which side of the engine the marks face.

**14** Unscrew and remove the main bearing cap bolts, and withdraw the bearing caps. If the bearing caps are stuck, tap them gently with a soft-faced mallet to free them. If the bearing shells are to be re-used, tape them to their respective caps.

**15** Lift the crankshaft from the crankcase **(see illustration)**.

**16** Extract the upper bearing shells, and identify them for position if they are to be re-used.

### 1.3 litre diesel engines

**Note:** *New cylinder block baseplate retaining bolts will be required for refitting.*

**17** Working in a diagonal sequence, progressively slacken the outer (M8) bolts securing the cylinder block baseplate to the cylinder block.

**18** When all the outer bolts have been slackened, repeat the procedure on the inner (M10) retaining bolts.

**19** Remove all the bolts and lift the cylinder block baseplate off the cylinder block **(see illustration)**. If the baseplate is initially tight to remove, carefully tap it free using a soft-faced mallet. Alternatively, use a spatula to break the seal between the baseplate and cylinder block.

**20** As the baseplate is withdrawn check that the lower main bearing shells come away with the baseplate. If they remain on the crankshaft journals, lift them off and refit them to their respective locations in the baseplate.

**21** Lift the crankshaft from the cylinder block and remove the crankshaft oil seal.

**22** Extract the upper bearing shells, and identify them for position if they are to be re-used.

### 1.7 litre diesel engines

**Note:** *New main bearing cap bolts will be required for reassembly.*

**23** Working as described in Chapter 2C, remove the oil pump/cover and oil pick-up pipe.

**24** Unbolt the crankshaft rear oil seal housing and remove it from the cylinder block. If the housing locating dowels are a loose fit, remove them and store them with the housing for safe-keeping.

**25** Undo the retaining bolts, and remove the oil baffle plate from the cylinder block **(see illustration)**.

**26** Remove the connecting rod bearing caps as described in Section 10.

**27** Unscrew the main bearing cap bolts and

**11.15 Lifting the crankshaft from the crankcase (Z14XE petrol engines)**

**11.19 Lift the cylinder block baseplate off the cylinder block (diesel engines)**

**11.25 Remove the oil baffle plate (1.7 litre diesel)**

**12.1  Coolant elbow on the front of the cylinder block**

**12.3a  Undo the retaining bolts and remove the piston oil spray nozzles (1.3 litre diesel engines)**

**12.3b  Oil spray nozzles (1.7 litre diesel)**

remove the bearing caps. Note that the caps should are numbered 1 to 5, Number 1 cap being at the timing belt end, and the arrow on each cap should point towards the timing belt end of the engine.

28  Carefully remove the crankshaft, and recover the thrustwasher halves from the sides of Number 2 main bearing.

## 12  Cylinder block – cleaning and inspection

### Cleaning

1  For complete cleaning, remove all external components (senders, sensors, brackets, oil pipes, coolant pipes, etc) from the cylinder block **(see illustration)**.

2  Scrape all traces of gasket and/or sealant from the cylinder block and cylinder block baseplate, taking particular care not to damage the cylinder head and sump mating faces.

3  Remove all oil gallery plugs, where fitted. The plugs are usually very tight – they may have to be drilled out and the holes retapped. Use new plugs when the engine is reassembled. On 1.3 litre diesel engines, undo the retaining bolts and remove the piston oil spray nozzles from inside the cylinder block **(see illustration)**. On 1.7 litre diesel engines, the oil spray nozzles are a push-fit **(see illustration)**. Also remove the timing chain oil spray pipe from the front face of the cylinder block.

4  If the block and baseplate (where applicable) are extremely dirty, they should be steam-cleaned.

5  If the components have been steam-cleaned, clean all oil holes and oil galleries one more time on completion. Flush all internal passages with warm water until the water runs clear. Dry the block and, where necessary, the baseplate thoroughly and wipe all machined surfaces with a light oil. If you have access to compressed air, use it to speed-up the drying process, and to blow out all the oil holes and galleries.

⚠ *Warning: Wear eye protection when using compressed air.*

6  If the block and baseplate are relatively clean, an adequate cleaning job can be achieved with hot soapy water and a stiff brush. Take plenty of time, and do a thorough job. Regardless of the cleaning method used, be sure to clean all oil holes and galleries very thoroughly, dry everything completely, and coat all cast-iron machined surfaces with light oil.

7  The threaded holes in the cylinder block and baseplate must be clean, to ensure accurate torque readings when tightening fixings during reassembly. Run the correct-size tap (which can be determined from the size of the relevant bolt) into each of the holes to remove rust, corrosion, thread sealant or other contamination, and to restore damaged threads. If possible, use compressed air to clear the holes of debris produced by this operation. Do not forget to clean the threads of all bolts and nuts which are to be re-used, as well.

8  Where applicable, apply suitable sealant to the new oil gallery plugs, and insert them into the relevant holes in the cylinder block. Tighten the plugs securely. On diesel engines, refit the oil spray nozzles into the block. Refit the timing chain oil spray pipe to the front face of the cylinder block and tighten the two bolts securely.

9  If the engine is to be left dismantled for some time, cover the cylinder block with a large plastic bag to keep it clean and prevent corrosion. Where applicable, refit the baseplate and tighten the bolts finger-tight.

### Inspection

10  Visually check the block for cracks, rust and corrosion. Look for stripped threads in the threaded holes. It's also a good idea to have the block checked for hidden cracks by an engine reconditioning specialist that has the equipment to do this type of work, especially if the vehicle had a history of overheating or using coolant. If defects are found, have the block repaired, if possible, or renewed.

11  If in any doubt as to the condition of the cylinder block, have it inspected and measured by an engine reconditioning specialist. If the

bores are worn or damaged, they will be able to carry out any necessary reboring (where possible), and supply appropriate oversized pistons, etc.

## 13  Piston/connecting rod assemblies – inspection

1  Before the inspection process can begin, the piston/connecting rod assemblies must be cleaned, and the original piston rings removed from the pistons. **Note:** *Always use new piston rings when the engine is reassembled.*

2  Carefully expand the old rings over the top of the pistons. The use of two or three old feeler gauges will be helpful in preventing the rings dropping into empty grooves **(see illustration)**. Take care, however, as piston rings are sharp.

3  Scrape away all traces of carbon from the top of the piston. A hand-held wire brush, or a piece of fine emery cloth, can be used once the majority of the deposits have been scraped away.

4  Remove the carbon from the ring grooves in the piston, using an old ring. Break the ring in half to do this (be careful not to cut your fingers – piston rings are sharp). Be very careful to remove only the carbon deposits – do not remove any metal, and do not nick or scratch the sides of the ring grooves.

5  Once the deposits have been removed, clean the piston/connecting rod assembly with paraffin or a suitable solvent, and dry

**13.2  Using a feeler gauge to aid removal of a piston ring**

thoroughly. Make sure that the oil return holes in the ring grooves are clear.

**6** If the pistons and cylinder bores are not damaged or worn excessively, and if the cylinder block does not need to be rebored, the original pistons can be refitted. Normal piston wear shows up as even vertical wear on the piston thrust surfaces, and slight looseness of the top ring in its groove. New piston rings should always be used when the engine is reassembled.

**7** Carefully inspect each piston for cracks around the skirt, at the gudgeon pin bosses, and at the piston ring lands (between the ring grooves).

**8** Look for scoring and scuffing on the thrust faces of the piston skirt, holes in the piston crown, and burned areas at the edge of the crown. If the skirt is scored or scuffed, the engine may have been suffering from overheating, and/or abnormal combustion ('pinking') which caused excessively-high operating temperatures. The cooling and lubrication systems should be checked thoroughly. A hole in the piston crown, or burned areas at the edge of the piston crown indicates that abnormal combustion (pre-ignition, 'pinking', knocking or detonation) has been occurring. If any of the above problems exist, the causes must be investigated and corrected, or the damage will occur again.

**9** Corrosion of the piston, in the form of pitting, indicates that coolant has been leaking into the combustion chamber and/or the crankcase. Again, the cause must be corrected, or the problem may persist in the rebuilt engine.

**10** If in any doubt as to the condition of the pistons and connecting rods, have them inspected and measured by an engine reconditioning specialist. If new parts are required, they will be able to supply and fit appropriate-sized pistons/rings, and rebore (where possible) or hone the cylinder block.

## 14 Crankshaft – inspection

**1** Clean the crankshaft using paraffin or a suitable solvent, and dry it, preferably with compressed air if available. Be sure to clean the oil holes with a pipe cleaner or similar probe, to ensure that they are not obstructed.

⚠ *Warning: Wear eye protection when using compressed air.*

**2** Check the main and big-end bearing journals for uneven wear, scoring, pitting and cracking.

**3** Big-end bearing wear is accompanied by distinct metallic knocking when the engine is running (particularly noticeable when the engine is pulling from low revs), and some loss of oil pressure.

**4** Main bearing wear is accompanied by severe engine vibration and rumble – getting progressively worse as engine revs increase – and again by loss of oil pressure.

**14.8 Transfer the crankshaft speed/position sensor pulse pick-up ring to the new crankshaft**

**5** Check the bearing journal for roughness by running a finger lightly over the bearing surface. Any roughness (which will be accompanied by obvious bearing wear) indicates that the crankshaft requires regrinding.

**6** If the crankshaft has been reground, check for burrs around the crankshaft oil holes (the holes are usually chamfered, so burrs should not be a problem unless regrinding has been carried out carelessly). Remove any burrs with a fine file or scraper, and thoroughly clean the oil holes as described previously.

**7** Have the crankshaft journals measured by an engine reconditioning specialist. If the crankshaft is worn or damaged, they may be able to regrind the journals and supply suitable undersize bearing shells. If no undersize shells are available and the crankshaft has worn beyond the specified limits, it will have to be renewed. Consult your Vauxhall dealer or engine reconditioning specialist for further information on parts availability.

**8** If a new crankshaft is to be fitted on petrol engines, undo the screws securing the crankshaft speed/position sensor pulse pick-up ring to the crankshaft, and transfer the ring to the new crankshaft **(see illustration)**.

## 15 Main and big-end bearings – inspection

**1** Even though the main and big-end bearings should be renewed during the engine overhaul, the old bearings should be retained for close examination, as they may reveal valuable information about the condition of the engine.

**2** Bearing failure occurs because of lack of lubrication, the presence of dirt or other foreign particles, overloading the engine, or corrosion **(see illustration)**. If a bearing fails, the cause must be found and eliminated before the engine is reassembled, to prevent the failure from happening again.

**3** To examine the bearing shells, remove them from the cylinder block, the cylinder block baseplate, the connecting rods and the big-end bearing caps, and lay them out on a clean surface in the same order as they were fitted to the engine. This will enable any

bearing problems to be matched with the corresponding crankshaft journal.

**4** Dirt and other foreign particles can enter the engine in a variety of ways. Contamination may be left in the engine during assembly, or it may pass through filters or the crankcase ventilation system. Normal engine wear produces small particles of metal, which can eventually cause problems. If particles find their way into the lubrication system, it is likely that they will eventually be carried to the bearings. Whatever the source, these foreign particles often end up embedded in the soft bearing material, and are easily recognised. Large particles will not embed in the bearing, and will score or gouge the bearing and journal. To prevent possible contamination, clean all parts thoroughly, and keep everything spotlessly-clean during engine assembly. Once the engine has been installed in the vehicle, ensure that engine oil and filter changes are carried out at the recommended intervals.

**5** Lack of lubrication (or lubrication breakdown) has a number of interrelated causes. Excessive heat (which thins the oil), overloading (which squeezes the oil from the bearing face), and oil leakage (from excessive bearing clearances, worn oil pump or high engine speeds) all contribute to lubrication breakdown. Blocked oil passages, which may be the result of misaligned oil holes in a bearing shell, will also starve a bearing of oil and destroy it. When lack of lubrication is the cause of bearing failure, the bearing material is wiped or extruded from the steel backing of the bearing. Temperatures may increase to the point where the steel backing turns blue from overheating.

**6** Driving habits can have a definite effect on bearing life. Full-throttle, low-speed operation (labouring the engine) puts very high loads on bearings, which tends to squeeze out the oil film. These loads cause the bearings to flex,

**15.2 Typical bearing failures**

**17.4 Measuring a piston ring end gap using a feeler gauge**

**17.9 Fitting an oil control spreader ring**

**17.11 Sectional view showing correct orientation of piston rings**

which produces fine cracks in the bearing face (fatigue failure). Eventually the bearing material will loosen in places, and tear away from the steel backing. Regular short journeys can lead to corrosion of bearings, because insufficient engine heat is produced to drive off the condensed water and corrosive gases which form inside the engine. These products collect in the engine oil, forming acid and sludge. As the oil is carried to the bearings, the acid attacks and corrodes the bearing material.

7 Incorrect bearing installation during engine assembly will also lead to bearing failure. Tight-fitting bearings leave insufficient bearing lubrication clearance, and will result in oil starvation. Dirt or foreign particles trapped behind a bearing shell results in high spots on the bearing which can lead to failure.

8 *Do not* touch any shell's bearing surface with your fingers during reassembly; there is a risk of scratching the delicate surface, or of depositing particles of dirt on it.

9 As mentioned at the beginning of this Section, the bearing shells should be renewed as a matter of course during engine overhaul; to do otherwise is false economy.

## 16 Engine overhaul – reassembly sequence

1 Before reassembly begins, ensure that all necessary new parts have been obtained (particularly gaskets, and various bolts which must be renewed), and that all the tools required are available. Read through the entire procedure to familiarise yourself with the work involved, and to ensure that all items necessary for reassembly of the engine are to hand. In addition to all normal tools and materials, a thread-locking compound will be required. A tube of suitable sealant will be required to seal certain joint faces which are not fitted with gaskets.

2 In order to save time and avoid problems, engine reassembly can be carried out in the following order:

### Petrol engines

a) *Piston rings (see Section 17).*
b) *Crankshaft (see Section 18).*
c) *Piston/connecting rod assemblies (see Section 19).*

d) *Timing chain and sprockets (see Chapter 2A).*
e) *Oil pump (see Chapter 2A or 2B).*
f) *Sump (see Chapter 2A or 2B).*
g) *Flywheel/driveplate (see Chapter 2A or 2B).*
h) *Cylinder head (see Chapter 2A or 2B).*
i) *Coolant pump (see Chapter 3).*
j) *Timing belt, sprockets and tensioner (see Chapter 2B).*
k) *Inlet and exhaust manifolds (see Chapter 4A or 4B).*

### Diesel engines

a) *Piston rings (see Section 17).*
b) *Crankshaft (see Section 18).*
c) *Pistons/connecting rod assemblies (see Section 19).*
d) *Flywheel (see Chapter 2C or 2D).*
e) *Inlet and exhaust manifolds (see Chapter 4C or 4D).*
f) *Cylinder head (see Chapter 2C or 2D).*
g) *Camshaft housing (see Chapter 2C or 2D).*
h) *Oil pump (see Chapter 2C or 2D).*
i) *Timing chain or belt and sprockets (see Chapter 2C or 2D).*
j) *Coolant pump (see Chapter 3).*
k) *Sump (see Chapter 2C or 2D).*

3 At this stage, all engine components should be absolutely clean and dry, with all faults repaired. The components should be laid out (or in individual containers) on a completely clean work surface.

## 17 Piston rings – refitting

1 Before refitting the new piston rings, the ring end gaps must be checked as follows.

2 Lay out the piston/connecting rod assemblies and the new piston ring sets, so that the ring sets will be matched with the same piston and cylinder during the end gap measurement and subsequent engine reassembly.

3 Insert the top ring into the first cylinder, and push it down the bore slightly using the top of the piston. This will ensure that the ring remains square with the cylinder walls

4 Measure the end gap using feeler gauges,

and compare the measurements with the figures given in the Specifications **(see illustration)**.

5 If the gap is too small (unlikely if genuine Vauxhall parts are used), it must be enlarged or the ring ends may contact each other during engine operation, causing serious damage. Ideally, new piston rings providing the correct end gap should be fitted, but as a last resort, the end gap can be increased by filing the ring ends very carefully with a fine file. Mount the file in a vice equipped with soft jaws, slip the ring over the file with the ends contacting the file face, and slowly move the ring to remove material from the ends – take care, as piston rings are sharp, and are easily broken.

6 With new piston rings, it is unlikely that the end gap will be too large. If they are too large, check that you have the correct rings for your engine and for the particular cylinder bore size.

7 Repeat the checking procedure for each ring in the first cylinder, and then for the rings in the remaining cylinders. Remember to keep rings, pistons and cylinders matched up.

8 Once the ring end gaps have been checked and if necessary corrected, the rings can be fitted to the pistons.

9 The oil control ring (lowest one on the piston) is composed of three sections, and should be installed first. Fit the lower steel ring, then the spreader ring, followed by the upper steel ring **(see illustration)**.

10 With the oil control ring components installed, the second (middle) ring can be fitted. It is usually stamped with a mark (TOP) which must face up, towards the top of the piston. **Note:** *Always follow the instructions supplied with the new piston ring sets – different manufacturers may specify different procedures. Do not mix up the top and middle rings, as they have different cross-sections.* Using two or three old feeler blades, as for removal of the old rings, carefully slip the ring into place in the middle groove.

11 Fit the top ring in the same manner, ensuring that, where applicable, the mark on the ring is facing up. If a stepped ring is being fitted, fit the ring with the smaller diameter of the step uppermost **(see illustration)**.

12 Repeat the procedure for the remaining pistons and rings.

**18.5a Main bearing shell (A) and central main bearing shell (B) with thrust flange (petrol engines shown)**

**18.5b Fitting a main bearing shell to the cylinder block**

**18.7 Liberally lubricate each bearing shell in the cylinder block then lower the crankshaft into position (petrol engines except Z14XE)**

## 18 Crankshaft – refitting

**1** Refitting the crankshaft is the first step in the engine reassembly procedure. It is assumed at this point that the cylinder block, baseplate (where applicable) and crankshaft have been cleaned, inspected and repaired or reconditioned as necessary.
**2** Position the cylinder block with the sump/baseplate mating face uppermost.
**3** Clean the bearing shells and the bearing recesses in both the cylinder block and the baseplate/caps. If new shells are being fitted, ensure that all traces of the protective grease are cleaned off using paraffin. Wipe the shells dry with a clean lint-free cloth.

**4** Note that the crankshaft endfloat is controlled by thrustwashers located on one of the main bearing shells. The thrustwashers are incorporated into, or attached to, the bearing shells themselves.
**5** If the original bearing shells are being re-used, they must be refitted to their original locations in the block and baseplate, or caps **(see illustrations)**.
**6** Fit the upper main bearing shells in place in the cylinder block.

### 1.0, 1.2 and 1.4 litre Z14XEP engines

**Note:** *New cylinder block baseplate bolts must be used when refitting the crankshaft. A tube of sealant (Loctite 5900 or equivalent) will be required when fitting the baseplate to the cylinder block.*
**7** Liberally lubricate each bearing shell in the

cylinder block, and lower the crankshaft into position **(see illustration)**.
**8** If necessary, seat the crankshaft using light taps from a soft-faced mallet on the crankshaft balance webs.
**9** Fit the bearing shells in the baseplate.
**10** Lubricate the crankshaft journals, and the bearing shells in the baseplate **(see illustration)**.
**11** Ensure that the cylinder block and baseplate mating surfaces are clean and dry, then apply a 2 mm diameter bead of sealant to the outside of the groove (not in the groove itself) in the baseplate **(see illustration)**.
**12** Locate the baseplate over the crankshaft and onto the cylinder block.
**13** Fit the new baseplate retaining bolts, then working progressively and in a diagonal sequence, tighten the inner (M8) bolts

**18.10 Lubricate the bearing shells in the baseplate (petrol engines except Z14XE)**

**18.11 Apply a 2 mm diameter bead of silicone sealant to the outside of the groove in the baseplate (petrol engines except Z14XE)**

**18.13a Fit the new baseplate inner bolts . . .**

**18.13b . . . and outer bolts (petrol engines except Z14XE)**

**18.13c Tighten the inner bolts to the specified Stage 1 torque setting using a torque wrench . . .**

**18.13d . . . then through the specified Stage 2 angle using an angle tightening gauge (petrol engines except Z14XE)**

18.13e Similarly tighten the outer bolts to the specified torque . . .

18.13f . . . and through the specified angle (petrol engines except Z14XE)

to the specified torque, then through the specified angle, in the two stages given in the Specifications. Now similarly tighten the outer (M6) retaining bolts **(see illustrations)**.

### 1.4 litre Z14XE engines

**Note:** *New main bearing cap bolts must be used when refitting the crankshaft. Suitable sealants will be required to coat the end main bearing caps.*

**14** Liberally lubricate each bearing shell in the cylinder block, and lower the crankshaft into position. Check that the oil seal is positioned correctly.

**15** If necessary, seat the crankshaft using light taps from a soft-faced mallet on the crankshaft balance webs.
**16** Fit the bearing shells into the bearing caps.
**17** Lubricate the bearing shells in the bearing caps, and the crankshaft journals, then fit Nos 2, 3 and 4 bearing caps, and tighten the new bolts as far as possible by hand **(see illustration)**.
**18** Fill the side grooves of the timing belt end (where applicable – not all engines have grooves in the timing belt end main bearing cap) and flywheel end main bearing caps with RTV jointing compound (Vauxhall part

No 15 03 295, or equivalent). Coat the lower surfaces of the bearing caps with sealing compound (Vauxhall part No 15 03 170, or equivalent). Fit the bearing caps, and tighten the new bolts as far as possible by hand **(see illustrations)**. Ensure that the timing belt end main bearing cap is exactly flush with the end face of the cylinder block.
**19** Working from the centre main bearing cap outwards, tighten the bearing cap bolts to the specified torque in the three stages given in the Specifications; ie, tighten all bolts to Stage 1, then tighten all bolts to Stage 2, and so on **(see illustrations)**.

18.17 Fitting the centre main bearing cap (Z14XE petrol engines)

18.18a Fill the side grooves of the flywheel end main bearing cap with RTV jointing compound . . .

18.18b . . . and coat the lower surfaces with sealing compound (Z14XE petrol engines)

18.19a Tighten the main bearing cap bolts to the specified torque . . .

18.19b . . . then through the specified angle (Z14XE petrol engines)

18.21a Liberally lubricate each bearing shell in the cylinder block . . .

18.21b . . . and lower the crankshaft into position (diesel engines)

18.23 Fit the bearing shells in the baseplate . . .

18.24 . . . then lubricate the crankshaft journals, and the bearing shells (diesel engines)

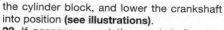

18.25a Apply a bead of sealant to the cylinder block mating face . . .

J46154

18.25b . . . ensuring the sealant is applied around the inside of the bolt holes as shown (diesel engines)

**20** When all bolts have been fully tightened, inject further RTV jointing compound into the side grooves of the timing belt end (where applicable) and flywheel end main bearing caps until it is certain that they are full.

### 1.3 litre diesel engines

**Note:** *New cylinder block baseplate bolts must be used when refitting the crankshaft. A tube of sealant (Loctite 5900 or equivalent) will be required when fitting the baseplate to the cylinder block.*

**21** Liberally lubricate each bearing shell in

the cylinder block, and lower the crankshaft into position **(see illustrations)**.

**22** If necessary, seat the crankshaft using light taps from a soft-faced mallet on the crankshaft balance webs.

**23** Fit the bearing shells in the baseplate **(see illustration)**.

**24** Lubricate the crankshaft journals, and the bearing shells in the baseplate **(see illustration)**.

**25** Ensure that the cylinder block and baseplate mating surfaces are clean and dry, then apply a 2.5 mm diameter bead of sealant to the cylinder block face **(see illustrations)**.

**26** Locate the baseplate over the crankshaft and onto the cylinder block.

**27** Fit the new baseplate retaining bolts, then working progressively and in sequence, tighten the inner (M10) bolts to the specified torque, then through the specified angle, in the two stages given in the Specifications. Now similarly tighten the outer (M8) retaining bolts to the specified torque in sequence **(see illustrations)**.

18.27a Tightening sequence for cylinder block baseplate inner (M10) bolts . . .

18.27b . . . and outer (M8) bolts (diesel engines)

**18.27c Tighten the M10 bolts to the specified torque . . .**

**18.27d . . . then through the specified angle . . .**

**18.27e . . . and tighten the outer M8 bolts to the specified torque (diesel engines)**

**18.28 Lower the crankshaft into position (1.7 litre diesel)**

**18.31 Tighten the main bearing cap bolts to the specified torque (1.7 litre diesel)**

**18.33 Apply sealant to the oil seal housing mating surface (1.7 litre diesel)**

### 1.7 litre diesel engines

**28** Lubricate the upper shells with clean engine oil then lower the crankshaft into position (see illustration).
**29** If necessary, seat the crankshaft using light taps from a soft-faced mallet on the crankshaft balance webs.
**30** Ensure the bearing shells are correctly located in the caps, then lubricate the shells and refit the caps to the cylinder block. Ensure the caps are fitted in their correct locations, with Number 1 cap at the timing belt end, and are fitted the correct way around so that the arrows all point towards the timing belt end of the engine. Prior to refitting No 1 cap, apply a smear of sealant to its mating surface.
**31** Apply a smear of clean engine oil to the threads and underneath the heads of the new main bearing cap bolts. Fit the bolts tightening them all by hand then working in a diagonal sequence from the centre outwards, evenly and progressively tighten them to the specified torque setting (see illustration).
**32** Ensure that the mating surfaces of the crankshaft rear oil seal housing and cylinder block are clean and dry. Note the correct fitted depth of the oil seal then tap/lever the seal out of the housing.
**33** Apply a smear of sealant to the oil seal housing mating surface, and make sure that the locating dowels are in position (see illustration). Slide the housing over the end of the crankshaft, and into position on the cylinder block. Put a drop of locking compound on the threads, then tighten the retaining bolts securely.

**34** Refit the oil pump/cover together with new gaskets with reference to Chapter 2D.

### All engines

**35** Now rotate the crankshaft, and check that it turns freely, with no signs of binding or tight spots.
**36** Check the crankshaft endfloat with reference to Section 11.
**37** Fit a new crankshaft flywheel end oil seal as described in Chapter 2A, 2B, 2C or 2D.
**38** Refit the pistons and connecting rods as described in Section 19.
**39** Refit the flywheel/driveplate as described in Chapter 2A, 2B or 2C.

### 19 Pistons/connecting rods – refitting

**1** Clean the backs of the big-end bearing shells and the recesses in the connecting rods and big-end caps. If new shells are being fitted, ensure that all traces of the protective grease are cleaned off using paraffin. Wipe the shells, caps and connecting rods dry with a lint-free cloth.
**2** Press the bearing shells into the connecting rods and caps in their correct positions (see illustration).
**Note:** *When finally refitting the piston/connecting rod assemblies, new big-end bearing cap bolts must be used. Ensure that the mating faces of the connecting rods and big-end bearing caps are clean before refitting (refer to Section 10).*
**3** Lubricate No 1 piston and piston rings,

and check that the ring gaps are correctly positioned. The gaps in the upper and lower steel rings of the oil control ring should be offset by 25 to 50 mm to the right and left of the spreader ring gap. The two upper compression ring gaps should be offset by 180° to each other.
**4** Liberally lubricate the cylinder bore with clean engine oil.
**5** Fit a ring compressor to No 1 piston, then insert the piston and connecting rod into the cylinder bore so that the base of the compressor stands on the block. With the crankshaft big-end bearing journal positioned at its lowest point, tap the piston carefully into the cylinder bore with the wooden handle of a hammer, and at the same time guide the connecting rod onto the bearing journal. Note that the arrow or notch (as applicable) on the piston crown must

**19.2 Press the bearing shells into the connecting rods and caps in their correct positions**

**19.5a Position the piston with the arrow or notch (as applicable) pointing towards the timing chain/belt end of the engine . . .**

**19.5b . . . then tap the piston carefully into the cylinder bore**

**19.7a Tighten the big-end bearing cap bolts to the specified torque . . .**

**19.7b . . . then through the specified angle**

point towards the timing chain/belt end of the engine (see illustrations).
6 Fit the bearing shells to the bearing caps.
7 Liberally lubricate the bearing journals and bearing shells, and fit the bearing cap in its original location. Tighten the new bearing cap bolts to the Stage 1 torque setting, then tighten all bolts through the specified angles (see illustrations).
8 After refitting each piston/connecting rod assembly, rotate the crankshaft, and check that it turns freely, with no signs of binding or tight spots.

9 Refit the following components.

### Petrol and 1.7 litre diesel engines

a) *Refit the oil baffle plate and tighten the retaining bolts securely.*
b) *Refit the sump and oil pick-up pipe as described in Chapter 2A, 2B or 2D.*
c) *Refit the cylinder head as described in Chapter 2A, 2B or 2D.*

### 1.3 litre diesel engines

a) *Refit the oil baffle plate and tighten the retaining bolts securely.*

b) *Refit the cylinder head as described in Chapter 2C.*
c) *Refit the camshaft housing as described in Chapter 2C.*
d) *Refit the timing chain, sprockets and tensioner as deccribed in Chapter 2C.*
e) *Refit the timing cover (which includes the sump refitting procedure) as described in Chapter 2C.*

## 20 Engine – initial start-up after overhaul

1 With the engine refitted in the vehicle, double-check the engine oil and coolant levels. Make a final check that everything has been reconnected, and that there are no tools or rags left in the engine compartment.
2 Start the engine, noting that this may take a little longer than usual. Make sure that the oil pressure warning light goes out.
3 While the engine is idling, check for fuel, water and oil leaks. Don't be alarmed if there are some odd smells and smoke from parts getting hot and burning off oil deposits.
4 Assuming all is well, keep the engine idling until hot water is felt circulating through the top hose, then switch off the engine.
5 After a few minutes, recheck the oil and coolant levels as described in *Weekly checks*, and top-up as necessary.
6 Note that there is no need to retighten the cylinder head bolts once the engine has first run after reassembly.
7 If new pistons, rings or crankshaft bearings have been fitted, the engine must be treated as new, and run-in for the first 600 miles. *Do not* operate the engine at full-throttle, or allow it to labour at low engine speeds in any gear. It is recommended that the oil and filter be changed at the end of this period.

# Chapter 3
# Cooling, heating and air conditioning systems

## Contents

## Degrees of difficulty

| Easy, suitable for novice with little experience  | Fairly easy, suitable for beginner with some experience | Fairly difficult, suitable for competent DIY mechanic | Difficult, suitable for experienced DIY mechanic | Very difficult, suitable for expert DIY or professional  |
|---|---|---|---|---|

## Specifications

### Thermostat

| | |
|---|---|
| Opening temperature | 92°C |

### Air conditioning compressor

| | |
|---|---|
| Lubricant capacity: | |
| Petrol engines | 150 cc |
| Diesel engines | 120 cc |
| Lubricant type (synthetic PAG fluid) | Vauxhall part number 90 510 419/19 49 874 |

### Torque wrench settings

| | Nm | lbf ft |
|---|---|---|
| Air conditioning: | | |
| Petrol engines: | | |
| Compressor lubricant drain bolt | 18 | 13 |
| Compressor mounting bolts | 20 | 15 |
| Compressor clutch to shaft | 11 | 8 |
| Safety valve to compressor | 8 | 6 |
| Diesel engines: | | |
| Compressor lubricant drain bolt | 15 | 11 |
| Compressor mounting bolts | 22 | 16 |
| Compressor clutch to shaft | 20 | 15 |
| Safety valve to compressor | 10 | 7 |
| Automatic transmission fluid cooler banjo unions | 25 | 18 |
| Coolant pump blanking plug: | | |
| 1.0, 1.2 and 1.4 litre Z14XEP petrol engines | 15 | 11 |
| Coolant pump bolts: | | |
| Petrol engines. | 8 | 6 |
| Diesel engines | 9 | 7 |
| Coolant pump cover bolts: | | |
| 1.0, 1.2 and 1.4 litre Z14XEP petrol engines | 8 | 6 |
| Coolant pump pulley bolts: | | |
| 1.0, 1.2 and 1.4 litre Z14XEP petrol engines | 20 | 15 |
| Engine mounting-to-cylinder block retaining bolts: | | |
| 1.4 litre Z14XE petrol engines. | 50 | 37 |
| Radiator lower mounting brackets to crossmember | 15 | 11 |
| Thermostat housing/cover bolts: | | |
| Petrol engines. | 8 | 6 |
| Diesel engines | 25 | 18 |
| Timing belt guide roller retaining bolts: | | |
| 1.4 litre Z14XE petrol engines. | 25 | 18 |
| Timing belt tensioner roller retaining bolts: | | |
| 1.4 litre Z14XE petrol engines. | 20 | 15 |

## 1  General information and precautions

The cooling system is of pressurised type, comprising a pump driven by the auxiliary drivebelt on all engine types except the 1.4 litre Z14XE petrol engine, on which it is driven by the timing belt, an aluminium crossflow radiator, electric cooling fan, and a thermostat. The system functions as follows. Cold coolant from the radiator passes through the hose to the coolant pump, where it is pumped around the cylinder block and head passages. After cooling the cylinder bores, combustion surfaces and valve seats, the coolant reaches the underside of the thermostat, which is initially closed. The coolant passes through the heater, and is returned to the coolant pump.

When the engine is cold, the coolant circulates only through the cylinder block, cylinder head, expansion tank and heater. When the coolant reaches a predetermined temperature, the thermostat opens and the coolant passes through to the radiator. As the coolant circulates through the radiator, it is cooled by the inrush of air when the car is in forward motion. Airflow is supplemented by the action of the electric cooling fan when necessary. Once the coolant has passed through the radiator, and has cooled, the cycle is repeated.

The electric cooling fan, mounted on the rear of the radiator, is controlled by a thermostatic switch/sensor. At a predetermined coolant temperature, the fan is actuated.

An expansion tank is fitted to the left-hand side of the engine compartment to accommodate expansion of the coolant when it gets hot. The expansion tank is connected to the top of the radiator by a small bore rubber hose.

⚠ **Warning: Do not attempt to remove the expansion tank filler cap, or disturb any part of the cooling system, while the engine is hot; there is a high risk of scalding. If the expansion tank filler cap must be removed before the engine and radiator have fully cooled (even though this is not recommended) the pressure in the cooling system must** first be relieved. Cover the cap with a thick layer of cloth, to avoid scalding, and slowly unscrew the filler cap until a hissing sound can be heard. When the hissing has stopped, indicating that the pressure has reduced, slowly unscrew the filler cap until it can be removed; if more hissing sounds are heard, wait until they have stopped before unscrewing the cap completely. At all times, keep well away from the filler cap opening.

⚠ **Warning: Do not allow antifreeze to come into contact with skin, or with the painted surfaces of the vehicle. Rinse off spills immediately, with plenty of water. Never leave antifreeze lying around in an open container, or in a puddle on the driveway or garage floor. Children and pets are attracted by its sweet smell, but antifreeze can be fatal if ingested.**

⚠ **Warning: If the engine is hot, the electric cooling fan may start rotating even if the engine is not running and the ignition is not turned on; be careful to keep hands, hair and loose clothing well clear when working in the engine compartment.**

⚠ **Warning: Refer to Section 11 for precautions to be observed when working on models equipped with air conditioning.**

## 2  Cooling system hoses – disconnection and renewal

**Note:** *Refer to the warnings given in Section 1 of this Chapter before proceeding. Do not attempt to disconnect any hose while the system is still hot.*

1  If the checks described in Chapter 1A or 1B reveal a faulty hose, it must be renewed as follows.

2  First drain the cooling system (see Chapter 1A or 1B). If the coolant is not due for renewal, it may be re-used if it is collected in a clean container.

3  Before disconnecting a hose, first note its routing in the engine compartment, and whether it is secured by any additional retaining clips or cable ties. Use a pair of pliers to release the clamp-type clips, or a screwdriver to slacken the screw-type clips, then move the clips along the hose, clear of the relevant inlet/outlet union. Carefully work the hose free.

4  Note that the radiator inlet and outlet unions are fragile; do not use excessive force when attempting to remove the hoses. If a hose proves to be difficult to remove, try to release it by rotating the hose ends before attempting to free it.

> **HAYNES HiNT**  *If all else fails, cut the coolant hose with a sharp knife, then slit it so that it can be peeled off in two pieces. Although this may prove expensive if the hose is otherwise undamaged, it is preferable to buying a new radiator.*

5  When fitting a hose, first slide the clips onto the hose, then work the hose into position. If clamp-type clips were originally fitted, it is a good idea to use screw-type clips when refitting the hose. If the hose is stiff, use a little soapy water (washing-up liquid is ideal) as a lubricant, or soften the hose by soaking it in hot water.

6  Work the hose into position, checking that it is correctly routed and secured. Slide each clip along the hose until it passes over the flared end of the relevant inlet/outlet union, before tightening the clips securely.

7  Refill the cooling system with reference to Chapter 1A or 1B.

8  Check thoroughly for leaks as soon as possible after disturbing any part of the cooling system.

## 3  Radiator – removal, inspection and refitting

### Removal

#### Petrol engines

1  Disconnect the battery negative terminal (refer to *Disconnecting the battery* in the Reference Chapter).

2  Remove the front bumper as described in Chapter 11.

3  Drain the cooling system as described in Chapter 1A.

4  Slacken the retaining clips, and disconnect the coolant top hose and the expansion tank hose from the top of the radiator (see illustration).

5  Slacken the retaining clip, and disconnect the bottom hose from the radiator (see illustration).

6  On models with automatic transmission, undo the banjo union bolts and disconnect the fluid cooler hoses.

7  Remove the electric cooling fan from the radiator as described in Section 5.

8  On models equipped with air conditioning, undo the two bolts and separate the

**3.4  Release the retaining clips (arrowed) and disconnect the coolant hoses from the top of the radiator . . .**

**3.5  . . . and the coolant hose from the bottom of the radiator**

3.9a  Withdraw the radiator downwards . . .

3.9b  . . . disengaging it from the upper mountings (arrowed)

3.16a  Slacken the retaining clip (arrowed) . . .

condenser from the radiator. Suitably suspend the condenser from the radiator crossmember to avoid straining the refrigerant lines.

9  Undo the retaining bolts, and release the radiator mounting brackets from the bottom of the radiator. Lower the radiator out through the bottom of the vehicle, disengaging it from its upper mountings (see illustrations).

### Diesel engines

10  Disconnect the battery negative terminal (refer to *Disconnecting the battery* in the Reference Chapter).

11  Remove the front bumper as described in Chapter 11.

12  Drain the cooling system as described in Chapter 1B.

13  Slacken the retaining clips, and disconnect the coolant top hose and the expansion tank hose from the top of the radiator.

14  Slacken the retaining clip, and disconnect the bottom hose from the radiator.

15  Detach the air cleaner intake hose from the resonator, then undo the retaining screw, and slide the resonator to one side to release it from the radiator crossmember (see illustrations 5.3a and 5.3b).

16  Slacken the retaining clip, disconnect the quick-release fitting and remove the air hose from the turbocharger and intercooler charge air pipe, where fitted (see illustrations).

17  At the front left-hand side of the engine compartment, lift off the cover on the additional relay box and disconnect the two wiring connectors (see illustration).

18  Using a screwdriver, release the retaining lug and lift the additional relay box out of its mounting bracket. Place the box to one side.

19  Undo the bolt and detach the earth lead located just to the left of the ABS hydraulic modulator.

20  On models equipped with air conditioning, disconnect the auxiliary fan wiring connector and the air conditioning pressure switch wiring connector, located on the receiver-dryer. Undo the two bolts and separate the condenser from the radiator. Suitably suspend the condenser from the upper crossmember to avoid straining the refrigerant lines. Disconnect the compressor wiring connector.

21  Slacken the retaining clip, disconnect the quick-release fitting and remove the

3.16b  . . . then disconnect the quick-release fitting (arrowed) and remove the turbocharger air hose – diesel engines

two air hoses from the intercooler. Release the retaining clip each side and remove the intercooler from the radiator.

22  Undo the retaining bolts, and release the radiator mounting brackets from the bottom of the radiator. Lower the radiator out through the bottom of the vehicle, disengaging it from its upper mountings.

23  If required, the electric cooling fan and intercooler charge air pipe can be removed after undoing the mounting bolts and releasing the wiring harness.

### Inspection

24  If the radiator has been removed due to suspected blockage, reverse-flush it as described in Chapter 1A or 1B. Clean dirt and debris from the radiator fins, using an airline (in which case, wear eye protection) or a soft brush.

3.28a  Check the radiator upper mounting rubbers . . .

3.17  Disconnect the wiring connectors (arrowed) in the relay box – diesel engines

*Caution: Be careful, as the fins are easily damaged, and are sharp.*

25  If necessary, a radiator specialist can perform a 'flow test' on the radiator, to establish whether an internal blockage exists.

26  A leaking radiator must be referred to a specialist for permanent repair. Do not attempt DIY repairs to a leaking radiator, as damage may result.

27  In an emergency, minor leaks from the radiator can be cured by using a suitable radiator sealant (in accordance with its manufacturer's instructions) with the radiator *in situ*.

28  Inspect the radiator mounting rubbers, and renew them if necessary (see illustrations).

### Refitting

29  Refitting is a reversal of removal, bearing in mind the following points:

*a) Ensure that the lugs on the radiator are*

3.28b  . . . and lower mounting rubbers for signs of damage, and renew if necessary *correctly engaged with the mounting rubbers in the mounting bracket (see illustrations).*

b) *Ensure that all hoses are correctly reconnected, and their retaining clips securely tightened.*

c) *Where applicable, reconnect the automatic transmission fluid cooler banjo unions using new copper washers.*

d) *On completion, refill the cooling system as described in Chapter 1A or 1B.*

e) *On models with automatic transmission, check and, if necessary, top-up the automatic transmission fluid as described in Chapter 1A.*

## 4 Thermostat – removal, testing and refitting

### Removal

#### Petrol engines

**1** Disconnect the battery negative terminal (refer to *Disconnecting the battery* in the Reference Chapter).

**2** On 1.4 litre Z14XE engines, remove the oil filler cap, undo the two retaining bolts and remove the engine cover, refit the oil filler cap.

**3** Drain the cooling system (see Chapter 1A).

**4** Slacken the retaining clip, and disconnect the coolant hose from the thermostat housing cover (see illustration).

**5** On 1.4 litre Z14XE engines, slacken the retaining clip, and disconnect the small

**3.29a On refitting, ensure that the radiator pegs engage with lower mounting rubbers**

coolant hose from the thermostat housing cover.

**6** Slacken and remove the three retaining bolts, and remove the thermostat housing cover (see illustration).

**7** Remove the thermostat. Note on some models, the thermostat is an integral part of the housing cover, and cannot be renewed separately.

**8** Remove the sealing ring from the housing cover and discard it; a new one should be used on refitting (see illustration).

### 1.3 litre diesel engines

**9** Disconnect the battery negative terminal (refer to *Disconnecting the battery* in the Reference Chapter).

**10** Lift off the engine cover.

**11** Drain the cooling system (see Chapter 1B).

**12** Remove the fuel filter as described in Chapter 1B.

**13** Unclip the expansion tank coolant hose

**3.29b Slight adjustment can be made on the left-hand upper mounting bracket (arrowed) if required**

and the wiring harness from the fuel filter crash box, and disconnect the harness connector (see illustrations).

**14** Release the retaining clip, lift the coolant expansion tank from its location and place it to one side (see illustration).

**15** Unscrew the outer retaining nut, slacken the inner nut and remove the crash box from the bulkhead (see illustrations).

**16** Slacken the clip and disconnect the intercooler air hose from the inlet manifold charge air pipe. Undo the three bolts securing the charge air pipe to the inlet manifold, and the single bolt securing the pipe to the thermostat housing. Remove the charge air pipe from the engine. Remove the sealing ring from the pipe and discard it; a new one should be used on refitting.

**17** Slacken the retaining clips, and disconnect the four coolant hose from the thermostat housing.

**4.4 Release the clip (arrowed) and disconnect the hose from the thermostat housing cover – 1.0 litre petrol engine shown**

**4.6 Remove the thermostat housing cover from the coolant pump – 1.0 litre petrol engine shown**

**4.8 Remove the sealing ring from the thermostat cover – 1.0 litre petrol engine shown**

**4.13a Unclip the expansion tank coolant hose and the wiring harness from the crash box . . .**

**4.13b . . . and disconnect the harness connector – diesel engines**

**4.14 Release the retaining clip and lift the expansion tank from its location – diesel engines**

**4.15a Unscrew the outer retaining nut (arrowed) and slacken the inner nut . . .**

**4.15b . . . then remove the crash box from the bulkhead – diesel engines**

**4.19 Undo the two retaining bolts (arrowed) and remove the thermostat housing – diesel engines**

**4.20 Remove the sealing ring from the thermostat housing – diesel engines**

**4.25 Undo the two bolts (arrowed) and remove the wiring harness bracket from the thermostat housing cover**

**4.29 Testing the thermostat opening temperature**

**18** Disconnect the coolant temperature sensor wiring connector.

**19** Undo and remove the two retaining bolts, unclip the wiring harness and remove the thermostat housing from the engine **(see illustration)**.

**20** Remove the sealing ring from the housing and discard it; a new one should be used on refitting **(see illustration)**.

**21** Note that the thermostat is an integral part of the housing, and cannot be renewed separately.

### 1.7 litre diesel engines

**22** Disconnect the battery negative terminal (refer to *Disconnecting the battery* in the Reference Chapter).

**23** Drain the cooling system (see Chapter 1B).

**24** Slacken the retaining clip, and disconnect the coolant hose from the thermostat housing.

**25** Undo the retaining bolt(s) and detach the wiring harness bracket from the thermostat housing **(see illustration)**.

**26** Slacken and remove the two retaining bolts, and remove the thermostat housing from the engine **(see illustration 4.12)**.

**27** Withdraw the thermostat from coolant housing unit.

**28** Remove the gasket/sealing ring from the edge of the thermostat and discard it; a new one should be used on refitting.

### Testing

**Note:** *Frankly, if there is any question about*

*the operation of the thermostat, it's best to renew it – they are not usually expensive items. Testing involves heating in, or over, an open pan of boiling water, which carries with it the risk of scalding. A thermostat which has seen more than five years' service may well be past its best already.*

**29** Where it is possible to separate the ther-mostat from the cover, a rough test of the thermostat's operation may be made by suspending it with a piece of string in a container full of water. Heat the water to bring it to the boil – the thermostat must open by the time the water boils. If not, renew it **(see illustration)**.

**30** The opening temperature is marked on the thermostat. If a thermometer is available, the precise opening temperature of the thermostat may be determined, and compared with the value mark on the thermostat.

**31** A thermostat which fails to close as the water cools must also be renewed.

### Refitting

**32** Refitting is a reversal of removal, bearing in mind the following points:
a) *Fit the new sealing rings to all applicable mating faces.*
b) *Tighten the thermostat housing/cover bolts to the specified torque.*
c) *On 1.3 litre diesel engines, refit the fuel filter as described in Chapter 1B.*
d) *On completion, refill the cooling system as described in Chapter 1A or 1B.*

---

### 5  Electric cooling fan – removal and refitting

⚠️ *Warning: If the engine is hot, the cooling fan may start up at any time, even with the ignition off.* ***Take extra precautions when working in the vicinity of the fan.***

### Removal

#### Petrol engines

**1** Disconnect the battery negative terminal (refer to *Disconnecting the battery* in the Reference Chapter).

**2** On models with air conditioning, remove the front bumper as described in Chapter 11.

**3** Detach the air cleaner intake hose from the intake pipe, then undo the retaining screw, and

**5.3a Undo the retaining screw (arrowed) . . .**

**5.3b** . . . then slide the locating pegs (arrowed) out from the crossmember

**5.5** Disconnect the wiring block connector from the cooling fan motor

**5.6** Unclip the coolant hoses (arrowed) from the fan shroud

**5.7a** Undo the retaining bolts (right-hand side arrowed) . . .

**5.7b** . . . and withdraw the fan assembly out from the radiator

slide the intake pipe to one side to release it from the radiator crossmember **(see illustrations)**. **Note:** *Where applicable, withdraw the dipstick from its tube.*

**4** On models equipped with air conditioning, disconnect the wiring connectors at the air conditioning pressure switch and the compressor.

**5** Disconnect the cooling fan motor wiring connector(s), then unclip the wiring loom from the fan shroud **(see illustration)**.

**6** Unclip any hoses or additional wiring from the fan shroud **(see illustration)**.

**7** Unscrew the fan shroud retaining bolts, then tilt the assembly back slightly towards the engine, and withdraw it upwards away from the radiator **(see illustrations)**. Where necessary, push the coolant hoses aside to provide sufficient clearance for removal.

**8** To remove the fan motor, first release the retaining nut and remove the fan from the

motor. Retrieve the washer from the motor spindle for refitting **(see illustrations)**.

**9** Turn the fan assembly over and unscrew the three retaining nuts, then remove the fan motor from the shroud **(see illustration)**.

**5.8a** Undo the retaining nut, withdraw the fan from the motor . . .

**10** Undo the screw and detach the wiring plug and resistor from the shroud **(see illustrations)**.

**11** No spare parts are available for the motor, and if the unit is faulty, it must be renewed complete.

### Diesel engines

**12** Disconnect the battery negative terminal (refer to *Disconnecting the battery* in the Reference Chapter).

**13** Remove the front bumper as described in Chapter 11.

**14** Slacken the retaining clip, disconnect the quick-release fitting and remove the air hose from the turbocharger and intercooler charge air pipe, where fitted **(see illustrations 3.16a and 3.16b)**.

**15** Undo the upper bolt and the two lower bolts and remove the charge air pipe from the fan shroud, where fitted.

**5.8b** . . . and recover the washer

**5.9** Undo the retaining bolts (arrowed) to remove the motor from the shroud

**5.10a** Undo the retaining screw (arrowed) . . .

**5.10b** . . . and withdraw the fan resistor from the shroud

**5.26a Ensure the fan is located correctly in the sides of the radiator (arrowed) . . .**

**5.26b . . . the top of the radiator (arrowed) . . .**

**5.26c . . . and the bottom of the radiator (arrowed)**

**16** Disconnect the fan motor wiring connectors, then unclip the wiring loom from the fan shroud.

**17** Unclip any hoses or additional wiring from the fan shroud.

**18** Undo the retaining bolt and remove the upper right-hand radiator mounting bracket.

**19** Undo the two bolts securing the fan shroud to the radiator.

**20** Undo the rear bolts, and slacken the front bolts securing the radiator mounting brackets to the underbody on each side.

**21** Ease the fan shroud away from the radiator and lower it down and out from under the car.

**22** To remove the fan motor, first release the retaining nut and remove the fan from the motor. Retrieve the washer from the motor spindle for refitting **(see illustrations 5.8a and 5.8b)**.

**23** Turn the fan assembly over and unscrew the three retaining nuts, then remove the fan motor from the shroud **(see illustration 5.9)**.

**24** Undo the screw and detach the wiring plug and resistor from the shroud **(see illustrations 5.10a and 5.10b)**.

**25** No spare parts are available for the motor, and if the unit is faulty, it must be renewed complete.

## Refitting

**26** Refitting is a reversal of removal, ensuring that the shroud is correctly located in the radiator clips **(see illustrations)**.

**27** On completion, start the engine and run it until it reaches normal operating

temperature; continue to run the engine, and check that the cooling fan cuts in and functions correctly.

**6 Coolant temperature sensor
– testing, removal and refitting**

## Testing

**1** Testing of the coolant temperature sensor circuit is best entrusted to a Vauxhall dealer, who will have the necessary specialist diagnostic equipment.

## Removal

### Petrol engines

**2** On 1.0, 1.2 and 1.4 litre Z14XEP engines, the coolant temperature sensor is located at the top of the coolant pump housing **(see illustration)**. On 1.4 litre Z14XE engines, the sensor is located on the thermostat housing on the front right-hand side of the cylinder head.

**3** Drain the cooling system as described in Chapter 1A. Alternatively, remove the undertray from under the engine compartment, then position a suitable container beneath the sensor position to catch the spilled coolant.

**4** With the engine cold, unscrew the cap from the coolant expansion tank to release the pressure, then refit and tighten it. This will

reduce the loss of coolant when the sensor is removed. Have a suitable plug available to insert in the sensor hole.

**5** Where applicable, remove the cover from the top of the engine.

**6** Disconnect the wiring from the temperature sensor, then unscrew and remove it from the coolant pump or thermostat housing. If the cooling system has not been drained, either insert the new sensor or fit a blanking plug to prevent further loss of coolant.

### Diesel engines

**Note:** *Access on 1.3 litre engines is difficult. On 1.7 litre engines, access is slightly easier and some of the preliminary dismantling operations described here may not be necessary.*

**7** The coolant temperature sensor is located on the thermostat housing on the left-hand end of the cylinder head **(see illustrations)**.

**8** Disconnect the battery negative terminal (refer to *Disconnecting the battery* in the Reference Chapter).

**9** Lift off the engine cover.

**10** Drain the cooling system as described in Chapter 1B.

**11** Remove the fuel filter as described in Chapter 1B.

**12** Unclip the expansion tank coolant hose and the wiring harness from the fuel filter crash box, and disconnect the harness connector **(see illustrations 4.13a and 4.13b)**.

**13** Release the retaining clip, lift the coolant expansion tank from its location and place it to one side **(see illustration 4.14)**.

**6.2 Coolant temperature sensor location (arrowed) – 1.0 litre petrol engine shown**

**6.7a Coolant temperature sensor location (arrowed) – 1.3 litre diesel engines**

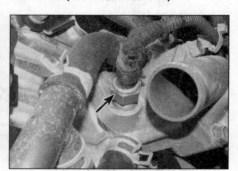

**6.7b Coolant sensor (arrowed) – 1.7 litre diesel engines**

**7.3 Slacken the three coolant pump pulley retaining bolts (arrowed) – 1.0 litre petrol engine shown**

**7.9a Release the clips (arrowed) and disconnect the hoses from the front . . .**

**7.9b . . . and rear (arrowed) of the coolant pump housing – 1.0 litre petrol engine shown**

**14** Unscrew the outer retaining nut, slacken the inner nut and remove the crash box from the bulkhead **(see illustrations 4.15a and 4.15b)**.

**15** Slacken the clip and disconnect the inlet manifold charge air pipe connection hose from the inlet manifold charge air pipe. Undo the three bolts securing the charge air pipe to the inlet manifold, and the single bolt securing the pipe to the thermostat housing. Remove the charge air pipe from the engine. Remove the sealing ring from the pipe and discard it; a new one should be used on refitting.

**16** Disconnect the wiring from the temperature sensor, then unscrew and remove it from the thermostat housing.

### *Refitting*

**17** Refitting is a reversal of removal, bearing in mind the following points:

 a) *Where applicable fit a new sealing O-ring to the sensor. Where the sensor is fitted without an O-ring, ensure the sensor threads are clean, and apply a smear of suitable sealant to them.*

 b) *On diesel engines, use a new sealing ring when refitting the charge air pipe.*

 c) *On diesel engines, refit the fuel filter as described in Chapter 1B.*

 d) *On completion, top-up/refill the cooling system as described in Chapter 1A or 1B.*

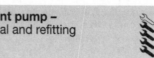

## 7  Coolant pump – removal and refitting

### *Removal*

#### 1.0, 1.2 and 1.4 litre Z14XEP engines

**1** Disconnect the battery negative terminal (refer to *Disconnecting the battery* in the Reference Chapter).

**2** Remove the air cleaner assembly and air intake ducts as described in Chapter 4A.

**3** Slacken the three coolant pump pulley retaining bolts **(see illustration)**.

**4** Remove the auxiliary drivebelt as described in Chapter 1A.

**5** Drain the cooling system as described in Chapter 1A.

**6** Support the engine and remove the right-hand engine mounting as described in Chapter 2A.

**7** Unscrew the previously-slackened coolant pump pulley bolts and withdraw the pulley from the pump.

**8** Disconnect the coolant temperature sensor wiring connector.

**9** Release the retaining clips and disconnect the hoses from the coolant pump and thermostat housing **(see illustrations)**.

**10** Unscrew the coolant pump retaining bolts, noting the locations of the three short bolts **(see illustration)**. The short bolts secure the pump to the timing cover, and the long bolts secure the pump and the timing cover to the cylinder block and cylinder head.

**11** Withdraw the coolant pump from the timing cover, noting that it may be necessary to tap the pump lightly with a soft-faced hammer to free it from the locating dowels. **Note:** *Coolant which is trapped in the cylinder block will leak out when the pump is removed.*

**12** Recover the pump sealing ring/gasket, and discard it; a new one must be used on refitting **(see illustration)**.

**13** Note that it is not possible to overhaul the pump. If it is faulty, the unit must be renewed complete.

**14** If the pump is being renewed, remove the thermostat (referring to the procedures in Section 4) and temperature sensor then transfer them to the new pump.

**15** Similarly, where applicable, unscrew the two bolts and withdraw the coolant pump top cover from the old pump and fit the cover to the new pump using a new seal. Tighten the cover bolts to the specified torque. Note that later engines have a modified coolant pump without a detachable top cover.

**7.10 Coolant pump short retaining bolt locations (arrowed) – 1.0 litre petrol engine shown with timing cover removed**

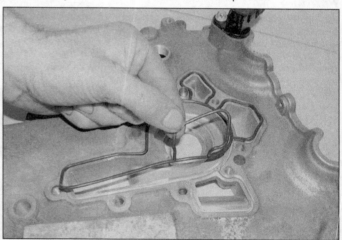

**7.12 Remove the sealing ring or gasket from the timing cover – 1.0 litre petrol engine shown with timing cover removed**

**7.30 Working through the pulley apertures, unscrew and remove the coolant pump retaining nuts – diesel engines**

**7.33 Undo the four retaining bolts (arrowed)**

**7.34 Withdraw the pulley from the coolant pump**

## 1.4 litre Z14XE engines

**16** Disconnect the battery negative terminal (refer to *Disconnecting the battery* in the Reference Chapter).

**17** Drain the cooling system with reference to Chapter 1A.

**18** Remove the timing belt as described in Chapter 2B.

**19** Undo the two timing belt guide roller centre bolts and remove them from the cylinder block.

**20** Undo the three retaining bolts and remove the engine mounting bracket from the cylinder block.

**21** Undo the timing belt tensioner roller centre bolt and remove it from the cylinder block.

**22** Remove the timing belt drive gear from the end of the crankshaft, then undo the retaining bolts and remove the timing belt rear cover from the lower part of the cylinder block.

**23** Unscrew and remove the three coolant pump securing bolts.

**24** Withdraw the coolant pump from the cylinder block, noting that it may be necessary to tap the pump lightly with a soft-faced hammer to free it from the cylinder block. **Note:** *Coolant which is trapped in the cylinder block will leak out when the pump is removed.*

**25** Recover the pump sealing ring, and discard it; a new one must be used on refitting.

**26** Note that it is not possible to overhaul the pump. If it is faulty, the unit must be renewed complete.

## All diesel engines

**27** Disconnect the battery negative terminal (refer to *Disconnecting the battery* in the Reference Chapter).

**28** Drain the cooling system with reference to Chapter 1B.

## 1.3 litre diesel engines

**29** Remove the auxiliary drivebelt as described in Chapter 1B.

**30** Working through the apertures in the pulley, unscrew and remove the four coolant pump retaining nuts **(see illustration)**.

## 1.7 litre diesel engines

**31** Remove the air filter assembly as described in Chapter 4C.

**32** Slacken the retaining bolts on the coolant

pump pulley, then remove the auxiliary drivebelt as described in Chapter 1B.

**33** Undo the four retaining bolts and remove the crankshaft pulley/vibration damper from the end of the crankshaft **(see illustration)**.

**34** Undo the retaining bolts and remove the coolant pump pulley from the coolant pump **(see illustration)**.

**35** Unscrew and remove the five coolant pump retaining bolts **(see illustration)**.

**36** Withdraw the coolant pump from the cylinder block studs. **Note:** *Coolant which is trapped in the cylinder block will leak out when the pump is removed.*

## All diesel engines

**37** Recover the pump sealing ring, and discard it; a new one must be used on refitting **(see illustration)**.

**38** Note that it is not possible to overhaul the pump. If it is faulty, the unit must be renewed complete.

## *Refitting*

### 1.0, 1.2 and 1.4 litre Z14XEP engines

**39** Ensure that the pump and timing cover mating faces are clean and dry and locate a new seal in the timing cover groove. Note that later engines utilise a flanged metal gasket instead of a rubber seal, and there is no groove in the timing cover. Ensure that the correct seal/gasket is being fitted, according to type.

**40** Check that the locating dowels are in place and locate the pump in position on the timing cover.

**7.35 Undo the five retaining bolts (arrowed) and remove the coolant pump – diesel engines**

**41** Refit the pump retaining bolts, ensuring that the short bolts are fitted to their correct locations **(see illustration 7.10)**. Tighten the bolts to the specified torque.

**42** Refit the coolant pump pulley and tighten the three bolts to the specified torque. To prevent the pulley turning as the bolts are tightened, hold the pulley using a screwdriver engaged with one of the bolts and the pump centre spindle. Alternatively, wait until the auxiliary drivebelt has been refitted and tighten the bolts then.

**43** Reconnect the coolant hoses and the coolant temperature sensor wiring connector.

**44** Refit the auxiliary drivebelt and refill the cooling system as described in Chapter 1A.

**45** If not already done, tighten the coolant pump pulley bolts to the specified torque. Refit the engine mounting with reference to Chapter 2A.

**46** Refit the air cleaner assembly and air intake ducts as described in Chapter 4A, then reconnect the battery.

**47** Refill the cooling system as described in Chapter 1A.

### 1.4 litre Z14XE engines

**48** Ensure that the pump and cylinder block mating surfaces are clean and dry, and apply a smear of silicone grease to the pump mating surface in the cylinder block. Vauxhall recommend the use of their grease (Part No 90 167 353); in the absence of this, ensure a good-quality equivalent is used.

**49** Fit a new sealing ring to the pump, and install the pump in the cylinder block. Carefully

**7.37 Remove the sealing ring from the coolant pump – diesel engines**

ease away the rear timing belt cover and turn the pump so that the edge of the pump flange is aligned with mark on the cylinder block.

**50** Refit the pump retaining bolts, tightening them to the specified torque setting.

**51** Refit the timing belt rear cover to the lower part of the cylinder block, then refit the timing belt drive gear to the end of the crankshaft.

**52** Refit the timing belt tensioner roller centre bolt and refit it to the cylinder block.

**53** Refit the engine mounting bracket to the cylinder block.

**54** Refit the timing belt guide roller to the cylinder block.

**55** Refit the timing belt as described in Chapter 2B.

**56** Reconnect the battery then refill the cooling system as described in Chapter 1A.

### Diesel engines

**57** Ensure that the pump and cylinder block mating surfaces are clean and dry.

**58** Fit a new sealing ring to the pump, and install the pump in the cylinder block.

**59** Refit the pump retaining nuts, tightening them to the specified torque setting.

**60** Refit the auxiliary drivebelt as described in Chapter 1B.

**61** Reconnect the battery then refill the cooling system as described in Chapter 1B.

## 8 Heater/ventilation system – general information

The heater/ventilation system consists of a four-speed blower motor which is inside the vehicle behind the facia to the left-hand side of the heater housing, face-level vents in the centre and at each end of the facia, and air ducts to the front footwells and windscreen.

The control unit is located in the facia to the right-hand side of the heater housing assembly. The controls operate flap valves to deflect and mix the air flowing through the various parts of the heater/ventilation system. The flap valves are contained in the air distribution housing, which acts as a central distribution unit, passing air to the various ducts and vents.

Cold air enters the system through the grille at the rear of the engine compartment. A pollen filter is fitted to the ventilation intake, to filter out dust, soot, pollen and spores from the air entering the vehicle.

The air (boosted by the blower fan if required) then flows through the various ducts, according to the settings of the controls. Stale air is expelled through ducts behind the doors. If warm air is required, the cold air is passed through the heater matrix, which is heated by the engine coolant.

A recirculation lever enables the outside air supply to be closed off, while the air inside the vehicle is recirculated. This can be useful to prevent unpleasant odours entering from outside the vehicle, but should only be used briefly, as the recirculated air inside the vehicle will soon deteriorate in quality.

**9.3a  Undo the retaining screw . . .**

**9.4  Carefully prise out the trim from the heater control panel**

## 9 Heater/ventilation system components – removal and refitting

### Heater control panel

#### Removal

**1** Disconnect the battery negative terminal (refer to *Disconnecting the battery* in the Reference Chapter).

**2** Working inside the vehicle, remove the glove-box (see Chapter 11, Section 26), this will help to gain access to the rear of the control panel.

**3** Remove the radio/cassette/CD player as described in Chapter 12, then undo the retaining screw and withdraw the radio/

**9.6  Undo the two retaining screws (arrowed) . . .**

**9.3b  . . . and withdraw the radio/cassette/ CD player housing**

**9.5  Unclip the direction control cable (arrowed) from the rear of the control panel**

cassette/CD player housing, disconnecting the wiring connectors from the rear of the housing on removal **(see illustrations)**.

**4** Carefully prise the trim from the heater control panel, starting at the top of the panel then working down each side, withdrawing the trim from the control panel, taking great care not to damage the panel **(see illustration)**.

**5** From inside the radio aperture, unclip the direction control cable from the rear of the control panel **(see illustration)**.

**6** From inside the radio aperture undo the two retaining screws from the top of the heater control panel **(see illustration)**.

**7** Release the locating lugs and withdraw the heater control panel from the facia panel until access can be gained to release the temperature control cable from the rear of the control panel **(see illustrations)**.

**9.7a  . . . then withdraw the control panel from the facia**

**9.7b  Unclip the remaining control cable (arrowed) from the rear of the control panel**

**9.9  Pull the control knobs, to release them from the control panel**

**9.12a  Undo the two retaining screws (arrowed) . . .**

**9.12b  . . . and the two retaining screws (arrowed) from the lower trim panel**

**9.13  Release the retaining clip to free the outer cable**

**9.17a  Undo the two retaining screws (arrowed) . . .**

8 Disconnect the wiring connectors from the control panel, noting the wiring's correct fitted location and routing.

9 If necessary, the control knobs can be removed by carefully prising them from the control panel **(see illustration)**.

### Refitting

10 Refitting is reversal of removal. Ensure that the wiring connectors and control cables are correctly routed and reconnected to the control panel, as noted before removal. Clip the outer cable(s) in position, and check the operation of each knob/lever before refitting the centre facia panel.

### *Temperature control cable*

#### Removal

11 Remove the heater control panel from the facia, as described above in paragraphs 1 to 9.

12 Undo the two retaining screws and remove the trim from the side of the heater unit, then

the two screws to remove the driver's side lower trim panel **(see illustrations)**.

13 Release the retaining clip and disconnect the cable from the control valve lever on the lower part of the heater control drive unit **(see illustration)**.

14 Follow the run of the cable behind the facia, taking note of its routing, and if not already removed, disconnect the cable from the lever on the rear of the control panel. Note that the method of fastening is the same as that used at the control drive unit.

#### Refitting

15 Refitting is reversal of removal. Ensure that the wiring connectors and control cables are correctly routed and reconnected to the control panel, as noted before removal. Clip the outer cable(s) in position, and check the operation of each knob/lever before refitting the centre facia panel.

### *Heater control unit and cable*

#### Removal

16 Remove the direction control cable from the rear of the control panel, as described above in paragraphs 1 to 5.

17 Undo the two retaining screws and remove the trim from the side of the heater unit, then the two screws to remove the driver's side lower trim panel **(see illustrations)**.

18 Release the retaining clip and disconnect the cable from the control valve lever on the lower part of the heater control drive unit **(see illustration)**.

19 Unclip the two operating levers from the air flap controls **(see illustration)**.

**9.17b  . . . and the two retaining screws from the lower trim panel and remove**

**9.18  Release the retaining clip (arrowed) to free the outer cable**

J44737

**9.19  Carefully lever the two linkage rods (arrowed) from the air flap control unit**

9.20 Undo the retaining bolt (arrowed)

9.21a Align the hole arrowed . . .

9.21b . . . then slide the cable from the housing

9.22 Align the peg (arrowed) on the housing with the slot in the cable

20 Undo the retaining bolt **(see illustration)** and withdraw the heater control drive unit from the heater housing, complete with direction control cable.

21 The cable can then be removed from the control drive unit, align the hole in the drive-shaft, then pull the cable out of its housing **(see illustrations)**.

9.25a Release the retaining clips from the heater hoses . . .

9.25b . . . then disengage the hoses from the heater matrix pipes

9.27a Withdraw the securing pin . . .

9.27b . . . and remove the heater air duct

### Refitting

22 Refitting is reversal of removal. Ensure that the wiring connectors and control cables are correctly routed and reconnected, as noted before removal **(see illustration)**. Clip the cables in position, and check the operation of each knob/lever before refitting the centre facia panel.

## Heater matrix

### Removal

23 With the engine cold, unscrew the expansion tank cap (referring to the warning note in Section 1) to release any pressure present in the cooling system, then securely refit the cap.

24 Clamp both heater hoses as close to the bulkhead as possible, to minimise coolant loss. Alternatively, drain the cooling system as described in Chapter 1A or 1B.

25 Working in the engine compartment, release the retaining clips, and disconnect both hoses from the heater matrix unions **(see illustrations)**.

26 Undo the two retaining screws and remove the trim from the side of the heater unit, then the two screws to remove the driver's side lower trim panel **(see illustrations 9.12a and 9.12b)**.

27 Release the retaining clip and remove the driver's side front footwell air duct **(see illustrations)**.

28 Cover the carpet directly underneath the air distribution housing, to catch any coolant which may be spilt from the matrix as it is removed. Alternatively, release the carpet fasteners, and fold the carpet back from the bulkhead so that any spilt coolant will go behind the carpet.

29 Undo the retaining screw and remove the bracket from the coolant pipes entering the air distribution housing, then undo the two retaining clips and disconnect the pipes from the heater matrix **(see illustration)**.

30 Slide the heater matrix out from the air distribution housing and remove the matrix from the vehicle. **Note:** *Keep the matrix unions uppermost as the matrix is removed, to prevent coolant spillage.* Mop-up any spilt coolant immediately, and wipe the affected area with a damp cloth to prevent staining.

31 Where necessary, recover the sealing

9.29 Undo the retaining screw (A), then the two retaining clips (B)

**9.36  Remove the passenger side heater air duct**

**9.37  Disconnect the wiring connector (arrowed) from the blower motor**

rings from the matrix unions and hoses, and renew them.

### Refitting

**32** Refitting is a reversal of the removal procedure, bearing in mind the following points:

a) *Apply a smear silicone grease to the matrix sealing rings, to ease installation.*

b) *Ensure that the heater hose retaining clips are securely pressed back into position.*

c) *On completion, top-up/refill the cooling system as described in Chapter 1A or 1B.*

## Heater blower motor

### Removal

**33** Disconnect the battery negative terminal (refer to *Disconnecting the battery* in the Reference Chapter).

**34** Working inside the vehicle, remove the glovebox as described in Chapter 11, Section 26.

**35** Remove the lower trim panel from the facia above the passenger side footwell and the lower trim panel from the centre of the facia.

**36** Release the retaining clip and remove the passenger side front footwell air duct **(see illustration)**.

**37** Disconnect the wiring connector from the fan motor, noting the correct routing of the wiring **(see illustration)**.

**38** Working your way around the fan motor

air distribution housing, undo the retaining screws, then unclip the motor from the housing **(see illustrations)**.

### Refitting

**39** Refitting is a reversal of the removal procedure, noting the following points:

a) *Make sure that the motor wiring is correctly routed.*

b) *Make sure that the blower motor covers are correctly engaged with each other, and clipped securely in position.*

## Heater blower motor resistor

### Removal

**40** Remove the fan motor as described above in paragraphs 33 to 38.

**9.38a  Undo the retaining screws (one arrowed) . . .**

**41** From inside the vehicle, reach up behind the air distribution housing, and disconnect the wiring connector from the underside of the blower motor resistor, which is on the left-hand side of the air distribution housing **(see illustration)**.

**42** Unclip the resistor from the air distribution housing **(see illustration)**.

### Refitting

**43** Refitting is the reverse of removal.

## Air distribution housing

**Note:** *On models with air conditioning, it is not possible to remove the air distribution housing without opening the refrigerant circuit (see Section 11). Therefore, this task must be carried out by qualified personnel.*

**9.38b  . . . then unclip the retaining clips (one arrowed) from around the motor housing . . .**

**9.38c  and withdraw the motor from the housing**

**9.41  Disconnecting the wiring connector from the blower motor resistor . . .**

**9.42  . . . and withdraw the blower motor resistor out of position**

**9.46a Undo the crossmember upper retaining bolt (right-hand side arrowed) . . .**

**9.46b . . . and the lower retaining bolt (right-hand side arrowed)**

**9.54 Undo the two retaining bolts (arrowed)**

## Removal

**44** Remove the centre console and facia assembly as described in Chapter 11.

**45** Unclip the wiring harness from the steering support crossmember, which is bolted across the front bulkhead behind the facia panel.

**46** With the both front doors open, undo the retaining bolts (two each side), and withdraw the crossmember from the bulkhead **(see illustrations)**.

**47** Drain the cooling system as described in Chapter 1A or 1B.

**48** Working in the engine compartment, release the retaining clips, and disconnect both hoses from the heater matrix unions **(see illustrations 9.25a and 9.25b)**.

**49** Remove the windscreen wipers and water deflector as described in Chapter 12.

**50** Remove the battery, then undo the four retaining bolts and withdraw the pollen filter housing from the bulkhead.

**51** On models with air conditioning, the refrigerant line block connection will need to be disconnected from the expansion valve (*this task **must** be carried out by qualified personnel* – see **Note**).

**52** Cover the carpet directly underneath the air distribution housing, to catch any coolant which may be spilt from the matrix as the housing assembly is removed.

**53** Disconnect the wiring connector from the blower motor resistor on the left-hand side of the housing.

**54** Working in the engine compartment, undo the two bolts where the heater hoses come out through the bulkhead and the one bolt

which is located under the pollen filter housing **(see illustration)**

**55** Working inside the vehicle withdraw the air distribution housing from the bulkhead. **Note:** *Keep the matrix unions uppermost as the housing is removed, to prevent coolant spillage.* Mop-up any spilt coolant immediately, and wipe the affected area with a damp cloth to prevent staining.

## Refitting

**56** Refitting is the reverse of removal. On completion, refill the cooling system as described in Chapter 1A or 1B. On models with air conditioning, have the system charged by the air conditioning engineer.

---

### 10 Heater/ventilation vents and ducts – removal and refitting

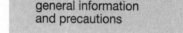

## Centre vents and housing

**1** Unclip the hazard warning light switch cover from between the centre air vents **(see illustration)**.

**2** Insert a small, flat-bladed screwdriver in through the gap, and carefully lever between the sides of the vent and the housing to release the vent from its locating pegs **(see illustration)**.

**3** Once the vent is free from both its locating pegs, it can be withdrawn from the facia.

**4** Undo the four retaining screws and remove the air vent trim surround **(see illustration)**. Disconnect the wiring block connector from the housing.

**5** On refitting, carefully manoeuvre the vent back into the facia, ensuring it is correctly engaged with the locating pegs.

### Side vents

**6** Remove the vents as described in para-graphs 2 and 3.

**7** Refitting is a reversal of the removal procedure, ensuring that the housing is correctly located with the duct.

---

### 11 Air conditioning system – general information and precautions

## General information

**1** Air conditioning is available on certain models. It enables the temperature of incoming air to be lowered, and also dehumidifies the air, which makes for rapid demisting and increased comfort.

**2** The cooling side of the system works in the same way as a domestic refrigerator. Refrigerant gas is drawn into a belt-driven compressor, and passes into a condenser mounted in front of the radiator, where it loses heat and becomes liquid. The liquid passes through an expansion valve to an evaporator, where it changes from liquid under high pressure to gas under low pressure. This change is accompanied by a drop in temperature, which cools the evaporator. The refrigerant returns to the compressor, and the cycle begins again.

**3** Air blown through the evaporator passes to the air distribution unit, where it is mixed

**10.1 Unclip the cover from the hazard switch**

**10.2 Carefully unclip the heater/ventilation ducts**

**10.4 Undo the four retaining screws and withdraw the vent housing from the facia**

with hot air blown through the heater matrix, to achieve the desired temperature in the passenger compartment.

**4** The heating side of the system works in the same way as on models without air conditioning (see Section 8).

**5** The operation of the system is controlled electronically. Any problems with the system should be referred to a Vauxhall dealer.

### Air conditioning service ports

**6** The high-pressure service port is located adjacent to the right-hand front suspension strut turret **(see illustration)**.

**7** The low-pressure service port is located just in front of the air cleaner housing **(see illustration)**.

### Precautions

**8** It is necessary to observe special precautions whenever dealing with any part of the system, its associated components, and any items which necessitate disconnection of the system.

⚠️ *Warning: The refrigeration circuit contains a liquid refrigerant. This refrigerant is potentially dangerous, and should only be handled by qualified persons. If it is splashed onto the skin, it can cause frostbite. It is not itself poisonous, but in the presence of a naked flame it forms a poisonous gas; inhalation of the vapour through a lighted cigarette could prove fatal. Uncontrolled discharging of the refrigerant is dangerous, and potentially damaging to the environment. It is therefore dangerous to disconnect any part of the system without specialised knowledge and equipment. If for any reason the system must be disconnected, entrust this task to your Vauxhall dealer or air conditioning specialist.*
*Caution: Do not operate the air conditioning system if it is known to be short of refrigerant, as this may damage the compressor.*

### 12 Air conditioning system components – removal and refitting

⚠️ *Warning: The air conditioning system is under high pressure. Do not loosen any fittings or remove any components until after the system has been discharged. Air conditioning refrigerant should be properly discharged into an approved type of container at a dealer service department or an automotive air conditioning repair facility capable of handling R134a refrigerant. Cap or plug the pipe lines as soon as they are disconnected, to prevent the entry of moisture. Always wear eye protection when disconnecting air conditioning system fittings.*
**Note:** *This Section refers to the components of the air conditioning system itself – refer to Sections 9 and 10 for details of components common to the heating/ventilation system.*

11.6 Air conditioning system high-pressure service port location (arrowed) . . .

### Condenser

#### Petrol engines

**1** Have the refrigerant discharged at a dealer service department or an automotive air conditioning repair facility.

**2** Disconnect the battery negative terminal (refer to *Disconnecting the battery* in the Reference Chapter).

**3** Firmly apply the handbrake, then jack up the front of the car and support it securely on axle stands (see *Jacking and vehicle support*).

**4** Remove the front bumper as described in Chapter 11.

**5** Disconnect the wiring connector at the air conditioning pressure switch, located on the receiver-dryer.

**6** With the system discharged, undo the retaining bolt and disconnect the refrigerant pipe connector block. Discard the O-ring seals – new ones must be used when refitting. Suitably cap the open fittings immediately to keep moisture and contamination out of the system.

**7** Slacken the two lower radiator mounting bracket bolts on the right-hand side.

**8** Undo the two bolts securing the condenser to the radiator. Lift the condenser (complete with the receiver-dryer) to disengage it from the radiator mounting brackets.

**9** Lower the condenser complete with receiver-dryer out from under the vehicle. Store it upright, to prevent fluid loss. Take care not to damage the condenser fins.

**10** Refitting is the reverse of removal. Renew the O-rings and lubricate with refrigerant oil.

**11** Have the system evacuated, charged and leak-tested by the specialist who discharged it.

#### Diesel engines

**12** Have the refrigerant discharged at a dealer service department or an automotive air conditioning repair facility.

**13** Disconnect the battery negative terminal (refer to *Disconnecting the battery* in the Reference Chapter).

**14** Firmly apply the handbrake, then jack up the front of the car and support it securely on axle stands (see *Jacking and vehicle support*).

**15** Remove the front bumper as described in Chapter 11.

**16** Slacken the two lower radiator mounting bracket bolts on the right-hand side.

11.7 . . . and low-pressure service port location (arrowed)

**17** Disconnect the auxiliary fan wiring connector. Push the two upper mounting lugs inwards and lift the auxiliary fan upwards and off the condenser.

**18** Disconnect the wiring connector at the air conditioning pressure switch, located on the receiver-dryer.

**19** With the system discharged, undo the retaining bolt and disconnect the refrigerant pipe connector block. Discard the O-ring seals – new ones must be used when refitting. Suitably cap the open fittings immediately to keep moisture and contamination out of the system.

**20** On models with an intercooler, slacken the retaining clip, disconnect the quick-release fitting and remove the two air hoses from the intercooler. Release the retaining clip each side and remove the intercooler from the radiator.

**21** Undo the two bolts securing the condenser to the radiator. Lift the condenser (complete with the receiver-dryer) to disengage it from the radiator mounting brackets.

**22** Lower the condenser complete with receiver-dryer out from under the vehicle. Store it upright, to prevent fluid loss. Take care not to damage the condenser fins.

**23** Refitting is the reverse of removal. Renew the O-rings and lubricate with refrigerant oil.

**24** Have the system evacuated, charged and leak-tested by the specialist who discharged it.

### Receiver-dryer

**25** Have the refrigerant discharged at a dealer service department or an automotive air conditioning repair facility.

**26** Disconnect the battery negative terminal (refer to *Disconnecting the battery* in the Reference Chapter).

**27** Firmly apply the handbrake, then jack up the front of the car and support it securely on axle stands (see *Jacking and vehicle support*).

**28** Remove the front bumper as described in Chapter 11.

**29** With the system discharged, undo the retaining bolt and disconnect the refrigerant pipe connector block. Discard the O-ring seals – new ones must be used when refitting. Suitably cap the open fittings immediately to keep moisture and contamination out of the system.

**30** Slacken the two lower radiator mounting bracket bolts on the right-hand side.

**31** Undo the clamp bolt and release the receiver-dryer from the condenser. Remove the receiver-dryer downwards and withdraw it from the vehicle.

**32** Refitting is the reverse of removal. Renew the O-rings and lubricate with refrigerant oil.

**33** Have the system evacuated, charged and leak-tested by the specialist who discharged it.

### Evaporator

**34** The evaporator is mounted inside the heater housing with the heater matrix. Apart from the need to have the refrigerant discharged, and to disconnect the refrigerant lines, the procedure is as described in Section 9 of this Chapter.

**35** Unbolt the heater unit assembly from the bulkhead to remove the evaporator. Refitting is the reverse of removal.

**36** Have the system evacuated, charged and leak-tested by the specialist who discharged it.

### Compressor

**37** Have the refrigerant discharged at a dealer service department or an automotive air conditioning repair facility.

**38** Disconnect the battery negative terminal (refer to *Disconnecting the battery* in the Reference Chapter).

**39** Firmly apply the handbrake, then jack up the front of the car and support it securely on axle stands (see *Jacking and vehicle support*).

**40** Remove the auxiliary drivebelt as described in Chapter 1A or 1B.

**41** With the system discharged, undo the retaining bolt(s) and disconnect the refrigerant pipes from the compressor. Discard the O-ring seals – new ones must be used when refitting. Suitably cap the open fittings immediately to keep moisture and contamination out of the system.

**42** Disconnect the compressor wiring connector.

**43** On 1.4 litre Z14XE petrol engines undo the three retaining bolts and remove the exhaust front pipe from the catalytic converter.

**44** Unbolt the compressor from the cylinder block/crankcase, then withdraw the compressor downwards from under the vehicle.

**45** Refit the compressor in the reverse order of removal; renew all seals disturbed.

**46** If you are installing a new compressor, refer to the compressor manufacturer's instructions for adding refrigerant oil to the system.

**47** Have the system evacuated, charged and leak-tested by the specialist that discharged it.

**48** After installing a new compressor, always observe the following running-in procedure:
  1) *Open all instrument panel air outlet flaps.*
  2) *Start vehicle engine and stabilise idle speed for approximately 5 seconds.*
  3) *Switch fan to maximum speed.*
  4) *Switch on the air conditioning and let it run for at least 2 minutes without interruption at engine speed under 1500 rpm. It might be necessary to have the car doors open, to keep the air conditioning running.*

### Auxiliary fan

**Note:** *An auxiliary fan is only fitted to diesel engine models.*

**49** Firmly apply the handbrake, then jack up the front of the car and support it securely on axle stands (see *Jacking and vehicle support*).

**50** Remove the front bumper as described in Chapter 11.

**51** Disconnect the auxiliary fan wiring connector. Push the two upper mounting lugs inwards and lift the auxiliary fan upwards and off the condenser.

**52** Refitting is the reverse of removal.

# Chapter 4 Part A:
## Fuel and exhaust systems –
## 1.0, 1.2 and 1.4 litre (Z14XEP) petrol engines

# Contents

# Degrees of difficulty

| Easy, suitable for novice with little experience | Fairly easy, suitable for beginner with some experience | Fairly difficult, suitable for competent DIY mechanic | Difficult, suitable for experienced DIY mechanic | Very difficult, suitable for expert DIY or professional |
|---|---|---|---|---|

# Specifications

### General

System type:
| | |
|---|---|
| 1.0 litre, 1.2 litre Z12XEP and 1.4 litre engines . . . . . . . . . . . . . . . . . | Bosch Motronic ME 7.6.1/2 sequential multipoint fuel injection |
| 1.2 litre Z12XE engine . . . . . . . . . . . . . . . . . . . . . . . . . . . . . . . . . . . | Bosch Motronic ME 1.5.5 sequential multipoint fuel injection |

### Fuel pump

| | |
|---|---|
| Type . . . . . . . . . . . . . . . . . . . . . . . . . . . . . . . . . . . . . . . . . . . . . . . . . | Electric, mounted in fuel tank |

### Fuel injection system data

| | |
|---|---|
| System pressure . . . . . . . . . . . . . . . . . . . . . . . . . . . . . . . . . . . . . . . . | 3.8 bars |
| Idle speed (not adjustable – for reference only): | |
| 1.0 litre engines . . . . . . . . . . . . . . . . . . . . . . . . . . . . . . . . . . . . . | 790 to 990 rpm |
| 1.2 litre engines: | |
| Z12XE . . . . . . . . . . . . . . . . . . . . . . . . . . . . . . . . . . . . . . . . . . . | 750 to 810 rpm |
| Z12XEP . . . . . . . . . . . . . . . . . . . . . . . . . . . . . . . . . . . . . . . . . . | 670 to 830 rpm |
| 1.4 litre engines . . . . . . . . . . . . . . . . . . . . . . . . . . . . . . . . . . . . . | 670 to 830 rpm |
| Idle mixture CO content (not adjustable – for reference only) . . . . . . . . | 0.4% maximum |

### Torque wrench settings

| | Nm | lbf ft |
|---|---|---|
| Camshaft position sensor to timing cover . . . . . . . . . . . . . . . . . . . . | 6 | 4 |
| Crankshaft speed/position sensor to cylinder block baseplate . . . . . . . | 8 | 6 |
| Exhaust front pipe to manifold* . . . . . . . . . . . . . . . . . . . . . . . . . . . . | 25 | 18 |
| Exhaust manifold securing nuts*: | | |
| 1.0 and 1.2 litre Z12XEP engines . . . . . . . . . . . . . . . . . . . . . . . . . | 20 | 15 |
| 1.2 litre Z12XE and 1.4 litre engines . . . . . . . . . . . . . . . . . . . . . . . | 15 | 11 |
| Exhaust tailpipe-to-intermediate pipe clamp . . . . . . . . . . . . . . . . . . | 50 | 37 |
| Fuel tank . . . . . . . . . . . . . . . . . . . . . . . . . . . . . . . . . . . . . . . . . . . . | 20 | 15 |
| Knock sensor . . . . . . . . . . . . . . . . . . . . . . . . . . . . . . . . . . . . . . . . . | 20 | 15 |
| Oxygen sensor: | | |
| Catalytic converter control . . . . . . . . . . . . . . . . . . . . . . . . . . . . . . | 40 | 30 |
| Mixture regulation . . . . . . . . . . . . . . . . . . . . . . . . . . . . . . . . . . . . | 40 | 30 |

* Use new nuts

## 1 General information and precautions

### General information

The fuel supply system consists of a fuel tank (which is mounted under the rear of the car, with an electric fuel pump immersed in it), a fuel filter, and fuel feed lines. The fuel pump supplies fuel to the fuel rail, which acts as a reservoir for the fuel injectors which inject fuel into the inlet tracts. The fuel filter incorporated in the feed line from the pump to the fuel rail ensures that the fuel supplied to the injectors is clean. There is no return line from the engine compartment to the fuel tank, only a short line from the fuel filter (on the side of the tank) to the tank. The fuel pressure regulator is located on the fuel pump.

The electronic control unit controls both the fuel injection system and the ignition system, integrating the two into a complete engine management system. Refer to Section 8 for further information on the operation of the fuel system and to Chapter 5B for details of the ignition side of the system.

The 1.0 litre, 1.2 litre Z12XEP and 1.4 litre engines utilise a 'Twinport' inlet manifold configuration. Vacuum-operated flap valves located in the inlet manifold are opened or closed according to engine operating conditions, to create a variable venturi manifold arrangement. This layout has significant advantages in terms of engine power, fuel economy and reduced exhaust emissions. The Z12XE engine utilises a conventional single tract inlet manifold without the twinport system.

The exhaust manifold incorporates an integral catalytic converter to reduce harmful exhaust gas emissions. The remaining exhaust system is in two sections. Further details can be found in Part E of this Chapter, along with details of the other emission control systems and components.

### Precautions

**Note:** *Refer to Part D of this Chapter for general information and precautions relating to the catalytic converter.*

• Before disconnecting any fuel lines, or working on any part of the fuel system, the system must be depressurised as described in Section 4.

• Care must be taken when disconnecting the fuel lines. When disconnecting a fuel union or hose, loosen the union or clamp screw slowly, to avoid sudden uncontrolled fuel spillage. Take adequate fire precautions.

• When working on fuel system components, scrupulous cleanliness must be observed, and care must be taken not to introduce any foreign matter into fuel lines or components.

• After carrying out any work involving disconnection of fuel lines, it is advisable to check the connections for leaks; pressurise the system by switching the ignition on and off several times.

• Electronic control units are very sensitive components, and certain precautions must be taken to avoid damage to these units as follows.

a) When carrying out welding operations on the vehicle using electric welding equipment, the battery and alternator should be disconnected.

b) Although the underbonnet-mounted control units will tolerate normal under-bonnet conditions, they can be adversely affected by excess heat or moisture. If using welding equipment or pressure-washing equipment in the vicinity of an electronic control unit, take care not to direct heat, or jets of water or steam at the unit. If this cannot be avoided, remove the control unit from the vehicle, and protect its wiring plug with a plastic bag.

c) Before disconnecting any wiring, or removing components, always ensure that the ignition is switched off.

d) Do not attempt to improvise fault diagnosis procedures using a test light or multimeter, as irreparable damage could be caused to the control unit.

e) After working on fuel injection/engine management system components, ensure that all wiring is correctly reconnected before reconnecting the battery or switching on the ignition.

⚠ **Warning: Many of the procedures in this Chapter require the disconnection of fuel line connections, and the removal of components, which may result in some fuel spillage. Before carrying out any operation on the fuel system, refer to the precautions given in 'Safety first!' at the beginning of this manual, and follow them implicitly. Petrol is a highly-dangerous and volatile liquid, and the precautions necessary when handling it cannot be overstressed.**

## 2 Air cleaner assembly – removal and refitting

### Removal

1 Release the hose clamp and disconnect the breather hose from the side of the airbox or air inlet trunking **(see illustration)**.

2 On 1.2 litre Z12XE engines, undo the two bolts and lift off the airbox and inlet trunking from the throttle body. On all other engines, slacken the clamp screw and lift the inlet trunking from the throttle body **(see illustrations)**.

3 Disconnect the wiring connector from the air mass meter, then slacken the clamp and withdraw the air mass meter from the air cleaner cover **(see illustrations 10.9, 10.10a and 10.10b)**. Lift the air mass meter and inlet trunking off the engine.

4 Unclip the purge valve from the side of the air cleaner cover **(see illustration)**.

5 Undo the screws, lift off the air cleaner cover, and lift out the air cleaner element **(see illustrations)**.

6 Disconnect the air inlet duct from the front of the air cleaner **(see illustration)**.

**2.1 Disconnecting the breather hose**

**2.2a On 1.2 litre Z12XE engines, undo the bolts . . .**

**2.2b . . . and lift the airbox from the throttle body**

**2.2c On all other engines, slacken the clamp screw (arrowed) and lift the inlet trunking from the throttle body**

**2.4  Unclip the purge valve from the side of the air cleaner cover**

**2.5a  Undo the screws . . .**

**2.5b  . . . lift off the air cleaner cover . . .**

**2.5c  . . . then lift out the element**

**2.6  Removing the front inlet duct from the air cleaner**

**2.7a  Remove the screw . . .**

**7** Unscrew the crossbar mounting screw at the rear of the air cleaner, and release the crossbar rubber mountings from the mounting pegs. Note that the screw retains the purge valve-to-carbon canister line support **(see illustrations)**.

**8** Pull the air cleaner body rearwards from the front mounting rubber **(see illustration)**, and withdraw from the engine compartment.
**9** To remove the intake pipe from the crossmember, undo the retaining screw, and slide the intake pipe to one side to

release it from the radiator crossmember **(see illustrations)**. **Note:** *Where applicable, withdraw the dipstick from its tube.*

### Refitting

**10** Refitting is a reversal of removal.

**3  Accelerator pedal/ position sensor –** removal and refitting

### Removal

**1** Disconnect the battery negative terminal (refer to *Disconnecting the battery* in the Reference Chapter).
**2** Working in the driver's footwell under the facia, disconnect the wiring from the top of the accelerator pedal/position sensor **(see illustration)**. Where necessary, pull back the footwell carpet first.

**2.7b  . . . and release the crossbar from the mounting pegs**

**2.8  Pull the air cleaner from the front mounting rubber**

**3.2  Disconnecting the wiring connector (arrowed) from the accelerator pedal/ position sensor**

**2.9a  To remove the front intake pipe, undo the retaining screw (arrowed) . . .**

**2.9b  . . . then slide the locating pegs (arrowed) out from the crossmember**

**4.2 Undo the two screws and remove the cover over the fuel rail**

3 Unscrew the three mounting nuts, and withdraw the sensor from the bulkhead.

### Refitting

4 Refitting is a reversal of removal.

### 4 Fuel system – depressurising

**Warning: The fuel system is pressurised all the time the ignition is switched on, and a high pressure will remain in the system even 20 minutes after switching off. It is therefore essential to depressurise the system before disconnecting fuel lines, or carrying out any work on the fuel system components. Failure to do this before carrying out work may result in a sudden release of pressure which may cause fuel spray – this constitutes a fire hazard, and a health risk. Note that, even when the system has been depressurised, fuel will still be present in the system fuel lines and components, and adequate precautions should still be taken when carrying out work.**

1 The fuel system referred to in this Section is defined as the tank-mounted fuel pump and pressure regulator, the fuel filter, the fuel injectors, the fuel rail, and the metal pipes and flexible hoses of the fuel lines between these components. All these contain fuel which will be under pressure while the engine is running, and/or while the ignition is switched on. High pressure will remain for at least 20 minutes after the ignition has been switched off, and

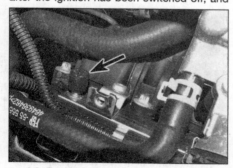

**4.3 Fuel pressure testing point valve (arrowed)**

must be relieved in a controlled fashion when any of these components are disturbed for servicing work.

2 Undo the two screws and remove the cover over the fuel rail (where fitted) **(see illustration)**.

3 Unscrew the cap from the fuel pressure testing point valve on the fuel rail and position a container beneath the valve **(see illustration)**. Note that the valve will be located either on the top right-hand side of the fuel rail, or on the left-hand end.

4 Hold a wad of rag over the valve and relieve the pressure in the fuel system by depressing the valve core with a suitable screwdriver. Be prepared for the squirt of fuel as the valve core is depressed and catch it with the rag. Hold the valve core down until no more fuel is expelled from the valve.

5 Once all pressure is relieved, refit the valve cap and dispose of the expelled fuel and the rag safely.

### 5 Fuel tank – removal and refitting

**Note:** Refer to the precautions in Section 1 before proceeding. Since a fuel tank drain plug is not provided, it is preferable to carry out this work when the tank is nearly empty.

### Removal

1 Depressurise the fuel system (see Section 4).

2 Disconnect the battery negative terminal (refer to Disconnecting the battery in the Reference Chapter).

3 Hand-pump any remaining fuel in the tank out through the filler pipe into a clean metal container which can be sealed.

4 Chock the front wheels then jack up the rear of the vehicle and support on axle stands (see Jacking and vehicle support). Remove both rear wheels.

5 Refer to Chapter 9 and disconnect the front ends of the rear (secondary) handbrake cables from the underbody clips after backing off the primary cable adjustment. Unclip the cables from the underbody and the right-hand side of the fuel tank, then tie them to one side, away from the fuel tank. Where necessary on ECO models, remove the underbody air guide plate.

6 Disconnect the rear of the exhaust system from its rubber mountings, and lower the system, then move it to one side sufficiently to enable removal of the fuel tank. Alternatively, remove the exhaust system completely to provide greater clearance (refer to Section 13).

7 Disconnect the wiring from the fuel pump and fuel gauge sender at the connector on the underbody.

8 Disconnect the fuel feed line and the evaporative vent line at the quick-release connectors on the underbody (if necessary, detach the line retaining bracket from the underbody). Be prepared for some loss of fuel.

A Vauxhall special tool is available to release the fuel line connectors, but provided care is taken, the connectors can be released using a pair of long-nosed pliers, or a similar tool, to depress the retaining tangs.

9 Unscrew the lower filler hose mounting bolt, then unclip the ventilation and carbon canister purge hoses from the bottom of the fuel tank.

10 Loosen the clip and disconnect the fuel filler hose from the fuel tank.

11 Support the weight of the fuel tank on a jack with interposed block of wood.

12 Unbolt and remove the two securing straps from the fuel tank.

13 Lower the tank sufficiently to enable access to the fuel hoses on the tank, then disconnect them. Be prepared for some loss of fuel.

14 Continue to lower the tank until it can be removed from under the vehicle.

15 Plug or clamp the fuel and vent hoses to prevent entry of dust and dirt.

16 If necessary, remove the fuel lines and hoses, heat shield and wiring from the tank for transfer to the new tank. If a new tank is being fitted, it is recommended that the filter is renewed at the same time.

17 If the tank contains sediment or water, it may cleaned out with two or three rinses of clean fuel. Remove the fuel gauge sender unit and fuel pump as described in Sections 6 and 7 respectively. Shake the tank vigorously, and change the fuel as necessary to remove all contamination from the tank.

**Warning: This procedure should be carried out in a well-ventilated area, and it is vital to take adequate fire precautions.**

18 Any repairs to the fuel tank should be carried out by a professional. Do not under any circumstances attempt any form of DIY repair to a fuel tank.

### Refitting

19 Refitting is a reversal of removal, bearing in mind the following points:
a) Ensure that all hoses are securely reconnected to their correct locations.
b) Check the handbrake cable adjustment, as described in Chapter 9.
c) On completion, fill the fuel tank, then run the engine and check for leaks. If leakage is evident, stop the engine immediately and rectify the problem without delay.

### 6 Fuel gauge sender unit – removal and refitting

**Note 1:** Refer to the precautions given in Section 1 before proceeding.
**Note 2:** The fuel tank should be as empty as possible when carrying out this procedure.

### Removal

1 Depressurise the fuel system as described in Section 4.

**6.5a  Prise the plastic cover from the floor . . .**

**6.5b  . . . to expose the fuel pump cover. Locking ring arrowed**

**6.6  Disconnect the fuel gauge sender wiring plug**

**2** Disconnect the battery negative terminal (refer to *Disconnecting the battery* in the Reference Chapter).

**3** Hand-pump any remaining fuel in the tank out through the filler pipe into a clean metal container which can be sealed.

**4** Remove the rear seat as described in Chapter 11.

**5** Fold up the acoustic insulation, then, using a screwdriver, carefully lever out the plastic cover to expose the fuel pump cover **(see illustrations)**.

**6** Disconnect the main wiring plug from the cover **(see illustration)**.

**7** Identify the position of the two fuel lines, then disconnect the quick-release fittings. Be prepared for some loss of fuel. A Vauxhall special tool is available to release the fuel line connectors, but provided care is taken, the connectors can be released using a pair of long-nosed pliers, or a similar tool, to depress the retaining tangs. Clamp or plug the open ends of the hoses, to prevent dirt ingress and further fuel spillage.

**8** Release the fuel pump cover locking ring. A special tool (Vauxhall tool No KM-797) is available for this, but the ring can be removed by tapping anti-clockwise until the locking clips release.

>  **Warning: To prevent the possibility of any sparks which could ignite fuel vapour, use a plastic, wooden or brass tool to release the locking ring.**

**9** Remove the locking ring, then carefully lift the cover from the top of the pump, noting the location of the wiring and hose connections.

**10** Disconnect the sender unit wiring and the fuel pump wiring from the bottom of the cover.

**11** Where applicable, disconnect the earth wiring from the pressure regulator.

**12** Release the clip and disconnect the fuel supply hose from the cover.

**13** Disconnect the fuel return hose from the pressure regulator, and withdraw the cover.

**14** Remove the cover sealing ring.

**15** Press the retaining hook outwards and pull the sender unit from the clips on the side of the fuel pump housing **(see illustration)**.

### Refitting

**16** Refitting is a reversal of removal, bearing in mind the following points:

a) *Ensure that the sender unit engages correctly with the clips on the fuel pump housing.*

b) *Check the condition of the sealing ring on the underside of the fuel pump cover, and renew if necessary.*

c) *Refit the fuel pump cover locking ring by tapping it clockwise until the locking clips 'click' into position.*

## 7  Fuel pump –
testing, removal and refitting

### Testing

**1** If the pump is functioning, it should be possible to hear it 'buzzing' by listening under the rear of the vehicle when the ignition is switched on. Unless the engine is started, the fuel pump should switch off after approximately two seconds. If the noise produced is excessive, this may indicate a faulty pump.

**2** If the pump appears to have failed completely, check the wiring to the pump, and check the appropriate fuse and relay.

**3** To test the performance of the pump, special equipment is required, and it is recommended that any suspected faults are referred to a Vauxhall dealer.

### Removal

**Note:** *Refer to the precautions in Section 1 before proceeding. The fuel tank should be as empty as possible when carrying out this procedure.*

**4** Depressurise the fuel system as described in Section 4.

**5** Disconnect the battery negative terminal (refer to *Disconnecting the battery* in the Reference Chapter).

**6** Hand-pump any remaining fuel in the tank out through the filler pipe into a clean metal container which can be sealed.

**7** Remove the rear seat as described in Chapter 11.

**8** Fold up the acoustic insulation then, using a screwdriver, carefully lever out the plastic cover to expose the fuel pump cover.

**9** Disconnect the main wiring plug from the cover **(see illustration)**.

**6.15  Carefully pull the sender unit from the fuel pump housing**

**10** Identify the position of the two fuel lines, then disconnect the quick-release fittings. Be prepared for some loss of fuel. A Vauxhall special tool is available to release the fuel line connectors, but provided care is taken, the connectors can be released using a pair of long-nosed pliers, or a similar tool, to depress the retaining tangs. Clamp or plug the open ends of the hoses, to prevent dirt ingress and further fuel spillage.

**11** Release the fuel pump cover locking ring. A special tool (Vauxhall tool No KM-797) is available for this, but the ring can be removed by tapping anti-clockwise until the locking clips release **(see illustration)**.

>  **Warning: To prevent the possibility of any sparks which could ignite fuel vapour, use a plastic, wooden or brass tool to release the locking ring.**

**12** Remove the locking ring, then carefully lift

**7.9  Disconnect the fuel pump wiring plug**

7.11 Releasing the fuel pump locking ring using a brass drift

7.13 Disconnect the wiring plugs from the underside of the cover

7.18a Press the three retaining lugs (1 – one shown), and pull the housing from the tank using a hook on the eyelet (2)

7.18b Withdrawing the fuel pump housing from the fuel tank

7.19 Removing the fuel filter from the base of the fuel pump

the cover from the top of the pump, noting the location of the wiring and hose connections.

13 Disconnect the sender unit wiring and the fuel pump wiring from the bottom of the cover **(see illustration)**.

14 Where applicable, disconnect the earth wiring from the pressure regulator.

15 Release the clip and disconnect the fuel supply hose from the cover.

16 Disconnect the fuel return hose from the pressure regulator, and withdraw the cover.

17 Remove the cover sealing ring.

18 Press the three pump housing retaining lugs to release them, and simultaneously pull the pump housing from the tank using a wire hook engaged with the eyelet provided **(see illustrations)**.

19 To remove the pump from the housing, first pull the filter from the base of the pump **(see illustration)** and disconnect the wires from the pump. Note the wire locations to ensure correct refitting.

20 Compress the three locking tabs, and pull the pump mounting plate and the pump from the housing **(see illustrations)**.

21 Disconnect the wiring and if necessary, remove the filter from the bottom of the fuel pump.

## Refitting

22 Refitting is a reversal of removal, bearing in mind the following points:

a) *Before refitting the filter to the bottom of the pump, inspect the filter for contamination or blockage, and renew if necessary.*

b) *Ensure that the pump mounting plate engages correctly with the retaining clips on the housing.*

c) *Check the condition of the sealing ring on the underside of the fuel pump cover, and renew if necessary.*

d) *Refit the fuel pump cover locking ring by tapping it clockwise until the locking clips 'click' into position.*

7.20a Compress the three locking tabs (arrowed) . . .

7.20b . . . and withdraw the pump from the housing

## 8 Fuel injection system – general information

The fuel injection system is integrated with the ignition system to form a combined engine management system under the control of one electronic control unit (ECU). The two Motronic systems covered in this Chapter are virtually identical in terms of their sensors and actuators, the main difference lies in the software contained in the ECU.

Fuel is supplied from the rear-mounted tank, via a pressure regulator and fuel filter, to the fuel rail. The fuel rail acts as a reservoir for the fuel injectors, which inject fuel into the cylinder inlet tracts, upstream of the inlet valves. The Motronic systems are of the 'sequential' injection type, which means that each of the three (1.0 litre engines), or four (1.2 and 1.4 litre engines) fuel injectors is triggered individually, just before the inlet valve on the relevant cylinder opens.

The duration of the electrical pulses to the fuel injectors determines the quantity of fuel injected. The pulse duration is computed by the ECU on the basis of information received from the following sensors:

a) *Accelerator pedal position sensor – informs the ECU of accelerator pedal position, and the rate of throttle opening/ closing.*

b) *Air mass meter – informs the ECU of the load on the engine (expressed in terms of the mass of air passing from the air cleaner to the throttle body).*

c) *Crankshaft speed/position sensor – informs the ECU of the crankshaft speed and position.*

d) *Camshaft position sensor – informs the ECU when No 1 cylinder is at top dead centre (TDC) on the firing stroke (expressed in terms of the position of the inlet camshaft).*

e) *Coolant temperature sensor – informs the ECU of engine temperature.*

f) *Exhaust gas oxygen sensors (two) – inform the ECU of the oxygen content of the exhaust gases (explained in greater detail in Chapter 4E).*

g) *Knock sensor – informs the ECU when*

engine 'knock' (pre-ignition) occurs (explained in greater detail in Chapter 5B).

h) Wheel speed sensor – informs the ECU of the vehicle speed (explained in greater detail in Chapter 9).

The signals from the various sensors are processed by the ECU, and the optimum fuelling and ignition settings are selected for the prevailing engine operating conditions.

Idle speed and throttle position is controlled by the throttle valve control motor, which is an integral part of the throttle body. The motor is controlled by the electronic control unit, in conjunction with signals received from the accelerator pedal position sensor.

A catalytic converter is incorporated in the exhaust manifold, to reduce harmful exhaust gas emissions. Details of this and other emissions control system equipment are given in Chapter 4E.

If certain sensors fail, and send abnormal signals to the ECU, the ECU has a back-up programme. In this event, the abnormal signals are ignored, and a preprogrammed value is substituted for the sensor signal, allowing the engine to continue running, albeit at reduced efficiency. If the ECU enters its back-up mode, a warning light on the instrument panel will illuminate, and a fault code will be stored in the ECU memory. This fault code can be read using suitable specialist test equipment.

## 9  Fuel injection system components – testing

**1** If a fault appears in the engine management system, first ensure that all the system wiring connectors are securely connected and free of corrosion. Ensure that the fault is not due to poor maintenance; ie, check that the air cleaner filter element is clean, the spark plugs are in good condition and correctly gapped, the cylinder compression pressures are correct and that the engine breather hoses are clear and undamaged, referring to Chapters 1A and 2A for further information.

**2** If these checks fail to reveal the cause of the problem, the vehicle should be taken to a suitably-equipped Vauxhall dealer or engine management diagnostic specialist for testing. A diagnostic socket is located in the centre of the facia, above the centre console, to which a fault code reader or other suitable test equipment can be connected **(see illustration)**. By using the code reader or test equipment, the engine management ECU can be interrogated, and any stored fault codes can be retrieved. Live data can also be captured from the various system sensors and actuators, indicating their operating parameters. This will allow the fault to be quickly and simply traced, alleviating the need to test all the system components individually, which is a time-consuming operation that carries a risk of damaging the ECU.

**9.2  Diagnostic socket location in the centre of the facia**

## 10  Fuel injection system components – removal and refitting

### Throttle body

#### Removal

**1** Disconnect the battery negative terminal (refer to *Disconnecting the battery* in the Reference Chapter).

**2** Remove the air cleaner cover, inlet trunking and airbox from the top of the throttle body, with reference to Section 2.

**3** Disconnect the wiring from the throttle valve control motor **(see illustration)**.

**4** Partially drain the cooling system as described in Chapter 1A (drain sufficient coolant to empty the coolant expansion tank).

**5** Release the retaining clips and disconnect

**10.3  Disconnect the wiring from the throttle valve control motor**

**10.9  Air mass meter wiring connector (arrowed)**

the two coolant hoses from the rear of the throttle body.

**6** Undo the four bolts and lift the throttle body off the inlet manifold **(see illustration)**. Recover the gasket.

**7** It is not possible to obtain the throttle valve control motor or throttle valve position sensor separately, so if either is faulty, the complete throttle body must be renewed.

#### Refitting

**8** Refitting is a reversal of removal, but thoroughly clean the mating faces and use a new gasket. Tighten the bolts progressively and securely. Top-up the coolant level as described in *Weekly checks*. Finally, switch on the ignition for 30 seconds without starting the engine.

### Air mass meter

#### Removal

**9** Disconnect the wiring from the air mass meter at the right-hand rear corner of the engine compartment **(see illustration)**.

**10** Slacken the retaining clamps and remove the air mass meter from the air cleaner cover and inlet trunking **(see illustrations)**.

#### Refitting

**11** Refitting is a reversal of removal, but ensure that the arrow on the air mass meter body points toward the throttle body when fitted.

### Fuel injectors and fuel rail

**Note:** *Refer to the precautions given in Section 1 before proceeding. The seals at both ends of the fuel injectors must be renewed on refitting.*

**10.6  Throttle body retaining bolts (arrowed)**

**10.10a  Slacken the retaining clamps . . .**

10.10b ... and remove the air mass meter

10.17 Fuel injector wiring connectors (arrowed)

10.23 Fit new O-rings (arrowed) to the fuel injectors before refitting

## Removal

**12** Depressurise the fuel system as described in Section 4.

**13** Disconnect the battery negative terminal (refer to *Disconnecting the battery* in the Reference Chapter).

**14** Remove the throttle body as described previously in this Section, although, it is not necessary to drain the cooling system, as the body can be placed to one side with the hoses still attached.

**15** Loosen the clip and disconnect the engine breather hose from the camshaft cover.

**16** Undo the two screws and remove the cover over the fuel rail (where fitted) **(see illustration 4.2)**.

**17** Disconnect the wiring connector from each fuel injector **(see illustration)**.

**18** Disconnect the fuel feed hose quick-release connector at the fuel rail. Be prepared for some loss of fuel. A Vauxhall special tool is available to release the connector, but provided care is taken, it can be released using a pair of long-nosed pliers, or a similar tool, to depress the retaining tangs. Clamp or plug the open end of the hose, to prevent dirt ingress and further fuel spillage.

**19** Unscrew the mounting bolts, then lift the fuel rail complete with the injectors off of the inlet manifold.

**20** To remove an injector from the fuel rail, prise out the metal securing clip using a screwdriver or a pair of pliers, and pull the injector from the fuel rail. Remove and discard the injector sealing rings; new ones must be fitted on refitting.

**21** Overhaul of the fuel injectors is not possible, as no spares are available. If faulty, an injector must be renewed.

## Refitting

**22** Before refitting, clean thoroughly the mating surfaces of the throttle body and inlet manifold.

**23** Commence refitting by fitting new O-ring seals to both ends of the fuel injectors **(see illustration)**. Coat the seals with a thin layer of petroleum jelly before fitting.

**24** Refitting is a reversal of removal, bearing in mind the following points:

a) *When refitting the injectors to the fuel rail, note that the groove in the metal securing clip must engage with the lug on the injector body.*

b) *Make sure that the quick-release connector audibly engages on the fuel rail.*

c) *Refit the throttle body as described previously in this Section.*

d) *Ensure that all wiring connectors are securely reconnected, and that the wiring is secured in the relevant clips and brackets.*

## *Crankshaft speed/position sensor*

**Note:** *A new O-ring seal must be used on refitting.*

### Removal

**25** The crankshaft speed/position sensor is located at the rear left-hand end of the cylinder block baseplate, below the starter motor **(see illustration)**.

**26** Apply the handbrake, then jack up the front of the vehicle and support it on axle stands (see *Jacking and vehicle support*). On ECO models, remove the engine undertray.

**27** Disconnect the sensor wiring connector, then undo the retaining bolt and withdraw the sensor from the cylinder block baseplate.

### Refitting

**28** Refitting is a reversal of removal, but ensure that the mating surfaces of the sensor and baseplate are clean and fit a new O-ring seal to the sensor before refitting. Tighten the bolt to the specified torque.

## *Camshaft position sensor*

### Removal

**29** The camshaft position sensor is located on the timing cover, on the inlet camshaft side.

**30** Disconnect the sensor wiring connector.

**31** Undo the retaining bolt and withdraw the sensor from the timing cover.

### Refitting

**32** Refitting is a reversal of removal, but ensure that the mating surfaces of the sensor and timing cover are clean before fitting.

## *Coolant temperature sensor*

**33** The coolant temperature sensor is located in the top of the coolant pump housing **(see illustration)**.

**34** Removal and refitting procedures are given in Chapter 3.

## *Oxygen sensor – mixture regulation*

**Caution: The sensor will be very hot if the engine has been running within 10 or 15 minutes.**

### Removal

**35** The mixture regulation oxygen sensor is located on the exhaust manifold/catalytic converter **(see illustration)**.

**36** First, trace the wiring back from the sensor to the connector next to the oil filter, and disconnect it.

**37** Release the wiring from the clip.

**38** Unscrew the sensor from the exhaust manifold. Ideally, a special 'split' socket should be used, as this will locate over the sensor wiring.

10.25 Crankshaft speed/position sensor location

10.33 Coolant temperature sensor (arrowed) located in the top of the coolant pump housing

## Refitting

**39** Clean the threads of the sensor then coat them with Vauxhall special grease for oxygen sensors. If a new sensor is being fitted, it will be supplied with the threads already coated with the special grease to prevent it seizing in the manifold.

**40** Screw the sensor into the exhaust manifold/catalytic converter and tighten to the specified torque.

**41** Reconnect the wiring and clip it in place.

### *Oxygen sensor – catalytic converter control*

**Caution: The sensor will be very hot if the engine has been running within 10 or 15 minutes.**

### Removal

**42** The catalytic converter control oxygen sensor is located in the exhaust front pipe, just behind the flexible section **(see illustration)**.

**43** First, apply the handbrake, then jack up the front of the vehicle and support it on axle stands (see *Jacking and vehicle support*).

**44** Trace the wiring back from the sensor to the connector above the right-hand driveshaft, and disconnect it. Release the wiring from the clip.

**45** Unscrew the sensor from the exhaust front pipe. Ideally, a special 'split' socket should be used, as this will locate over the sensor wiring.

### Refitting

**46** Clean the threads of the sensor then coat them with Vauxhall special grease for oxygen sensors. If a new sensor is being fitted, it will be supplied with the threads already coated with the special grease to prevent it seizing in the pipe.

**47** Screw the sensor into the exhaust front pipe and tighten to the specified torque.

**48** Reconnect the wiring and clip it in place.

### *Knock sensor*

### Removal

**49** The knock sensor is located on the rear of the cylinder block, just above the starter motor.

**50** Disconnect the battery negative terminal (refer to *Disconnecting the battery* in the Reference Chapter).

**51** Apply the handbrake, then jack up the front of the vehicle and support it on axle stands (see *Jacking and vehicle support*). On ECO models, remove the engine undertray.

**52** On the left-hand side of the engine, disconnect the wiring connectors for the engine electronic control unit by releasing them in the direction of the arrow marked on the connector.

**53** Unscrew the bolt securing the earth wire to the cylinder head, then unbolt and remove the electronic control unit.

**54** Reach up behind the engine and disconnect the wiring from the knock sensor.

**55** Note its position, then unscrew the bolt and remove the knock sensor from the block.

## Refitting

**56** Clean the contact surfaces of the sensor and block. Also clean the threads of the sensor mounting bolt.

**57** Locate the sensor on the block and insert the mounting bolt. Position the sensor as previously noted, then tighten the bolt to the specified torque. Note that the torque setting is critical for the sensor to function correctly.

**58** Reconnect the wiring, then refit the engine control unit together with its wiring and earth wire.

**59** Refit the engine undertray where applicable, lower the vehicle to the ground and reconnect the battery.

### *Electronic control unit (ECU)*

### Removal

**60** The engine management electronic control unit is located on the rear, left-hand side of the engine.

**61** Disconnect the battery negative terminal (refer to *Disconnecting the battery* in the Reference Chapter).

**62** Disconnect the wiring connectors for the electronic control unit by releasing them in the direction of the arrow marked on the connector **(see illustration)**.

**63** Unscrew the bolt securing the earth wire to the cylinder head, then unbolt and remove the control unit.

### Refitting

**64** Refitting is a reversal of removal.

### *Wheel speed sensor*

**65** Refer to the anti-lock braking system information contained in Chapter 9.

### 11 Inlet manifold – removal and refitting

### *Removal*

**1** Apply the handbrake, then jack up the front of the vehicle and support it on axle stands (see *Jacking and vehicle support*). On ECO models, remove the engine undertray.

**10.42 Exhaust gas oxygen sensor for catalytic converter control (arrowed) located in the exhaust front pipe**

**10.35 Exhaust gas oxygen sensor for mixture regulation (arrowed)**

**2** Disconnect the battery negative terminal (refer to *Disconnecting the battery* in the Reference Chapter).

**3** Drain the coolant as described in Chapter 1A.

**4** Remove the throttle body as described in Section 10.

**5** Disconnect the fuel evaporation system hose from the inlet manifold.

**6** Depressurise the fuel system as described in Section 4.

**7** Disconnect the fuel supply line from the fuel rail and release it from the support clip. A quick-release connector is fitted and Vauxhall technicians use a special tool to release it, however, provided care is taken, the connector can be released using a pair of long-nosed pliers, or a similar tool, to depress the retaining tangs.

**8** Disconnect the crankcase ventilation hose from the camshaft cover, and the brake servo vacuum line from the inlet manifold.

**9** Disconnect the wiring from the injectors and engine electronic control unit, also unbolt the earth cable and unclip the wiring conduit. Place the wiring harness to one side.

**10** Working beneath the vehicle, disconnect the wiring from the starter motor and release it from the supports on the inlet manifold.

**11** Unbolt the EGR valve pipe from the EGR valve housing and position to one side. Discard the gasket; a new one must be used for refitting.

**12** Unscrew the nuts and withdraw the inlet manifold from the cylinder head. Discard the seals; new ones must be used for refitting.

**10.62 Disconnect the wiring connectors from the electronic control unit. Note the location of the earth lead (arrowed)**

## Refitting

**13** Thoroughly clean the mating face of the inlet manifold and cylinder head, then locate the new rubber seals in the grooves in the manifold mating face **(see illustration)**.

**14** Locate the inlet manifold over the cylinder head studs and secure with the nuts tightened progressively and securely.

**15** Refit the EGR valve pipe together with a new gasket, and tighten the bolts securely.

**16** Reconnect the wiring to the starter, injectors and engine control unit, and tighten the earth cable bolt.

**17** Reconnect the brake servo vacuum line and crankcase ventilation hose.

**18** Reconnect the fuel supply line to the fuel rail, making sure that an audible click is heard as it engages.

**19** Reconnect the fuel evaporation system hose to the inlet manifold.

**20** Refit the throttle body with reference to Section 10.

**21** Where applicable, refit the cover over the fuel rail.

**22** Refit the engine undertray where necessary, then lower the vehicle to the ground.

**23** Reconnect the battery negative, then refill and bleed the cooling system with reference to Chapter 1A.

## 12 Exhaust manifold/ catalytic converter – removal and refitting

**Note 1:** *New manifold retaining nuts, a new*

**12.4 Exhaust front pipe-to-manifold/ catalytic converter joint**

**12.10a Remove the exhaust manifold heat shield . . .**

**11.13 Fit new individual rubber seals to the grooves in the inlet manifold**

*manifold gasket, exhaust front pipe gasket and oil dipstick guide tube O-rings must be used on refitting.*

**Note 2:** *Either a cast iron, or a pressed steel manifold may be fitted according to engine type. The following procedures are applicable to both types, but the pressed steel manifold does not have a separate heat shield.*

## Removal

**1** Apply the handbrake, then jack up the front of the vehicle and support it on axle stands (see *Jacking and vehicle support*).

**2** Disconnect the battery negative lead (refer to *Disconnecting the battery* in the Reference Chapter).

**3** On models with air conditioning, unbolt the compressor from the front of the engine with reference to Chapter 3, and support it to one side. **Do not** disconnect the refrigerant lines from the compressor.

**12.8 Remove the engine lifting bracket from the front of the cylinder head**

**12.10b . . . then undo the exhaust manifold retaining nuts . . .**

**4** Refer to Section 10 and disconnect the wiring from the mixture regulation oxygen sensor on the catalytic converter, then unbolt the exhaust front pipe from the exhaust manifold/catalytic converter, taking care to support the flexible section **(see illustration)**. **Note:** *Angular movement in excess of 10° can cause permanent damage to the flexible section.* Recover the gasket.

**5** Release the mounting rubbers and support the front of the exhaust pipe to one side.

**6** Where applicable, undo the two lower exhaust manifold support bolts.

**7** Remove the mixture regulation oxygen sensor from the exhaust manifold as described in Section 10.

**8** Unbolt the engine lifting eye from the cylinder head **(see illustration)**.

**9** Unbolt and remove the oil dipstick guide tube, and withdraw it from the baseplate. Remove and discard the O-ring seals.

**10** Unbolt the heat shield (where fitted), then undo the retaining nuts and withdraw the exhaust manifold/catalytic converter downwards from the cylinder head studs **(see illustrations)**. Recover the gasket.

## Refitting

**11** Thoroughly clean the mating face of the exhaust manifold and cylinder head, then locate a new gasket over the studs.

**12** Locate the exhaust manifold/catalytic converter over the cylinder head studs and secure with the (new) nuts tightened progressively to the specified torque.

**13** Refit the heat shield and tighten the retaining bolts.

**14** Fit the new O-ring seals to the oil dipstick guide tube, then insert the tube in the baseplate. Insert and tighten the retaining bolt.

**15** Refit the left-hand lifting eye and tighten the bolt.

**16** Refer to Section 10 and refit the mixture regulation oxygen sensor to the manifold/ catalytic converter. Tighten to the specified torque.

**17** Where applicable, refit the two lower exhaust manifold support bolts.

**18** Refit the exhaust front pipe to the manifold/catalytic converter together with a new gasket, then tighten the (new) nuts to the specified torque.

**12.10c . . . and withdraw the manifold from the cylinder head studs**

**19** On air conditioning models, refit the compressor to the front of the engine with reference to Chapter 3.

**20** Lower the vehicle to the ground, then reconnect the battery negative lead.

## 13 Exhaust system – general information and component renewal

### General information

**1** The exhaust system is in two sections. The front section includes the catalytic converter control oxygen sensor, silencer and intermediate pipe. The rear section consists of the tailpipe and silencer.

**2** Periodically, the exhaust system should be checked for signs of leaks or damage. Also inspect the system rubber mountings, and renew if necessary.

**3** Small holes or cracks can be repaired using proprietary exhaust repair products.

**4** Before renewing an individual section of the exhaust system, it is wise to inspect the remaining section. If corrosion or damage is evident, it may prove more economical to renew the entire system.

### Component renewal

**5** If either part of the system is to be renewed, it is important to ensure that the correct component is obtained.

**6** To remove the rear tailpipe and silencer, chock the front wheels then jack up the rear of the vehicle and support on axle stands (see *Jacking and vehicle support*). Loosen the clamp securing the intermediate pipe to the tailpipe, then release the rubber mountings and slide the tailpipe from the intermediate pipe. If the tailpipe is rusted onto the intermediate pipe, apply liberal amounts of penetrating oil and tap around the joint with a hammer to free it. Twist the tailpipe in both directions while holding the intermediate pipe.

**7** To remove the front section of the exhaust, jack up the front and rear of the vehicle and support it on axle stands (see *Jacking and vehicle support*). Remove the tailpipe and silencer as described in paragraph 6, then remove the oxygen sensor from the front pipe as described in Section 10. Unbolt

**13.7 Exhaust front pipe-to-catalytic converter/exhaust manifold joint**

the exhaust front pipe from the catalytic converter/exhaust manifold **(see illustration)**, taking care to support the flexible section. **Note:** *Angular movement in excess of 10° can cause permanent damage to the flexible section.* Recover the gasket. Release the rubber mountings and withdraw the exhaust from under the vehicle.

**8** Refitting is a reversal of removal, but renew all gaskets and tighten the clamp and front pipe flange nuts to the specified torque.

# Chapter 4 Part B:
# Fuel and exhaust systems –
# 1.4 litre (Z14XE) petrol engines

## Contents

## Degrees of difficulty

| **Easy,** suitable for novice with little experience  | **Fairly easy,** suitable for beginner with some experience | **Fairly difficult,** suitable for competent DIY mechanic | **Difficult,** suitable for experienced DIY mechanic | **Very difficult,** suitable for expert DIY or professional |
|---|---|---|---|---|

## Specifications

### General
System type . . . . . . . . . . . . . . . . . . . . . . . . . . . . . . . . . . . . . . .    Multec S(F) sequential multipoint fuel injection

### Fuel pump
Type . . . . . . . . . . . . . . . . . . . . . . . . . . . . . . . . . . . . . . . . . . . .    Electric, mounted in fuel tank

### Fuel injection system data
System pressure . . . . . . . . . . . . . . . . . . . . . . . . . . . . . . . . . . . .    3.8 bars
Idle speed (not adjustable – for reference only) . . . . . . . . . . . . . . . . .    710 to 930 rpm
Idle mixture CO content (not adjustable – for reference only) . . . . . . . .    0.4 % maximum

### Torque wrench settings

| | Nm | lbf ft |
|---|---|---|
| Accelerator pedal/position sensor . . . . . . . . . . . . . . . . . . . . . . . . . . . | 9 | 7 |
| Coolant flange to inlet manifold . . . . . . . . . . . . . . . . . . . . . . . . . . . | 20 | 15 |
| Crankshaft speed/position sensor . . . . . . . . . . . . . . . . . . . . . . . . . . | 8 | 6 |
| EGR valve to lower inlet manifold . . . . . . . . . . . . . . . . . . . . . . . . . . | 20 | 15 |
| Engine electronic control unit . . . . . . . . . . . . . . . . . . . . . . . . . . . . . | 8 | 6 |
| Exhaust front pipe-to-manifold/catalytic converter nuts . . . . . . . . . . . | 25 | 18 |
| Exhaust manifold/catalytic converter securing nuts* . . . . . . . . . . . . . | 22 | 16 |
| Exhaust tailpipe-to-intermediate pipe clamp . . . . . . . . . . . . . . . . . . . | 50 | 37 |
| Fuel tank . . . . . . . . . . . . . . . . . . . . . . . . . . . . . . . . . . . . . . . . . . | 20 | 15 |
| Inlet manifold lower section-to-cylinder head nuts* . . . . . . . . . . . . . . . | 20 | 15 |
| Inlet manifold support: | | |
|    To inlet manifold . . . . . . . . . . . . . . . . . . . . . . . . . . . . . . . . . . . | 20 | 15 |
|    To cylinder block . . . . . . . . . . . . . . . . . . . . . . . . . . . . . . . . . . . | 35 | 26 |
| Inlet manifold upper section to lower section . . . . . . . . . . . . . . . . . . | 8 | 6 |
| Knock sensor . . . . . . . . . . . . . . . . . . . . . . . . . . . . . . . . . . . . . . . | 20 | 15 |
| Manifold absolute pressure sensor . . . . . . . . . . . . . . . . . . . . . . . . . | 8 | 6 |
| Oxygen sensor: | | |
|    Catalytic converter control . . . . . . . . . . . . . . . . . . . . . . . . . . . . . | 30 | 22 |
|    Mixture regulation . . . . . . . . . . . . . . . . . . . . . . . . . . . . . . . . . . . | 30 | 22 |

* Use new nuts

## 1 General information and precautions

### General information

The fuel supply system consists of a fuel tank (which is mounted under the rear of the car, with an electric fuel pump immersed in it), a fuel filter, and fuel feed lines. The fuel pump supplies fuel to the fuel rail, which acts as a reservoir for the fuel injectors which inject fuel into the inlet tracts. The fuel filter incorporated in the feed line from the pump to the fuel rail ensures that the fuel supplied to the injectors is clean. There is no return line from the engine compartment to the fuel tank, only a short line from the fuel filter (on the side of the tank) to the tank. The fuel pressure regulator is located on the fuel pump.

The electronic control unit controls both the fuel injection system and the ignition system, integrating the two into a complete engine management system. Refer to Section 8 for further information on the operation of the fuel system and to Chapter 5B for details of the ignition side of the system.

The exhaust manifold incorporates an integral catalytic converter to reduce harmful exhaust gas emissions. The remaining exhaust system is in two sections. Further details can be found in Part E of this Chapter, along with details of the other emission control systems and components.

### Precautions

**Note:** *Refer to Part D of this Chapter for general information and precautions relating to the catalytic converter.*

• Before disconnecting any fuel lines, or working on any part of the fuel system, the system must be depressurised as described in Section 4.
• Care must be taken when disconnecting the fuel lines. When disconnecting a fuel union or hose, loosen the union or clamp screw slowly, to avoid sudden uncontrolled fuel spillage. Take adequate fire precautions.
• When working on fuel system components, scrupulous cleanliness must be observed, and care must be taken not to introduce any foreign matter into fuel lines or components.
• After carrying out any work involving disconnection of fuel lines, it is advisable to check the connections for leaks; pressurise the system by switching the ignition on and off several times.
• Electronic control units are very sensitive components, and certain precautions must be taken to avoid damage to these units as follows.
 a) *When carrying out welding operations on the vehicle using electric welding equipment, the battery and alternator should be disconnected.*
 b) *Although the underbonnet-mounted control units will tolerate normal underbonnet conditions, they can be adversely affected by excess heat or moisture. If using welding equipment or pressure-washing equipment in the vicinity of an electronic control unit, take care not to direct heat, or jets of water or steam, at the unit. If this cannot be avoided, remove the control unit from the vehicle, and protect its wiring plug with a plastic bag.*
 c) *Before disconnecting any wiring, or removing components, always ensure that the ignition is switched off.*
 d) *Do not attempt to improvise fault diagnosis procedures using a test light or multimeter, as irreparable damage could be caused to the control unit.*
 e) *After working on fuel injection/engine management system components, ensure that all wiring is correctly reconnected before reconnecting the battery or switching on the ignition.*

⚠ **Warning: Many of the procedures in this Chapter require the disconnection of fuel line connections, and the removal of components, which may result in some fuel spillage. Before carrying out any operation on the fuel system, refer to the precautions given in 'Safety first!' at the beginning of this manual, and follow them implicitly. Petrol is a highly-dangerous and volatile liquid, and the precautions necessary when handling it cannot be overstressed.**

## 2 Air cleaner assembly – removal and refitting

### Removal

**1** Unscrew the oil filler cap, then unscrew the engine top cover securing bolts and lift off the cover. Screw the cap back into the camshaft cover.
**2** Disconnect the wiring from the air temperature sensor and evaporative system purge valve. Unclip the valve from the side of the air cleaner cover.
**3** Loosen the clip and disconnect the airbox crankcase ventilation hose from the camshaft cover.
**4** Loosen the clip and remove the airbox from

**3.2 Disconnecting the wiring connector (arrowed) from the accelerator pedal/ position sensor**

the throttle body. Loosen the clip and separate the airbox and duct from the air cleaner cover.
**5** Disconnect the air inlet duct from the front of the air cleaner.
**6** Unscrew the crossbar mounting bolt from the rear of the air cleaner, then pull the air cleaner body rearwards from the front mounting rubber, and withdraw from the engine compartment.
**7** If necessary, release the securing clips and lift off the air cleaner cover. Lift out the air cleaner element.
**8** To remove the intake pipe from the crossmember, undo the retaining screw, and slide the intake pipe to one side to release it from the radiator crossmember.

### Refitting

**9** Refitting is a reversal of removal.

## 3 Accelerator pedal/ position sensor – removal and refitting

### Removal

**1** Disconnect the battery negative terminal (refer to *Disconnecting the battery* in the Reference Chapter).
**2** Working in the driver's footwell under the facia, disconnect the wiring from the top of the accelerator pedal/position sensor **(see illustration)**. Where necessary, pull back the footwell carpet first.
**3** Unscrew the three mounting nuts, and withdraw the sensor from the bulkhead.

### Refitting

**4** Refitting is a reversal of removal.

## 4 Fuel system – depressurising

⚠ **Warning: The fuel system is pressurised all the time the ignition is switched on, and a high pressure will remain in the system even 20 minutes after switching off. It is therefore essential to depressurise the system before disconnecting fuel lines, or carrying out any work on the fuel system components. Failure to do this before carrying out work may result in a sudden release of pressure which may cause fuel spray – this constitutes a fire hazard, and a health risk. Note that, even when the system has been depressurised, fuel will still be present in the system fuel lines and components, and adequate precautions should still be taken when carrying out work.**

**1** The fuel system referred to in this Section is defined as the tank-mounted fuel pump and pressure regulator, the fuel filter, the fuel injectors, the fuel rail, and the metal pipes and flexible hoses of the fuel lines between these components. All these contain fuel which will be under pressure while the engine is running, and/or while the ignition is switched on. High pressure will remain for at least 20 minutes after the ignition has been switched off, and must be relieved in a controlled fashion when any of these components are disturbed for servicing work.

2 Unscrew the cap from the fuel pressure testing point valve on the fuel rail and position a container beneath the valve. Hold a wad of rag over the valve and relieve the pressure in the fuel system by depressing the valve core with a suitable screwdriver. Be prepared for the squirt of fuel as the valve core is depressed and catch it with the rag. Hold the valve core down until no more fuel is expelled from the valve.

4 Once all pressure is relieved, refit the valve cap and dispose of the expelled fuel and the rag safely.

## 5  Fuel tank –
### removal and refitting
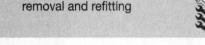

**Note 1:** *Refer to the precautions given in Section 1 before proceeding.*
**Note 2:** *The fuel tank should be as empty as possible when carrying out this procedure.*

### Removal

1 Depressurise the fuel system as described in Section 4.
2 Disconnect the battery negative terminal (refer to *Disconnecting the battery* in the Reference Chapter).
3 Hand-pump any remaining fuel in the tank out through the filler pipe into a clean metal container which can be sealed.
4 Chock the front wheels then jack up the rear of the vehicle and support on axle stands (see *Jacking and vehicle support*). Remove both rear wheels.
5 Refer to Chapter 9 and disconnect the front ends of the rear (secondary) handbrake cables from the underbody clips after backing off the primary cable adjustment. Unclip the cables from the underbody and the right-hand side of the fuel tank, then tie them to one side, away from the fuel tank.
6 Disconnect the rear of the exhaust system from its rubber mountings, and lower the system, then move it to one side sufficiently to enable removal of the fuel tank. Alternatively,

remove the exhaust system completely to provide greater clearance (refer to Section 13).
7 Disconnect the wiring from the fuel pump and fuel gauge sensor, at the connector on the underbody.
8 Disconnect the fuel feed line and the evaporative vent line at the quick-release connectors on the underbody (if necessary, detach the line retaining bracket from the underbody). Be prepared for some loss of fuel. A Vauxhall special tool is available to release the fuel line connectors, but provided care is taken, the connectors can be released using a pair of long-nosed pliers, or a similar tool, to depress the retaining tangs.
9 Loosen the clip and disconnect the fuel filler hose from the fuel tank.
10 Support the weight of the fuel tank on a jack with interposed block of wood.
11 Unbolt and remove the two securing straps from the fuel tank.
12 Lower the tank sufficiently to enable access to the fuel hoses on the tank, then disconnect them. Be prepared for some loss of fuel.
13 Continue to lower the tank until it can be removed from under the vehicle.
14 Plug or clamp the fuel and vent hoses to prevent entry of dust and dirt.
15 If necessary, remove the fuel lines and hoses, heat shield and wiring from the tank for transfer to the new tank. If a new tank is being fitted, it is recommended that the filter is renewed at the same time.

### Refitting

16 If the tank contains sediment or water, it may cleaned out with two or three rinses of clean fuel. Remove the fuel gauge sender unit and fuel pump as described in Sections 6 and 7 respectively. Shake the tank vigorously, and change the fuel as often as is necessary to remove all contamination from the tank. *This procedure should be carried out in a well-ventilated area, and it is vital to take adequate fire precautions.*
17 Any repairs to the fuel tank should be carried out by a professional. Do not under any circumstances attempt any form of DIY repair to a fuel tank.
18 Refitting is a reversal of removal, bearing in mind the following points:
 a) *Ensure that all hoses are securely*

reconnected to their correct locations.
 b) *Check the handbrake cable adjustment, as described in Chapter 9.*
 c) *On completion, fill the fuel tank, then run the engine and check for leaks. If leakage is evident, stop the engine immediately and rectify the problem without delay.*

## 6  Fuel gauge sender unit
### – removal and refitting

**Note:** *Refer to the precautions in Section 1 before proceeding.*
**Note:** *The fuel tank should be as empty as possible when carrying out this procedure.*

### Removal

1 Depressurise the fuel system as described in Section 4.
2 Disconnect the battery negative terminal (refer to *Disconnecting the battery* in the Reference Chapter).
3 Hand-pump any remaining fuel in the tank out through the filler pipe into a clean metal container which can be sealed.
4 Remove the rear seat as described in Chapter 11.
5 Fold up the acoustic insulation then, using a screwdriver, carefully lever out the plastic cover to expose the fuel pump cover **(see illustrations)**.
6 Disconnect the main wiring plug from the cover **(see illustration)**.
7 Identify the position of the two fuel lines, then disconnect the quick-release fittings. Be prepared for some loss of fuel. A Vauxhall special tool is available to release the fuel line connectors, but provided care is taken, the connectors can be released using a pair of long-nosed pliers, or a similar tool, to depress the retaining tangs. Clamp or plug the open ends of the hoses, to prevent dirt ingress and further fuel spillage.
8 Release the fuel pump cover locking ring. A special tool (Vauxhall tool No KM-797) is available for this, but the ring can be removed by tapping anti-clockwise until the locking clips release.

⚠️ **Warning: To prevent the possibility of any sparks which could ignite fuel vapour, use a plastic, wooden or brass tool to release the locking ring.**

**6.5a  Prise the plastic cover from the floor . . .**

**6.5b  . . . to expose the fuel pump cover. Locking ring arrowed**

**6.6  Disconnect the fuel gauge sender wiring plug**

**6.15 Carefully pull the sender unit from the fuel pump housing**

9 Remove the locking ring, then carefully lift the cover from the top of the pump, noting the location of the wiring and hose connections.

10 Disconnect the sender unit wiring and the fuel pump wiring from the bottom of the cover.

11 Where applicable, disconnect the earth wiring from the pressure regulator.

12 Release the clip and disconnect the fuel supply hose from the cover.

13 Disconnect the fuel return hose from the pressure regulator, and withdraw the cover.

14 Remove the cover sealing ring.

15 Press the retaining hook outwards and pull the sender unit from the clips on the side of the fuel pump housing **(see illustration)**.

### Refitting

16 Refitting is a reversal of removal, bearing in mind the following points:

a) Ensure that the sender unit engages

correctly with the clips on the fuel pump housing.

b) Check the condition of the sealing ring on the underside of the fuel pump cover, and renew if necessary.

c) Refit the fuel pump cover locking ring by tapping it clockwise until the locking clips 'click' into position.

## 7 Fuel pump – testing, removal and refitting

### Testing

1 If the pump is functioning, it should be possible to hear it 'buzzing' by listening under the rear of the vehicle when the ignition is switched on. Unless the engine is started, the fuel pump should switch off after approximately two seconds. If the noise produced is excessive, this may indicate a faulty pump.

2 If the pump appears to have failed completely, check the wiring to the pump, and check the appropriate fuse and relay.

3 To test the performance of the pump, special equipment is required, and it is recommended that any suspected faults are referred to a Vauxhall dealer.

### Removal

**Note:** Refer to the precautions in Section 1 before proceeding.

4 Depressurise the fuel system as described in Section 4.

5 Disconnect the battery negative terminal

(refer to Disconnecting the battery in the Reference Chapter).

6 Hand-pump any remaining fuel in the tank out through the filler pipe into a clean metal container which can be sealed.

7 Remove the rear seat as described in Chapter 11.

8 Fold up the acoustic insulation, then, using a screwdriver, carefully lever out the plastic cover to expose the fuel pump cover.

9 Disconnect the main wiring plug from the cover **(see illustration)**.

10 Identify the position of the two fuel lines, then disconnect the quick-release fittings. Be prepared for some loss of fuel. A Vauxhall special tool is available to release the fuel line connectors, but provided care is taken, the connectors can be released using a pair of long-nosed pliers, or a similar tool, to depress the retaining tangs. Clamp or plug the open ends of the hoses, to prevent dirt ingress and further fuel spillage.

11 Release the fuel pump cover locking ring. A special tool (Vauxhall tool No KM-797) is available for this, but the ring can be removed by tapping anti-clockwise until the locking clips release **(see illustration)**.

⚠️ *Warning: To prevent the possibility of any sparks which could ignite fuel vapour, use a plastic, wooden or brass tool to release the locking ring.*

12 Remove the locking ring, then carefully lift the cover from the top of the pump, noting the location of the wiring and hose connections.

13 Disconnect the sender unit wiring and the fuel pump wiring from the bottom of the cover **(see illustration)**.

14 Where applicable, disconnect the earth wiring from the pressure regulator.

15 Release the clip and disconnect the fuel supply hose from the cover.

16 Disconnect the fuel return hose from the pressure regulator, and withdraw the cover.

17 Remove the cover sealing ring.

18 Press the three pump housing retaining lugs to release them, and simultaneously pull the pump housing from the tank using a wire hook engaged with the eyelet provided **(see illustrations)**.

19 To remove the pump from the housing, first pull the filter from the base of the pump **(see illustration)**, and disconnect the wires

**7.9 Disconnect the fuel pump wiring plug**

**7.11 Releasing the fuel pump locking ring using a brass drift**

**7.13 Disconnect the wiring plugs from the underside of the cover**

**7.18a Press the three retaining lugs (1 – one shown), and pull the housing from the tank using a hook on the eyelet (2)**

**7.18b Withdrawing the fuel pump housing from the fuel tank**

**7.19  Removing the fuel filter from the base of the fuel pump**

**7.20a  Compress the three locking tabs (arrowed) . . .**

**7.20b  . . . and withdraw the pump from the housing**

from the pump. Note the wire locations to ensure correct refitting.

**20** Compress the three locking tabs, and pull the pump mounting plate and the pump from the housing **(see illustrations)**.

**21** Disconnect the wiring and, if necessary, remove the filter from the bottom of the fuel pump.

### Refitting

**22** Refitting is a reversal of removal, bearing in mind the following points:

a) *Before refitting the filter to the bottom of the pump, inspect the filter for contamination or blockage, and renew if necessary.*

b) *Ensure that the pump mounting plate engages correctly with the retaining clips on the housing.*

c) *Check the condition of the sealing ring on the underside of the fuel pump cover, and renew if necessary.*

d) *Refit the fuel pump cover locking ring by tapping it clockwise until the locking clips 'click' into position.*

## 8  Fuel injection system – general information

The fuel injection system is integrated with the ignition system to form a combined engine management system under the control of one electronic control unit (ECU).

Fuel is supplied from the rear-mounted tank, via a pressure regulator and fuel filter, to the fuel rail. The fuel rail acts as a reservoir for the four fuel injectors, which inject fuel into the cylinder inlet tracts, upstream of the inlet valves. The Multec S(F) system is a 'sequential' fuel injection system. This means that each of the four fuel injectors is triggered individually, just before the inlet valve on the relevant cylinder opens.

The duration of the electrical pulses to the fuel injectors determines the quantity of fuel injected. The pulse duration is computed by the Multec electronic control unit (ECU) on the basis of information received from the following sensors:

a) *Accelerator pedal position sensor – informs the ECU of accelerator pedal*

position, and the rate of throttle opening/closing.

b) *Manifold absolute pressure (MAP) sensor – informs the ECU of the load on the engine (expressed in terms of inlet manifold vacuum).*

c) *Inlet air temperature sensor – informs the ECU of the temperature of the air passing through the air inlet ducting.*

d) *Crankshaft speed/position sensor – informs the ECU of the crankshaft speed and position.*

e) *Camshaft position sensor – informs the ECU when No 1 cylinder is at top dead centre (TDC) on the firing stroke (expressed in terms of the position of the exhaust camshaft).*

f) *Coolant temperature sensor – informs the ECU of engine temperature.*

g) *Exhaust gas oxygen sensors (two) – inform the ECU of the oxygen content of the exhaust gases (explained in greater detail in Chapter 4E).*

h) *Knock sensor – informs the ECU when engine 'knock' (pre-ignition) occurs (explained in greater detail in Chapter 5B).*

i) *Wheel speed sensor – informs the ECU of the vehicle speed (explained in greater detail in Chapter 9).*

The signals from the various sensors are processed by the ECU, and the optimum fuelling and ignition settings are selected for the prevailing engine operating conditions.

Idle speed and throttle position is controlled by the throttle valve control motor, which is an integral part of the throttle body. The motor is controlled by the electronic control unit, in conjunction with signals received from the accelerator pedal position sensor.

A catalytic converter is incorporated in the exhaust manifold to reduce harmful exhaust gas emissions. Details of this and other emissions control system equipment are given in Chapter 4E.

If certain sensors fail, and send abnormal signals to the ECU, the ECU has a back-up programme. In this event, the abnormal signals are ignored, and a preprogrammed value is substituted for the sensor signal, allowing the engine to continue running, albeit at reduced efficiency. If the ECU enters its back-up mode, a warning light on the instrument panel will illuminate, and a fault code will be stored in

the ECU memory. This fault code can be read using suitable specialist test equipment.

## 9  Fuel injection system components – testing

**1** If a fault appears in the engine management system, first ensure that all the system wiring connectors are securely connected and free of corrosion. Ensure that the fault is not due to poor maintenance; ie, check that the air cleaner filter element is clean, the spark plugs are in good condition and correctly gapped, the cylinder compression pressures are correct and that the engine breather hoses are clear and undamaged, referring to Chapters 1A and 2B for further information.

**2** If these checks fail to reveal the cause of the problem, the vehicle should be taken to a suitably-equipped Vauxhall dealer or engine management diagnostic specialist for testing. A diagnostic socket is located in the centre of the facia, above the centre console, to which a fault code reader or other suitable test equipment can be connected **(see illustration)**. By using the code reader or test equipment, the engine management ECU can be interrogated, and any stored fault codes can be retrieved. Live data can also be captured from the various system sensors and actuators, indicating their operating parameters. This will allow the fault to be quickly and simply traced, alleviating the need to test all the system components individually, which is a time-consuming operation that carries a risk of damaging the ECU.

**9.2  Diagnostic socket location in the centre of the facia**

**10.29a Disconnect the wiring plug . . .**

**10.29b . . . then remove the securing clip . . .**

**10.29c . . . and withdraw the injector**

## 10 Fuel injection system components – removal and refitting

### Throttle body

#### Removal

**1** Disconnect the battery negative terminal (refer to *Disconnecting the battery* in the Reference Chapter).

**2** Remove the air cleaner cover, inlet trunking and airbox from the top of the throttle body, with reference to Section 2.

**3** Disconnect the wiring from the throttle body module.

**4** Partially drain the cooling system as described in Chapter 1A (drain sufficient coolant to empty the coolant expansion tank).

**5** Release the retaining clips and disconnect the two coolant hoses from the rear of the throttle body.

**6** Disconnect the crankcase ventilation hose and carbon canister vent hose from the throttle body.

**7** Undo the four bolts and lift the throttle body off the upper section of the inlet manifold. Recover the gasket.

**8** It is not possible to obtain the throttle valve control motor or throttle valve position sensor separately, so if either is faulty, the complete throttle body must be renewed.

#### Refitting

**9** Refitting is a reversal of removal, but thoroughly clean the mating faces and use a new gasket. Tighten the bolts progressively and securely. Top-up the coolant level as described in *Weekly checks*. Finally, switch on the ignition for 30 seconds without starting the engine.

### Manifold absolute pressure sensor

#### Removal

**10** The sensor is located on the inlet manifold on the front of the cylinder head.

**11** Disconnect the wiring from the sensor.

**12** Unscrew the clamp nut, remove the clamp plate, and withdraw the sensor from the cylinder head.

#### Refitting

**13** Refitting is a reversal of removal, but clean the contact faces of the sensor and manifold, and tighten the clamp nut to the specified torque.

### Air temperature sensor

#### Removal

**14** Disconnect the wiring from the air temperature sensor located on the rear of the air cleaner-to-throttle body duct.

**15** Twist and pull the sensor from the duct, and recover the seal.

#### Refitting

**16** Refitting is a reversal of removal, but renew the seal.

### Fuel injectors and fuel rail

**Note:** *Refer to the precautions in Section 1 before proceeding. The seals at both ends of the fuel injectors must be renewed on refitting.*

#### Removal

**17** Depressurise the fuel system as described in Section 4.

**18** Disconnect the battery negative terminal (refer to *Disconnecting the battery* in the Reference Chapter).

**19** Unscrew the oil filler cap, then unscrew the engine top cover securing bolts and lift off the cover. Screw the cap back into the camshaft cover.

**20** Disconnect the wiring from the air temperature sensor on the rear of the air cleaner air duct, then loosen the clip and disconnect the crankcase ventilation hose from the camshaft cover.

**21** Loosen the clip and remove the airbox and duct from the throttle body. Place the duct to one side.

**22** Disconnect the wiring from the oil pressure switch on the front of the cylinder block.

**23** Unscrew the union bolt and disconnect the fuel feed line from the fuel rail. Tape over or plug the rail aperture and the end of the line.

**24** Disconnect the wiring from the following components:
a) *Engine management ECU.*
b) *Carbon canister purge valve located behind the air cleaner.*
c) *Coolant temperature sensor.*
d) *Camshaft position sensor.*
e) *Throttle body module.*
f) *Knock sensor.*
g) *Inlet manifold absolute pressure (MAP) sensor.*

**25** Remove the catalytic converter control oxygen sensor as described later in this Section.

**26** Remove the EGR valve as described in Chapter 4E, then release the wiring harness from the cable ties.

**27** Release the heater hose for the throttle body from the bracket on the camshaft cover.

**28** Unscrew the two mounting bolts and remove the fuel rail, together with the injectors and wiring conduit, from the lower section of the inlet manifold.

**29** To remove an injector from the fuel rail and wiring conduit, first note the fitted position of the clips. Prise out the metal securing clip using a screwdriver or a pair of pliers, then release the wiring plug by carefully pulling the retaining spring clip downwards. Pull the injector from the fuel rail **(see illustrations)**. Remove and discard the injector sealing rings; new ones must be fitted on refitting.

**30** Overhaul of the fuel injectors is not possible, as no spares are available. If faulty, an injector must be renewed.

#### Refitting

**31** Commence refitting by fitting new O-ring seals to both ends of the fuel injectors. Coat the seals with a thin layer of petroleum jelly before fitting.

**32** Refitting is a reversal of removal, bearing in mind the following points:
a) *When refitting the injectors to the fuel rail, note that the groove in the metal securing clip must engage with the lug on the injector body (see illustration).*
b) *Tighten the fuel rail mounting and fuel line union bolts securely.*
c) *Ensure that all wiring connectors are securely reconnected, and that the wiring is secured in the relevant clips and brackets.*

### Crankshaft speed/position sensor

**Note:** *A new O-ring seal must be used on refitting.*

## Removal

**33** The crankshaft speed/position sensor is located at the front left-hand end of the cylinder block, below the oil filter. Access is most easily obtained from beneath the vehicle.

**34** Apply the handbrake, then jack up the front of the vehicle and support it on axle stands (see *Jacking and vehicle support*). Where necessary, remove the engine undertray.

**35** Disconnect the sensor wiring connector, then unscrew the retaining bolt and withdraw the sensor from the block.

## Refitting

**36** Refitting is a reversal of removal, but ensure that the mating surfaces of the sensor and block are clean and fit a new O-ring seal to the sensor before refitting. Tighten the bolt to the specified torque.

### Camshaft position sensor

#### Removal

**37** The camshaft position sensor is located next to the right-hand side of the throttle body.

**38** Disconnect the wiring, then unscrew the mounting bolt and withdraw the sensor.

#### Refitting

**39** Refitting is a reversal of removal.

### Coolant temperature sensor

**40** The coolant temperature sensor is located on the right-hand front end of the cylinder head.

**41** Removal and refitting procedures are in Chapter 3.

### Oxygen sensor – mixture regulation

*Caution: The sensor will be very hot if the engine has been running within 10 or 15 minutes.*

#### Removal

**42** The mixture regulation oxygen sensor is located on the exhaust manifold/catalytic converter.

**43** With the engine top cover removed, trace the wiring back from the sensor to the connector located on the left-hand side of the cylinder head, and disconnect it.

**44** Unscrew the sensor from the exhaust manifold/catalytic converter. Ideally, a special 'split' socket should be used, as this will locate over the sensor wiring.

#### Refitting

**45** Clean the threads of the sensor then coat them with Vauxhall special grease for oxygen sensors. If a new sensor is being fitted, it will be supplied with the threads already coated with the special grease to prevent it seizing in the manifold.

**46** Screw the sensor into the exhaust manifold/catalytic converter and tighten to the specified torque.

**47** Reconnect the wiring and clip it in place.

10.32 **The metal securing clip must engage with the lug on the injector body**

### Oxygen sensor – catalytic converter control

*Caution: The sensor will be very hot if the engine has been running within 10 or 15 minutes.*

#### Removal

**48** The catalytic converter control oxygen sensor is located in the exhaust front pipe, just behind the flexible section.

**49** First, apply the handbrake, then jack up the front of the vehicle and support it on axle stands (see *Jacking and vehicle support*).

**50** Trace the wiring back from the sensor to the connector located on the bracket, and disconnect it.

**51** Unclip the wiring from the bracket.

**52** Unscrew the sensor from the exhaust front pipe. Ideally, a special 'split' socket should be used, as this will locate over the sensor wiring.

#### Refitting

**53** Clean the threads of the sensor then coat them with Vauxhall special grease for oxygen sensors. If a new sensor is being fitted, it will be supplied with the threads already coated with the special grease to prevent it seizing in the pipe.

**54** Screw the sensor into the exhaust front pipe and tighten to the specified torque.

**55** Reconnect the wiring and clip it in place.

### Knock sensor

#### Removal

**56** The knock sensor is located on the rear, left-hand side of the cylinder block, just above the starter motor.

**57** Apply the handbrake, then jack up the front of the vehicle and support it on axle stands (see *Jacking and vehicle support*).

**58** Unscrew the oil filler cap, then unscrew the engine top cover securing bolts and lift off the cover. Screw the cap back into the camshaft cover.

**59** Disconnect the wiring from the air temperature sensor located on the rear of the air cleaner-to-throttle body duct.

**60** Loosen the clip and disconnect the airbox crankcase ventilation hose from the camshaft cover.

**61** Loosen the clip and remove the airbox from the throttle body, then loosen the clip and separate the airbox and duct from the air cleaner cover.

**62** Disconnect the knock sensor wiring at the connector on the top of the engine, then feed the wire between the fuel rail and wiring trough.

**63** Note its position, then unscrew the mounting bolt and withdraw the sensor from the block.

#### Refitting

**64** Clean the contact surfaces of the sensor and block. Also clean the threads of the sensor mounting bolt.

**65** Locate the sensor on the block and insert the mounting bolt. Position the sensor as previously noted, then tighten the bolt to the specified torque. Note that the torque setting is critical for the sensor to function correctly.

**66** Reconnect the wiring, making sure that it is routed as previously noted.

**67** Refit the airbox and duct and tighten the clips.

**68** Reconnect the airbox crankcase ventilation hose, and reconnect the wiring to the air temperature sensor.

**69** Refit the engine top cover and tighten the bolts.

**70** Lower the vehicle to the ground.

### Electronic control unit (ECU)

#### Removal

**71** The electronic control unit is located on the rear, left-hand side of the engine.

**72** Disconnect the battery negative terminal (refer to *Disconnecting the battery* in the Reference Chapter).

**73** Unscrew the oil filler cap, then unscrew the engine top cover securing bolts and lift

**11.13  Disconnecting the breather hose from the camshaft cover**

off the cover. Screw the cap back into the camshaft cover.

**74** Disconnect the wiring from the following components:

 a) *Mixture regulating oxygen sensor.*
 b) *Ignition module.*
 c) *Combination plug.*
 d) *Control unit.*

**75** Unscrew the bolt securing the earth wire to the control unit, then unbolt and remove the engine control unit.

### Refitting

**76** Refitting is a reversal of removal.

## Wheel speed sensor

**77** Refer to the anti-lock braking system information contained in Chapter 9.

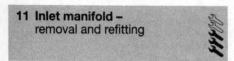

## 11  Inlet manifold –
removal and refitting

**Note:** *A new manifold gasket must be used on refitting.*

## Upper section

### Removal

**1** Disconnect the battery negative terminal (refer to *Disconnecting the battery* in the Reference Chapter).

**2** Apply the handbrake, then jack up the front of the vehicle and support it on axle stands (see *Jacking and vehicle support*). Remove the right-hand front roadwheel and the wheel arch liner for access to the crankshaft pulley.

**11.18  Disconnecting the brake servo vacuum hose from the upper section of the inlet manifold**

**3** Partially drain the cooling system as described in Chapter 1A so that the coolant level is below the throttle body.

**4** Remove the auxiliary drivebelt as described in Chapter 1A. Mark the drivebelt to indicate its running direction and ensure it is refitted correctly.

**5** Unscrew and remove the inlet manifold support bracket upper bolt, then loosen only the lower bolt. Move the bracket to one side.

**6** Disconnect the wiring from the oil pressure switch and release the wiring from the cable tie.

**7** Unscrew the oil filler cap, then unscrew the engine top cover securing bolts and lift off the cover. Screw the cap back into the camshaft cover.

**8** Remove the air cleaner assembly as described in Section 2.

**9** Depressurise the fuel system as described in Section 4.

**10** Unscrew the union bolt and disconnect the fuel feed line from the fuel rail. Tape over or plug the rail aperture and the end of the line.

**11** Disconnect the wiring from the following components, and release the wiring from the cable ties:

 a) *Coolant temperature sensor.*
 b) *Camshaft position sensor.*
 c) *Throttle body.*
 d) *Knock sensor.*
 e) *Manifold absolute pressure (MAP) sensor.*
 f) *Catalytic converter oxygen sensor.*
 g) *EGR valve.*

**12** Release the retaining clips and disconnect the two coolant hoses from the rear of the throttle body.

**13** Disconnect the crankcase ventilation hose from the throttle body and camshaft cover **(see illustration)**.

**14** Unscrew the two mounting bolts and remove the fuel rail, together with the injectors and wiring conduit, from the lower section of the inlet manifold.

**15** Unbolt the wiring harness bracket from the alternator.

**16** Unscrew the three bolts and remove the upper mounting bracket from the alternator. Loosen the lower mounting bolt. Swivel the alternator to the rear.

**17** Unbolt the bracket and unclip the wiring harness from the rear right-hand side of the inlet manifold.

**18** Disconnect the brake vacuum hose from the upper section of the inlet manifold **(see illustration)**.

**19** Disconnect the carbon canister purge hose from the throttle body, then unbolt and remove the throttle body from the manifold. Recover the gasket.

**20** Unscrew the securing bolts, and withdraw the upper section of the inlet manifold. Recover the gasket.

### Refitting

**21** Commence refitting by checking the condition of the rubber gasket which fits

between the upper and lower sections of the inlet manifold. Renew the gasket if necessary. Thoroughly clean the mating surfaces of the manifolds.

**22** Refit the upper section of the inlet manifold, ensuring that the gasket between the upper and lower manifold sections locates correctly. Insert and tighten the securing bolts progressively to the specified torque.

**23** Refit the throttle body with reference to Section 10, and reconnect the purge hose.

**24** Reconnect the brake vacuum hose.

**25** Refit the wiring harness and bracket and tighten the bolts.

**26** Refit the alternator bracket and tighten the bolts. Also refit the wiring harness bracket.

**27** Refit the fuel rail and injectors with reference to Section 10.

**28** Reconnect the crankcase ventilation hose and the two coolant hoses.

**29** Reconnect the wiring to the components listed in paragraph 11.

**30** Refit the fuel feed line to the fuel rail and tighten the union bolt securely.

**31** Refit the air cleaner assembly and engine top cover.

**32** Reconnect the wiring to the oil pressure switch and secure with a new cable tie.

**33** Refit the inlet manifold support bracket and tighten the bolts.

**34** Refit the auxiliary drivebelt with reference to Chapter 1A.

**35** Top-up the cooling system with reference to *Weekly checks*.

**36** Refit the wheel arch liner and front wheel and lower the vehicle to the ground.

**37** Reconnect the battery negative terminal.

## Lower section

### Removal

**38** Remove the upper section of the inlet manifold as described previously in this Section. It should be noted however, that the cooling system should be drained completely.

**39** Unbolt and remove the engine lifting eye.

**40** Unbolt and remove the coolant flange.

**41** Remove the coolant hose, then unscrew the 9 nuts and remove the lower section of the inlet manifold. The manufacturers recommend that the nuts are renewed.

**42** Unbolt the EGR valve from the inlet manifold. Discard the gasket and obtain a new one.

### Refitting

**43** Thoroughly clean the mating surfaces of the manifolds, cylinder head, coolant flange and EGR valve.

**44** Refit the EGR valve together with a new gasket, and tighten the bolts to the specified torque.

**45** Refit the lower section of the inlet manifold together with a new gasket, and progressively tighten the nuts to the specified torque.

**46** Reconnect the coolant hose and tighten the clip.

**47** Refit the coolant flange and tighten the bolts to the specified torque.

J44618

**13.5  Exhaust system components**

1  *Front exhaust pipe with flexible section*
2  *Front silencer*
3  *Intermediate exhaust pipe*
4  *Tail pipe and silencer*

**13.7a  Exhaust system rubber mounting spring clip (arrowed)**

**13.7b  Removing the exhaust front pipe gasket**

**48** Refit the engine lifting eye and tighten the bolt.

**49** Refit the upper section of the inlet manifold as described earlier in this Section.

## 12  Exhaust manifold –
removal and refitting

**Note:** *A new gasket must be used on refitting.*

### Removal

**1** Disconnect the battery negative lead (refer to *Disconnecting the battery* in the Reference Chapter).

**2** Unscrew the oil filler cap, then unscrew the engine top cover securing bolts and lift off the cover. Screw the cap back into the camshaft cover.

**3** Apply the handbrake, then jack up the front of the vehicle and support it on axle stands (see *Jacking and vehicle support*).

**4** Refer to Section 10 and disconnect the wiring from the mixture regulation oxygen sensor on the exhaust manifold/catalytic converter, then unbolt the exhaust front pipe from the exhaust manifold, taking care to support the flexible section. **Note:** *Angular movement in excess of 10° can cause permanent damage to the flexible section.* Recover the gasket.

**5** Release the mounting rubbers and support the front of the exhaust pipe to one side.

**6** Remove the mixture regulation oxygen sensor from the exhaust manifold as described in Section 10.

**7** Unbolt the hot air shroud from the exhaust manifold. Also remove the engine oil dipstick.

**8** Unscrew the retaining nuts and carefully withdraw the exhaust manifold upwards from the engine. Recover the manifold gasket. The manufacturers recommend that the nuts are renewed.

### Refitting

**9** Thoroughly clean the mating surfaces of the exhaust manifold and cylinder head.

**10** Refit the exhaust manifold to the cylinder head together with a new gasket. Tighten the (new) nuts progressively to the specified torque.

**11** Refit the oil dipstick, then refit the heat shield to the manifold and tighten the bolts.

**12** Refit the mixture regulation oxygen sensor to the exhaust manifold as described in Section 10.

**13** Refit the front pipe to the manifold together with a new gasket and tighten the nuts to the specified torque. Reconnect the mounting rubbers.

**14** Reconnect the wiring for the catalytic converter control oxygen sensor.

**15** Lower the vehicle to the ground.

**16** Refit the engine top cover, and reconnect the battery negative lead (refer to *Disconnecting the battery* in the Reference Chapter). Finally, it may be necessary to have a Vauxhall dealer program all volatile memories.

## 13  Exhaust system –
general information
and component renewal

### General information

**1** The exhaust system is in two sections. The front section includes the catalytic converter control oxygen sensor, silencer and intermediate pipe. The rear section consists of the tailpipe and silencer.

**2** Periodically, the exhaust system should be checked for signs of leaks or damage. Also inspect the system rubber mountings, and renew if necessary.

**3** Small holes or cracks can be repaired using proprietary exhaust repair products.

**4** Before renewing an individual section of the exhaust system, it is wise to inspect the remaining section. If corrosion or damage is evident, it may prove more economical to renew the entire system.

### Component renewal

**5** If either part of the system is to be renewed, it is important to ensure that the correct component is obtained **(see illustration)**.

**6** To remove the rear tailpipe and silencer, chock the front wheels then jack up the rear of the vehicle and support on axle stands (see *Jacking and vehicle support*). Loosen the clamp securing the intermediate pipe to the tailpipe, then release the rubber mountings and slide the tailpipe from the intermediate pipe. If the tailpipe is rusted onto the intermediate pipe, apply liberal amounts of penetrating oil and tap around the joint with a hammer to free it. Twist the tailpipe in both directions while holding the intermediate pipe.

**7** To remove the front section of the exhaust, jack up the front and rear of the vehicle and support it on axle stands (see *Jacking and vehicle support*). Remove the tailpipe and silencer as described in paragraph 6, then remove the oxygen sensor from the front pipe as described in Section 10. Unbolt the exhaust front pipe from the catalytic converter/ exhaust manifold **(see illustrations)**, taking care to support the flexible section. **Note:** *Angular movement in excess of 10° can cause permanent damage to the flexible section.* Recover the gasket. Release the rubber mountings and withdraw the exhaust from under the vehicle.

**8** Refitting is a reversal of removal, but renew all gaskets and tighten the clamp and front pipe flange nuts to the specified torque.

# Chapter 4 Part C:
## Fuel and exhaust systems – 1.3 litre diesel engines

## Contents

## Degrees of difficulty

| **Easy,** suitable for novice with little experience | 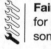 | **Fairly easy,** suitable for beginner with some experience | **Fairly difficult,** suitable for competent DIY mechanic | **Difficult,** suitable for experienced DIY mechanic | **Very difficult,** suitable for expert DIY or professional |  |

## Specifications

### General
System type ............................................. Magneti-Marelli 6JF high-pressure direct injection 'common-rail' system incorporating an electronically controlled fuel injection pump and injectors
Firing order............................................. 1–3–4–2 (No 1 at timing chain end)
Fuel system operating pressure............................ 1400 bar at 2200 rpm
Idle speed.............................................. 850 rpm – controlled by ECU
Maximum speed......................................... 5200 rpm – controlled by ECU

### High-pressure fuel pump
Type ................................................... Bosch CP1

### Fuel supply pump
Type ................................................... Electric, mounted in fuel tank
Delivery pressure ....................................... 3.3 bar (maximum)

### Injectors
Type ................................................... Bosch CRIP 1-MI

## Torque wrench settings

| | Nm | lbf ft |
|---|---|---|
| Catalytic converter to turbocharger | 25 | 18 |
| Catalytic converter support bracket to sump reinforcement bracket | 25 | 18 |
| Camshaft position sensor retaining bolt | 7 | 5 |
| Coolant pipe-to-heat exchanger bolts | 9 | 7 |
| Crankshaft speed/position sensor retaining bolt | 9 | 7 |
| EGR valve bolts | 22 | 16 |
| Exhaust manifold nuts*: | | |
|     Stage 1 | 15 | 11 |
|     Stage 2 | Angle-tighten a further 30° | |
| Exhaust system clamp nuts | 50 | 37 |
| Fuel injector clamp bracket nuts | 20 | 15 |
| Fuel pressure regulating valve to fuel rail | 9 | 7 |
| Fuel pressure sensor to fuel rail | 70 | 52 |
| Fuel rail-to-mounting bracket bolts | 25 | 18 |
| Fuel rail mounting bracket-to-camshaft housing bolts | 25 | 18 |
| High-pressure fuel pipe unions: | | |
|     M12 union nuts | 25 | 18 |
|     M14 union nuts | 28 | 21 |
| High-pressure fuel pump mounting bolts | 15 | 11 |
| Inlet manifold bolts | 25 | 18 |
| Injection pump to camshaft housing | 15 | 11 |
| Injector retaining clamp nut | 20 | 15 |
| Oil filter housing-to-cylinder block | 9 | 7 |
| Turbocharger oil return pipe bolts | 9 | 7 |
| Turbocharger oil supply pipe banjo union bolts | 12 | 9 |
| Turbocharger to exhaust manifold | 25 | 18 |

* Use new nuts

## 1 General information

The diesel engine covered in this manual is equipped with a High-pressure Diesel injection (HDi) system which incorporates the very latest in diesel injection technology. On the HDi system, the high-pressure fuel pump is used purely to provide the pressure required for the injection system and has no control over the injection timing (unlike conventional diesel injection systems). The injection timing is controlled by the electronic control unit (ECU) via the electrically-operated injectors. The system operates as follows.

The fuel system consists of a fuel tank (which is mounted under the rear of the car, with an electric fuel supply pump immersed in it, a fuel filter with integral water separator, a high-pressure fuel pump, injectors and associated components.

Fuel is supplied by the tank-mounted supply pump to the fuel filter housing which is located at the rear left-hand side of the engine compartment. The fuel filter removes all foreign matter and water and ensures that the fuel supplied to the high-pressure pump is clean. Excess fuel is returned from the outlet on the filter housing lid to the tank via the fuel cooler. The fuel cooler is fitted to the underside of the vehicle and is cooled by the passing airflow to ensure the fuel is cool before it enters the fuel tank.

The fuel is heated to ensure no problems occur when the ambient temperature is very low. An electrically-operated fuel heater is fitted to the fuel filter housing, and the heater is controlled by the ECU.

The high-pressure fuel pump is driven directly from the rear of the exhaust camshaft. The high pressure required in the system (up to 1400 bar) is produced by the three pistons in the pump. The pump supplies high pressure fuel to the fuel rail, which acts as a reservoir for the four injectors.

The electrical control system consists of the ECU, along with the following sensors:

a) *Accelerator pedal/position sensor – informs the ECU of the accelerator pedal position, and the speed of pedal travel.*

b) *Coolant temperature sensor – informs the ECU of engine temperature.*

c) *Air mass meter – informs the ECU of the amount and temperature of air passing through the inlet duct.*

d) *Crankshaft speed/position sensor – informs the ECU of the crankshaft position and speed of rotation.*

e) *Camshaft position sensor – informs the ECU of the positions of the pistons.*

f) *Fuel pressure sensor – informs the ECU of the fuel pressure present in the fuel rail.*

g) *Manifold pressure sensor – informs the ECU of the load on the engine.*

h) *Wheel speed sensors – informs the ECU of the vehicle speed.*

All the above signals (in addition to signals from various other systems on the vehicle) are analysed by the ECU which selects the fuelling response appropriate to those values. The ECU controls the fuel injectors (varying the pulse width – the length of time the injectors are held open – to provide a richer or weaker mixture, as appropriate). The mixture is constantly varied by the ECU, to provide the best setting for cranking, starting (with either a hot or cold engine), warm-up, idle, cruising and acceleration.

The ECU also has full control over the fuel pressure present in the system via the pressure regulating valve located on the fuel rail. To reduce the fuel pressure, the ECU opens the pressure regulating valve which allows the excess fuel to return directly to the fuel tank.

The ECU also controls the exhaust gas recirculation (EGR) system, described in detail in Part E of this Chapter, and the engine cooling fan.

A turbocharger is fitted to increase engine efficiency. It does this by raising the pressure in the inlet manifold above atmospheric pressure. Instead of the air simply being sucked into the cylinders, it is forced in.

Energy for the operation of the turbocharger comes from the exhaust gas. The gas flows through a specially-shaped housing (the turbine housing) and in so doing, spins the turbine wheel. The turbine wheel is attached to a shaft, at the end of which is another vaned wheel known as the compressor wheel. The compressor wheel spins in its own housing, and compresses the inlet air on the way to the inlet manifold. The turbo shaft is pressure-lubricated by an oil feed pipe from the main oil gallery. The shaft 'floats' on a cushion of oil. A drain pipe returns the oil to the sump. Boost pressure (the pressure in the inlet manifold) is limited by a wastegate, which diverts the exhaust gas away from the turbine wheel in response to a pressure-sensitive actuator.

If there is an abnormality in any of the readings obtained from the various sensors, the ECU enters its back-up mode. In this event, it ignores the abnormal sensor signal and assumes a preprogrammed value which will allow the engine to continue running (albeit at reduced efficiency). If the ECU enters this back-up mode, the warning light on the instrument panel will come on, and the relevant fault code will be stored in the ECU memory. This fault code can be read using specialist test equipment connected to the diagnostic socket located in the centre of the facia, above the centre console.

## 2 High-pressure Diesel injection system – special information

### Warnings and precautions

**1** It is essential to observe strict precautions when working on the fuel system components, particularly the high-pressure side of the system. Before carrying out any operations on the fuel system, refer to the precautions given in *Safety first!* at the beginning of this manual, and to the following additional information.

• Do not carry out any repair work on the high-pressure fuel system unless you are competent to do so, have all the necessary tools and equipment required, and are aware of the safety implications involved.

• Before starting any repair work on the fuel system, wait at least 30 seconds after switching off the engine to allow the fuel circuit to return to atmospheric pressure.

• Never work on the high-pressure fuel system with the engine running.

• Keep well clear of any possible source of fuel leakage, particularly when starting the engine after carrying out repair work. A leak in the system could cause an extremely high-pressure jet of fuel to escape, which could result in severe personal injury.

• Never place your hands or any part of your body near to a leak in the high-pressure fuel system.

• Do not use steam cleaning equipment or compressed air to clean the engine or any of the fuel system components.

### Repair procedures and general information

**2** Strict cleanliness must be observed at all times when working on any part of the fuel system. This applies to the working area in general, the person doing the work, and the components being worked on.

**3** Before working on the fuel system components,

**2.4 Typical plastic plug and cap set for sealing disconnected fuel pipes and components**

they must be thoroughly cleaned with a suitable degreasing fluid. Cleanliness is particularly important when working on the fuel system connections at the following components:
a) Fuel filter.
b) High-pressure fuel pump.
c) Fuel rail.
d) Fuel injectors.
e) High-pressure fuel pipes.

**4** After disconnecting any fuel pipes or components, the open union or orifice must be immediately sealed to prevent the entry of dirt or foreign material. Plastic plugs and caps in various sizes are available in packs from motor factors and accessory outlets, and are particularly suitable for this application **(see illustration)**. Fingers cut from disposable rubber gloves should be used to protect components such as fuel pipes, fuel injectors and wiring connectors, and can be secured in place using elastic bands.

**5** The torque wrench settings given in the

**3.1a  Disconnect the wiring connector from the air mass meter . . .**

**2.5 Two crow-foot adapters will be necessary for tightening the fuel pipe unions**

Specifications must be strictly observed when tightening component mountings and connections. This is particularly important when tightening the high-pressure fuel pipe unions. To enable a torque wrench to be used on the fuel pipe unions, two crow-foot adapters are required. Suitable types are available from motor factors and accessory outlets **(see illustration)**.

## 3 Air cleaner assembly and intake ducts – removal and refitting

### Air cleaner assembly

**1** Disconnect the wiring connector from the air mass meter, then slacken the clamp and withdraw the air mass meter from the air cleaner cover **(see illustrations)**.

**2** Undo the screws, lift off the air cleaner cover, and lift out the air cleaner element **(see illustrations)**.

**3.1b  . . . then slacken the clamp and withdraw the air mass meter from the air cleaner cover**

**3.2a  Undo the screws . . .**

**3.2b  . . . lift off the air cleaner cover . . .**

**3.2c  . . . then lift out the element**

**3.3 Removing the front intake duct from the air cleaner**

**3.4a Unscrew the crossbar mounting screw (arrowed) at the rear of the air cleaner . . .**

**3.4b . . . and release the crossbar from the mounting pegs**

**3** Disconnect the air intake duct from the front of the air cleaner (**see illustration**).

**4** Unscrew the crossbar mounting screw at the rear of the air cleaner, and release the crossbar rubber mountings from the mounting pegs (**see illustrations**).

**5** Pull the air cleaner body rearwards from the front mounting rubber, and withdraw from the engine compartment.

**6** Refitting is a reversal of removal.

### Air intake ducts

**7** Various flexible ducts and rigid pipes are used to circulate the intake air through the air cleaner, turbocharger, intercooler and inlet manifold (**see illustration**). Depending on the particular duct or pipe being removed, it may be necessary to move aside or disconnect additional components for access, and to release cable ties and harness clips to allow complete removal of the duct. Refer to the accompanying illustrations and proceed as described under the relevant sub-heading below.

### Resonator

**8** Detach the air cleaner intake duct from the resonator, then undo the retaining screw, and slide the resonator to one side to release it from the radiator crossmember (**see illustrations**).

**9** Refitting is a reversal of removal.

### Air cleaner intake duct

**10** The intake duct at the front of the air cleaner is removed by simply disengaging each end from the resonator and air cleaner.

### Upper intake duct

**11** Slacken the clamp and disconnect the right-hand end of the duct from the air mass meter. Slacken the clamp at the other end, withdraw the duct from the turbocharger charge air pipe and remove the duct from the engine (**see illustrations**).

**12** Refitting is a reversal of removal ensuring the clamps are tightened securely.

### Turbocharger charge air pipe

**13** Lift off the plastic cover over the top of the engine.

**14** Slacken the clamp and disconnect the upper intake duct from turbocharger charge air pipe.

**3.7 Air intake duct arrangement**

1 Air cleaner assembly
2 Air mass meter
3 Upper intake duct
4 Inlet manifold charge air pipe
5 Turbocharger charge air pipe
6 Inlet manifold charge air pipe connection hose
7 Intercooler

8 Intercooler charge air pipe hose connection
9 Charge air hose
10 Charge air hose
11 Resonator
12 Air cleaner intake duct
13 Inlet manifold
14 Turbocharger

**3.8a Undo the retaining screw (arrowed) . . . .**

**3.8b . . . then slide the locating pegs (arrowed) out from the crossmember**

**3.11a Slacken the clamp (arrowed) and disconnect the right-hand end of the upper intake duct from the air mass meter**

**3.11b Slacken the clamp at the other end (arrowed) and withdraw the duct from the turbocharger charge air pipe**

**3.15 Slacken the clamp and disconnect the lower end of the charge air pipe (arrowed) from the turbocharger**

**3.16a Release the wiring harness retaining clips from the charge air pipe supports at the top . . .**

**3.16b . . . and at the front . . .**

**3.16c . . . then release the fuel hose from the retaining clip**

**15** Slacken the clamp and disconnect the lower end of the charge air pipe from the turbocharger **(see illustration)**. Collect the spacing sleeve.

**16** Working along the charge air pipe, release the wiring harness retaining clips from the pipe supports and release the fuel hose from the retaining clips **(see illustrations)**.

**17** Release the locking clip and disconnect the crankcase breather hose at the quick-release connection on the charge air pipe **(see illustration)**.

**18** Undo the two mounting bolts and remove the charge air pipe from the engine **(see illustration)**.

**19** Refitting is a reversal of removal ensuring the clamps are tightened securely, and that the wiring harness and fuel hose are correctly located in their respective clips and supports.

### Charge air hose

**20** Lift off the plastic cover over the top of the engine.

**21** Slacken the retaining clip, extract the locking clip to disconnect the quick-release fitting, and remove the charge air hose from the turbocharger and intercooler charge air pipe **(see illustrations)**.

**22** Refitting is a reversal of removal ensuring the clamp is tightened securely and the quick-release fitting is fully engaged.

### Intercooler charge air pipe

**23** Remove the front bumper as described in Chapter 11.

**24** Extract the locking clip to disconnect the quick-release fitting, and detach the charge

air hose from the intercooler charge air pipe **(see illustration 3.21b)**.

**25** Slacken the clamp and disconnect the charge air pipe from the intercooler hose connection.

**3.17 Release the locking clip and disconnect the crankcase breather hose quick-release connection**

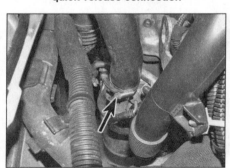

**3.21a Slacken the retaining clip (arrowed) . . .**

**26** Undo the upper bolt and the two lower bolts and remove the charge air pipe from the radiator cooling fan shroud.

**27** Refitting is a reversal of removal ensuring the clamp is tightened securely and the quick-

**3.18 Undo the two mounting bolts (arrowed) and remove the charge air pipe**

**3.21b . . . then disconnect the quick-release fitting (arrowed) and remove the turbocharger charge air hose**

**3.34a Unclip the expansion tank coolant hose and the wiring harness from the crash box . . .**

**3.34b . . . and disconnect the harness connector**

**3.35 Release the retaining clip and lift the expansion tank from its location**

**3.36a Unscrew the outer retaining nut (arrowed) and slacken the inner nut . . .**

**3.36b . . . then remove the crash box from the bulkhead**

box, and disconnect the harness connector **(see illustrations)**.

**35** Release the retaining clip, lift the coolant expansion tank from its location and place it to one side **(see illustration)**.

**36** Unscrew the outer retaining nut, slacken the inner nut and remove the crash box from the bulkhead **(see illustrations)**.

**37** Working below the thermostat housing, slacken the clamp and disconnect the connection hose from the charge air pipe.

**38** Undo the three bolts securing the charge air pipe to the inlet manifold flange, and the bolt securing the pipe support to the thermostat housing. Manipulate the charge air pipe out from its location and recover the sealing ring **(see illustrations)**.

**39** Refitting is a reversal of removal ensuring the clamp is tightened securely. Refit the fuel filter as described in Chapter 1B.

**3.38a Unbolt the charge air pipe from the inlet manifold and undo the bolt (arrowed) . . .**

**3.38b . . . then manipulate the charge air pipe (arrowed) out from its location and recover the sealing ring**

release fitting is fully engaged. Refit the front bumper with reference to Chapter 11.

### Inlet manifold charge air pipe connection hose

**28** Remove the front bumper as described in Chapter 11.

**29** Lift off the plastic cover over the top of the engine.

**30** Working below the thermostat housing, slacken the clamp and disconnect the connection hose from the inlet manifold charge air pipe.

**31** Extract the locking clip to disconnect the quick-release fitting, and detach the connection hose from the intercooler. Manipulate the hose out from the engine compartment.

**32** Refitting is a reversal of removal ensuring the clamp is tightened securely and the quick-release fitting is fully engaged.

### Inlet manifold charge air pipe

**33** Remove the fuel filter as described in Chapter 1B.

**34** Unclip the expansion tank coolant hose and the wiring harness from the fuel filter crash

**4.2 Disconnecting the wiring connector (arrowed) from the accelerator pedal/ position sensor**

| 4 | Accelerator pedal/ position sensor – removal and refitting | 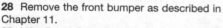 |

### Removal

**1** Disconnect the battery negative terminal (refer to *Disconnecting the battery* in the Reference Chapter).

**2** Working in the driver's footwell under the facia, disconnect the wiring from the top of the accelerator pedal/position sensor **(see illustration)**. Where necessary, pull back the footwell carpet first.

**3** Unscrew the three mounting nuts, and withdraw the sensor from the bulkhead.

### Refitting

**4** Refitting is a reversal of removal.

| 5 | Fuel system – priming and bleeding |  |

**1** It is not necessary to manually prime and bleed the fuel system after any operation on the system components. Start the engine, noting that this may take longer than usual, especially if the fuel system has been allowed to run dry. Operate the starter in ten second bursts with 5 seconds rest in between each operation, for a maximum of 40 seconds. When the engine starts, run it at a fast idle speed for a minute or so to purge any trapped air from the fuel lines. After this time the engine should idle smoothly at a constant speed.

**2** If the engine idles roughly, then there is still some air trapped in the fuel system. Increase the engine speed again for another minute or so then recheck the idle speed. Repeat this procedure as necessary until the engine is idling smoothly.

### 6  Fuel gauge sender unit – removal and refitting

**Note 1:** *Refer to the information contained in Section 2 before proceeding.*
**Note 2:** *The fuel tank should be as empty as possible when carrying out this procedure.*

#### Removal

**1** Disconnect the battery negative terminal (refer to *Disconnecting the battery* in the Reference Chapter).
**2** Hand-pump any remaining fuel in the tank out through the filler pipe into a clean metal container which can be sealed.
**3** Remove the rear seat as described in Chapter 11.

**6.4  Prise the plastic cover from the floor for access to the fuel gauge sender cover**

**4** Fold up the acoustic insulation, then, using a screwdriver, carefully lever out the plastic cover to expose the fuel gauge sender cover **(see illustration)**.
**5** Identify the position of the fuel feed and return lines, then disconnect the quick-release fittings. Be prepared for some loss of fuel. A Vauxhall special tool is available to release the fuel line connectors **(see illustration)**, but provided care is taken, the connectors can be released using a pair of long-nosed pliers, or a similar tool, to depress the retaining tangs. Clamp or plug the open ends of the hoses, to prevent dirt ingress and further fuel spillage.
**6** Disconnect the main wiring plug from the cover **(see illustration)**.

**6.5  Using the special tool to release the fuel line connectors**

**7** Release the fuel gauge sender cover locking ring. A special tool (Vauxhall tool No KM-797) is available for this, but the ring can be removed by tapping anti-clockwise until the locking clips release **(see illustration)**.
**8** Remove the locking ring, then carefully lift off the cover, noting the location of the wiring and hose connections **(see illustration)**.
**9** Disconnect the sender unit wiring from the bottom of the cover **(see illustration)**.
**10** Release the clip and disconnect the fuel supply hose from the cover **(see illustration)**.
**11** Disconnect the fuel return hose, and withdraw the cover.
**12** Remove the cover sealing ring **(see illustration)**.

**6.6  Disconnecting the main wiring plug**

**6.7  Tapping the locking ring anti-clockwise to release it**

**6.8  Removing the locking ring**

**6.9  Disconnect the fuel gauge sender wiring plug**

**6.10  Disconnecting the fuel supply hose from the cover**

**6.12 Removing the cover sealing ring**

**6.13a Depress the hook . . .**

**6.13b . . . pull the sender unit from the housing**

**13** Depress the hook and pull the sender unit from the clips on the side of the housing **(see illustrations)**.

### Refitting

**14** Refitting is a reversal of removal, bearing in mind the following points:
  a) *Check the condition of the sealing ring on the underside of the fuel pump cover, and renew if necessary.*
  b) *Refit the fuel pump cover locking ring by tapping it clockwise until the locking clips 'click' into position.*

## 7 Fuel tank –
removal and refitting

**Note 1:** *Refer to the information contained in Section 2 before proceeding.*
**Note 2:** *The fuel tank should be as empty as possible when carrying out this procedure.*

### Removal

**1** Disconnect the battery negative terminal (refer to *Disconnecting the battery* in the Reference Chapter).
**2** Hand-pump any remaining fuel in the tank out through the filler pipe into a clean metal container which can be sealed.
**3** Chock the front wheels then jack up the rear of the vehicle and support on axle stands (see *Jacking and vehicle support*). Remove both rear wheels.
**4** Refer to Chapter 9 and disconnect the front ends of the rear (secondary) handbrake cables from the underbody clips after backing off the primary cable adjustment. Unclip the cables from the underbody and the right-hand side of the fuel tank, then tie them to one side, away from the fuel tank.
**5** Disconnect the rear of the exhaust system from its rubber mountings, and lower the system, then move it to one side sufficiently to enable removal of the fuel tank. Alternatively, remove the exhaust system completely to provide greater clearance (refer to Section 19).
**6** Disconnect the wiring from the fuel gauge sensor, at the connector on the underbody.
**7** Disconnect the fuel feed and return lines at the quick-release connectors on the underbody (if necessary, detach the line

retaining bracket from the underbody). Be prepared for some loss of fuel. A Vauxhall special tool is available to release the fuel line connectors, but provided care is taken, the connectors can be released using a pair of long-nosed pliers, or a similar tool, to depress the retaining tangs.
**8** Unscrew the lower filler hose mounting bolt, then unclip the ventilation hose from the bottom of the fuel tank.
**9** Loosen the clip and disconnect the fuel filler hose from the fuel tank.
**10** Support the weight of the fuel tank on a jack with interposed block of wood.
**11** Unbolt and remove the two securing straps from the fuel tank.
**12** Lower the tank sufficiently to enable access to the fuel hoses on the tank, then disconnect them. Be prepared for some loss of fuel.
**13** Continue to lower the tank until it can be removed from under the vehicle.
**14** Plug or clamp the fuel and vent hoses to prevent entry of dust and dirt.
**15** If necessary, remove the fuel lines and hoses, heat shield and wiring from the tank for transfer to the new tank. If a new tank is being fitted, it is recommended that the filter is renewed at the same time.

### Refitting

**16** If the tank contains sediment or water, it may cleaned out with two or three rinses of clean fuel. Remove the fuel gauge sender unit as described in Section 6. Shake the tank vigorously, and change the fuel as necessary to remove all contamination from the tank. *This procedure should be carried out in a well-ventilated area, and it is vital to take adequate fire precautions.*
**17** Any repairs to the fuel tank should be carried out by a professional. Do not under any circumstances attempt any form of DIY repair to a fuel tank.
**18** Refitting is a reversal of removal, bearing in mind the following points:
  a) *Ensure that all hoses are securely reconnected to their correct locations.*
  b) *Check the handbrake cable adjustment, as described in Chapter 9.*
  c) *On completion, fill the fuel tank, then run the engine and check for leaks. If leakage*

*is evident, stop the engine immediately and rectify the problem without delay.*

## 8 Fuel supply pump –
testing, removal and refitting

### Testing

**1** If the pump is functioning, it should be possible to hear it 'buzzing' by listening under the rear of the vehicle when the ignition is switched on. Unless the engine is started, the fuel pump should switch off after approximately two seconds. If the noise produced is excessive, this may indicate a faulty pump.
**2** If the pump appears to have failed completely, check the wiring to the pump, and check the appropriate fuse and relay.
**3** To test the performance of the pump, special equipment is required, and it is recommended that any suspected faults are referred to a Vauxhall dealer.

### Removal

**Note 1:** *Refer to the information contained in Section 2 before proceeding.*
**Note 2:** *The fuel tank should be as empty as possible when carrying out this procedure.*
**4** Disconnect the battery negative terminal (refer to *Disconnecting the battery* in the Reference Chapter).
**5** Hand-pump any remaining fuel in the tank out through the filler pipe into a clean metal container which can be sealed.
**6** Remove the rear seat as described in Chapter 11.
**7** Fold up the acoustic insulation then, using a screwdriver, carefully lever out the plastic cover to expose the fuel pump cover.
**8** Disconnect the main wiring plug from the cover **(see illustration)**.
**9** Identify the position of the two fuel lines, then disconnect the quick-release fittings. Be prepared for some loss of fuel. A Vauxhall special tool is available to release the fuel line connectors, but provided care is taken, the connectors can be released using a pair of long-nosed pliers, or a similar tool, to depress the retaining tangs. Clamp or plug the open ends of the hoses, to prevent dirt ingress and further fuel spillage.

**8.8  Disconnect the fuel pump wiring plug**

**8.10  Releasing the fuel pump locking ring**

**8.12  Disconnect the wiring plugs from the underside of the cover**

**8.17a  Press the three retaining lugs (1 – one shown), and pull the housing from the tank using a hook on the eyelet (2)**

**8.17b  Withdrawing the fuel pump housing from the fuel tank**

**10**  Release the fuel pump cover locking ring. A special tool (Vauxhall tool No KM-797) is available for this, but the ring can be removed by tapping anti-clockwise until the locking clips release **(see illustration)**.

**11**  Remove the locking ring, then carefully lift the cover from the top of the pump, noting the location of the wiring and hose connections.

**12**  Disconnect the sender unit wiring and the fuel pump wiring from the bottom of the cover **(see illustration)**.

**13**  Where applicable, disconnect the earth wiring from the pressure regulator.

**14**  Release the clip and disconnect the fuel supply hose from the cover.

**15**  Disconnect the fuel return hose from the pressure regulator, and withdraw the cover.

**16**  Remove the cover sealing ring.

**17**  Press the three pump housing retaining lugs to release them, and simultaneously pull the pump housing from the tank using a wire hook engaged with the eyelet provided **(see illustrations)**.

**18**  To remove the pump from the housing, first pull the filter from the base of the pump **(see illustration)** and disconnect the wires

from the pump. Note the wire locations to ensure correct refitting.

**19**  Compress the three locking tabs, and pull the pump mounting plate and the pump from the housing **(see illustrations)**.

**20**  Disconnect the wiring and if necessary, remove the filter from the bottom of the fuel pump.

### Refitting

**21**  Refitting is a reversal of removal, bearing in mind the following points:

*a) Before refitting the filter to the bottom*

**8.18  Removing the fuel filter from the base of the fuel pump**

**8.19a  Compress the three locking tabs (arrowed) . . .**

**8.19b  . . . and withdraw the pump from the housing**

of the pump, inspect the filter for contamination or blockage, and renew if necessary.

b) Ensure that the pump mounting plate engages correctly with the retaining clips on the housing.

c) Check the condition of the sealing ring on the underside of the fuel pump cover, and renew if necessary.

d) Refit the fuel pump cover locking ring by tapping it clockwise until the locking clips 'click' into position.

### 9  Injection system electrical components – removal and refitting

### Testing

1  If a fault is suspected in the electronic control side of the system, first ensure that all the wiring connectors are securely connected and free of corrosion. Ensure that the suspected problem is not of a mechanical nature, or due to poor maintenance; ie, check that the air cleaner filter element is clean, the engine breather hoses are clear and undamaged, and that the cylinder compression pressures are correct, referring to Chapters 1B and 2C for further information.

2  If these checks fail to reveal the cause of the problem, the vehicle should be taken to a Vauxhall dealer or suitably-equipped engine management diagnostic specialist for testing.

3  A diagnostic socket is located in the centre of the facia, above the centre console, to which a fault code reader or other suitable test equipment can be connected (see illustration). By using the code reader or test equipment, the engine management ECU (and the various other vehicle system ECUs) can be interrogated, and any stored fault codes can be retrieved. This will allow the fault to be quickly and simply traced, alleviating the need to test all the system components individually, which is a time-consuming operation that carries a risk of damaging the ECU.

### Removal and refitting

#### Air mass meter

4  Disconnect the wiring from the air mass meter at the right-hand rear corner of the engine compartment (see illustration).

5  Slacken the retaining clamps and remove the air mass meter from the air cleaner cover and upper intake duct (see illustration).

6  Refitting is a reversal of removal, but ensure that the arrow on the air mass meter body points away from the air cleaner when refitting.

#### Crankshaft speed/position sensor

7  Lift off the plastic cover over the top of the engine.

8  The crankshaft speed/position sensor is located on the front of the cylinder block, in line with the flywheel.

9  Disconnect the sensor wiring connector, then undo the retaining bolt and remove the sensor from the cylinder block (see illustration).

10  Refitting is a reversal of removal, tightening the retaining bolt securely.

#### Camshaft position sensor

11  Lift off the plastic cover over the top of the engine.

12  The camshaft position sensor is located on the front right-hand side of the camshaft housing, above the exhaust camshaft (see illustration).

13  Disconnect the sensor wiring connector, then undo the retaining bolt and remove the sensor from the camshaft housing.

14  Refitting is a reversal of removal, tightening the retaining bolt securely.

#### Fuel pressure sensor

15  Lift off the plastic cover over the top of the engine.

16  The fuel pressure sensor is located at the right-hand end of the fuel rail.

17  Disconnect the sensor wiring connector, then unscrew the sensor from the fuel rail (see illustration 11.2a).

18  Refitting is a reversal of removal, tightening the sensor to the specified torque.

#### Manifold pressure sensor

19  Lift off the plastic cover over the top of the engine.

20  The manifold pressure sensor is located on the upper face of the inlet manifold, near the centre. For improved access, remove the turbocharger charge air pipe as described in Section 3.

21  Using a small screwdriver, lift up the locking catch and disconnect the sensor wiring connector (see illustration).

22  Undo the retaining bolt and withdraw the sensor from the manifold. Recover the sealing O-ring.

9.3  Diagnostic socket location in the centre of the facia

9.4  Disconnect the air mass meter wiring connector (arrowed)

9.5  Slacken the retaining clamps (arrowed) and remove the air mass meter

9.9  Undo the retaining bolt and remove the crankshaft speed/position sensor from the cylinder block

9.12  Camshaft position sensor location (arrowed)

9.21  Lift up the locking catch to disconnect the manifold pressure sensor wiring connector

**23** Renew the sealing O-ring, then refit the sensor and tighten the retaining bolt securely. Reconnect the wiring connector and secure with the locking catch.

**24** If removed, refit the charge air pipe as described in Section 3, then refit the engine cover.

### Electronic control unit (ECU)

**Note:** *If a new ECU is to be fitted, this work must be entrusted to a Vauxhall dealer or suitably-equipped specialist. It is necessary to initialise the new ECU after installation, which requires the use of dedicated Vauxhall diagnostic equipment.*

**25** Disconnect the battery negative terminal (refer to *Disconnecting the battery* in the Reference Chapter).

**26** Unclip the expansion tank coolant hose and the wiring harness from the fuel filter crash box, and disconnect the harness connector **(see illustrations 3.34a and 3.34b)**.

**27** Release the retaining clip, lift the coolant expansion tank from its location and place it to one side **(see illustration 3.35)**.

**28** Withdraw the locking plates, lift the locking levers and disconnect the two wiring connectors from the ECU **(see illustrations)**.

**29** Undo the two nuts securing each end of the ECU mounting frame to the body **(see illustration)**.

**30** Move the wiring harness to one side and lift the ECU and mounting frame from the engine compartment.

**31** Undo the four nuts and separate the ECU from the mounting frame.

**32** Refitting is a reversal of removal, ensuring that the wiring connectors are securely connected and locked with the locking levers.

### Coolant temperature sensor

**33** Refer to the procedures contained in Chapter 3, Section 6.

### Wheel speed sensors

**34** Refer to the anti-lock braking system information contained in Chapter 9.

---

## 10 High-pressure fuel pump – removal and refitting

---

**Warning: Refer to the information contained in Section 2 before proceeding.**

### Removal

**1** Remove the braking system vacuum pump as described in Chapter 9.

**2** Thoroughly clean the fuel pipe unions on the fuel pump and fuel rail. Using an open-ended spanner, unscrew the union nuts securing the high-pressure fuel pipe to the fuel pump and fuel rail. Counterhold the unions on the pump with a second spanner, while unscrewing the union nuts. Withdraw the high-pressure fuel pipe and plug or cover the open unions to prevent dirt entry.

**9.28a Withdraw the locking plates . . .**

**9.29a ECU mounting frame front retaining nut (arrowed) . . .**

**3** Release the retaining clip and disconnect the fuel return hose, either at the pump or at the fuel rail. Cover the hose end to prevent dirt entry.

**4** Release the fuel supply hose from the support clip on the turbocharger charge air pipe.

**5** Unscrew the three mounting bolts and withdraw the pump from the camshaft housing. Recover the sealing O-ring **(see illustrations)**.

*Caution: The high-pressure fuel pump is manufactured to extremely close tolerances and must not be dismantled in any way. No parts for the pump are available separately and if the unit is in any way suspect, it must be renewed.*

### Refitting

**6** Thoroughly clean the fuel pump and camshaft housing mating faces.

**7** Locate a new sealing O-ring on the pump

**10.5b . . . withdraw the fuel pump from the camshaft housing . . .**

**9.28b . . . then lift the locking levers and disconnect the ECU wiring connectors**

**9.29b . . . and rear retaining nut (arrowed)**

flange and lubricate the O-ring with clean diesel fuel.

**8** Align the pump drive dog with the slot on the camshaft, then place the pump in position. Refit the three mounting bolts and tighten them to the specified torque.

**10.5a Unscrew the three mounting bolts (arrowed) . . .**

**10.5c . . . and recover the sealing O-ring**

**11.2a Disconnect the wiring connector at the fuel pressure sensor . . .**

**11.2b . . . and fuel pressure regulating valve**

**11.3a Unscrew the union nuts securing the high-pressure fuel pipes to the fuel injectors . . .**

**11.3b . . . and the fuel rail**

**11.4a Unscrew the union nuts securing the high-pressure fuel pipe to the fuel pump . . .**

**11.4b . . . and fuel rail**

**9** Locate the fuel supply hose in its clip on the turbocharger charge air pipe.

**10** Reconnect the fuel return hose and secure with the retaining clip.

**11** Remove the blanking plugs from the fuel pipe unions on the pump and fuel rail. Locate high-pressure fuel pipe over the unions and screw on the union nuts finger tight at this stage.

**12** Using a torque wrench and crow-foot adapter, tighten the fuel pipe union nuts to the specified torque. Counterhold the unions on the pump with an open-ended spanner, while tightening the union nuts.

**13** Refit the braking system vacuum pump as described in Chapter 9.

**14** Observing the precautions listed in Section 2, prime the fuel system as described in Section 5, then start the engine and allow it to idle. Check for leaks at the high-pressure fuel pipe unions with the engine idling. If

satisfactory, increase the engine speed to 4000 rpm and check again for leaks. Take the car for a short road test and check for leaks once again on return. If any leaks are detected, obtain and fit a new high-pressure fuel pipe.

**15** Refit the engine cover on completion.

## 11 Fuel rail – removal and refitting

> ⚠️ **Warning: Refer to the information contained in Section 2 before proceeding.**

### Removal

**1** Remove the turbocharger charge air pipe as described in Section 3.

**2** Disconnect the wiring connectors at the at the fuel pressure sensor and fuel pressure regulating valve on the fuel rail **(see illustrations)**.

**3** Thoroughly clean all the high-pressure fuel pipe unions on the fuel rail, fuel pump and injectors. Using two spanners, hold the unions and unscrew the union nuts securing the high-pressure fuel pipes to the fuel injectors. Unscrew the union nuts securing the high-pressure fuel pipes to the fuel rail, withdraw the pipes and plug or cover the open unions to prevent dirt entry **(see illustrations)**. It is advisable to lable each fuel pipe (1 to 4) to avoid confusion when refitting.

**4** Using an open-ended spanner, unscrew the union nuts securing the high-pressure fuel pipe to the fuel pump and fuel rail. Counterhold the unions on the pump with a second spanner, while unscrewing the union nuts **(see illustrations)**. Withdraw the high-pressure fuel pipe and plug or cover the open unions to prevent dirt entry.

**5** Release the retaining clip and disconnect the upper fuel return hose at the fuel rail **(see illustration)**. Cover the hose end to prevent dirt entry.

**6** Release the lower fuel return hose at the quick-release connector at the fuel rail. A Vauxhall special tool is available to release the connector, but provided care is taken, it can be released using a pair of long-nosed pliers, two small screwdrivers, or similar, to depress the retaining tangs **(see illustration)**. Plug or cover the open unions to prevent dirt entry.

**7** Disconnect the fuel leak-off hose connection at each injector by extracting the locking clip and lifting out the hose fitting **(see illustrations)**. Refit the locking clips to the injectors after disconnecting the hose fitting. Slip a plastic bag over the disconnected

**11.5 Disconnect the upper fuel return hose at the fuel rail**

**11.6 Using two screwdrivers to release the lower fuel return hose quick-release connector (arrowed)**

**11.7a Extract the locking clip . . .**

**11.7b . . . and disconnect the fuel leak-off hose connection at each injector**

**11.7c Slip a plastic bag over the disconnected leak-off hose to prevent dirt entry**

**11.8a Undo the two fuel rail retaining bolts (arrowed) . . .**

**11.8b . . . and lift the fuel rail off the mounting bracket**

**11.9a Fuel pressure sensor (arrowed)**

leak-off hose to prevent dirt entry **(see illustration)**.

**8** Undo the two retaining bolts and lift the fuel rail off the mounting bracket **(see illustrations)**.

**9** If required, the fuel return hose banjo union can be removed after unscrewing the union bolt and collecting the two copper washers. The fuel pressure sensor can be unscrewed from the end of the fuel rail and the pressure regulating valve can be removed after unscrewing the two retaining bolts **(see illustrations)**. Recover the sealing O-rings from the pressure sensor and pressure regulating valve.

### Refitting

**10** If removed, refit the fuel pressure sensor and pressure regulating valve to the fuel rail using new sealing O-rings lubricated with clean diesel fuel. Tighten the pressure sensor and the pressure regulating bolts to the specified torque. Similarly refit the fuel return banjo union using new copper washers and tightening the banjo union bolt securely.

**11** Locate the fuel rail on the mounting bracket, refit the two retaining bolts and tighten them to the specified torque.

**12** Reconnect the fuel leak-off hose fittings to the injectors by pushing in the locking clip,

attaching the fitting, then releasing the locking clip. Ensure that each fitting is securely connected and retained by the clip.

**13** Refit the lower fuel return hose quick-release connector, then refit the upper return hose and secure with the retaining clip.

**14** Working on one fuel injector at a time, remove the blanking plugs from the fuel pipe unions on the fuel rail and the relevant injector. Locate the high-pressure fuel pipe over the unions and screw on the union nuts finger tight. Tighten the union nuts to the specified torque using a torque wrench and crow-foot adapter **(see illustration)**. Counterhold the union on the injector with an open-ended spanner, while

**11.9b Fuel pressure regulating valve retaining bolts (A) and fuel return hose banjo union (B)**

**11.14 Tighten the fuel pipe union nuts using a torque wrench and crow-foot adapter**

**12.5 Disconnect the injector wiring, while moving the wiring harness guide forward**

**12.8a Unscrew the retaining nut . . .**

**12.8b . . . then remove the upper washer . . .**

**12.8c . . . and lower washer from the injector clamp brackets**

tightening the union nut. Repeat this operation for the remaining three injectors.

**15** Similarly, fit the high-pressure fuel pipe to the fuel pump and fuel rail, and tighten the union nuts to the specified torque. Counterhold the union on the pump with an open-ended spanner, while tightening the union nut.

**16** Reconnect the wiring connectors at the fuel pressure sensor and pressure regulating valve.

**17** Refit the turbocharger charge air pipe as described in Section 3.

**18** Observing the precautions listed in Section 2, prime the fuel system as described in Section 5, then start the engine and allow it to idle. Check for leaks at the high-pressure fuel pipe unions with the engine idling. If satisfactory, increase the engine speed to 4000 rpm and check again for leaks. Take the car for a short road test and check for leaks once again on return. If any leaks are

detected, obtain and fit a new high-pressure fuel pipe(s).

**19** Refit the engine cover on completion.

## 12 Fuel injectors –
removal and refitting

⚠️ **Warning: Refer to the information contained in Section 2 before proceeding.**

**Note:** *The following procedure describes the removal and refitting of the injectors as a complete set, however the injectors may be removed in pairs if required. New copper sealing washers will be required for each disturbed injector when refitting.*

### Removal

**1** Remove the turbocharger charge air pipe as described in Section 3.

**2** Thoroughly clean all the high-pressure fuel pipe unions on the fuel rail and injectors.

**3** Disconnect the wiring connector at the camshaft position sensor on the top of the camshaft housing.

**4** Unscrew the three bolts securing the plastic wiring harness guide to the top of the camshaft housing.

**5** Release the locking catches securing the wiring connectors to the four injectors, then disconnect the injector wiring, while at the same time moving the wiring harness guide forward **(see illustration)**.

**6** Using two spanners, hold the unions and unscrew the union nuts securing the high-pressure fuel pipes to the fuel injectors. Unscrew the union nuts securing the high-pressure fuel pipes to the fuel rail, withdraw the pipes and plug or cover the open unions to prevent dirt entry **(see illustrations 11.3a and 11.3b)**. It is advisable to lable each fuel pipe (1 to 4) to avoid confusion when refitting.

**7** Disconnect the fuel leak-off hose connection at each injector by extracting the locking clip and lifting out the hose fitting **(see illustrations 11.7a and 11.7b)**. Refit the locking clips to the injectors after disconnecting the hose fitting. Slip a plastic bag over the disconnected leak-off hose to prevent dirt entry **(see illustration 11.7c)**.

**8** Unscrew the retaining nut then remove the two washers from the injector clamp brackets **(see illustrations)**. There are two clamp brackets, one securing injectors one and two, and the other securing injectors three and four.

**9** Working on one pair of injectors at a time (one and two, or three and four) withdraw the two injectors together with the clamp bracket from the camshaft housing and cylinder head. If difficulty is experienced removing the injectors, liberally apply penetrating oil to the base of each injector and allow time for the oil to penetrate. If the injectors are still reluctant to free, it will be necessary to use a small slide hammer engaged under the flange of the injector body casting, and gently tap them free. Note that it is not possible to twist the injectors from side-to-side to free them due to the design of the clamp bracket which positively engages in slots in the injector body **(see illustrations)**.

**12.9a If necessary, use a slide hammer to free the injectors . . .**

**12.9b . . . then withdraw the two injectors together with the clamp bracket**

**12.9c The clamp bracket engages with slots in the injector body**

**10** Once the injector pair has been removed, separate them from the clamp bracket and remove the copper washer from each injector **(see illustration)**. The copper washers may have remained in place at the base of the injector orifice in the cylinder head. If so, hook them out with a length of wire. Remove the upper injector seals from the camshaft housing.

**11** Examine each injector visually for any signs of obvious damage or deterioration. If any defects are apparent, renew the injector(s).

*Caution: The injectors are manufactured to extremely close tolerances and must not be dismantled in any way. Do not unscrew the fuel pipe union on the side of the injector, or separate any parts of the injector body. Do not attempt to clean carbon deposits from the injector nozzle or carry out any form of ultrasonic or pressure testing.*

**12** If the injectors are in a satisfactory condition, plug the fuel pipe union (if not already done) and suitably cover the electrical element and the injector nozzle.

**13** Prior to refitting, obtain a new copper washer and camshaft housing seal for each removed injector.

### Refitting

**14** Locate a new copper washer on the base of each injector, and fit a new seal to the injector location in the camshaft housing.

**15** Place the injector clamp bracket in the slot on each injector body and refit the injectors to the cylinder head in pairs. Guide the clamp bracket over the mounting stud as each injector pair is inserted.

**16** Fit the two washers and the injector clamp bracket retaining nut to the mounting stud of each injector pair. Tighten the nuts finger tight only at this stage.

**17** Working on one fuel injector at a time, remove the blanking plugs from the fuel pipe unions on the fuel rail and the relevant injector. Locate the high-pressure fuel pipe over the unions and screw on the union nuts. Take care not to cross-thread the nuts or strain the fuel pipes as they are fitted. Once the union nut threads have started, tighten the nuts moderately tight only at this stage.

**18** When all the fuel pipes are in place, tighten the injector clamp bracket retaining nuts to the specified torque.

**19** Tighten the fuel pipe union nuts to the specified torque using a torque wrench and crow-foot adapter **(see illustration 11.14)**. Counterhold the union on the injector with an open-ended spanner, while tightening the union nut. Repeat this operation for the remaining three injectors.

**20** Reconnect the fuel leak-off hose fittings to the injectors by pushing in the locking clip, attaching the fitting, then releasing the locking clip. Ensure that each fitting is securely connected and retained by the clip.

**21** Reconnect the fuel injector wiring connectors and secure with the locking catches.

**12.10  Remove the copper washer from each injector**

**22** Refit the three bolts securing the plastic wiring harness guide to the top of the camshaft housing.

**23** Reconnect the camshaft position sensor wiring connector.

**24** Refit the turbocharger charge air pipe as described in Section 3.

**25** Observing the precautions listed in Section 2, prime the fuel system as described in Section 5, then start the engine and allow it to idle. Check for leaks at the high-pressure fuel pipe unions with the engine idling. If satisfactory, increase the engine speed to 4000 rpm and check again for leaks. Take the car for a short road test and check for leaks once again on return. If any leaks are detected, obtain and fit a new high-pressure fuel pipe(s).

**26** Refit the engine cover on completion.

### 13  Fuel pressure regulating valve – removal and refitting

⚠️ *Warning: Refer to the information contained in Section 2 before proceeding.*

### Removal

**1** The fuel pressure regulating valve is located on the left-hand end of the fuel rail.

**2** Lift off the plastic cover over the top of the engine.

**3** Disconnect the pressure regulating valve wiring connector **(see illustration 11.2b)**.

**4** Undo the two retaining bolts and remove

**14.6  Undo the retaining bolt and detach the crankcase ventilation hose attachment**

the valve from the fuel rail. Recover the sealing O-ring.

### Refitting

**5** Thoroughly clean the fuel rail and pressure regulating valve mating faces.

**6** Locate a new sealing O-ring on the pressure regulating valve and lubricate the O-ring with clean diesel fuel.

**7** Refit the valve to the fuel rail and secure with the two retaining bolts tightened to the specified torque.

**8** Reconnect the wiring connector and refit the engine cover.

### 14  Inlet manifold – removal and refitting

### Removal

**1** Disconnect the battery negative terminal (refer to *Disconnecting the battery* in the Reference Chapter).

**2** Remove the air cleaner assembly and turbocharger charge air pipe as described in Section 3.

**3** Remove the exhaust gas recirculation (EGR) valve as described in Chapter 4E.

**4** Withdraw the engine oil dipstick, then undo the retaining bolt securing the dipstick guide tube to the inlet manifold.

**5** Using a small screwdriver, lift up the locking catch and disconnect the manifold pressure sensor wiring connector **(see illustration 9.21)**.

**6** Undo the retaining bolt and detach the crankcase ventilation hose attachment at the timing cover **(see illustration)**.

**7** Undo the two bolts and free the crankcase ventilation system oil separator from the inlet manifold **(see illustration)**.

**8** Undo the nine retaining bolts (noting their different lengths) and remove the inlet manifold from the cylinder head. Remove the rubber gasket from the manifold flange **(see illustrations)**.

### Refitting

**9** Thoroughly clean the inlet manifold and cylinder head mating faces, then locate a new rubber gasket on the inlet manifold flange.

**10** Locate the manifold in position and refit the

**14.7  Undo the two bolts (arrowed) and free the oil separator from the inlet manifold**

14.8a Undo the retaining bolts (arrowed) and remove the inlet manifold . . .

14.8b . . . then remove the rubber gasket from the manifold flange

retaining bolts. Diagonally and progressively, tighten the bolts to the specified torque.

11 Refit the crankcase ventilation system oil separator to the inlet manifold.

12 Refit the crankcase ventilation hose attachment to the timing cover and secure with the retaining bolt, securely tightened.

13 Refit the wiring connector to the manifold pressure sensor.

14 Refit and tighten the bolt securing the oil dipstick guide tube to the manifold, then re-insert the dipstick.

15 Refit the exhaust gas recirculation (EGR) valve as described in Chapter 4E.

16 Refit the air cleaner assembly and turbocharger charge air pipe as described in Section 3.

17 On completion, reconnect the battery negative terminal.

## 15 Intercooler – removal and refitting

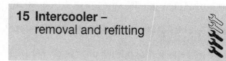

### Removal

1 Remove the front bumper as described in Chapter 11.

2 Slacken the retaining clip, disconnect the quick-release fitting and remove the charge air pipe and charge air pipe connection hose from each side of the intercooler.

3 Release the retaining clip each side and remove the intercooler from the radiator.

### Refitting

4 Refitting is a reversal of removal.

16.5 Undo nut and two bolts (arrowed) and remove the oil filter heat shield

16.7 Engine lifting bracket retaining bolt (A) and heat shield centre retaining nut (B)

16.8 Undo the two bolts (arrowed) securing the coolant pipe to the heat exchanger

16.9 Unscrew the turbocharger oil supply pipe banjo union bolt (arrowed) from the oil filter housing

## 16 Exhaust manifold – removal and refitting

**Note:** *New manifold retaining nuts, a new manifold gasket, coolant pipe gasket, catalytic converter gasket, oil filter housing rubber seal, catalytic converter retaining bolt locking plate and turbocharger oil supply pipe banjo union copper washers will be required for refitting.*

### Removal

1 Disconnect the battery negative terminal (refer to *Disconnecting the battery* in the Reference Chapter).

2 Referring to the procedures contained in Section 19, separate the exhaust system front section from the catalytic converter.

3 Drain the cooling system as described in Chapter 1B.

4 Remove the turbocharger charge air pipe and the charge air hose as described in Section 3.

5 Undo the upper nut and two lower bolts and remove the oil filter heat shield **(see illustration)**.

6 Disconnect the wiring connector from the oil pressure switch located at the left-hand end of the cylinder head.

7 Undo the bolt securing the engine lifting bracket to the exhaust manifold and the central nut securing the heat shield to the manifold **(see illustration)**. Remove the lifting bracket, then manipulate the heat shield off the manifold.

8 Undo the two bolts securing the coolant pipe to the heat exchanger on the oil filter housing **(see illustration)**. Release the retaining clip securing the other end of the pipe to the hose on the thermostat housing. Undo the pipe support bracket bolt, release the wiring harness from the retaining clip and remove the coolant pipe from the engine. Recover the gasket noting that a new one will be required for refitting.

9 Unscrew the banjo union bolt and release the turbocharger oil supply pipe from the oil filter housing **(see illustration)**. Recover the two copper washers from the banjo union, and suitable cover the end of the pipe to prevent dirt entry. Note that new copper washers will be required for refitting.

10 Slacken the retaining clip and disconnect the radiator bottom hose from the outlet at the base of the oil filter housing.

11 Undo the three bolts securing the heat shield support bracket to the heat exchanger on the oil filter housing **(see illustration)**.

12 Undo the remaining bolt and remove the oil filter housing and heat exchanger assembly from the cylinder block. Recover the rubber seal from the rear of the housing. Note that a new seal will be required for refitting.

13 From under the car, undo the bolt securing the catalytic converter support bracket to the sump reinforcement bracket.

14 Suitably support the weight of the catalytic

**16.11 Undo the three bolts (arrowed) securing the heat shield support bracket to the heat exchanger**

**16.14 Unscrew the three bolts (arrowed) securing the catalytic converter to the turbocharger**

**16.15 Separate the catalytic converter from the turbocharger and recover the gasket**

converter on blocks or on a jack. Bend back the locking plate tabs and unscrew the three bolts securing the catalytic converter flange to the turbocharger **(see illustration)**. Remove the bolts and locking plate, noting that a new locking plate will be required for refitting.

**15** Separate the catalytic converter from the turbocharger and recover the gasket **(see illustration)**. Carefully lower the converter and remove it from under the car. Note that a new gasket will be required for refitting.

**16** Undo the two bolts securing the turbocharger oil return pipe to the cylinder block **(see illustration)**. Disconnect the vacuum hose from the turbocharger waste gate actuator.

**17** Undo the ten nuts securing the exhaust manifold to the cylinder head. Withdraw the manifold from the cylinder head studs and

remove it, complete with turbocharger, from the engine. Recover the manifold gasket and the gasket on the turbocharger oil return pipe flange **(see illustrations)**. Note that a new manifold gasket, oil return pipe gasket and new manifold retaining nuts will be required for refitting.

**18** If required, the turbocharger can be removed from the manifold after undoing the three retaining nuts.

### Refitting

**19** If removed, thoroughly clean the mating faces of the turbocharger and exhaust manifold, then locate the turbocharger over the manifold studs. Refit the three retaining nuts and tighten to the specified torque.

**20** Locate a new gasket over the turbocharger

oil return pipe flange and bend over the tabs of the gasket to retain it on the flange **(see illustrations)**.

**21** Thoroughly clean the mating face of the exhaust manifold and cylinder head, then locate a new gasket over the studs.

**22** Locate the exhaust manifold/turbocharger over the cylinder head studs and secure with the new nuts tightened progressively to the specified torque.

**23** Refit the two bolts securing the turbocharger oil return pipe to the cylinder block and tighten them to the specified torque. Reconnect the vacuum hose to the turbocharger waste gate actuator.

**24** Using a new gasket, position the catalytic converter on the turbocharger. Insert the three retaining bolts, with a new locking plate and tighten the bolts to the specified torque. Bent

**16.16 Undo the two bolts securing the turbocharger oil return pipe to the cylinder block**

**16.17a Undo the exhaust manifold retaining nuts . . .**

**16.17b . . . withdraw the manifold from the cylinder head studs . . .**

**16.17c . . . and remove the gasket**

**16.20a Locate a new gasket over the turbocharger oil return pipe . . .**

**16.20b . . . and bend over the gasket tabs to retain it on the flange**

**16.26 Place a new rubber seal on the oil filter housing, ensuring it fully engages with the housing grooves**

over the tabs of the locking plate to retain the bolts.

25 From under the car, refit the bolt securing the catalytic converter support bracket to the sump reinforcement bracket and tighten the bolt to the specified torque.

26 Place a new rubber seal on the oil filter housing, ensuring the seal is fully engaged with the housing grooves **(see illustration)**.

27 Position the oil filter housing on the cylinder block and fit the lower left retaining bolt finger tight. Place the heat shield support bracket in position and fit the remaining three retaining bolts. Tighten the four bolts securely.

28 Connect the radiator bottom hose to the outlet at the base of the oil filter housing and secure with the retaining clip.

29 Using a new copper washer on each side of the banjo union, refit the turbocharger oil supply pipe and screw in the banjo union bolt. Tighten the bolt to the specified torque.

30 Locate a new gasket over the heat exchanger coolant pipe and bend over the tabs of the gasket to retain it on the flange **(see illustration)**.

31 Engage the coolant pipe with the hose on the thermostat housing, then position the pipe flange on the heat exchanger. Refit the two bolts and tighten them to the specified torque. At the other end of the pipe, tighten the hose retaining clip, refit and tighten the pipe support bracket bolt and secure the wiring harness with the retaining clip.

32 Place the heat shield in position over the top of the exhaust manifold. Refit the engine

**18.3a Undo the oil return pipe outer bolt, slacken the inner bolt and slide out the pipe flange**

**16.30 Locate a new gasket over the heat exchanger coolant pipe and bend over the tabs to retain it on the flange**

lifting bracket and tighten the retaining bolt finger tight.

33 Place the heat shield over the oil filter, refit the two lower bolts and tighten them finger tight. Refit the two upper nuts securing the heat shield(s), then tighten the engine lifting bracket bolt, the manifold heat shield upper nuts and the oil filter heat shield lower bolts securely.

34 Reconnect the oil pressure switch wiring connector.

35 Refit the turbocharger charge air pipe and the charge air hose as described in Section 3.

36 Refit the exhaust system components with reference to Section 19.

37 Lower the vehicle to the ground, then reconnect the battery negative lead.

38 Refill the cooling system as described in Chapter 1B.

## 17 Turbocharger – description and precautions

### Description

1 The turbocharger increases engine efficiency by raising the pressure in the inlet manifold above atmospheric pressure. Instead of the air simply being sucked into the cylinders, it is forced in.

2 Energy for the operation of the turbocharger comes from the exhaust gas. The gas flows through a specially-shaped housing (the turbine housing) and, in so doing, spins the turbine wheel. The turbine wheel is attached to

**18.3b Unscrew the return pipe inner bolt and remove the gasket**

a shaft, at the end of which is another vaned wheel known as the compressor wheel. The compressor wheel spins in its own housing, and compresses the inlet air on the way to the inlet manifold.

3 Boost pressure (the pressure in the inlet manifold) is limited by a wastegate, which diverts the exhaust gas away from the turbine wheel in response to a pressure-sensitive actuator.

4 The turbo shaft is pressure-lubricated by an oil feed pipe from the main oil gallery. The shaft 'floats' on a cushion of oil. A drain pipe returns the oil to the sump.

### Precautions

5 The turbocharger operates at extremely high speeds and temperatures. Certain precautions must be observed, to avoid premature failure of the turbo, or injury to the operator.

6 Do not operate the turbo with any of its parts exposed, or with any of its hoses removed. Foreign objects falling onto the rotating vanes could cause excessive damage, and (if ejected) personal injury.

7 Do not race the engine immediately after start-up, especially if it is cold. Give the oil a few seconds to circulate.

8 Always allow the engine to return to idle speed before switching it off – do not blip the throttle and switch off, as this will leave the turbo spinning without lubrication.

9 Allow the engine to idle for several minutes before switching off after a high-speed run.

10 Observe the recommended intervals for oil and filter changing, and use a reputable oil of the specified quality. Neglect of oil changing, or use of inferior oil, can cause carbon formation on the turbo shaft, leading to subsequent failure.

## 18 Turbocharger – removal, inspection and refitting

### Removal

1 Carry out the operations described in Section 16, paragraphs 1 to 16.

2 Undo the three retaining nuts, then remove the turbocharger from the exhaust manifold.

3 If required, remove the oil return pipe from the turbocharger as follows. Undo the outer bolt, slacken the inner bolt and slide the pipe out from its location (the inner bolt hole in the pipe flange is slotted to allow removal). With the pipe removed, unscrew the inner bolt and recover the gasket **(see illustrations)**.

4 If required, unscrew the banjo union bolt and release the turbocharger oil supply pipe. Recover the two copper washers from the banjo union, noting that new copper washers will be required for refitting.

### Inspection

5 With the turbocharger removed, inspect the housing for cracks or other visible damage.

6 Spin the turbine or the compressor wheel,

**19.7 Removing the exhaust system front section from the catalytic converter**

to verify that the shaft is intact and to feel for excessive shake or roughness. Some play is normal, since in use, the shaft is 'floating' on a film of oil. Check that the wheel vanes are undamaged.

**7** If oil contamination of the exhaust or induction passages is apparent, it is likely that turbo shaft oil seals have failed.

**8** No DIY repair of the turbo is possible and none of the internal or external parts are available separately. If the turbocharger is suspect in any way a complete new unit must be obtained.

### Refitting

**9** Thoroughly clean the turbocharger and exhaust manifold mating faces.

**10** If removed, refit the oil return pipe inner mounting bolt to the turbocharger, together with a new gasket, and screw the bolt in two or

three turns. Slide the oil return pipe into place, align the gasket and fit the outer retaining bolt. Tighten both retaining bolts securely.

**11** Also, if removed, refit the oil supply pipe, using a new copper washer on each side of the banjo union, refit the banjo union bolt and tighten the bolt to the specified torque.

**12** Engage the turbocharger mounting studs with the exhaust manifold, refit the three retaining nuts and tighten to the specified torque.

**13** Refit the exhaust manifold and turbocharger assembly as described in Section 16, paragraphs 20 to 38.

## 19 Exhaust system – general information and component renewal

### General information

**1** The exhaust system is in two sections. The front section includes the silencer and intermediate pipe. The rear section consists of the tailpipe and silencer.

**2** Periodically, the exhaust system should be checked for signs of leaks or damage. Also inspect the system rubber mountings, and renew if necessary.

**3** Small holes or cracks can be repaired using proprietary exhaust repair products.

**4** Before renewing an individual section of the exhaust system, it is wise to inspect the remaining section. If corrosion or damage is evident, it may prove more economical to renew the entire system.

### Component renewal

**5** If either part of the system is to be renewed, it is important to ensure that the correct component is obtained.

**6** To remove the rear tailpipe and silencer, chock the front wheels then jack up the rear of the vehicle and support on axle stands (see *Jacking and vehicle support*). Loosen the clamp securing the intermediate pipe to the tailpipe, then release the rubber mountings and slide the tailpipe from the intermediate pipe. If the tailpipe is rusted onto the intermediate pipe, apply liberal amounts of penetrating oil and tap around the joint with a hammer to free it. Twist the tailpipe in both directions while holding the intermediate pipe.

**7** To remove the front section of the exhaust, jack up the front and rear of the vehicle and support it on axle stands (see *Jacking and vehicle support*). Remove the tailpipe and silencer as described in paragraph 6. Loosen the clamp securing the exhaust front section to the catalytic converter then release the rubber mountings and slide the front section from the catalytic converter **(see illustration)**. While doing this, take care to support the flexible section. **Note:** *Angular movement in excess of 10° can cause permanent damage to the flexible section.* If the front section is rusted onto the catalytic converter, apply liberal amounts of penetrating oil and tap around the joint with a hammer to free it. Twist the front section in both directions until free.

**8** Refitting is a reversal of removal, tightening the clamp nuts to the specified torque.

# Notes

# Chapter 4 Part D:
# Fuel and exhaust systems –
# 1.7 litre diesel engines

## Contents

## Degrees of difficulty

| Easy, suitable for novice with little experience  | Fairly easy, suitable for beginner with some experience  | Fairly difficult, suitable for competent DIY mechanic | Difficult, suitable for experienced DIY mechanic  | Very difficult, suitable for expert DIY or professional  |
|---|---|---|---|---|

## Specifications

### General

System type . . . . . . . . . . . . . . . . . . . . . . . . . . . . . . . . . . . . . . . . . . . . ECD V5 direct injection system incorporating an electronically-controlled Nippon Denso V5 distributor fuel injection pump with integral transfer pump. Two stage injectors with pilot and post injection. Turbocharger fitted to all models and intercooler on Y17DT engined models

### Adjustment data

Idle speed . . . . . . . . . . . . . . . . . . . . . . . . . . . . . . . . . . . . . . . . . . . . . 825 to 875 rpm – controlled by ECU
Maximum speed . . . . . . . . . . . . . . . . . . . . . . . . . . . . . . . . . . . . . . . . 5060 to 5180 rpm – controlled by ECU

### Injection pump

Direction of rotation . . . . . . . . . . . . . . . . . . . . . . . . . . . . . . . . . . . . . Clockwise, viewed from sprocket end
Pump timing (static):
  Checking . . . . . . . . . . . . . . . . . . . . . . . . . . . . . . . . . . . . . . . . . . . . 0.28 to 0.33 mm pump plunger travel @ TDC
  Setting . . . . . . . . . . . . . . . . . . . . . . . . . . . . . . . . . . . . . . . . . . . . . . 0.33 mm pump plunger travel @ TDC
Transfer fuel pump pressure . . . . . . . . . . . . . . . . . . . . . . . . . . . . . . . 8.0 ± 0.1 bars at 2200 rpm

### Injectors

Opening pressure . . . . . . . . . . . . . . . . . . . . . . . . . . . . . . . . . . . . . . . 175 bar (1st stage) to 335 bar (2nd stage)

### Torque wrench settings

| | Nm | lbf ft |
|---|---|---|
| Accelerator pedal/position sensor . . . . . . . . . . . . . . . . . . . . . . . . . . | 9 | 7 |
| Air conditioning compressor bracket . . . . . . . . . . . . . . . . . . . . . . . . | 43 | 32 |
| Air conditioning compressor . . . . . . . . . . . . . . . . . . . . . . . . . . . . . . | 22 | 16 |
| Charge pressure sensor . . . . . . . . . . . . . . . . . . . . . . . . . . . . . . . . . | 10 | 7 |
| Coolant temperature sensor . . . . . . . . . . . . . . . . . . . . . . . . . . . . . . | 22 | 16 |
| Crankshaft sensor . . . . . . . . . . . . . . . . . . . . . . . . . . . . . . . . . . . . . | 10 | 7 |
| Electronic control unit . . . . . . . . . . . . . . . . . . . . . . . . . . . . . . . . . . . | 6 | 4 |

## Torque wrench settings (contnued)

| | Nm | lbf ft |
|---|---|---|
| Exhaust front pipe-to-turbocharger nuts . . . . . . . . . . . . . . . . . . . . . . | 67 | 49 |
| Exhaust manifold: | | |
|    Retaining nuts and bolts. . . . . . . . . . . . . . . . . . . . . . . . . . . . . . . . | 24 | 18 |
|    Support bracket bolts. . . . . . . . . . . . . . . . . . . . . . . . . . . . . . . . . . | 51 | 38 |
| Fuel injector return pipe unions . . . . . . . . . . . . . . . . . . . . . . . . . . . . | 15 | 11 |
| Fuel injectors . . . . . . . . . . . . . . . . . . . . . . . . . . . . . . . . . . . . . . . . . | 22 | 16 |
| Fuel pipe union nuts. . . . . . . . . . . . . . . . . . . . . . . . . . . . . . . . . . . . . | 23 | 17 |
| Fuel tank. . . . . . . . . . . . . . . . . . . . . . . . . . . . . . . . . . . . . . . . . . . . . | 20 | 15 |
| Injection pump: | | |
|    Central bleed screw . . . . . . . . . . . . . . . . . . . . . . . . . . . . . . . . . . | 25 | 18 |
|    Pump bracket to cylinder block . . . . . . . . . . . . . . . . . . . . . . . . . | 54 | 40 |
|    Pump to pump bracket. . . . . . . . . . . . . . . . . . . . . . . . . . . . . . . . | 18 | 13 |
|    Pump to timing cover . . . . . . . . . . . . . . . . . . . . . . . . . . . . . . . . . | 20 | 15 |
|    Timing belt sprocket nut. . . . . . . . . . . . . . . . . . . . . . . . . . . . . . . | 69 | 51 |
| Inlet manifold nuts and bolts*. . . . . . . . . . . . . . . . . . . . . . . . . . . . . . | 25 | 18 |
| Oil pressure switch. . . . . . . . . . . . . . . . . . . . . . . . . . . . . . . . . . . . . . | 21 | 15 |
| Oil return line banjo . . . . . . . . . . . . . . . . . . . . . . . . . . . . . . . . . . . . . | 15 | 11 |
| Turbocharger: | | |
|    Exhaust flange nuts . . . . . . . . . . . . . . . . . . . . . . . . . . . . . . . . . . | 27 | 20 |
|    Oil feed line adaptor to block . . . . . . . . . . . . . . . . . . . . . . . . . . . | 21 | 15 |
|    Oil feed line to turbocharger/block adaptor . . . . . . . . . . . . . . . . | 10 | 7 |
|    Turbocharger-to-manifold nuts. . . . . . . . . . . . . . . . . . . . . . . . . . | 27 | 20 |

* Use new fasteners

## 1  General information and precautions

### General information

**1** The fuel supply system consists of a fuel tank (which is mounted under the rear of the car), a fuel filter with integral water separator (in the engine compartment), an electronically-controlled distributor fuel injection pump with integral transfer pump, injectors and associated components.

**2** Fuel is drawn from the fuel tank by the fuel injection pump. Before reaching the pump, the fuel passes through a fuel filter, where foreign matter and water are removed. Excess fuel lubricates the moving components of the pump, and is then returned to the tank.

**3** The fuel injection pump is driven at half-crankshaft speed by the timing belt. The high pressure required to inject the fuel into the compressed air in the cylinder is achieved by radial plungers.

**4** The injection pump is electronically-controlled to meet the latest emission standards. The system consists of the engine electronic control unit, the injection electronic control unit, and the following sensors:

a) *Accelerator pedal position sensor – informs the ECUs of the accelerator pedal position.*

b) *Coolant temperature sensor – informs the ECUs of engine temperature.*

c) *Intake air temperature sensor – informs the ECUs of the temperature of the air passing through the intake duct.*

d) *Hot film mass airflow meter – informs the ECUs of the amount of air passing through the intake duct.*

e) *Crankshaft sensor – informs the ECUs of engine speed and crankshaft position.*

f) *Charge pressure sensor – informs ECUs of the pressure in the inlet manifold.*

g) *ABS control unit – informs the ECUs of the vehicle speed.*

h) *Atmospheric pressure sensor – informs the ECUs of the atmospheric pressure.*

i) *Fuel temperature sensor – informs the ECUs of the fuel temperature.*

j) *Injection pump shaft sensor – used by the ECUs to determine the exact injection timing.*

k) *Oil pressure switch – used by the engine ECU to control the instrument cluster oil warning lamp.*

l) *Clutch switch – used by the ECUs for cruise control functions.*

m) *Air conditioning system compressor switch (where fitted) – informs the ECUs when the air conditioning system is switched on.*

**5** All the above information is analysed by the ECUs and, based on this, the ECUs determine the appropriate injection requirements for the engine. The engine ECU controls the injection pump timing, via the pump control unit, to provide the best setting for cranking, starting (with either a hot or cold engine), warm-up, idle, cruising, and acceleration.

**6** Basic injection timing is determined when the pump is fitted. When the engine is running, it is varied automatically to suit the prevailing engine speed by a mechanism which turns the cam plate or ring – controlled by the ECU.

**7** The engine ECU also controls the exhaust gas recirculation (EGR) system (see Chapter 4E) and the pre-heating system (see Chapter 5C).

**8** The four fuel injectors produce a spray of fuel directly into the cylinders. The injectors are calibrated to open and close at critical pressures to provide efficient and even combustion. Each injector needle is lubricated by fuel which accumulates in the spring chamber and is channelled to the injection pump return hose by leak-off pipes.

**9** The inlet manifold is a two-part assembly sealed by a metal gasket. The EGR (exhaust gas recirculation) valve and charge pressure sensor are mounted to the upper part of the manifold.

**10** A turbocharger is fitted to increase engine efficiency by raising the pressure in the inlet manifold above atmospheric pressure. Instead of the air simply being sucked into the cylinders, it is forced in. Additional fuel is supplied by the injection pump in proportion to the increased air intake.

**11** Energy for the operation of the turbocharger comes from the exhaust gas. The gas flows through a specially-shaped housing (the turbine housing) and in so doing, spins the turbine wheel. The turbine wheel is attached to a shaft, at the end of which is another vaned wheel known as the compressor wheel. The compressor wheel spins in its own housing, and compresses the inlet air on the way to the inlet manifold.

**12** Between the turbocharger and the inlet manifold, the compressed air passes through an intercooler (except Y17DTL engine). This is an air-to-air heat exchanger mounted next to the radiator, and supplied with cooling air from the front of the vehicle. The purpose of the intercooler is to remove some of the heat gained in being compressed from the inlet air. Because cooler air is denser, removal of this heat further increases engine efficiency.

2.1a Air cleaner and ducting – 17DTL engine

| | | | | | |
|---|---|---|---|---|---|
| 1 | Air cleaner housing | 3 | Air intake hose | 6 | Charge air hose |
| 2 | Hot film mass airflow | 4 | Air intake manifold | 7 | Resonator/air intake pipe |
| | meter | 5 | Charge air pipe | 8 | Connecting hose |

**Caution:** *Do not operate the engine if any of air intake ducts are disconnected or the filter element is removed. Any debris entering the engine will cause severe damage to the turbocharger.*

**Caution:** *To prevent damage to the turbocharger, do not race the engine immediately after start-up, especially if it is cold. Allow it to idle smoothly to give the oil a few seconds to circulate around the turbocharger bearings. Always allow the engine to return to idle speed before switching it off – do not blip the throttle and switch off, as this will leave the turbo spinning without lubrication.*

**Caution:** *Observe the recommended intervals for oil and filter changing, and use oil of the specified quality. Neglect of oil changing, or use of inferior oil, can cause carbon formation on the turbo shaft, leading to subsequent failure.*

## 2 Air cleaner assembly and intake ducts – removal and refitting

**Note:** *The intercooler is only fitted to the Y17DT engine.*

### Removal

**1** Disconnect the wiring from the hot film mass airflow meter by releasing it towards the air cleaner cover **(see illustrations)**.

**13** Charge pressure (the pressure in the inlet manifold) is limited by a wastegate, which diverts the exhaust gas away from the turbine wheel in response to a pressure-sensitive actuator. A pressure-operated switch operates a warning light on the instrument panel in the event of excessive charge pressure developing.

**14** The turbo shaft is pressure-lubricated by an oil feed pipe from the engine main oil so that the shaft 'floats' on a cushion of oil. A drain pipe returns the oil to the sump.

**15** The charge pressure wastegate is controlled by the ECU via a solenoid valve.

**16** If there is an abnormality in any of the readings obtained from any sensor, the ECU enters its back-up mode. In this event, the ECU ignores the abnormal sensor signal, and assumes a preprogrammed value which will allow the engine to continue running (albeit at reduced efficiency). If the ECU enters this back-up mode, the warning light on the instrument panel will come on, and the relevant fault code will be stored in the ECU memory.

**17** If the warning light comes on, the vehicle should be taken to a Vauxhall dealer at the earliest opportunity. A complete test of the injection system can then be carried out, using a special electronic diagnostic test unit which is simply plugged into the system's diagnostic connector. The connector is located behind the centre of the facia.

### Precautions

⚠ **Warning:** *It is necessary to take certain precautions when working on the fuel system components, particularly the fuel injectors. Before carrying out any operations on the fuel system, refer to the precautions given in 'Safety first!' at the beginning of this manual, and to any additional warning notes at the start of the relevant Sections.*

2.1b Air cleaner and ducting – 17DT engine

| | | | | | |
|---|---|---|---|---|---|
| 1 | Air cleaner housing | 5 | Upper charge air pipe | 10 | Lower charge air pipe |
| 2 | Hot film mass airflow | 6 | Charge air hose | 11 | Centre charge air pipe |
| | meter | 7 | Charge air hose | 12 | Resonator/air intake |
| 3 | Air intake hose | 8 | Intercooler | | pipe |
| 4 | Air intake manifold | 9 | Charge air hose | 13 | Connecting hose |

2.2a Loosen the clip . . .

2.2b . . . and disconnect the mass airflow meter from the air cleaner cover

2.2c Disconnecting the air duct from the pipe at the rear of the engine

2.3a Undo the screws . . .

2.3b . . . and lift the cover from the air cleaner

2.4 Removing the element

**2** Loosen the clip and disconnect the hot film mass airflow meter from the air cleaner cover. Similarly, disconnect the duct from the intermediate pipe at the rear of the engine **(see illustrations)**.

**3** Undo the screws and lift the cover from the air cleaner **(see illustrations)**.

**4** Lift out the element **(see illustration)**.

**5** Disconnect the air inlet duct from the front of the air cleaner **(see illustration)**.

**6** Unscrew the crossbar mounting bolt from the rear of the air cleaner, and release the crossbar from the rear rubber mountings **(see illustration)**.

**7** Pull the air cleaner body rearwards from the front mounting rubber, and withdraw from the engine compartment **(see illustration)**.

**8** The remaining ducts linking the turbocharger, intercooler and inlet manifold can be removed once their retaining clips and (where necessary) bolts have been slackened.

### Refitting

**9** Refitting is the reverse of removal, ensuring that all intake ducts are properly reconnected and their retaining clips securely tightened.

### 3 Accelerator pedal and position sensor – removal and refitting

#### Removal

**1** Disconnect the battery negative lead (refer to *Disconnecting the battery* at the end of this manual).

**2** Working in the driver's footwell under the facia, disconnect the wiring from the top of the accelerator pedal/position sensor. Where necessary, pull back the footwell carpet first.

**3** Unscrew the three mounting nuts, and withdraw the sensor from the bulkhead.

### Refitting

**4** Refitting is a reversal of removal. After reconnecting the battery, have a Vauxhall dealer reprogram the volatile memories.

### 4 Fuel system – priming and bleeding

**1** It is not necessary to manually prime and bleed the fuel system after any operation on the system components. Start the engine, noting that this may take longer than usual, especially if the fuel system has been allowed to run dry. Operate the starter in ten second bursts with 5 seconds rest in between each operation, for a maximum of 40 seconds. When the engine starts, run it at a fast idle speed for a minute or so to purge any trapped air from the fuel lines. After this time the

2.5 Removing the air inlet duct from the front of the air cleaner

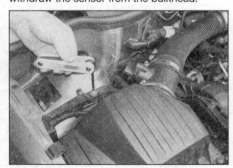

2.6 Removing the mounting crossbar from the rear of the air cleaner

2.7 Removing the air cleaner assembly

**5.4  Prise the plastic cover from the floor for access to the fuel gauge sender cover**

**5.5  Using the special tool to release the fuel line connectors**

**5.6  Disconnecting the main wiring plug**

**5.7  Tapping the locking ring anti-clockwise to release it**

**5.8  Removing the locking ring**

**5.9  Disconnect the fuel gauge sender wiring plug**

engine should idle smoothly at a constant speed.

**2** If the engine idles roughly, then there is still some air trapped in the fuel system. Increase the engine speed again for another minute or so then recheck the idle speed. Repeat this procedure as necessary until the engine is idling smoothly.

## 5  Fuel gauge sender unit – removal and refitting

**Note:** *Refer to the precautions given in Section 1 before proceeding.*
**Note:** *The fuel tank should be as empty as possible when carrying out this procedure.*

### Removal

**1** Disconnect the battery negative lead (refer to *Disconnecting the battery* at the end of this manual).

**2** Syphon out any remaining fuel in the tank through the filler pipe into a clean metal container which can be sealed.

**3** On Hatchback models, remove the rear seat as described in Chapter 11. On standard Van models, fold up the rear seat. On Combo Van models, unbolt the tank cover flap from the rear floor.

**4** Fold up the acoustic insulation, then, using a screwdriver, carefully lever out the plastic cover to expose the fuel gauge sender cover **(see illustration)**.

**5** Identify the position of the fuel feed and return lines, then disconnect the quick-release fittings. Be prepared for some loss of fuel. A Vauxhall special tool is available to release the fuel line connectors **(see illustration)**, but provided care is taken, the connectors can be released using a pair of long-nosed pliers, or

a similar tool, to depress the retaining tangs. Clamp or plug the open ends of the hoses, to prevent dirt ingress and further fuel spillage.

**6** Disconnect the main wiring plug from the cover **(see illustration)**.

**7** Release the fuel gauge sender cover locking ring. A special tool (Vauxhall tool No KM-797) is available for this, but the ring can be removed by tapping anti-clockwise until the locking clips release **(see illustration)**.

**8** Remove the locking ring, then carefully lift off the cover, noting the location of the wiring and hose connections **(see illustration)**.

**9** Disconnect the sender unit wiring from the bottom of the cover **(see illustration)**.

**10** Release the clip and disconnect the fuel supply hose from the cover **(see illustration)**.

**11** Disconnect the fuel return hose, and withdraw the cover.

**12** Remove the cover sealing ring **(see illustration)**.

**5.10  Disconnecting the fuel supply hose from the cover**

**5.12  Removing the cover sealing ring**

**5.13a  Depress the hook . . .**

**5.13b . . . pull the sender unit from the housing**

13 Depress the hook and pull the sender unit from the clips on the side of the housing **(see illustrations)**.

### Refitting

14 Refitting is a reversal of removal, bearing in mind the following points:
  a) *Check the condition of the sealing ring on the underside of the fuel pump cover, and renew if necessary.*
  b) *Refit the fuel pump cover locking ring by tapping it clockwise until the locking clips 'click' into position.*

## 6  Fuel tank –
### removal and refitting

**Note:** *Refer to the precautions given in Section 1 before proceeding.*
**Note:** *The fuel tank should be as empty as possible when carrying out this procedure.*

### Removal

1 Disconnect the battery negative lead (refer to *Disconnecting the battery* at the end of this manual).
2 Syphon out any remaining fuel in the tank through the filler pipe into a clean metal container which can be sealed.
3 Chock the front wheels then jack up the rear of the vehicle and support on axle stands (see *Jacking and vehicle support*). Remove both rear wheels.

**8.1  Slide the lock to disconnect the wiring from the mass airflow meter**

4 Refer to Chapter 9 and disconnect the front ends of the rear (secondary) handbrake cables from the underbody clips after backing off the primary cable adjustment. Unclip the cables from the underbody and the right-hand side of the fuel tank, then tie them to one side, away from the fuel tank.
5 Disconnect the rear of the exhaust system from its rubber mountings, and lower the system, then move it to one side sufficiently to enable removal of the fuel tank. Alternatively, remove the exhaust system completely to provide greater clearance (refer to Section 16).
6 Disconnect the wiring from the fuel gauge sensor, at the connector on the underbody.
7 Disconnect the fuel feed and return lines at the quick-release connectors on the underbody (if necessary, detach the line retaining bracket from the underbody). Be prepared for some loss of fuel. A Vauxhall special tool is available to release the fuel line connectors, but provided care is taken, the connectors can be released using a pair of long-nosed pliers, or a similar tool, to depress the retaining tangs.
8 Unscrew the lower filler hose mounting bolt, then unclip the ventilation hose from the bottom of the fuel tank.
9 Loosen the clip and disconnect the fuel filler hose from the fuel tank.
10 Support the weight of the fuel tank on a jack with interposed block of wood.
11 Unbolt and remove the two securing straps from the fuel tank.
12 Lower the tank sufficiently to enable access to the fuel hoses on the tank, then disconnect them. Be prepared for some loss of fuel.
13 Continue to lower the tank until it can be removed from under the vehicle.
14 Plug or clamp the fuel and vent hoses to prevent entry of dust and dirt.
15 If necessary, remove the fuel lines and hoses, heat shield and wiring from the tank for transfer to the new tank. If a new tank is being fitted, it is recommended that the filter is renewed at the same time.

### Refitting

16 If the tank contains sediment or water, it may cleaned out with two or three rinses of clean fuel. Remove the fuel gauge sender unit as described in Section 5. Shake the tank vigorously, and change the fuel as necessary to remove all contamination from the tank. *This procedure should be carried out in a well-ventilated area, and it is vital to take adequate fire precautions.*
17 Any repairs to the fuel tank should be carried out by a professional. Do not under any circumstances attempt any form of DIY repair to a fuel tank.
18 Refitting is a reversal of removal, bearing in mind the following points:
  a) *Ensure that all hoses are securely reconnected to their correct locations.*
  b) *Check the handbrake cable adjustment, as described in Chapter 9.*

  c) *On completion, fill the fuel tank, then run the engine and check for leaks. If leakage is evident, stop the engine immediately and rectify the problem without delay.*

## 7  Maximum speed –
### checking and adjustment

*Caution: The maximum speed is controlled by the ECU and cannot be adjusted by the home mechanic. The speed can be checked using a tachometer as described below, but if adjustment is needed it will be necessary to take the vehicle to a Vauxhall dealer. They will have access to the necessary diagnostic equipment required to test and adjust the settings.*
1 Run the engine to normal operating temperature.
2 Have an assistant fully depress the accelerator pedal, and check that the maximum engine speed is as given in the Specifications. Do not keep the engine at maximum speed for more than two or three seconds.

## 8  Injection system
### electrical components –
### removal and refitting

### Hot film mass airflow meter

**Note:** *The intake air temperature sensor is built into the airflow meter.*

#### Removal

1 Ensure the ignition is switched off and disconnect the wiring plug from the hot film mass airflow meter. To do this, slide the lock towards the air cleaner **(see illustration)**.
2 Release the retaining clips then free the airflow meter from the air cleaner cover and intake duct. Remove it from the engine compartment.

#### Refitting

3 Refitting is the reverse of removal, ensuring the airflow meter is correctly seated in the air cleaner and duct and the retaining clips are securely tightened.

### Crankshaft sensor

#### Removal

4 Apply the handbrake, then jack up the front of the vehicle and support it on axle stands (see *Jacking and vehicle support*). Remove the engine undertray.
5 The sensor is located on the rear of the cylinder block, beneath the starter motor. Working from under the vehicle, disconnect the wiring plug from the sensor.
6 Undo the retaining bolt and remove the sensor. Recover the sealing ring **(see illustration)**.

8.6  Crankshaft position sensor

8.9  Engine coolant temperature sensor

8.18  Undo the bolts and remove the charge pressure sensor

### Refitting

7  Refitting is a reversal of removal. If necessary renew the sealing ring and tighten the sensor retaining bolt to the specified torque.

## Coolant temperature sensor

### Removal

8  With reference to Chapter 3, drain the coolant system, or be prepared for coolant spillage.

9  The coolant temperature sensor is located in the thermostat housing at the left-hand end of the cylinder head. Disconnect the wiring plug from the sensor (see illustration).

10  Unscrew the sensor from the thermostat housing. Mop up any spilled coolant.

### Refitting

11  Apply a little locking compound to the threads of the sensor, and refit the sensor to the housing. Tighten the sensor to the specified torque.

12  Reconnect the wiring plug to the sensor.

13  Top-up the coolant system (see Weekly checks or Chapter 3).

## Charge pressure sensor

### Removal

14  The charge pressure sensor is located on the right-hand rear end of the inlet manifold.

15  Loosen the clips and remove the air intake hose from above the inlet manifold.

16  Remove the exhaust gas recirculation (EGR) solenoid valve from the inlet manifold as described in Part D of this Chapter.

17  Disconnect the wiring plug from the sensor.

18  Unscrew the mounting bolt and remove the sensor (see illustration).

### Refitting

19  Refitting is a reversal of removal. Tighten the sensor retaining bolt to the specified torque.

## Oil pressure switch

### Removal

20  The signal from the oil pressure switch is used by the injection control unit to determine whether or not to illuminate the oil pressure warning light.

21  The oil pressure switch is located at the left-hand, rear end of the cylinder block. For improved access, remove the battery and battery tray as described in Chapter 5A.

22  Unclip the coolant expansion tank hose and position to one side.

23  Disconnect the wiring plug from the switch.

24  Unscrew the switch from the cylinder block. Be prepared for some oil spillage (see illustration).

### Refitting

25  Apply some suitable silicone sealant (available from Vauxhall dealers) to the threads, and screw the switch into place. Tighten the switch to the specified torque.

26  Reconnect the wiring plug, locate the expansion tank hose in the clip, and refit the battery tray and battery where removed.

27  Start the vehicle and check for oil leaks.

8.24  Oil pressure switch

## Engine electronic control unit (ECU)

### Removal

28  The engine control unit is located on top of the engine above the exhaust gas recirculation valve.

29  Disconnect the battery negative lead (refer to Disconnecting the battery in the Reference Chapter).

30  Disconnect the wiring plugs from the ECU. The two main plugs are unlocked by lifting up the metal levers, and this is best achieved using two screwdrivers (see illustrations).

31  Unbolt and remove the wiring harness bracket from the top of the ECU.

32  Unscrew the mounting bolts and nuts, and remove the ECU from the mounting bracket.

33  Release the glow plug wiring, then unscrew the two mounting bolts and single nut, and remove the ECU mounting bracket.

8.30a  Using two screwdrivers to lift the metal lock levers . . .

8.30b  . . . in order to disconnect the main plugs from the engine ECU

8.30c  Disconnecting the central wiring

**8.38 Wiring plug on the injection electronic control unit**

**8.39 Unscrew the injection ECU retaining bolts**

**8.41 Fuel injection pump**

1  Spill valve
2  Fuel return line
3  Fuel temperature sensor
4  Fuel supply line
5  Programmable read-only memory
6  Timing control solenoid
7  Injection pump shaft position sensor

### Refitting

**34** Refitting is a reversal of removal. Tighten the ECU retaining bolts/nuts to the specified

**8.43 Screw the fuel temperature sensor into the injection pump**

torque. The ECU wiring plugs are shaped such that each plug will only fit its correct socket. The plug from the left-hand side of the engine compartment connects to the rearmost socket. Take great care when refitting the plugs, as the terminals are very delicate and easily damaged. Finally, it may be necessary to have a Vauxhall dealer program all volatile memories.

### Injection electronic control unit (ECU)

#### Removal

**35** The injection ECU is located on the rear of the engine, beneath the injection pump. Access is best from beneath the vehicle.
**36** Disconnect the battery negative lead (refer to *Disconnecting the battery* in the Reference Chapter).

**37** Apply the handbrake, then jack up the front of the vehicle and support it on axle stands (see *Jacking and vehicle support*). Remove the engine undertray.
**38** Working under the vehicle, disconnect the ECU wiring plug **(see illustration)**.
**39** Undo the retaining bolts, and remove the ECU **(see illustration)**.

#### Refitting

**40** Refitting is a reversal of removal, but tighten the bolts to the specified torque. Finally, it may be necessary to have a Vauxhall dealer program all volatile memories.

### Fuel temperature sensor

#### Removal

**41** The fuel temperature sensor is fitted to the right-hand top of the injection pump **(see illustration)**.
**42** To remove the sensor, disconnect the wiring plug and unscrew the sensor from the top of the injection pump.

#### Refitting

**43** With a new seal fitted, screw the sensor into the injection pump and tighten the nut securely **(see illustration)**.
**44** Reconnect the wiring plug.

### Injection pump shaft position sensor

**45** The sensor is located on the side of the fuel injection pump.
**46** The sensor may not be available as a separate item. Check with a Vauxhall dealer prior to any attempt to remove the sensor.

### Injection commencement sensor

**47** The sensor is located on the underside of the fuel injection pump at the flywheel end.
**48** The sensor may not be available as a separate item. Check with a Vauxhall dealer prior to any attempt to remove the sensor.

### Fuel cut-off solenoid

**49** The fuel cut-off solenoid is located on top of the fuel injection pump, at the flywheel end.
**50** The solenoid may not be available as a separate item. Check with a Vauxhall dealer prior to any attempt to remove the sensor.

**9  Fuel injection pump – removal and refitting**

*Caution: Be careful not to allow dirt into the injection pump or injector pipes during this procedure.*

### Removal

**1** Disconnect the battery negative lead (refer to *Disconnecting the battery* in the Reference Chapter).
**2** Apply the handbrake, then jack up the front of the vehicle and support it on axle stands (see *Jacking and vehicle support*). Remove the right-hand front roadwheel and the inner

wheel arch liner for access to the crankshaft pulley. Remove the engine compartment undertray.

**3** Remove the timing belt and injection pump sprocket as described in Chapter 2C.

**4** Disconnect the wiring plugs from the engine electronic control unit (ECU) located on the top of the engine. The two main plugs are unlocked by lifting up the metal levers.

**5** Disconnect the crankcase ventilation hose from the camshaft cover then unscrew the mounting bolts and disconnect the air intake pipe from the turbocharger. Also disconnect the clips and remove the centre charge air hose.

**6** Remove the engine electronic control unit (ECU) and mounting bracket as described in Section 8.

**7** Unscrew the nuts and remove the starter/ alternator wiring harness bracket from the EGR valve.

**8** Unscrew the studs and bolts and remove the centre charge air metal pipe.

**9** Disconnect the wiring from the glow plugs.

**10** Remove the EGR valve and EGR solenoid valve as described in Part E of this Chapter.

**11** Unbolt and remove the right-hand engine lifting eye.

**12** Remove the charge pressure sensor as described in Section 8.

**13** Place a suitable container beneath the oil filter housing, then unscrew the cover and remove the filter element.

**14** Release the clip and disconnect the oil return line from the oil filter housing.

**15** Remove the protective insulator (where fitted), then unscrew the bolts and remove the three clamps from the injector lines **(see illustrations)**. Also, unscrew the union nuts and remove the lines from the injection pump and injectors.

**16** Unscrew the union bolt and the mounting bolt securing the oil return line to the cylinder head, then release the clip and disconnect the oil return hose.

**17** Disconnect the three wiring plugs from the injection pump **(see illustration)**.

**18** Progressively unscrew the mounting bolts and nuts, and remove the inlet manifolds from the cylinder head. Recover the gaskets.

**19** Disconnect the fuel supply and return hoses from the injection pump.

**20** Note its location, then carefully unscrew the fuel return check valve from the injection pump **(see illustration)**. Do not unscrew the check valve from the banjo bolt. Tape over or plug the fuel return aperture to prevent entry of dust and dirt.

**21** Unscrew the bolt and remove the injection pump outer insulation, then disconnect and unclip the engine management wiring, and carefully lever off the inner insulation. Note the routing of the various wiring looms.

**22** Unbolt the mounting bracket from the left-hand end of the pump **(see illustration)**.

**23** Disconnect the PROM (Programmable Read-Only Memory) wiring harness plug, then unscrew the two retaining nuts, and manoeuvre the injection pump from the

**9.15a  Fuel injection pump protective insulator**

**9.15b  Injector line clamp**

**9.17  Injection pump wiring plugs**

**9.20  Fuel return check valve**

timing case. Recover the foam insulator from between the pump and cylinder block.

*Caution: Never attempt to dismantle the pump assembly. If there is a problem, take the pump to a Vauxhall dealer/diesel injection specialist for testing/repair.*

### Refitting

**24** To refit the pump, hold the correct piece of foam insulator against the cylinder block, engage the pump shaft with the corresponding hole in the timing case, and fit the two retaining nuts. Hand-tighten the nuts at this stage.

**25** Refit the pump mounting bracket to the cylinder block, and tighten the bolts to the specified torque. Fit the bolts securing the bracket to the pump, then fully tighten the pump mounting nuts and bolts to the specified torque. Refit the foam insulation pieces around the pump **(see illustration)**. **Note:** *Reconnect*

*the wiring plug to the PROM on the side of the pump before fitting the rearmost foam insulation piece.*

**26** Reconnect the wiring and insulation, and tighten the bolt.

**27** Refit the fuel return check valve and tighten the banjo bolt securely.

**28** Reconnect the fuel supply and return hoses.

**29** Refit the inlet manifolds together with new gaskets, and tighten the nuts and bolts to the specified torque.

**30** Reconnect the pump wiring, then refit the oil return line and hose.

**31** Reconnect the oil return line to the oil filter housing.

**32** Insert a new oil filter element, then refit the cover and tighten.

**33** Refit the charge pressure sensor with reference to Section 8.

**34** Refit the engine lifting eye.

**9.22  Fuel injection pump mounting bracket and bolts**

**9.25  Refit the foam insulation pieces**

**10.4 Remove the central bleed screw**

**35** Refer to Part E and refit the EGR solenoid valve and EGR valve.
**36** Reconnect the wiring to the glow plugs.
**37** Refit the timing belt and injection pump sprocket as described in Chapter 2C.
**38** Carry out the injection timing checking and adjustment procedure described in Section 10.
**39** Refit the injector lines and clamps.
**40** Refit the centre charge air metal pipe, and starter/alternator wiring harness bracket.
**41** Refit the engine electronic control unit (ECU) and mounting bracket with reference to Section 8.
**42** Reconnect the centre charge air hose, turbocharger air intake pipe and crankcase ventilation hose.
**43** Reconnect the wiring plugs to the ECU.
**44** Refit the wheel arch liner and roadwheel, and lower the vehicle to the ground.
**45** Reconnect the battery negative lead (refer to *Disconnecting the battery* in the Reference Chapter).
**46** Finally, it may be necessary to have a Vauxhall dealer program all volatile memories.

## 10 Injection timing –
checking and adjustment

**Note:** *Although on these models the injection timing is determined by the engine ECU, the basic injection timing has to be set when the pump is fitted. Actual checking of the injection system can only be carried out using specialist diagnostic equipment.*

**10.5 Screw the adapter into the pump and mount the dial gauge**

*Caution: Be careful not to allow dirt into the injection pump or injector pipes during this procedure.*
*Caution: Some of the injection pump settings and access plugs may be sealed by the manufacturers at the factory, using paint or locking wire and lead seals. Do not disturb the seals if the vehicle is still within the warranty period, otherwise the warranty will be invalidated. Also do not attempt the timing procedure unless accurate instrumentation is available.*
**1** Remove the air cleaner housing and ducting (Section 2)
**2** Undo the unions and remove the fuel injection delivery pipes. We found it necessary to remove the oil cooler housing retaining bolt (see Chapter 2D) and push the housing to the rear, to allow sufficient access to the rear of the pump. Be prepared for fluid spillage.
**3** With reference to Chapter 2D, position the crankshaft at approximately 45° before TDC for No 1 piston.
**4** Remove the central bleed screw from the centre of the four fuel delivery unions at the left-hand end of the injection pump **(see illustration)**. Recover the seal.
**5** Screw the adapter into the rear of the pump and mount the dial gauge in the adapter **(see illustration)**. The special adapter and dial gauge (Vauxhall tool No KM-798) can be purchased from most good motor factors. Position the dial gauge so that its plunger is at the mid-point of its travel and securely tighten the adapter locknut.
**6** Slowly rotate the crankshaft back-and-forth whilst observing the dial gauge, to determine when the injection pump plunger is at the bottom of its travel (BDC). When the pump plunger is correctly positioned, zero the dial gauge.
**7** Rotate the crankshaft slowly in the correct direction until the crankshaft pulley TDC mark is correctly aligned with the pointer (No 1 cylinder at TDC on its compression stroke).
**8** The reading obtained on the dial gauge should be equal to the specified pump timing measurement given in the Specifications at the start of this Chapter. If adjustment is necessary, slacken the pump front mounting nuts and rear mounting bolts and slowly rotate the pump body until the point is found where the specified reading is obtained. **Note:** *If necessary remove the upper timing belt cover for access to the nuts and bolts.* If the reading is too large turn the pump towards the engine, and if the reading is too small turn the pump away from the engine. When the pump is correctly positioned, tighten both its front and rear mounting nuts and bolts to the specified torque.
**9** Rotate the crankshaft through one and three quarter rotations in the normal direction of rotation. Find the injection pump plunger BDC as described in paragraph 6 and zero the dial gauge.
**10** Rotate the crankshaft slowly in the correct direction of rotation until the crankshaft pulley

mark is realigned with the pointer (bringing the No 1 cylinder piston back to TDC). Recheck the timing measurement.
**11** If adjustment is necessary, slacken the pump mounting nuts and bolts and repeat the operations in paragraphs 8 to 10.
**12** When the pump timing is correctly set unscrew the adapter and remove the dial gauge.
**13** Inspect the seal and renew if necessary, then refit the central bleed screw and tighten it to the specified torque.
**14** Refit the fuel injection pipes, tightening the unions to the specified torque, and refit the oil cooler housing and retaining bolt (if removed).
**15** Where removed, refit the upper timing belt cover, then refit the air filter housing and ducting.
**16** The fuel system should 'self-bleed' as the engine is cranked, although it may take longer than normal to restart. Check for fuel leaks from the disturbed pipes and unions.

## 11 Fuel injectors –
removal and refitting

⚠ *Warning: Exercise extreme caution when working on the fuel injectors. Never expose the hands or any part of the body to injector spray, as the high working pressure can cause the fuel to penetrate the skin, with possibly fatal results. You are strongly advised to have any work which involves testing the injectors under pressure carried out by a dealer or fuel injection specialist.*
*Caution: Be careful not to allow dirt into the injection pump, injectors or pipes during this procedure.*
*Caution: Take care not to drop the injectors, or allow the needles at their tips to become damaged. The injectors are precision-made to fine limits, and must not be handled roughly. In particular, never mount them in a bench vice.*

### Removal

**1** Remove the camshaft cover as described in Chapter 2D.
**2** Drain the cooling system as described in Chapter 1B. **Note:** *This is recommended by the manufacturers as a precaution against coolant entering the combustion chambers when the fuel injectors are removed, as a result of the injector heat sleeves becoming displaced.*
**3** Undo the five bolts and remove the inner fuel leak-back pipe. Recover the copper washers **(see illustrations)**.
**4** Slacken and remove the retaining nuts, and remove the injector clamps **(see illustration)**.
**5** Lift the injectors out of the cylinder head. Discard the rubber seals and copper washers; new seals/washers must be fitted prior to reassembly. Do not attempt to dismantle the injectors any further.

**6** Testing of the injectors requires the use of special equipment. If any injector is thought to be faulty have it tested and, if necessary, reconditioned by a diesel engine specialist or Vauxhall dealer.

## Refitting

**7** Commence reassembly by ensuring that the injector and cylinder head mating faces are clean, and fitting new copper sealing washers and rubber seals to each injector. Note the correct orientation of the copper washers **(see illustration)**.

**8** Carefully fit each injector into the cylinder head, and secure them in place by fitting the injector clamps. Tighten the clamp retaining nuts to the specified torque.

**9** Refit the inner fuel leak-back pipe to the injectors and the camshaft housing. The larger diameter bolt secures the leak-back pipe to the camshaft housing. Note that new copper washers should be fitted to the top of each injector, and the underside of each bolt. Reconnect the pipe to the camshaft housing using new copper washers. Tighten the bolts to the specified torque.

**10** Refit the camshaft cover as described in Chapter 2D.

**11** Refill the cooling system as described in Chapter 1B.

**12** Restart the engine and check for leaks.

## 12 Turbocharger – removal and refitting

### Removal

**1** Remove the exhaust manifold, together with the turbocharger assembly, as described in Section 15.

**2** With the assembly on the bench, unbolt the turbocharger heat shield **(see illustration)**.

**3** Undo the retaining nuts and remove the exhaust connection flange and gasket from the turbocharger **(see illustration)**.

**4** Undo the union and remove the oil feed pipe along with the sealing washers which are fitted on each side of the pipe union **(see illustration)**.

**5** Unscrew the retaining bolts and remove

**11.3a Copper washers fit either side of the fuel leak-back pipe unions on the injectors . . .**

**11.4 The injector clamp washer fits dished with the side facing down**

the oil return pipe union and gasket **(see illustration)**.

**6** Slacken and remove the four mounting nuts then remove the turbocharger and gasket from the manifold **(see illustration)**.

**12.2 Turbocharger heat shield**

**11.3b . . . and the union on the camshaft housing**

**11.7 Note the rubber seal and copper washer**

**7** Unscrew the bolts securing the wastegate unit to the turbocharger. Release the clip and disconnect the control rod.

**8** Do not attempt to dismantle the turbocharger any further. If the unit is thought to be faulty

**12.3 Exhaust flange connection nuts**

**12.4 Turbocharger oil feed pipe union**

**12.5 Turbocharger oil return union**

**12.6 Undo the nuts and separate the turbocharger from the exhaust manifold**

**14.17a Remove the rear section of the manifold . . .**

**14.17b . . . and the front section**

take it to a turbo specialist or Vauxhall dealer for testing and examination. They will be able to inform you if the unit can be overhauled or will need renewing.

### Refitting

**9** Refitting is the reverse of removal, using new gaskets and sealing washers, and tightening the fasteners to their specified torque settings (where given). Refit the manifold and turbocharger assembly as described in Section 15.

### 13 Intercooler –
removal and refitting

**Note:** *The intercooler is only fitted to the Y17DT engine.*

### Removal

**1** The intercooler is located in front of the lower part of the radiator.
**2** Remove the front bumper with reference to Chapter 11.
**3** Carefully unclip the air duct from the front of the radiator, and lift upwards from behind the front crossmember.
**4** Loosen the clips and disconnect the two air hoses from the intercooler.
**5** Release the retaining clamps and withdraw the intercooler from the front of the radiator.

### Refitting

**6** Refitting is a reversal of removal.

**15.3a Engine oil level dipstick tube upper mounting bolt . . .**

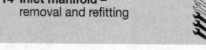

### 14 Inlet manifold –
removal and refitting

**Note:** *New manifold retaining nuts will be required on refitting*
**Note:** *The intercooler is only fitted to the Y17DT engine.*

### Removal

**1** Disconnect the battery negative lead (refer to *Disconnecting the battery* in the Reference Chapter).
**2** Remove the air cleaner assembly as described in Section 2.
**3** Remove the engine electronic control unit (ECU) as described in Section 8.
**4** Loosen the clip and disconnect the crankcase ventilation hose from the left-hand end of the camshaft cover. Unscrew the intercooler-to-turbocharger air pipe mounting bolts, then disconnect the pipe from the turbocharger and withdraw from the engine.
**5** Unscrew the nuts and remove the starter/alternator wiring harness bracket from the EGR valve.
**6** Loosen the clips and disconnect the charge air hose from the centre air pipe, then unbolt the centre air pipe from the inlet manifold.
**7** Disconnect the wiring from the glow plugs.
**8** Remove the EGR valve and gaskets with reference to Chapter 4E. To do this, unbolt the pipe then unscrew the studs and bolts, disconnect the vacuum hose and remove the valve. Recover the gaskets.

**15.3b . . . and lower mounting bolts**

**9** Disconnect the vacuum hose from the EGR solenoid valve, then disconnect the wiring and unbolt the solenoid valve.
**10** Unbolt the rear engine lifting eye.
**11** Disconnect the wiring then unbolt the clamp and remove the charge pressure sensor.
**12** Place a suitable container beneath the oil filter housing, then unscrew the cover and remove the filter element.
**13** Release the clip and disconnect the oil return line from the oil filter housing.
**14** Unscrew the bolts and remove the three clamps from the injector lines, then unscrew the union nuts and remove the lines from the injection pump and injectors.
**15** Unscrew the union bolt and the mounting bolt securing the oil return line to the cylinder head, then release the clip and disconnect the oil return hose.
**16** Disconnect the three wiring plugs from the injection pump.
**17** Progressively unscrew the mounting bolts and nuts, and remove the inlet manifold rear and front sections from the cylinder head **(see illustrations)**. Recover the gaskets.

### Refitting

**18** Clean the cylinder head and manifold(s) gasket faces, and fit a new gasket(s) in place.
**19** The remainder of the refitting procedure is a reversal of removal, but tighten all nuts and bolts to the correct torque setting where specified. After reconnecting the battery, have a dealer reprogram the volatile memories.

### 15 Exhaust manifold –
removal and refitting

**Note:** *The intercooler is only fitted to the Y17DT engine.*

### Removal

**1** The exhaust manifold is removed together with the turbocharger, then separated on the bench. First, apply the handbrake, then jack up the front of the vehicle and support it on axle stands (see *Jacking and vehicle support*). Remove the right-hand front roadwheel and the inner wheel arch liner for access to the crankshaft pulley. Remove the engine compartment undertray.
**2** Disconnect the battery negative lead (refer to *Disconnecting the battery* in the Reference Chapter). Remove the air cleaner and ducting as described in Section 2.
**3** Unscrew the upper and lower mounting bolts and remove the oil level dipstick tube from the sump. Note the wiring and hose supports on the tube **(see illustrations)**.
**4** Remove the auxiliary drivebelt as described in Chapter 1B. Prior to removal, mark the direction of rotation on the belt to ensure the belt is refitted the same way around.
**5** At the rear of the alternator, loosen the clips and remove the brake vacuum pump oil return hose from the pump and block.

**15.6 Exhaust front pipe-to-turbocharger joint**

**15.7 Unbolt the turbocharger from the cylinder block mounting bracket**

**15.8 Disconnect the oil return hose**

**6** Unbolt the exhaust front pipe from the turbocharger, taking care to support the flexible section **(see illustration)**. Note: *Angular movement in excess of 10° can cause permanent damage to the flexible section.* Release the mounting rubbers and support the front of the exhaust pipe to one side.

**7** Unscrew and remove the turbocharger mounting bracket bolt **(see illustration)**.

**8** Loosen the clips and remove the turbocharger oil return hose **(see illustration)**.

**9** While counterholding the block adapter with one spanner, unscrew the domed nut from the oil feed line union on the block **(see illustration)**.

**10** Disconnect the vacuum hose from the wastegate actuator on the turbocharger **(see illustration)**.

**11** Loosen the clips securing the air intake pipe to the turbocharger and intercooler **(see illustration)**, then unscrew the mounting bolt and remove the air intake pipe.

**12** On models equipped with air conditioning, disconnect the compressor wiring plug, undo the compressor mounting bolts, and move the compressor to one side. Secure the compressor with cable ties. Do not open the refrigerant hoses.

**13** Undo the three bolts and remove the air conditioning compressor mounting bracket.

**14** Unscrew the nuts securing the oil dipstick guide tube bracket to the camshaft cover, then unbolt the guide tube from the block, release the vacuum hoses and remove the bracket and guide tube **(see illustration)**.

**15** Unscrew the bolt, loosen the clip and remove the centre charge air pipe.

**16** Unbolt the heat shield from the exhaust manifold **(see illustration)**.

**17** Disconnect the wiring from the engine electronic control unit.

**18** Disconnect the crankcase ventilation hose from the camshaft cover then unscrew the

mounting bolts and disconnect the air intake pipe from the turbocharger. Also disconnect the clips and remove the centre charge air hose.

**19** Unscrew the oil feed banjo bolt on the turbocharger and recover the seals.

**20** The EGR (exhaust gas recirculation) pipe is mounted at the left-hand end of the manifold. Undo the two retaining bolts, and recover the gasket **(see illustration)**.

**21** Undo the exhaust manifold retaining nuts/ bolts, unscrew and remove the two manifold studs, and remove the exhaust manifold.

**22** The manifold can now be separated from the turbocharger as described in Section 12.

### Refitting

**23** Refitting is the reverse of removal, but clean the mating surfaces and renew all gaskets/sealing washers. Tighten all nuts and bolts to their specified torques, where given.

**15.9 Remove the oil feed pipe from the cylinder block**

**15.10 Wastegate actuator vacuum pipe**

**15.11 Turbocharger air intake pipe**

**15.14 Remove the oil dipstick guide tube mounting bolt from the block**

**15.16 Exhaust manifold heat shield**

**15.20 EGR pipe flange on the exhaust manifold**

**16.5 Exhaust system**

| | | |
|---|---|---|
| 1 Front exhaust pipe with flexible section | 2 Catalytic converter | 4 Rear silencer |
| | 3 Intermediate exhaust pipe | 5 Tail pipe |

## 16 Exhaust system – general information, removal and refitting

### General information

1 The exhaust system is in two sections. The front section includes the catalytic converter, oxygen sensor and intermediate pipe. The rear section consists of the tailpipe and silencer.

2 Periodically, the exhaust system should be checked for signs of leaks or damage. Also inspect the system rubber mountings, and renew if necessary.

3 Small holes or cracks can be repaired using proprietary exhaust repair products.

4 Before renewing an individual section of the exhaust system, it is wise to inspect the remaining section. If corrosion or damage is evident, it may prove more economical to renew the entire system.

### Component renewal

5 If either part of the system is to be renewed, it is important to ensure that the correct component is obtained **(see illustration)**.

6 To remove the rear tailpipe and silencer, chock the front wheels then jack up the rear of the vehicle and support on axle stands (see *Jacking and vehicle support*). Loosen the clamp securing the intermediate pipe to the tailpipe, then release the rubber mountings and slide the tailpipe from the intermediate pipe **(see illustrations)**. If the tailpipe is rusted onto the intermediate pipe, tap around the joint with a hammer to free it. Twist the tailpipe in both directions while holding the intermediate pipe.

7 To remove the front section of the exhaust, jack up the front and rear of the vehicle and support it on axle stands (see *Jacking and vehicle support*). Remove the tailpipe and silencer as described in paragraph 6, then unbolt the exhaust front pipe from the turbocharger, taking care to support the flexible section. **Note:** *Angular movement in excess of 10° can cause permanent damage to the flexible section.* Recover the gasket. Release the rubber mountings and withdraw the exhaust from under the vehicle **(see illustration)**.

8 Refitting is a reversal of removal, but renew all gaskets and tighten the clamp and front pipe flange nuts to the specified torque, where given.

**16.6a Tailpipe-to-intermediate pipe exhaust clamp**

**16.6b One of the tailpipe rubber mountings**

**16.7 Exhaust front section rubber mountings**

# Chapter 4 Part E:
# Emissions control systems

## Contents

## Degrees of difficulty

| Easy, suitable for novice with little experience | Fairly easy, suitable for beginner with some experience | Fairly difficult, suitable for competent DIY mechanic | Difficult, suitable for experienced DIY mechanic | Very difficult, suitable for expert DIY or professional |
|---|---|---|---|---|

## Specifications

| Torque wrench settings | Nm | lbf ft |
|---|---|---|
| **Models up to September 2003** | | |
| EGR pipe-to-exhaust manifold (1.7 litre diesel) . . . . . . . . . . . . . . . . . . | 28 | 21 |
| EGR pipe-to-valve union nut (1.7 litre diesel) . . . . . . . . . . . . . . . . . . . | 44 | 33 |
| EGR valve-to-inlet manifold: | | |
|   1.4 litre petrol . . . . . . . . . . . . . . . . . . . . . . . . . . . . . . . . . . . . . . . | 20 | 15 |
|   1.7 litre diesel . . . . . . . . . . . . . . . . . . . . . . . . . . . . . . . . . . . . . . . | 25 | 18 |
| **Models from October 2003** | | |
| EGR valve to cylinder head (diesel engines) . . . . . . . . . . . . . . . . . . . | 22 | 16 |
| EGR valve to inlet manifold (petrol engines) . . . . . . . . . . . . . . . . . . . | 20 | 15 |

## 1 General information and precautions

**1** All petrol engine models use unleaded petrol and also have various other features built into the fuel/exhaust system to help minimise harmful emissions. All models are equipped with a crankcase emission control system, a catalytic converter, an exhaust gas recirculation (EGR) system and an evaporative emission control system to keep fuel vapour/exhaust gas emissions down to a minimum.

**2** Diesel engine models are also designed to meet strict emission requirements. A crankcase emission control system and a catalytic converter are fitted to keep exhaust emissions down to a minimum. An exhaust gas recirculation (EGR) system is also used to further decrease exhaust emissions.

**3** The emission control systems function as follows.

### Petrol models

### Crankcase emissions control

**4** To reduce the emission of unburned hydrocarbons from the crankcase into the atmosphere, the engine is sealed and the blow-by gases and oil vapour are drawn from the camshaft cover into the inlet manifold to be burned by the engine during normal combustion.

**5** The gases are forced out of the crankcase by the relatively higher crankcase pressure; if the engine is worn, the raised crankcase pressure (due to increased blow-by) will cause some of the flow to return under all manifold conditions.

### Exhaust emission control

**6** To minimise the amount of pollutants which escape into the atmosphere, all models are fitted with a catalytic converter which is integral with the exhaust manifold. The system is of the closed-loop type, in which oxygen sensors in the exhaust system provide the fuel injection/ignition system ECU with constant feedback, enabling the ECU to adjust the mixture to provide the best possible conditions for the converter to operate.

**7** On all engines covered by this manual, there are two heated oxygen sensors fitted to the exhaust system. The sensor on the top of the exhaust manifold/catalytic converter determines the residual oxygen content of the exhaust gases for mixture correction. The sensor in the exhaust front pipe (after the catalytic converter) monitors the function of the catalytic converter to give the driver a warning signal if there is a fault.

**8** The oxygen sensor's tip is sensitive to oxygen and sends the ECU a varying voltage depending on the amount of oxygen in the exhaust gases; if the intake air/fuel mixture is too rich, the exhaust gases are low in oxygen so the sensor sends a low-voltage signal, the voltage rising as the mixture weakens and the amount of oxygen rises in the exhaust gases. Peak conversion efficiency of all major pollutants occurs if the intake air/fuel mixture is maintained at the chemically-correct ratio for the complete combustion of petrol of 14.7 parts (by weight) of air to 1 part of fuel (the 'stoichiometric' ratio). The sensor output voltage alters in a large step at this point, the ECU using the signal change as a reference point and correcting the intake air/fuel mixture accordingly by altering the fuel injector pulse width.

### Fuel evaporation emission control

**9** To minimise the escape into the atmosphere of unburned hydrocarbons, a fuel evaporation emission control system is fitted. The fuel tank filler cap is sealed and a charcoal canister is mounted behind the right-hand front wing. The canister collects the petrol vapours generated in the tank when the car is parked and stores them until they can be cleared from the canister (under the control of the fuel injection/ignition system ECU) via the purge valve into the inlet manifold to be burned by the engine during normal combustion.

**10** To ensure that the engine runs correctly when it is cold and/or idling and to protect the catalytic converter from the effects of an over-rich mixture, the purge control valve is not opened by the ECU until the engine has warmed-up, and the engine is under load; the valve solenoid is then modulated on and off to allow the stored vapour to pass into the inlet manifold.

### Exhaust gas recirculation system

**11** This system is designed to recirculate small quantities of exhaust gas into the inlet manifold, and therefore into the combustion process. This reduces the level of unburnt hydrocarbons present in the exhaust gas before it reaches the catalytic converter. The system is controlled by the fuel injection/ignition ECU, using the information from its various sensors, via the electrically-operated EGR solenoid valve mounted on a housing bolted to the left-hand end of the cylinder head. A metal pipe from the EGR housing links the exhaust ports in the cylinder head to the inlet manifold on the rear of the head.

## Diesel models

### Crankcase emission control

**12** Refer to paragraphs 4 and 5.

### Exhaust emission control

**13** To minimise the level of exhaust pollutants released into the atmosphere, a catalytic converter is fitted in the exhaust system.

**14** The catalytic converter consists of a canister containing a fine mesh impregnated with a catalyst material, over which the hot exhaust gases pass. The catalyst speeds up the oxidation of harmful carbon monoxide, unburned hydrocarbons and soot, effectively reducing the quantity of harmful products released into the atmosphere via the exhaust gases.

### Exhaust gas recirculation system

**15** This system is designed to recirculate small quantities of exhaust gas into the inlet manifold, and therefore into the combustion process. This reduces the level of unburnt hydrocarbons present in the exhaust gas before it reaches the catalytic converter. The system is controlled by the injection system ECU, using the information from its various sensors, via the electrically-operated EGR valve.

---

**2  Petrol engine emissions control systems** – testing and component renewal

---

## Crankcase emission control

**1** The components of this system require no attention other than to check that the hose(s) are clear and undamaged at regular intervals.

**J44723**

**2.5  Charcoal canister location**

| 1 | Charcoal canister | 2 | Purge hose |
|---|---|---|---|
|   |   | 3 | Mounting bolt |

## Evaporative emission control

### Testing

**2** If the system is thought to be faulty, disconnect the hoses from the charcoal canister and purge control valve and check that they are clear by blowing through them. Full testing of the system can only be carried out using specialist electronic equipment which is connected to the engine management system diagnostic wiring connector (see Chapter 4A or 4B). If the purge control valve or charcoal canister are thought to be faulty, they must be renewed.

### Charcoal canister renewal

**3** At the right-hand rear corner of the engine compartment, disconnect the quick-release connector connecting the charcoal canister to the inlet manifold. A Vauxhall special tool is available to release the connectors, but provided care is taken, the connectors can be released using a pair of long-nosed pliers, or a similar tool, to depress the retaining tangs.

**4** Apply the handbrake, then jack up the front of the vehicle and support it on axle stands (see *Jacking and vehicle support*). Remove the right-hand front roadwheel.

**5** Remove the wheel arch liner for access to

**2.10  Purge valve for the evaporative emission system**

the charcoal canister which is located on the inner wing **(see illustration)**.

**6** Unbolt the charcoal canister from the mounting bracket, then disconnect the purge valve hose from the top outlet.

**7** Withdraw the canister, together with the ventilation inlet hose from the inner wing.

**8** Where necessary, transfer the ventilation hose to the new charcoal canister. Refitting is a reversal of the removal procedure. Make sure the hoses are correctly and securely reconnected.

### Purge valve renewal

**9** The purge valve is mounted on the rear of the air cleaner cover.

**10** Disconnect the wiring from the purge valve **(see illustration)**.

**11** Release the purge valve from the air cleaner cover.

**12** Disconnect the inlet manifold vacuum hose from the purge valve.

**13** Disconnect the canister hose and withdraw the purge valve.

**14** Note that, if a new valve is being fitted, it is supplied complete with purge and vacuum hoses, therefore it will be necessary to disconnect these from the canister and throttle body.

**15** Refitting is a reversal of the removal procedure, ensuring the valve is fitted the correct way around and the hoses are securely connected. Check the hoses carefully for cracking and damage, and where evident, renew them. **Note:** *A cracked ventilation hose is potentially a fire hazard.*

## Exhaust emission control

### Testing

**16** The performance of the catalytic converter can be checked only by measuring the exhaust gases using a good-quality, carefully-calibrated exhaust gas analyser.

**17** If the CO level at the tailpipe is too high, the vehicle should be taken to a Vauxhall dealer so that the complete fuel injection and ignition systems, including the oxygen sensors, can be thoroughly checked using the special diagnostic equipment. Once these have been checked and are known to be free from faults, the fault must be in the catalytic converter, which must be renewed.

### Catalytic converter renewal

**18** The catalytic converter is welded to the exhaust manifold, and the removal and refitting procedure is described in Chapter 4A or 4B.

### Oxygen sensor renewal

**19** Removal and refitting of both oxygen sensors is described in Chapter 4A or 4B.

## Exhaust gas recirculation system

### Testing

**20** Comprehensive testing of the system can only be carried out using specialist electronic equipment which is connected to the engine management system diagnostic wiring connector (see Chapter 4A or 4B). If the EGR valve is thought to be faulty, it must be renewed.

2.21 EGR valve location (arrowed)

2.22 Disconnecting the wiring from the EGR valve

2.24 EGR valve coolant hose (1), wiring plug (2) and coolant temperature sensor wiring connector (3)

### EGR valve renewal – 1.0, 1.2 and 1.4 litre Z14XEP engines

21 The exhaust gas recirculation valve is bolted to the left-hand end of the cylinder head (see illustration). First drain the cooling system as described in Chapter 1A.

22 Disconnect the wiring connector from the EGR valve (see illustration).

23 Disconnect the wiring from the ignition module, then unclip the wiring harness and position it to one side.

24 Release the clip and disconnect the coolant hose from the EGR valve (see illustration).

25 Unscrew the bolts securing the EGR pipe to the EGR valve (see illustration). Recover the gasket and seal.

26 Unbolt the EGR valve/housing from the cylinder block and recover the gasket (see illustration).

27 Refitting is a reversal of removal, but clean the mating surfaces, fit new gaskets, and tighten all bolts securely. Refill the cooling system with reference to Chapter 1A.

### EGR valve renewal – 1.4 litre Z14XE engines

28 The exhaust gas recirculation valve is located on top of the inlet manifold. First, remove the engine top cover.

29 Disconnect the wiring from the EGR valve. Unclip the wiring harness and position it to one side.

30 Unscrew the mounting bolts and remove the EGR valve from the inlet manifold. Recover the gasket.

31 Refitting is a reversal of removal, but clean the mating surfaces, fit a new gasket, and tighten the bolts securely.

### 3 Diesel engine emissions control systems – testing and component renewal

### *Crankcase emission control*

1 The components of this system require no attention other than to check that the hose(s) are clear and undamaged at regular intervals.

2.25 EGR pipe-to-EGR valve housing securing bolts (arrowed)

### *Exhaust emission control*

#### Testing

2 The performance of the catalytic converter can only be checked by measuring the exhaust gases using a good-quality, carefully-calibrated exhaust gas analyser.

3 If the catalytic converter is thought to be faulty, first check the problem is not due to faulty injectors.

#### Catalytic converter renewal

4 The catalytic converter is located between the turbocharger and the exhaust front pipe. on 1.3 litre models. On 1.7 litre models it is an integral part of the exhaust system front pipe. Removal and refitting details are in Chapter 4C or 4D.

### *Exhaust gas recirculation system*

#### Testing

5 Comprehensive testing of the system can

3.10a Unclip the expansion tank coolant hose and the wiring harness from the crash box . . .

2.26 EGR valve housing securing bolts (arrowed)

only be carried out using specialist electronic equipment which is connected to the injection system diagnostic wiring connector (see Chapter 4C or 4D). If the EGR valve or solenoid valve are thought to be faulty, they must be renewed.

### EGR valve renewal – 1.3 litre engines

6 The exhaust gas recirculation valve is bolted to the rear, left-hand side of the cylinder head.

7 Disconnect the battery negative terminal (refer to *Disconnecting the battery* in the Reference Chapter).

8 Drain the cooling system as described in Chapter 1B.

9 Remove the fuel filter as described in Chapter 1B.

10 Unclip the expansion tank coolant hose and the wiring harness from the fuel filter crash box, and disconnect the harness connector (see illustrations).

11 Release the retaining clip, lift the coolant

3.10b . . . and disconnect the harness connector

**3.11 Release the retaining clip and lift the expansion tank from its location**

**3.12a Unscrew the outer retaining nut (arrowed) and slacken the inner nut . . .**

**3.12b . . . then remove the crash box from the bulkhead**

**3.14a Unbolt the charge air pipe from the inlet manifold and undo the bolt (arrowed) . . .**

**3.14b . . . then manipulate the charge air pipe (arrowed) out from its location and recover the sealing ring**

**3.17 Slacken the retaining screw and release the EGR pipe clamp**

expansion tank from its location and place it to one side (see illustration).

12 Unscrew the outer retaining nut, slacken the inner nut and remove the crash box from the bulkhead (see illustrations).

13 Working below the thermostat housing, slacken the retaining clip and disconnect the air hose connecting the intercooler to the inlet manifold charge air pipe.

14 Undo the three bolts securing the charge air pipe to the inlet manifold flange, and the bolt securing the pipe support to the thermostat housing. Manipulate the charge air pipe out from its location and recover the sealing ring (see illustrations).

15 Slacken the retaining clips, or disconnect the quick-release fittings and detach the two coolant hoses for the EGR valve heat exchanger.

16 Disconnect the wiring connector from the top of the EGR valve.

17 Slacken the retaining screw and release the clamp securing the EGR pipe to the inlet manifold (see illustration).

18 Undo the two mounting bolts and remove the EGR valve and heat exchanger assembly from the engine (see illustration). Recover the gasket.

19 Refit the EGR valve assembly using the reversal of removal, but bearing in mind the following points:

a) Thoroughly clean the mating faces and use a new gasket. It will be necessary to insert the mounting bolts into the valve prior to refitting, to retain the gasket in position.

b) Tighten the mounting bolts to the specified torque.

c) Refit the fuel filter and refill the cooling system as described in Chapter 1B.

### EGR valve renewal – 1.7 litre engines

20 The exhaust gas recirculation valve is bolted to the top of the inlet manifold, at the rear of the engine.

21 At the rear of the cylinder head, disconnect the middle and rear wiring connectors from the engine control unit (ECU).

22 Release the wiring harnesses from the air intake pipe at the left-hand rear of the engine, then unscrew the intake pipe mounting bolts.

23 Release the clamps and disconnect the crankcase ventilation hose from the intake pipe and camshaft cover.

24 Release the clamps and disconnect the intake pipe from the mass airflow meter and

**3.18 Undo the two bolts (arrowed) and remove the EGR valve and heat exchanger assembly**

turbocharger, then withdraw the intake pipe complete from the engine.

25 Unscrew the nuts, and position the alternator wiring bracket to one side.

26 Unbolt the support clamp and unscrew the mounting nut and bolt, then remove the charge air pipe.

27 Depressurise the cooling system by carefully removing then retightening the expansion tank filler cap.

28 Loosen the clip securing the coolant hose to the thermostat housing, then carefully push the hose back by approximately 1.0 cm. Do not disconnect the hose, or coolant will be lost.

29 Remove the EGR pipe support bracket from the camshaft housing.

30 Unscrew the bolts securing the EGR pipe to the exhaust manifold, then unscrew the union nut and remove the EGR pipe from the EGR valve (see illustration). Recover the gasket.

**3.30 Undo the large EGR valve union nut – 1.7 litre diesel models**

**3.35 EGR valve retaining bolts (arrowed) – 1.7 litre diesel models**

**3.39 Vacuum hoses on the EGR solenoid valve**

**3.40 EGR solenoid valve retaining bolts (arrowed) – 1.7 litre diesel models**

**31** Disconnect the three wiring plugs from the engine control unit (ECU) located over the inlet manifold at the rear of the engine. The two main plugs are unlocked by lifting up the metal levers.

**32** Unbolt and remove the wiring harness bracket from the top of the ECU.

**33** Unscrew the mounting bolts and nuts, and remove the ECU from the mounting bracket.

**34** Release the glow plug wiring, then unscrew the two mounting bolts and single nut, and remove the ECU mounting bracket.

**35** Disconnect the vacuum hose, then unbolt the EGR valve from the inlet manifold **(see illustration)**. Recover the gasket.

**36** If the EGR valve is faulty, it must be renewed.

**37** Refitting is a reversal of removal, but clean the mating surfaces, use new gaskets and tighten all nuts and bolts to the specified torque, where given.

### EGR solenoid valve renewal

**38** At the rear of the engine, loosen the clips and remove the convoluted hose leading from the mass airflow meter to the metal air pipe.

**39** Disconnect the wiring, then note the locations of the vacuum hoses and disconnect them from the EGR solenoid valve **(see illustration)**.

**40** Unscrew the mounting bolts and remove the EGR solenoid valve from the inlet manifold **(see illustration)**.

**41** Refitting is a reversal of removal.

### 4 Catalytic converter – general information and precautions

The catalytic converter is a reliable and simple device which needs no maintenance in itself, but there are some facts of which an owner should be aware if the converter is to function properly for its full service life.

### Petrol models

a) *DO NOT use leaded petrol or LRP – the lead will coat the precious metals and reduce their efficiency, and will eventually destroy the converter.*

b) *Always keep the ignition and fuel systems well-maintained in accordance with the manufacturer's schedule.*

c) *If the engine develops a misfire, do not drive the car at all (or at least as little as possible) until the fault is cured.*

d) *DO NOT push- or tow-start the car.*

e) *Remember that the catalytic converter is FRAGILE – do not strike it with tools during servicing work.*

f) *The catalytic converter, used on a well-maintained and well-driven car, should last for between 50 000 and 100 000 miles – if the converter is no longer effective it must be renewed.*

### Diesel models

a) *Always keep the fuel system well-maintained in accordance with the manufacturer's schedule.*

b) *If the engine develops a misfire, do not drive the car at all (or at least as little as possible) until the fault is cured.*

c) *DO NOT push- or tow-start the car.*

d) *Remember that the catalytic converter is FRAGILE – do not strike it with tools during servicing work.*

e) *The catalytic converter, used on a well-maintained car, should last for between 50 000 and 100 000 miles – if the converter is no longer effective it must be renewed.*

# Notes

# Chapter 5 Part A:
## Starting and charging systems

## Contents

## Degrees of difficulty

| **Easy,** suitable for novice with little experience | **Fairly easy,** suitable for beginner with some experience | **Fairly difficult,** suitable for competent DIY mechanic | **Difficult,** suitable for experienced DIY mechanic | **Very difficult,** suitable for expert DIY or professional |
|---|---|---|---|---|

## Specifications

### General
Electrical system type ............................................... 12 volt negative earth

### Battery
| | |
|---|---|
| Type | Lead-acid, 'maintenance-free' (sealed for life) |
| Battery capacity | 36, 44, 55 or 60 Ah (depending on model) |
| Charge condition: | |
| Poor | 12.5 volts |
| Normal | 12.6 volts |
| Good | 12.7 volts |

### Alternator
| | |
|---|---|
| Type | Bosch or Delco-Remy |
| Regulated voltage | 13.7 to 14.7 volts (approximately) |

### Starter motor
| | |
|---|---|
| Type | Pre-engaged, Delco-Remy or Valeo |

### Torque wrench settings

| | Nm | lbf ft |
|---|---|---|
| Alternator: | | |
| 1.0, 1.2 and 1.4 litre Z14XEP petrol engines | 35 | 26 |
| 1.4 litre Z14XE petrol engine: | | |
| Top shackle | 20 | 15 |
| Mounting bolt | 35 | 26 |
| Diesel engines: | | |
| Upper bolt | 25 | 18 |
| Lower bolts | 22 | 16 |
| Auxiliary drivebelt tensioner: | | |
| 1.0, 1.2 and 1.4 litre Z14XEP petrol engines: | | |
| M8 bolt | 20 | 15 |
| M10 bolt | 55 | 41 |
| 1.4 litre Z14XE petrol engines | 35 | 26 |
| Diesel engines | 50 | 37 |
| Oil pressure warning light switch: | | |
| Petrol engines: | | |
| 1.0, 1.2 and 1.4 litre Z14XEP | 20 | 15 |
| 1.4 litre Z14XE | 30 | 22 |
| Diesel engines | 32 | 24 |
| Starter motor | 25 | 18 |

## 1 General information, precautions and battery disconnection

### General information

The engine electrical system consists mainly of the charging and starting systems. Because of their engine-related functions, these components are covered separately from the body electrical devices such as the lights, instruments, etc (which are covered in Chapter 12). On petrol engine models refer to Part B for information on the ignition system, and on diesel models refer to Part C for information on the preheating system.

The electrical system is of 12 volt negative earth type.

The battery is of low-maintenance or maintenance-free (sealed for life) type, and is charged by the alternator, which is belt-driven from the crankshaft pulley.

The starter motor is of pre-engaged type incorporating an integral solenoid. On starting, the solenoid moves the drive pinion into engagement with the flywheel/driveplate ring gear before the starter motor is energised. Once the engine has started, a one-way clutch prevents the motor armature being driven by the engine until the pinion disengages.

Further details of the various systems are given in the relevant Sections of this Chapter. While some repair procedures are given, the usual course of action is to renew the component concerned. The owner whose interest extends beyond mere component renewal should obtain a copy of the *Automotive Electrical & Electronic Systems Manual*, available from the publishers of this manual.

### Precautions

It is necessary to take extra care when working on the electrical system to avoid damage to semi-conductor devices (diodes and transistors), and to avoid the risk of personal injury. In addition to the precautions given in *Safety first!* at the beginning of this manual, observe the following when working on the system:

• Always remove rings, watches, etc, before working on the electrical system. Even with the battery disconnected, capacitive discharge could occur if a component's live terminal is earthed through a metal object. This could cause a shock or nasty burn.

• Do not reverse the battery connections. Components such as the alternator, electronic control units, or any other components having semi-conductor circuitry could be irreparably damaged.

• If the engine is being started using jump leads and a slave battery, connect the batteries positive-to-positive and negative-to-negative (see *Jump starting*). This also applies when connecting a battery charger but in this case both of the battery terminals should first be disconnected.

• Never disconnect the battery terminals, the alternator, any electrical wiring or any test instruments when the engine is running.

• Do not allow the engine to turn the alternator when the alternator is not connected.

• Never test for alternator output by flashing the output lead to earth.

• Never use an ohmmeter of the type incorporating a hand-cranked generator for circuit or continuity testing.

• Always ensure that the battery negative lead is disconnected when working on the electrical system.

• Before using electric-arc welding equipment on the car, disconnect the battery, alternator and components such as the fuel injection/ignition electronic control unit to protect them from the risk of damage.

### Battery disconnection

Refer to the precautions listed in *Disconnecting the battery* in the Reference Chapter.

## 2 Electrical fault finding – general information

Refer to Chapter 12.

## 3 Battery – testing and charging

### Testing

#### Traditional and low-maintenance battery

**1** If the vehicle covers a small annual mileage, it is worthwhile checking the specific gravity of the electrolyte every three months to determine the state of charge of the battery. Use a hydrometer to make the check and compare the results with the following table. Note that the specific gravity readings assume an electrolyte temperature of 15°C; for every 10°C below 15°C subtract 0.007. For every 10°C above 15°C add 0.007.

**3.5 Battery condition indicator (arrowed)**

| | Ambient temperature | |
|---|---|---|
| | above 25°C | below 25°C |
| **Fully-charged** | 1.210 to 1.230 | 1.270 to 1.290 |
| **70% charged** | 1.170 to 1.190 | 1.230 to 1.250 |
| **Discharged** | 1.050 to 1.070 | 1.110 to 1.130 |

**2** If the battery condition is suspect, first check the specific gravity of electrolyte in each cell. A variation of 0.040 or more between any cells indicates loss of electrolyte or deterioration of the internal plates.

**3** If the specific gravity variation is 0.040 or more, the battery should be renewed. If the cell variation is satisfactory but the battery is discharged, it should be charged as described later in this Section.

#### Maintenance-free battery

**4** Where a 'sealed for life' maintenance-free battery is fitted, topping-up and testing of the electrolyte in each cell is not possible. The condition of the battery can therefore only be tested using a battery condition indicator or a voltmeter.

**5** Later models are fitted with a maintenance-free battery with a built-in 'magic-eye' charge condition indicator. The indicator is located in the top of the battery casing, and indicates the condition of the battery from its colour **(see illustration)**. If the indicator shows green, then the battery is in a good state of charge. If the indicator turns darker, eventually to black, then the battery requires charging, as described later in this Section. If the indicator shows clear/yellow, then the electrolyte level in the battery is too low to allow further use, and the battery should be renewed. Do not attempt to charge, load or jump start a battery when the indicator shows clear/yellow.

#### All battery types

**6** If testing the battery using a voltmeter, connect the voltmeter across the battery and compare the result with those given in the Specifications under 'charge condition'. The test is only accurate if the battery has not been subjected to any kind of charge for the previous six hours. If this is not the case, switch on the headlights for 30 seconds, then wait four to five minutes before testing the battery after switching off the headlights. All other electrical circuits must be switched off, so check that the doors and tailgate are fully shut when making the test.

**7** If the voltage reading is less than 12.2 volts, then the battery is discharged, whilst a reading of 12.2 to 12.4 volts indicates a partially-discharged condition.

**8** If the battery is to be charged, remove it from the vehicle (Section 4) and charge it as described later in this Section.

### Charging

**Note:** *The following is intended as a guide only. Always refer to the manufacturer's recommendations (often printed on a label attached to the battery) before charging a battery.*

## Traditional
## and low-maintenance battery

**9** Charge the battery at a rate of 3.5 to 4 amps and continue to charge the battery at this rate until no further rise in specific gravity is noted over a four hour period.

**10** Alternatively, a trickle charger charging at the rate of 1.5 amps can safely be used overnight.

**11** Specially rapid 'boost' charges which are claimed to restore the power of the battery in 1 to 2 hours are not recommended, as they can cause serious damage to the battery plates through overheating.

**12** While charging the battery, note that the temperature of the electrolyte should never exceed 38°C.

## Maintenance-free battery

**13** This battery type takes considerably longer to fully recharge than the standard type, the time taken being dependent on the extent of discharge, but it will take anything up to three days.

**14** A constant voltage type charger is required, to be set, when connected, to 13.9 to 14.9 volts with a charger current below 25 amps. Using this method, the battery should be usable within three hours, giving a voltage reading of 12.5 volts, but this is for a partially-discharged battery and, as mentioned, full charging can take considerably longer.

**15** If the battery is to be charged from a fully-discharged state (condition reading less than 12.2 volts), have it recharged by your Vauxhall dealer or local automotive electrician, as the charge rate is higher and constant supervision during charging is necessary.

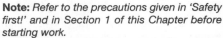

## 4 Battery –
### removal and refitting

**Note:** *Refer to 'Disconnecting the battery' in the Reference Chapter before proceeding.*

### Removal

**1** On right-hand drive models, the battery is located on the left-hand side of the engine compartment bulkhead, beneath the windscreen cowl panel **(see illustration)**. On left-hand drive models, the battery is located on the right-hand side of the bulkhead.

**2** Pull off the rubber seal from the bulkhead at the rear of the engine compartment.

**3** Remove the water deflector from in front of the windscreen by first removing the windscreen wiper arms then undoing the retaining screws. Also disconnect the hose from the windscreen washer nozzle.

**4** Disconnect the lead(s) at the negative (–) terminal by unscrewing the retaining nut and removing the terminal clamp. If necessary, the auxiliary lead may also be unbolted from the terminal. Note that the battery negative (–) and positive (+) terminal connections are stamped on the battery case.

**5** Disconnect the lead(s) at the positive (+) terminal by unscrewing the retaining nut and removing the terminal clamp. If necessary, the auxiliary lead may also be unbolted from the terminal.

**6** On the inner side of the battery, unscrew the bolt and remove the retaining clamp.

**7** Carefully lift the battery from its location and remove from the car. Make sure the battery is kept upright at all times.

### Refitting

**Note:** *As a precaution, before refitting the battery check that all doors are unlocked.*

**8** Refitting is a reversal of removal, but smear petroleum jelly on the terminals after reconnecting the leads to reduce corrosion, and always reconnect the positive lead first, followed by the negative lead.

## 5 Charging system –
### testing

**Note:** *Refer to the precautions given in 'Safety first!' and in Section 1 of this Chapter before starting work.*

**1** If the ignition no-charge warning light fails to illuminate when the ignition is switched on, first check the alternator wiring connections for security. If satisfactory, check that the warning light bulb has not blown, and that the bulbholder is secure in its location in the instrument panel. If the light still fails to illuminate, check the continuity of the warning light feed wire from the alternator to the bulbholder. If all is satisfactory, the alternator is at fault, and should be renewed, or taken to an auto-electrician for testing and repair.

**2** If the ignition warning light illuminates when the engine is running, stop the engine and check that the drivebelt is correctly tensioned (see Chapter 1A or 1B) and that the alternator connections are secure. If all is so far satisfactory, have the alternator checked by an auto-electrician for testing and repair.

**3** If the alternator output is suspect even though the warning light functions correctly, the regulated voltage may be checked as follows.

**4** Connect a voltmeter across the battery terminals, and start the engine.

**5** Increase the engine speed until the voltmeter reading remains steady; the reading should be approximately 12 to 13 volts, and no more than 14 volts.

**6** Switch on as many electrical accessories (eg, the headlights, heated rear window and heater blower) as possible, and check that the alternator maintains the regulated voltage at around 13.5 to 14.5 volts.

**7** If the regulated voltage is not as stated, the fault may be due to worn brushes, weak brush springs, a faulty voltage regulator, a faulty diode, a severed phase winding, or worn or

**4.1 Battery position (arrowed) on RHD models**

damaged slip-rings. The alternator should be renewed or taken to an auto-electrician for testing and repair.

## 6 Auxiliary drivebelt –
### removal and refitting

Refer to Chapter 1A or 1B.

## 7 Auxiliary drivebelt tensioner
### – removal and refitting

### Removal

**1** Remove the auxiliary drivebelt as described in Chapter 1A or 1B.

**2** On 1.0, 1.2 and 1.4 litre Z14XEP petrol engine models, unscrew the upper and lower mounting bolts and withdraw the tensioner pulley and spring assembly **(see illustration)**.

**3** On 1.4 litre Z14XE petrol and 1.7 litre diesel engine models, unscrew the pivot bolt and withdraw the tensioner pulley and spring housing **(see illustration)**.

**4** On 1.3 litre diesel engine models, unscrew the tensioner body retaining bolt and withdraw the tensioner assembly **(see illustration)**.

### Refitting

**5** Refitting is a reversal of removal, but tighten the mounting bolt(s) to the specified torque.

**7.2 Auxiliary drivebelt tensioner mounting bolts – 1.0, 1.2 and 1.4 litre Z14XEP petrol engine models**

J44601

**7.3  Auxiliary drivebelt tensioner –
1.4 litre Z14 XE petrol engine models**

1  *Pivot bolt*          2  *Locking bolt*

On 1.3 litre diesel engine models, ensure that
the lug on the tensioner body engages with
the corresponding hole on the cylinder block
as the tensioner is refitted **(see illustration)**.

### 8  Alternator –
removal and refitting

## 1.0, 1.2 and
## 1.4 litre Z14XEP engines

### Removal

**1** The alternator is located on the rear of the
cylinder block. First, apply the handbrake,
then jack up the front of the vehicle and
support it on axle stands (see *Jacking and
vehicle support*). Remove the right-hand
front roadwheel and the wheel arch liner
cover for access to the right-hand side of the
engine. Where necessary, remove the engine
undertray.
**2** Disconnect the battery negative terminal
(refer to *Disconnecting the battery* in the
Reference Chapter).

**8.7  Alternator upper and lower mounting
bolts/nuts (arrowed) – 1.0, 1.2 and
1.4 litre Z14XEP petrol engine models**

**7.4  Unscrew the tensioner body retaining
bolt and withdraw the tensioner assembly
– diesel engine models**

**3** With reference to Chapter 4A, remove the
air cleaner housing.
**4** Remove the auxiliary drivebelt tensioner as
described in Section 7.
**5** Unscrew the nuts and disconnect the two
wires from the rear of the alternator.
**6** On 1.0 litre models, unscrew the nuts and
remove the oxygen sensor wiring harness
bracket. On 1.2 litre models, disconnect the
plug and release the harness from the cable
ties.
**7** Unscrew the upper and lower mounting
bolts/nuts and withdraw the alternator
downwards from the block **(see illustration)**.

### Refitting

**8** Refitting is a reversal of removal, but tighten
the mounting bolts to the specified torque.

## 1.4 litre Z14XE engines

### Removal

**9** The alternator is located on the rear of the
cylinder block. First, apply the handbrake,
then jack up the front of the vehicle and
support it on axle stands (see *Jacking and
vehicle support*). Remove the right-hand front
roadwheel and the wheel arch liner cover for
access to the right-hand side of the engine.
**10** Disconnect the battery negative terminal
(refer to *Disconnecting the battery* in the
Reference Chapter).

**7.5  Ensure that the lug on the tensioner
body (arrowed) engages with the cylinder
block – diesel engine models**

**11** With reference to Chapter 4B, remove the
air cleaner housing.
**12** Remove the auxiliary drivebelt as
described in Chapter 1A.
**13** Unbolt the inlet manifold support bracket,
noting the location of the earth cable.
**14** Disconnect the wiring from the oil pressure
switch and unclip the harness.
**15** Depressurise the fuel system with reference
to Chapter 4B, then disconnect the fuel hose
from the fuel rail. Tape over or plug the hose.
**16** Disconnect the following engine
management wiring connectors, and release
the support cable ties:

a)  *Coolant temperature sensor.*
b)  *Camshaft position sensor.*
c)  *Throttle body module.*
d)  *Knock sensor.*
e)  *Intake pipe pressure sensor.*
f)  *Oxygen sensor.*
g)  *EGR valve.*

**17** Disconnect the hoses from the throttle
body and the crankcase ventilation hose from
the camshaft cover.
**18** Remove the fuel rail, together with the
injectors and wiring harness.
**19** Unbolt the wiring harness bracket from
the alternator.
**20** Unscrew the three bolts and remove
the alternator top mounting shackle **(see
illustration)**. Swivel the alternator rearwards.

H.28149

**8.20  Upper alternator mounting shackle (1) – 1.4 litre Z14 XE petrol engine models**

**8.25 Alternator lower mounting bracket – 1.4 litre Z14 XE petrol engine models**

A   Models without air conditioning

B   Models with air conditioning

1   Alternator lower mounting bracket

**21** Unbolt the engine management wiring harness from above the alternator. Also unclip the brake vacuum hose.

**22** Disconnect the evaporative carbon canister hose from the throttle body.

**23** Unbolt and remove the inlet manifold from the cylinder head and recover the gasket.

**24** Unscrew the nuts and disconnect the wiring from the rear of the alternator.

**25** Unscrew the lower mounting bolt then lift the alternator from the rear of the engine **(see illustration)**.

### Refitting

**26** Refitting is a reversal of removal, but fit a new inlet manifold gasket and tighten all nuts and bolts to the specified torque, where given.

## 1.3 litre diesel engines

### Removal

**27** The alternator is located on the rear of the cylinder block. First, apply the handbrake, then jack up the front of the vehicle and support it on axle stands (see *Jacking and vehicle support*). Remove the right-hand front roadwheel and the wheel arch liner cover for access to the right-hand side of the engine.

**28** Disconnect the battery negative terminal (refer to *Disconnecting the battery* in the Reference Chapter).

**29** With reference to Chapter 4C, remove the air cleaner housing.

**30** Remove the auxiliary drivebelt as described in Chapter 1A.

**31** Unscrew the nuts and disconnect the two wires from the rear of the alternator.

**32** Unscrew the upper mounting bolt and the two lower mounting bolts, then withdraw the

alternator downwards from the block **(see illustration)**.

### Refitting

**33** Refitting is a reversal of removal, but tighten the mounting bolts to the specified torque.

## 1.7 litre diesel engines

### Removal

**34** The alternator is located on the front right-hand side of the cylinder block. First, apply the handbrake, then jack up the front of the vehicle and support it on axle stands (see *Jacking and vehicle support*). Remove the right-hand front roadwheel and the wheel arch liner cover for access to the right-hand side of the engine.

**35** Disconnect the battery negative lead (refer to *Disconnecting the battery* in the Reference Chapter).

**36** With reference to Chapter 4C, remove the air cleaner housing.

**37** On models with air conditioning, carry out the following procedures:

a)  *Unclip the brake servo vacuum line from the 5 brackets and position to one side.*

b)  *Loosen the clips and remove the charge air hose from the turbocharger and centre charge air pipe.*

c)  *Unbolt and remove the centre charge air pipe.*

d)  *Remove the front bumper as described in Chapter 11.*

e)  *Remove the auxiliary drivebelt with reference to Chapter 1B.*

f)  *Loosen the clip then unbolt and remove the lower charge air pipe.*

g)  *The condenser refrigerant pipe obstructs removal of the alternator. As an alternative to evacuating the air conditioning system, the engine may be lowered after removing the right-hand engine mounting, or alternatively, the condenser may be moved to one side (refer to Chapter 3).*

**38** Detach the vacuum hoses from the brake vacuum pump located on the rear of the alternator **(see illustration)**.

**8.32 Alternator mounting bolts (arrowed) – diesel engine models**

**8.38 Vacuum hose connection on the brake vacuum pump**

**8.39a Disconnecting the battery cable . . .**

**8.39b . . . and wiring plug from the alternator**

## 9 Alternator – testing and overhaul

If the alternator is thought to be suspect, it should be removed from the vehicle and taken to an auto-electrician for testing. Most auto-electricians will be able to supply and fit brushes at a reasonable cost. However, check on the cost of repairs before proceeding as it may prove more economical to obtain a new or exchange alternator.

## 10 Starting system – testing

**39** Unscrew the nut and disconnect the battery cable from the alternator. Also disconnect the wiring plug **(see illustrations)**.
**40** Position a container beneath the alternator, then unscrew the banjo bolt and detach the oil feed line from the vacuum pump. If necessary, the feed line may be unbolted from the cylinder block **(see illustrations)**.
**41** Disconnect the vacuum pump oil return hose.
**42** Unscrew the upper and lower mounting bolts **(see illustrations)**, then withdraw the alternator. Unscrew the nut and remove the

brake vacuum servo vacuum line.
**43** With the alternator on the bench, unbolt the vacuum pump and recover the seal **(see illustration)**.

### Refitting

**44** Refitting is a reversal of removal, but fit a new vacuum pump seal, and tighten all nuts and bolts to the specified torque, where given. After reconnecting the battery leads, it may be necessary to have any volatile memories reprogrammed by a Vauxhall dealer.

**Note:** *Refer to the precautions given in 'Safety first!' and in Section 1 of this Chapter before starting work.*
**1** If the starter motor fails to operate when the ignition key is turned to the appropriate position, the possible causes are as follows:
  a) *The battery is faulty.*
  b) *The electrical connections between the switch, solenoid, battery and starter motor are somewhere failing to pass*

**8.40a Vacuum pump oil feed pipe bolt (A) and return pipe (B) on diesel engines**

**8.40b Oil feed line on the cylinder block**

**8.42a Alternator upper mounting bolt . . .**

**8.42b . . . and lower mounting bolt on diesel engines**

**8.43 Inner view of the vacuum pump on diesel engines**

**11.5 Battery positive cable connection on the starter motor (arrowed) – petrol engine models**

**11.10 Extract the rubber plug from the bellhousing for access to the starter upper mounting bolt – diesel engine models**

*the necessary current from the battery through the starter to earth.*
*c) The solenoid is faulty.*
*d) The starter motor is mechanically or electrically defective.*

2 To check the battery, switch on the headlights. If they dim after a few seconds, this indicates that the battery is discharged – recharge (see Section 3) or renew the battery. If the headlights glow brightly, operate the starter switch while watching the headlights. If they dim, then this indicates that current is reaching the starter motor, therefore the fault must lie in the starter motor. If the lights continue to glow brightly (and no clicking sound can be heard from the starter motor solenoid), this indicates that there is a fault in the circuit or solenoid – see the following paragraphs. If the starter motor turns slowly when operated, but the battery is in good condition, then this indicates either that the starter motor is faulty, or there is considerable resistance somewhere in the circuit.

3 If a fault in the circuit is suspected, disconnect the battery leads (including the earth connection to the body), the starter/solenoid wiring and the engine/transmission earth strap. Thoroughly clean the connections, and reconnect the leads and wiring. Use a voltmeter or test light to check that full battery voltage is available at the battery positive lead

connection to the solenoid. Smear petroleum jelly around the battery terminals to prevent corrosion – corroded connections are among the most frequent causes of electrical system faults.

4 If the battery and all connections are in good condition, check the circuit by disconnecting the switched feed wire from the solenoid (the thinner wire). Connect a voltmeter or test light between the wire end and a good earth (such as the battery negative terminal), and check that the wire is live when the ignition switch is turned to the 'start' position. If it is, then the circuit is sound – if not, there is a fault in the ignition/starter switch or wiring.

5 The solenoid contacts can be checked by connecting a voltmeter or test light between the battery positive feed connection on the starter side of the solenoid and earth. When the ignition switch is turned to the 'start' position, there should be a reading or lighted bulb, as applicable. If there is no reading or lighted bulb, the solenoid is faulty and should be renewed.

6 If the circuit and solenoid are proved sound, the fault must lie in the starter motor. Begin checking the starter motor by removing it (see Section 11), and checking the brushes (see Section 12). If the fault does not lie in the brushes, the motor windings must be faulty. In this event, the starter motor must be

renewed, unless an auto-electrical specialist can be found who will overhaul the unit at a cost significantly less than that of a new or exchange starter motor.

**11 Starter motor –**
**removal and refitting**

### Petrol engines

#### Removal

1 Disconnect the battery negative terminal (refer to *Disconnecting the battery* in the Reference Chapter).
2 Apply the handbrake, then jack up the front of the vehicle and support it on axle stands (see *Jacking and vehicle support*).
3 On 1.0 litre engines, remove the alternator as described in Section 8.
4 On 1.4 litre Z14XE engines, unbolt the inlet manifold support bracket, noting the location of the earth cable.
5 Unscrew the two nuts and disconnect the battery positive cable and the starter trigger wire from the starter **(see illustration)**.
6 Unscrew the two mounting bolts and withdraw the starter motor from the rear of the engine.

#### Refitting

7 Refitting is a reversal of removal, but tighten the mounting bolts to the specified torque. On 1.0 litre engines, refit the alternator as described in Section 8.

### 1.3 litre diesel engines

#### Removal

8 On models equipped with the Easytronic transmission, first remove the transmission shift module as described in Chapter 7C.
9 Disconnect the battery negative terminal (refer to *Disconnecting the battery* in the Reference Chapter).
10 Extract the rubber plug at the top of the transmission bellhousing for access to the starter upper mounting bolt **(see illustration)**.
11 Using a long socket bit inserted through the access hole, unscrew and remove the upper mounting bolt **(see illustration)**. Take great care not to drop the bolt in the bellhousing.
12 Apply the handbrake, then jack up the front of the vehicle and support it on axle stands (see *Jacking and vehicle support*).
13 Undo the nut and disconnect the wiring from the starter solenoid **(see illustration)**.
14 Unscrew the lower mounting bolt and withdraw the starter motor from the engine.

#### Refitting

15 Refitting is a reversal of removal, but tighten the mounting bolts to the specified torque. On models equipped with the Easytronic transmission, refit the transmission shift module as described in Chapter 7C.

**11.11 Working through the access hole, unscrew and remove the starter upper mounting bolt – diesel engine models**

**11.13 Battery positive cable connection on the starter motor (arrowed) – diesel engine models**

**11.18 Earth cable on the starter motor upper mounting bolt**

**11.24 Starter motor wiring**

**11.25 Starter motor lower mounting bolt**

### *1.7 litre diesel engines*

#### Removal

**16** Disconnect the battery negative lead (refer to *Disconnecting the battery* in the Reference Chapter).

**17** Apply the handbrake, then jack up the front of the vehicle and support it on axle stands (see *Jacking and vehicle support*).

**18** At the rear left-hand end of the engine, unscrew the starter motor upper mounting bolt, noting that the engine earth cable is located beneath the head of the bolt **(see illustration)**.

**19** Remove the gearchange bracket from the rear of the engine subframe. To do this, extract the circlip and release the gearchange link, then unbolt the bracket and remove from the splines.

**20** Disconnect the wiring from the crankshaft pulse pick-up.

**21** Disconnect the vacuum hose from the charge pressure control solenoid valve.

**22** Place a container beneath the cylinder block, then release the clip and disconnect the oil return hose from the block.

**23** Unscrew the two bolts and remove the atmospheric pressure sensor bracket.

**24** Undo the screw and nut and disconnect the wiring from the starter motor **(see illustration)**.

**25** Unscrew the lower mounting bolt and withdraw the starter motor from the engine **(see illustration)**.

#### Refitting

**26** Refitting is a reversal of removal, but tighten the mounting bolts to the specified torque. After reconnecting the battery leads, it may be necessary to have any volatile memories reprogrammed by a Vauxhall dealer.

### 12 Starter motor –
testing and overhaul

If the starter motor is thought to be suspect, it should be removed from the vehicle and taken to an auto-electrician for testing. Most auto-electricians will be able to supply and fit brushes at a reasonable cost. However, check on the cost of repairs before proceeding as it may prove more economical to obtain a new or exchange motor.

### 13 Ignition switch –
removal and refitting

The switch is integral with the steering column lock, and removal and refitting is described in Chapter 10.

### 14 Oil pressure
warning light switch
– removal and refitting

#### *Removal*

**1** On 1.0, 1.2 litre and 1.4 litre Z14XEP petrol engines, the oil pressure warning light switch is screwed into the front right-hand side of the cylinder head **(see illustration)**. On the 1.4 litre Z14XE petrol engine, it is screwed in the end of the oil pump, on the inlet manifold side of the engine **(see illustration)**. On diesel engines it is screwed into the front left-hand end of the cylinder head. (1.3 litre engines) or the left-hand end of the cylinder block (1.7 litre engines) **(see illustration)**.

**2** Pull back the cover and disconnect the wiring from the switch.

**3** Place some cloth rags beneath the switch, then unscrew the switch from the block.

#### *Refitting*

**4** Refitting is a reversal of removal, but tighten the switch to the specified torque.

**14.1a Oil pressure warning light switch location (arrowed) – 1.0, 1.2 and 1.4 litre Z14XEP petrol engine models**

**14.1b Oil pressure warning light switch location (arrowed) – 1.4 litre Z14 XE petrol engine models**

**14.1c Oil pressure warning light switch location on the 1.7 litre diesel engine**

# Chapter 5 Part B:
# Ignition system – petrol engines

## Contents

## Degrees of difficulty

| Easy, suitable for novice with little experience | Fairly easy, suitable for beginner with some experience | Fairly difficult, suitable for competent DIY mechanic | Difficult, suitable for experienced DIY mechanic | Very difficult, suitable for expert DIY or professional |
|---|---|---|---|---|

## Specifications

### General

System type . . . . . . . . . . . . . . . . . . . . . . . . . . . . . . . . . . . . . . . . . . . . . . Distributorless ignition system
System application:
    1.0 litre, 1.2 litre Z12XEP and 1.4 litre Z14XEP engines . . . . . . . . . . Bosch Motronic ME 7.6.1/2
    1.2 litre Z12XE engine. . . . . . . . . . . . . . . . . . . . . . . . . . . . . . . . . . . . . Bosch Motronic ME 1.5.5
    1.4 litre Z14XE engine. . . . . . . . . . . . . . . . . . . . . . . . . . . . . . . . . . . . . GM Multec-S(F)
Location of No 1 cylinder . . . . . . . . . . . . . . . . . . . . . . . . . . . . . . . . . . . Timing chain/timing belt end of engine
Firing order:
    All except 1.0 litre engines . . . . . . . . . . . . . . . . . . . . . . . . . . . . . . . . . 1-3-4-2
    1.0 litre engines . . . . . . . . . . . . . . . . . . . . . . . . . . . . . . . . . . . . . . . . . 1-2-3

| Torque wrench setting | Nm | lbf ft |
|---|---|---|
| Ignition module. . . . . . . . . . . . . . . . . . . . . . . . . . . . . . . . . . . . . . . . . . | 8 | 6 |

## 1 General information

The ignition system is integrated with the fuel injection system to form a combined engine management system under the control of one ECU (See Chapter 4A or 4B for further information). The ignition side of the system is of the distributorless type, and consists of the ignition module (mounted on top of the cylinder head) and the knock sensor (mounted on the rear of the cylinder block).

The ignition module consists of four ignition coils, one per cylinder, in one casing mounted directly above the spark plugs. This module eliminates the need for any HT leads as the coils locate directly onto the relevant spark plug. The ECU uses its inputs from the various sensors to calculate the required ignition advance setting.

The knock sensor is mounted onto the cylinder block and informs the ECU when the engine is 'pinking' under load. The sensor is sensitive to vibration and detects the knocking which occurs when the engine starts to 'pink' (pre-ignite). The knock sensor sends an electrical signal to the ECU which in turn retards the ignition advance setting until the 'pinking' ceases.

The Bosch and Multec ignition systems operate in a similar fashion under the overall control of the engine management electronic control unit. The systems comprise various sensors (whose inputs also provide data to control the fuel injection system), and the electronic control unit, in addition to the ignition module and spark plugs. Details of the system sensors and the electronic control unit are given in Chapter 4A and 4B.

The electronic control unit selects the optimum ignition advance setting based on the information received from the various sensors, and fires the relevant ignition coil accordingly. The degree of advance can thus be constantly varied to suit the prevailing engine operating conditions.

**⚠ Warning: Due to the high voltages produced by the electronic ignition system, extreme care must be taken when working on the system with the ignition switched on. Persons with surgically-implanted cardiac pacemaker devices should keep well clear of the ignition circuits, components and test equipment.**

## 2 Ignition system – testing

1 If a fault appears in the engine management system, first ensure that all the system wiring connectors are securely connected and free of corrosion. Ensure that the fault is not due to poor maintenance; ie, check that the air cleaner filter element is clean, the spark plugs are in good condition and correctly gapped, the cylinder compression pressures are correct and that the engine breather hoses are clear and undamaged, referring to Chapters 1A, 2A and 2B for further information.

**2.2 Diagnostic socket location in the centre of the facia**

**2** If these checks fail to reveal the cause of the problem, the vehicle should be taken to a suitably-equipped Vauxhall dealer or engine management diagnostic specialist for testing. A diagnostic socket is located in the centre of the facia, above the centre console, to which a fault code reader or other suitable test equipment can be connected **(see illustration)**. By using the code reader or test equipment, the engine management ECU can be interrogated, and any stored fault codes can be retrieved. This will allow the fault to be quickly and simply traced, alleviating the need to test all the system components individually, which is a time-consuming operation that carries a risk of damaging the ECU.

**3** The only ignition system checks which can be carried out by the home mechanic are those described in Chapter 1A relating to the spark plugs. If necessary, the system

wiring and wiring connectors can be checked as described in Chapter 12, ensuring that the ECU wiring connector(s) have first been disconnected.

### 3  Ignition module – removal and refitting

#### Removal

**1** The ignition module is mounted in the centre of the camshaft cover, directly above the spark plugs.

**2** On all except 1.4 litre Z14XE engines, remove the cover from the ignition module by sliding it towards the transmission **(see illustrations)**. On 1.4 litre Z14XE engines, remove the engine top cover by unscrewing the oil filler cap and the two mounting bolts. Refit the filler cap.

**3** Disconnect the wiring plug from the end of the module **(see illustration)**.

**4** Unscrew the ignition module mounting bolts – four on 1.4 litre Z14XE engines, two on all other engines **(see illustration)**.

**5** Vauxhall technicians use two special tools to lift the module from the spark plugs, however, as an alternative, two threaded rods may be screwed into the special holes. Pull on the rods to release the module from the tops of the spark plugs **(see illustration)**. The module may also be removed by carefully easing it upwards using a screwdriver. Take care to keep the module level as it is released

from the spark plugs to avoid damage to the module connectors and the upper ceramic part of the spark plugs.

#### Refitting

**6** Refitting is a reversal of removal, but tighten the mounting bolts to the specified torque.

### 4  Knock control system – general information

The knock control system forms part of the ignition system, and allows the ignition timing to be advanced to the point at which 'knocking' or pre-ignition is about to occur. This contributes to improved engine efficiency and reduced exhaust emission levels, as it allows the engine to run as close as possible to the 'knock limit' (the point at which pre-ignition or 'pinking' occurs) without the risk of engine damage. The ignition timing is set to a predetermined value (stored in the memory of the engine management electronic control unit), which is very close to the knock limit for the engine. Due to slight changes in the combustion process during varying engine operating conditions, and possible slight fuel irregularities, engine knock may occur, and this is detected and controlled by the knock control system.

The system comprises a knock sensor and the Multec or Motronic engine management electronic control unit (see Chapter 4A or 4B). On all engines the knock module is an integral part of the engine management electronic control unit (ECU).

The knock sensor is located on the cylinder block, and contains a piezo-electric crystal, which has a resonance frequency which corresponds to the engine knock frequency. Mechanical vibrations in the cylinder block are converted by the sensor into an electrical signal. The output signal provided by the sensor increases with an increase in the vibrations in the cylinder block. If the signal increases beyond a preset limit, the sensor indicates the onset of 'knock' to the knock module.

The knock module acts as a signal processor, and modifies the signal produced

**3.2a Release the ignition module cover by sliding it towards the transmission . . .**

**3.2b . . . then remove it**

**3.3 Disconnecting the DIS module wiring plug**

**3.4 Undo the retaining bolts . . .**

**3.5 . . . then screw two threaded rods into the ignition module and lift it upwards off the spark plugs**

by the sensor before providing an output to the ECU.

The ECU processes the signals received from the knock module, and retards the ignition timing to prevent knock. From the signals provided by other engine management sensors (see Chapter 4A or 4B), the ECU can determine the cylinder which fired most recently before the knocking occurred, and hence can trace the knocking to that particular cylinder. The ignition timing for the particular cylinder concerned is thus retarded ('selective knock control'), giving independent ignition timing control over all cylinders. Once knocking has been detected and prevented, the ignition timing is progressively advanced to the predetermined value, or until knocking recurs. The system processes signals many times per second, and is able to react to changes sufficiently quickly to prevent engine damage, with no perceptible effect on engine performance.

If the system develops a fault, the ignition timing is automatically retarded by a predetermined amount as a safety precaution, and this may be detected as a slight reduction in engine performance.

## 5  Knock sensor – removal and refitting

Refer to Chapter 4A or 4B as applicable.

## 6  Ignition timing – checking and adjustment

Due to the nature of the ignition system, the ignition timing is constantly being monitored and adjusted by the engine management ECU.

The only way in which the ignition timing can be checked is by using specialist diagnostic test equipment, connected to the engine management system diagnostic socket. No adjustment of the ignition timing is possible. Should the ignition timing be incorrect, then a fault is likely to be present in the engine management system.

**Notes**

# Chapter 5 Part C:
# Pre/post-heating system - diesel engines

## Contents

## Degrees of difficulty

| | | | | |
|---|---|---|---|---|
| **Easy,** suitable for novice with little experience  | **Fairly easy,** suitable for beginner with some experience | **Fairly difficult,** suitable for competent DIY mechanic | **Difficult,** suitable for experienced DIY mechanic | **Very difficult,** suitable for expert DIY or professional |

## Specifications

| Torque wrench setting | Nm | lbf ft |
|---|---|---|
| Glow plugs: | | |
| 1.3 litre engines | 10 | 7 |
| 1.7 litre engines | 20 | 15 |

---

### 1 Pre/post-heating system – description and testing

#### Description

**1** Each cylinder of the engine is fitted with a heater plug (commonly called a glow plug) screwed into it. The plugs are electrically-operated before and during start-up when the engine is cold. Electrical feed to the glow plugs is controlled via the pre/post-heating system control unit.

**2** A warning light in the instrument panel tells the driver that pre/post-heating is taking place. When the light goes out, the engine is ready to be started. The voltage supply to the glow plugs continues for several seconds after the light goes out. If no attempt is made to start, the timer then cuts off the supply, in order to avoid draining the battery and overheating the glow plugs.

**3** The glow plugs also provide a 'post-heating' function, whereby the glow plugs remain switched on after the engine has started. The length of time 'post-heating' takes place

is also determined by the control unit, and is dependent on engine temperature.

**4** The fuel filter is fitted with a heating element to prevent the fuel 'waxing' in extreme cold temperature conditions and to improve combustion. The heating element is located in the fuel filter housing and is controlled by the pre/post-heating system control unit.

#### Testing

**5** If the system malfunctions, testing is ultimately by substitution of known good units, but some preliminary checks may be made as follows.

**6** Connect a voltmeter or 12 volt test lamp between the glow plug supply cable and earth (engine or vehicle metal). Make sure that the live connection is kept clear of the engine and bodywork.

**7** Have an assistant switch on the ignition, and check that voltage is applied to the glow plugs. Note the time for which the warning light is lit, and the total time for which voltage is applied before the system cuts out. Switch off the ignition.

**8** At an underbonnet temperature of 20°C, typical times noted should be approximately 3

seconds for warning light operation. Warning light time will increase with lower temperatures and decrease with higher temperatures.

**9** If there is no supply at all, the control unit or associated wiring is at fault.

**10** To locate a defective glow plug, disconnect the wiring connector from each plug.

**11** Use a continuity tester, or a 12 volt test lamp connected to the battery positive terminal, to check for continuity between each glow plug terminal and earth. The resistance of a glow plug in good condition is very low (less than 1 ohm), so if the test lamp does not light or the continuity tester shows a high resistance, the glow plug is certainly defective.

**12** If an ammeter is available, the current draw of each glow plug can be checked. After an initial surge of 15 to 20 amps, each plug should draw 12 amps. Any plug which draws much more or less than this is probably defective.

**13** As a final check, the glow plugs can be removed and inspected as described in the following Section.

### 2 Glow plugs – removal, inspection and refitting

*Caution: If the pre/post-heating system has just been energised, or if the engine has been running, the glow plugs will be very hot.*

#### Removal
##### 1.3 litre engines

**1** The glow plugs are located at the front of the cylinder head above the exhaust manifold.

**2** Lift off the engine cover, then disconnect the wiring from the glow plugs by squeezing the connectors with thumb and forefinger, and pulling them from the plugs **(see illustrations)**.

**2.2a Lift off the engine cover . . .**

**2.2b . . . then disconnect the wiring from the glow plugs (No 1 glow plug arrowed)**

**3** Unscrew the glow plugs and remove them from the cylinder head.

### 1.7 litre engines

**4** Disconnect the battery negative lead (refer to *Disconnecting the battery* in the Reference Chapter).

**5** Remove the air cleaner assembly as described in Chapter 4D.

**6** Remove the engine electronic control unit and mounting bracket as described in Chapter 4D, Section 8.

**7** Disconnect the wiring from the glow plugs by squeezing the connectors with thumb and forefinger, and pulling them from the plugs.

**8** Unscrew the glow plugs and remove them from the cylinder head **(see illustration)**.

### Inspection

**9** Inspect each glow plug for physical damage. Burnt or eroded glow plug tips can be caused by a bad injector spray pattern. Have the injectors checked if this type of damage is found.

**10** If the glow plugs are in good physical con-dition, check them electrically using a 12 volt test lamp or continuity tester as described in the previous Section.

**11** The glow plugs can be energised by applying 12 volts to them to verify that they heat up evenly and in the required time. Observe the following precautions.

 a) *Support the glow plug by clamping it carefully in a vice or self-locking pliers. Remember it will become red-hot.*
 b) *Make sure that the power supply or test lead incorporates a fuse or overload trip to protect against damage from a short-circuit.*
 c) *After testing, allow the glow plug to cool for several minutes before attempting to handle it.*

**12** A glow plug in good condition will start to glow red at the tip after drawing current

for 5 seconds or so. Any plug which takes much longer to start glowing, or which starts glowing in the middle instead of at the tip, is defective.

### Refitting

#### 1.3 litre engines

**13** Carefully refit the plugs and tighten to the specified torque. Do not overtighten, as this can damage the glow plug element.

**14** Push the electrical connectors firmly onto the glow plugs and refit the engine cover.

**15** Check the operation of the glow plugs.

#### 1.7 litre engines

**16** Carefully refit the plugs and tighten to the specified torque. Do not overtighten, as this can damage the glow plug element.

**17** Push the electrical connectors firmly onto the glow plugs.

**18** Refit the electronic control unit and bracket with reference to Chapter 4D.

**19** Refit the air cleaner assembly with reference to Chapter 4D.

**20** Reconnect the battery negative lead (refer to *Disconnecting the battery* in the Reference Chapter). It may be necessary to have the engine management memory reprogrammed by a Vauxhall dealer after reconnecting the battery.

**21** Check the operation of the glow plugs.

| 3 | Pre/post-heating system control unit – removal and refitting |
|---|---|

### Removal

**1** The pre/post-heating system control unit is located on the left-hand side of the engine compartment where it is mounted beneath the fuse/relay box on the inner wing panel.

**2.8 Removing the glow plugs from the cylinder head**

**2** Disconnect the battery negative terminal (refer to *Disconnecting the battery* in the Reference Chapter).

**3** Remove the engine management electronic control unit (ECU) as described in Chapter 4C or 4D.

**4** Disconnect the wiring connector on the top of the fuel filter housing.

**5** Unclip the expansion tank coolant hose and the wiring harness from the fuel filter crash box, and disconnect the harness connector **(see illustrations)**.

**6** Release the retaining clip, lift the coolant expansion tank from its location and place it to one side **(see illustration)**.

**7** Remove the cover from the fuse/relay box, then unclip the pre/post-heating system control unit wiring harness.

**8** Detach the fuse/relay box from the inner wing panel, then carefully push the fuse/relay box to one side.

**9** Unclip the pre/post-heating control unit and disconnect the wiring harness plug. Withdraw the unit from the vehicle.

### Refitting

**10** Refitting is a reversal of removal.

**3.5a Unclip the expansion tank coolant hose and the wiring harness from the crash box . . .**

**3.5b . . . and disconnect the harness connector**

**3.6 Release the retaining clip and lift the expansion tank from its location**

# Chapter 6
# Clutch

## Contents

## Degrees of difficulty

| Easy, suitable for novice with little experience | Fairly easy, suitable for beginner with some experience | Fairly difficult, suitable for competent DIY mechanic | Difficult, suitable for experienced DIY mechanic | Very difficult, suitable for expert DIY or professional |
|---|---|---|---|---|

## Specifications

Type . . . . . . . . . . . . . . . . . . . . . . . . . . . . . . . . . . . . . . . . . . . . . . . . . Single dry plate with diaphragm spring, hydraulically-operated

**Friction disc**

Diameter:
| | |
|---|---|
| 1.0 and 1.2 litre petrol engines: | |
| Standard transmission | 190 mm |
| Easytronic transmission | 200 mm |
| 1.4 litre petrol engines: | |
| Standard transmission | 200 mm |
| Easytronic transmission | 200 mm |
| 1.3 litre diesel engines: | |
| Standard transmission | 216 mm |
| Easytronic transmission | 216 mm |
| 1.7 litre diesel engines | 205 mm |

New lining thickness:
| | |
|---|---|
| 1.0 and 1.4 litre petrol engines | 7.65 mm |
| 1.2 litre petrol engines: | |
| Standard transmission | 8.0 mm |
| Easytronic transmission | 7.65 mm |
| Diesel engines | 7.2 mm |

| Torque wrench settings | Nm | lbf ft |
|---|---|---|
| Clutch master cylinder retaining nuts* | 20 | 15 |
| Pedal mounting bracket nuts* | 20 | 15 |
| Pressure plate retaining bolts*: | | |
| M7 bolts | 15 | 11 |
| M8 bolts | 28 | 21 |

* Use new self-locking bolts/nuts

## 1 General information

### Standard clutch

**1** The clutch consists of a friction disc, a pressure plate assembly, and the hydraulic release cylinder (which incorporates the release bearing); all of these components are contained in the large cast-aluminium alloy bellhousing, sandwiched between the engine and the transmission **(see illustration)**.

**2** The friction disc is fitted between the engine flywheel and the clutch pressure plate, and is allowed to slide on the transmission input shaft splines.

**3** The pressure plate assembly is bolted to the engine flywheel. When the engine is running, drive is transmitted from the crankshaft, via the flywheel, to the friction disc (these components being clamped securely together by the pressure plate assembly) and from the friction disc to the transmission input shaft.

**4** To interrupt the drive, the spring pressure must be relaxed. This is achieved using a hydraulic release mechanism which consists of the master cylinder, the release cylinder and the pipe/hose linking the two components. Depressing the pedal pushes on the master cylinder pushrod which hydraulically forces the release cylinder piston against the pressure plate spring fingers. This causes the springs to deform and releases the clamping force on the friction disc.

**5** The clutch is self-adjusting and requires no manual adjustment.

### Easytronic semi-automatic clutch

**6** Models equipped with the Easytronic MTA (Manual Transmission with Automatic shift), are fitted with a Semi Automatic Clutch (SAC). The clutch may be operated either fully automatically or semi-automatically by means of the gear selector lever. There is no conventional clutch pedal fitted.

**7** The Easytronic system essentially consists of a conventional manual gearbox and clutch fitted with electrical and hydraulic controls, the clutch being operated by a clutch module attached to the side of the transmission casing. Refer to Chapter 7C for more information. The clutch component removal and refitting procedures are included in this Chapter as they are very similar to those for the standard manual transmission.

**1.1 Standard clutch components**

| | | | |
|---|---|---|---|
| 1 Pressure line | 5 Clutch pedal assembly | 8 Release cylinder | 11 Pressure plate |
| 2 Damper | 6 Clutch pedal switch (where fitted) | 9 Release cylinder pressure line | 12 Friction disc |
| 3 Supply hose | 7 O-ring | 10 Pressure plate bolt | 13 Assembly guide |
| 4 Master cylinder | | | 14 Fastening sleeve |

J44620

## 2 Clutch hydraulic system – bleeding

⚠️ **Warning: Hydraulic fluid is poisonous; wash off immediately and thoroughly in the case of skin contact, and seek immediate medical advice if any fluid is swallowed or gets into the eyes. Certain types of hydraulic fluid are flammable, and may ignite when allowed into contact with hot components; when servicing any hydraulic system, it is safest to assume that the fluid is flammable, and to take precautions against the risk of fire as though it is petrol that is being handled. Hydraulic fluid is also an effective paint stripper, and will attack plastics; if any is spilt, it should be washed off immediately, using copious quantities of fresh water. Finally, it is hygroscopic (it absorbs moisture from the air) – old fluid may be contaminated and unfit for further use. When topping-up or renewing the fluid, always use the recommended type, and ensure that it comes from a freshly-opened sealed container.**

**Note:** On models with the Easytronic semi-automatic clutch (SAC), the following manual method of bleeding the clutch is not possible since the hydraulic control unit is integral with the transmission. On these models, bleeding is carried out using the Vauxhall TECH2 diagnostic instrument, therefore this work should be entrusted to a Vauxhall dealer.

### General information

**1** The correct operation of any hydraulic system is only possible after removing all air from the components and circuit; this is achieved by bleeding the system.

**2** The manufacturer's stipulate that the system must be initially bled by the 'back-bleeding' method using Vauxhall special bleeding equipment. This entails connecting a pressure bleeding unit containing fresh brake fluid to the release cylinder bleed screw, with a collecting vessel connected to the brake fluid master cylinder reservoir. The pressure bleeding unit is then switched on, the bleed screw is opened and hydraulic fluid is delivered under pressure, backwards, to be expelled from the reservoir into the collecting vessel. Final bleeding is then carried out in the conventional way.

**3** In practice, this method would normally only be required if new hydraulic components have been fitted, or if the system has been completely drained of hydraulic fluid. If the system has only been disconnected to allow component removal and refitting procedures to be carried out, such as removal and refitting of the transmission (for example for clutch renewal) or engine removal and refitting, then it is quite likely that normal bleeding will be sufficient.

**4** Our advice would therefore be as follows:

a) If the hydraulic system has only been partially disconnected, try bleeding by the conventional methods described in paragraphs 10 to 15, or 16 to 19.

b) If the hydraulic system has been completely drained and new components have been fitted, try bleeding by using the pressure bleeding method described in paragraphs 20 to 22.

c) If the above methods fail to produce a firm pedal on completion, it will be necessary to 'back-bleed' the system using Vauxhall bleeding equipment, or suitable alternative equipment as described in paragraphs 23 to 28.

**5** During the bleeding procedure, add only clean, unused hydraulic fluid of the recommended type; never re-use fluid that has already been bled from the system. Ensure that sufficient fluid is available before starting work.

**6** If there is any possibility of incorrect fluid being already in the system, the hydraulic circuit must be flushed completely with uncontaminated, correct fluid.

**7** If hydraulic fluid has been lost from the system, or air has entered because of a leak, ensure that the fault is cured before continuing further.

**8** The bleed screw is located in the hose end fitting which is situated on the top of the transmission housing **(see illustration)**. On some models access to the bleed screw is limited and it may be necessary to jack up the front of the vehicle and support it on axle stands so that the screw can be reached from below, or remove the inlet air trunking (see Chapter 4A, 4B or 4C) so that the screw can be reached from above.

**9** Check that all pipes and hoses are secure, unions tight and the bleed screw is closed. Clean any dirt from around the bleed screw.

### Bleeding procedure

#### Conventional method

**10** Collect a clean glass jar, a suitable length of plastic or rubber tubing which is a tight fit over the bleed screw, and a ring spanner to fit the screw. The help of an assistant will also be required.

**11** Unscrew the master cylinder fluid reservoir cap (the clutch shares the same fluid reservoir as the braking system), and top the master cylinder reservoir up to the upper (MAX) level line. Ensure that the fluid level is maintained at least above the lower level line in the reservoir throughout the procedure.

**12** Remove the dust cap from the bleed screw. Fit the spanner and tube to the screw, place the other end of the tube in the jar, and pour in sufficient fluid to cover the end of the tube.

**13** Have the assistant fully depress the clutch pedal several times to build-up pressure, then maintain it on the final down stroke.

**14** While pedal pressure is maintained, unscrew the bleed screw (approximately one turn) and allow the compressed fluid and air to flow into the jar. The assistant should

**2.8 Clutch bleed screw (arrowed)**

maintain pedal pressure and should not release it until instructed to do so. When the flow stops, tighten the bleed screw again, have the assistant release the pedal slowly, and recheck the reservoir fluid level.

**15** Repeat the steps given in paragraphs 13 and 14 until the fluid emerging from the bleed screw is free from air bubbles. If the master cylinder has been drained and refilled allow approximately five seconds between cycles for the master cylinder passages to refill.

#### Conventional method using a one-way valve kit

**16** As their name implies, these kits consist of a length of tubing with a one-way valve fitted, to prevent expelled air and fluid being drawn back into the system; some kits include a translucent container, which can be positioned so that the air bubbles can be more easily seen flowing from the end of the tube.

**17** The kit is connected to the bleed screw, which is then opened.

**18** The user returns to the driver's seat, depresses the clutch pedal with a smooth, steady stroke, and slowly releases it; this is repeated until the expelled fluid is clear of air bubbles.

**19** Note that these kits simplify work so much that it is easy to forget the clutch fluid reservoir level; ensure that this is maintained at least above the lower level line at all times.

#### Pressure-bleeding method

**20** These kits are usually operated by the reservoir of pressurised air contained in the spare tyre. However, note that it will probably be necessary to reduce the pressure to a lower level than normal; refer to the instructions supplied with the kit.

**21** By connecting a pressurised, fluid-filled container to the clutch fluid reservoir, bleeding can be carried out simply by opening the bleed screw and allowing the fluid to flow out until no more air bubbles can be seen in the expelled fluid.

**22** This method has the advantage that the large reservoir of fluid provides an additional safeguard against air being drawn into the system during bleeding.

#### 'Back-bleeding' method

**23** The following procedure describes the bleeding method using Vauxhall equipment.

**3.4 Slide out the retaining clip and free the hydraulic pipe from the connector**

Alternative equipment is available and should be used in accordance with the maker's instructions.

**24** Connect the pressure hose (MKM-6174-1) to the bleed screw located in the hose end fitting situated on the top of the transmission housing **(see illustration 2.8)**. Connect the other end of the hose to a suitable pressure bleeding device set to operate at approximately 2.0 bar.

**25** Attach the cap (MKM-6174-2) to the master cylinder reservoir, and place the hose in a collecting vessel.

**26** Switch on the pressure bleeding equipment, open the bleed screw, and allow fresh hydraulic fluid to flow from the pressure bleeding unit, through the system and out through the top of the reservoir and into the collecting vessel. When fluid, free of air bubbles appears in the reservoir, close the bleed screw and switch off the bleeding equipment.

**27** Disconnect the bleeding equipment from the bleed screw and reservoir.

**28** Carry out a final conventional bleeding procedure as described in paragraphs 10 to 15, or 16 to 19.

### All methods

**29** When bleeding is complete, no more bubbles appear and correct pedal feel is restored, tighten the bleed screw securely (do not overtighten). Remove the tube and spanner, and wash off any spilt fluid. Refit the dust cap to the bleed screw.

**30** Check the hydraulic fluid level in the

**4.2a Clutch release cylinder hydraulic pipe union nut (A) and retaining bolts (B)**

master cylinder reservoir, and top-up if necessary (see *Weekly checks*).

**31** Discard any hydraulic fluid that has been bled from the system; it will not be fit for re-use.

**32** Check the operation of the clutch pedal. If the clutch is still not operating correctly, air must still be present in the system, and further bleeding is required. Failure to bleed satisfactorily after a reasonable repetition of the bleeding procedure may be due to worn master cylinder/release cylinder seals.

### 3 Clutch master cylinder – removal and refitting

**Note:** *This procedure does not apply to models fitted with the Easytronic semi-automatic transmission.*

### Removal

**1** Remove the clutch pedal and bracket as described in Section 5. Note that the clutch master cylinder retaining nuts are removed during the bracket removal.

**2** Remove the brake/clutch hydraulic fluid reservoir filler cap, and tighten it down onto a piece of polythene. This will reduce the loss of fluid when the master cylinder is removed. Alternatively, detach the clutch master cylinder fluid supply hose from the brake fluid reservoir, and plug the apertures.

**3** Working in the engine compartment, remove all traces of dirt from the outside of the master cylinder and position some cloth beneath the cylinder to catch any spilt fluid.

**4** Slide out the retaining clip, and free the hydraulic pipe from the connector in the end of the master cylinder at the engine compartment bulkhead. Plug the pipe end and master cylinder port to minimise fluid loss and

**4.2b Clutch release cylinder hydraulic pipe quick-release connector (1), adaptor (2) and outer sealing ring (3)**

*Also note the inner sealing ring (arrowed)*

prevent the entry of dirt. Recover the sealing ring from the union and discard it; a new one must be used on refitting **(see illustration)**. Gently squeeze the two legs of the retaining clip together, and re-insert the clip into the pipe end fitting.

**5** Working in the engine compartment, withdraw the clutch master cylinder from the bulkhead.

### Refitting

**6** Ensure the mating surfaces are clean and dry, then locate the master cylinder on the bulkhead.

**7** Using a new sealing ring, push the hydraulic pipe into the connector until the retaining clip engages.

**8** Where applicable, reconnect the fluid supply hose to the brake fluid reservoir.

**9** Refit the clutch pedal and bracket with reference to Section 5.

**10** Bleed the clutch hydraulic system as described in Section 2.

### 4 Release cylinder – removal and refitting

**Note 1:** *Due to the amount of work necessary to remove and refit clutch components, it is usually considered good practice to renew the clutch friction disc, pressure plate assembly and release bearing as a matched set, even if only one of these is actually worn enough to require renewal. It is also worth considering the renewal of the clutch components on a preventative basis if the engine and/or transmission have been removed for some other reason.*

**Note 2:** *Refer to the warning concerning the dangers of asbestos dust at the beginning of Section 6.*

### Removal

**1** Unless the complete engine/transmission unit is to be removed from the car and separated for major overhaul (see Chapter 2D), the clutch release cylinder can be reached by removing the transmission only, as described in Chapter 7A or 7C.

**2** Wipe clean the outside of the release cylinder then either unscrew the union nut or release the quick-release connector and disconnect the hydraulic pipe **(see illustrations)**. Wipe up any spilt fluid with a clean cloth.

**3** Unscrew the three retaining bolts and slide the release cylinder from the transmission input shaft. Remove the sealing ring which is fitted between the cylinder and transmission housing and discard it; a new one must be used on refitting.

**4** The release cylinder is a sealed unit and cannot be overhauled. If the cylinder seals leak or the release bearing is noisy or rough in operation, then the complete unit must be renewed.

### Refitting

**5** Ensure the release cylinder and transmission mating surfaces are clean and dry and fit the new sealing ring to the transmission recess.

**6** Lubricate the release cylinder seal with a smear of transmission oil then carefully ease the cylinder along the input shaft and into position. **Note:** *Vauxhall technicians use a special tapered sleeve on the input shaft to prevent damage to the seal. If necessary, wrap suitable tape around the end of the shaft.* Ensure the sealing ring is still correctly seated in its groove then refit the release cylinder retaining bolts and tighten them securely.

**7** Reconnect the hydraulic pipe to the release cylinder, making sure that the quick-release connector engages correctly. It should make an audible 'click'.

**8** Refit the transmission unit as described in Chapter 7A or 7C.

**9** Bleed the clutch hydraulic system as described in Section 2.

**10** On Easytronic (semi-automatic transmission) models, a Vauxhall dealer must carry out a Contact Point Determination program, using the TECH2 diagnostic instrument.

### 5 Clutch pedal and bracket – removal and refitting

### Removal

**1** Remove the lower facia panel from the driver's footwell, then remove the air duct.

**2** Remove the steering column as described in Chapter 10.

**3** Where fitted (according to model), remove the clutch switch from the pedal bracket, and unclip the wiring harness bracket.

**4** Disconnect the return spring from the clutch pedal, then remove the clip securing the pedal to the master cylinder piston rod. Vauxhall technicians use a special tool to do this, however, the clip may be released using screwdrivers. **Note:** *Do not remove the ballhead clip at the master cylinder end.*

**5** Remove the windscreen wiper motor from the bulkhead as described in Chapter 12.

**6** In the engine compartment, unscrew the pedal support strut bolt from the bulkhead (behind the wiring harness), then unscrew the nuts in the driver's footwell and remove the support strut.

**7** Unscrew the two self-locking nuts securing the clutch master cylinder to the bulkhead. Discard the nuts and obtain new ones.

**8** Unscrew the three remaining self-locking nuts, and withdraw the clutch pedal and bracket from inside the vehicle **(see illustration)**. Discard the nuts and obtain new ones. To prevent any damage, make sure that all wiring is moved to one side.

**9** Check the pedal and bracket for excessive wear and damage. It is not possible to renew the pedal pivot bushes separately, so if they are worn, the complete assembly must be renewed.

### Refitting

**10** Manoeuvre the pedal and bracket assembly into position, making sure that the surrounding wiring is not trapped. Screw on the new retaining nuts, including the master cylinder ones, and tighten to the specified torque. The pedal bracket nuts should be tightened before the master cylinder nuts.

**11** Refit the pedal support strut and tighten the bolts/nuts.

**12** Refit the windscreen wiper motor with reference to Chapter 12.

**13** Reconnect the clutch pedal to the master cylinder piston rod, making sure that an audible 'click' is heard as the clip engages.

**14** Reconnect the clutch return spring.

**15** Where applicable, refit the clutch switch and clip the wiring harness in place.

**16** Refit the steering column with reference to Chapter 10.

**17** Refit the air duct and lower facia panel to the driver's footwell.

### 6 Clutch assembly (Standard) – removal, inspection and refitting

⚠️ **Warning: Dust created by clutch wear and deposited on the clutch components may contain asbestos, which is a health hazard. DO NOT blow it out with compressed air, or inhale any of it. DO NOT use petrol or petroleum-based solvents to clean off the dust. Brake system cleaner or methylated spirit should be used to flush the dust into a suitable receptacle. After the clutch components are wiped clean with rags, dispose of the contaminated rags and cleaner in a sealed, marked container.**

**Note:** *To prevent possible damage to the ends of the pressure plate diaphragm spring fingers, Vauxhall recommend the use of a special jig (KM-6263) to remove the clutch assembly, however, with care it is possible to carry out the work without the jig.*

### Removal

**1** Unless the complete engine/transmission unit is to be removed from the car and separated for major overhaul (see Chapter 2D), the clutch can be reached by removing the transmission as described in Chapter 7A.

**2** Before disturbing the clutch, use chalk or a marker pen to mark the relationship of the pressure plate assembly to the flywheel.

**3** At this stage, Vauxhall technicians fit the special jig KM-6263 to the rear of the engine and compress the diaphragm spring fingers until the friction disc is released **(see illustrations)**. The pressure plate mounting bolts are then unscrewed, and the jig spindle backed off.

**4** If the jig is not available, progressively unscrew the pressure plate retaining bolts in diagonal sequence by half a turn at a time, until spring pressure is released and the bolts can be unscrewed by hand.

J44616

**5.8 Clutch pedal and master cylinder**

| | | |
|---|---|---|
| 1 Clutch master cylinder | 3 Seal | 5 Foot pad |
| 2 Clutch pedal and bracket | 4 Support strut | 6 Pedal stop/bumper |

**5** Remove the pressure plate assembly and collect the friction disc, noting which way round the disc is fitted. It is recommended that new pressure plate retaining bolts are obtained.

### Inspection

**Note:** *Due to the amount of work necessary to remove and refit clutch components, it is usually considered good practice to renew the clutch friction disc and pressure plate assembly as a matched set, even if only one of these is actually worn enough to require renewal. It is also worth checking the release cylinder and thrust bearing for wear.*

**6** Wipe clean the clutch components, however, read the warning at the beginning of this Section. Remove dust using a clean, dry cloth, and working in a well-ventilated area.

**7** Check the friction disc linings for signs of wear, damage or oil contamination. If the friction material is cracked, burnt, scored or damaged, or if it is contaminated with oil or grease (shown by shiny black patches), the friction disc must be renewed.

**8** If the friction material is still serviceable, check that the centre boss splines are unworn, that the torsion springs are in good condition and securely fastened, and that all the rivets are tight. If any wear or damage is found, the friction disc must be renewed.

**9** If the friction material is fouled with oil, this must be due to an oil leak from the crankshaft oil seal, from the sump-to-cylinder block joint, or from the release cylinder assembly (either the main seal or the sealing ring). Renew the

crankshaft oil seal or repair the sump joint as described in the relevant part of Chapter 2, before installing the new friction disc. The clutch release cylinder work is covered in Section 4.

**10** Check the pressure plate assembly for obvious signs of wear or damage by shaking it to check for loose internal components. If the diaphragm spring is worn or damaged, or if its pressure is in any way suspect, the pressure plate assembly should be renewed.

**11** Check that the machined surfaces of the pressure plate and flywheel are clean, completely flat, and free from scratches or scoring. If either is discoloured from excessive heat, or shows signs of cracks, it should be renewed.

**12** Check that the release cylinder bearing rotates smoothly and easily, with no sign of noise or roughness. Also check that the surface itself is smooth and unworn, with no signs of cracks, pitting or scoring. If there is any doubt about its condition, the clutch release cylinder should be renewed (it is not possible to renew the bearing separately).

### Refitting

**13** On reassembly, ensure that the friction surfaces of the flywheel and pressure plate are completely clean, smooth, and free from oil or grease. Use solvent to remove any protective grease from new components.

**14** Lightly grease the teeth of the friction disc hub with high melting-point grease. Do not apply too much, otherwise it may eventually contaminate the friction disc linings.

### Using the Vauxhall jig

**15** Fit the special Vauxhall guide bush to the centre of the crankshaft, and locate the friction disc on it, making sure that the lettering 'transmission side' points towards the transmission.

**16** Locate the pressure plate on the special centring pins on the flywheel, then compress the diaphragm spring fingers with the jig, until the friction disc is in full contact with the flywheel.

**17** Insert new pressure plate retaining bolts, and progressively tighten them to the specified torque. If necessary, hold the flywheel stationary while tightening the bolts, using a screwdriver engaged with the teeth of the starter ring gear.

**18** Back off the jig spindle so that the diaphragm spring forces the pressure plate against the friction disc and flywheel, then remove the jig and guide bush from the engine.

**19** Refit the transmission as described in Chapter 7A.

### Without using the Vauxhall jig

**20** Locate the friction disc on the flywheel, making sure that the lettering 'transmission side' points towards the transmission.

**21** Refit the pressure plate assembly, aligning the marks made on dismantling (if the original pressure plate is re-used). Fit new pressure plate bolts, but tighten them only finger-tight so that the friction disc can still be moved.

**22** The friction disc must now be centralised so that, when the transmission is refitted, its

**6.3a Vauxhall special jig (4) for removing the clutch pressure plate and friction disc**

*1, 3 and 6   Bolts securing the jig to the engine*
*2 and 5       Bolts for adjusting the jig to the centre of the crankshaft*

**6.3b Thrust piece (1) in contact with the diaphragm spring fingers (3) of the pressure plate (2)**

**6.23 Centralise the friction disc using a clutch aligning tool or similar**

input shaft will pass through the splines at the centre of the friction disc.

**23** Centralisation can be achieved by passing a screwdriver or other long bar through the friction disc and into the hole in the crankshaft. The friction disc can then be moved around until it is centred on the crankshaft hole. Alternatively, a clutch-aligning tool can be used to eliminate the guesswork; these can be obtained from most accessory shops **(see illustration)**.

**24** When the friction disc is centralised, tighten the pressure plate bolts evenly and in a diagonal sequence to the specified torque setting.

**25** Refit the transmission as described in Chapter 7A.

---

### 7 Clutch assembly (Easytronic) – removal, inspection and refitting

**Note 1:** *After fitting the clutch assembly, a Vauxhall dealer must carry out a Contact Point Determination program, using the TECH2 diagnostic instrument.*

**Note 2:** *To prevent possible damage to the pressure plate diaphragm spring fingers, Vauxhall recommend the use of a special jig KM-6263 to remove the clutch assembly. Additionally, Vauxhall tool KM-6289 will be required when removing the pressure plate. The following procedure assumes these tools are available.*

### Removal

**1** Unless the complete engine/transmission unit is to be removed from the car and separated for major overhaul (see Chapter 2D), the clutch can be reached by removing the transmission as described in Chapter 7C.

**2** Prepare Vauxhall tool KM-6289 in accordance with the clutch diameter, then fit the tool onto the outside of the pressure plate, making sure that the two inner pins are in contact with the pressure plate adjusting ring. Insert the two spring hooks in the pressure plate **(see illustrations)**.

**3** Fit the Vauxhall jig KM-6263 to the engine, and compress the diaphragm spring fingers until the friction disc is released. Check that

**7.2a Vauxhall tool KM-6289 required to hold the adjusting ring when removing the pressure plate**

A  *Tool*
B  *Attach pin for pretensioning spring*
C  *Pins adjusted for clutch diameter*

D  *Attach pin for pretensioning spring*
1, 2 and 3  *Connection points for different diameter clutches*

as the fingers are compressed, tool KM-6289 rotates the pressure plate anti-clockwise.

**4** Progressively unscrew and remove the pressure plate retaining bolts, then back off the jig spindle and remove the pressure plate, together with the friction disc.

**5** Remove tool KM-6289 if the pressure plate

is to be renewed and fit it to the new pressure plate, otherwise leave it in position on the original pressure plate.

### Inspection

**6** Refer to Section 6, paragraphs 6 to 12.

**7.2b Vauxhall tool KM-6289 fitted to the pressure plate**

1  *Tool*
2  *Hooks*

3  *Pressure plate*
4  *Pins*

5  *Adjusting ring contact*

## Refitting

**7** On reassembly, ensure that the friction surfaces of the flywheel and pressure plate are completely clean, smooth, and free from oil or grease. Use solvent to remove any protective grease from new components.

**8** Lightly grease the teeth of the friction disc hub with high melting-point grease. Do not apply too much, otherwise it may eventually contaminate the friction disc linings.

**9** Fit the special Vauxhall guide bush to the centre of the crankshaft, and locate the friction disc on it, making sure that the lettering 'transmission side' points towards the transmission.

**10** Locate the pressure plate on the special centring pins on the flywheel, then compress the diaphragm spring fingers with the jig, until the friction disc is in full contact with the flywheel.

**11** Insert new pressure plate retaining bolts, and progressively tighten them to the specified torque. If necessary, hold the flywheel stationary while tightening the bolts, using a screwdriver engaged with the teeth of the starter ring gear.

**12** Back off the jig spindle so that the diaphragm spring forces the pressure plate against the friction disc and flywheel, then remove the jig and guide bush from the engine.

**13** Remove Vauxhall tool KM-6289 from the pressure plate.

**14** Refit the transmission as described in Chapter 7C.

# Chapter 7 Part A:
# Manual transmission

## Contents

## Degrees of difficulty

| | | | | |
|---|---|---|---|---|
| **Easy,** suitable for novice with little experience  | **Fairly easy,** suitable for beginner with some experience  | **Fairly difficult,** suitable for competent DIY mechanic | **Difficult,** suitable for experienced DIY mechanic | **Very difficult,** suitable for expert DIY or professional 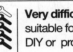 |

## Specifications

### General

Type . . . . . . . . . . . . . . . . . . . . . . . . . . . . . . . . . . . . . . . . . . . . . . Five forward speeds and one reverse, synchromesh on all forward gears. Integral differential

Manufacturer's designation:
  Petrol engines . . . . . . . . . . . . . . . . . . . . . . . . . . . . . . . . . . . . . . F 13/5 CR
  Diesel engine:
    Without intercooler . . . . . . . . . . . . . . . . . . . . . . . . . . . . . . . . F 13/5 WR
    With intercooler . . . . . . . . . . . . . . . . . . . . . . . . . . . . . . . . . . F 17/5 WR

### Gear ratios

F 13/5 CR transmission:
  1st . . . . . . . . . . . . . . . . . . . . . . . . . . . . . . . . . . . . . . . . . . . . . . 3.73:1
  2nd . . . . . . . . . . . . . . . . . . . . . . . . . . . . . . . . . . . . . . . . . . . . . 2.14:1
  3rd . . . . . . . . . . . . . . . . . . . . . . . . . . . . . . . . . . . . . . . . . . . . . 1.41:1
  4th . . . . . . . . . . . . . . . . . . . . . . . . . . . . . . . . . . . . . . . . . . . . . 1.12:1
  5th . . . . . . . . . . . . . . . . . . . . . . . . . . . . . . . . . . . . . . . . . . . . . 0.89:1
  Reverse . . . . . . . . . . . . . . . . . . . . . . . . . . . . . . . . . . . . . . . . . 3.31:1
F 13/5 WR and F 17/5 WR transmissions:
  1st . . . . . . . . . . . . . . . . . . . . . . . . . . . . . . . . . . . . . . . . . . . . . . 3.73:1
  2nd . . . . . . . . . . . . . . . . . . . . . . . . . . . . . . . . . . . . . . . . . . . . . 1.96:1
  3rd . . . . . . . . . . . . . . . . . . . . . . . . . . . . . . . . . . . . . . . . . . . . . 1.31:1
  4th . . . . . . . . . . . . . . . . . . . . . . . . . . . . . . . . . . . . . . . . . . . . . 0.95:1
  5th . . . . . . . . . . . . . . . . . . . . . . . . . . . . . . . . . . . . . . . . . . . . . 0.76:1
  Reverse . . . . . . . . . . . . . . . . . . . . . . . . . . . . . . . . . . . . . . . . . 3.31:1

### Final drive ratios

F 13/5 CR transmission:
  1.0 and 1.2 litre petrol engines . . . . . . . . . . . . . . . . . . . . . . . . . 3.74:1 or 3.94:1
  1.4 litre petrol engine . . . . . . . . . . . . . . . . . . . . . . . . . . . . . . . . 3.94:1
F 13/5 WR and F 17/5 WR transmissions:
  Except Combo models . . . . . . . . . . . . . . . . . . . . . . . . . . . . . . . 3.55:1
  Combo models . . . . . . . . . . . . . . . . . . . . . . . . . . . . . . . . . . . . . 3.74:1

### Torque wrench settings

| | Nm | lbf ft |
|---|---|---|
| Differential housing cover plate bolts: | | |
|   Alloy plate | 18 | 13 |
|   Steel plate | 30 | 22 |
| Gearchange mechanism selector rod clamp bolt: | | |
|   Stage 1 | 12 | 9 |
|   Stage 2 | Angle-tighten a further 225° | |
| Left-hand engine mounting | See Chapter 2A, 2B, 2C or 2D | |
| Reversing light switch | 20 | 15 |
| Transmission-to-engine/sump bolts | See Chapter 2A, 2B, 2C or 2D | |
| Vehicle speed sensor retaining plate bolt | 4 | 3 |

J44619

**1.1 Transmission and gearchange**

1 Linkage guide components
2 Gear lever/housing assembly

3 Housing
4 Control rod
5 Shift guide bearing support

6 Gear shift guide lever
7 Shift guide rod

## 1 General information

**1** One of three different CR (close ratio) or WR (wide ratio) manual transmissions may be fitted, depending on model and engine fitted (see Specifications); there are only minor internal differences between the transmission types **(see illustration)**.
**2** Drive from the clutch is transmitted to the input shaft, which runs in parallel with the mainshaft. The input shaft and mainshaft gears are in constant mesh, and selection of gears is by sliding synchromesh hubs, which lock the appropriate mainshaft gear to the mainshaft.
**3** The 5th speed gear components are located in an extension housing at the end of the transmission.
**4** Reverse gear is obtained by sliding an idler gear into mesh with two straight-cut gears on the input shaft and mainshaft.
**5** The differential is mounted in the main transmission casing, and drive is transmitted to the differential by a pinion gear on the end of the mainshaft. The inboard ends of the

driveshafts locate directly into the differential. The transmission and differential unit share the same lubricating oil.
**6** Gear selection is by a floor-mounted gearchange lever, via a remote control linkage.

## 2 Transmission oil – draining and refilling

**Note:** Changing the transmission oil is not a

**2.3 Differential cover plate securing bolts**

routine job, however, it may be considered necessary if the vehicle has completed a high mileage or if a second-hand transmission is being fitted. No drain plug is fitted.

### Draining

**1** Apply the handbrake, then jack up the front of the vehicle and support it on axle stands (see Jacking and vehicle support). Remove the engine undertray where fitted.
**2** Unbolt the rear engine torque link from the transmission and pivot it to one side.
**3** Place a suitable container under the differential cover plate. Unscrew the securing bolts and withdraw the cover plate, allowing the transmission oil to drain into the container **(see illustration)**. Recover the gasket and, if necessary, renew it.
**4** Refit the differential cover plate together with the gasket, and tighten the securing bolts, then refit the rear engine torque link and tighten the bolts.

### Refilling

**5** Wipe clean the area around the level plug. The level plug is located behind the driveshaft inner joint on the left-hand side of the transmission **(see illustration)**. Unscrew the plug and clean it.

**2.5 Transmission oil level hole**

**2.6 Fill the transmission through the reversing light switch aperture**

**3.3 Gear selector rod-to-clamp sleeve clamp nut**

**3.5 Insert a 5 mm drill or punch through the clamp and into the locating hole**

**3.6 Lock the selector mechanism by pressing in the spring-loaded locking pin**

**6** The transmission is refilled via the reversing light switch aperture **(see illustration)**. Wipe clean the area around the reversing light switch, and remove the switch as described in Section 7. Refill the transmission with the specified grade of oil given in *Lubricants and fluids*, until it reaches the bottom of the level plug aperture. Allow any excess oil to drain, then refit and tighten the level plug. **Note:** *When new, the transmission is originally filled by weight, and the level may be 20 mm below the level hole.*

**7** Refit the reversing light switch with reference to Section 7, then refit the engine undertray (where fitted) and lower the vehicle to the ground.

### 3 Gearchange linkage/ mechanism – adjustment

**Note:** *A 5 mm drill or metal rod will be required to carry out this procedure.*

**1** Adjustment of the gearchange linkage/ mechanism is not a routine operation and should only be needed if the mechanism has been disconnected or removed. The mechanism is adjusted on the clamp bolt which secures the selector rod to the transmission linkage at the rear of the engine compartment. Access is best from under the vehicle.

**2** Apply the handbrake, then jack up the front of the vehicle and support it on axle stands (see *Jacking and vehicle support*). Remove the engine undertray where fitted.

**3** Slacken the gearchange selector rod clamp bolt which is situated at the front of the rod **(see illustration)**. Do not remove the bolt completely.

**4** From inside the vehicle, unclip the gear lever gaiter from the console and fold it back.

**5** Push the gear lever to the left in neutral, then insert a 5 mm drill or metal rod through the special hole in the lever base to lock it in the adjusting position **(see illustration)**.

**6** Working in the engine compartment, with the selector mechanism in neutral, turn the selector shaft anti-clockwise against the spring pressure towards the third gear position, and lock the selector mechanism

by pressing in the spring-loaded locking pin which is located on the top of the transmission unit **(see illustration)**.

**7** With both the lever and transmission locked in position, tighten the selector rod clamp bolt to the specified torque Stage 1, then through the Stage 2 angle.

**8** Remove the locking rod from the gear lever and check the operation of the gearchange mechanism; the transmission locking pin will automatically release when the lever is moved into the reverse position.

**9** Ensure the transmission locking pin has released, then refit the engine undertray (where necessary) and lower the vehicle to the ground.

**10** Finally check that all gears can be engaged easily, first with the engine off, then with the engine running and the clutch disengaged.

### 4 Gearchange linkage/ mechanism – removal and refitting

**1** The gearchange mechanism consists of the gear lever, the selector rod and the linkage assembly on the transmission. The lever and selector rod and the linkage assembly can be removed separately.

### Gear lever

**Note:** *To remove the gear lever, it is necessary to destroy the ball socket. Obtain a new socket before carrying out the work.*

### Removal

**2** Ensure that the lever is in neutral, then carefully unclip the edge of the gearchange lever gaiter from the centre console. There are two retaining lugs at the front and two at the rear of the centre console aperture. Pull the gaiter upwards over the gear lever knob, then release the cable tie and remove it completely.

**3** Using a screwdriver, depress the tabs at the bottom of the gear lever housing to release the ball socket from the housing **(see illustration)**. Pull up the gear lever together with the ball socket.

**4.3 Depress the tabs at the bottom of the gear lever housing to release the ball socket from the housing**

**4.4 Lever the ball socket from the bottom of the gear lever**

**4** Using a screwdriver, lever the ball socket from the bottom of the gear lever **(see illustration)**. Note that this will destroy the socket.

**5** Withdraw the gear lever from the gearchange rod guide.

### Refitting

**6** Wipe clean all lubricant from the bearing surfaces of the gear lever and guide, then apply new silicone grease to the surfaces.

**7** Insert the gear lever through the gearchange rod guide, then press the new ball socket firmly onto the end of the gear lever until it engages. Note that the lugs on the ball end

**4.21 Driving the knob from the gear lever**

**4.22 Correct position of the gear lever knob**

*A = 8.0 to 10.0 mm*

**4.7 The lugs on the ball end must be aligned with the grooves of the ball socket**

must be aligned with the grooves of the ball socket **(see illustration)**.

**8** Align the gear lever with the gearchange rod guide, then press the ball socket firmly into the housing. Note that the retaining clips must be heard to engage.

**9** Refit the gaiter to the gear lever, using a new cable tie, then clip the edge of the gaiter firmly into the centre console. To prevent any subsequent noise, the loose end of the cable tie should be cut off.

## Lever housing and control rod

### Removal

**10** Apply the handbrake, then jack up the front of the vehicle and support it on axle stands (see *Jacking and vehicle support*). Where fitted, remove the engine undertray.

**11** Reach up behind the transmission and loosen the clamp bolt of the shift guide clamp (do not remove it). Push the control rod rearwards and separate it from the shift guide.

**12** Prise the gaiter from the bulkhead and withdraw from the control rod.

**13** Remove the centre console as described in Chapter 11.

**14** Unscrew the nut and release the wiring trough from the left-hand side of the gear lever housing.

**15** Unscrew the four bolts, then withdraw the gear lever housing and control rod assembly from the vehicle.

**4.26 Shift guide viewed from the top of the transmission**

**16** If necessary, the control rod may be removed from the housing.

### Refitting

**17** Clean the bush guide in the housing, and apply some silicone grease. Insert the control rod through the guide.

**18** The remaining refitting procedure is a reversal of removal, tightening the housing mounting bolts securely, and adjusting the linkage as described in Section 3.

## Gear lever knob

### Renewal

**19** Using a small screwdriver, carefully prise the position indicator plate from the top of the gear lever knob.

**20** Remove the gear lever as described earlier in this Section.

**21** Make sure you note the fitted position of the knob, and also check that the pressure spring fitted below the knob stays in place. Mount the gear lever in a soft-jawed vice, then drive the knob from the lever using a suitable spanner and mallet **(see illustration)**.

**22** Locate the new knob on the lever and drive into position with the mallet. The distance from the lower edge of the lever guide to the lower edge of the stop lever with reverse gear button lock applied, must be between 8.0 and 10.0 mm **(see illustration)**.

**23** Refit the gear lever as described earlier in this Section.

**24** Place the position indicator plate on the gear lever knob with the tab and knob groove aligned with each other, then press firmly into position.

## Gearchange shift guide

### Removal

**25** Apply the handbrake, then jack up the front of the vehicle and support it on axle stands (see *Jacking and vehicle support*). Where fitted, remove the engine undertray.

**26** Reach up behind the transmission and loosen the clamp bolt of the shift guide clamp (do not remove it). Push the control rod rearwards and separate it from the shift guide **(see illustration)**.

**27** Remove the two clips and disconnect the linkage from the shift guide bracket **(see illustration)**.

**4.27 Shift guide bracket**

**28** Depress the retaining spring and lever out the pin. Detach the universal joint from the shift rod **(see illustration)**.
**29** Withdraw the shift pivot together with the shift guide.

### Refitting

**30** Refitting is a reversal of removal, but adjust the linkage as described in Section 3.

---

### 5 Vehicle speed sensor – removal and refitting

**Note:** *On later models (with or without ABS), a wheel speed sensor provides the engine ECU(s) with vehicle speed data. On these vehicles no speed sensor is fitted to the transmission.*

### Removal

**1** The sensor is located on the rear of the transmission casing, above the left-hand driveshaft. Working in the engine compartment, reach down and disconnect the wiring plug from the top of the sensor.
**2** Unscrew the retaining bolt and remove the sensor from the casing **(see illustration)**.

### Refitting

**3** With a new sealing ring fitted, insert the sensor into the transmission casing aperture.
**4** Tighten the retaining bolt to the specified torque and reconnect the wiring plug.

---

### 6 Oil seals – renewal

### *Driveshaft oil seals*

**1** Apply the handbrake, then jack up the front of the vehicle and support it on axle stands (see *Jacking and vehicle support*). Remove the relevant front roadwheel.
**2** Drain the transmission oil as described in Section 2 or be prepared for oil loss as the seal is changed.
**3** Disconnect the inner end of the relevant driveshaft from the differential as described in Chapter 8. There is no need to disconnect the driveshaft from the swivel hub. Support the driveshaft by suspending it with wire or string – do not allow the driveshaft to hang down under its own weight, or the joints may be damaged.
**4** Prise the now-exposed oil seal from the differential housing, using a screwdriver or similar instrument **(see illustration)**.
**5** Smear the sealing lip of the new oil seal with a little transmission oil, then using a metal tube or socket of suitable diameter, drive the new seal into the differential casing until the outer surface of the seal is flush with the outer surface of the differential casing **(see illustration)**.
**6** Reconnect the driveshaft to the differential as described in Chapter 8.

**4.28 Gearchange shift guide removal**

*Arrow shows position of hollow pin retaining spring*

**7** Refill or top up the transmission oil level with reference to Section 2.
**8** Refit the roadwheel, then lower the vehicle to the ground.

### *Input shaft oil seal*

**9** The input shaft oil seal is an integral part of the clutch release cylinder; if the seal is leaking the complete release cylinder assembly must be renewed. Before condemning the release cylinder, check that the leak is not coming from the sealing ring which is fitted between the cylinder and the transmission housing; the sealing ring can be renewed once the release cylinder assembly has been

**5.2 Vehicle speed sensor and retaining bolt**

**6.5 Fitting a new driveshaft oil seal using a socket as a tubular drift**

removed. Refer to Chapter 6 for removal and refitting details.

### *Selector rod oil seal*

**10** Renewal of the selector rod oil seal requires the selector mechanism cover to be unbolted from the transmission and dismantled. This task is considered to be beyond the scope of the DIY mechanic, and should therefore be entrusted to a Vauxhall dealer or specialist.

---

### 7 Reversing light switch – testing, removal and refitting

### *Testing*

**1** The reversing light circuit is operated by a plunger-type switch, mounted on the upper/front of the transmission casing.
**2** To test the switch, disconnect the wiring **(see illustration)**, and use a suitable meter or a battery-and-bulb test circuit to check for continuity between the switch terminals. Continuity should only exist when reverse gear is selected. If this is not the case, and there are no obvious breaks or other damage to the wires, the switch is faulty and must be renewed.

### *Removal*

**3** The reversing light switch is located on the front of the transmission casing, and is accessible from the left-hand side of the engine compartment or from beneath the vehicle.

**6.4 Prising out a driveshaft oil seal**

**7.2 Disconnecting the wiring from the reversing light switch**

**7.5 Removing the reversing light switch and sealing washer**

**4** On Y17DT diesel engine models, remove the air duct leading to the intercooler for access to the top of the transmission. If necessary, also remove the engine undertray.

**5** Disconnect the wiring from the switch, then unscrew the switch from the transmission **(see illustration)**. Recover the O-ring seal.

### Refitting

**6** Refitting is a reversal of removal, but tighten the switch to the specified torque.

## 8 Manual transmission – removal and refitting

**Note:** *This is an involved procedure, and it may well prove easier to remove the transmission complete with the engine as an assembly (see Chapter 2E), then separate the transmission. However, this Section describes removing the transmission leaving the engine in position. Suitable equipment will be required to support the engine and transmission, and the help of an assistant will be required.*

### Removal

**1** Apply the handbrake, then jack up the front of the vehicle and support it on axle stands (see *Jacking and vehicle support*). Allow sufficient working room to remove the transmission from under the left-hand side of the engine compartment. Remove both front roadwheels then, where necessary, undo the retaining clips/screws and remove the engine

undertray. Also remove the engine top cover where fitted.

**2** Remove the air cleaner housing and intake trunking (see Chapter 4A, 4B, 4C or 4D).

**3** Drain the transmission oil as described in Section 2 or be prepared for oil loss as the transmission is removed.

**4** On diesel engines, remove the crash box from the rear of the engine compartment **(see illustration)**. To do this, first remove the fuel filter as described in Chapter 1B, then unscrew the nut and remove the add-on heater from the crash box. Release the coolant hose from the bracket on the front of the crash box. Next to the crash box, release the coolant expansion tank and position to one side. Unscrew the mounting nuts and withdraw the crash box from the bulkhead. Note that it is only necessary to loosen the outer mounting nut.

**5** Remove the filler cap from the brake/clutch fluid reservoir on the bulkhead, then tighten it onto a piece of polythene. This will reduce the loss of fluid when the clutch hydraulic hose is disconnected. Alternatively, fit a hose clamp to the flexible hose next to the clutch hydraulic connection on the transmission housing.

**6** Place some cloth rags beneath the hose, then prise out the retaining clip securing the clutch hydraulic pipe/hose end fitting to the top of the transmission bellhousing and detach the end fitting from the transmission **(see illustration)**. Gently squeeze the two legs of the retaining clip together and re-insert the retaining clip back into position in the end fitting. Discard the sealing ring from the pipe end; a new sealing ring must be used on refitting. Plug/cover both the union and pipe ends to minimise fluid loss and prevent the entry of dirt into the hydraulic system. **Note:** *Whilst the hose/pipe is disconnected, do not depress the clutch pedal.*

**7** Disconnect the wiring from the reversing lamp switch on the front of the transmission.

**8** Unscrew and remove the three upper bolts securing the transmission to the rear of the engine. Where necessary, pull up the coolant hoses and secure them away from the transmission using plastic cable ties.

**9** Tie the radiator to the engine compartment front crossmember in preparation for lowering the front subframe.

**10** Remove the hub caps, then extract the split pins and unscrew the driveshaft outer hub nuts while holding the hubs stationary. To do this, temporarily insert the wheel bolts and have an assistant depress the brake pedal while the nuts are loosened.

**11** Remove the front brake discs with reference to Chapter 9.

**12** Refer to Chapter 10 and disconnect the track rods from the hub carrier steering arms. Also detach the anti-roll bar links from the front suspension struts, and detach the front suspension lower arms from the hub carriers.

**13** Disconnect the driveshafts from the hub carriers by carefully tapping them through the hubs while pulling out the carriers. Do not allow the driveshafts to hang down under their own weight, or the joints may be damaged – support the driveshafts with wire or string.

**14** On models with air conditioning, remove the auxiliary drivebelt (Chapter 1A or 1B), then unbolt the compressor from the engine **without disconnecting the refrigerant lines** and support the compressor to one side.

**15** Remove the exhaust system as described in Chapter 4A, 4B, 4C or 4D.

**16** Refer to Section 4 and disconnect the gearchange/selector rod from the transmission.

**17** Support the front suspension subframe on trolley jacks, then mark the position of the subframe on the front underbody **(see Haynes Hint)**, and unscrew the four mounting bolts. Discard the bolts as new ones must be used for refitting. Unscrew and remove the bolt securing the engine rear torque link to the subframe. With the help of an assistant, carefully lower the subframe to the ground and withdraw from under the vehicle.

**18** Attach a suitable hoist and lifting tackle to the lifting bracket located on the left-hand side of the cylinder head, and support the weight of the engine/transmission. Alternatively, the engine can be supported using a jack and interposed block of wood under the sump, however, great care must be taken when removing the transmission not to move the engine off the jack.

**8.4 Crash box and fuel filter on the bulkhead**

**8.6 Prise out the clip to disconnect the clutch hydraulic hose from the release cylinder pipe**

**HAYNES HINT**

*To ensure correct repositioning, we bolted two lengths of metal bar to the subframe, and marked their position on the underbody.*

**19** Unbolt and remove the left-hand mounting bracket from the transmission and body with reference to Chapter 2A, 2B, 2C or 2D.

**20** Lower the engine and transmission by approximately 5 cm making sure that the coolant hoses and wiring harnesses are not stretched.

**21** Disconnect the gearchange linkage from the transmission with reference to Section 4.

**22** Refer to Chapter 8 and remove the driveshafts from the transmission. To do this, disconnect the front suspension lower arm balljoints from the hub carriers, and also disconnect the steering track rod ends from the steering arms. It is not necessary to remove the driveshafts from the hub carriers. Tie the driveshafts to one side.

**23** On diesel engine models, unbolt and remove the front left-hand engine mounting with reference to Chapter 2C or 2D.

**24** Unbolt and remove the rear engine mounting torque link with reference to Chapter 2A, 2B, 2C or 2D.

**25** Unscrew the four lower bolts securing the transmission to the engine sump.

**26** Support the weight of the transmission on a trolley jack, then unscrew the remaining transmission-to-engine bolts, noting the location of the earth cable **(see illustration)**.

**27** Make a final check that all components have been disconnected, and are positioned clear of the transmission so that they will not hinder the removal procedure.

**28** With the help of an assistant, carefully withdraw the transmission from the engine, taking care not to allow the weight of the transmission to hang on the input shaft otherwise the clutch friction disc hub may be damaged. Note that there are two locating dowels which may be tight, and it may be necessary to rock the transmission from side-to-side to release it from them. Once the transmission is free, lower the jack and manoeuvre the unit out from under the car.

### Refitting

**29** Commence refitting by positioning the transmission on the trolley jack beneath the engine compartment. With the help of an assistant, raise the transmission and locate it on the engine, making sure that the input shaft engages accurately with the splines of the friction disc hub. With the transmission located on the dowels, insert all of the retaining bolts and tighten to the specified torque.

**30** The remaining refitting procedure is a reversal of removal, noting the following points:

a) Tighten all nuts and bolts to the specified torque (where given). Note that the torque for the transmission-to-sump bolts is different than the bolts to the rest of the engine.

b) Renew the driveshaft oil seals (see Section 6) before refitting the driveshafts.

c) Refit the front subframe assembly with reference to Chapter 10.

d) Fit a new sealing ring to the transmission clutch hydraulic pipe before clipping the hose/pipe end fitting into position. Ensure the end fitting is securely retained by its clip then bleed the hydraulic system as described in Chapter 6.

e) Refill the transmission with the specified type and quantity of oil, as described in Section 2.

f) On completion, adjust the gearchange linkage/mechanism as described in Section 3.

**8.26 Earth cable on a transmission mounting bolt**

### 9 Manual transmission overhaul – general information

**1** Overhauling a manual transmission unit is a difficult and involved job for the DIY home mechanic. In addition to dismantling and reassembling many small parts, clearances must be precisely measured and, if necessary, changed by selecting shims and spacers. Internal transmission components are also often difficult to obtain, and in many instances, extremely expensive. Because of this, if the transmission develops a fault or becomes noisy, the best course of action is to have the unit overhauled by a specialist repairer, or to obtain an exchange reconditioned unit.

**2** Nevertheless, it is not impossible for the more experienced mechanic to overhaul the transmission, provided the special tools are available, and the job is done in a deliberate step-by-step manner, so that nothing is overlooked.

**3** The tools necessary for an overhaul include internal and external circlip pliers, bearing pullers, a slide hammer, a set of pin punches, a dial test indicator, and possibly a hydraulic press. In addition, a large, sturdy workbench and a vice will be required.

**4** During dismantling of the transmission, make careful notes of how each component is fitted, to make reassembly easier and more accurate **(see illustration overleaf)**.

**5** Before dismantling the transmission, it will help if you have some idea what area is malfunctioning. Certain problems can be closely related to specific areas in the transmission, which can make component examination and replacement easier. Refer to the *Fault finding* Section of this manual for more information.

H23097

**9.4 Exploded view of the transmission**

# Chapter 7 Part B:
# Automatic transmission

## Contents

## Degrees of difficulty

| **Easy,** suitable for novice with little experience | **Fairly easy,** suitable for beginner with some experience | **Fairly difficult,** suitable for competent DIY mechanic | **Difficult,** suitable for experienced DIY mechanic | **Very difficult,** suitable for expert DIY or professional |
|---|---|---|---|---|

## Specifications

### General
Type . . . . . . . . . . . . . . . . . . . . . . . . . . . . . . . . . . . . . . . . . . . . . . . .     Hydrodynamic torque converter with electronically-controlled mechanical lock-up system, two epicyclic gearsets giving four forward speeds and reverse, integral final drive. Gearchanging under full electronic control, with three selectable 'driving' modes

Manufacturer's designation . . . . . . . . . . . . . . . . . . . . . . . . . . . . . . .     AF 13 II

### Gear ratios
1st. . . . . . . . . . . . . . . . . . . . . . . . . . . . . . . . . . . . . . . . . . . . . . . . . . . .     2.81:1
2nd . . . . . . . . . . . . . . . . . . . . . . . . . . . . . . . . . . . . . . . . . . . . . . . . . .     1.48:1
3rd . . . . . . . . . . . . . . . . . . . . . . . . . . . . . . . . . . . . . . . . . . . . . . . . . .     1.00:1
4th . . . . . . . . . . . . . . . . . . . . . . . . . . . . . . . . . . . . . . . . . . . . . . . . . .     0.74:1
Reverse . . . . . . . . . . . . . . . . . . . . . . . . . . . . . . . . . . . . . . . . . . . . . .     2.77:1
Final drive . . . . . . . . . . . . . . . . . . . . . . . . . . . . . . . . . . . . . . . . . . . .     4.12:1

### Torque wrench settings

| | Nm | lbf ft |
|---|---|---|
| Engine/transmission mountings . . . . . . . . . . . . . . . . . . . . . . . . . . . . | See Chapter 2B | |
| Fluid cooler pipe union bolts . . . . . . . . . . . . . . . . . . . . . . . . . . . . . . | 25 | 18 |
| Fluid filler tube support. . . . . . . . . . . . . . . . . . . . . . . . . . . . . . . . . . | 60 | 44 |
| Selector lever position switch hub-to-shaft nut . . . . . . . . . . . . . . . . | 8 | 6 |
| Selector lever position switch to transmission. . . . . . . . . . . . . . . . . | 25 | 18 |
| Selector lever to selector lever shaft . . . . . . . . . . . . . . . . . . . . . . . . | 16 | 12 |
| Torque converter-to-driveplate bolts* . . . . . . . . . . . . . . . . . . . . . . . | 50 | 37 |
| Transmission-to-engine bolts. . . . . . . . . . . . . . . . . . . . . . . . . . . . . . | See Chapter 2B | |

* Use new bolts

## 1 General information

**1** A 4-speed fully-automatic transmission is available as an option on certain 1.4 litre petrol engine models. The transmission consists of a torque converter, an epicyclic geartrain, and hydraulically-operated clutches and brakes. The differential is integral with the transmission, and is similar to that used in manual gearbox models **(see illustration)**.

**2** The torque converter provides a fluid coupling between the engine and transmission which acts as an automatic 'clutch', and also provides a degree of torque multiplication when accelerating.

**3** The epicyclic geartrain provides either one of the four forward gear ratios, or reverse gear, according to which of its component parts are held stationary or allowed to turn.

The components of the geartrain are held or released by brakes and clutches, which are activated by a hydraulic control unit. A fluid pump within the transmission provides the necessary hydraulic pressure to operate the brakes and clutches.

**4** The transmission is electronically-controlled, and three driving modes – Economy, Sport and Winter – are provided. The transmission electronic control unit (ECU) operates in conjunction with the engine management ECU

**1.1 Cutaway view of the AF 13 II automatic transmission**

| | | |
|---|---|---|
| 1 *Gear assembly* | 4 *Multi-plate clutch* | 7 *Freewheel assembly* | 10 *Brake band* |
| 2 *Multi-disc brake* | 5 *Multi-plate clutch* | 8 *Multi-plate clutch* | 11 *Fluid pump* |
| 3 *Multi-plate clutch* | 6 *Freewheel assembly* | 9 *Differential* | 12 *Torque converter* |

to control the gearchanges. The transmission ECU receives information on transmission fluid temperature, throttle position, engine coolant temperature, and input-versus-output speed. The ECU controls the hydraulically-operated clutches and brakes via four solenoids. The control system can also retard the engine ignition timing, via the engine management ECU, to permit smoother gearchanges.

5 Due to the complexity of the automatic transmission, any repair or overhaul work must be entrusted to a Vauxhall dealer, who will have the necessary specialist equipment and knowledge for fault diagnosis and repair. Refer to the *Fault finding* section at the end of this manual for further information.

## 2 Automatic transmission fluid renewal

Refer to Chapter 1A.

## 3 Selector cable – removal, refitting and adjustment

### Removal

1 Apply the handbrake, then jack up the front of the vehicle and support it on axle stands (see *Jacking and vehicle support*). Where applicable, remove the engine undertray.
2 Remove the centre console as described in Chapter 11.
3 Release the wiring trough from the front of the selector housing.
4 Using a screwdriver, prise the inner selector cable end fitting off the selector lever then extract the retaining clip and release the outer selector cable from the mounting bracket.
5 Working in the engine compartment, press the inner cable end fitting from the lever on the position switch.
6 Using a screwdriver, prise off the retaining clip and release the outer selector cable from the mounting bracket on the transmission.
7 Working beneath the vehicle, pull the selector cable through the rubber grommet in the bulkhead and withdraw. Do not remove the grommet.

### Refitting and adjustment

8 Apply soapy water solution to the outer cable, then insert it through the rubber grommet into the passenger compartment.
9 The remaining refitting procedure is a reversal of removal, but adjust the cable as follows before lowering the vehicle to the ground.
10 In the engine compartment, use a screwdriver to prise up the locking clamp at the support mounting on the transmission (see illustration).
11 Move the selector lever inside the vehicle to position P. Check that the lever has engaged properly by moving it back-and-forth without depressing the lock knob.

12 Working at the transmission, move the lever on the position switch clockwise as far as it will go, then rotate the front wheels until the parking lock pawl engages.
13 Press down the locking clamp to lock the cable in position.
14 Check the adjustment by selecting P, R, N, D, 3, 2, 1 and checking that the relative positions on the transmission are engaged.

## 4 Selector lever housing – removal and refitting

### Removal

1 Remove the centre console as described in Chapter 11.
2 Release the wiring trough from the front of the selector housing.
3 On the left-hand side of the housing, use a screwdriver to lever off the cable end fitting from the selector lever.
4 Release the clip and remove the outer selector cable from the mounting bracket.
5 Disconnect the wiring from the right-hand front of the housing.
6 Unscrew the mounting bolts and withdraw the selector lever housing from the floor.

### Refitting

7 Refitting is a reversal of removal, but tighten the mounting bolts securely, and adjust the cable as described in Section 3.

## 5 Selector lever lock components – removal and refitting

### General

1 The transmission selector lever assembly incorporates an electrically-operated selector lever lock mechanism that prevents the lever being moved out of the P position unless the ignition is switched on and the brake pedal or handbrake operated. The components associated with the system are as follows:
  a) *Selector lever lock contact switch.*
  b) *Selector lever lock solenoid switch.*
  c) *Ignition key contact switch.*
  d) *Footbrake stop-light switch.*
  e) *Handbrake 'on' switch.*
2 Apart from the footbrake and handbrake switches, all the components are located on the selector lever housing, and removal and refitting is described in the following sub-Sections. Stop-light and handbrake 'on' switch removal and refitting procedures are given in Chapters 9 and 12.
3 If the selector lever is in the P position and there is an interruption of the power supply to the ignition switch (ie, if the battery is disconnected, or if the battery is flat) it will not be possible to move the selector lever out of position P by the normal means. To overcome this problem, it is possible, in an emergency,

J44730

**3.10 Selector cable locking clamp (1)**

to manually release the selector lever lock solenoid switch as described in *Lever lock manual override* later in this Section.

### Lever lock contact switch

**Note:** *New contact switch retaining clip washers will be required for refitting.*

#### Removal

4 Remove the selector lever housing as described in Section 4.
5 Remove the cable tie then disconnect the earth lead from the earth terminal on the base of the selector lever housing (see illustration overleaf).
6 Disconnect the wiring connector from the solenoid switch for the lock lever.
7 Release the two securing clip washers and press the selector lever contact switch out of the housing. Note that new clip washers will be required for refitting.

#### Refitting

8 Locate the switch on the housing ensuring that it is positioned correctly and secure with two new clip washers.
9 Reconnect the wiring connector and the earth lead. Secure the earth lead with a new cable tie.
10 Refit the selector lever housing as described in Section 4.

### Lever lock solenoid switch

#### Removal

11 Remove the selector lever housing as described in Section 4.
12 Unbolt the lever lock solenoid switch from the housing and disconnect the wiring, noting its location.

#### Refitting

13 Refitting is a reversal of removal.

### Ignition lock release switch

#### Removal

14 Remove the selector lever housing as described in Section 4.
15 Release the two securing clip washers

**5.5 Selector lever lock contact switch details**

*1 Selector lever lock contact switch*
*2 Securing clip washers*

*3 Wiring connector*
*Arrow indicates earth lead connection*

and press the ignition lock release contact switch out of the housing. Note that new clip washers will be required for refitting.
**16** Remove the cable ties from the wiring harness.
**17** Release the switch wiring contact pin from the wiring connector (pin 1 in the connector). Vauxhall special tool MKM-923-22 is available for releasing the contact pin, but it should be possible to carefully release the pin using conventional tools.
**18** Disconnect the relevant earth cable, then remove the contact switch.

### Refitting

**19** Refitting is a reversal of removal.

**5.22 To release the selector lever lock, depress the plunger on the selector lever lock solenoid switch**

### Lever lock manual override

**20** If it is not possible to move the selector lever out of the P position due to a disconnected or flat battery, proceed as follows.
**21** Carefully prise up the indicator cover from the base of the selector lever.
**22** Using a ballpoint pen or small screwdriver, push the release lever on the solenoid switch forwards and hold in this position **(see illustration)**. Now depress the knob and move the selector lever out of the P position.
**23** Refit the indicator cover.

## 6 Transmission input/ output speed sensors – removal and refitting

### Removal

**1** The input and output speed sensors are located on the rear of the transmission casing, above the left-hand driveshaft **(see illustration)**. Working in the engine compartment, reach down and disconnect the wiring plug from the top of the sensor.
**2** Unscrew the retaining bolt and remove the sensor from the casing.

### Refitting

**3** With a new sealing ring fitted, insert the sensor into the transmission casing aperture.
**4** Tighten the retaining bolt securely and reconnect the wiring plug.

## 7 Driveshaft oil seals – renewal

**1** Apply the handbrake, then jack up the front of the vehicle and support it on axle stands (see *Jacking and vehicle support*). Remove the relevant front roadwheel.
**2** Drain the transmission fluid as described in Chapter 1A or be prepared for fluid loss as the seal is changed.
**3** Disconnect the inner end of the relevant driveshaft from the differential as described in Chapter 8. There is no need to disconnect the driveshaft from the swivel hub. Support the driveshaft by suspending it with wire or string – do not allow the driveshaft to hang down under its own weight, or the joints may be damaged.
**4** Prise the now-exposed oil seal from the differential housing, using a screwdriver or similar instrument.
**5** Smear the sealing lip of the new oil seal with a little transmission oil, then using a metal tube or socket of suitable diameter, drive the new seal into the differential casing until the outer surface of the seal is flush with the outer surface of the differential casing.
**6** Reconnect the driveshaft to the differential as described in Chapter 8.
**7** Refill or top-up the transmission fluid level with reference to Chapter 1A.
**8** Refit the roadwheel, then lower the vehicle to the ground.

## 8 Fluid cooler – general information

**1** The transmission fluid cooler is an integral part of the radiator assembly; radiator removal and refitting is described in Chapter 3.
**2** The hoses running from the transmission to the cooler should be checked at regular intervals, and renewed if there is any doubt about their condition.

**6.1 Transmission output (1) and input (2) speed sensors**

**3** Always take note of the pipe and hose connections before disturbing them, and take note of the hose routing.

**4** To minimise the loss of fluid, and to prevent the entry of dirt into the system, clamp the hoses before disconnecting them, and plug the unions once the hoses have been disconnected.

**5** When reconnecting the hoses, ensure that they are connected to their original locations, and route them so that they are not kinked or twisted.

**6** Always renew the sealing washers if the banjo union bolts (where fitted) are disturbed, and tighten the bolts to their specified torque wrench setting. Be particularly careful when tightening the cooler unions.

## 9 Selector lever position switch – adjustment, removal and refitting

### Adjustment

**1** Adjustment of the switch entails the use of Vauxhall special tool KM-962, which is then connected to the selector lever position switch wiring connector on the transmission. The tool contains a series of LEDs (light emitting diodes), that illuminate in sequence, with the ignition switched on, as each selector position is engaged. If the LEDs do not illuminate correctly in each selector lever position, the position switch securing screws must be slackened and the switch repositioned accordingly. As accurate adjustment of the position switch can only be carried out using this tool, the work should be entrusted to a Vauxhall dealer.

### Removal

**Note:** *It will be necessary to have the adjustment of the switch carried out by a Vauxhall dealer on completion (see adjustment above). Bearing this in mind, it may be beneficial to have the complete operation (removal, refitting and adjustment) carried out by the dealer at the same time.*

**2** Remove the transmission electronic control unit as described in Section 11. Also remove the control unit mounting bracket.

**3** Working in the engine compartment, press the cable end fitting from the lever on the position switch.

**4** Using a screwdriver, prise off the retaining clip and release the outer selector cable from the mounting bracket on the transmission.

**5** Remove the wiring harness plug bracket, and disconnect the wiring from the lever position switch.

**6** Unscrew the nut and remove the lever from the transmission selector shaft.

**7** Bend up the lockplate, then unscrew the switch hub retaining nut and withdraw from the shaft. It is recommended that the lockplate is renewed.

**8** Mark the position of the selector lever position switch, then unscrew the adjustment lockbolts and withdraw the switch from the transmission **(see illustration)**.

### Refitting

**9** Locate the position switch over the shaft and onto the transmission in the previously-noted position. Insert the adjustment lock-bolts and tighten them to the specified torque.

**10** Refit the switch hub nut together with a new lockplate and tighten to the specified torque. Bend the lockplate onto the nut to lock it.

**11** Locate the lever on selector shaft and tighten the nut to the specified torque.

**12** Reconnect the wiring and refit the bracket.

**13** Refit the outer cable to the bracket and secure with the clip.

**14** Press the cable end fitting onto the lever on the position switch.

**15** Refit the electronic control unit and bracket with reference to Section 11.

**16** Have a Vauxhall dealer adjust the switch.

## 10 Transmission 'mode' switches – removal and refitting

### Economy/Sport switch

**1** Removal of the Economy/Sport mode switch entails complete dismantling of the selector lever housing so that the switch can be pushed out of the selector lever using a length of welding rod, or similar. The switch wires must then be unsoldered from the switch. It is recommended that this operation is entrusted to a Vauxhall dealer.

### Winter switch

#### Removal

**2** Remove the centre console as described in Chapter 11.

**3** Remove the selector lever housing as described in Section 4.

**4** Unclip the indicator cover, then press out the winter mode switch upwards.

**5** Cut free the cable ties and remove the harness from the bracket.

**6** Release the relevant switch wiring contact pins from the wiring connector, noting their location. Vauxhall special tool MKM-923-22 is available for releasing the contact pins, but it should be possible to carefully release the pin using conventional tools.

**7** Remove the winter mode switch through the hole in the indicator cover.

#### Refitting

**8** Refitting is a reversal of removal.

## 11 Electronic control unit – removal and refitting

**Note:** *The electronic control units vary according to model, and it is important that the correct unit if fitted.*

**9.8 Selector lever position switch (3)**

*1 Adjustment lock bolts*
*2 Switch hub retaining nut*

### Removal

**1** The automatic transmission electronic control unit is located on the left-hand side of the engine compartment, on the side of the ABS unit.

**2** Disconnect the battery negative terminal (refer to *Disconnecting the battery* in the Reference Chapter).

**3** Disconnect the wiring plugs from the front and rear of the electronic control unit **(see illustration).**

**11.3 Automatic transmission electronic control unit**

*1 Rear wiring plug*     *3 Front wiring plug*
*2 ECU retaining tab*

**4** At the front of the unit, press out the retaining tab, then withdraw the control unit forwards from the mounting bracket.

### Refitting

**5** Refitting is a reversal of removal.

## 12 Automatic transmission
– removal and refitting

**Note:** *This is an involved procedure, and it may prove easier in many cases to remove the transmission complete with the engine as an assembly, as described in Chapter 2E. If removing the transmission on its own, it is suggested that this Section is read through thoroughly before commencing work. Suitable equipment will be required to support the engine and transmission, and the help of an assistant will be required. New torque converter-to-driveplate bolts must be used on refitting, and if the original torque converter is being used, an M10 x 1.25 mm tap will be required.*

### Removal

**1** Apply the handbrake, then jack up the front of the vehicle and support it on axle stands (see *Jacking and vehicle support*). Allow sufficient working room to remove the transmission from under the left-hand side of the engine compartment. Remove both front roadwheels then, where necessary, undo the retaining clips/screws and remove the engine undertray. Also remove the engine top cover where fitted.

**2** Drain the transmission fluid as described in Chapter 1A.

**3** Remove the engine control unit from the top of the engine as described in Chapter 4B.

**4** On the top of the transmission, unclip the selector lever cable, then unbolt the cable bracket.

**5** Release the wiring plug and selector lever position switch from the bracket, then disconnect and separate them.

**6** Pull the bleeder hose from the top of the transmission.

**7** Unscrew and remove the two uppermost bolts securing the transmission to the rear of the engine. Note that the front one secures the fluid filler tube. Withdraw the filler tube and dipstick upwards from the engine.

**8** Attach a suitable hoist and lifting tackle to the lifting bracket(s) located on the left-hand side of the cylinder head, and support the weight of the engine/transmission.

**9** Refer to Chapter 10 and remove the front subframe.

**10** Disconnect the inner ends of both driveshafts from the differential as described in Chapter 8. There is no need to disconnect the driveshafts from the swivel hubs. Support the driveshafts by suspending them with wire or string – do not allow the driveshafts to hang down under their own weight, or the joints may be damaged.

**11** Unbolt and remove the rear engine/transmission mounting torque link bracket with reference to Chapter 2B.

**12** Place a suitable container beneath the transmission quick-release fluid cooler hose connections at the transmission. Clamp the transmission fluid cooler hoses, then lever off the retaining clamps and disconnect them from the transmission, noting their locations. Be prepared for fluid spillage, and plug the

open ends of the hoses and transmission, to minimise fluid loss and prevent dirt ingress. Tie the lines to one side.

**13** Prise out the two access covers from the transmission housing.

**14** Working through the bellhousing access holes, unscrew the three torque converter-to-driveplate bolts. It will be necessary to turn the engine, using a suitable spanner or socket on the crankshaft pulley or sprocket bolt (as applicable), to gain access to each bolt in turn through the aperture. Use a screwdriver or a similar tool to jam the driveplate ring gear, preventing the driveplate from rotating as the bolts are loosened. Discard the bolts.

**15** Unbolt and remove the left-hand engine/transmission mounting bracket from the transmission with reference to Chapter 2B.

**16** Lower the engine and transmission by approximately 5 cm making sure that the coolant hoses and wiring harnesses are not stretched.

**17** Disconnect the wiring from the crankshaft speed/position sensor at the left-hand front of the engine.

**18** Support the weight of the transmission on a trolley jack. Ensure that the engine is adequately supported as previously described.

**19** Unscrew and remove the transmission-to-engine bolts.

**20** Make a final check that all components have been disconnected, and are positioned clear of the transmission so that they will not hinder the removal procedure.

**21** With the help of an assistant, carefully withdraw the transmission from the rear of the engine, taking care to ensure that the torque converter remains firmly in place in the

H.26703

**12.23 Torque converter-to-driveplate bolt threads must be recut on refitting**

J44609

**12.24 Check that the torque converter is fully entered**

1  *Straight-edge*
2  *Vernier calipers on bolt hole*
3  *Torque converter centre stub*

transmission. Note that there are two locating dowels in the rear of the engine which may be tight, and it may be necessary to rock the transmission from side-to-side to release it from them. If this precaution is not taken, the torque converter could fall out, resulting in fluid spillage and possible damage.

**22** Lower the transmission to the ground and withdraw it from under the vehicle. Retain the torque converter while the transmission is removed by bolting a strip of metal across the transmission bellhousing end face.

### Refitting

**23** If the original torque converter is being refitted, commence refitting by recutting the torque converter-to-driveplate bolt threads in the torque converter using an M10 x 1.25 mm tap **(see illustration)**. Clean any rust from the centre stub of the torque converter and the hole in the centre of the driveplate. Apply a little grease to the contact surfaces.

**24** Check that the torque converter is fully entered inside the transmission bellhousing by measuring the distance from the flange to the bolt holes in the torque converter, using a straight-edge and vernier calipers **(see illustration)**. The distance must measure approximately 12.0 mm.

**25** If a new transmission is being fitted, the manufacturers recommend that the radiator's fluid cooler passages are flushed clean before the new transmission is installed. Ideally, compressed air should be used (in which case, ensure that adequate safety precautions are taken; in particular, eye protection should be worn). Alternatively, the cooler can be flushed with clean automatic transmission fluid until all the old fluid has been removed, and fresh fluid runs clear from the cooler outlet.

**26** Position the transmission under the front of the vehicle, and support with the trolley jack. Remove the strip of metal retaining the torque converter in the transmission, and hold the torque converter in position as the transmission is located on the engine.

**27** With the help of an assistant, raise the transmission and locate it on the rear of the engine. Refit all of the engine-to-transmission bolts hand-tight with the exception of the one which secures the fluid filler tube support bracket, then tighten them to their specified torque.

**28** Raise the engine and transmission, then refit the left-hand mounting and bracket with reference to Chapter 2B. Remove the hoist and lifting tackle.

**29** Align the holes of the torque converter with the holes in the driveplate. Apply locking fluid to the threads of the new bolts, then insert them separately and tighten to the specified torque while holding the driveplate ring gear stationary with the screwdriver. Refit the two access covers to the transmission housing.

**30** Reconnect the wiring to the crankshaft speed/position sensor.

**31** Reconnect the driveshafts to the transmission with reference to Chapter 8.

**32** Reconnect the quick-release fluid cooler hoses together with new O-ring seals to the transmission.

**33** Refit the rear engine/transmission mounting torque link bracket with reference to Chapter 2B.

**34** Refit the front subframe assembly with reference to Chapter 10.

**35** Refit the fluid filler tube together with a new O-ring seal to the cylinder block. Insert the dipstick, then fit the final transmission-to-engine bolt (which also secures the filler tube support) and tighten to the specified torque.

**36** Refit the bleeder hose, selector lever position switch and selector lever cable with bracket.

**37** Refit the engine control unit with reference to Chapter 4B.

**38** Refill the transmission with the specified fluid with reference to Chapter 1A.

**39** Where fitted, refit the engine undertray, then refit the roadwheels and lower the vehicle to the ground. Refit the engine top cover where applicable.

### 13 Automatic transmission overhaul – general information

**1** In the event of a fault occurring on the transmission, it is first necessary to determine whether it is of an electrical, mechanical or hydraulic nature, and to achieve this special test equipment is required. It is therefore essential to have the work carried out by a Vauxhall dealer if a transmission fault is suspected.

**2** Do not remove the transmission from the car for possible repair before professional fault diagnosis has been carried out, since most tests require the transmission to be in the vehicle.

# Chapter 7 Part C:
## Easytronic transmission

## Contents

## Degrees of difficulty

| Easy, suitable for novice with little experience | Fairly easy, suitable for beginner with some experience | Fairly difficult, suitable for competent DIY mechanic | Difficult, suitable for experienced DIY mechanic | Very difficult, suitable for expert DIY or professional |

## Specifications

### General

Type . . . . . . . . . . . . . . . . . . . . . . . . . . . . . . . . . . . . . . . . . . . . . . . . . . Five forward speeds and one reverse, automatic or manual selection. Integral differential

Manufacturer's designation:
  Petrol engines . . . . . . . . . . . . . . . . . . . . . . . . . . . . . . . . . . . . . . . . F 13 MTA
  Diesel engines . . . . . . . . . . . . . . . . . . . . . . . . . . . . . . . . . . . . . . . F 17+ MTA

### Gear ratios

F 13 MTA (close ratio) transmissions:
  1st . . . . . . . . . . . . . . . . . . . . . . . . . . . . . . . . . . . . . . . . . . . . . . . . 3.73:1
  2nd . . . . . . . . . . . . . . . . . . . . . . . . . . . . . . . . . . . . . . . . . . . . . . . 2.14:1
  3rd . . . . . . . . . . . . . . . . . . . . . . . . . . . . . . . . . . . . . . . . . . . . . . . . 1.41:1
  4th . . . . . . . . . . . . . . . . . . . . . . . . . . . . . . . . . . . . . . . . . . . . . . . . 1.12:1
  5th . . . . . . . . . . . . . . . . . . . . . . . . . . . . . . . . . . . . . . . . . . . . . . . . 0.89:1
  Reverse . . . . . . . . . . . . . . . . . . . . . . . . . . . . . . . . . . . . . . . . . . . . 3.31:1
F 13 MTA and F 17+ MTA (wide ratio) transmissions:
  1st . . . . . . . . . . . . . . . . . . . . . . . . . . . . . . . . . . . . . . . . . . . . . . . . 3.73:1
  2nd . . . . . . . . . . . . . . . . . . . . . . . . . . . . . . . . . . . . . . . . . . . . . . . 1.96:1
  3rd . . . . . . . . . . . . . . . . . . . . . . . . . . . . . . . . . . . . . . . . . . . . . . . . 1.31:1
  4th . . . . . . . . . . . . . . . . . . . . . . . . . . . . . . . . . . . . . . . . . . . . . . . . 0.95:1
  5th . . . . . . . . . . . . . . . . . . . . . . . . . . . . . . . . . . . . . . . . . . . . . . . . 0.76:1
  Reverse . . . . . . . . . . . . . . . . . . . . . . . . . . . . . . . . . . . . . . . . . . . . 3.31:1

### Final drive ratios

F 13 MTA transmissions . . . . . . . . . . . . . . . . . . . . . . . . . . . . . . . . . . 3.74:1 or 3.94:1
F 17+ MTA transmissions . . . . . . . . . . . . . . . . . . . . . . . . . . . . . . . . 3.55:1

### Torque wrench settings

| | Nm | lbf ft |
|---|---|---|
| Clutch module with MTA control unit | 11 | 8 |
| Differential housing cover plate bolts: | | |
| Alloy plate | 18 | 13 |
| Steel plate | 30 | 22 |
| Engine/transmission mountings | See Chapter 2A, 2B or 2C | |
| Transmission oil level plug: | | |
| Stage 1 | 4 | 3 |
| Stage 2 | Angle-tighten a further 45° to 135° | |
| Transmission shift module | 11 | 8 |
| Transmission-to-engine bolts | See Chapter 2A, 2B or 2C | |
| Transmission vent plug: | | |
| Stage 1 | 4 | 3 |
| Stage 2 | Angle-tighten a further 45° to 135° | |

J44733

**1.1 Easytronic (MTA) transmission**

1  *Transmission shift module*
2  *Wiring harness*
3  *Hydraulic fluid reservoir*
4  *Clutch control module*

5  *Hydraulic supply line to clutch control module*
6  *Wiring harness for clutch control module*
7  *Hydraulic pressure line to clutch release cylinder*

## 1  General information

1  The Easytronic MTA transmission (Manual Transmission Automatic-shift) is essentially a conventional manual transmission with the addition of a clutch module and shift module, used in conjunction with a self-adjusting clutch plate **(see illustration)**.
2  The description of the MTA transmission is basically as for the manual transmission given in Chapter 7A, but with an electronically-operated hydraulic clutch control module and gear selection module. The transmission can be switched between fully automatic and manual mode, even while driving.
3  The clutch control module incorporates its own master cylinder and pushrod, which is operated electrically by a worm gear.
4  The gear selection module is fitted with a shifting motor and a selector motor, which together position the selector lever to move the selector forks in the transmission. It is located in exactly the same position as the gear selection cover fitted to the conventional manual transmission.
5  Since the transmission is electronically-controlled, in the event of a problem, in the

first instance the vehicle should be taken to a Vauxhall dealer or diagnostic specialist who will have the TECH2 diagnostic equipment (or equivalent) necessary to pin-point the faulty area. Note also that if the transmission assembly, shift module or clutch module are renewed, the vehicle must be taken to a Vauxhall dealer or diagnostic specialist in order to have the fault memory erased and new parameters programmed into the ECU.

## 2  Transmission oil – draining and refilling

**Note:** *Changing the transmission oil is not a specified service operation, however, it may be considered necessary if the vehicle has covered a high mileage or if a new transmission is being fitted. No drain plug is fitted.*

### Draining

1  Apply the handbrake, then jack up the front of the vehicle and support it on axle stands (see *Jacking and vehicle support*). Remove the engine undertray where fitted.
2  Unbolt the rear engine/transmission mounting torque link bracket from the transmission and pivot it to one side. If necessary, for improved access, undo the bolt securing the rear engine/transmission mounting torque link to the subframe and remove the torque link and bracket assembly.
3  Place a suitable container under the differential cover plate. Unscrew the securing bolts and withdraw the cover plate, allowing the transmission oil to drain into the container **(see illustration)**. Recover the gasket and, if necessary, renew it.
4  Refit the differential cover plate together with the gasket, and tighten the securing bolts to the specified torque. Refit the rear engine/transmission mounting torque link and tighten the bolts to the specified torque.

### Refilling

5  Wipe clean the area around the level plug.

**2.3  Differential cover plate securing bolts (arrowed)**

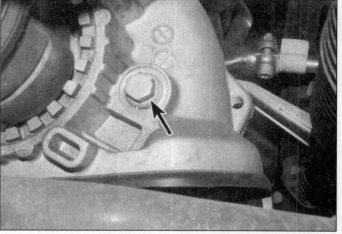

**2.5  Transmission oil level plug (arrowed)**

The level plug is located behind the driveshaft inner joint on the left-hand side of the transmission (see illustration). Unscrew the plug and clean it.

6 The transmission is refilled through the vent on top of the transmission. Wipe clean the area around the vent, then unscrew and remove it. Refill the transmission with the specified grade of oil given in *Lubricants and fluids*, until it reaches the bottom of the level plug aperture. Allow any excess oil to drain, then refit and tighten the level plug. **Note:** *When new, the transmission is originally filled by weight, and the level may be 20 mm below the level hole.*

7 Refit and tighten the vent, then refit the engine undertray (where fitted) and lower the vehicle to the ground.

## 3 Selector lever assembly – removal and refitting

### Removal

1 Remove the centre console as described in Chapter 11.

2 Disconnect the wiring from the selector lever.

3 Unscrew the mounting bolts and withdraw the selector lever assembly from the floor.

4 If required, the panel may be removed from the top of the gear lever using a small screwdriver.

### Refitting

5 Refitting is a reversal of removal.

## 4 Transmission shift module – removal and refitting

### Removal

1 Switch on the ignition, then depress the footbrake pedal and move the selector lever to position N. Switch off the ignition.

2 On diesel engine models, refer to the procedures contained in Section 7 and remove the fuel filter crash box from the engine compartment bulkhead.

3 Disconnect the two wiring plugs and release the harness from the support cable ties on the top of the transmission.

4 Unbolt and remove the transmission shift module from the top of the transmission. To do this, lift it and tilt it slightly forwards before removing. Recover the gasket.

5 If the module cannot be removed because of internal jamming, unbolt the selector motor followed by the shifting motor (see illustration), and use a screwdriver to move the selector lever to its neutral position first. The selector motor is the uppermost unit. **Note:** *The manufacturers recommend that the shift module assembly is never re-used if dismantled.*

4.5  Shift motor (1) and selector motor (2) on the transmission shift module

4.7a  Neutral mark (1) and shift lever shaft (2) on the transmission shift module

### Refitting

6 Clean the gasket faces of the module and transmission, and obtain a new gasket.

7 Make sure that the selector lever is in neutral, by checking that the mark on the segment is aligned with the pinion tooth. Check also that the lever is fully extended so that the annular groove is visible. The shift forks in the transmission must also be in neutral – use a screwdriver to move them if necessary (see illustrations).

8 Refit the shift module together with a new gasket, then insert the bolts and tighten to the specified torque.

9 Reconnect the wiring and secure with new cable ties.

10 Finally, it may be necessary to have a Vauxhall dealer or diagnostic specialist reprogramme all volatile control unit memories. If a new control unit has been fitted, a Vauxhall dealer or diagnostic specialist must programme the unit specifically for the model to which it is fitted.

## 5 Clutch module with MTA control unit – removal and refitting

**Note:** *Bleeding the module is carried out using the Vauxhall TECH2 diagnostic instrument, therefore this work should be entrusted to a Vauxhall dealer or diagnostic specialist.*

### Removal

1 Apply the handbrake, then jack up the front of the vehicle and support it on axle stands (see *Jacking and vehicle support*). Where necessary, remove the engine undertray.

2 Disconnect the wiring from the Easytronic transmission and release it from the cable tie supports.

3 Place a suitable container beneath the front of the transmission to catch spilt hydraulic fluid.

4 Fit a hose clamp to the hydraulic hose leading from the hydraulic fluid reservoir to the clutch control unit, then disconnect the hose.

4.7b  Groove (3) visible when the shift module is in neutral

4.7c  Using a screwdriver to move the transmission shift forks into neutral

**7.4a Disconnect the wiring connector (arrowed) from the fuel filter cover . . .**

**7.4c Unclip the expansion tank coolant hose and the wiring harness from the crash box . . .**

5 Disconnect the hydraulic quick-release pressure hose from the clutch control unit.
6 Unscrew the mounting bolts and remove the clutch module with MTA control unit from the transmission.

**7.4d . . . and disconnect the harness connector**

**7.4f Unscrew the outer retaining nut (arrowed) and slacken the inner nut . . .**

**7.4b . . . then depress the retaining clip and lift the filter from the crash box**

### Refitting

7 Refitting is a reversal of removal, but tighten the mounting bolts to the specified torque. Make sure that the quick-release pressure hose is fully engaged – it must make an audible sound. Bleed the hydraulic circuit. Finally, it may be necessary to reprogramme all volatile control unit memories. If a new control unit has been fitted, a Vauxhall dealer or diagnostic specialist must programme the unit specifically for the model to which it is fitted.

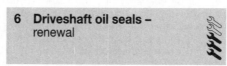

**6  Driveshaft oil seals –**
renewal

1 Apply the handbrake, then jack up the front of the vehicle and support it on axle stands

**7.4e Release the retaining clip and lift the expansion tank from its location**

**7.4g . . . then remove the crash box from the bulkhead**

(see *Jacking and vehicle support*). Remove the relevant front roadwheel.
2 Drain the transmission oil as described in Section 2 or be prepared for oil loss as the seal is changed.
3 Disconnect the inner end of the relevant driveshaft from the differential as described in Chapter 8. There is no need to disconnect the driveshaft from the swivel hub. Support the driveshaft by suspending it with wire or string – do not allow the driveshaft to hang down under its own weight, or the joints may be damaged.
4 Prise the now-exposed oil seal from the differential housing, using a screwdriver or similar instrument.
5 Smear the sealing lip of the new oil seal with a little transmission oil, then using a metal tube or socket of suitable diameter, drive the new seal into the differential casing until the outer surface of the seal is flush with the outer surface of the differential casing.
6 Reconnect the driveshaft to the differential as described in Chapter 8.
7 Refill or top-up the transmission oil level with reference to Section 2.
8 Refit the roadwheel, then lower the vehicle to the ground.

**7  Easytronic transmission**
– removal and refitting

**Note:** *This is an involved procedure, and it may well prove easier to remove the transmission complete with the engine as an assembly (see Chapter 2E), then separate the transmission. However, this Section describes removing the transmission leaving the engine in position. Suitable equipment will be required to support the engine and transmission, and the help of an assistant will be required.*

### Removal

1 Apply the handbrake, then jack up the front of the vehicle and support it on axle stands (see *Jacking and vehicle support*). Allow sufficient working room to remove the transmission from under the left-hand side of the engine compartment. Remove both front roadwheels then, where necessary, undo the retaining clips/screws and remove the engine undertray. Also remove the engine top cover where fitted.
2 Remove the air cleaner housing and intake ducts (see Chapter 4A, 4B or 4C).
3 Drain the transmission oil as described in Section 2 or be prepared for oil loss as the transmission is removed.
4 On diesel engine models, remove the fuel filter crash box from the rear of the engine compartment. To do this, disconnect the wiring connector from the fuel filter cover, depress the retaining clip and lift the filter from the crash box. Place the filter to one side. Unclip the expansion tank coolant hose and the wiring harness from the crash box, and disconnect the harness connector. Release

the retaining clip, lift the expansion tank from its location and place it to one side. Unscrew the outer retaining nut, slacken the inner nut and remove the crash box from the bulkhead (see illustrations).

**5** Attach a suitable hoist and lifting tackle to the lifting bracket(s) located on the left-hand side of the cylinder head, and support the weight of the engine/transmission.

**6** Refer to Chapter 10 and remove the front subframe.

**7** Disconnect the inner ends of both driveshafts from the differential as described in Chapter 8. There is no need to disconnect the driveshafts from the swivel hub. Support the driveshafts by suspending them with wire or string – do not allow the driveshafts to hang down under their own weight, or the joints may be damaged.

**8** Unbolt and remove the rear (and on diesel engine models, the front) engine/transmission mounting torque link brackets with reference to Chapter 2A , 2B or 2C.

**9** Disconnect the wiring from the transmission clutch and shift modules, and release the wiring from the support cables.

**10** Unbolt and remove the left-hand engine/transmission mounting bracket from the trans-mission with reference to Chapter 2A, 2B or 2C.

**11** Lower the engine and transmission by approximately 5 cm making sure that the coolant hoses and wiring harnesses are not stretched.

**12** Unscrew and remove the upper bolts securing the transmission to the rear of the engine. Where necessary, pull up the coolant hoses and secure them away from the transmission using plastic cable ties.

**13** Support the weight of the transmission on a trolley jack, then unscrew the remaining transmission-to-engine bolts.

**14** Make a final check that all components have been disconnected, and are positioned clear of the transmission so that they will not hinder the removal procedure.

**15** With the help of an assistant, carefully withdraw the transmission (and adapter plate on diesel engine models) from the engine. Take care not to allow the weight of the transmission to hang on the input shaft otherwise the clutch friction disc hub may be damaged. Note that there are two locating dowels which may be tight, and it may be necessary to rock the transmission from side-to-side to release it from them. Once the transmission is free, lower the jack and manoeuvre the unit out from under the car.

### Refitting

**16** Commence refitting by positioning the transmission on the trolley jack beneath the engine compartment. With the help of an assistant, raise the transmission and locate it on the engine (together with the adapter plate on diesel engine models), making sure that the input shaft engages accurately with the splines of the friction disc hub. With the transmission located on the dowels, insert all of the retaining bolts and tighten to the specified torque.

**17** The remaining refitting procedure is a reversal of removal, noting the following points:
a) *Tighten all nuts and bolts to the specified torque (where given).*
b) *Renew the driveshaft oil seals (see Section 6) before refitting the driveshafts.*
c) *Refit the front subframe assembly with reference to Chapter 10.*
d) *Refill or top-up the transmission with the specified type and quantity of oil, as described in Section 2.*
e) *Finally, it may be necessary to have a dealer or diagnostic specialist reprogramme all volatile control unit memories.*

## 8  Easytronic transmission overhaul – general information

In the event of a fault occurring on the transmission, it is first necessary to determine whether it is of an electrical, mechanical or hydraulic nature, and to achieve this, special test equipment is required. It is therefore essential to have the work carried out by a Vauxhall dealer if a transmission fault is suspected.

Do not remove the transmission from the car for possible repair before professional fault diagnosis has been carried out, since most tests require the transmission to be in the vehicle.

# Chapter 8
# Driveshafts

## Contents

## Degrees of difficulty

| Easy, suitable for novice with little experience | Fairly easy, suitable for beginner with some experience | Fairly difficult, suitable for competent DIY mechanic | Difficult, suitable for experienced DIY mechanic | Very difficult, suitable for expert DIY or professional |
|---|---|---|---|---|

## Specifications

### Type
1.0 litre models. . . . . . . . . . . . . . . . . . . . . . . . . . . . . . . . . . . . . . . . . . . Unequal length shafts with outer ball-and-cage type and inner tripod type constant velocity joints

All except 1.0 litre models . . . . . . . . . . . . . . . . . . . . . . . . . . . . . . . . . Unequal length shafts with ball-and-cage type constant velocity joint at each end

### Lubrication (overhaul only – see text)
Lubricant type/specification. . . . . . . . . . . . . . . . . . . . . . . . . . . . . . . . . Use only special grease supplied in sachets with gaiter kits – joints are otherwise prepacked with grease and sealed

### Torque wrench settings

| | Nm | lbf ft |
|---|---|---|
| Driveshaft retaining nut*: | | |
| Stage 1 . . . . . . . . . . . . . . . . . . . . . . . . . . . . . . . . . . . . . | 120 | 89 |
| Stage 2 . . . . . . . . . . . . . . . . . . . . . . . . . . . . . . . . . . . . . | Slacken the nut completely | |
| Stage 3 . . . . . . . . . . . . . . . . . . . . . . . . . . . . . . . . . . . . . | 20 | 15 |
| Stage 4 . . . . . . . . . . . . . . . . . . . . . . . . . . . . . . . . . . . . . | Angle-tighten through a further 90° | |
| Drop link retaining nut* . . . . . . . . . . . . . . . . . . . . . . . . . . | 65 | 48 |
| Lower arm balljoint clamp bolt nut* . . . . . . . . . . . . . . . . . | 60 | 44 |
| Roadwheel bolts. . . . . . . . . . . . . . . . . . . . . . . . . . . . . . . . | 110 | 81 |

* Use new nuts/bolts.

---

## 1  General information

Drive is transmitted from the differential to the front wheels by means of two solid steel driveshafts of unequal length. The right-hand driveshaft is longer than the left-hand one, due to the position of the transmission unit.

Both driveshafts are splined at their outer ends to accept the wheel hubs, and are threaded so that each hub can be fastened by a large nut. The inner end of each driveshaft is splined to accept the differential sun gear. On some models, a vibration damper is attached to the right-hand driveshaft.

Constant velocity (CV) joints are fitted to each end of the driveshafts, to ensure the smooth and efficient transmission of drive at all the angles possible as the roadwheels move up-and-down with the suspension, and as they turn from side-to-side under steering. Both inner and outer constant velocity joints are of the ball-and-cage type on all except 1.0 litre models; on these vehicles, the inner constant velocity joints are of the tripod type.

**2.2  Extract the split pin from the driveshaft retaining nut**

## 2  Driveshafts – removal and refitting

**Note:** *A new driveshaft retaining nut, split pin and balljoint clamp bolt nut will be needed on refitting.*

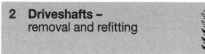

**HAYNES HiNT**  *If work is being carried out without the aid of an assistant, remove the wheel trim/hub cap (as applicable) then withdraw the split pin and slacken the driveshaft retaining nut with the vehicle resting on its wheels.*

### Removal

**1** Firmly apply the handbrake, then jack up the front of the car and support it securely on

**2.6  Unscrew the nut, and withdraw the clamp bolt from the swivel hub**

**2.8  Push down the lower suspension arm to free the balljoint from the swivel hub**

**2.3  Using a fabricated tool to hold the front hub stationary whilst the driveshaft retaining nut is slackened**

axle stands (see *Jacking and vehicle support*). Remove the relevant front roadwheel.

**2** Extract the split pin from the driveshaft retaining nut and discard it; a new one must be used on refitting **(see illustration)**.

**3** Refit at least two roadwheel bolts to the front hub, and tighten them securely. Have an assistant firmly depress the brake pedal to prevent the front hub from rotating, then using a socket and extension bar, slacken and remove the driveshaft retaining nut. Alternatively, a tool can be fabricated from two lengths of steel strip (one long, one short) and a nut an bolt; the nut and bolt forming the pivot of a forked tool. Bolt the tool to the hub using two wheel bolts, and hold the tool to prevent the hub from rotating as the driveshaft retaining nut is undone **(see illustration)**.

**4** Unscrew the driveshaft retaining nut, and remove the washer. Discard the nut; a new one must be used on refitting.

**2.7  Using a chisel to expand the bottom of the swivel hub**

**2.9a  Use a soft-faced hammer to drive the driveshaft from the hub splines . . .**

**2.5  Holding the anti-roll bar drop link joint stub with an open-ended spanner**

**5** Unscrew and remove the nut securing the anti-roll bar drop link to the strut, while holding the joint stub on the flats provided with a further spanner **(see illustration)**. Release the link from the strut and move it to one side.

**6** Unscrew and remove the lower arm balljoint clamp bolt nut, and withdraw the clamp bolt from the swivel hub **(see illustration)**. Discard the clamp bolt nut; a new one must be used on refitting.

**7** Use a chisel or screwdriver as a wedge to expand the lower portion of the swivel hub **(see illustration)**.

**8** Using a lever, push down on the lower arm to free the balljoint from the swivel hub **(see illustration)**, then move the swivel hub to one side and release the balljoint, taking care not to damage the balljoint rubber boot.

**9** The swivel hub must now be freed from the end of the driveshaft. It should be possible to pull the hub off the driveshaft, but if the end of the driveshaft is tight in the hub, then tap the end of the driveshaft with a soft-faced hammer while pulling outwards on the swivel hub **(see illustrations)**. Support the driveshaft by suspending it with wire or string; **Do not allow the driveshaft to hang down under its own weight, or the joints may be damaged.**

**10** Where fitted, remove the splash shield from under the engine compartment. Position a container beneath the transmission to catch any oil that may be spilt.

**11** A suitable lever will now be required to release the inner end of the driveshaft from the differential. To release the right-hand driveshaft, a flat steel bar with a good chamfer on one end can be used. The left-hand driveshaft may prove

**2.9b  . . . then pull the swivel hub outwards**

**2.12 Lever the driveshaft CV joint out from the transmission to release its circlip from the differential**

**2.15 Prior to refitting, ensure that the circlip (arrowed) is correctly located in the inner CV joint groove**

**2.18 Using a punch on the CV joint weld bead to drive the joint into the differential until the circlip engages positively**

more difficult to release, and a suitable square- or rectangular-section bar may be required.

12 Lever between the driveshaft and the differential housing to release the driveshaft circlip from the differential. Carefully withdraw the driveshaft from the transmission unit, taking great care not to damage the driveshaft oil seal, and remove the driveshaft from underneath the vehicle **(see illustration)**.

13 Plug the opening in the differential, to prevent further oil loss and dirt ingress.

*Caution: Do not allow the vehicle to rest on its wheels with one or both driveshaft(s) removed, as damage to the wheel bearing(s) may result. If the vehicle must be moved on its wheels, clamp the wheel bearings using a long threaded rod and spacers to take the place of the outer driveshaft joint through the hub.*

### Refitting

14 Before installing the driveshaft, examine the driveshaft oil seal in the transmission for signs of damage or deterioration. Renew if necessary, referring to the relevant part of Chapter 7 for further information.

15 Remove the circlip from the end of the inner constant velocity joint splines and discard it. Fit a new circlip, making sure it is correctly seated in its groove **(see illustration)**.

16 Thoroughly clean the driveshaft splines, and the apertures in the transmission unit and hub assembly. Apply a thin film of grease to the oil seal lips, and to the driveshaft splines and shoulders. Check that all gaiter clips are securely fastened.

17 Remove the plug from the transmission (see paragraph 13) and offer up the driveshaft. Locate the joint splines with those of the differential sun gear, taking great care not to damage the oil seal.

18 Place a screwdriver or similar tool on the slot/weld bead on the inner driveshaft joint, not the rubber cover, and drive the shaft into the differential until the retaining circlip engages positively **(see illustration)**. Pull on the joint, not the shaft, to make sure that the joint is securely retained by the circlip.

19 Locate the outer constant velocity joint splines with those of the swivel hub, and slide the joint back into position in the hub.

20 Using the lever, push down on the lower suspension arm, then relocate the balljoint and release the arm. Make sure that the balljoint stub is fully entered in the swivel hub.

21 Insert the balljoint clamp bolt to the swivel hub, so that its threads are facing to the rear of the vehicle. Fit a new nut to the clamp bolt, and tighten it to the specified torque setting.

22 Refit the anti-roll bar drop link to the strut, and tighten the nut to the specified torque while holding the joint on its flats using a spanner.

23 Refit the washer to the end of the driveshaft, then screw on a new nut. Using the method employed on removal to prevent rotation, tighten the new driveshaft retaining nut through the stages given in the Specifications at the start of this Chapter **(see illustration)**.

24 With the nut correctly tightened, secure it in position with a new split pin (see

illustrations). If the holes in the driveshaft are not aligned with any of the slots in the nut, loosen **(do not tighten)** the nut by the *smallest possible amount* until the split pin can be inserted.

25 Refit the splash shield under the engine (where fitted), then refit the roadwheel, then lower the vehicle to the ground and tighten the roadwheel bolts to the specified torque.

26 Check and if necessary top-up the transmission oil level, using the information given in the relevant part of Chapter 7.

### 3 Driveshaft rubber gaiters – renewal

### *Ball-and-cage type joint*

**Note:** *If both driveshaft gaiters are to renewed at the same time, it is only necessary to remove one of the constant velocity joints. The second gaiter can then be slid along and removed from the exposed end of the driveshaft. The inner and outer CV joints are identical (except 1.0 litre model inner joints) and the following procedure can be used for either joint.*

#### All joints except 1.0 litre models inner

1 Remove the driveshaft from the car as described in Section 2.

2 Secure the driveshaft in a vice equipped with soft jaws, and release the two retaining clips on the gaiter which is to be renewed. If necessary, the retaining clips can be cut to release them.

**2.23 Refit the washer and a new retaining nut**

**2.24a Insert a new split pin . . .**

**2.24b . . . and secure in position by bending over the split pin ends**

3.4a  The CV joint circlip (arrowed) . . .

3.4b  . . . can be expanded using circlip pliers to release the joint from the shaft

3.9  Examine the constant velocity joint balls and cage for signs of wear or damage

**3** Slide the rubber gaiter down the shaft to expose the constant velocity joint. Scoop out any excess grease.

**4** Using circlip pliers, expand the circlip which secures the joint to the driveshaft **(see illustrations)**.

**5** Using a soft-faced mallet, tap the joint off the end of the driveshaft.

**6** Slide the rubber gaiter off the driveshaft, and discard it.

**7** If both gaiters are to be renewed, release the retaining clips, then slide the second gaiter along the driveshaft and remove it. If the driveshaft is fitted with a vibration damper, mark the damper fitted position, then remove it from the driveshaft (see Section 5).

**8** Wipe away as much of the old grease as possible (do not use any solvent) to allow the joint components to be inspected.

**9** Move the inner splined driving member from side-to-side, to expose each ball in turn

at the top of its track. Examine the balls for cracks, flat spots, or signs of surface pitting **(see illustration)**.

**10** Inspect the ball tracks on the inner and outer members. If the tracks have widened, the balls will no longer be a tight fit. At the same time, check the ball cage windows for wear or cracking between the windows.

**11** If on inspection any of the constant velocity joint components are found to be worn or damaged, it will be necessary to renew the complete joint assembly. If the joint is in satisfactory condition, obtain a repair kit consisting of a new gaiter and retaining clips, a constant velocity joint circlip, and the correct type and quantity of grease **(see illustration)**.

**12** Wind tape around the splines on the end of the driveshaft, to protect the gaiter as it is slid into place.

**13** Where both gaiters have been removed,

slide on the first gaiter and proceed as described in paragraphs 15 to 18.

**14** Slide the (second) gaiter onto the end of the driveshaft **(see illustration)**, then remove the tape from the driveshaft splines.

**15** Fit a new circlip to the constant velocity joint, then tap the joint onto the driveshaft until the circlip engages in its groove **(see illustrations)**. Make sure that the joint is securely retained by the circlip, by pulling on the joint, not the shaft.

**16** Pack the joint with the specified type of grease **(see illustration)**. Work the grease well into the bearing tracks whilst twisting the joint, and fill the rubber gaiter with any excess.

**17** Ease the gaiter over the joint, and ensure that the gaiter lips are correctly located in the grooves on both the driveshaft and constant velocity joint. Lift the outer sealing lip of the gaiter, to equalise air pressure within the gaiter.

3.11  Components required for driveshaft gaiter renewal

3.14  Slide the gaiter onto the end of the driveshaft

3.15a  Fit a new circlip . . .

3.15b  . . . ensuring it is correctly located in the joint inner member

3.15c  Slide the joint onto the driveshaft until the circlip is correctly located in the driveshaft groove

3.16  Pack the CV joint and gaiter with the grease supplied

**3.18a Hook the large outer retaining clip ends together . . .**

**3.18b . . . then secure the clip in position by compressing the raised section of the clip**

**3.18c Small inner retaining clip is secured in position in the same way**

**18** Fit the large metal retaining clip to the gaiter. Pull the clip as tight as possible, and locate the hooks on the clip in their slots. Remove any slack in the gaiter retaining clip by carefully compressing the raised section of the clip. In the absence of the special tool, a pair of side-cutters may be used. Secure the small retaining clip using the same procedure **(see illustrations)**.

**19** Check that both constant velocity joints move freely in all directions then, where applicable, refit the vibration damper to its original position on the driveshaft (see Section 5). On completion, refit the driveshaft to the car as described in Section 2.

### *Tripod joints*

#### 1.0 litre models inner

**20** Remove the driveshaft from the car as described in Section 2.

**21** The outer CV joint on 1.0 litre models is of the same ball-and-cage type as used on all other models. Both rubber gaiters can therefore be renewed after removing the outer CV joint as described previously in paragraphs 1 to 19.

**22** If the inner rubber gaiter is being renewed, and an initial inspection indicates possible wear in the inner joint, remove the joint for a detailed inspection as follows.

**23** With the rubber gaiter released from the joint, mark the joint outer member in relation to the driveshaft, to ensure correct refitting. Withdraw the joint outer member from the tripod and driveshaft. As the outer member is withdrawn, take precautions to prevent the bearing rollers falling off the tripod. Wipe away all excess grease and, if necessary, wrap tape around the tripod joint to secure the rollers in position.

**24** Prise the circlip from the end of the drive-shaft, then using a punch, paint or a suitable marker pen, make alignment marks between the tripod joint and driveshaft, and also identify which way round the tripod is fitted **(see illustrations)**. Remove the tripod joint assembly from the end of the shaft, if the joint is a tight fit, it maybe necessary to use a puller to draw it off the shaft – if a puller is used, take great care not to damage the rollers.

**25** Slide the gaiter off the end of the driveshaft.

**26** Where applicable, remove the tape from the joint, and wipe away as much of the old grease as possible (do not use any solvent).

**27** Check the spider, rollers and outer member for signs of wear, pitting or scuffing on their bearing surfaces. Also check that the spider rollers rotate smoothly and easily, with no traces of roughness.

**28** If any of the constant velocity joint components are found to be worn or damaged, it will be necessary to renew the complete joint assembly. If the joint is in satisfactory condition, obtain a repair kit consisting of a new gaiter and retaining clips, circlips, and the correct type and quantity of grease.

**29** Clean the driveshaft, and tape over the splines on its inner end to protect the new gaiter as it is fitted.

**30** Slide the new gaiter onto the driveshaft then remove the tape from the driveshaft end.

**31** If necessary, again wind tape around the tripod to retain the rollers then, with the previously-made marks on the tripod and driveshaft aligned, push the tripod onto the driveshaft splines. If necessary use a soft-faced mallet to drive the tripod fully onto the splines. Secure the tripod in position using the new circlip, making sure that the circlip locates correctly in the driveshaft groove.

**32** Where applicable, remove the tape from around the tripod, then work the grease supplied with the repair kit fully into the roller bearings. Fill the joint outer member with any excess grease.

**33** Locate the outer member over the tripod,

**3.24a Prise the circlip from the end of the driveshaft. . .**

making sure that the previously-made marks are aligned.

**34** Slide the gaiter along the driveshaft, and locate it in the recesses on the driveshaft and joint outer member.

**35** Ensure that the gaiter is not twisted or distorted, then carefully lift the lip of the gaiter at the outer member end to equalise air pressure in the gaiter.

**36** Fit the large metal retaining clip to the gaiter. Remove any slack in the gaiter retaining clip by carefully compressing the raised section of the clip. In the absence of the special tool, a pair of side-cutters may be used. Secure the small retaining clip using the same procedure.

**37** The driveshaft can now be refitted to the car as described in Section 2.

---

**4  Driveshaft joint –**
checking and renewal

### *Checking*

**1** First carry out the checks described in Chapter 1A or 1B, to reveal if there is any wear in one of the driveshaft joints.

**2** Check the split pin is in position and the driveshaft nut is tight. If in doubt, the only alternative is to obtain a new nut and split pin, then fit and tighten the nut using the procedures described in Section 2. Once tightened, secure the nut in position with the new split pin, and refit the centre cap or trim. Repeat this check on the other driveshaft nut.

**3.24b . . . then make alignment marks between the tripod joint and the driveshaft**

**5.0 Vibration damper fitted to the right-hand driveshaft on certain models**

3 Road test the vehicle, and listen for a metallic clicking noise from the front as the vehicle is driven slowly in a circle on full-lock. If evident, this indicates wear in the outer constant velocity joint which must be renewed.

4 To check for wear on the inner joint, apply the handbrake then jack up the front of the vehicle and support it on axle stands (see *Jacking and vehicle support*). Attempt to move the inner end of the driveshaft up-and-down, then hold the joint with one hand and attempt to rotate the driveshaft with the other. If excessive wear is evident, the joint must be renewed. **Note:** *If vibration, consistent with roadspeed, is felt through the car when accelerating, there is a possibility of wear in the inner constant velocity joints.*

**5.6 The vibration damper (1) must be secured in position with a new retaining clip (2)**

*Dimension I = 22.5 cm ± 5 mm*

### Renewal

**Note:** *It may not be possible to renew the tripod type inner joint individually (as fitted to the 1.0 litre model), check with your local Vauxhall dealer for the availability of parts.*

5 To renew the ball-and-cage type constant velocity joint, follow the procedures in Section 3. If the old gaiter is going to be re-used, it can be left on the driveshaft, take care not to damage the gaiter when removing the retaining clips.

## 5 Vibration damper (right-hand driveshaft) – removal and refitting

**Note:** *On some models a vibration damper*

is fitted to the right-hand driveshaft **(see illustration)**. *The vibration damper can only be separated from the driveshafts that are made by GKN. On any other make of driveshaft the complete driveshaft will have to be renewed if there is a fault with the vibration damper.*

### Removal

1 Remove the driveshaft from the car as described in Section 2.

2 Remove the transmission side constant velocity joint and gaiter as described in Section 3.

3 Clean around the vibration damper, then mark the damper's fitted position on the driveshaft.

4 Cut the retaining clip from around the collar of the vibration damper and discard it, a new one will be required on refitting.

5 Spray the shaft with penetrating oil, and pull the vibration damper from the driveshaft.

### Refitting

6 Refitting is a reversal of removal, bearing in mind the following points:

a) *Fit the vibration damper to the driveshaft using the measurement shown* **(see illustration)**.

b) *Refit the constant velocity joint to the driveshaft as described in Section 3.*

c) *Refit the the driveshaft to the vehicle as described in Section 2.*

# Chapter 9
# Braking system

## Contents

## Degrees of difficulty

**Easy,** suitable for novice with little experience

**Fairly easy,** suitable for beginner with some experience

**Fairly difficult,** suitable for competent DIY mechanic

**Difficult,** suitable for experienced DIY mechanic

**Very difficult,** suitable for expert DIY or professional

## Specifications

### Front brakes

| | New | Minimum |
|---|---|---|
| Type . . . Disc, with single-piston sliding caliper | | |
| Disc diameter: | | |
| 1.0 and 1.2 litre petrol models | 240 mm | |
| 1.4 litre petrol models | 260 mm | |
| Diesel engines: | | |
| 1.3 litre models | 260 mm | |
| 1.7 litre models: | | |
| Y17DT | 260 mm | |
| Y17DTL | 240 mm | |
| Disc thickness: | | |
| 1.0 and 1.2 litre petrol models : | | |
| With ABS | 20.0 mm | 17.0 mm |
| Without ABS | 11.0 mm | 8.0 mm |
| 1.4 litre petrol models | 24.0 mm | 21.0 mm |
| Diesel engines: | | |
| 1.3 litre models | 24.0 mm | 21.0 mm |
| 1.7 litre models: | | |
| Y17DT | 24.0 mm | 21.0 mm |
| Y17DTL | 20.0 mm | 17.0 mm |
| Maximum disc run-out | 0.03 mm | |
| Brake pad thickness: | | |
| New (including backing plate): | | |
| 1.0 and 1.2 litre petrol models | 15.0 mm | |
| 1.4 litre petrol models | 16.0 mm | |
| Diesel models | 16.0 mm | |
| Minimum thickness (including backing plate) | 7.0 mm | |
| Brake caliper piston diameter: | | |
| 1.0 and 1.2 litre petrol models | 48.0 mm | |
| 1.4 litre petrol models | 54.0 mm | |
| Diesel models | 54.0 mm | |

## Rear brakes

| | New | Maximum |
|---|---|---|
| Type . . . . . . . . . . . . . . . . . . . . . . . . . . . . . . . . . . . . . . . . . . . . Single leading shoe drum | | |
| Drum diameter (inner): | | |
|   Corsa and Corsavan models: | | |
|     All models except Y17DTL diesel engines . . . . . . . . . . . . . . . . . | 200 mm | 201 mm |
|     Y17DTL diesel engines (also some Y17DT engines) . . . . . . . . . . | 230 mm | 231 mm |
|   Combo Van models . . . . . . . . . . . . . . . . . . . . . . . . . . . . . . . . . | 230 mm | 231 mm |
| Drum width: | | |
|   Corsa and Corsavan models: | | |
|     All models except Y17DTL diesel engines | | |
|       With ABS . . . . . . . . . . . . . . . . . . . . . . . . . . . . . . . . . . . . | 45.0 mm | |
|       Without ABS . . . . . . . . . . . . . . . . . . . . . . . . . . . . . . . . . | 28.0 mm | |
|     Y17DTL diesel engines (also some Y17DT engines) . . . . . . . . . . | 40.0 mm | |
|   Combo Van models . . . . . . . . . . . . . . . . . . . . . . . . . . . . . . . . . | 40.0 mm | |
| Maximum drum out-of-round. . . . . . . . . . . . . . . . . . . . . . . . . . . . . | 0.8 mm | |
| Brake shoes thickness: | | |
|   New (without backing plate) . . . . . . . . . . . . . . . . . . . . . . . . . . . | 5.0 mm | |
|   Minimum thickness. . . . . . . . . . . . . . . . . . . . . . . . . . . . . . . . . . | 2.5 mm | |
| Wheel cylinder nominal diameter . . . . . . . . . . . . . . . . . . . . . . . . . . | 19.05 mm | |

## Torque wrench settings

| | Nm | lbf ft |
|---|---|---|
| ABS components: | | |
|   ECU-to-modulator retaining screws* . . . . . . . . . . . . . . . . . . . . . . . | 3 | 2 |
|   Front wheel speed sensor bolt. . . . . . . . . . . . . . . . . . . . . . . . . . . . | 8 | 6 |
|   Modulator block retaining nuts. . . . . . . . . . . . . . . . . . . . . . . . . . . | 10 | 7 |
| Brake hose-to-caliper union bolt . . . . . . . . . . . . . . . . . . . . . . . . . . . | 40 | 30 |
| Brake pedal bracket bolt and nuts* . . . . . . . . . . . . . . . . . . . . . . . . . | 20 | 15 |
| Brake pipe union nut . . . . . . . . . . . . . . . . . . . . . . . . . . . . . . . . . . . | 16 | 12 |
| Front brake caliper: | | |
|   Guide bolts* . . . . . . . . . . . . . . . . . . . . . . . . . . . . . . . . . . . . . . . . | 27 | 20 |
|   Mounting bracket-to-swivel hub bolts . . . . . . . . . . . . . . . . . . . . . . | 100 | 74 |
| Front brake disc retaining screw . . . . . . . . . . . . . . . . . . . . . . . . . . . | 7 | 5 |
| Master cylinder mounting nuts* . . . . . . . . . . . . . . . . . . . . . . . . . . . . | 25 | 18 |
| Pressure-regulating valve: | | |
|   Mounting bolts . . . . . . . . . . . . . . . . . . . . . . . . . . . . . . . . . . . . . . | 20 | 15 |
|   Tension spring clamping screw . . . . . . . . . . . . . . . . . . . . . . . . . . | 11 | 8 |
| Rear drum hub nut* . . . . . . . . . . . . . . . . . . . . . . . . . . . . . . . . . . . . | 175 | 129 |
| Rear wheel cylinder bolts. . . . . . . . . . . . . . . . . . . . . . . . . . . . . . . . | 9 | 7 |
| Roadwheel bolts. . . . . . . . . . . . . . . . . . . . . . . . . . . . . . . . . . . . . . | 110 | 81 |
| Vacuum pump mounting bolts: | | |
|   Stage 1 . . . . . . . . . . . . . . . . . . . . . . . . . . . . . . . . . . . . . . . . . . . | 5 | 4 |
|   Stage 2 . . . . . . . . . . . . . . . . . . . . . . . . . . . . . . . . . . . . . . . . . . . | 20 | 15 |
| Vacuum servo unit mounting nuts* . . . . . . . . . . . . . . . . . . . . . . . . . | 20 | 15 |

*Use new nuts/bolts*

---

## 1 General information

The braking system is of the servo-assisted, dual-circuit hydraulic type. The arrangement of the hydraulic system is such that each circuit operates one front and one rear brake from a tandem master cylinder. Under normal circumstances, both circuits operate in unison. However, in the event of hydraulic failure in one circuit, full braking force will still be available at two wheels.

All models covered in this manual have front disc brakes and rear drum brakes (rear discs are fitted to the 1.8 litre petrol engines – not covered in this manual). An Anti-lock Braking System (ABS) is fitted as standard or an optional extra to all vehicles covered in this manual. Refer to Section 19 for further information on ABS operation.

The front disc brakes are actuated by single-piston sliding type calipers, which ensure that equal pressure is applied to each disc pad.

The rear drum brakes incorporate leading and trailing shoes, which are actuated by twin-piston wheel cylinders. A self-adjust mechanism is incorporated to automatically compensate for brake shoe wear. As the brake shoe linings wear, the footbrake operation automatically operates the adjuster mechanism, which effectively lengthens the shoe strut, and repositions the brake shoes to maintain the lining-to-drum clearance.

On models without ABS, there are pressure-regulating valves situated in the hydraulic lines to control the pressure applied to the rear brakes. The regulating valves are of the pressure-dependent type and help to prevent rear wheel lock-up during emergency braking.

The cable-operated handbrake provides an independent mechanical means of rear brake application.

**Note:** *When servicing any part of the system, work carefully and methodically; also observe scrupulous cleanliness when overhauling any part of the hydraulic system. Always renew components (in axle sets, where applicable) if in doubt about their condition, and use only genuine Vauxhall parts, or at least those of known good quality. Note the warnings given in 'Safety first!' and at relevant points in this Chapter concerning the dangers of asbestos dust and hydraulic fluid.*

## 2 Hydraulic system – bleeding

⚠ *Warning: Hydraulic fluid is poisonous; wash off immediately and thoroughly in the case of skin contact, and seek immediate medical advice if any fluid is swallowed or gets into the eyes. Certain types of hydraulic fluid are inflammable, and may ignite when allowed into contact with hot components. When servicing any hydraulic system, it is safest to assume that the fluid IS inflammable, and to take precautions against the risk of fire as though it is petrol that is being handled. Hydraulic fluid is also an effective paint stripper, and will attack plastics; if any is spilt, it should be washed off immediately using copious quantities of water. Finally, it is hygroscopic (it absorbs moisture from the air) – old fluid may be contaminated, and unfit for further use. When topping-up or renewing the fluid, always use the recommended type, and ensure that it comes from a freshly-opened sealed container.*

## General

**1** Any hydraulic system will only function correctly once all the air has been removed from the components and circuit; this is achieved by bleeding the system.

**2** During the bleeding procedure, add only clean, fresh hydraulic fluid of the recommended type; never use old fluid, nor re-use any which has already been bled from the system. Ensure that sufficient fresh fluid is available before starting work.

**3** If there is any possibility of the wrong fluid being in the system, the brake components and circuit must be flushed completely with uncontaminated, correct fluid, and new seals should be fitted to the various components.

**4** If hydraulic fluid has been lost from the system (or if air has entered) because of a leak, ensure that the fault is cured before proceeding further.

**5** Park the vehicle on level ground, switch off the engine and select first or reverse gear, then chock the wheels and release the handbrake.

**6** Check that all pipes and hoses are secure, that the pipe unions are tight, and that the bleed screws are closed. Clean any dirt from around the bleed screws.

**7** Unscrew the master cylinder reservoir cap, and top the master cylinder reservoir up to the MAX level line; refit the cap loosely, and remember to maintain the fluid level at least above the MIN level line throughout the procedure, to avoid the risk of further air entering the system.

**8** There is a number of one-man, do-it-yourself brake bleeding kits currently available from motor accessory shops. It is recommended that one of these kits is used whenever possible, as they greatly simplify the bleeding operation, and also reduce the risk of expelled air and fluid being drawn back into the system. If such a kit is not available, the basic (two-man) method must be used, which is described in detail below.

*Caution: Vauxhall recommend using a pressure bleeding kit for this operation (see paragraphs 24 to 27).*

**9** If a kit is to be used, prepare the vehicle as described previously, and follow the kit manufacturer's instructions, as the procedures may vary slightly according to the type being used; generally, they will be as outlined below in the relevant sub-Section.

**10** Whichever method is used, the same sequence must be followed (paragraphs 11 and 12) to ensure the removal of all air from the system.

## Bleeding sequence

**11** If the system has been only partially disconnected, and suitable precautions were taken to minimise fluid loss, it should only be necessary to bleed that part of the system (ie, the primary or secondary circuit).

**12** If the complete system is to be bled, then it should be done working in the following sequence:

   a) *Left-hand front brake.*
   b) *Right-hand front brake.*
   c) *Left-hand rear brake.*
   d) *Right-hand rear brake.*

## Bleeding

### Basic (two-man) method

**13** Collect a clean glass jar, a suitable length of plastic or rubber tubing which is a tight fit over the bleed screw, and a ring spanner to fit the bleed screw. The help of an assistant will also be required.

**14** Remove the dust cap from the first screw in the sequence. Fit the spanner and tube to the screw, place the other end of the tube in the jar, and pour in sufficient fluid to cover the end of the tube.

**15** Ensure that the master cylinder reservoir fluid level is maintained at least above the MIN level line throughout the procedure.

**16** Have the assistant fully depress the brake pedal several times to build-up pressure, then maintain it on the final stroke.

**17** While pedal pressure is maintained, unscrew the bleed screw (approximately one turn) and allow the compressed fluid and air to flow into the jar. The assistant should maintain pedal pressure, following it down to the floor if necessary, and should not release it until instructed to do so. When the flow stops, tighten the bleed screw again; the pedal should then be released slowly, and the reservoir fluid level checked and topped-up.

**18** Repeat the steps given in paragraphs 16 and 17 until the fluid emerging from the bleed screw is free from air bubbles. If the master cylinder has been drained and refilled, and air is being bled from the first screw in the

**2.22 Using a one-way valve kit to bleed the rear brake**

sequence, allow approximately five seconds between cycles for the master cylinder passages to refill.

**19** When no more air bubbles appear, tighten the bleed screw securely, remove the tube and spanner, and refit the dust cap. Do not overtighten the bleed screw.

**20** Repeat the procedure on the remaining screws in the sequence, until all air is removed from the system and the brake pedal feels firm again.

### Using a one-way valve kit

**21** As their name implies, these kits consist of a length of tubing with a one-way valve fitted, to prevent expelled air and fluid being drawn back into the system; some kits include a translucent container, which can be positioned so that the air bubbles can be more easily seen flowing from the end of the tube.

**22** The kit is connected to the bleed screw, which is then opened **(see illustration)**. The user returns to the driver's seat, depresses the brake pedal with a smooth, steady stroke, then slowly releases it; this is repeated until the expelled fluid is clear of air bubbles.

**23** These kits simplify work so much that it is easy to forget the master cylinder reservoir fluid level; ensure that this is maintained at least above the MIN level line at all times, or air will be drawn into the system.

### Using a pressure bleeding kit

**24** These kits are usually operated by the reservoir of pressurised air contained in the spare tyre, noting that it will probably be necessary to reduce the pressure to less than normal; refer to the instructions supplied with the kit.

**25** By connecting a pressurised, fluid-filled container to the master cylinder reservoir, bleeding can be carried out simply by opening each screw in turn (in the specified sequence) and allowing the fluid to flow out until no more air bubbles can be seen in the expelled fluid.

**26** This method has the advantage that the large reservoir of fluid provides an additional safeguard against air being drawn into the system during bleeding.

**27** Pressure bleeding is particularly effective when bleeding 'difficult' systems, or when bleeding the complete system at the time of routine fluid renewal.

### All methods

**28** When bleeding is complete and firm pedal feel is restored, wash off any spilt fluid, tighten the bleed screws securely, and refit their dust caps.

**29** Check the hydraulic fluid level, and top-up if necessary (see *Weekly checks*).

**30** Discard any hydraulic fluid that has been bled from the system; it will not be fit for re-use. Bear in mind that this fluid may be inflammable.

**31** Check the feel of the brake pedal. If it feels at all spongy, air must still be present in the system, and further bleeding is required. Failure to bleed satisfactorily after a reasonable repetition of the bleeding procedure may be due to worn master cylinder seals.

## 3 Hydraulic pipes and hoses – renewal

**Note:** *Before starting work, refer to the warning note at the beginning of Section 2 concerning the dangers of hydraulic fluid.*

1 If any pipe or hose is to be renewed, minimise fluid loss by first removing the master cylinder reservoir cap and screwing it down onto a piece of polythene. Alternatively, flexible hoses can be sealed, if required, using a proprietary brake hose clamp. Metal brake pipe unions can be plugged (if care is taken not to allow dirt into the system) or capped immediately they are disconnected. Place a wad of rag under any union that is to be disconnected, to catch any spilt fluid.

2 If a flexible hose is to be disconnected, unscrew the brake pipe union nut before removing the spring clip which secures the hose to its mounting bracket. Where applicable, unscrew the banjo union bolt securing the hose to the caliper and recover the copper washers.

3 To unscrew the union nuts, it is preferable to obtain a brake pipe spanner of the correct size; these are available from most large motor accessory shops. Failing this, a close-fitting open-ended spanner will be required, though if the nuts are tight or corroded, their flats may be rounded-off if the spanner slips. In such a case, a self-locking wrench is often the only way to unscrew a stubborn union,

but it follows that the pipe and the damaged nuts must be renewed on reassembly. Always clean a union and surrounding area before disconnecting it. If disconnecting a component with more than one union, make a careful note of the connections before disturbing any of them.

4 If a brake pipe is to be renewed it can be obtained, cut to length and with the union nuts and end flares in place, from Vauxhall dealers. All that is then necessary is to bend it to shape, following the line of the original, before fitting it to the car. Alternatively, most motor accessory shops can make up brake pipes from kits, but this requires very careful measurement of the original to ensure that the new one is of the correct length. The safest answer is usually to take the original to the shop as a pattern.

5 On refitting, securely tighten the union nuts but do not overtighten (it is not necessary to exercise brute force to obtain a sound joint).

6 When refitting hoses to the calipers, always use new copper washers and tighten the banjo union bolts to the specified torque. Make sure that the hoses are positioned so that they will not touch surrounding bodywork or the roadwheels.

7 Ensure that the pipes and hoses are correctly routed, with no kinks, and that they are secured in the clips or brackets provided. After fitting, remove the polythene from the reservoir, and bleed the hydraulic system as described in Section 2. Wash off any spilt fluid, and check carefully for fluid leaks.

## 4 Front brake pads – renewal

**⚠ Warning: Renew BOTH sets of front brake pads at the same time – NEVER renew the pads on only one wheel, as uneven braking may result. Note that the dust created by wear of the pads may contain asbestos, which is a health hazard. Never blow it out with compressed air, and don't inhale any of it. An approved filtering mask should be worn when working on the brakes. DO NOT use petroleum-based solvents to clean brake parts – use brake cleaner or methylated spirit only.**

**Note:** *A new brake caliper lower guide bolt will be required for refitting.*

1 Firmly apply the handbrake, then jack up the front of the car and support it securely on axle stands (see *Jacking and vehicle support*). Remove the front roadwheels.

2 Push in the caliper piston by sliding the caliper body towards the outside of the vehicle by hand.

3 Follow the accompanying photos (**illustrations 4.3a to 4.3n**) for the actual pad renewal procedure, bearing in mind the additional points listed below. Be sure to stay in order and read the caption under each illustration. Note that if the old pads are to be refitted, ensure that they are identified so that they can be returned to their original positions.

4 If the original brake pads are still serviceable, carefully clean them using a clean, fine wire

4.3a **Unscrew the lower guide bolt from the caliper . . .**

4.3b **. . . lift the caliper upwards to gain access to the brake pads . . .**

4.3c **. . . and tie the caliper in the raised position using string or wire**

4.3d **Lift out the outer brake pad . . .**

4.3e **. . . and the inner brake pad . . .**

4.3f **. . . then remove the pad wear warning spring from the outer pad**

4.3g Remove the anti-rattle springs from the caliper mounting bracket, noting their fitted position

4.3h Measure the thickness of the pad friction material and backing plate. If any are worn down to the specified minimum, or fouled with oil or grease, all four pads must be renewed

4.3i If new pads are to be fitted, before refitting the caliper, push back the caliper piston whilst opening the bleed screw. This is to prevent any dirt/debris being forced back up the hydraulic circuit in the ABS modulator

4.3j Apply a smear of high-temperature grease to the contact areas of the backing plates

4.3k Refit the anti-rattle springs to the caliper mounting bracket, then place the inner pad in position. The inner pad can be identified by the projecting (arrowed) on the backing plate

4.3l Fit the pad wear warning spring to the outer pad . . .

brush or similar, paying particular attention to the sides and back of the metal backing plate. Clean out the grooves in the friction material, and pick out any large embedded particles of dirt or debris. Carefully clean the pad locations in the caliper body/mounting bracket.

5 Prior to fitting the pads, check that the guide pins are a snug fit in the caliper mounting bracket. Brush the dust and dirt from the caliper and piston, but do not inhale it, as it is injurious to health. Inspect the dust seal around the piston for damage, and the piston for evidence of fluid leaks, corrosion

or damage. If attention to any of these components is necessary, refer to Section 8.

6 If new brake pads are to be fitted, the caliper piston must be pushed back into the cylinder to allow for the extra pad thickness. Either use a G-clamp or similar tool, or use suitable pieces of wood as levers. Clamp off the flexible brake hose leading to the caliper then connect a brake bleeding kit to the caliper bleed screw. Open the bleed screw as the piston is retracted, the surplus brake fluid will then be collected in the bleed kit vessel **(see illustration 4.3i)**. Close the bleed screw

just before the caliper piston is pushed fully into the caliper. This should ensure no air enters the hydraulic system.

Note: *The ABS unit contains hydraulic components that are very sensitive to impurities in the brake fluid. Even the smallest particles can cause the system to fail through blockage. The pad retraction method described here prevents any debris in the brake fluid expelled from the caliper from being passed back to the ABS hydraulic unit, as well as preventing any chance of damage to the master cylinder seals.*

7 With the brake pads installed, depress the

4.3m . . . then place the outer pad in position

4.3n Lower the caliper and secure with a new guide bolt tightened to the specified torque

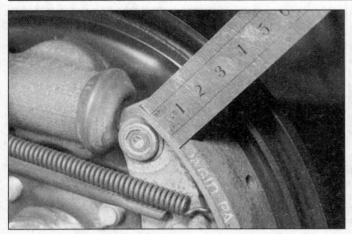

**5.3a Measure the thickness of the brake shoe friction material at several points. If any are worn down to the specified minimum, or fouled with oil or grease, all four shoes must be renewed**

**5.3b Prior to disturbing the shoes, note the correct fitted locations of all components, paying particular attention to the adjuster strut components**

**5.3c Unhook the upper return spring, and remove it from the brake shoes**

**5.3d Prise the adjusting lever retaining spring out of the leading brake shoe . . .**

**5.3e . . . then remove the return spring . . .**

**5.3f . . . and the adjusting lever**

**5.3g Prise the brake shoes apart and remove the adjuster strut**

**5.3h Remove the leading shoe retainer spring cup by depressing and turning it through 90°. With the cup removed, lift off the spring and withdraw the retainer pin**

brake pedal repeatedly, until normal (non-assisted) pedal pressure is restored, and the pads are pressed into firm contact with the brake disc.

**8** Repeat the above procedure on the remaining front brake caliper.

**9** Refit the roadwheels, then lower the vehicle to the ground and tighten the roadwheel bolts to the specified torque setting.

**10** Check the hydraulic fluid level as described in *Weekly checks*.

*Caution: New pads will not give full braking efficiency until they have bedded-in. Be prepared for this, and avoid hard braking as far as possible for the first hundred miles or so after pad renewal.*

## 5 Rear brake shoes – renewal

⚠️ *Warning: Brake shoes must be renewed on BOTH rear wheels at the same time – NEVER renew the shoes on only one wheel, as uneven braking may result. The dust created as the shoes wear may contain asbestos, which is a health hazard. Never blow it out with compressed air, and don't inhale any of it. An approved filtering mask should be worn when working on the brakes. DO NOT use petroleum-based*

solvents to clean brake parts – use brake cleaner or methylated spirit only.

**1** Remove the brake drum as described in Section 7.

**2** Working carefully and taking the necessary precautions, remove all traces of brake dust from the brake drum, backplate and shoes.

**3** Follow the accompanying photos (illustrations 5.3a to 5.3w) for the actual brake shoe renewal procedure, bearing in mind the additional points listed below. Be sure to stay in order and read the caption under each illustration.

5.3i Remove the leading shoe from the backplate and unhook the return spring

5.3j Remove the trailing shoe retainer spring cup then lift off the spring and withdraw the retainer pin

5.3k Remove the trailing shoe from the backplate and unhook the handbrake cable

5.3l Use a cable tie or elastic band to retain the wheel cylinder pistons

5.3m The left-hand adjuster strut assembly is marked L (arrowed)

5.3n Dismantle and clean the adjuster strut and apply a smear of silicone-based grease to the adjuster threads

5.3o It may be necessary to transfer the adjusting lever pivot pin and clip (arrowed) from the original shoes to the new ones

5.3p With the brake shoes removed, check the wheel cylinder for hydraulic fluid leaks

5.3q Thoroughly clean the backplate, then apply a smear of high-temperature brake grease to the contact surfaces (arrowed)

5.3r Locate the handbrake cable under the clip (arrowed), then engage the trailing shoe with the cable. Locate the shoe on the backplate and secure with the retainer pin, spring and cup

5.3s Connect the lower return spring to both shoes (arrowed), then locate the leading shoe on the backplate and secure with the retainer pin, spring and cup

5.3t Refit the adjuster strut, noting that the shorter part of the fork (arrowed) must be to the front of the shoe

**5.3u Refit the adjusting lever and retaining spring . . .**

**5.3v . . . then refit the return spring, making sure that the spring is correctly engaged in the correct hole (arrowed)**

**5.3w Cut the plastic cable tie from the wheel cylinder after fitting the brake shoes**

**4** If both brake assemblies are dismantled at the same time, take care not to mix up the components. Note that the left-hand and right-hand adjuster components are marked as such; the threaded rod is marked L or R, and the other 'handed' components are colour-coded black for the left-hand side, and silver for the right-hand side.

**5** If a new handbrake operating lever was not supplied with the new shoes (where applicable), transfer the lever from the old shoes. The lever may be secured with a pin and circlip, or by a rivet, which will have to be drilled out. It may also be necessary to transfer the adjusting lever pivot pin and clip from the original front shoe to the new shoe.

**6** Prior to refitting the adjuster strut, screw the adjuster wheel fully onto the forked end of the adjuster, so that the adjuster strut is set to its shortest possible length. Back the wheel off a half a turn, and check that it is free to rotate easily.

**7** On completion, ensure that the handbrake operating lever stop peg is correctly positioned against the edge of the shoe web, then refit the brake drum as described in Section 7.

**8** Repeat the operation on the remaining brake.

**9** Once both sets of rear shoes have been renewed, with the handbrake fully released, adjust the lining-to-drum clearance by repeatedly depressing the brake pedal 20 to 25 times. Whilst depressing the pedal, have an assistant listen to the rear drums, to check that the adjuster strut is functioning correctly; if so, a clicking sound will be emitted by the strut as the pedal is depressed.

**10** Check and, if necessary, adjust the handbrake as described in Section 14.

**11** Refit the roadwheels, then lower the vehicle to the ground and tighten the roadwheel bolts to the specified torque setting.

**12** Check the hydraulic fluid level as described in *Weekly checks*.

*Caution: New brake shoes will not give full braking efficiency until they have bedded-in. Be prepared for this, and avoid hard braking as far as possible for the first hundred miles or so after shoe renewal.*

### 6 Front brake disc – inspection, removal and refitting

**Note:** *Before starting work, refer to the warning at the beginning of Section 4 concerning the dangers of asbestos dust.*

#### Inspection

**Note:** *If either disc requires renewal, BOTH should be renewed at the same time, to ensure even and consistent braking.*

**1** Firmly apply the handbrake, then jack up the front of the car and support it securely on axle stands (see *Jacking and vehicle support*). Remove the appropriate front roadwheel.

**2** Slowly rotate the brake disc so that the full area of both sides can be checked; remove the brake pads if better access is required to the inner surface. Light scoring is normal in the area swept by the brake pads, but if heavy scoring is found, the disc must be renewed.

**3** It is normal to find a lip of rust and brake dust around the disc's perimeter; this can be scraped off if required. If, however, a lip has formed due to excessive wear of the brake pad swept area, then the disc's thickness must be measured using a micrometer. Take measurements at several places around the disc, at the inside and outside of the pad swept area; if the disc has worn at any point to the specified minimum thickness or less, the disc must be renewed.

**4** If the disc is thought to be warped, it can be checked for run-out either using a dial gauge mounted on any convenient fixed point, while the disc is slowly rotated, or by using feeler gauges to measure (at several points all around the disc) the clearance between the disc and a fixed point such as the caliper mounting bracket. To ensure that the disc is squarely seated on the hub, fit two wheel bolts, complete with spacers approximately 10 mm thick, and tighten them securely. If the measurements obtained are at the specified maximum or beyond, the disc is excessively warped and must be renewed; however, it is worth checking first that the hub bearing is in good condition (Chapter 1A or 1B).

**5** Check the disc for cracks, especially around the wheel bolt holes, and for any other wear or damage, and renew if necessary.

#### Removal

**6** Unscrew the two bolts securing the brake caliper assembly to the swivel hub, and slide the caliper assembly off the disc **(see illustrations)**. Using a piece of wire or string, tie the caliper to the front suspension coil spring, to avoid placing any strain on the hydraulic brake hose.

**6.6a Slacken and remove the two bolts securing the brake caliper mounting bracket to the hub . . .**

**6.6b . . . then slide the caliper assembly off the brake disc**

**6.7 Undo the retaining screw and remove the brake disc from the hub**

**7** Remove the screw securing the brake disc to the hub, and remove the disc. If it is tight, lightly tap its rear face with a hide or plastic mallet **(see illustration)**.

## Refitting

**8** Refitting is the reverse of the removal procedure, noting the following points:

a) *Ensure that the mating surfaces of the disc and hub are clean and flat.*

b) *Tighten the disc retaining screw to the specified torque setting.*

c) *If a new disc has been fitted, use a suitable solvent to wipe any preservative coating from the disc before refitting the caliper.*

d) *Remove all traces of old thread-locking compound from the brake caliper bolts and holes in the swivel hub, ideally by running a tap of the correct size and pitch through them. Apply a suitable thread-locking compound to the threads of the caliper mounting bracket bolts. Slide the caliper assembly into position over the disc, then fit the mounting bolts and tighten them to the specified torque setting.*

e) *Refit the roadwheel, then lower the vehicle to the ground and tighten the roadwheel bolts to the specified torque. On completion, repeatedly depress the brake pedal until normal (non-assisted) pedal pressure returns.*

## 7  Rear brake drum – removal, inspection and refitting

**Note:** *Before starting work, refer to the warning at the beginning of Section 5 concerning the dangers of asbestos dust. A new hub nut and dust cap will be required on refitting.*

## Removal

**1** Chock the front wheels, then jack up the rear of the vehicle and support it on axle stands. Remove the appropriate rear wheel and release the handbrake. Proceed as described under the relevant sub-heading.

### Corsa and Corsavan

**2** Use a chisel to prise out the cap from the centre of the drum **(see illustration)**.

**3** Slacken and remove the rear hub nut, then withdraw the brake drum assembly from the stub axle by hand. It may be difficult to remove the drum, due to the brake shoes binding on the inner circumference of the drum. If the brake shoes are binding, first check that the handbrake is fully released, then proceed as follows.

**4** Referring to Section 14 for further information, fully slacken the handbrake cable adjuster nut to obtain maximum free play in the cable.

**5** Remove the plug from the inspection hole in the brake backplate, and push the handbrake operating lever outwards away from the brake shoe. This will release the handbrake lever

**7.2  Remove the cap from the centre of the drum to gain access to the hub nut**

**7.5b  . . . release the handbrake lever stop-peg by inserting a screwdriver in through the hole in the rear of the backplate . . .**

stop-peg from the edge of the brake shoe, and further collapse the shoes **(see illustrations)**. The brake drum can then be withdrawn from the stub axle.

### Combo Van

**6** Slacken and remove the drum retaining screw, and remove the drum from the vehicle **(see illustrations)**. It may be difficult to remove the drum due to the brake shoes binding on the inner circumference of the drum. If the brake shoes are binding, first check that the handbrake is fully released, then proceed as described above in paragraphs 4 and 5.

## Inspection

**Note:** *If either drum requires renewal, BOTH should be renewed at the same time, to ensure even and consistent braking.*

**7** Working carefully, remove all traces of

**7.6a  Remove the securing screw . . .**

**7.5a  Remove the rubber plug (arrowed) from the brake backplate . . .**

**7.5c  . . . and use screwdriver (A) to push the handbrake lever away from the brake shoe in the direction of arrow (B) – shown with drum removed**

brake dust from the drum, but *avoid inhaling the dust, as it is a health-hazard.*

**8** Scrub clean the outside of the drum, and check it for obvious signs of wear or damage (such as cracks around the roadwheel bolt holes); renew the drum if necessary.

**9** Examine the inside of the drum carefully. Light scoring of the friction surface is normal, but if heavy scoring is found, the drum must be renewed. It is usual to find a lip on the drum's inboard edge which consists of a mixture of rust and brake dust; this should be scraped away, to leave a smooth surface which can be polished with fine (120- to 150-grade) emery paper. If, however, the lip is due to the friction surface being recessed by excessive wear, then the drum must be renewed.

**10** If the drum is thought to be excessively worn, or oval, its internal diameter must be

**7.6b  . . . and withdraw the brake drum**

**7.12 Prior to refitting the drum, check that the handbrake lever is correctly positioned on the shoe**

measured at several points using an internal micrometer. Take measurements in pairs, the second at right-angles to the first, and compare the two to check for signs of ovality. Provided that it does not enlarge the drum to beyond the specified maximum diameter, it may be possible to have the drum refinished by skimming or grinding; if this is not possible, the drums on both sides must be renewed. Note that if the drum is to be skimmed, both drums must be refinished, to maintain a consistent internal diameter on both sides.

### Refitting

**11** If a new brake drum is to be installed, use a suitable solvent to remove any preservative coating that may have been applied to its interior. Note that it may also be necessary to shorten the adjuster strut length by rotating the strut wheel, to allow the new drum to pass over the brake shoes.

#### Corsa and Corsavan

**12** Ensure that the handbrake lever stop-peg is correctly repositioned against the edge of the brake shoe web **(see illustration)**.
**13** Slide the drum into position, then fit a new hub nut, and tighten it to the specified torque setting.
**14** Fit the new dust cap to the centre of the brake drum.
**15** With the handbrake fully released, adjust the lining-to-drum clearance by repeatedly depressing the brake pedal 20 to 25 times. Whilst depressing the pedal, have an assistant listen to the rear drums, to check that the adjuster strut is functioning correctly; if so, a

**8.7 Removing the piston seal from the caliper body**

clicking sound will be emitted by the strut as the pedal is depressed.
**16** With the lining-to-drum clearance set, check and, if necessary, adjust the handbrake as described in Section 14.
**17** Refit the roadwheel, aligning the marks made on removal, then lower the vehicle to the ground and tighten the roadwheel bolts to the specified torque setting.

#### Combo Van

**18** Ensure that the drum and hub flange mating surfaces are clean and dry, and remove all traces of corrosion.
**19** Ensure that the handbrake lever stop-peg is correctly repositioned against the edge of the brake shoe web, and locate the drum on the hub. Refit the drum retaining screw, and tighten it securely.
**20** Carry out the operations described in paragraphs 15 to 17.

---

## 8 Front brake caliper – removal, overhaul and refitting

**Note:** *New caliper guide bolts and brake hose sealing washers will be required when refitting. Before starting work, refer to the warning at the beginning of Section 2 concerning the dangers of hydraulic fluid, and to the warning at the beginning of Section 4 concerning the dangers of asbestos dust.*

### Removal

**1** Firmly apply the handbrake, then jack up the front of the car and support it securely on axle stands (see *Jacking and vehicle support*). Remove the appropriate roadwheel.
**2** Minimise fluid loss by first removing the master cylinder reservoir cap, then tightening it down onto a piece of polythene to obtain an airtight seal. Alternatively, use a brake hose clamp, a G-clamp or a similar tool to clamp the flexible hose.
**3** Clean the area around the caliper brake hose union **(see illustration)**. Slacken and remove the union bolt, and recover the sealing washer from either side of the hose union. Discard the washers; new ones must be used on refitting. Plug the hose end and caliper hole, to minimise fluid loss and prevent the ingress of dirt into the hydraulic system.

**8.3 Slacken the brake hose union (A), then undo the caliper guide bolts (B)**

**4** Slacken and remove the lower and upper caliper guide bolts and remove the brake caliper from the vehicle **(see illustration 8.3)**.

### Overhaul

**Note:** *Before starting work, check with your local dealer for the availability of parts to overhaul the caliper.*
**5** With the caliper on the bench, wipe away all traces of dust and dirt, but *avoid inhaling the dust, as it is a health hazard.*
**6** Withdraw the partially-ejected piston from the caliper body, and remove the dust seal. The piston can be withdrawn by hand, or if necessary pushed out by applying compressed air to the brake hose union hole. Only low pressure should be required, such as is generated by a foot pump, and as a precaution a block of wood should be positioned to prevent any damage to the piston.
**7** Using a small screwdriver, carefully remove the piston seal from the caliper, taking great care not mark the bore **(see illustration)**.
**8** Carefully press the guide bushes out of the caliper body.
**9** Thoroughly clean all components, using only methylated spirit, isopropyl alcohol or clean hydraulic fluid as a cleaning medium. Never use mineral-based solvents such as petrol or paraffin, which will attack the hydraulic system's rubber components. Dry the components immediately, using compressed air or a clean, lint-free cloth. If compressed air is available, use it to blow through the fluid passages to make sure they are clear

 *Warning: Always wear eye protection when using compressed air.*

**10** Check all components, and renew any that are worn or damaged. Check particularly the cylinder bore and piston; these should be renewed (note that this means the renewal of the complete body assembly) if they are scratched, worn or corroded in any way. Similarly check the condition of the guide bushes and bolts; both bushes and bolts should be undamaged and (when cleaned) a reasonably tight sliding fit in each other. If there is any doubt about the condition of any component, renew it.
**11** If the assembly is fit for further use, obtain the necessary components from your Vauxhall dealer. Renew the caliper seals as a matter of course; these should never be re-used.
**12** On reassembly, ensure that all components are absolutely clean and dry.
**13** Soak the piston and the new piston (fluid) seal in clean hydraulic fluid. Smear clean fluid on the cylinder bore surface.
**14** Fit the new piston (fluid) seal, using only the fingers to manipulate it into the cylinder bore groove.
**15** Fit the new dust seal to the piston, refit it to the cylinder bore using a twisting motion, and ensure that the piston enters squarely into the bore. Press the dust seal fully into the caliper body, and push the piston fully into the caliper bore.

9.4 Brake pipe union nut (A) and wheel cylinder retaining bolt (B)

H.2815B

9.7 Exploded view of a rear brake wheel cylinder

**16** Ease the guide bushes into position in the caliper body.

### Refitting

**17** Using new guide bolts, refit the caliper and brake pads (where removed) as described in Section 4.

**18** Position a new sealing washer on each side of the hose union, and connect the brake hose to the caliper. Ensure that the hose is correctly positioned against the caliper body lug, then install the union bolt and tighten it to the specified torque setting.

**19** Remove the brake hose clamp or the polythene, where fitted, and bleed the hydraulic system as described in Section 2. Note that, providing the precautions described were taken to minimise brake fluid loss, it should only be necessary to bleed the relevant front brake.

**20** Refit the roadwheel, then lower the vehicle to the ground and tighten the roadwheel bolts to the specified torque.

## 9  Rear wheel cylinder – removal, overhaul and refitting

**Note:** *Before starting work, refer to the warning at the beginning of Section 2 concerning the dangers of hydraulic fluid, and to the warning at the beginning of Section 5 concerning the dangers of asbestos dust.*

### Removal

**1** Remove the brake drum as described in Section 7.

**2** Using pliers, carefully unhook the upper brake shoe return spring, and remove it from both brake shoes **(see illustration 5.3c)**. Pull the upper ends of the shoes away from the wheel cylinder to disengage them from the pistons.

**3** Minimise fluid loss by first removing the master cylinder reservoir cap, then tightening it down onto a piece of polythene to obtain an airtight seal. Alternatively, use a brake hose clamp, a G-clamp or a similar tool to clamp the flexible hose at the nearest convenient point to the wheel cylinder.

**4** Wipe away all traces of dirt around the brake pipe union at the rear of the wheel cylinder, and unscrew the union nut. Carefully ease the pipe out of the wheel cylinder, and plug or tape over its end to prevent dirt entry. Wipe off any spilt fluid immediately **(see illustration)**.

**5** Unscrew the wheel cylinder retaining bolt from the rear of the backplate **(see illustration 9.4)**, and remove the cylinder, taking great care not to allow surplus hydraulic fluid to contaminate the brake shoe linings.

### Overhaul

**Note:** *Before starting work, check with your local dealer for the availability of parts to overhaul the wheel cylinder.*

**6** Brush the dirt and dust from the wheel cylinder, but take care not to inhale it.

**7** Pull the rubber dust seals from the ends of the cylinder body **(see illustration)**.

**8** The pistons will normally be ejected by the pressure of the coil spring, but if they are not, tap the end of the cylinder body on a piece of wood, or apply low air pressure (eg, from a foot pump) to the hydraulic fluid union hole to eject the pistons from their bores.

**9** Inspect the surfaces of the pistons and their bores in the cylinder body for scoring, or evidence of metal-to-metal contact. If evident, renew the complete wheel cylinder assembly.

**10** If the pistons and bores are in good condition, discard the seals and obtain a repair kit, which will contain all the necessary renewable items.

**11** Lubricate the piston seals with clean brake fluid, and insert them into the cylinder bores, with the spring between them, using finger pressure only.

**12** Dip the pistons in clean brake fluid, and insert them into the cylinder bores.

**13** Fit the dust seals, and check that the pistons can move freely in their bores.

### Refitting

**14** Ensure that the backplate and wheel cylinder mating surfaces are clean, then spread the brake shoes and manoeuvre the wheel cylinder into position.

**15** Engage the brake pipe, and screw in the union nut two or three turns to ensure that the thread has started.

**16** Insert the wheel cylinder retaining bolt, and tighten it to the specified torque setting. Now tighten the brake pipe union nut to the specified torque.

**17** Remove the clamp from the flexible brake hose, or the polythene from the master cylinder reservoir (as applicable).

**18** Ensure that the brake shoes are correctly located against the cylinder pistons, then carefully refit the brake shoe upper return spring, using a screwdriver to stretch the spring into position.

**19** Refit the brake drum as described in Section 7.

**20** Bleed the brake hydraulic system as described in Section 2. Providing suitable precautions were taken to minimise loss of fluid, it should only be necessary to bleed the relevant rear brake.

## 10  Master cylinder – removal, overhaul and refitting

**Note:** *New master cylinder retaining nuts will be required when refitting. Before starting work, refer to the warning at the beginning of Section 2 concerning the dangers of hydraulic fluid.*

### Removal

**1** Remove the master cylinder reservoir cap, and syphon the hydraulic fluid from the reservoir. **Note:** *Do not syphon the fluid by mouth, as it is poisonous; use a syringe or an old hydrometer.* Alternatively, open any convenient bleed screw in the system, and

10.4a Peel the bonnet seal off the engine compartment bulkhead . . .

10.4b . . . then unclip the cover from the battery cables

10.5 Release the battery cables from the water deflector

10.6a Undo the retaining screw (arrowed) from the right-hand side of the water deflector . . .

10.6b . . . the retaining screw (arrowed) from the left-hand side of the water deflector . . .

10.6c . . . and the retaining screw from the middle of the water deflector

gently pump the brake pedal to expel the fluid through a plastic tube connected to the screw (see Section 2).

**2** Disconnect the battery negative terminal (refer to *Disconnecting the battery* in the Reference Chapter).

**3** Remove both windscreen wiper arms as described in Chapter 12.

**4** Peel the bonnet seal off the engine compartment bulkhead, then unclip the cover from the battery cables **(see illustrations)**.

**5** Unclip the battery cables from the wind deflector, and move them to one side **(see illustration)**.

**6** Undo the three retaining screws – one at each end and one in the middle **(see illustrations)**. Remove both halves of the wind deflector trim, release the trim from the engine

compartment bulkhead and wiper spindles. Disconnect the washer pipe for the washer jets as the trim is removed from the vehicle.

**7** Unclip the rubber guide/grommet from the bulkhead for the brake pipes.

**8** Disconnect the wiring connector from the brake fluid level sender unit **(see illustration)**.

**9** Detach the fluid supply hose for the clutch master cylinder from the reservoir.

**10** Wipe clean the area around the brake pipe unions on the side of the master cylinder, and place absorbent rags beneath the pipe unions to catch any surplus fluid. Make a note of the correct fitted positions of the unions, then unscrew the union nuts and carefully withdraw the pipes **(see illustration)**. Plug or tape over the pipe ends and master cylinder orifices, to minimise the loss of brake fluid and to prevent

the entry of dirt into the system. Wash off any spilt fluid immediately with cold water.

**11** Slacken and remove the two nuts securing the master cylinder to the vacuum servo unit and discard them; new ones must be used on refitting **(see illustration)**. Withdraw the master cylinder assembly from the engine compartment.

**12** Where applicable, recover the seal which is fitted between the master cylinder and servo.

### Overhaul

**13** At the time of writing, master cylinder overhaul is not possible as no spares are available.

**14** The only parts available individually are the fluid reservoir, its mounting seals, the filler cap and the master cylinder mounting seals. The reservoir can be unclipped **(see**

10.8 Disconnecting the master cylinder brake fluid level sender wiring connector

10.10 Slacken and remove the brake pipes (arrowed) from the brake master cylinder

10.11 Undo the two retaining nuts (arrowed) and remove the master cylinder from the servo unit

illustration), then the seals can be removed from the master cylinder.

**15** If the master cylinder is worn excessively, it must be renewed.

### Refitting

**16** Remove all traces of dirt from the master cylinder and servo unit mating surfaces. Inspect the master cylinder seal for signs of wear or damage, and renew if necessary.

**17** Where applicable, fit a new seal to the servo and refit the master cylinder, ensuring that the pushrod enters the master cylinder bore centrally. Fit the new master cylinder mounting nuts, and tighten them to the specified torque.

**18** Wipe clean the brake pipe unions, refit them to the master cylinder ports, and tighten them to the specified torque.

**19** Ensure that the brake pipes are correctly clipped back into position in the bulkhead rubber guide/grommet.

**20** Reconnect the wiring connector to the brake fluid level sender unit.

**21** Fill the master cylinder reservoir with new fluid, and bleed the complete hydraulic system as described in Section 2.

**22** Install the components removed for access by reversing the removal procedure.

## 11 Brake pedal – removal and refitting

### Removal

**1** Remove the clutch pedal as described in Chapter 6.

**2** Working in the engine compartment, unscrew the brake pedal mounting bracket upper retaining bolt **(see illustration)**.

**3** From inside the vehicle, remove the stop-light switch as described in Section 18.

**4** Unhook the return spring from the brake pedal, then slide off the spring clip, and withdraw the clevis pin securing the pedal to the servo unit pushrod **(see illustration)**.

**5** Undo the mounting bracket retaining nuts and remove the pedal and support bracket assembly from the vehicle **(see illustration)**.

**6** Inspect the pedal pivot bush and shaft for signs of wear, and renew if necessary.

### Refitting

**7** Apply a smear of multi-purpose grease to the pedal pivot bush, then manoeuvre the pedal and support bracket assembly into place, fitting new retaining nuts.

**8** Make sure that the brake servo pushrod fits correctly in the brake pedal bracket.

**9** Align the pedal hole with the pushrod end, and insert the clevis pin. Secure the pin in position with the spring clip **(see illustration)**.

**10** Refit the return spring to the brake pedal.

**11** Refit the stop-light switch as described in Section 18.

**12** Working in the engine compartment, refit the brake pedal mounting bracket upper retaining bolt.

**10.14 Where necessary, unclip the reservoir (arrowed) from the master cylinder**

**11.4 Unhook the pedal return spring (A), then withdraw the locking clip (B) and remove the clevis pin from the pedal/pushrod**

**13** Refit the clutch pedal as described in Chapter 6.

## 12 Vacuum servo unit – testing, removal and refitting

### Testing

**1** To test the operation of the servo unit, with the engine off, depress the footbrake several times to exhaust the vacuum. Now start the engine, keeping the pedal firmly depressed. As the engine starts, there should be a noticeable 'give' in the brake pedal as the vacuum builds-up. Allow the engine to run for at least two minutes, then switch it off. The brake pedal should now feel normal, but further applications should result in the pedal feeling firmer, the pedal stroke decreasing with each application.

**11.9 Ensure that the servo pushrod clevis pin is securely retained by its spring clip**

**11.2 Slacken and remove the brake pedal upper retaining bolt (arrowed)**

**11.5 Remove the pedal mounting assembly retaining nuts (arrowed)**

**2** If the servo does not operate as described, first inspect the servo unit check valve as described in Section 13.

**3** If the servo unit still fails to operate satisfactorily, the fault lies within the unit itself. Repairs to the unit are not possible; if faulty, the servo unit must be renewed.

### Removal

**4** Remove the master cylinder as described in Section 10. On some models, it may prove sufficient to unbolt the master cylinder and position it clear of the servo, taking great care not to strain the brake pipes. This removes the need to disconnect the brake pipes and open the hydraulic system.

**5** Carefully ease the vacuum hose out of the servo unit, taking care not to displace the sealing grommet **(see illustration)**.

**6** Working from inside the vehicle, unhook the return spring, slide off the spring clip and

**12.5 Carefully ease the vacuum hose (arrowed) out of the servo unit**

withdraw the clevis pin securing the brake pedal to the servo unit pushrod **(see illustration)**.

**7** Slacken and remove the nuts securing the servo unit to the pedal mounting bracket **(see illustration)**.

**8** Return to the engine compartment, and lift the servo unit out of position. Where fitted, recover the gasket from the rear of the servo unit. Discard the gasket and retaining nuts; new ones should be used on refitting.

### Refitting

**9** Inspect the servo unit check valve sealing grommet for signs of damage or deterioration, and renew if necessary.

**10** Ensure that the servo and bulkhead mating surfaces are clean and dry.

**11** Fit a new gasket to the rear of the servo, and reposition the unit in the engine compartment.

**12** From inside the vehicle, ensure that the servo unit pushrod is correctly engaged with the brake pedal, then fit the new servo unit mounting nuts. Tighten the nuts to the specified torque setting.

**13** Refit the servo unit pushrod-to-brake pedal clevis pin, and secure it in position with the spring clip.

**14** Refit the return spring to the brake pedal.

**15** Ease the vacuum hose end piece into place in the servo unit, taking great care not to displace or damage the grommet.

**16** Refit the master cylinder as described in Section 10.

**17** On completion, start the engine and check for air leaks at the vacuum hose-to-servo unit connection. Check the operation of the braking system.

**13.1 Vacuum servo unit check valve is integral with the hose, and cannot be renewed separately**

**14.3 Unclipping the cover from around the handbrake lever**

**12.6 Unhook the pedal return spring (A), then withdraw the locking clip (B) and remove the clevis pin**

### 13 Vacuum servo unit check valve – removal, testing and refitting

**1** The check valve is located in the vacuum hose running from the inlet manifold (or vacuum pump on diesel engine models) to the brake servo. If the valve is faulty, it will need to be renewed with the hose as a complete assembly **(see illustration)**.

### Removal

**2** Carefully ease the vacuum hose out of the servo unit, taking care not to displace the grommet **(see illustration)**.

**3** Note the correct routing of the hose, then undo the union nut, or disconnect the quick-release fitting, securing the hose to the inlet manifold or vacuum pump. Remove the hose assembly from the vehicle.

**13.2 Ease the vacuum hose out from the servo unit, taking care not to displace the grommet (arrowed)**

**14.4 Adjusting the handbrake cable**

**12.7 Servo unit retaining nuts (arrowed)**

### Testing

**4** Examine the check valve and vacuum hose for signs of damage, and renew if necessary.

**5** The valve may be tested by blowing through it in both directions. Air should flow through the valve in one direction only: when blown through from the servo unit end of the valve. Renew the valve if this is not the case.

**6** Examine the servo unit rubber sealing grommet for signs of damage or deterioration, and renew as necessary.

### Refitting

**7** Ensure that the sealing grommet is correctly fitted to the servo unit.

**8** Ease the hose union into position in the servo, taking great care not to displace or damage the grommet.

**9** Ensure that the hose is correctly routed, and connect it to the inlet manifold or vacuum pump, tightening its union nut securely (where applicable).

**10** On completion, start the engine and check for air leaks at the check valve-to-servo unit connection.

### 14 Handbrake – adjustment

**1** To check the handbrake adjustment, fully release the handbrake lever, and apply the footbrake firmly several times. This will establish correct shoe-to-drum clearance, and ensure that the self-adjust mechanism is fully adjusted. Applying normal, moderate pressure, pull the handbrake lever to the fully-applied position, counting the number of clicks emitted from the handbrake ratchet mechanism. If adjustment is correct, there should be 7 clicks before the handbrake is fully applied; if this is not the case, adjust as follows.

**2** Chock the front wheels then jack up the rear of the car and securely support it on axle stands (see *Jacking and vehicle support*).

**3** The handbrake cable adjuster nut is situated is situated by the handbrake lever inside the vehicle, unclip the cover from around the handbrake lever **(see illustration)**.

**4** With the handbrake set on the third notch of the ratchet mechanism, rotate the adjusting nut until a reasonable amount of force is required to turn each wheel/hub **(see illustration)**.

**15.4 Unclip the storage tray from the rear of the centre console**

**15.5 Disconnect the wiring connector from the handbrake warning light switch**

**15.6 Slacken and remove the handbrake cable adjuster nut**

**Note:** *The force required should be equal for each wheel.* Once this is so, fully release the handbrake lever and check that the wheels/hubs rotate freely. Check the adjustment by applying the handbrake fully whilst counting the clicks emitted from the handbrake ratchet and, if necessary, re-adjust.

**5** On completion of adjustment, check the handbrake cables for free movement, and apply a little grease to the exposed cable ends to prevent corrosion.

**6** Refit the handbrake lever cover and lower the vehicle to the ground. If the roadwheels have been removed, tighten the roadwheel bolts to the specified torque setting.

### 15 Handbrake lever – removal and refitting

#### Removal

**1** Chock the front wheels then jack up the rear of the car and securely support it on axle stands (see *Jacking and vehicle support*).

**2** Disengage the exhaust system from the rubber mountings and lower it until it comes to rest on the rear axle. Disconnect the wiring block connectors to the oxygen sensor(s).

**3** Undo the retaining nuts, and remove the exhaust heat shield from underneath the vehicle to gain access to the underside of the handbrake lever.

**4** From inside the vehicle, unclip the storage tray from the rear of the centre console **(see illustration)**.

**5** Unclip the cover from around the handbrake lever and disconnect the wiring connector from the handbrake warning light switch **(see illustration)**.

**6** Fully slacken and remove the handbrake cable adjuster nut **(see illustration)**.

**7** Unscrew the four handbrake lever mounting bolts **(see illustration)**.

**8** From under the vehicle, disconnect the front handbrake cable from the handbrake lever connecting bracket.

**9** The handbrake lever can now be withdrawn from inside the vehicle. The warning light switch can be removed from the lever assembly after unscrewing its retaining bolt **(see illustration)**.

**15.7 Unscrew the four retaining bolts (arrowed), then lift the handbrake lever out of position**

#### Refitting

**10** Refitting is a reversal of the removal procedure, adjusting the cable as described in Section 14.

### 16 Handbrake cables – removal and refitting

#### Corsa and Corsavan

**1** The handbrake cable consists of two main sections, a long cable linking the handbrake lever to the left-hand drum brake, and a short cable linking the right-hand drum brake to the equaliser. The equaliser links both cables together, and is situated above the rear axle crossmember. Each cable can be renewed individually as follows. **Note:** *There are also two short rear sections of cable which attach*

**16.1 Handbrake cable connector (arrowed) in front of the rear brake drum assembly on each side**

**15.9 To remove the warning light switch from the handbrake lever, undo the retaining bolt (arrowed)**

*the main cables to the brake shoes* **(see illustration)**.

#### Long cable

**2** Undo the retaining nuts, and remove the exhaust heat shield from underneath the vehicle to gain access to the underside of the handbrake lever.

**3** Unscrew the handbrake cable adjuster nut, from inside the vehicle (see Section 14).

**4** Remove the left-hand rear brake drum as described in Section 7.

**5** Referring to Section 5, remove the upper and lower return springs, then remove the spring cup, spring and retainer pin, and remove the rear brake shoe. Note that the front shoe and adjuster strut mechanism can be left in position on the backplate.

**6** Free the handbrake cable from the retaining clip on the shoe lower pivot, then remove the retaining clip and withdraw the cable from the rear of the backplate **(see illustration)**.

**16.6 Each handbrake cable is secured to the backplate on the inside by a retaining clip**

7 Work back along the cable, releasing it from any relevant retaining clips and guides, whilst noting its correct routing (**see illustration**).

8 Detach the front end of the cable from the handbrake lever assembly, then remove the rubber grommet from around the equaliser link and withdraw the cable from underneath the vehicle (**see illustration**).

9 On refitting, attach the front end of the cable to the handbrake lever, then hook the cable through the equaliser link. Secure the cable in position with the rubber grommet.

10 Work back along the cable, securing it in position with all the relevant clips and guides, and routing it as noted on removal.

11 Insert the cable through the backplate, and secure it in position with the clip.

12 Ensure that the cable is securely retained by the clip on the shoe lower pivot point (**see illustration**), and refit the rear brake shoe as described in Section 5.

13 Ensure that the brake shoes and adjuster strut components are correctly fitted, then refit the brake drum as described in Section 7.

14 Adjust the handbrake cable as described in Section 14.

### Short cable

15 Remove the cable as described above in paragraphs 3 to 7, removing the right-hand brake drum instead of the left-hand drum. Remove the rubber grommet from around the equaliser link and withdraw the cable.

16 Attach the front end of the cable to the equaliser link, securing the cable in position with the rubber grommet. Refit the cable as described in paragraphs 10 to 14.

### *Combo Van*

17 The handbrake cable consists of two sections of equal length, which run from each rear brake to the equaliser plate. The equaliser plate is secured to the handbrake lever by a short cable which is secured to the handbrake lever by the adjuster nut. The two cables from the rear brake assemblies can only be bought as a complete item and cannot be separated from the equaliser plate, therefore the cable arrangement can only be removed and refitted as an assembly (**see illustration**).

### Removal

18 Where applicable, undo the retaining nuts,

**16.7 Free the cable from any relevant clips or guides (arrowed) securing it to the vehicle underbody**

and remove the exhaust heat shield from underneath the vehicle to gain access to the underside of the handbrake lever.

19 Unscrew the handbrake cable adjuster nut from inside the vehicle (see Section 14).

20 Remove the left-hand rear brake drum as described in Section 7.

21 Referring to Section 5, remove the upper and lower return springs, then remove the spring cup, spring and retainer pin, and remove the rear brake shoe. Note that the front shoe and adjuster strut mechanism can be left in position on the backplate.

22 Free the handbrake cable from the retaining clip on the shoe lower pivot, then remove the retaining clip and withdraw the cable from the rear of the backplate.

23 Repeat the operations in paragraphs 20 to 22 on the right-hand rear brake.

24 Work back along both cables, releasing them from any relevant retaining clips and ties, whilst noting the correct routing. Remove the cable/ equaliser plate assembly from the underneath the vehicle, releasing it from the short cable to the handbrake lever (**see illustration**).

### Refitting

25 Connect the equaliser plate to the short front handbrake cable, and screw on the adjuster nut.

26 Work back along both cables, securing them in position with all the relevant clips and ties, and routing them as noted on removal.

27 Insert the cable through the left-hand backplate, and secure it in position with the clip.

**16.8 Remove the rubber grommet (arrowed) and withdraw the cable**

28 Ensure that the cable is securely retained by the clip on the shoe lower pivot point, and refit the rear brake shoe as described in Section 5.

29 Ensure that the brake shoes and adjuster strut components are correctly fitted, then refit the left-hand brake drum as described in Section 7. **Note**: *Do not apply the brake pedal until the right-hand drum has also been installed.*

30 Repeat the operations in paragraphs 27 to 29 on the right-hand brake.

31 Once both drums are in position, with the handbrake fully released, adjust the lining-to-drum clearance by repeatedly depressing the brake pedal 20 to 25 times. Whilst depressing the pedal, have an assistant listen to the rear drums, to check that the adjuster strut is functioning correctly; if so, a clicking sound will be emitted by the strut as the pedal is depressed.

32 Adjust the handbrake cable as described in Section 14.

## 17 Rear brake pressure-regulating valve(s) – removal and refitting

**Note 1:** *Rear brake pressure regulating valves are only fitted to models without ABS. On models with ABS, the pressure regulation is carried out by the ABS hydraulic modulator.*

**Note 2:** *Before starting work, refer to the warning at the beginning of Section 2 concerning the dangers of hydraulic fluid.*

**16.12 Make sure the handbrake cable is located behind the clip (arrowed) correctly**

**16.17 Handbrake linkage/equaliser plate on the Combo Van model**

**16.24 Twist the handbrake short cable (arrowed), to release it from the equaliser plate**

**17.1 Rear brake pressure-regulating valves (arrowed) – 1.0 and 1.2 litre models**

**17.7 Rear brake pressure-regulating valve assembly – Corsa and Corsavan models**

**17.9 Undo the two retaining nuts (arrowed) and remove the spring securing bracket**

## 17 Rear brake pressure-regulating valve(s) – removal and refitting

**Note:** *Before starting work, refer to the warning at the beginning of Section 2 concerning the dangers of hydraulic fluid.*

### Removal

#### 1.0 and 1.2 litre models

1 The rear brake pressure-regulating valves are of the pressure-dependent type, and are located underneath the bonnet of the vehicle, directly above the transmission on the left-hand side of the vehicle **(see illustration)**. There are two valves, one for each rear brake. The purpose of the valves is to prevent the rear wheels locking up under heavy braking.

2 Minimise fluid loss by first removing the master cylinder reservoir cap and screwing it down onto a piece of polythene.

3 Wipe clean the area around the brake pipe unions on the relevant valve, and place absorbent rags beneath the pipe unions to catch any surplus fluid.

4 Retain the relevant pressure-regulating valve with a suitable open-ended spanner, slacken the union nuts and disconnect both brake pipes, and remove the valve from the vehicle. Plug or tape over the pipe ends and valve orifices, to minimise the loss of brake fluid and to prevent the entry of dirt into the system. Wash off any spilt fluid immediately with cold water.

5 Where necessary, remove the other valve in the same way.

6 If renewal is necessary, both valves should be renewed as a matched pair.

#### All other models

7 The pressure-regulating valve is of the load-dependent type, and is mounted underneath the rear of the vehicle. The valve is mounted onto the vehicle underbody, and is connected to the rear axle by a spring **(see illustration)**. As the load being carried by the vehicle is altered, the suspension moves in relation to the vehicle body, altering the tension in the spring. The spring then adjusts the pressure-regulating valve lever so that the correct pressure is applied to the rear brakes to suit the load being carried. The purpose of the valve is to prevent the rear wheels locking up under heavy braking.

8 Minimise fluid loss by first removing the master cylinder reservoir cap and screwing it down onto a piece of polythene.

9 Undo the two retaining nuts from the spring securing bracket **(see illustration)**, then carefully unhook the spring and detach it from the valve.

10 Wipe clean the area around the brake pipe unions on the brake pressure-regulating valve, and place absorbent rags beneath the pipe unions to catch any surplus fluid. Make identification marks on the brake pipes; these marks can then be used on refitting to ensure that each pipe is correctly reconnected **(see illustration)**.

11 Slacken the union nuts, and disconnect the brake pipes from the valve. Plug or tape over the pipe ends and valve orifices, to minimise the loss of brake fluid and to prevent

the entry of dirt into the system. Wash off any spilt fluid immediately with cold water.

12 Undo the two bolts, and remove the pressure-regulating valve from underneath the vehicle **(see illustration)**.

### Refitting

#### 1.0 and 1.2 litre models

13 Refitting is the reverse of the removal procedure, tightening the pipe union nuts to the specified torque setting. On completion, bleed the complete hydraulic system as described in Section 2.

#### All other models

14 Refitting is the reverse of the removal procedure, noting the following points:

   a) *Tighten the valve mounting bolts to the specified torque.*
   b) *Ensure that the brake pipes are correctly connected to the valve, and tighten the union nuts to the specified torque settings.*
   c) *Coat the ends of the spring with grease prior to installation.*
   d) *Bleed the complete hydraulic system as described in Section 2.*

15 On completion, adjust the valve as follows.

16 With the vehicle completely unladen and approximately 5 litres of fuel in the fuel tank, position the car over an inspection pit, or drive it onto ramps so that it is resting on all four wheels.

17 Make sure the spring on the pressure-regulating valve is not under any tension.

18 Remove the clamping screw from the pressure-regulating valve spring **(see illustration)**.

**17.10 Brake pipe unions (arrowed) on the valve**

**7.12 Undo the two retaining bolts (arrowed) to remove the valve**

**17.18 Slacken the clamping screw (arrowed) to adjust the spring**

**18.4a Pull out the centre actuating pin arrowed (switch removed for clarity) . . .**

**18.4b . . . and unclip the locking sleeve (arrowed) . . .**

**18.5 . . . then withdraw the switch from the pedal bracket**

**19** Move the spring forwards or backwards until it lies against the regulator lever without tension. Refit the clamping screw (using thread locking compound) and tighten to specified torque. Repeat procedure if required.

## 18 Stop-light switch –
removal and refitting

### Removal

**1** The stop-light switch is located on the pedal bracket in the driver's footwell, behind the facia.
**2** To remove the switch, the lower facia trim will have to be removed for improved access (see Chapter 11), then remove the securing clip and withdraw the heating duct.
**3** Disconnect the wiring plug from the stop-light switch.
**4** Push the brake pedal down, pull out the brake switch actuating pin, then unclip the locking sleeve from around the actuating pin **(see illustrations)**.
**5** Release the securing clips and pull the switch to disengage it from the pedal mounting bracket **(see illustration)**.

### Refitting

**6** Refitting is a reversal of removal, making sure the locking sleeve is located correctly.

## 19 Anti-lock Braking System (ABS) –
general information

The Bosch 8.0 anti-lock braking system comprises a hydraulic modulator unit and the four wheel speed sensors. The modulator unit contains the electronic control unit (ECU), the hydraulic solenoid valves and the electrically-driven return pump. The purpose of the system is to prevent the wheel(s) locking during heavy braking. This is achieved by automatic release of the brake on the relevant wheel, followed by re-application of the brake.

The solenoid valves are controlled by the ECU, which itself receives signals from the four wheel speed sensors which monitor the speed of rotation of each wheel. By comparing these signals, the ECU can determine the speed at which the vehicle is travelling. It can then use this speed to determine when a wheel is decelerating at an abnormal rate, compared to the speed of the vehicle, and therefore predicts when a wheel is about to lock. During normal operation, the system functions in the same way as a non-ABS braking system.

If the ECU senses that a wheel is about to lock, it closes the relevant outlet solenoid valves in the hydraulic unit, which then isolates the relevant brake(s) on the wheel(s) which is/are about to lock from the master cylinder, effectively sealing-in the hydraulic pressure.

If the speed of rotation of the wheel continues to decrease at an abnormal rate, the ECU opens the inlet solenoid valves on the relevant brake(s), and operates the electrically-driven return pump which pumps the hydraulic fluid back into the master cylinder, releasing the brake. Once the speed of rotation of the wheel returns to an acceptable rate, the pump stops; the solenoid valves switch again, allowing the hydraulic master cylinder pressure to return to the caliper or wheel cylinder, which then re-applies the brake. This cycle can be carried out many times a second.

The action of the solenoid valves and return pump creates pulses in the hydraulic circuit. When the ABS system is functioning, these pulses can be felt through the brake pedal.

The operation of the ABS system is entirely dependent on electrical signals. To prevent the system responding to any inaccurate signals, a built-in safety circuit monitors all signals received by the ECU. If an inaccurate signal or low battery voltage is detected, the ABS system is automatically shut-down, and the warning light on the instrument panel is illuminated, to inform the driver that the ABS system is not operational. Normal braking should still be available, however.

Additional safety features are also incorporated into the ABS system. These include electronic brake force distribution, which automatically apportions braking effort between the front and rear wheels, and emergency brake assist, which guarantees full braking effort in the event of an emergency stop by monitoring the rate at which the brake pedal is depressed.

Should a fault develop in the system, the ECU illuminates a warning light on the instrument panel constantly. To facilitate fault diagnosis, the system is provided with an on-board diagnostic facility. In the event of a fault, the ECU stores a series of fault codes for subsequent read-out and diagnosis. If the instrument panel warning light remains on after the engine has been started, the vehicle must be taken to a Vauxhall dealer or suitably-equipped diagnostic specialist for fault diagnosis and repair.

## 20 Anti-lock Braking System (ABS) components –
removal and refitting

### Hydraulic modulator assembly

**Note:** *Before starting work, refer to the note at the beginning of Section 2 concerning the dangers of hydraulic fluid.*

**Removal**

**1** Disconnect the battery negative terminal (refer to *Disconnecting the battery* in the Reference Chapter).
**2** Pull up the locking bar and disconnect the wiring harness multiplug connector from the electronic control unit located on the hydraulic modulator **(see illustrations)**.
**3** Unscrew the master cylinder reservoir filler cap, and top-up the reservoir to the MAX mark (see *Weekly checks*). Place a piece of polythene over the filler neck, and secure the polythene with the filler cap. This will minimise brake fluid loss during subsequent

**20.2 Pull up the locking bar and disconnect the multiplug connector from the electronic control unit**

20.17 Disconnect the wiring connector . . .

20.18a . . . then undo the retaining bolt (arrowed) . . .

20.18b . . . and remove the front wheel speed sensor from the vehicle

operations. As a precaution, place absorbent rags beneath the modulator brake pipe unions when unscrewing them.

4 Wipe clean the area around the modulator brake pipe unions, then make a note of how the pipes are arranged, to use as a reference on refitting. Unscrew the union nuts, and carefully withdraw the pipes.

5 Plug or tape over the pipe ends and modulator orifices, to minimise the loss of brake fluid and to prevent the entry of dirt into the system. Wash off any spilt fluid immediately with cold water.

6 Slacken and remove the two mounting nuts, and release the modulator assembly from its mounting bracket. Remove the assembly from the engine compartment.

### Refitting

7 Refitting is the reverse of the removal procedure, noting the following points:

a) Tighten the modulator block mounting nuts to the specified torque setting.

b) Refit the brake pipes to their respective unions, and tighten the union nuts to the specified torque.

c) Ensure that the wiring is correctly routed, and that the multiplug connector is firmly pressed into position and secured with the locking bar.

d) On completion, and prior to refitting the battery, bleed the complete hydraulic system as described in Section 2. Ensure that the system is bled in the correct order, to prevent air entering the modulator return pump.

### Electronic control unit (ECU)

**Caution: Separation of the ECU from the hydraulic modulator is not recommended by the manufacturers of the ABS system (Bosch). Information on this operation is, however, given by Vauxhall. If difficulties are experienced when refitting the ECU to the modulator, it may be necessary to renew the complete assembly.**

**Note:** New ECU retaining screws will be required for refitting.

### Removal

8 Remove the hydraulic modulator from the car as described previously in this Section.

9 Undo the four retaining screws and carefully withdraw the ECU upwards and off the hydraulic modulator. Recover the gasket.

### Refitting

10 Prior to refitting, clean and then carefully inspect, the condition of the gasket sealing surfaces on the ECU and hydraulic modulator. If the surfaces are in any way deformed, damaged, or rough to the extent that a perfect gasket seal cannot be maintained, the complete modulator and ECU assembly must be renewed.

11 With the gasket in position, and holding the ECU by the outer edges, carefully lower it over the solenoid valves on the modulator, keeping it square and level.

12 Fit the four new retaining screws, and tighten them evenly and progressively until they all just make contact with the ECU body. Continue tightening the screws alternately and progressively until the ECU body just makes contact with the hydraulic modulator.

13 Progressively, and working in a diagonal sequence, tighten the screws to the specified torque. The ECU must make complete contact with the hydraulic modulator, with no visible gap around any of the sealing area. If this cannot be achieved, release all the screws and tighten them progressively again. If it is still not possible to obtain correct seating of the unit, the complete assembly must be renewed.

14 On completion, refit the hydraulic modulator as described previously in this Section.

### Front wheel speed sensor

**Note:** The front wheel speed sensors also provide the vehicle roadspeed signal to the various system ECUs as required. One, or both wheel speed sensors are therefore also fitted to models without ABS.

### Removal

15 Disconnect the battery negative terminal (refer to Disconnecting the battery in the Reference Chapter).

16 Firmly apply the handbrake, then jack up the front of the car and support it securely on axle stands (see Jacking and vehicle support). Remove the appropriate front roadwheel.

17 Trace the wheel speed sensor wiring back

to its wiring connector, and release it from its retaining clip. Disconnect the connector **(see illustration)**, and work back along the sensor wiring, freeing it from all the relevant retaining clips and ties.

18 Slacken and remove the bolt securing the sensor to the mounting bracket, and remove the sensor and lead assembly from the vehicle **(see illustrations)**.

### Refitting

19 Prior to refitting, apply a thin coat of multipurpose grease to the sensor mounting bracket.

20 Ensure that the sensor and mounting bracket sealing faces are clean, then fit the sensor to the hub. Refit the retaining bolt, and tighten it to the specified torque.

21 Ensure that the sensor wiring is correctly routed, and retained by all the necessary clips. Reconnect it to its wiring connector, and fit the connector into the retaining clip.

22 Refit the roadwheel, aligning the marks made on removal, then lower the vehicle to the ground and tighten the roadwheel bolts to the specified torque.

### Rear wheel speed sensor

23 The rear wheel sensors is part of the rear hub/stub axle assembly. At the time of writing, the sensor could not be bought separately; see your local Vauxhall dealer.

24 To remove the hub/stub axle units, refer to the relevant Section in Chapter 10.

### Front wheel speed sensor toothed rings

25 The front toothed rings are an integral part of the driveshaft outer constant velocity (CV) joints, and cannot be renewed separately. Examine the rings for such damage as chipped or missing teeth. If renewal is necessary, the complete outer constant velocity joint must be renewed, as described in Chapter 8.

### Rear wheel speed sensor toothed rings

### Removal

26 The rear sensor pick-up rings are on the inside of the rear brake drums, remove the rear brake drum as described in Section 7.

27 Examine the rings for signs of damage

**21.2a Unclip the expansion tank coolant hose and the wiring harness from the crash box . . .**

**21.2b . . . and disconnect the harness connector**

**21.3 Release the retaining clip and lift the expansion tank from its location**

**21.4a Unscrew the outer retaining nut (arrowed) and slacken the inner nut . . .**

**21.4b . . . then remove the crash box from the bulkhead**

such as chipped or missing teeth, use a puller to withdraw the ring from the inside of the brake drum.

### Refitting

**28** Refit the sensor pick-up ring to the inside of the brake drum, taking care not to damage it as it is being pressed onto the hub assembly. Refitting is the reverse of the removal procedure.

## 21 Vacuum pump (diesel engine models) – removal and refitting

### Removal

**1** Remove the fuel filter as described in Chapter 1B.
**2** Unclip the expansion tank coolant hose and the wiring harness from the fuel filter crash box, and disconnect the harness connector **(see illustrations)**.
**3** Release the retaining clip, lift the coolant expansion tank from its location and place it to one side **(see illustration)**.
**4** Unscrew the outer retaining nut, slacken the inner nut and remove the crash box from the bulkhead **(see illustrations)**.

**5** Disconnect the vacuum hose at the quick-release fitting on the pump **(see illustration)**.
**6** Unscrew the two mounting bolts and remove the vacuum pump from the camshaft housing **(see illustration)**. Recover the gasket.
**7** Thoroughly clean the mating faces on the cylinder head and vacuum pump and obtain a new gasket for refitting.

### Refitting

**8** Place a new gasket in position on the vacuum pump. Turn the pump shaft to align the drive dog with the slots in the end of the camshaft, then locate the pump on the cylinder head.
**9** Refit the two pump mounting bolts and tighten them to the specified Stage 1 torque setting, then to the Stage 2 setting.
**10** Reconnect the vacuum hose to the pump outlet.
**11** Refit the fuel filter crash box and the expansion tank.
**12** Reconnect the wiring connector, then secure the harness and coolant hose in position on the crash box.
**13** Refit the fuel filter as described in Chapter 1B.

**21.5 Disconnect the vacuum hose (arrowed) at the quick-release fitting on the pump**

**21.6 Unscrew the two mounting bolts (arrowed) and remove the vacuum pump from the camshaft housing**

# Chapter 10
# Suspension and steering

## Contents

## Degrees of difficulty

| Easy, suitable for novice with little experience | Fairly easy, suitable for beginner with some experience | Fairly difficult, suitable for competent DIY mechanic | Difficult, suitable for experienced DIY mechanic | Very difficult, suitable for expert DIY or professional |
|---|---|---|---|---|

## Specifications

**Front suspension**

Type . . . . . . . . . . . . . . . . . . . . . . . . . . . . . . . . . . . . . . . . . . . Independent, with MacPherson struts and anti-roll bar

**Rear suspension**

Type . . . . . . . . . . . . . . . . . . . . . . . . . . . . . . . . . . . . . . . . . . . Semi-independent torsion beam, with trailing arms, coil springs and
telescopic shock absorbers. Anti-roll bar on some models

**Steering**

Type . . . . . . . . . . . . . . . . . . . . . . . . . . . . . . . . . . . . . . . . . . . Rack-and-pinion. Electric motor in EPS steering column

**Front wheel alignment and steering angles**

Camber angle:
  All models except Sport:
    Corsa and Corsavan. . . . . . . . . . . . . . . . . . . . . . . . . . . . . . . -1°10' ± 45'
    Corsa ECO . . . . . . . . . . . . . . . . . . . . . . . . . . . . . . . . . . . . -1°25' ± 45'
    Combo Van. . . . . . . . . . . . . . . . . . . . . . . . . . . . . . . . . . . . -1°05' ± 45'
  Sport models . . . . . . . . . . . . . . . . . . . . . . . . . . . . . . . . . . . -1°20' ± 45'
  Maximum difference between sides. . . . . . . . . . . . . . . . . . . . . 1°
Castor angle:
  All models except Sport:
    Corsa and Corsavan. . . . . . . . . . . . . . . . . . . . . . . . . . . . . . . 1°35' ± 1°
    Corsa ECO . . . . . . . . . . . . . . . . . . . . . . . . . . . . . . . . . . . . 1°40' ± 1°
    Combo Van. . . . . . . . . . . . . . . . . . . . . . . . . . . . . . . . . . . . 1°25' ± 1°
    Combo Van with increased pay load . . . . . . . . . . . . . . . . . . . 1°15' ± 1°
  Sport models . . . . . . . . . . . . . . . . . . . . . . . . . . . . . . . . . . . 1°30' ± 1°
  Maximum difference between sides. . . . . . . . . . . . . . . . . . . . . 1°
Toe setting:
  Corsa and Corsavan. . . . . . . . . . . . . . . . . . . . . . . . . . . . . . . +0°10' ± 10'
  Combo Van. . . . . . . . . . . . . . . . . . . . . . . . . . . . . . . . . . . . -0°10' ± 10'

## Rear wheel alignment

Camber angle (not adjustable):
| | |
|---|---|
| Corsa and Corsavan . . . . . . . . . . . . . . . . . . . . . . . . . . . . . . . . . . . . . . . . . . . . . . . | -1°30' ± 30' |
| Combo Van . . . . . . . . . . . . . . . . . . . . . . . . . . . . . . . . . . . . . . . . . . . . . . . . . . . . . | -1°40' ± 30' |
| Maximum difference between sides . . . . . . . . . . . . . . . . . . . . . . . . . . | 35' |

Toe setting (not adjustable):
| | |
|---|---|
| Corsa and Corsavan . . . . . . . . . . . . . . . . . . . . . . . . . . . . . . . . . . . . . . . . . . . . . . | +0°10' +30' / -15' |
| Combo Van . . . . . . . . . . . . . . . . . . . . . . . . . . . . . . . . . . . . . . . . . . . . . . . . . . . . . | +0°00' +30' / -15' |
| Maximum difference between sides . . . . . . . . . . . . . . . . . . . . . . . . . . | 15' |

## Torque wrench settings

| | Nm | lbf ft |
|---|---|---|
| **Steering** | | |
| Airbag unit to steering wheel . . . . . . . . . . . . . . . . . . . . . . . . . . . . . . . . | 8 | 6 |
| Intermediate shaft-to-steering pinion clamp bolts . . . . . . . . . . . . . . . | 24 | 18 |
| Steering column mounting bolts . . . . . . . . . . . . . . . . . . . . . . . . . . . . . | 22 | 16 |
| Steering column-to-intermediate shaft clamp bolt: | | |
| Stage 1 . . . . . . . . . . . . . . . . . . . . . . . . . . . . . . . . . . . . . . . . . . . . . . . . | 24 | 18 |
| Stage 2 . . . . . . . . . . . . . . . . . . . . . . . . . . . . . . . . . . . . . . . . . . . . . . . . | Angle tighten a further 60° | |
| Steering gear-to-front axle body bolts*: | | |
| Stage 1 . . . . . . . . . . . . . . . . . . . . . . . . . . . . . . . . . . . . . . . . . . . . . . . . | 45 | 33 |
| Stage 2 . . . . . . . . . . . . . . . . . . . . . . . . . . . . . . . . . . . . . . . . . . . . . . . . | Angle tighten a further 45° | |
| Stage 3 . . . . . . . . . . . . . . . . . . . . . . . . . . . . . . . . . . . . . . . . . . . . . . . . | Angle tighten a further 15° | |
| Steering wheel bolt . . . . . . . . . . . . . . . . . . . . . . . . . . . . . . . . . . . . . . . | 25 | 18 |
| Track rod axial joint to steering rack . . . . . . . . . . . . . . . . . . . . . . . . . . | 70 | 52 |
| Track rod balljoint locknut . . . . . . . . . . . . . . . . . . . . . . . . . . . . . . . . . . | 50 | 37 |
| Track rod balljoint-to-swivel hub nut* . . . . . . . . . . . . . . . . . . . . . . . . . | 35 | 26 |
| | | |
| **Front suspension** | | |
| Anti-roll bar clamp bolts . . . . . . . . . . . . . . . . . . . . . . . . . . . . . . . . . . . | 20 | 15 |
| Balljoint-to-lower arm bolts/nuts* . . . . . . . . . . . . . . . . . . . . . . . . . . . | 55 | 41 |
| Brake caliper mounting bracket-to-swivel hub bolts . . . . . . . . . . . . . | 100 | 74 |
| Driveshaft retaining nut*: | | |
| Stage 1 . . . . . . . . . . . . . . . . . . . . . . . . . . . . . . . . . . . . . . . . . . . . . . . . | 120 | 89 |
| Stage 2 . . . . . . . . . . . . . . . . . . . . . . . . . . . . . . . . . . . . . . . . . . . . . . . . | Slacken the nut completely | |
| Stage 3 . . . . . . . . . . . . . . . . . . . . . . . . . . . . . . . . . . . . . . . . . . . . . . . . | 20 | 15 |
| Stage 4 . . . . . . . . . . . . . . . . . . . . . . . . . . . . . . . . . . . . . . . . . . . . . . . . | Angle-tighten a further 90° | |
| Front subframe mounting bolts*: | | |
| Stage 1 . . . . . . . . . . . . . . . . . . . . . . . . . . . . . . . . . . . . . . . . . . . . . . . . | 90 | 66 |
| Stage 2 . . . . . . . . . . . . . . . . . . . . . . . . . . . . . . . . . . . . . . . . . . . . . . . . | Angle-tighten a further 45° | |
| Stage 3 . . . . . . . . . . . . . . . . . . . . . . . . . . . . . . . . . . . . . . . . . . . . . . . . | Angle-tighten a further 15° | |
| Link rod-to-strut nut* . . . . . . . . . . . . . . . . . . . . . . . . . . . . . . . . . . . . . | 65 | 48 |
| Link rod-to-anti-roll bar nut* . . . . . . . . . . . . . . . . . . . . . . . . . . . . . . . . | 65 | 48 |
| Lower arm balljoint clamp bolt nut* . . . . . . . . . . . . . . . . . . . . . . . . . . | 60 | 44 |
| Lower arm pivot bolts/nut to engine subframe*: | | |
| Stage 1 . . . . . . . . . . . . . . . . . . . . . . . . . . . . . . . . . . . . . . . . . . . . . . . . | 90 | 66 |
| Stage 2 . . . . . . . . . . . . . . . . . . . . . . . . . . . . . . . . . . . . . . . . . . . . . . . . | Angle-tighten a further 75° | |
| Stage 3 . . . . . . . . . . . . . . . . . . . . . . . . . . . . . . . . . . . . . . . . . . . . . . . . | Angle-tighten a further 15° | |
| Lower arm-to-inner front bush bolts/nuts* . . . . . . . . . . . . . . . . . . . . | 55 | 41 |
| Suspension strut piston rod upper mounting nut* . . . . . . . . . . . . . . . | 50 | 37 |
| Suspension strut-to-swivel hub bolts*: | | |
| Stage 1 . . . . . . . . . . . . . . . . . . . . . . . . . . . . . . . . . . . . . . . . . . . . . . . . | 80 | 59 |
| Stage 2 . . . . . . . . . . . . . . . . . . . . . . . . . . . . . . . . . . . . . . . . . . . . . . . . | Angle-tighten a further 60° | |
| Stage 3 . . . . . . . . . . . . . . . . . . . . . . . . . . . . . . . . . . . . . . . . . . . . . . . . | Angle-tighten a further 15° | |
| Suspension strut upper mounting nut . . . . . . . . . . . . . . . . . . . . . . . . . | 55 | 41 |
| Wheel sensor retaining bracket bolt . . . . . . . . . . . . . . . . . . . . . . . . . . | 8 | 6 |
| **Rear suspension – Corsa and Corsavan models** | | |
| Anti-roll bar bolts*: | | |
| Stage 1 . . . . . . . . . . . . . . . . . . . . . . . . . . . . . . . . . . . . . . . . . . . . . . . . | 60 | 44 |
| Stage 2 . . . . . . . . . . . . . . . . . . . . . . . . . . . . . . . . . . . . . . . . . . . . . . . . | Angle-tighten a further 15° | |
| Drum/hub nut* . . . . . . . . . . . . . . . . . . . . . . . . . . . . . . . . . . . . . . . . . . | 175 | 129 |
| Shock absorber: | | |
| Lower bolt: | | |
| M10 x 1.25 bolt . . . . . . . . . . . . . . . . . . . . . . . . . . . . . . . . . . . . . . . | 65 | 48 |
| M14 x 1.50 bolt . . . . . . . . . . . . . . . . . . . . . . . . . . . . . . . . . . . . . . . | 110 | 81 |
| Upper nut . . . . . . . . . . . . . . . . . . . . . . . . . . . . . . . . . . . . . . . . . . . . . | 20 | 15 |

## Torque wrench settings (continued)

| | Nm | lbf ft |
|---|---|---|
| **Rear suspension – Corsa and Corsavan models (continued)** | | |
| Stub axle bolts*: | | |
| Stage 1 . . . . . . . . . . . . . . . . . . . . . . . . . . . . . . . . . . . . . . . . . . . . . . . . | 50 | 37 |
| Stage 2 . . . . . . . . . . . . . . . . . . . . . . . . . . . . . . . . . . . . . . . . . . . . . . . . | Angle-tighten a further 30° | |
| Stage 3 . . . . . . . . . . . . . . . . . . . . . . . . . . . . . . . . . . . . . . . . . . . . . . . . | Angle-tighten a further 15° | |
| Trailing arm pivot bolts*: | | |
| Stage 1 . . . . . . . . . . . . . . . . . . . . . . . . . . . . . . . . . . . . . . . . . . . . . . . . | 50 | 37 |
| Stage 2 . . . . . . . . . . . . . . . . . . . . . . . . . . . . . . . . . . . . . . . . . . . . . . . . | Angle-tighten a further 45° | |
| Stage 3 . . . . . . . . . . . . . . . . . . . . . . . . . . . . . . . . . . . . . . . . . . . . . . . . | Angle-tighten a further 15° | |
| **Rear suspension – Combo Van models** | | |
| Shock absorber: | | |
| Lower bolt . . . . . . . . . . . . . . . . . . . . . . . . . . . . . . . . . . . . . . . . . . . . . | 110 | 81 |
| Upper bolt . . . . . . . . . . . . . . . . . . . . . . . . . . . . . . . . . . . . . . . . . . . . . | 90 | 66 |
| Stub axle/bearing unit bolts*: | | |
| Stage 1 . . . . . . . . . . . . . . . . . . . . . . . . . . . . . . . . . . . . . . . . . . . . . . . . | 50 | 37 |
| Stage 2 . . . . . . . . . . . . . . . . . . . . . . . . . . . . . . . . . . . . . . . . . . . . . . . . | Angle-tighten a further 30° | |
| Stage 3 . . . . . . . . . . . . . . . . . . . . . . . . . . . . . . . . . . . . . . . . . . . . . . . . | Angle-tighten a further 15° | |
| Trailing arm mounting bolts*: | | |
| Stage 1 . . . . . . . . . . . . . . . . . . . . . . . . . . . . . . . . . . . . . . . . . . . . . . . . | 90 | 66 |
| Stage 2 . . . . . . . . . . . . . . . . . . . . . . . . . . . . . . . . . . . . . . . . . . . . . . . . | Angle-tighten a further 30° | |
| Stage 3 . . . . . . . . . . . . . . . . . . . . . . . . . . . . . . . . . . . . . . . . . . . . . . . . | Angle-tighten a further 15° | |
| Trailing arm pivot centre bolt*: | | |
| Stage 1 . . . . . . . . . . . . . . . . . . . . . . . . . . . . . . . . . . . . . . . . . . . . . . . . | 90 | 66 |
| Stage 2 . . . . . . . . . . . . . . . . . . . . . . . . . . . . . . . . . . . . . . . . . . . . . . . . | Angle-tighten a further 60° | |
| Stage 3 . . . . . . . . . . . . . . . . . . . . . . . . . . . . . . . . . . . . . . . . . . . . . . . . | Angle-tighten a further 15° | |
| **Roadwheels** | | |
| Roadwheel bolts . . . . . . . . . . . . . . . . . . . . . . . . . . . . . . . . . . . . . . . . | 110 | 81 |

*Use new nuts/bolts.*

## 1  General information

The independent front suspension is of the MacPherson strut type, incorporating coil springs and integral telescopic shock absorbers. The MacPherson struts are located by transverse lower suspension arms, which utilise rubber inner mounting bushes, and incorporate a balljoint at the outer ends. The front swivel hubs, which carry the wheel bearings, brake calipers and the hub/disc assemblies, are bolted to the MacPherson struts, and connected to the lower arms via the balljoints. A front anti-roll bar is fitted, which has link rods with balljoints at each end to connect it to the strut.

The rear suspension is of semi-independent type, consisting of a torsion beam axle and trailing arms, with double-conical coil springs and telescopic shock absorbers. The front ends of the trailing arms are attached to the vehicle underbody by horizontal bushes; the rear ends are located by the shock absorbers, which are bolted to the underbody at their upper ends. The coil springs are mounted independently of the shock absorbers, and act directly between the trailing arms and the underbody. Certain models are fitted with an anti-roll bar, which is bolted onto the underside of each trailing arm.

The steering column is linked to the steering gear by an intermediate shaft. The intermediate shaft has a universal joint fitted to its upper end, and is secured to the column by a clamp bolt. The lower end of the intermediate shaft is attached to the steering gear pinion by means of a clamp bolt.

The rack-and-pinion type steering gear is rubber-mounted onto the engine compartment bulkhead, and is connected by two track rods, with balljoints at their outer ends, to the steering arms projecting rearwards from the swivel hubs. The track rod ends are threaded, to facilitate adjustment.

Electric power-assisted steering is fitted as standard, whereby an electric motor, drive gear assembly and torque sensor incorporated in the upper steering column provide a variable degree of power assistance according to roadspeed. The system is controlled by an electronic control unit with self-diagnostic capability, located on the steering column.

**2.2  Extract the split pin from the driveshaft retaining nut**

## 2  Front swivel hub assembly – removal and refitting

**Note:** *New retaining nuts and/or bolts will be required for most attachments when refitting (see text).*

 **HAYNES HiNT**  *If work is being carried out without the aid of an assistant, remove the wheel trim/hub cap (as applicable), then withdraw the split pin and slacken the driveshaft retaining nut prior to jacking up the vehicle.*

### Removal

**1** Firmly apply the handbrake, then jack up the front of the car and support it securely on axle stands (see *Jacking and vehicle support*). Remove the appropriate front roadwheel.
**2** Where fitted, remove the dust cap from the centre of the hub assembly, then extract the split pin from the driveshaft retaining nut and discard it; a new one must be used on refitting **(see illustration)**.
**3** Refit at least two roadwheel bolts to the

**2.3 Using a fabricated tool to hold the front hub stationary whilst the driveshaft retaining nut is slackened**

**2.6 Undo the bolt (arrowed) and remove the wheel speed sensor – where applicable**

**2.8 Withdraw the clamp bolt, and free the lower arm balljoint from the swivel hub**

front hub, and tighten them securely. Have an assistant firmly depress the brake pedal to prevent the front hub from rotating, then using a socket and extension bar, slacken and remove the driveshaft retaining nut. Alternatively, a tool can be fabricated from two lengths of steel strip (one long, one short) and a nut and bolt; the nut and bolt forming the pivot of a forked tool. Bolt the tool to the hub using two wheel bolts, and hold the tool to prevent the hub from rotating as the driveshaft retaining nut is undone **(see illustration)**.

4 Unscrew the driveshaft retaining nut, and remove the washer. Discard the nut and washer; new ones must be used on refitting.

5 Remove the brake disc as described in Chapter 9. The procedure involves removing the brake caliper, using a piece of wire or string, tie the caliper to the front suspension coil spring to avoid placing any strain on the hydraulic brake hose.

6 Where applicable, undo the bolt securing the wheel speed sensor mounting bracket to the swivel hub, and position the sensor assembly clear of the hub **(see illustration)**.

7 Slacken and remove the nut securing the steering gear track rod balljoint to the swivel hub, and release the balljoint tapered shank using a universal balljoint separator. Discard the nut; it should be renewed whenever it is disturbed.

8 Unscrew and remove the lower arm balljoint clamp bolt nut, and withdraw the clamp bolt from the swivel hub, noting which way round it is fitted **(see illustration)**. Discard the clamp bolt nut; a new one must be used on refitting.

9 Using a suitable lever, push down the lower

arm to separate the balljoint from the swivel hub. When releasing the lower arm, take care not to damage the balljoint rubber boot; if necessary protect it with a piece of card or plastic. **Note:** *If the balljoint stub is tight in the swivel hub, use a screwdriver or cold chisel as a wedge to force the clamp apart.*

10 Slacken and remove the two nuts and bolts securing the suspension strut to the swivel hub, noting which way around the bolts are inserted **(see illustration)**. Discard the nuts and bolts; they should be renewed whenever they are disturbed.

11 Carefully pull the swivel hub assembly outwards, and withdraw the driveshaft outer constant velocity joint from the hub assembly. If necessary, the shaft can be tapped out of the hub using a soft-faced mallet. Support the driveshaft by suspending it with wire or string, and do not allow it to hang under its own weight. Remove the hub assembly from the vehicle.

### Refitting

12 Ensure that the driveshaft outer constant velocity joint and hub splines are clean, then slide the hub onto the driveshaft splines. Fit the washer and new driveshaft retaining nut, tightening it by hand only at this stage **(see illustration)**.

13 Engage the swivel hub with the suspension strut, and insert the new bolts from the front of the strut so that their threads are facing to the rear. Fit the new nuts, tightening them by hand only at this stage.

14 Locate the lower arm balljoint in the swivel hub. Insert the clamp bolt from the front of the

swivel hub, so that its threads are facing to the rear. Fit the new nut to the clamp bolt, and tighten it to the specified torque setting.

15 With the hub correctly located, tighten the strut-to-swivel hub bolts through the various stages given in the Specifications at the start of this Chapter.

16 Engage the track rod balljoint in the swivel hub, then fit the new retaining nut and tighten it to the specified torque setting.

17 Refit the brake disc and caliper to the swivel hub, referring to Chapter 9 for further information.

18 Where necessary, refit the ABS wheel speed sensor to the hub, making sure it is located correctly, and tighten the retaining bolt to the specified torque.

19 Using the method employed on removal to prevent rotation, tighten the driveshaft retaining nut through the stages given in the Specifications.

20 With the nut correctly tightened, secure it in position with a new split pin. If the holes in the driveshaft are not aligned with any of the slots in the nut, loosen **(do not tighten)** the nut by the *smallest possible amount* until the split pin can be inserted.

21 Refit the roadwheel, then lower the vehicle to the ground and tighten the roadwheel bolts to the specified torque. Refit the wheel trim/hub cap, where applicable.

### 3 Front hub bearings – renewal

**Note 1:** *The bearing is sealed, pre-adjusted and pre-lubricated. Never overtighten the driveshaft nut beyond the specified torque setting in an attempt to 'adjust' the bearing.*
**Note 2:** *A press will be required to dismantle and rebuild the assembly; if such a tool is not available, a large bench vice and spacers (such as large sockets) will serve as an adequate substitute. The bearing's inner races are an interference fit on the hub; if the inner race remains on the hub flange when it is pressed out of the swivel hub, a knife-edged bearing puller will be required to remove it.*

1 Remove the swivel hub assembly as described in Section 2.

**2.10 Unscrew the nuts and withdraw the bolts securing the suspension strut to the swivel hub**

**2.12 Engage the swivel hub with the driveshaft constant velocity joint**

**3.2 Disc shield retaining screws are accessed through holes in the hub flange**

**3.3a Using a socket to drift out the hub flange from the bearing**

**3.3b Use a chisel to remove the inner bearing race from the hub flange**

**3.4 Use circlip pliers to remove the circlip**

**3.5 Using a drift to remove the bearing from the swivel hub**

**3.8 Use a threaded rod and spacers to press the bearing squarely into position . . .**

**2** Align the holes in the hub and undo the screws, to remove the brake disc shield from the hub **(see illustration)**.

**3** Support the swivel hub securely on blocks or in a vice. Using a tubular spacer/socket which bears only on the inner end of the hub flange, press the hub flange out of the bearing. If the bearing's outboard inner race remains on the hub, remove it using a bearing puller – see note above **(see illustrations)**.

**4** Extract the bearing retaining circlip from the swivel hub assembly **(see illustration)**.

**5** Using a drift or tubular spacer which bears only on the inner race, press the complete bearing assembly out of the swivel hub **(see illustration)**.

**6** Thoroughly clean the hub and swivel hub, removing all traces of dirt and grease. Polish away any burrs or raised edges which might hinder reassembly. Check both assemblies for

cracks or any other signs of wear or damage, and renew as necessary. Renew the circlip regardless of its apparent condition.

**7** On reassembly, apply a light film of oil to the bearing outer race and hub flange shaft, to aid installation of the bearing. Remove all traces of old thread-locking compound from the disc shield retaining screw holes, ideally by running a tap of the correct size and pitch through them.

**8** Securely support the swivel hub, and locate the bearing in the hub. Press the bearing fully into position, ensuring that it enters the hub squarely, using the old wheel bearing or a tubular spacer which bears only on the bearing outer race **(see illustration)**.

**9** Once the bearing is correctly seated, secure the bearing in position with the new inner circlip. Make sure that the circlip is correctly located in its groove **(see illustration)**.

**10** Securely support the swivel hub in a vice,

then locate the hub flange into the bearing inner race. Press the flange into the swivel hub bearing, using a tubular spacer/sockets and threaded rod, until it seats against the hub shoulder **(see illustration)**. Check that the hub flange rotates freely, and wipe off any excess oil or grease.

**11** Fit the disc shield to the hub assembly **(see illustration)**, and apply a few drops of thread-locking compound to the new screws. Fit the screws, and tighten them securely.

**12** Refit the swivel hub assembly as described in Section 2.

**4   Front strut –**
removal, overhaul and refitting

**Note:** *When refitting, new strut-to-swivel hub bolts and nuts, and strut link rod nut, will be required.*

**3.9 . . . then refit the circlip securely into the groove (arrowed)**

**3.10 Using a threaded rod and spacers/ sockets to press the hub flange into the bearing**

**3.11 Refit the disc shield to the hub assembly**

**4.2 Hold the joint stub with an open-ended spanner and undo the retaining nut (arrowed)**

**4.4 Unscrew the nuts and withdraw the bolts (arrowed) securing the suspension strut to the swivel hub**

**4.5a Remove the plastic cap, unscrew the mounting nut (arrowed) . . .**

**4.5b . . . and withdraw the upper retaining plate**

**4.6 Release the lower end of the strut from the swivel hub**

## Removal

**1** Firmly apply the handbrake, then jack up the front of the car and support it securely on axle stands (see *Jacking and vehicle support*). Remove the appropriate roadwheel.

**2** Unscrew the retaining nut and disconnect

the anti-roll bar link rod from the strut, discard it; a new one should be used on refitting. Use a spanner on the flats to hold the link while the nut is being loosened **(see illustration)**.

**3** Where applicable, release the front wheel

speed sensor wiring from its clip on the suspension strut.

**4** Slacken and remove the two nuts and bolts securing the suspension strut to the swivel hub. Discard both nuts and bolts; these must be renewed whenever they are disturbed **(see illustration)**.

**5** Support the front strut assembly then, from within the engine compartment, remove the plastic cap from the upper strut mounting. Unscrew the suspension strut upper mounting nut and remove the retaining plate **(see illustrations)**.

**6** Release the strut from the swivel hub, and withdraw it from under the wheel arch **(see illustration)**.

## Overhaul

**Note:** *A spring compressor tool will be required for this operation. Before overhaul, mark the position of each component in relationship with each other for reassembly.*

**7** With the suspension strut resting on a bench, or clamped in a vice, fit a spring compressor tool, and compress the coil spring to relieve the pressure on the spring seats. Ensure that the compressor tool is securely located on the spring, in accordance with the tool manufacturer's instructions **(see illustration)**.

**8** Mark the position of the spring relevant to the top and bottom mountings, then counter-hold the strut piston rod with a spanner, and unscrew the piston rod nut **(see illustration)**.

**9** Remove the upper damping ring with support bearing and upper spring seat **(see illustration)**.

**10** Remove the spring and buffer from the strut **(see illustrations)**.

**4.7 Ensure that the compressor tool is securely located on the spring**

**4.8 Counterhold the strut piston rod with a spanner, and unscrew the piston rod nut**

**4.9 Withdraw the upper damping ring . . .**

**4.10a . . . and the coil spring . . .**

**4.10b . . . then the buffer**

**4.15 Locate the spring against the raised stop (arrowed) in the strut**

**11** With the strut assembly now completely dismantled, examine all the components for wear, damage or deformation, and check the support bearing for smoothness of operation. Renew any of the components as necessary.
**12** Examine the strut for signs of fluid leakage. Check the strut piston for signs of pitting along its entire length, and check the strut body for signs of damage. While holding it in an upright position, test the operation of the strut by moving the piston through a full stroke, and then through short strokes of 50 to 100 mm. In both cases, the resistance felt should be smooth and continuous. If the resistance is jerky or uneven or if there is any visible sign of wear or damage to the strut, renewal is necessary.
**13** If any doubt exists as to the condition of the coil spring, carefully remove the spring compressors and check the spring for distortion and signs of cracking. Renew the spring if it is damaged or distorted, or if there is any doubt as to its condition.
**14** Inspect all other components for damage or deterioration, and renew any that are suspect.
**15** With the spring compressed with the compressor tool, locate the spring on the strut making sure that it is correctly seated with its lower end against the raised stop **(see illustration)**.
**16** Refit the buffer, upper spring seat, and upper damping ring.
**17** Refit the piston rod nut and tighten it to the specified torque while counterholding the piston rod with a spanner.

**18** Slowly slacken the spring compressor tool to relieve the tension in the spring. Check that the ends of the spring locate correctly against the stops on the spring seats. If necessary, turn the spring and the upper seat so that the components locate correctly before the compressor tool is removed. Remove the compressor tool when the spring is fully seated.

### Refitting

**19** Manoeuvre the strut assembly into position, ensuring that the top mounting is correctly located in the inner wing panel. Fit the upper mounting plate and retaining nut, and tighten it to the specified torque setting.
**20** Engage the lower end of the strut with the swivel hub. Insert the new bolts from the front of the strut so that their threads are facing to the rear. Fit the new nuts to the bolts, and tighten them through the various stages given in the Specifications at the start of this Chapter.
**21** Refit the anti-roll bar link rod to the strut, using a new retaining nut. Use a spanner on the flats to hold the link, while the nut is being tightened to the specified torque setting.
**22** Where applicable, clip the wheel speed sensor wiring back into its retaining clip.
**23** Refit the roadwheel, then lower the vehicle to the ground and tighten the roadwheel bolts to the specified torque.

### 5  Front lower arm – removal, overhaul and refitting

**Note:** *When refitting, new pivot bolt/nuts, and new lower arm-to-balljoint nut/bolt, will be required.*

### Removal

**1** Firmly apply the handbrake, then jack up the front of the car and support it securely on axle stands (see *Jacking and vehicle support*). Remove the appropriate front roadwheel.
**2** Unscrew and remove the lower arm balljoint clamp bolt nut, and withdraw the clamp bolt from the swivel hub, noting which way round it is fitted **(see illustration)**. Discard the clamp bolt nut; a new one must be used on refitting.
**3** Using a suitable lever, push down the lower

arm to separate the balljoint from the swivel hub. When releasing the lower arm, take care not to damage the balljoint rubber boot; if necessary protect it with a piece of card or plastic. **Note:** *If the balljoint stub is tight in the swivel hub, use a screwdriver or cold chisel as a wedge to force the clamp apart.*
**4** Unscrew the nut and withdraw the pivot bolt securing the front of the lower arm to the front subframe **(see illustration)**. Discard the bolt/nut; new ones should be used on refitting.
**5** Undo the securing bolt and withdraw it from the lower arm rear mounting to the front subframe **(see illustration)**. Discard the bolt; a new one should be used on refitting. Remove the lower arm from the vehicle.

### Overhaul

**6** Thoroughly clean the lower arm and the area around the arm mountings, removing all traces of dirt and underseal if necessary. Check carefully for cracks, distortion, or any other signs of wear or damage, paying particular attention to the pivot bushes. If rear bush renewal is necessary, the lower arm should be taken to a Vauxhall dealer or suitably-equipped garage. A hydraulic press and spacers are required to press the bushes out of the arm, and to install the new ones. To renew the lower arm balljoint or front inner bush see Section 6.

### Refitting

**7** Offer up the lower arm, aligning the inner end of the arm with its mountings, insert new pivot bolt and nut to the front and rear mounting points. **Note:** *Only tighten the mounting bolts/nut hand tight at this stage.*
**8** Locate the lower balljoint stub fully in the bottom of the swivel hub, then refit the clamp bolt and tighten to the specified torque. Make sure the bolt head is facing the front of the vehicle.
**9** The lower arm inner mounting bolts/nut can now be tightened through the various stages given in the Specifications at the start of this Chapter.
**10** Refit the roadwheel, lower the vehicle to the ground, and tighten the roadwheel bolts to the specified torque setting.
**11** Have the front wheel alignment settings checked by a suitably-equipped garage.

**5.2 Slacken and remove the nut and clamp bolt . . .**

**5.4 . . . the front lower arm pivot bolt (arrowed) . . .**

**5.5 . . . and the rear lower arm retaining bolt**

**6.2 Drill out the balljoint securing rivets (arrowed) using a 10 mm drill bit**

**6.6 Drill out the front bush securing rivets (arrowed) using a 10 mm drill bit**

**7.2 Unscrew the bolt (arrowed) securing the bottom of the steering column intermediate shaft**

## 6 Front lower arm balljoint and inner front bush – removal and refitting

**Note:** *When refitting, a new clamp bolt/nut and new balljoint-to-lower arm nuts and bolts will be required.*

### Balljoint

#### Removal

1 Remove the front lower arm assembly as described in Section 5.
2 Using a 10mm drill bit, drill out the three rivets which hold the balljoint to the lower arm **(see illustration)**, and remove the balljoint. Coat the holes in the lower arm where the rivets had been with anti-corrosion paint.

#### Refitting

3 Align the new balljoint with the lower arm, then insert the new special bolts (supplied by the dealer) from the top downwards through the lower arm. Fit the new nuts to the bolts, tightening them to the specified torque setting at the beginning of this Chapter.
4 Refit the front lower arm assembly as described in Section 5.

### Inner front bush (Hydro-bush)

#### Removal

5 Remove the front lower arm assembly as described in Section 5.

6 Using a 10mm drill bit, drill out the three rivets which hold the bush to the lower arm **(see illustration)**, and remove the bush. Coat the holes in the lower arm where the rivets had been with anti-corrosion paint.

#### Refitting

7 Align the new bush with the lower arm, then insert the new special bolts (supplied by the dealer) from the top downwards through the lower arm. Fit the new nuts to the bolts, tightening them to the specified torque setting at the beginning of this Chapter.
8 Refit the front lower arm assembly as described in Section 5.

## 7 Front subframe – removal and refitting

**Note:** *Vauxhall technicians use special jigs to ensure that the front subframe is correctly aligned. Without the use of these tools it is important to note the position of the subframe accurately before removal.*

### Removal

1 Set the front wheels in the straight-ahead position, then remove the ignition key and lock the column by turning the steering wheel as required.
2 In the driver's footwell, unscrew the bolt securing the bottom of the steering column

intermediate shaft to the steering gear pinion **(see illustration)**. Use paint or a suitable marker pen to make alignment marks between the intermediate shaft and the steering gear pinion, then pull the shaft from the pinion and position to one side.
3 Apply the handbrake, then jack up the front of the vehicle and support it on axle stands (see *Jacking and vehicle support*). Remove both front wheels.
4 Remove the front bumper as described in Chapter 11, then detach the wheel arch liner from the subframe on the right-hand side.
5 Connect a hoist to the engine/transmission assembly and support its weight. If available, the type of support bar which locates in the engine compartment side channels is to be preferred, as this will ensure correct repositioning during refitting. Where applicable, remove the engine upper cover.
6 Use cable-ties to secure the top mountings on each side of the radiator to prevent the radiator dropping when the subframe is removed **(see illustration)**.
7 Disconnect the steering track rod balljoints from the swivel hubs by unscrewing the nuts and using a balljoint separator tool **(see illustration)**.
8 Unscrew the nuts and disconnect the anti-roll bar link rods from the struts on both sides. Use a further spanner to hold the studs while the nuts are being loosened **(see illustration)**.
9 Unscrew and remove the lower arm balljoint clamp bolt nut, and withdraw the clamp bolt from the swivel hub on each side, noting which

**7.6 Use cable-ties to prevent the radiator dropping**

**7.7 Using a balljoint separator tool to free the balljoint**

**7.8 Holding the joint stub with an open-ended spanner, while removing the retaining nut**

**7.9 Withdraw the clamp bolt, and free the lower arm balljoint from the swivel hub**

**7.13a Undo the centre bolt (arrowed) from the rear torque link mounting**

**7.13b On diesel models, remove the mounting bolt (arrowed) from the front torque link**

way round they are fitted (see illustration). Discard the clamp bolt nuts; new ones must be used on refitting.

**10** Using a suitable lever, push down the lower arms to separate the balljoints from the swivel hubs. When releasing the lower arms, take care not to damage the balljoint rubber boots; if necessary protect them with a piece of card or plastic. **Note:** *If the balljoint stub is tight in the swivel hub, use a screwdriver or cold chisel as a wedge to force the clamp apart.*

**11** On petrol models, disconnect the oxygen sensor wiring and position to one side.

**12** Remove the exhaust system as described in the relevant part of Chapter 4.

**13** Undo the centre bolt from the torque link mounting at the rear of the engine/transmission (see illustration). **Note:** *On diesel models, there is a torque link mounting bolt on the front of the engine/transmission that will also need to be removed (see illustration).*

**14** Remove the retaining clip and release the gearchange guide bracket (see illustration).

**15** Support the subframe with a cradle across a trolley jack. Alternatively, two trolley jacks and the help of an assistant will be required.

**16** Accurately mark the position of the subframe in relation with the mounting points

to ensure correct refitting (see Haynes Hint). Note that Vauxhall technicians use a special jig with guide pins located through the alignment holes in the subframe and underbody.

**17** Unscrew the four subframe mounting bolts and carefully lower the subframe to the ground (see illustrations). As the subframe is lowered, make sure there are no cables or wiring still attached.

**18** Remove the lower suspension arms from the subframe with reference to Section 5, the anti-roll bar with reference to Section 8, the rear engine mounting with reference to the relevant part of Chapter 2, and the steering gear with reference to Section 20.

### Refitting

**19** Refitting is a reversal of removal, bearing in mind the following points:
a) Tighten all nuts and bolts to the specified torque and, where necessary, in the stages given. Ensure that new nuts/bolts are used where indicated.
b) Make sure that the subframe is correctly aligned with the underbody before fully tightening the mounting bolts.
c) Refer to the procedures contained in Section 19 when connecting the steering column intermediate shaft to the steering gear pinion.

**7.14 Release the retaining clip from the gearchange guide bracket**

## 8 Front anti-roll bar – removal and refitting

### Removal

**1** Firmly apply the handbrake, then jack up the front of the car and support it securely on axle stands (see *Jacking and vehicle support*).

**2** Remove the front subframe assembly as described in Section 7.

**3** Prior to removal of the anti-roll bar, mark the position of each anti-roll bar mounting clamp rubber.

**4** Unscrew the retaining nut and disconnect the link rod from the ends of the anti-roll bar,

**HAYNES HINT**

*To ensure correct repositioning, we bolted two lengths of metal bar to the subframe (one each side) and marked their positions on the underbody.*

**7.17a Unscrew the rear mounting bolts (one side arrowed) . . .**

**7.17b . . . and the front mounting bolts (one side shown)**

**8.4 Undo the link rod retaining nut (arrowed) from the end of the anti-roll bar**

**8.5 Unscrew and remove the anti-roll bar clamp retaining bolts (arrowed)**

**8.6 Remove and inspect the mounting clamp rubbers**

discard the retaining nut; a new one should be used on refitting **(see illustration)**. Use a spanner on the flats to hold the link while the nut is being loosened.

**5** Unscrew the two bolts from each mounting clamp, and remove the clamp **(see illustration)**. As the last clamp is removed, support the anti-roll bar and remove it from the subframe.

**6** Inspect the mounting clamp rubbers for signs of damage and deterioration, and renew if necessary **(see illustration)**.

### Refitting

**7** Align the mounting rubbers with the marks made on the anti-roll bar prior to removal.

**8** Refit the anti-roll bar to the subframe, and fit the mounting clamps. Ensure that the clamp half is correctly engaged with the anti-roll bar rubbers, then tighten each clamp retaining bolt, by hand only at this stage.

**9** With the two clamps loosely installed, check

the position of the anti-roll bar to the marks made on removal, then tighten the clamp bolts to the specified torque setting.

**10** Refit the link rods to the ends of the anti-roll bar using new retaining nuts, tighten to the specified torque setting.

**11** Refit the front subframe assembly as described in Section 7.

**12** Refit the roadwheels if not already done, then lower the vehicle to the ground and tighten the roadwheel bolts to the specified torque setting.

### 9  Rear hub assembly – removal and refitting

### Removal

#### Corsa and Corsavan models

**1** On these models, the rear hub is an integral part of the brake drum **(see illustration)**. Refer to Chapter 9 for drum removal and refitting details.

**2** Check the hub bearing for signs of roughness or damage, and renew if necessary as described in Section 10.

**3** With the hub removed, examine the stub axle shaft for signs of wear or damage **(see illustration)**, if necessary, renew it as described in Section 11.

#### Combo Van models

**4** Remove the rear brake drum as described in Chapter 9.

**5** On models with ABS, disconnect the wiring for the wheel speed sensor, located on the rear of the brake backplate.

**6** Support the hub assembly then undo the four retaining nuts from the rear of the trailing arm. Withdraw the hub assembly from the vehicle **(see illustration)**.

### Refitting

#### Corsa and Corsavan models

**7** Refit the brake drum as described in Chapter 9.

#### Combo Van models

**8** Ensure that the backplate is clean, then locate the hub assembly onto the trailing arm and fit new retaining nuts to secure.

**9** Tighten the new retaining nuts to the specified torque and angles in the stages given at the beginning of this Chapter.

**10** Where applicable, reconnect the wiring for the wheel speed sensor.

**11** Refit the brake drum as described in Chapter 9.

### 10  Rear hub bearings – renewal

**Note:** *On Combo Van models, the bearing and hub assembly can only be bought as a complete unit (see your local dealer for availability of parts). To remove the hub/bearing assembly on the Combo Van see Section 9.*

**1** Remove the rear brake drum as described in Chapter 9, Section 7.

**2** Extract the bearing retaining circlip from the inside of the brake drum assembly **(see illustration)**.

**9.1 The drum and hub assembly on the Corsa and Corsavan models**

**9.3 Examine the stub axle shaft (arrowed) for signs of wear or damage**

**9.6 Undo the four retaining nuts (arrowed) from the rear of the trailing arm**

**10.2 Use circlip pliers to remove the circlip**

10.6a Press the bearing squarely into position . . .

10.6b . . . then use a threaded rod and spacers to press the bearing into the hub

10.7 Refit the circlip securely into the groove (arrowed)

**3** Turn the drum/hub over, then supporting it on two blocks of wood, use a drift to tap the complete bearing out of the hub.

**4** Thoroughly clean the hub, removing all traces of dirt and grease. Polish away any burrs or raised edges which might hinder reassembly. Check the drum/hub surface for cracks or any other signs of wear or damage, and renew it if necessary. The bearings must be renewed whenever they are disturbed, as removal will almost certainly damage the outer races. Obtain new bearings from your Vauxhall dealer.

**5** On reassembly, apply a light film of clean engine oil to each bearing outer race, to aid installation.

**6** Securely support the drum/hub, and locate the bearing in the hub. Press the bearing fully into position, ensuring that it enters the hub squarely. Use a tubular spacer/sockets which bears only on the bearing outer race and threaded rod to press the bearing into position **(see illustrations)**.

**HAYNES HINT** *The old wheel bearing can be used to press the new bearing into the hub.*

**7** Once the bearing is correctly seated, secure the bearing in position with the new inner circlip. Make sure that the circlip is correctly located in its groove **(see illustration)**.

**8** Refit the brake drum as described in Chapter 9, Section 7.

## 11 Rear stub axle – removal and refitting

**Note 1:** *On Combo Van models, the stub axle/bearing hub assembly is one unit. Refer to Section 9 to remove the hub bearing assembly.*

**Note 2:** *When refitting, new stub axle retaining bolts/nuts must be used.*

### Removal

**1** Remove the brake drum as described in Chapter 9.

**2** On models with ABS, disconnect the rear wheel speed sensor at the wiring connector and free the sensor wiring from the retaining clip on the brake pipe **(see illustration)**. Release the sensor wiring grommet from the brake backplate.

**3** Position a jack underneath the relevant trailing arm, and raise the jack until it is just supporting the weight of the arm.

**4** Undo the lower shock absorber mounting bolt **(see illustration)**, and swing the shock absorber away from the trailing arm to gain access to the stub axle retaining bolts.

**5** Slacken and remove the retaining bolts, and remove the stub axle from the trailing arm **(see illustration)**. Discard the retaining bolts; new ones must be used on refitting.

**6** Inspect the stub axle surface for signs of damage such as scoring, and renew if necessary.

### Refitting

**7** Ensure that the mating surfaces of the stub axle and backplate are clean and dry. Check the backplate for signs of damage, and remove any burrs with a fine file or emery cloth.

**8** Offer up the stub axle, and fit the new retaining bolts. Tighten the retaining bolts through the various stages given in the Specifications.

**9** Align the shock absorber with the trailing arm, then fit its lower mounting bolt, tightening it to the specified torque.

**10** Where applicable refit the wheel speed sensor wiring grommet to the backplate, then reconnect the wiring connector and secure the wiring with the retaining clip.

**11** Remove the jack from underneath the trailing arm, and refit the brake drum as described in Chapter 9.

## 12 Rear shock absorber – removal, testing and refitting

**Note:** *Always renew shock absorbers in pairs and the correct version for model, to maintain good handling.*

### Removal

#### Corsa and Corsavan models

**1** Chock the front wheels then jack up the rear of the car and support it on axle stands (see *Jacking and vehicle support*).

11.2 Disconnect the rear wheel speed sensor at the wiring connector (arrowed)

11.4 Remove the lower mounting bolt then free the shock absorber from the trailing arm

11.5 Undo the four retaining bolts (arrowed) from the rear of the trailing arm

**12.3 Remove the cap (arrowed) to gain access to the shock absorber upper mounting nut**

**12.4 Slacken the mounting nut (A) whilst retaining the piston (B) with an open-ended spanner**

**12.5 Remove the lower mounting bolt (arrowed) then manoeuvre the shock absorber out from under the vehicle**

**2** Position a jack underneath the relevant trailing arm, and raise the jack until it is just supporting the weight of the arm.

**3** Working in the luggage compartment, unclip the trim cover cap to gain access to the shock absorber upper mounting nut **(see illustration).**

**4** Slacken and remove the nut, and lift off the plate and rubber mounting damper, noting their fitted position. If necessary, to prevent the shock absorber piston rotating as the nut is slackened, retain it using an open-ended spanner on the flats on the upper end of the piston **(see illustration).**

**5** Slacken and remove the lower shock absorber mounting bolt, then lower the shock absorber out of position and remove it from underneath the vehicle **(see illustration).**

### Combo Van

**6** Chock the front wheels then jack up the rear of the car and support it on axle stands (see *Jacking and vehicle support*).

**7** Position a jack underneath the axle, and raise the jack until it is just supporting the weight of the axle.

**8** Note the orientation of the shock absorber, then slacken and remove the upper and lower shock absorber mounting bolts, and remove the shock absorber from underneath the vehicle **(see illustrations).**

### Testing

**9** Examine the shock absorber for signs of fluid

leakage or damage. Test the operation of the strut, while holding it in an upright position, by moving the piston through a full stroke, and then through short strokes of 50 to 100 mm. In both cases, the resistance felt should be smooth and continuous. If the resistance is jerky, or uneven, or if there is any visible sign of wear or damage to the strut, renewal is necessary. Also check the rubber mounting bush(es) for damage and deterioration. If the bushes are damaged or worn, the complete shock absorber will have to be renewed, as the mounting bushes are not available separately. Inspect the shanks of the mounting bolts for signs of wear or damage, and renew as necessary.

**10** On Corsa and Corsavan models, examine the upper mounting rubber dampers for signs of damage or deterioration, and renew if necessary.

### *Refitting*

#### Corsa and Corsavan

**11** Manoeuvre the shock absorber into position, ensuring that the piston is correctly located in the hole in the vehicle body.

**12** Insert the shock absorber lower mounting bolt, and tighten it to the specified torque setting.

**13** From inside the luggage compartment, refit the rubber mounting damper and plate to the piston. Fit the upper mounting nut, and tighten it to the specified torque setting. If necessary, prevent the piston rotating as

described in paragraph 4. Refit the trim cover cap.

**14** Lower the vehicle to the ground and withdraw the jack from underneath the trailing arm.

#### Combo Van

**15** Operate the shock absorber fully through several strokes to prime it, then manoeuvre it into position underneath the vehicle.

**16** Ensure that the shock absorber is positioned the correct way up, and insert both the upper and lower mounting bolts. Tighten both mounting bolts to their specified torque settings.

**17** Lower the vehicle to the ground and withdraw the jack from underneath the trailing arm.

### 13 Rear coil spring – removal and refitting

**Note:** *Always renew coil springs in pairs and the correct version for model, to maintain good handling.*

### *Removal*

**1** Chock the front wheels then jack up the rear of the car and support it on axle stands (see *Jacking and vehicle support*). Remove both rear roadwheels.

**12.8a On Combo Van models, slacken and remove the upper (arrowed) . . .**

**12.8b . . . and lower mounting bolts (arrowed)**

**13.4a Lower the rear axle, then remove the coil spring (noting which way around it is installed) . . .**

**13.4b . . . then recover the lower . . .**

**13.4c . . . and upper damping rings/spring seats**

## Corsa and Corsavan

**2** Position a jack underneath the relevant trailing arm, and raise the jack until it is just supporting the weight of the arm.

**3** Undo the shock absorber lower mounting bolt, and disengage the shock absorber from the trailing arm.

**4** Slowly lower the jack, keeping watch on the brake pipes to ensure no excess strain is placed on them, until it is possible to withdraw the coil spring. Note which way around the spring is installed, and recover the upper damping ring and lower spring seat **(see illustrations)**.

**5** If the vehicle is to be left for some time with the spring removed, lift up the trailing arms and refit the shock absorber lower mounting bolts. **Note:** *Do not allow the rear axle assembly to hang unsupported.*

**6** Inspect the springs closely for signs of damage, such as cracking, and check the spring seats and damping ring for signs of wear or damage. Renew worn components as necessary.

## Combo Van

**Note:** *A spring compressor tool will be required for this operation.*

**7** Fit the spring compressor tool, and compress the coil spring to relieve the pressure on the spring seats. Ensure that the compressor tool is securely located on the spring, in accordance with the tool manufacturer's instructions.

**8** Withdraw the coil spring, noting which way around the spring is installed, and recover the upper damping ring and lower spring seat.

**9** Inspect the springs closely for signs of damage, such as cracking, and check the

spring seats and damping ring for signs of wear or damage. Renew worn components as necessary.

## Refitting

### All models

**10** Refitting is a reversal of removal, but note the following points.
   a) *Ensure that the spring locates correctly on the upper and lower seats, as well as on the trailing arm and underbody.*
   b) *On Corsa and Corsavan models, tighten the shock absorber lower mounting bolt to the specified torque.*
   c) *If the spring is being renewed, repeat the procedure on the remaining side of the vehicle.*
   d) *Refit the roadwheels, then lower the vehicle to the ground, and tighten the roadwheel bolts to the specified torque.*

## 14 Rear axle –
removal and refitting

**Note:** *Vauxhall technicians use special jigs to ensure that the rear axle is correctly aligned. Without the use of these tools it is important to note the position of the axle mounting points accurately before removal. New trailing arm pivot bolts and nuts will be required when refitting.*

## Removal

**1** Chock the front wheels then jack up the rear of the car and support it on axle stands (see *Jacking and vehicle support*). Remove

both rear roadwheels, marking the position in relation with the hub for refitting.

**2** Unscrew the brake master cylinder fluid reservoir cap and screw it down onto a piece of polythene to minimise fluid loss during the following procedure. Proceed as described under the relevant sub-heading.

## Corsa and Corsavan models

**3** On models with ABS, disconnect the rear wheel speed sensors at the wiring connectors. Free the sensor wiring from all its retaining clips, so that it is free to be removed with the axle.

**4** Follow the brake pipes and ABS wiring and disconnect from any retaining clips along the axle.

**5** With the handbrake lever in the off position, unscrew the handbrake cable adjuster nut (referring to Chapter 9), then detach the handbrake cable at the centre of the rear axle, unclipping it from the guide on the axle.

**6** On ECO models, undo the retaining screws and remove the cover from under the rear of the vehicle.

**7** Trace the brake pipes back from the backplates to their unions situated directly above the axle. A brake hose clamp or similar can be used to clamp the nearest flexible hose. Slacken the union nuts, and disconnect the pipes. Plug the pipe ends, to minimise fluid loss and prevent the entry of dirt into the hydraulic system. Remove the retaining clips, and release the pipes from the axle/vehicle body **(see illustrations)**.

**8** Where applicable, undo the two retaining nuts and disconnect the brake pressure-regulating valve spring bracket from the axle **(see illustration)**.

**14.7a Slacken the union nut (arrowed) . . .**

**14.7b . . . and disconnect the brake pipe**

**14.8 Undo the two retaining nuts (arrowed) to release the bracket from the axle**

**14.11 Slacken and remove the front pivot bolt**

**14.13a Using a drift to remove the trailing arm bush (note the fitted position)**

**14.13b Using a threaded rod and spacers to press the bush into the trailing arm**

**9** Remove the rear coil springs as described in Section 13, then place the jack underneath the centre of the axle.

**10** Accurately mark the position of the axle mounting points in relation with the vehicle underbody to ensure correct refitting. Note that Vauxhall technicians use a special jig with guide pins located through alignment holes in the underbody.

**11** Slacken and remove the nut and pivot bolt securing each trailing arm to the vehicle underbody **(see illustration)**. Discard the nuts and bolts; new ones should be used on refitting.

**12** Make a final check that all necessary components have been disconnected and positioned so that they will not hinder the removal procedure. Carefully lower the axle assembly out of position, and remove it from underneath the vehicle.

**14.14 Detach the handbrake cable from the connector (arrowed)**

**13** Inspect the trailing arm bushes for signs of damage or deterioration, and renew if necessary. The bushes can be pressed out of the axle and new ones fitted **(see illustrations)**. Always mark the position of the bush before removal, so that the new bushes can be refitted in the same position.

### Combo Van

**14** With the handbrake lever in the off position, unscrew the handbrake cable adjuster nut (referring to Chapter 9), then detach the handbrake cables at each side from the connections at the rear hub units **(see illustration)**.

**15** Remove the rear coil springs as described in Section 13.

**16** On vehicles with ABS fitted, disconnect the wiring connectors from each of the sensors on the rear hub units.

**17** Disconnect the brake pipes from the brake cylinders at their unions on the back-plates **(see illustration)**. Slacken the union nuts, and disconnect the pipes. Plug the pipe ends, to minimise fluid loss and prevent the entry of dirt into the hydraulic system.

**18** Follow the brake pipes and ABS wiring and disconnect any brackets or unclip from any retaining clips along the axle **(see illustration)**.

**19** Position a jack beneath the centre of the axle, and raise the jack until it is supporting the weight of the axle.

**20** Unscrew both the rear shock absorber

lower mounting bolts, and free both shock absorbers from the axle.

**21** Accurately mark the position of the axle mounting points in relation with the vehicle underbody to ensure correct refitting. Note that Vauxhall technicians use a special jig with guide pins located through alignment holes in the underbody.

**22** Unscrew the three retaining bolts (at each side) for the axle front mounting brackets to vehicle underbody **(see illustration)**.

**23** Make a final check that all necessary components have been disconnected and positioned so that they will not hinder the removal procedure. Carefully lower the axle assembly out of position, and remove it from underneath the vehicle.

### *Refitting*

#### Corsa and Corsavan models

**24** Refitting is a reverse of the removal procedure, bearing in mind the following points:

a) Ensure that the trailing arm and mounting bracket surfaces are clean and dry. Lubricate the bushes with 'red grease' see Vauxhall dealer for specification of grease. Raise the axle assembly into position, and insert the new trailing arm pivot bolts, tightening them by hand only at this stage.

b) Raise the axle until the distance between the lower coil spring mounting on the axle and the upper coil spring mounting on

**14.17 Slacken and remove the brake pipe (arrowed) from the brake cylinders**

**14.18 Undo the retaining bolt (arrowed) to disconnect the bracket from the axle**

**14.22 The axle front mounting bracket retaining bolts (arrowed) – one side shown**

**14.24 The height (arrowed) should be set at 100 mm ± 5 mm (172 mm ± 10 mm for Combo Van)**

**15.2 Prior to removal, mark the position of the rubber damper (arrowed) on the axle crossmember**

**15.3 Slacken and remove the nut and bolt (arrowed) securing the anti-roll bar to each trailing arm . . .**

the vehicle underbody is 100 ± 5mm **(see illustration)**.

c) The axle front mounting retaining bolts can now be tightened to their specified torque setting.

d) Refit the rear coil springs as described in Section 13,

e) Ensure that the brake pipes, handbrake cables and wiring (as applicable) are correctly routed, and retained by all the necessary retaining clips.

f) Tighten all the brake pipe union nuts to the specified torque, and bleed the braking system, with reference to Chapter 9.

g) Adjust the handbrake cable as described in Chapter 9. Where applicable, also adjust the rear brake pressure-regulating valve once the vehicle is on the ground.

h) Tighten the shock absorber lower mounting bolts to the specified torque.

i) On completion, lower the vehicle to the ground, and tighten the roadwheel bolts to the specified torque.

### Combo Van models

**25** Refitting is a reverse of the removal procedure, bearing in mind the following points:

a) Ensure that the trailing arm and mounting bracket surfaces are clean and dry. Raise the axle assembly into position, and insert the new trailing arm retaining bolts, tightening them by hand only at this stage. Make sure that the alignment holes in the mounting bracket and underbody are correctly aligned

b) Raise the axle until the distance between the lower coil spring mounting on the axle and the upper coil spring mounting on the vehicle underbody is 172 ± 10mm **(see illustration 14.24)**.

c) The axle front mounting retaining bolts can now be tightened to their specified torque setting.

d) Refit the rear coil springs as described in Section 13.

e) Ensure that the brake pipes, handbrake cables and wiring (as applicable) are correctly routed and retained by all the necessary retaining clips.

f) Tighten all the brake pipe union nuts to the specified torque, and bleed the braking system, with reference to Chapter 9.

**15.4a . . . then withdraw the anti-roll bar . . .**

g) Adjust the handbrake cable and rear brake pressure-regulating valve (where applicable) as described in Chapter 9.

h) Tighten the shock absorber lower mounting bolts to the specified torque.

i) On completion, lower the vehicle to the ground, and tighten the roadwheel bolts to the specified torque.

### 15 Rear anti-roll bar – removal and refitting

**Note:** New retaining bolts will be required on refitting.

### Removal

**1** Chock the front wheels then jack up the rear of the car and support it on axle stands (see *Jacking and vehicle support*). Remove both rear roadwheels, marking the position in relation with the hub for refitting.

**2** Prior to removal, mark the position of the rubber dampers on the axle crossmember **(see illustration)**.

**3** Slacken and remove the bolts securing the ends of the anti-roll bar to the trailing arms, noting the fitted position **(see illustration)**. Discard the bolts; new ones must be used on refitting.

**4** Withdraw the anti-roll bar from one side of the rear axle, if the bar is tight, drift the bar out using a hammer and soft metal drift from the opposite side. Recover the dampers from the bar as they are released **(see illustrations)**.

**5** Inspect the rubber dampers for signs

**15.4b . . . and recover the rubber damper**

of damage or deterioration, and renew as necessary.

### Refitting

**6** Insert the anti-roll bar in through the trailing arm, and locate the rubber dampers on the bar. Align the rubber dampers with the marks made prior to removal, and seat them in the axle crossmember.

**7** Slide the anti-roll bar fully into position, so that it is correctly engaged in the opposite trailing arm.

**8** Install the new retaining bolts in the same position as noted on removal. Tighten both bolts first to the specified torque, and then through the specified angle given in the Specifications at the start of this Chapter.

**9** Refit the roadwheel(s), aligning the marks made on removal. Lower the vehicle to the ground, and tighten the roadwheel bolts to the specified torque.

### 16 Steering wheel – removal and refitting

⚠️ **Warning: Make sure that the airbag safety recommendations given in Chapter 12 are followed, to prevent personal injury.**

### Removal

**1** Remove the airbag as described in Chapter 12.

**2** Set the front wheels in the straight-ahead position, then lock the column in position after removing the ignition key.

**16.3 Disconnect the wiring connectors . . .**

**16.4 . . . then remove the steering wheel retaining bolt**

**16.5 If not already marked, make alignment marks (arrowed)**

**16.7 Carefully guide the wiring (arrowed) for the contact unit through the hole in the steering wheel**

**16.8a Unclip the horn button cover . . .**

**16.8b . . . then remove the switch and wiring from the steering wheel**

**3** Release the horn wiring connector and, where fitted, the radio remote control wiring from the steering wheel, and disconnect the connectors **(see illustration)**.
**4** Unscrew the Torx retaining bolt securing the steering wheel to the column **(see illustration)**.
**5** Make alignment marks between the steering wheel and the steering column shaft **(see illustration)**. Refit the steering wheel retaining bolt back into the steering column approximately two full turns.
**6** Grip the steering wheel with both hands and carefully rock it from side-to-side to release it from the splines on the steering column.
**7** With the steering wheel loose on the splines, the retaining bolt can now be completely removed. As the steering wheel is being removed, guide the wiring for the contact unit through the hole, taking care not to damage the wiring contact unit **(see illustration)**.

**8** To remove the horn switch from the steering wheel, unclip the cover, then withdraw the switch and wiring from the steering wheel **(see illustrations)**.

### Refitting

**9** Refit the steering wheel, aligning the marks made prior to removal. Route the wiring connectors through the steering wheel aperture. **Note:** *Make sure the steering wheel centre hub locates correctly with the contact unit on the steering column.*
**10** Clean the threads on the retaining bolt and the threads in the steering column. Coat the retaining bolt with locking compound, then fit the retaining bolt and tighten to the specified torque setting **(see illustration)**.
**11** Reconnect the horn wiring connector and, where fitted, the radio remote control wiring, then clip the connectors into the steering wheel recess **(see illustration)**.

**12** Release the steering lock, and refit the airbag as described in Chapter 12.

## 17 Ignition switch/steering column lock – removal and refitting

### Removal

**1** Disconnect the battery negative terminal (refer to *Disconnecting the battery* in the Reference Chapter).
**2** Remove the steering wheel as described in Section 16.
**3** Unclip the upper steering column shroud from the lower shroud **(see illustration)**.
**4** Where necessary, undo the retaining screw and release the steering column adjustment handle from under the steering column.
**5** Undo the two upper retaining screws and the lower retaining screw and remove the

**16.10 Tighten the retaining bolt to the specified torque setting**

**16.11 Clip the wiring connector (arrowed) into the recess in the steering wheel**

**17.3 Unclipping the upper steering column shroud**

**17.5a Undo the two upper retaining screws (arrowed) . . .**

**17.5b . . . then the lower shroud retaining screw**

**17.6 Depress the retaining clips (arrowed) and slide the combination switch out from the column**

lower steering column shroud from the vehicle **(see illustrations)**.

6 Remove the windscreen wiper switch by releasing the upper and lower lugs and sliding the switch out of its mounting bracket **(see illustration)**.

### Lock cylinder

7 Remove the rubber trim from around the lock cylinder. Insert the ignition key into the ignition switch/lock, and turn it to position I.

8 Insert a thin rod into the hole in the lock housing, press the rod to release the detent spring, and pull out the lock cylinder using the key **(see illustration)**.

### Ignition switch wiring block

9 Release the securing clip and disconnect the wiring connector from the ignition switch wiring block **(see illustration)**.

10 Press the two lugs in (one at each side) and slide the switch wiring block down out of its mounting bracket **(see illustration)**.

### *Refitting*

### Lock cylinder

11 With the wiring block in position, insert the ignition switch/lock into the lock housing, while the key is in position I.

12 Ensure that the centre of the ignition

switch wiring block is correctly aligned with the lock cylinder rod flats. If necessary, rotate the switch centre using a suitable screwdriver **(see illustration)**. If the steering column lock has been actuated, release the lock by depressing the locking mechanism recess in the column housing.

13 Press the lock cylinder into the housing until the detent spring clicks into position, then check the operation of the lock cylinder and steering lock.

14 Refit the rubber trim around the lock cylinder **(see illustration)**. Refit the lower steering column shroud, tightening its

**17.8 Insert a thin rod (arrowed) into the hole in the lock housing to release the detent spring**

**17.9 Release the locking clip (arrowed) and disconnect the wiring connector**

**17.10 Depress the retaining clips (arrowed) and slide downwards out from the column**

**17.12 Align the lock cylinder recess (arrowed) in the switch housing**

**17.14 Refit the rubber trim to the lock cylinder**

**18.3a  Release the locking clip (arrowed) and disconnect the wiring connector from the switch . . .**

retaining screws securely, then clip the upper shroud back in position.

**15**  Where necessary, refit the steering column adjustment handle under the steering column.

**18.4a  Release the locking clips (arrowed) and withdraw the storage tray**

**18.4c  . . . then release the lower facia panel . . .**

**18.5b  . . . and withdraw the heater duct from the driver's footwell**

**18.3b  . . . and the immobiliser control unit**

**16**  Refit the steering wheel as described in Section 16, and check the operation of the switch.

**Ignition switch wiring block**

**17**  Slide the switch wiring block back up into

**18.4b  Undo the two retaining screws (arrowed) . . .**

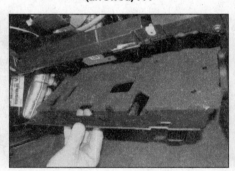

**18.4d  . . . and the lower trim above the pedal assembly**

**18.6a  Undo the retaining bolts and remove the crossmember, then cut the trim in the places arrowed**

its mounting bracket on the steering column, making sure it is located correctly.

**18**  Reconnect the wiring connector to switch wiring block.

**19**  Refit the ignition/lock cylinder as described in paragraphs 11 to 16.

## 18  Steering column – removal and refitting

### *Removal*

**1**  Disconnect the battery negative terminal (refer to *Disconnecting the battery* in the Reference Chapter).

**2**  Remove the airbag wiring contact unit as described in Chapter 12.

**3**  Release the securing clips and disconnect the wiring connectors from the ignition switch wiring block, the immobiliser control unit and the horn contact, then release the wiring cables from the steering column **(see illustrations)**.

**4**  Unclip the driver's side lower storage tray, then undo the retaining screws and remove the driver's side lower trim panels **(see illustrations)**.

**5**  Release the retaining clip and withdraw the air duct from the driver's side footwell **(see illustrations)**.

**6**  Undo the four retaining bolts and remove the crossmember from the footwell on the driver's side, then cut the facia panel padding web from the footwell on the driver's side **(see illustrations)**.

**18.5a  Remove the retaining clip (arrowed) . . .**

**18.6b  Using a junior hacksaw to remove the trim section**

**18.7  Disconnect the wiring connectors (arrowed) from the EPS control unit**

**18.8  Remove the clamp bolt (arrowed) securing the intermediate shaft to the steering column**

**18.10  Steering column lower mounting bolts (arrowed) . . .**

**7** Disconnect the wiring connectors from the EPS control unit on the steering column **(see illustration)**.

**8** Using paint or similar, make alignment marks between the steering column and intermediate shaft, then slacken and remove the clamp bolt securing the intermediate shaft to the steering column **(see illustration)**.

**9** If applicable, make sure the steering column adjustment handle is in the locked position.

**10** Unscrew the lower mounting nuts securing the steering column to the bulkhead **(see illustration)**.

**11** Two fasteners must now be extracted from the column upper mounting bracket, and the bolts at the middle of the steering column must be removed too **(see illustration)**.

**12** Release the column assembly from its mountings, then detach it from the intermediate shaft and remove it from the vehicle. DO NOT release the steering lock while the steering column is off the vehicle, as it will alter the position of the angular adjustment setting for refitting.

### Refitting

**13** Manoeuvre the steering column into position, and engage it with the intermediate shaft universal joint, aligning the marks made on removal.

**14** Refit the column upper, lower and middle mounting nut/bolts. Tighten all bolts by hand only at this stage.

**15** Align the intermediate shaft bolt hole with the steering column shaft cut-out so that the clamp bolt can be slid into position (use

thread-locking compound). Tighten the bolt by hand only.

**16** With the steering column in position, tighten the column mounting bolts to the specified torque setting. Start at the lower bolts first, then the middle, and finally the upper bolts.

**17** Tighten the intermediate shaft upper clamp bolt to the specified torque setting.

**18** The remainder of refitting is reverse of the removal procedure, noting the following points:

a) *Ensure that the wiring is correctly routed, and reconnect to the ignition switch, horn, EPS control unit and, where applicable, the immobiliser.*

b) *Clip the left-and right-hand switches back into position, and reconnect their wiring connectors.*

c) *Refit the contact unit to the top of the steering column, making sure it is located correctly (see Chapter 12).*

d) *Refit the trim panels to the driver's side lower footwell and the upper and lower steering column shrouds.*

e) *Refit the steering column adjustment handle under the steering column.*

f) *Refit the steering wheel and airbag as described in Section 16.*

g) *Reconnect the battery negative terminal.*

### 19  Steering column intermediate shaft – removal, inspection and refitting

**Note:** *Vauxhall use a special tool (locating*

*pin) to set the intermediate shaft length compensator when refitting.*

### Removal

**1** Set the front wheels in the straight-ahead position. Undo the retaining screws and remove the driver's side lower storage tray panel and instrument panel lower padding as described in Section 18, paragraph 4.

**2** If there are no alignment marks on the joints, use paint or a suitable marker pen to make alignment marks between the intermediate shaft joints and the steering column and steering gear shafts.

**3** Slacken and remove the upper clamp bolt and the lower clamp bolt and nut **(see illustrations)**. Discard the nut from the lower joint, as a new one will be required when refitting.

**4** Disengage the shaft universal joint from the steering column, then slide the shaft from the steering gear pinion and remove it from the vehicle.

### Inspection

**5** The steering column intermediate shaft incorporates a telescopic safety section; in the event of a front-end crash, the shaft shortens on the splines and prevents the steering wheel injuring the driver. Inspect the intermediate shaft universal joint for excessive wear or damage. If either joint is worn or damaged in any way, the complete shaft assembly must be renewed.

### Refitting

**6** Check that the front wheels are still in the

**18.11  . . . and upper mounting bolts (arrowed)**

**19.3a  Remove the upper clamp bolt (arrowed) . . .**

**19.3b  . . . and the lower clamp bolt (arrowed)**

**19.9 Locate the hole in the length compensator, then insert the locating pin**

**20.3a Undo the right-hand mounting bolt (arrowed) . . .**

**20.3b . . . and left-hand mounting bolt (arrowed)**

straight-ahead position, and that the steering wheel is correctly positioned.

**7** Aligning the marks made on removal, locate the upper universal joint onto the steering column.

**8** Install the steering column upper clamp bolt (use thread-locking compound) and tighten to the specified torque setting.

**9** Aligning the marks made on removal, locate the lower universal joint onto the steering gear pinion. Push the joint down onto the steering gear pinion until the hole in the length compensator is in line, then insert the locating pin (Vauxhall tool No KM-6181) **(see illustration)**. If the Vauxhall tool is not available, a suitable drill bit or a length of welding rod can be used.

**10** Install the lower clamp bolt and new retaining nut, then tighten to the specified torque setting.

**11** Remove the Vauxhall tool (locating pin) from the intermediate shaft after the lower retaining bolt has been tightened in the correct position.

**12** The remainder of refitting is reverse of the removal procedure

### 20 Steering gear assembly – removal, inspection and refitting

**Note:** *New track rod balljoint-to-swivel hub nuts and steering gear-to-subframe nuts, bolts and washers will be required when refitting.*

**22.2a Release the gaiter outer retaining clip (arrowed) . . .**

### Removal

**1** Firmly apply the handbrake, then jack up the front of the car and support it securely on axle stands (see *Jacking and vehicle support*). Remove both front roadwheels.

**2** Remove the front subframe as described in Section 7.

**3** Slacken and remove the two bolts, nuts and washers securing the steering gear to the subframe **(see illustrations)**, then remove the steering gear from the subframe. Discard the bolts, nuts and washers as new ones will be required when refitting.

**4** If a new steering gear is to be fitted, then the track rod balljoints will need to be removed from each end of the steering track rod arms (see Section 23).

### Inspection

**5** Examine the steering gear assembly for signs of wear or damage, and check that the rack moves freely throughout the full length of its travel, with no signs of roughness or excessive free play between the steering gear pinion and rack. Check with your Vauxhall dealer to see if it is possible to overhaul the steering gear assembly. The only components which can be renewed easily by the home mechanic are the steering gear gaiters, the track rod balljoints and the track rods. Steering gear gaiter, track rod balljoint and track rod renewal procedures are covered in Sections 22, 23 and 24 respectively.

### Refitting

**6** Refitting is a reverse of the removal procedure, bearing in mind the following points:

**22.2b . . . and inner retaining clip (arrowed)**

a) *Set the steering gear in the straight-ahead position prior to refitting the front subframe.*

b) *Refit the front subframe as described in Section 7.*

c) *Locate the track rod balljoints in position using new nuts, and tighten them to the specified torque.*

d) *On completion, have the front wheel alignment checked and, if necessary, adjusted – see Section 25 for general information.*

### 21 Electronic Power-assisted Steering components – information, removal and refitting

### EPS motor

**1** The electronic power-assisted steering motor is part of the steering column assembly, at the time of writing the motor was not available separately and could only be bought as a complete unit with the steering column.

**2** To remove the steering column, follow the procedures as described in Section 18.

### EPS control unit

**3** Disconnect the battery negative terminal (refer to *Disconnecting the battery* in the Reference Chapter).

**4** Unclip the driver's side lower storage tray, then undo the retaining screws and remove the driver's side lower trim panels.

**5** Disconnect the wiring connectors from the EPS control unit on the steering column **(see illustration 18.7)**.

**6** Undo the retaining bolts and remove the control unit from the steering column.

**7** Refitting is a reversal of removal.

### 22 Steering gear rubber gaiters – renewal

**1** Remove the track rod balljoint as described in Section 23.

**2** Mark the correct fitted position of the gaiter on the track rod, then release the retaining clips **(see illustrations)**, and slide the gaiter off the steering gear housing and track rod end.

**23.3 Use an open-ended spanner to hold the track rod arm, then slacken the locknut**

**23.4a Using a universal balljoint separator . . .**

**23.4b . . . release the track rod balljoint from the swivel hub**

3 Thoroughly clean the track rod and the steering gear housing, clean off any corrosion, burrs or sharp edges which might damage the new gaiter's sealing lips on installation. Scrape off all the old grease, and apply new grease to the track rod inner balljoint.

4 Carefully slide the new gaiter onto the track rod end, and locate it on the steering gear housing. Align the outer edge of the gaiter with the mark made on the track rod prior to removal, then secure it in position with new retaining clips.

5 Refit the track rod balljoint as described in Section 23.

## 23 Track rod balljoint – removal and refitting

**Note:** *A new track rod balljoint-to-swivel hub nut will be required when refitting.*

### Removal

1 Firmly apply the handbrake, then jack up the front of the car and support it securely on axle stands (see *Jacking and vehicle support*). Remove the appropriate front roadwheel.

2 If the balljoint is to be re-used, use a scriber, or similar, to mark its relationship to the track rod.

3 Hold the track rod arm, and unscrew the balljoint locknut by a quarter of a turn **(see illustration)**.

4 Slacken and remove the nut securing the track rod balljoint to the swivel hub, and release the balljoint tapered shank using a universal balljoint separator **(see illustrations)**. Discard the nut; a new one must be used of refitting.

5 Counting the exact number of turns necessary to do so, unscrew the balljoint from the track rod arm.

6 Count the number of exposed threads between the end of the track rod and the locknut, and record this figure. If a new gaiter is to be fitted, unscrew the locknut from the track rod.

7 Carefully clean the balljoint and the track rod threads. Renew the balljoint if there is excessive free play of the balljoint shank, or if the shank is excessively stiff. If the balljoint

gaiter is damaged, the complete balljoint assembly must be renewed; it is not possible to obtain the gaiter separately.

### Refitting

8 If it was removed, screw the locknut onto the track rod threads, and position it so that the same number of exposed threads are visible as was noted prior to removal.

9 Screw the balljoint on to the track rod by the number of turns noted on removal. This should bring the balljoint locknut to within approximately quarter of a turn from the locknut, with the alignment marks that were noted on removal.

10 Refit the balljoint shank to the swivel hub, then fit a new retaining nut and tighten it to the specified torque setting. If the balljoint stud turns as the nut is being tightened, press down on the track rod balljoint to force the tapered part of the stud into the arm on the swivel hub.

11 Tighten the track rod balljoint securing locknut on the track rod arm while holding the track rod arm stationary with a second spanner on the flats provided **(see illustration 23.3)**. **Note:** *If possible tighten the nut to the specified torque using a special crow's-foot adapter for the torque wrench.*

12 Refit the roadwheel, then lower the vehicle to the ground and tighten the roadwheel bolts to the specified torque setting.

13 Have the front wheel alignment checked and if necessary, adjusted at the earliest opportunity. See Section 25 for general information on wheel alignment

## 24 Track rod – renewal

**Note:** *When refitting, a new track rod balljoint-to-swivel hub nut and new gaiter retaining clips will be required. Vauxhall use a special socket to tighten the track rod inner balljoint to the end of the steering rack.*

1 Remove the track rod balljoint as described in Section 23.

2 Release the retaining clips, and slide the steering gear gaiter off the end of the track rod as described in Section 22.

3 Turn the steering on full lock, so that the rack protrudes from the steering gear housing on the relevant side, slide the cover (where fitted) off the inner balljoint.

4 Prevent the rack from rotating using an open-ended spanner located on the rack flats, then unscrew and remove the track rod inner balljoint from the end of the steering rack. Where fitted remove any spacers/washers noting the correct position for refitting.

5 Remove the track rod assembly, and examine the track rod inner balljoint for signs of slackness or tight spots. Check that the track rod itself is straight and free from damage. If necessary, renew the track rod; it is also recommended that the steering gear gaiter/dust cover is renewed.

6 Where applicable, locate the spacer on the end of the steering rack, and screw the balljoint into the end of the steering rack. Tighten the track rod inner balljoint to the specified torque, whilst retaining the steering rack with an open-ended spanner.

7 Install the steering gaiter and track rod balljoint as described in Sections 22 and 23.

## 25 Wheel alignment and steering angles – general information

### Definitions

1 A car's steering and suspension geometry is defined in four basic settings – all angles are expressed in degrees; the steering axis is defined as an imaginary line drawn through the axis of the suspension strut, extended where necessary to contact the ground.

2 **Camber** is the angle between each roadwheel and a vertical line drawn through its centre and tyre contact patch, when viewed from the front or rear of the car. Positive camber is when the roadwheels are tilted outwards from the vertical at the top; negative camber is when they are tilted inwards. The camber angle is not adjustable.

3 **Castor** is the angle between the steering axis and a vertical line drawn through each roadwheel's centre and tyre contact patch,

when viewed from the side of the car. Positive castor is when the steering axis is tilted so that it contacts the ground ahead of the vertical; negative castor is when it contacts the ground behind the vertical. The castor angle is not adjustable.

**4 Toe** is the difference, viewed from above, between lines drawn through the roadwheel centres and the car's centre-line. 'Toe-in' is when the roadwheels point inwards, towards each other at the front, while 'toe-out' is when they splay outwards from each other at the front.

**5** The front wheel toe setting is adjusted by screwing the track rod in or out of its balljoints, to alter the effective length of the track rod assembly. The rear wheel toe setting is not adjustable.

### Checking and adjustment

**6** Due to the special measuring equipment necessary to check the wheel alignment and steering angles, and the skill required to use it properly, the checking and adjustment of these settings is best left to a Vauxhall dealer or similar expert. Note that most tyre-fitting shops now possess sophisticated checking equipment.

# Chapter 11
# Bodywork and fittings

## Contents

## Degrees of difficulty

| | | | | |
|---|---|---|---|---|
| **Easy,** suitable for novice with little experience  | **Fairly easy,** suitable for beginner with some experience  | **Fairly difficult,** suitable for competent DIY mechanic 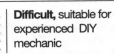 | **Difficult,** suitable for experienced DIY mechanic  | **Very difficult,** suitable for expert DIY or professional  |

## Specifications

| Torque wrench settings | Nm | lbf ft |
|---|---|---|
| Facia-to-bulkhead nuts . . . . . . . . . . . . . . . . . . . . . . . . . . . . . . . . . . . . . . | 22 | 16 |
| Front seat bolts . . . . . . . . . . . . . . . . . . . . . . . . . . . . . . . . . . . . . . . . . . . . | 20 | 15 |
| Rear seat: | | |
|   Corsa and Corsavan (split rear seat): | | |
|     Seat back-to-bracket bolts. . . . . . . . . . . . . . . . . . . . . . . . . . . . . . . . | 30 | 22 |
|     Seat back-to-centre bearing bolts . . . . . . . . . . . . . . . . . . . . . . . . . | 20 | 15 |
|     Seat back-to-hinge bolts . . . . . . . . . . . . . . . . . . . . . . . . . . . . . . . . . | 20 | 15 |
|   Combo Van: | | |
|     Seat back bolts. . . . . . . . . . . . . . . . . . . . . . . . . . . . . . . . . . . . . . . . . | 20 | 15 |
| Seat belt anchorage bolts . . . . . . . . . . . . . . . . . . . . . . . . . . . . . . . . . . . | 35 | 26 |
| Seat belt height adjuster ratchet bolts . . . . . . . . . . . . . . . . . . . . . . . . . | 20 | 15 |
| Seat belt inertia reel bolt. . . . . . . . . . . . . . . . . . . . . . . . . . . . . . . . . . . . . | 35 | 26 |

## 1 General information

The bodyshell is made of pressed-steel sections, and is available in three- and five-door Hatchback versions, as well as two different forms of Van. Most components are welded together, but some use is made of structural adhesives; the front wings are bolted on.

The bonnet, doors, and some other vulnerable panels, are made of zinc-coated metal, and are further protected by being coated with an anti-chip primer, prior to being sprayed.

Extensive use is made of plastic materials, mainly on the interior, but also in exterior components. The front and rear bumpers are injection-moulded from a synthetic material which is very strong and yet light. Plastic components such as wheel arch liners are fitted to the underside of the vehicle, to improve the body's resistance to corrosion.

## 2 Maintenance – bodywork and underframe

The general condition of a vehicle's body-work is the one thing that significantly affects its value. Maintenance is easy, but needs to be regular. Neglect, particularly after minor damage, can lead quickly to further deterioration and costly repair bills. It is important also to keep watch on those parts of the vehicle not immediately visible, for instance the underside, inside all the wheel arches, and the lower part of the engine compartment.

The basic maintenance routine for the bodywork is washing – preferably with a lot of water, from a hose. This will remove all the loose solids which may have stuck to the vehicle. It is important to flush these off in such a way as to prevent grit from scratching the finish. The wheel arches and underframe need washing in the same way, to remove any accumulated mud, which will retain moisture and tend to encourage rust. Paradoxically enough, the best time to clean the underframe and wheel arches is in wet weather, when the mud is thoroughly wet and soft. In very wet weather, the underframe is usually cleaned of large accumulations automatically, and this is a good time for inspection.

Periodically, except on vehicles with a wax-based underbody protective coating, it is a good idea to have the whole of the underframe of the vehicle steam-cleaned, engine compartment included, so that a thorough inspection can be carried out to see what minor repairs and renovations are necessary. Steam-cleaning is available at many garages, and is necessary for the removal of the accumulation of oily grime, which sometimes is allowed to become thick in certain areas. If steam-cleaning facilities are not available, there are some excellent grease solvents available which can be brush-applied; the dirt can then be simply hosed off. Note that these methods should not be used on vehicles with wax-based underbody protective coating, or the coating will be removed. Such vehicles should be inspected annually, preferably just prior to Winter, when the underbody should be washed down, and any damage to the wax coating repaired. Ideally, a completely fresh coat should be applied. It would also be worth considering the use of such wax-based protection for injection into door panels, sills, box sections, etc, as an additional safeguard against rust damage, where such protection is not provided by the vehicle manufacturer.

After washing paintwork, wipe off with a chamois leather to give an unspotted clear finish. A coat of clear protective wax polish will give added protection against chemical pollutants in the air. If the paintwork sheen has dulled or oxidised, use a cleaner/polisher combination to restore the brilliance of the shine. This requires a little effort, but such dulling is usually caused because regular washing has been neglected. Care needs to be taken with metallic paintwork, as special non-abrasive cleaner/polisher is required to avoid damage to the finish. Always check that the door and ventilator opening drain holes and pipes are completely clear, so that water can be drained out. Brightwork should be treated in the same way as paintwork. Windscreens and windows can be kept clear of the smeary film which often appears, by the use of proprietary glass cleaner. Never use any form of wax or other body or chromium polish on glass.

## 3 Maintenance of upholstery and carpets – general

Mats and carpets should be brushed or vacuum-cleaned regularly, to keep them free of grit. If they are badly stained, remove them from the vehicle for scrubbing or sponging, and make quite sure they are dry before refitting. Seats and interior trim panels can be kept clean by wiping with a damp cloth. If they do become stained (which can be more apparent on light-coloured upholstery), use a little liquid detergent and a soft nail brush to scour the grime out of the grain of the material. Do not forget to keep the headlining clean in the same way as the upholstery. When using liquid cleaners inside the vehicle, do not over-wet the surfaces being cleaned. Excessive damp could get into the seams and padded interior, causing stains, offensive odours or even rot.

If the inside of the vehicle gets wet accidentally, it is worthwhile taking some trouble to dry it out properly, particularly where carpets are involved. Do not leave oil or electric heaters inside the vehicle for this purpose.

## 4 Minor body damage – repair

### Minor scratches

If the scratch is very superficial, and does not penetrate to the metal of the bodywork, repair is very simple. Lightly rub the area of the scratch with a paintwork renovator, or a very fine cutting paste, to remove loose paint from the scratch, and to clear the surrounding bodywork of wax polish. Rinse the area with clean water.

Apply touch-up paint to the scratch using a fine paint brush; continue to apply fine layers of paint until the surface of the paint in the scratch is level with the surrounding paintwork. Allow the new paint at least two weeks to harden, then blend it into the surrounding paintwork by rubbing the scratch area with a paintwork renovator or a very fine cutting paste. Finally, apply wax polish.

Where the scratch has penetrated right through to the metal of the bodywork, causing the metal to rust, a different repair technique is required. Remove any loose rust from the bottom of the scratch with a penknife, then apply rust-inhibiting paint to prevent the formation of rust in the future. Using a rubber or nylon applicator, fill the scratch with bodystopper paste. If required, this paste can be mixed with cellulose thinners to provide a very thin paste which is ideal for filling narrow scratches. Before the stopper-paste in the scratch hardens, wrap a piece of smooth cotton rag around the top of a finger. Dip the finger in cellulose thinners, and quickly sweep it across the surface of the stopper-paste in the scratch; this will ensure that the surface of the stopper-paste is slightly hollowed. The scratch can now be painted over as described earlier in this Section.

### Dents

When deep denting of the vehicle's bodywork has taken place, the first task is to pull the dent out, until the affected bodywork almost attains its original shape. There is little point in trying to restore the original shape completely, as the metal in the damaged area will have stretched on impact, and cannot be reshaped fully to its original contour. It is better to bring the level of the dent up to a point which is about 3 mm below the level of the surrounding bodywork. In cases where the dent is very shallow anyway, it is not worth trying to pull it out at all. If the underside of the dent is accessible, it can be hammered out gently from behind, using a mallet with a wooden or plastic head. Whilst doing this, hold a suitable block of wood firmly against the outside of the panel, to absorb the impact from the hammer blows and thus prevent a large area of the bodywork from being 'belled-out'.

Should the dent be in a section of the

bodywork which has a double skin, or some other factor making it inaccessible from behind, a different technique is called for. Drill several small holes through the metal inside the area – particularly in the deeper section. Then screw long self-tapping screws into the holes, just sufficiently for them to gain a good purchase in the metal. Now the dent can be pulled out by pulling on the protruding heads of the screws with a pair of pliers.

The next stage of the repair is the removal of the paint from the damaged area, and from an inch or so of the surrounding 'sound' bodywork. This is accomplished most easily by using a wire brush or abrasive pad on a power drill, although it can be done just as effectively by hand, using sheets of abrasive paper. To complete the preparation for filling, score the surface of the bare metal with a screwdriver or the tang of a file, or alternatively, drill small holes in the affected area. This will provide a really good 'key' for the filler paste.

To complete the repair, see the Section on filling and respraying.

## Rust holes or gashes

Remove all paint from the affected area, and from an inch or so of the surrounding 'sound' bodywork, using an abrasive pad or a wire brush on a power drill. If these are not available, a few sheets of abrasive paper will do the job most effectively. With the paint removed, you will be able to judge the severity of the corrosion, and therefore decide whether to renew the whole panel (if this is possible) or to repair the affected area. New body panels are not as expensive as most people think, and it is often quicker and more satisfactory to fit a new panel than to attempt to repair large areas of corrosion.

Remove all fittings from the affected area, except those which will act as a guide to the original shape of the damaged bodywork (eg headlight shells etc). Then, using tin snips or a hacksaw blade, remove all loose metal and any other metal badly affected by corrosion. Hammer the edges of the hole inwards, in order to create a slight depression for the filler paste.

Wire-brush the affected area to remove the powdery rust from the surface of the remaining metal. Paint the affected area with rust-inhibiting paint, if the back of the rusted area is accessible, treat this also.

Before filling can take place, it will be necessary to block the hole in some way. This can be achieved by the use of aluminium or plastic mesh, or aluminium tape.

Aluminium or plastic mesh, or glass-fibre matting, is probably the best material to use for a large hole. Cut a piece to the approximate size and shape of the hole to be filled, then position it in the hole so that its edges are below the level of the surrounding bodywork. It can be retained in position by several blobs of filler paste around its periphery.

Aluminium tape should be used for small or very narrow holes. Pull a piece off the roll, trim it to the approximate size and shape required, then pull off the backing paper (if used) and stick the tape over the hole; it can be overlapped if the thickness of one piece is insufficient. Burnish down the edges of the tape with the handle of a screwdriver or similar, to ensure that the tape is securely attached to the metal underneath.

## Filling and respraying

Before using this Section, see the Sections on dent, deep scratch, rust holes and gash repairs.

Many types of bodyfiller are available, but generally speaking, those proprietary kits which contain a tin of filler paste and a tube of resin hardener are best for this type of repair. A wide, flexible plastic or nylon applicator will be found invaluable for imparting a smooth and well-contoured finish to the surface of the filler.

Mix up a little filler on a clean piece of card or board – measure the hardener carefully (follow the maker's instructions on the pack), otherwise the filler will set too rapidly or too slowly. Using the applicator, apply the filler paste to the prepared area; draw the applicator across the surface of the filler to achieve the correct contour and to level the surface. As soon as a contour that approximates to the correct one is achieved, stop working the paste – if you carry on too long, the paste will become sticky and begin to 'pick-up' on the applicator. Continue to add thin layers of filler paste at 20-minute intervals, until the level of the filler is just proud of the surrounding bodywork.

Once the filler has hardened, the excess can be removed using a metal plane or file. From then on, progressively-finer grades of abrasive paper should be used, starting with a 40-grade production paper, and finishing with a 400-grade wet-and-dry paper. Always wrap the abrasive paper around a flat rubber, cork, or wooden block – otherwise the surface of the filler will not be completely flat. During the smoothing of the filler surface, the wet-and-dry paper should be periodically rinsed in water. This will ensure that a very smooth finish is imparted to the filler at the final stage.

At this stage, the 'dent' should be surrounded by a ring of bare metal, which in turn should be encircled by the finely 'feathered' edge of the good paintwork. Rinse the repair area with clean water, until all of the dust produced by the rubbing-down operation has gone.

Spray the whole area with a light coat of primer – this will show up any imperfections in the surface of the filler. Repair these imperfections with fresh filler paste or bodystopper, and once more smooth the surface with abrasive paper. Repeat this spray-and-repair procedure until you are satisfied that the surface of the filler, and the feathered edge of the paintwork, are perfect. Clean the repair area with clean water, and allow to dry fully.

The repair area is now ready for final spraying. Paint spraying must be carried out in a warm, dry, windless and dust-free atmosphere. This condition can be created artificially if you have access to a large indoor working area, but if you are forced to work in the open, you will have to pick your day very carefully. If you are working indoors, dousing the floor in the work area with water will help to settle the dust which would otherwise be in the atmosphere. If the repair area is confined to one body panel, mask off the surrounding panels; this will help to minimise the effects of a slight mis-match in paint colours. Bodywork fittings (eg chrome strips, door handles etc) will also need to be masked off. Use genuine masking tape, and several thicknesses of newspaper, for the masking operations.

Before commencing to spray, agitate the aerosol can thoroughly, then spray a test area (an old tin, or similar) until the technique is mastered. Cover the repair area with a thick coat of primer; the thickness should be built up using several thin layers of paint, rather than one thick one. Using 400-grade wet-and-dry paper, rub down the surface of the primer until it is really smooth. While doing this, the work area should be thoroughly doused with water, and the wet-and-dry paper periodically rinsed in water. Allow to dry before spraying on more paint.

Spray on the top coat, again building up the thickness by using several thin layers of paint. Start spraying at one edge of the repair area, and then, using a side-to-side motion, work until the whole repair area and about 2 inches of the surrounding original paintwork is covered. Remove all masking material 10 to 15 minutes after spraying on the final coat of paint.

Allow the new paint at least two weeks to harden, then, using a paintwork renovator, or a very fine cutting paste, blend the edges of the paint into the existing paintwork. Finally, apply wax polish.

## Plastic components

With the use of more and more plastic body components by the vehicle manufacturers (eg bumpers. spoilers, and in some cases major body panels), rectification of more serious damage to such items has become a matter of either entrusting repair work to a specialist in this field, or renewing complete components. Repair of such damage by the DIY owner is not really feasible, owing to the cost of the equipment and materials required for effecting such repairs. The basic technique involves making a groove along the line of the crack in the plastic, using a rotary burr in a power drill. The damaged part is then welded back together, using a hot-air gun to heat up and fuse a plastic filler rod into the groove. Any excess plastic is then removed, and the area rubbed down to a smooth finish. It is important that a filler rod of the correct plastic is used, as body components can be made of a variety of different types (eg polycarbonate, ABS, polypropylene).

**6.2a undo the retaining nut . . .**

**6.2b . . . and release the wheel arch trim panel from the end of the bumper**

Damage of a less serious nature (abrasions, minor cracks etc) can be repaired by the DIY owner using a two-part epoxy filler repair material. Once mixed in equal proportions, this is used in similar fashion to the bodywork filler used on metal panels. The filler is usually cured in twenty to thirty minutes, ready for sanding and painting.

If the owner is renewing a complete component himself, or if he has repaired it with epoxy filler, he will be left with the problem of finding a suitable paint for finishing which is compatible with the type of plastic used. At one time, the use of a universal paint was not possible, owing to the complex range of plastics encountered in body component applications. Standard paints, generally speaking, will not bond to plastic or rubber satisfactorily. However, it is now possible to obtain a plastic body parts finishing kit which consists of a pre-primer treatment, a primer

and coloured top coat. Full instructions are normally supplied with a kit, but basically, the method of use is to first apply the pre-primer to the component concerned, and allow it to dry for up to 30 minutes. Then the primer is applied, and left to dry for about an hour before finally applying the special-coloured top coat. The result is a correctly-coloured component, where the paint will flex with the plastic or rubber, a property that standard paint does not normally possess.

## 5 Major body damage repair – general

Where serious damage has occurred, or large areas need renewal due to neglect, it means that complete new panels will need

welding-in, and this is best left to professionals. If the damage is due to impact, it will also be necessary to check completely the alignment of the bodyshell, and this can only be carried out accurately by a Vauxhall dealer, using special jigs. If the body is left misaligned, it is primarily dangerous as the car will not handle properly, and secondly, uneven stresses will be imposed on the steering, suspension and possibly transmission, causing abnormal wear, or complete failure, particularly to such items as the tyres.

## 6 Front bumper – removal and refitting

### Models up to September 2003

**1** Firmly apply the handbrake, then jack up the front of the car and support it securely on axle stands (see *Jacking and vehicle support*).
**2** Remove the two retaining nuts (one on each side) securing either end of the bumper to the vehicle **(see illustrations)**.
**3** Undo the four screws (two on either side) securing the ends of the bumper to the wheel arch liner **(see illustration)**.
**4** Unscrew the three bolts securing the top of the radiator grille to the crossmember **(see illustration)**. Note the radiator grille is part of the bumper assembly.
**5** Withdraw the centre pins, then release the three clips securing the bottom of the bumper to the vehicle body **(see illustrations)**.
**6** Where applicable, disconnect any wiring block connector(s) from the rear of the bumper **(see illustration)**.
**7** With the aid of an assistant, release the bumper ends from the wheel arch outer trim covers, and remove the bumper from the front of the vehicle. On models with headlight washers, note that it will be necessary to disconnect the supply hose from the T-piece as it becomes accessible.
**8** Refitting is a reversal of the removal procedure, ensuring that all bumper fasteners are securely tightened.

### Models from October 2003

**9** Firmly apply the handbrake, then jack up the front of the car and support it securely on

**6.3 Undo the screws (arrowed) securing the inner wheel arch trim to the bumper (two on each side)**

**6.4 Front grille to crossmember securing bolts (arrowed)**

**6.5a Release the centre pins . . .**

**6.5b . . . then withdraw the lower bumper retaining clips (arrowed)**

**6.6 Disconnect the wiring block connector as the bumper is removed**

**6.10a Undo the retaining nut . . .**

**6.10b . . . and release the wheel arch trim from the corner of the bumper**

**6.11a Undo the screw (arrowed) securing the lower corner of the bumper . . .**

**6.11b . . . and the side of the bumper to the wheel arch liner**

**6.12 Radiator grille-to-crossmember securing bolts (arrowed)**

**6.13a Release the centre pins . . .**

**6.13b . . . then withdraw the lower bumper retaining clips (arrowed)**

**6.14 Disconnect the wiring block connector as the bumper is removed**

axle stands (see *Jacking and vehicle support*).
**10** Working under the wheel arch, undo the two retaining nuts (one on each side) securing the wheel arch trim and the upper corner of the bumper to the vehicle **(see illustrations)**.
**11** Undo the four screws (two on each side) securing the lower corners and sides of the bumper to the wheel arch liner **(see illustrations)**.
**12** Unscrew the three bolts securing the top of the radiator grille to the crossmember **(see illustration)**. Note the radiator grille is part of the bumper assembly.
**13** Withdraw the centre pins, then release the three clips securing the bottom of the bumper to the vehicle body **(see illustrations)**.
**14** Where applicable, disconnect any wiring block connector(s) from the rear of the bumper **(see illustration)**.
**15** With the aid of an assistant, release the bumper ends from the wheel arch trim, and

remove the bumper from the front of the vehicle. On models with headlight washers, note that it will be necessary to disconnect the supply hose from the T-piece as it becomes accessible.

**16** Refitting is a reversal of the removal procedure, ensuring that all bumper fasteners are securely tightened.

## 7 Rear bumper – removal and refitting

### Models up to September 2003

#### Corsa and Corsavan

**1** Open the tailgate, and undo the four screws securing the top of the bumper to the vehicle **(see illustration)**.
**2** Withdraw the centre pins, then remove the two plastic securing clips from the bottom of the bumper to the vehicle body **(see illustration)**.
**3** Undo the two retaining screws (one on

**7.1 Undo the rear bumper upper retaining screws (arrowed)**

**7.2 Release the centre pins, then withdraw the lower bumper retaining clips**

7.3 Undo the retaining screws (one side arrowed) from the bumper inner wing panel

7.4 Carefully ease the wheel arch trim covers away from the vehicle to release the bumper

7.5 Disconnect the wiring block connector as the bumper is removed

7.8 Release the centre pins, then withdraw the upper bumper retaining clips

7.9 Undo the retaining nut and release the wheel arch trim panel from the end of the bumper

either side) securing the ends of the bumper to the wheel arch liner (see illustration).

4 Remove the two retaining nuts (one on each side) securing either end of the bumper to the vehicle (see illustration).

5 With the aid of an assistant, unclip the bumper ends from the wheel arch outer trim covers, and remove the bumper from the rear of the vehicle. Disconnect the wiring connector as the bumper is being removed (see illustration).

6 Refitting is a reverse of the relevant removal procedure, ensuring that all disturbed fasteners are securely tightened. Before finally bolting the bumper in position, ensure that any wiring is securely connected.

### Combo Van

7 Remove both rear light units as described in Chapter 12, Section 7.

8 Prise out the centre pins, then release the two clips (one each side) securing the top of the bumper to the vehicle body (see illustration).

9 Remove the two retaining nuts (one on each side) securing either end of the bumper to the vehicle (see illustration).

10 Undo the six fasteners securing the bottom of the bumper to the vehicle, and the four screws (two each side) securing the bumper to the inner wing panels.

11 Lift the bumper away from the rear of the vehicle. If necessary, slide the foam wedges

out from between the bumper mountings, and unbolt the mountings from the vehicle body.

12 Refitting is a reverse of the relevant removal procedure, ensuring that all disturbed fasteners are securely tightened. Before finally bolting the bumper in position, ensure that any wiring is securely connected.

### *Models from October 2003*

13 Open the tailgate, and undo the four screws securing the top of the bumper to the vehicle (see illustration).

14 From under the wheel arch on each side, undo the upper plastic nut and lower retaining screw, and withdraw the foglight cover panel (see illustrations).

7.13 Undo the rear bumper upper retaining screws (arrowed)

7.14a Undo the upper plastic nut (arrowed) . . .

7.14b . . . and lower retaining screw (arrowed) . . .

7.14c . . . and withdraw the foglight cover panel

7.15 Disconnect the wiring connector from the foglight bulbholder

7.16 Release the centre pins, then withdraw the lower bumper retaining clips

7.17 Carefully ease the wheel arch trim covers away from the vehicle to release the bumper

15 Disconnect the wiring connector from the foglight bulbholder **(see illustration)**.

16 Withdraw the centre pins, then remove the two plastic retaining clips securing the bottom of the bumper to the vehicle body **(see illustration)**.

17 Undo the two retaining nuts (one on each side) securing the wheel arch trim and the upper corner of the bumper to the vehicle **(see illustration)**.

18 With the aid of an assistant, unclip the bumper ends from the wheel arch trim, and remove the bumper from the rear of the vehicle. Disconnect the wiring connector as the bumper is being removed **(see illustration)**.

19 Refitting is a reverse of the relevant removal procedure, ensuring that all disturbed fasteners are securely tightened. Before finally bolting the bumper in position, ensure that any wiring is securely connected.

## 8 Bonnet – removal, refitting and adjustment

### Removal

1 Open the bonnet, and have an assistant support it. It may be useful, to mark the outline position of each bonnet hinge relative to the

bonnet (using a pencil or felt-tip pen), to use as a guide on refitting.

2 Undo the bonnet retaining bolts **(see illustration)**, two each side, then with the help of an assistant, carefully lift the bonnet clear. Store the bonnet out of the way, in a safe place.

3 Inspect the hinge for signs of wear or damage. If hinge renewal is necessary, the lower hinge bolts (three each side) will need to be removed from the inner wing panel.

### Refitting and adjustment

4 With the aid of an assistant, offer up the bonnet, and loosely fit the retaining bolts. Align

7.18 Disconnect the wiring block connector as the bumper is removed

8.2 Undo the bonnet retaining bolts (arrowed) and lift the bonnet away from the vehicle

the hinges with the marks made on removal, then tighten the retaining bolts securely.

5 Close the bonnet, and check for alignment with the adjacent panels. If necessary, slacken the bonnet support bolts, and realign the bonnet to suit. Once the bonnet is correctly aligned, securely tighten the bolts.

6 Once the bonnet is correctly aligned, check that the bonnet fastens and releases in a satisfactory manner, and if necessary adjust the lock striker as described in Section 10.

9.2a Undo the retaining bolts (one side arrowed) . . .

9.2b . . . and remove the crossmember

## 9  Bonnet release cable –
removal and refitting

### Removal

1 Open the bonnet, and unscrew the three bolts securing the top of the radiator grille to the crossmember (see illustration 6.4).

2 Carefully pull back the top of the grille, to access the crossmember securing bolts (three on each side). Slacken and remove the bolts (see illustrations), then lift the crossmember to one side. Note: Bonnet release cable will still be attached.

3 Undo the two retaining bolts and remove the cover from the lock assembly (see illustrations).

4 Unscrew the clamp bolt from the crossmember and release the outer cable, then detach the inner cable from the lock spring (see illustrations).

5 Work back along the cable, releasing it from all the relevant retaining clips and ties, whilst noting its correct routing. Release the rubber sealing grommet from the engine compartment bulkhead, and tie a piece of string to the cable end, this can then be used to draw the cable back into position.

6 From inside the vehicle, release the retaining clip, then withdraw the bonnet release lever from the side of the driver's footwell (see illustrations).

7 Withdraw the lever and cable assembly from inside the vehicle. Once the cable end appears, untie the string and leave it in position in the vehicle.

### Refitting

8 Refitting is a reverse of the relevant removal procedure, noting the following points:

a) Tie the string to the end of the cable, and use the string to draw the bonnet release cable through from inside the vehicle into the engine compartment. Once the cable is through, untie the string.

b) Ensure that the cable is correctly routed and retained by all the relevant clips and ties, then seat the outer cable grommet in the engine compartment bulkhead.

c) Connect the inner cable to the lock spring, and seat the outer cable in its retaining clamp. Position the outer cable so that all free play is removed from the inner cable, then securely tighten its clamp screw.

d) Refit the crossmember, then check the operation of the bonnet release lever before shutting the bonnet.

9.3a Undo the two retaining bolts (arrowed) . . .

9.3b . . . and remove the cover from the lock assembly

9.4a Slacken the bonnet release cable clamp screw . . .

9.4b . . . then unhook the inner cable from the spring

9.6a Release the retaining clip (arrowed), slide the mounting bracket forwards . . .

9.6b . . . and withdraw the bonnet release lever

**10.1 Bonnet lock hook is removed by drilling out its pivot pin (arrowed)**

**10 Bonnet lock components – removal and refitting**

### Bonnet lock hook

1 Drill out the pivot pin, and remove the lock hook and return spring from the bonnet **(see illustration)**.
2 On refitting, locate the hook and spring in the bonnet bracket, and insert a new pivot pin. Secure the pin in position by flattening its end with a suitable pair of pliers.

### Lock striker

3 Slacken the striker locknut, then unscrew the striker from the bonnet and recover the washer. If necessary, unscrew the locknut from the end of the striker, and remove the spring and spring seats.
4 Where necessary, fit the spring and spring seats to the striker, and screw on the locknut. Fit the washer to the striker, and screw the striker into position in the bonnet, tightening it only lightly at this stage.
5 Hold the locknut, and adjust the position of the striker so that the distance from the lower spring seat to the inside of the bonnet is 40 to 45 mm **(see illustration)**.
6 When the striker is correctly positioned, securely tighten the locknut.

### Lock spring

7 Unhook the bonnet release cable from the spring (see Section 9), then free the spring

**11.3 Undo the retaining bolt (arrowed) securing the door check link to the door pillar**

**10.5 When refitting, adjust the position of the bonnet lock striker as described in text**

from the body crossmember and remove it from the vehicle **(see illustration)**.
8 On refitting, ensure that the spring is correctly engaged with the cable and crossmember. Check the operation of the bonnet release lever before shutting the bonnet.

**11 Door – removal, refitting and adjustment**

### Removal

#### All front and Corsa rear doors

1 Open the door to gain access to the wiring connector which is fitted to the front edge of the door.
2 On the front doors, slide the locking clip

**11.2a On front doors, release the locking clip in the direction of the arrow**

**11.4a Remove the lower plastic cover . . .**

**10.7 Free the spring from the crossmember**

out, then rotate the wiring connector to disconnect it from the front edge of the door **(see illustration)**. On the rear doors, slide the locking collar in, then carefully withdraw the wiring connector to disconnect it from the front edge of the door **(see illustration)**.
3 Undo the retaining bolt securing the door check link to the door pillar **(see illustration)**.
4 Remove the plastic covers (where fitted) from the door hinge pins. Have an assistant support the door, then drive both hinge pins out of position using a hammer and suitable punch **(see illustrations)**. Remove the door from the vehicle.
5 Inspect the hinge pins for signs of wear or damage, and renew if necessary.

#### Combo Van rear door

6 Open the rear door, and release the check link spring from the door pin **(see illustration)**.

**11.2b On the rear doors, slide the locking collar (arrowed) inwards**

**11.4b . . . and upper plastic cover . . .**

11.6 Release the check link spring (arrowed) from the door pin

11.7 Release the wiring grommet from the door pillar

11.8a Remove the upper hinge bolts (arrowed) . . .

11.8b . . . and lower hinge bolts (arrowed)

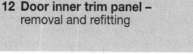

11.13 Door lock striker retaining bolts (arrowed)

**7** Where necessary, trace the wiring back into the door to its wiring connectors. Disconnect the wiring connectors, then free the grommet from the door **(see illustration)**, and withdraw the wiring loom so that it is free from the door.
**8** Have an assistant support the door, then slacken and remove the four hinge retaining bolts and remove the door from the vehicle **(see illustrations)**. It may be useful to mark the outline position of each hinge relative to the body (using a pencil or felt-tip pen), to use as a guide on refitting.
**9** If necessary, the hinge(s) can then be unbolted and removed from the door.

### Refitting

#### All front and Corsa rear doors

**10** Refitting is the reversal of removal procedure, tightening the check link bolts

securely, and ensuring that the wiring is securely reconnected.

#### Combo Van rear door

**11** Refitting is a reversal of the removal procedure, tightening the hinge bolts securely, and ensuring that the wiring is securely reconnected.

### Adjustment

#### All front and Corsa rear doors

**12** Adjustment of the door position is not possible; the hinges are welded to the vehicle body and door, and cannot be repositioned. Misalignment of the door can only be caused by accident damage or wear of the hinge pins.
**13** Door closure may be adjusted by altering the position of the door lock striker on the

body. Slacken the striker retaining bolts, reposition the striker as required, then securely retighten the bolts **(see illustration)**.

#### Combo Van rear door

**14** Slight adjustment of the doors can be achieved by slackening the hinge retaining bolts and repositioning the hinge/door.
**15** Door closure may be adjusted by altering the position of the upper and lower door lock strikers on the door/body (as applicable). Slacken the striker retaining bolts, reposition the striker as required, then securely retighten the bolts **(see illustrations)**.

### 12 Door inner trim panel – removal and refitting

### Removal

#### Front door

**1** Carefully unclip the exterior mirror inner trim panel from the door. On models with manually-operated mirrors, it will be necessary to pull the knob off the adjusting lever in order to remove the panel **(see illustrations)**. Depending on vehicle model, disconnect any wiring connectors as they become accessible.
**2** Lift the inner door lock handle, and carefully prise the handle trim cover out from the door trim panel **(see illustration)**.
**3** Unclip the electric window switch assembly from the door trim panel, then disconnect the wiring connector **(see illustration)**.

11.15a Rear upper door lock catch retaining bolts (arrowed) – Combo Van

11.15b Slacken the retaining bolt (arrowed) to adjust the door striker – Combo Van

12.1a Unclip the exterior mirror inner trim panel from the door . . .

12.1b . . . and disconnect the wiring connector

12.2 Unclip the trim cover from the door inner handle

12.3 Carefully unclip the electric window switch from the door trim panel

12.4 Prise out the window sealing strip from the top of the door

12.5a Undo the retaining screws (arrowed) from the door handle . . .

12.5b . . . the trim panel lower retaining screws (arrowed) . . .

**4** Carefully prise the window inner sealing strip from the top edge of the door trim panel **(see illustration)**.

**5** Unscrew the door grab handle retaining screws, the two lower trim panel screws and the upper trim panel securing screw **(see illustrations)**.

**6** Working your way around the door, carefully unclip the door trim panel, and remove it from the door **(see illustration)**.

### Rear door

**7** Undo the retaining screws, and remove the handle from the rear door **(see illustration)**.

**8** Lift the inner door lock handle, and carefully prise the handle trim cover out from the door trim panel, then undo the retaining screw from the trim panel **(see illustrations)**.

**9** On models with manually-operated windows, release the securing clip, and remove the window regulator handle. To

release the securing clip, either use a special forked tool, or insert a length of wire with a hooked end between the handle and the trim bezel on the door trim panel, and manipulate it to free the securing clip from the handle.

12.5c . . . and the trim panel front retaining screw

Take care not to damage the door trim panel. Recover the trim bezel **(see illustrations)**.

**10** Carefully prise the triangle trim panel away from the top of the door inner trim panel **(see illustration)**.

12.6 Remove the trim panel from the door

12.7 Undo the two screws, and remove the handle from the rear door

12.8a Unclip the trim cover from the door inner handle . . .

12.8b . . . and undo the retaining screw

**12.9a  Using a special forked tool to release the securing clip**

**12.9b  Recover the bezel from the door trim panel**

**12.10  Unclip the inner trim panel from the rear door . . .**

**12.11  . . . then prise out the window sealing strip from the top of the door**

**12.12a  Remove the trim panel lower retaining screws . . .**

**12.12b  . . . and remove the trim panel from the door**

**11**  Carefully prise the window inner sealing strip from the top edge of the door trim panel **(see illustration)**.

**12**  Undo the lower trim panel securing screw, then working your way around the

**12.13  Fit the clip (arrowed) to the regulator handle before fitting the handle to the door**

door, carefully unclip the door trim panel, and remove it from the door **(see illustrations)**.

### Refitting

**13**  Refitting is the reverse of the relevant removal procedure. On models with manual windows, fit the retaining clip to the regulator handle before fitting the handle onto the regulator **(see illustration)**.

## 13  Door handle and lock components – removal and refitting

### Removal

#### Interior handle

**1**  Remove the door inner trim panel as described in Section 12.

**2**  Peel the polythene weathershield away from the door to gain access to the inner handle components **(see illustration)**.

**3**  Slide the inner handle towards the rear of the door to release it from the door panel **(see illustration)**.

**4**  Pull the operating cable to release it from the inner handle assembly, and remove the inner handle from the door **(see illustration)**.

#### Front exterior handle

**5**  Remove the door inner trim panel as described in Section 12, then peel back the weathershield (see paragraph 2).

**6**  With the window fully raised, disconnect the wiring connector from the central locking unit, then undo the retaining bolts and remove the shield from around the door locking mechanism **(see illustrations)**.

**13.2  Carefully peel the weathershield away from the door to gain access to the lock components**

**13.3  Slide the interior handle forwards to release it from door**

**13.4  Release the outer cable (arrowed) from the inner handle assembly**

**13.6a Release the securing clip and disconnect the wiring block connector . . .**

**13.6b . . . then remove the shield from the door locking mechanism**

**13.7a Undo the two nuts . . .**

**7** Undo the two retaining nuts from the inside of the door handle, and remove the handle from the outside of the door **(see illustration)**.

### Front lock cylinder

**8** Remove the exterior door handle as described above, then unhook the inner door handle shell from the link rod **(see illustration)**.

**9** Unclip the locking washer from the rear of the lock cylinder, and remove the lever and springs, note the fitted position of the lever and springs for refitting **(see illustrations)**.

**10** Insert the key into the lock cylinder, then remove the roll-pin from the lock housing **(see illustration)**.

**11** Turn the lock housing anti-clockwise and

**13.7b . . . then withdraw the door handle from the vehicle**

**13.8 Unhook the link rod (arrowed) from the door lock lever**

carefully remove the lock cylinder upwards out of the housing **(see illustration)**.

**12** Remove the key, then withdraw the lock barrel from the housing, taking care the

tumblers do not fall out of the barrel **(see illustrations)**.

**13** If the collar is removed from the lock shell, note the position for refitting. Make sure the

**13.9a Remove the C-clip (arrowed) . . .**

**13.9b . . . then lift off the lever. . .**

**13.9c . . . and spring, noting the correct fitted position**

**13.10 Use long-nose pliers to remove the roll-pin**

**13.11 Remove the lock cylinder out of the housing**

**13.12a Remove the key . . .**

13.12b  . . . then withdraw the lock barrel from the housing

13.13a  Remove the collar from the lock shell . . .

13.13b  . . . then the ball-bearings (arrowed) . . .

13.13c  . . . and the locating ring

13.15  Undo the three retaining screws (arrowed)

two ball-bearings and locating ring are located correctly when refitting **(see illustrations)**.

### Front lock assembly

**14** Remove the exterior door handle as described in paragraphs 5 to 7, then unhook the inner door handle shell from the link rod to the lock assembly.

**15** Undo the three retaining screws, and manoeuvre the lock assembly to gain access to the operating cables **(see illustration)**.

**16** Release the retaining clips, and free the operating cables from the lock assembly **(see illustrations)**.

**17** Withdraw the lock assembly from the door frame **(see illustration)**.

### Corsa rear exterior handle

**18** Remove the door inner trim panel as described in Section 12, and peel back the weathershield (see paragraph 2).

**19** Wind the window fully down, and release the window sealing strip from the rear of the door and window guide **(see illustration)**.

**20** Undo the window guide retaining bolts, and manoeuvre the window guide upwards and out from the door **(see illustrations)**.

**21** Wind the window fully up, then undo the two nuts, and free the mounting plate

13.16a  Release the outer cable . . .

13.16b  . . . then unclip the inner cable

13.16c  Release the outer cable and unclip the inner cable

13.17  Withdraw the lock assembly from the door frame

13.19  Free the sealing strip from the rear of the door

13.20a  Slacken and remove the retaining bolts (arrowed) . . .

13.20b ... then manoeuvre the guide upwards and out of the rear door

13.21  Undo the two nuts, and free the mounting plate assembly

13.22a  Withdraw the handle from the door . . .

13.22b ... the link rod length can be adjusted by turning the plastic stop nut (arrowed)

13.23  Unhook the operating cable from the door handle lever

13.25  Undo the three retaining screws (arrowed)

assembly from the rear of the handle **(see illustration)**.

22  Remove the handle from the outside of the door, freeing its link rod from the lock assembly **(see illustrations)**.

### Corsa rear lock assembly

23  Remove the interior handle as described in paragraphs 1 to 4 above **(see illustration)**.

24  Undo the window guide retaining bolts, and manoeuvre the window guide out from the door **(see illustrations 13.20a and 13.20b)**.

25  Undo the three retaining screws, and manoeuvre the lock assembly to gain access to the central locking wiring connector **(see illustration)**.

26  Slide the locking clip out and disconnect the central locking wiring connector from the lock assembly **(see illustration)**.

27  Undo the retaining screw and unclip the

operating cables from the door and withdraw the lock assembly from door frame complete with operating cables **(see illustrations)**.

28  Release the cable from the lock assembly by unclipping the outer cable and disconnecting

the inner cable from the operating lever on the lock assembly, the link rod can be removed by pivoting the retaining clip away from the link rod, and free the link rod from the lock assembly **(see illustrations)**.

13.26  Release the securing clip (arrowed) and disconnect the wiring block connector

13.27a  Undo the retaining screw . . .

13.27b ... and unclip the operating cables (arrowed)

13.28a  Release the outer cable and unclip the inner cable . . .

13.28b ... then release the securing clip and disconnect the link rod

13.29a Release the securing clip using a special forked tool . . .

13.29b . . . then withdraw the handle

13.30 Remove the trim panel from the door

## Combo Van rear lock assembly

**29** Release the securing clip, and remove the door handle. To release the securing clip, either use a special forked tool, or insert a length of

13.32 Release the securing clips and disconnect the linkage rods (arrowed)

wire with a hooked end between the handle and the door trim panel, and manipulate it to free the securing clip from the handle. Take care not to damage the door trim panel **(see illustrations)**.

**30** Carefully unclip the inner trim panel, and remove it from the rear door **(see illustration)**.
**31** Remove the upper and lower latches as described in paragraphs 40 to 42.
**32** Release the retaining clips from the link rods, and free both link rods from the lock mechanism **(see illustration)**.
**33** Undo the three retaining screws from the lock assembly **(see illustration)**.
**34** Disconnect the central locking wiring connector from the lock assembly.
**35** Withdraw the actuation unit complete with the operating cables. To detach the cables from the unit, first unclip the covers, then release the outer cables from the bracket and unclip the inner cables from the linkage **(see illustrations)**.

## Combo Van rear handle

**36** Remove the lock assembly as described in paragraphs 29 to 35.
**37** Undo the two retaining nuts and remove the inner door handle shell from the door handle. Withdraw and remove the handle from the outside of the door **(see illustration)**.

## Combo Van rear lock cylinder

**38** Remove the rear handle as described in paragraphs 36 and 37.
**39** Remove the lock cylinder as described in paragraphs 8 to 13.

## Combo Van rear latches

**40** Undo the two bolts securing the latch to the door, and guide the latch out of position **(see illustration)**.

13.33 Undo the retaining screws (arrowed)

13.35a Withdraw the lock assembly from the door . . .

13.35b . . . unclip the cover . . .

13.35c . . . and disconnect the operating cables (arrowed) from the lever

13.37 Undo the two nuts (arrowed) and free the mounting plate assembly

13.40 Undo the two bolts and remove the latch from the door . . .

**13.41 . . . then disconnect the operating cable from the lever**

**41** Release the operating cable and free it from the latch assembly **(see illustration)**.
**42** If necessary, remove the second latch in the same way.

## Refitting

**43** Refitting is the reverse of the removal sequence, noting the following points:
a) *If a lock cylinder has been removed, on refitting ensure that all the components are refitted in the correct position, as noted on removal and are securely held in place by the C-clip. Check the operation of the lock cylinder, making sure that the spring returns the cylinder to its central position, before refitting the plate to the door.*
b) *Ensure that all link rods are securely held in position by their retaining clips.*
c) *Apply grease to all lock and link rod pivot points.*
d) *Before installing the relevant trim panel,*
*thoroughly check the operation of all the door lock handles and, where necessary, the central locking system, and ensure that the weathershield is correctly positioned.*
e) *Make sure the polythene weathershield fitted behind the trim panel is undamaged and perfectly sealed to the door around its complete contact area. If a perfect seal cannot be made, renew the weathershield.*

## 14 Door window glass and regulator – removal and refitting

## Removal

**1** Remove the door inner trim panel as described in Section 12.
**2** Peel the polythene weathershield away from the door to gain access to the door lock components. Proceed as described under the relevant sub-heading.

### Front window glass

**3** Remove the regulator assembly as described below. The glass can then be lifted out from the door **(see illustration)**.

### Rear window glass

**4** Carefully prise the window outer sealing strip from the top edge of the door trim panel **(see illustration)**.
**5** Wind the window fully down, and release the window sealing strip from the rear of the door and window guide **(see illustration 13.19)**.

**6** Undo the window guide retaining bolts, and manoeuvre the window guide upwards and out from the door **(see illustrations 13.20b)**.
**7** Tilt the window glass forwards, and free the window guide from the regulator mechanism (it may be necessary to raise the window mechanism slightly to disengage the window guide). The glass can then be manoeuvred out from the door **(see illustration)**.

### Front regulator

**Note:** *A pop-rivet gun and suitable rivets will be required when refitting. The rivet heads should be approximately 4.8 mm in diameter and 11 mm in length.*
**8** With the window set in the raised position, secure the window glass in position, then undo the retaining bolts from the base of the window guide **(see illustration)**.
**9** Using an 8.5 mm drill bit, drill out the rivets securing the regulator assembly and the guide rails to the door, taking great care not to damage the door panel **(see illustrations)**.
**10** With all the rivets removed, free the regulator rollers from the ends of the window glass guide rail, and manoeuvre the guide rails and regulator assembly out through the door aperture **(see illustrations)**.
**11** On models with electric windows, disconnect the wiring connector from the regulator as it becomes accessible.

### Rear regulator

**Note:** *A pop-rivet gun and suitable rivets will be required when refitting. The rivet heads should be approximately 4.8 mm in diameter and 11 mm in length.*

**14.3 Removing the front door window glass**

**14.4 Prise out the window sealing strip from the top of the door**

**14.7 Removing the rear door window glass**

**14.8 Undo the two retaining bolts (arrowed)**

**14.9a Using a suitable drill . . .**

**14.9b . . . carefully drill out the rivets (arrowed)**

**14.10a  Free the regulator rollers from the window glass runner . . .**

**14.10b  . . . and remove the regulator assembly from the door**

**14.13  Drill out the rivets (arrowed)**

**14.15a  Engage the regulator at the front (arrowed) . . .**

**14.15b  . . . and at the rear (arrowed)**

### Refitting

**15** Refitting is the reverse of the removal procedure, noting the following points:

a) *Where the regulator has been removed, remove the remains of the old rivets before fitting the regulator to the door. Engage the regulator in position on the door* **(see illustrations)** *and with the window glass, and secure it with new pop-rivets.*

b) *Check the window moves smoothly and easily up-and-down, without any sign of tight spots. If the window movement is stiff, trace and rectify the cause. On the front window, movement is adjustable by slackening the regulator guide bolts and moving them in the slotted holes. Find the position where the window movement is the easiest, then securely tighten the bolts.*

c) *Refit the weathershield, making sure it is securely stuck to the door, then install the trim panel as described in Section 12.*

**12** Remove the rear window glass as described in paragraphs 4 to 7.

**13** Using an 8.5 mm drill bit, drill out the rivets securing the regulator assembly to the door, taking great care not to damage the door panel **(see illustration)**.

**14** With all the rivets removed, manoeuvre the regulator out through the door aperture. On models with electric windows, disconnect the wiring connector from the regulator as it becomes accessible.

### 15  Tailgate and support struts – removal and refitting

### Removal

#### Tailgate

**1** Disconnect the battery negative terminal (refer to *Disconnecting the battery* in the Reference Chapter).

**2** Open the tailgate, and detach the parcel shelf cords from the tailgate. Undo the four retaining screws from the tailgate trim panel.

**3** Carefully prise the inner trim panel from the tailgate, taking care not to break the retaining clips on removal **(see illustration)**.

**4** Disconnect the wiring block connector from the tailgate. Tie a suitable length of string to the end of the wiring loom block connector, then free the grommet from the top of the tailgate and withdraw the wiring loom **(see illustrations)**. When the end of the loom appears, untie the string and leave it in position in the tailgate; it can then be used to draw the wiring back into position when refitting.

**5** Prise out the washer jet from the top of the tailgate, and disconnect it from the washer hose **(see illustration)**. Tie a suitable length

**15.3  Unclip the inner trim panel from the tailgate**

**15.4a  Disconnect the wiring block connector . . .**

**15.4b  . . . then remove the grommet and withdraw the wiring from the tailgate**

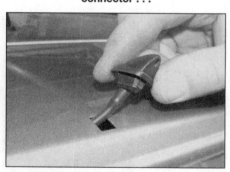

**15.5  Remove the washer jet out from the tailgate**

of string to the hose end, then withdraw the hose, leaving the string in position in the same way as for the wiring.

**6** Have an assistant support the tailgate, then raise the spring clips and pull the support struts off their balljoint mountings on the tailgate (see paragraphs 8 and 9). Prise out the hinge pin retaining clips, then tap both hinge pins out of position and remove the tailgate from the vehicle **(see illustrations)**.

**7** Examine the hinge pins for signs of wear or damage, and renew if necessary.

### Support struts

**8** Support the tailgate in the open position using a suitable piece of wood, or with the help of an assistant.

**9** Raise the spring clips, and pull the support strut off its balljoint mountings on the tailgate and vehicle body **(see illustrations)**.

### Refitting

#### Tailgate

**10** Refitting is a reversal of the removal procedure, noting the following points:

a) *Prior to refitting, apply a smear of multi-purpose grease to the hinge pins.*

b) *Ensure that the hinge pins are securely retained by their clips, and that the support struts are securely held in position by their spring clips.*

c) *Use the string to draw the wiring loom and washer hose through into position, and ensure that the wiring connector is securely reconnected.*

#### Support struts

**11** Refitting is a reverse of the removal procedure, ensuring that the strut is securely retained by its spring clips.

| 16 | Tailgate lock components – removal and refitting |
|---|---|

### Removal

**1** Open the tailgate, and detach the parcel shelf cords from the tailgate. Undo the four retaining screws from the tailgate trim panel.

**2** Carefully prise the inner trim panel from the tailgate, taking care not to break the retaining clips on removal **(see illustration 15.3)**.

**3** Proceed as described under the relevant sub-heading.

### Lock assembly

**4** From inside the tailgate, release the retaining clip by pivoting it away from the link rod, and detach the rod from the lock assembly **(see illustration)**.

**5** Slacken and remove the three screws, and remove the lock, complete with link rod, from the tailgate **(see illustrations)**.

### Lock cylinder assembly

**6** From inside the tailgate, release the

**15.6a Remove the retaining clips . . .**

**15.6b . . . then drift out the hinge pin and lift off the tailgate**

**15.9a Lift the retaining clip**

**15.9b . . . and free the support strut from its balljoints**

retaining clip by pivoting it away from the link rod, and detach the rod from the lock cylinder **(see illustration)**.

**7** Release the retaining clip and detach the

central locking wiring connector from the servo unit on the lock cylinder assembly **(see illustration)**.

**8** Undo the two nuts and the lock cylinder

**16.4 Release the retaining clip (arrowed) and detach the link rod from the tailgate lock**

**16.5a Remove the three screws (arrowed) . . .**

**16.5b . . . and withdraw the lock from the tailgate**

**16.6 Release the retaining clip (arrowed) and detach the link rod**

assembly can then be manoeuvred out of the tailgate **(see illustration)**. **Note:** *The lock cylinder assembly can only be replaced as a complete unit, check with your local Vauxhall dealer for the availability of parts.*

### Refitting

**9** Refitting is a reverse of the removal procedure.

### 17 Central locking components
– removal and refitting

### *Front door servo*

**1** The servo motor is part of the lock assembly and can only be purchased as a complete assembly. Remove the lock assembly as described in Section 13.

**17.4a Undo the two retaining screws (arrowed) . . .**

**17.7 Slide the wiring connector away from the lock cylinder to release it from the bracket**

**17.8b . . . and unclip the servo unit from the lock cylinder lever**

**16.7 Release the retaining clip (arrowed) and disconnect the wiring connector**

### *Rear door servo*

#### Corsa

**2** The servo motor is part of the lock assembly and can only be purchased as a complete

**17.4b . . . and disconnect the servo unit from the lock mechanism**

**17.8a Undo the two retaining screws (arrowed) . . .**

**17.11a Undo the two retaining screws (arrowed) . . .**

**16.8 Undo the nuts (arrowed) and remove the lock assembly**

assembly. Remove the lock assembly as described in Section 13.

#### Combo Van

**3** Remove the lock assembly as described in Section 13.
**4** Undo the two retaining screws and remove the servo unit from the lock assembly, detaching its actuating arm from the lock mechanism **(see illustrations)**.
**5** Refitting is the reverse of removal. Prior to installing the trim panel, check the operation of the servo unit.

### *Tailgate servo*

**6** Remove the tailgate lock cylinder assembly as described in Section 16.
**7** Release the wiring harness plug from the bracket by sliding it away from the lock cylinder **(see illustration)**.
**8** Undo the two retaining screws, withdraw the circlip (where fitted) from the actuating rod and unclip the servo unit from the lock cylinder assembly **(see illustrations)**.
**9** Refitting is the reverse of removal, ensuring that the actuating rod is correctly engaged with the lock mechanism. Prior to installing the trim panel, check the operation of the servo unit.

### *Fuel filler cap servo*

#### Corsa

**10** Open the fuel filler flap and remove the fuel tank cap.
**11** Undo the two retaining screws from the fuel filler flap catch and withdraw the servo unit assembly, disconnect the wiring connector as it becomes accessible **(see illustrations)**.

**17.11b . . . and withdraw the servo unit assembly**

**17.12 Unclip the servo unit and withdraw it from the housing**

**12** The servo motor can then be unclipped and withdrawn from the catch assembly **(see illustration)**.

**13** Refitting is the reverse of removal, ensuring that the servo unit assembly is correctly engaged in the filler neck aperture.

### Combo Van

**14** Remove the right-hand rear quarter inner trim panel.

**15** Release the servo retaining clips then manoeuvre the servo out from the rear quarter panel, disconnect the servo unit wiring connector.

**16** Refitting is the reverse of removal, ensuring that the servo unit is correctly engaged. Check the operation of the servo unit before refitting the inner trim panel.

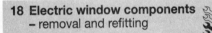

### 18 Electric window components – removal and refitting

**Note:** *Every time the battery is disconnected, or the electric window motors are disconnected, it will be necessary to reprogramme the motors to restore the one-touch function of the buttons. To do this, fully close both front windows. With the windows closed, depress the up button of the driver's side window for approximately 5 seconds, then release it and depress the passenger side window up button for approximately 5 seconds.*

**19.1 Unclip the exterior mirror inner trim panel from the door . . .**

**18.3a Undo the retaining screws (arrowed) . . .**

**18.4a Check the drive gear is located correctly on the motor . . .**

### Window switches

**1** Refer to Chapter 12.

### Window winder motors

**2** Remove the regulator mechanism as described in Section 14.

**3** With the regulator removed, slacken and remove the three retaining screws, and separate the motor and regulator **(see illustrations)**. Do not attempt to dismantle the motor assembly, as it is a sealed unit.

**4** Before refitting the motor, check the drive gear is located correctly on the motor, and the washer is clipped into place on the regulator assembly **(see illustrations)**.

**5** Fit the motor assembly to the regulator, and securely tighten its retaining screws.

**6** Install the regulator mechanism as described in Section 14.

**19.2 . . . and disconnect the wiring connector**

**18.3b . . . and remove the electric window motor**

**18.4b . . . and the washer is clipped into place on the regulator assembly**

### 19 Exterior mirror and associated components – removal and refitting

### Mirror assembly

**1** Unclip the exterior mirror inner trim panel from the door, on manually-adjusted mirrors detach the knob from the adjustment lever **(see illustration)**.

**2** Disconnect the wiring connector from the speaker in the trim panel **(see illustration)**.

**3** On electrically-operated mirrors, disconnect the wiring connector to the mirror assembly.

**4** Undo the three retaining bolts, and remove the mirror assembly from the outside of the door **(see illustrations)**.

**5** Refitting is a reverse of the removal procedure.

**19.4a Undo the retaining screws (arrowed) . . .**

19.4b ... and remove the exterior mirror

19.6a Press against the top face of the mirror ...

19.6b ... and carefully prise the glass from its balljoints

19.8 Ensure that the mirror is correctly located on the balljoint socket (A) and on each of its cable balljoints (B)

19.12a Carefully unclip the cover ...

19.12b ... and remove it from the mirror housing

### Mirror glass

6 While pressing against the top face of the mirror, insert a wide plastic or wooden wedge between the lower edge of the mirror glass and mirror housing, and carefully prise the glass from its balljoints (see illustrations). Take great care when removing the glass; do not use excessive force, as the glass is easily broken (use a rag or wear thick gloves, particularly if removing an already-broken mirror).

7 Remove the glass from the mirror. Where applicable, disconnect the wiring connector from the mirror heating element as it become accessible.

8 When refitting, carefully clip the glass back into position, ensuring that it is correctly located on each of its balljoints (see illustration).

### Mirror motor

9 Remove the mirror glass as described above.

10 Undo the three screws and remove the motor assembly, disconnecting its wiring connectors as they become accessible.

11 Refitting is the reverse of removal.

### Mirror cover

12 Fold the mirror in partially, then carefully unclip the cover from the mirror housing (see illustrations).

13 Refitting is the reverse of removal.

### Mirror switch

14 Refer to Chapter 12.

## 20 Windscreen, tailgate and fixed window glass – general information

These areas of glass are secured by the tight fit of the weatherstrip in the body aperture, and are bonded in position with a special adhesive. The removal and refitting of these areas of fixed glass is a difficult, messy and time-consuming task, which is considered beyond the scope of the home mechanic. It is difficult, unless one has plenty of practice, to obtain a secure, waterproof fit. Furthermore, the task carries a high risk of breakage; this applies especially to the laminated glass windscreen. In view of this, owners are strongly advised to have this sort of work carried out by one of the many specialist windscreen fitters, or a Vauxhall dealer.

## 21 Sunroof – general information

1 A manual or electric sunroof was offered as an optional extra on most models, and is fitted as standard equipment on some models.

2 Due to the complexity of the sunroof mechanism, considerable expertise is needed to repair, renew or adjust the sunroof components successfully. Removal of the roof first requires the headlining to be removed, which is a complex and tedious operation in itself, and not a task to be undertaken lightly (See Section 26). Therefore, any problems with the sunroof should be referred to a Vauxhall dealer.

3 On models with an electric sunroof, if the sunroof motor fails to operate, first check the relevant fuse. If the fault cannot be traced and rectified, the sunroof can be opened and closed manually using a suitable Allen wrench to turn the motor spindle. To gain access to the motor spindle, carefully prise out the trim cover situated at the rear of the sunroof. Insert the Allen key in the motor spindle, and turn to move the sunroof to the required position. A suitable Allen key is supplied with the vehicle, and should be found in the glovebox.

## 22 Body exterior fittings – removal and refitting

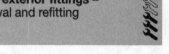

### Radiator grille

1 The radiator grille is part of the front bumper assembly, remove the bumper as described in Section 6.

### Wheel arch liners and body under-panels

2 The various plastic covers fitted to the underside of the vehicle are secured in position by a mixture of screws, nuts and retaining clips, and removal will be fairly obvious on inspection. Work methodically around the liner/panel, removing its retaining

screws and releasing its retaining clips until it is free to be removed from the underside of the vehicle. Most clips used on the vehicle, with the exception of the fasteners which are used to secure the wheel arch liners, are simply prised out of position. The wheel arch liner clips are released by tapping their centre pins through the clip, and then removing the outer section of the clip; new clips will be required on refitting if the centre pins are not recovered.

3 When refitting, renew any retaining clips that may have been broken on removal, and ensure that the panel is securely retained by all the relevant clips, nuts and screws. Vauxhall also recommend that plastic nuts (where used) are renewed, regardless of their apparent condition, whenever they are disturbed.

### Body trim strips and badges

4 The various body trim strips and badges are held in position with a special adhesive tape. Removal requires the trim/badge to be heated, to soften the adhesive, and then cut away from the surface. Due to the high risk of damage to the vehicle's paintwork during this operation, it is recommended that this task should be entrusted to a Vauxhall dealer.

## 23 Seats –
### removal and refitting

> ⚠️ **Warning:** The front seats are equipped with seat belt tensioners, and side airbags may be built into the outer sides of the seats. The seat belt tensioners and side airbags may cause injury if triggered accidentally. If the tensioner has been triggered due to a sudden impact or accident, the unit must be renewed, as it cannot be reset. If a seat is to be disposed of, the tensioner must be triggered before the seat is removed from the vehicle. Due to safety considerations, tensioner renewal or seat disposal must be entrusted to a Vauxhall dealer. Where side airbags are fitted, refer to Chapter 12 for the precautions which should be observed when dealing with an airbag system.

1 Disconnect the battery negative terminal (refer to *Disconnecting the battery* in the Reference Chapter). Wait 2 minutes for capacitors to discharge, before working on the seat electrics.

### Front seat removal

**Note:** *On Combo models, the front passenger seat needs a special Vauxhall tool (KM-6290) to slide the seat forwards, to access the rear mounting bolts. It is a bar which fits under the front of the seat and locates into the locking levers on the two seat guide rails. When the locking levers are released, the seat can slide forward to access the rear mounting bolts.*

2 Slide the seat adjustment fully to the rear.

23.2a Unclip the cover . . .

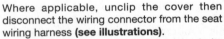

23.2c . . . and disconnect the wiring connector from the seat wiring harness

Where applicable, unclip the cover then disconnect the wiring connector from the seat wiring harness **(see illustrations)**.

3 Slacken and remove the seat retaining bolts from the front of the seat guide rails **(see illustration)**.

4 Slide the seat fully forwards, then slacken and remove the seat retaining bolts from rear of the guide rails **(see illustration)**. See note above for passenger seat in Combo models.

5 The seat can now be lifted out of the vehicle. On Combo models, note the position of any spacers under the seat guide rails on the floor panel.

### Rear seat removal

#### Cushion – Corsa and Corsavan

6 Pull the rear seat cushion forwards and fold it upwards.

7 Press the two hinge retaining rods towards

23.4 Undo the seat retaining bolts (one side arrowed) from the rear of the seat rails

23.2b . . . then release the locking clip . . .

23.3 Undo the seat retaining bolts (one side arrowed) from the front of the seat rails

the centre, to release them from the seat hinge brackets on the base of the seat cushion.

#### One-piece backrest – Corsa and Corsavan

8 Open up the tailgate, and remove the rear parcel shelf.

9 Fold the rear seat backrest forwards, and release the pivot pin from the left- and right-hand seat backrest pivot catch **(see illustration)**.

10 The seat backrest can then be manoeuvred out of the vehicle.

#### Two-piece backrest – Corsa and Corsavan

11 Open up the tailgate, and remove the rear parcel shelf.

12 Fold the left-hand backrest forward, unclip the trim cover from the right-hand seat backrest hinge and remove the retaining bolts.

23.9 Release the pivot pin (arrowed) from the seat backrest pivot catch

**23.12a Unclip the trim cover and remove the retaining bolts (arrowed)**

**23.12b Release the pivot pin (arrowed) from the seat backrest pivot catch**

**23.13 Unscrew the seat belt/stalk mounting bolt**

**23.14a Unclip the trim cover and remove the retaining bolts (arrowed)**

**23.14b Release the pivot pin (arrowed) from the seat backrest pivot catch**

**23.22 Press the end of the wiring block connector to secure**

Push the right-hand backrest to the right and detach it from the pivot bracket to withdraw the backrest **(see illustrations)**.

**13** Prise off the trim cover from the seat belt stalk/lap belt mounting bolt. Unscrew the mounting bolt, and recover the washer and spacer from behind the belt anchorage **(see illustration)**.

**14** Fold the left-hand backrest upwards, unclip the trim cover from the seat backrest hinge and remove the retaining bolts. Push the backrest to the left and detach it from the pivot bracket to withdraw the left-hand backrest **(see illustrations)**.

### Cushion – Combo Van

**15** Fold back the carpet from front of the seat to gain access to the seat pivot pins.

**16** Prise off the covers from each pin, then release the pins and remove the seat cushion from the vehicle.

### Backrest – Combo Van

**17** Where necessary, undo the retaining bolts and remove the luggage compartment grille from the vehicle.

**18** Fold the seat backrest forwards slightly, then unclip the cover at the centre seat to access the seat hinge bolts.

**19** Prise off the trim cover from the seat belt stalk/lap belt mounting bolts. Unscrew the mounting bolts, and recover the washer and spacer from behind the belt anchorage.

**20** Fold the left-hand backrest forward, push the right-hand backrest to the right and detach it from the pivot bracket to withdraw the backrest.

**21** Fold the left-hand backrest upwards, push the backrest to the left and detach it from the pivot bracket to withdraw the left-hand backrest.

### Refitting front seats

**22** Refitting is a reverse of the removal procedure, noting the following points:

a) *Remove all traces of old thread-locking compound from the threads of the seat retaining bolts, and clean the threaded holes in the vehicle floor, ideally by running a tap of the correct size and pitch down them.*

b) *Apply a suitable thread-locking compound to the threads of the seat bolts. Refit the bolts, and tighten them to the specified torque setting.*

c) *Reconnect the seat wiring block connector (see illustration) making sure it has locked securely, then reconnect the battery negative terminal.*

### Refitting rear seats

**23** Refitting is a reverse of the removal procedure, tightening the seat mounting bolts to the specified torque (where applicable).

## 24 Front seat belt tensioning mechanism – general information

All models covered in this manual are fitted with a front seat belt pyrotechnic tensioner system. The system is designed to instantaneously take up any slack in the seat

belt in the case of a sudden frontal impact, therefore reducing the possibility of injury to the front seat occupants. Each front seat is fitted with its own system, the components of which are mounted in the seat frame.

The seat belt tensioner is triggered by a frontal impact causing a deceleration of six times the force of gravity or greater. Lesser impacts, including impacts from behind, will not trigger the system.

When the system is triggered, a pretensioned spring draws back the seat belt via a cable which acts on the seat belt stalk. The cable can move by up to 80.0 mm, which therefore reduces the slack in the seat belt around the shoulders and waist of the occupant by a similar amount.

There is a risk of injury if the system is triggered inadvertently when working on the vehicle, and it is therefore strongly recommended that any work involving the seat belt tensioner system is entrusted to a Vauxhall dealer. Refer to the warning given at the beginning of Section 23 before contemplating any work on the front seats.

## 25 Seat belt components – removal and refitting

### Front belt removal

#### Three-door models

**1** Prise off the trim cover from the upper seat belt mounting. Unscrew the mounting bolt,

25.1a  Prise off the trim cover . . .

25.1b  . . . and unscrew the mounting bolt

25.2a  Remove the trim cap and unscrew the retaining bolt . . .

25.2b  . . . then disengage the seat belt mounting rail from the floor and seat belt, and remove it from the vehicle

25.4  Undo the retaining screw and release the sill trim panel

**4** Undo the retaining screw, and release the sill trim panel from the front edge of the rear seat side trim panel **(see illustration)**.
**5** Peel the door sealing strip away from the front edge of the rear seat side panel, then undo the two retaining screws, release the two securing clips and unclip the panel from the rear side panel of the vehicle **(see illustrations)**.
**6** Undo the two retaining screws, and remove the seat belt guide from the pillar **(see illustration)**.
**7** Undo the inertia reel retaining bolt, and remove the seat belt assembly from the vehicle **(see illustration)**.

**Five-door and Combo Van models**

**8** Unclip the storage tray from along the sill trim panel, then unclip the sill trim from the bottom of the door pillar **(see illustrations)**.

and recover any washer/spacers from behind the belt anchorage **(see illustrations)**.
**2** Slacken and remove bolt and washer securing the seat belt mounting rail to the

floor. Disengage the rail from the floor and the seat belt, and remove it **(see illustrations)**.
**3** Remove the rear seat backrest as described in Section 23.

25.5a  Peel the door sealing strip away from the panel . . .

25.5b  . . . undo the upper retaining screws (arrowed) . . .

25.5c  . . . unclip the lower rear trim clip . . .

25.5d  . . . unclip the lower front trim clip . . .

25.5e  . . . then unclip the trim panel from the vehicle

25.6  Undo the retaining screws (arrowed) and remove the seat belt guide from the pillar

**25.7 Undo the inertia reel retaining bolt (arrowed) and remove the seat belt assembly**

**25.8a Unclip the storage tray . . .**

**25.8b . . . then unclip the sill trim panel**

**25.9a Prise out the circular plug (where fitted) . . .**

**25.9b . . . then undo the retaining screw**

**25.10a Remove the trim from the outside of the door pillar . . .**

**9** Prise out the trim cap from upper trim panel and undo the retaining screw **(see illustrations)**. Peel the door sealing strip away from the door pillar.
**10** Remove the trim from the outside of the

door pillar to reveal the retaining nuts, then undo both bolts and free the upper inner trim panel **(see illustrations)**. Unclip the two panel sections, and remove them from the vehicle.
**11** Prise out the trim cap from the outside of

the door pillar to reveal the seat belt inertia reel mounting nut. Using a deep socket (Vauxhall use an extra long deep socket) unscrew the mounting nut and remove the inertia reel from inside the vehicle **(see illustrations)**.

**25.10b . . . undo the retaining nuts (arrowed) . . .**

**25.10c . . . and withdraw the inner trim panel**

**25.11a Remove the trim from the outside of the door pillar . . .**

**25.11b . . . undo the retaining nut, using a deep socket . . .**

**25.11c . . . and withdraw the inertia seat belt assembly**

**25.12a Unclip the trim panel . . .**

25.12b ... and remove the anchorage bolt (arrowed) from the seat frame

25.15a Unclip the trim/hook ...

25.15b ... undo the retaining screw ...

25.15c ... and remove the trim panel

25.17a Release the securing trim clips ...

25.17b ... unclip the height adjuster ...

**12** Unclip the trim panel from the side of the seat and remove the seat belt anchorage bolt from the seat frame (see illustrations).

### Height adjuster – three-door models

**13** Prise off the trim cover from the upper seat belt mounting. Unscrew the mounting bolt, and recover any washer/spacers from behind the belt anchorage (see illustrations 25.1a and 25.1b).
**14** Peel the door sealing strip away from the front edge of the rear seat side panel, then undo the two retaining screws and unclip the panel from the rear side panel of the vehicle (see illustrations 25.5a, 25.5b and 25.5e).
**15** Unclip the trim cap/hook at the top of the upper door trim panel and undo the retaining screw. Remove the trim panel and undo the two retaining bolts and withdraw the adjuster from the pillar (see illustrations).

### Height adjuster – five-door models

**16** Remove the upper B-pillar trim/height adjuster as described in paragraphs 9 and 10.
**17** Unclip the height adjuster from the trim panel, then feed the seat belt through the trim panel to remove (see illustrations).
**18** To remove the seat belt from the height adjuster, unscrew the mounting bolt, and recover the washer and spacer from behind the belt anchorage (see illustrations).

### Rear belt removal

#### Side belts

**19** Prise off the trim cover from the upper seat belt mounting. Unscrew the mounting bolt, and recover any washer/spacers from

behind the belt anchorage (see illustrations).
**20** Remove the rear seat backrest as described in Section 23. Unbolt the seat belt lower anchorage bolt from the floor panel (see illustration)

25.17c ... then feed the seat belt through the trim panel to remove

25.18b ... and recover the washer ...

**21** Peel the sealing strip away from the tailgate aperture and, on five-door vehicles, from the door aperture (see illustration).
**22** On five-door vehicles, undo the retaining screw at the rear of the upper trim panel, then

25.18a Unscrew the mounting bolt ...

25.18c ... and spacer from behind the belt anchorage

**25.19a Prise off the trim cover . . .**

**25.19b . . . and unscrew the mounting bolt**

**25.20 Unbolt the seat belt lower anchorage bolt**

**25.21 Peel the sealing strip away from the from the door aperture – 5-door models**

**25.22a Undo the retaining screw . . .**

unclip the trim and remove it from the vehicle **(see illustrations)**.

23 On three-door models, unclip the trim panel from the upper B-pillar trim panel **(see illustration)**.

24 Undo the two retaining bolts and remove the seat locking arm from the inner panel **(see illustration)**. Make alignment marks to aid the correct fitting of the arm.

25 Undo the retaining screws and unclip

the lower trim panel from the rear quarter panel. As the panel is removed feed the seat belt through the panel to disengage it **(see illustration)**. Disconnect wiring connectors for speakers or interior lights as they come into view.

26 Unscrew the inertia reel retaining bolt, free the belt and remove the belt reel from the vehicle **(see illustration)**.

### Centre buckles

27 Fold the rear seat cushion forwards, and unscrew the relevant bolt securing the buckle to the floor **(see illustration)**.

### Centre belt

28 Remove the rear seat backrest as described in Section 23.

29 Unclip the trim cover from around the rear seat locking button **(see illustrations)**.

30 With the aid of an assistant, unclip the

**25.22b . . . and unclip the panel from the vehicle**

**25.23 Unclip from the upper B-pillar trim panel – 3 door models**

**25.24 Undo the retaining bolts (arrowed) and remove the seat locking arm**

**25.25 Feed the seat belt through the trim panel**

**25.26 Unscrew the inertia reel retaining bolt**

**25.27 Unscrew the bolt (arrowed) to remove the seat belt buckle**

25.29a  Use a screwdriver to carefully release the trim cover . . .

25.29b  . . . then remove it from around the rear seat locking button

25.30a  Unclip the headrest locking sleeves from the seat . . .

25.30b  . . . press in at each side to release the locking tangs

25.31a  Carefully peel the seat cover from the seat frame . . .

25.31b  . . . then move the foam to one side to access the seat belt

headrest locking sleeves from the seat **(see illustrations)**.

**31** Working your way around the seat frame, unclip the seat cover from the seat frame, then pull back the foam cushion to access the inertia reel seat belt **(see illustrations)**.

**32** Undo the four retaining bolts and remove the bracket from around the inertia reel seat belt **(see illustration)**.

**33** Undo the inertia reel mounting bolt, then withdraw the reel and disconnect the cable from the bottom of the inertia reel **(see illustrations)**. *Note: This cable is a safety feature which is linked to the seat locking catches, if the seat is not located correctly on the seat catches then the seat belt will not operate correctly and will lock.*

### Refitting

**34** Refitting is a reversal of the removal procedure, ensuring that all the mounting

bolts are tightened to the specified torque, where applicable. Make sure that any trim panels disturbed during removal are securely retained by all the relevant retaining clips.

## 26 Interior trim – removal and refitting

### Interior trim panels

**1** The interior trim panels are secured using either screws or various types of trim fasteners, usually studs or clips.

**2** Check that there are no other panels overlapping the one to be removed; usually there is a sequence that has to be followed that will become obvious on close inspection.

**3** Remove all obvious fasteners, such as

screws. If the panel will not come free, it is held by hidden clips or fasteners. These are usually situated around the edge of the panel, and can be prised up to release them; note, however, that they can break quite easily, so new ones should be available. The best way of releasing such clips (in the absence of the correct type of tool) is to use a large flat-bladed screwdriver. Note in many cases that the adjacent sealing strip must be prised back to release a panel.

**4** When removing a panel, **never** use excessive force, or the panel may be damaged; always check carefully that all fasteners have been removed or released before attempting to withdraw a panel.

**5** Refitting is the reverse of the removal procedure; secure the fasteners by pressing them firmly into place, and ensure that all disturbed components are secured correctly, to prevent rattles.

25.32  Undo the four retaining bolts (arrowed)

25.33a  Undo the inertia reel mounting bolt . . .

25.33b  . . . then withdraw the reel and disconnect the locking cable

26.6 Undo the lower retaining screws (arrowed) . . .

26.7 . . . and the upper retaining screws (arrowed)

26.8a Pull out the two hinge pins . . .

26.8b . . . then unhook the guide rails

26.15a Release the retaining clip . . .

26.15b . . . and slide the mirror down out of the mounting plate

### Glovebox

6 Slacken and remove the two glovebox lower retaining screws (see illustration).
7 Open up the glovebox lid, and undo the two upper retaining screws situated inside the glovebox. Slide the glovebox out of position, disconnecting the wiring connector from the glovebox illumination light (where fitted) as it becomes accessible (see illustration).
8 To remove the lid from the glovebox housing, press out the two hinge pins (from the inside to the outside), then press the lugs on the guide rails upwards to release the lid from the glovebox housing (see illustrations).
9 Refitting is the reverse of removal.

### Carpets

10 The passenger compartment floor carpet is in one piece, and is secured at its edges by screws or clips, usually the same fasteners

used to secure the various adjoining trim panels.
11 Carpet removal and refitting is reasonably straightforward, but very time-consuming. All adjoining trim panels must be removed first, as must components such as the seats, the centre console and seat belt lower anchorages.

### Headlining

12 The headlining is clipped to the roof, and can only be withdrawn once all fittings such as the grab handles, sunvisors, sunroof (if fitted), windscreen and rear quarter windows and related trim panels have been removed, and the door, tailgate and sunroof aperture sealing strips have been prised clear.
13 Note that headlining removal requires considerable skill and experience if it is to be carried out without damage, and is therefore best entrusted to an expert.

### Interior mirror

14 On models with rain sensor fitted, unclip and remove the sensor trim panel and release the retaining clip(s) and disconnect the wiring connectors from the mirror assembly.
15 Press the retaining clip at the top of the interior mirror mounting bracket, then carefully release the interior mirror in the downwards direction to remove it from the windscreen (see illustrations).
16 Refitting is the reverse of removal.

### 27 Centre console – removal and refitting

### Removal

1 Unclip the handbrake lever gaiter from the centre console, and fold it back over the handbrake lever (see illustration).
2 On models with manual transmission, unclip the gear lever gaiter from the centre console, and fold it back over the gear lever (see illustration). On automatic models unclip the trim from around the gear lever.
3 Slide both front seats fully forwards and undo the two retaining screw from the rear of the centre console (see illustration).
4 Slide both front seats fully backwards, undo the four retaining screws (two at each side of the front of the centre console) and withdraw the front trim panels (see illustrations).
5 Unclip the switch panel from the front of

27.1 Unclip the handbrake lever gaiter . . .

27.2 . . . and the gear lever gaiter

**27.3  Remove the retaining screws from the rear of the centre console . . .**

**27.4a  . . . and the screws (arrowed) from the front of the console . . .**

**27.4b  . . . then release from the front trim panel**

the centre console and disconnect the wiring block connectors **(see illustration)**.

**6** On all models, slide the console to the rear to disengage it from its retaining clip, and lift it upwards and over the gear/selector lever and handbrake **(see illustration)**.

### Refitting

**7** Refitting is the reverse of removal.

## 28  Facia panel assembly –
   removal and refitting

**HAYNES HiNT** *Label each wiring connector as it is disconnected from its relevant component. The labels will prove useful when refitting, as a guide to routing the wiring and feeding it through the facia apertures.*

### Removal

**1** Disconnect the battery negative terminal (refer to *Disconnecting the battery* in the Reference Chapter).
**2** Undo the retaining screws and remove the two sill inner trim panels and the lower A-pillar trim panels – see Section 26.

**27.5  Unclip the switch panel from the centre console**

**3** Remove the steering column as described in Section 18 of Chapter 10.
**4** Remove the following components as described in Chapter 12:
  a) *Instrument panel.*
  b) *Windscreen wiper motor.*
  c) *Radio/cassette player.*
  d) *Clock/multi/function unit display.*
  e) *Light switch.*
  f) *Passenger side airbag.*
**5** Slide the light switch wiring connector out from its clip on the right-hand side of the facia.
**6** Undo the screw securing the radio/cassette mounting bracket in position, then slide out the bracket, freeing it from the

**27.6  Lift the console upwards and over the gear/selector lever and handbrake**

aerial lead and wiring connector **(see illustrations)**.
**7** Remove the glovebox as described in Section 26.
**8** Remove the centre console as described in Section 27.
**9** Remove the following components as described in Chapter 3:
  a) *Heater/ventilation control unit.*
  b) *Driver's side vent housing.*
  c) *Passenger side heater duct.*
**10** Release the retaining clips and, noting its correct routing, free the wiring loom from the metal frame of the facia panel. Also slide the instrument panel wiring connector out from its clip on the facia.

**28.6a  Undo the screw and slide the radio retaining bracket from the facia . . .**

**28.6b  . . . then free the aerial lead and wiring connector (arrowed)**

**28.11 Diagnostic plug wiring connector in the lower part of the facia at the centre**

**28.12 Undo the facia side retaining screws (one side arrowed)**

**11** Slide the diagnostic plug wiring connector out from its clip on the lower part of the facia **(see illustration)**.

**12** Undo the two retaining screws, one from the left-hand end and one from the right-hand end of the facia panel **(see illustration)**.

**13** Return to the engine compartment, and undo the two retaining nuts securing the facia to the bulkhead.

**14** The facia panel is now free to be removed.

Pull the panel away from the bulkhead, then remove the facia assembly, noting the correct routing of the wiring harnesses, and feeding the wiring back through the facia apertures.

### Refitting

**15** Refitting is a reversal of the removal procedure, noting the following points:

  a) Manoeuvre the facia into position and,

using the labels stuck on during removal, ensure that the wiring is correctly routed and fed through the relevant facia apertures.

  b) Clip the facia back into position, then refit all the facia fasteners and tighten them to their specified torque settings.

  c) On completion, reconnect the battery and check that all the electrical components and switches function correctly.

# Chapter 12
# Body electrical systems

## Contents

## Degrees of difficulty

| | | | | |
|---|---|---|---|---|
| **Easy,** suitable for novice with little experience  | **Fairly easy,** suitable for beginner with some experience | **Fairly difficult,** suitable for competent DIY mechanic | **Difficult,** suitable for experienced DIY mechanic | **Very difficult,** suitable for expert DIY or professional  |

## Specifications

| System type | 12 volt negative earth |
|---|---|

### Bulbs

| | Wattage |
|---|---|
| Direction indicator side repeater | 5 |
| Direction indicator | 21 |
| Front foglight | 55 |
| Headlight | 55 |
| Instrument panel illumination lights | 2 |
| Instrument panel warning lights | 1.2 |
| Interior lights | 10 |
| Number plate light | 10 |
| Rear foglight | 21 |
| Reversing light | 21 |
| Sidelight | 5 |
| Stop/tail-light | 21/5 |

### Torque wrench settings

| | Nm | lbf ft |
|---|---|---|
| Airbag unit retaining screws | 8 | 6 |
| Tailgate wiper arm nut | 9 | 7 |
| Windscreen wiper arm nut | 14 | 10 |

## 1 General information and precautions

⚠️ **Warning: Before carrying out any work on the electrical system, read through the precautions given in 'Safety first!' at the beginning of this manual, and in Chapter 5A.**

**1** The electrical system is of the 12 volt negative earth type. Power for the lights and all electrical accessories is supplied by a lead-acid type battery, which is charged by the engine-driven alternator.

**2** This Chapter covers repair and service procedures for the various electrical components not associated with the engine. Information on the battery, alternator and starter motor can be found in Chapter 5A.

**3** It should be noted that, prior to working on any component in the electrical system, the battery negative terminal should first be disconnected, to prevent the possibility of electrical short-circuits and/or fires.

*Caution: Before proceeding, refer to 'Disconnecting the battery' in the Reference Chapter for further information.*

## 2 Electrical fault finding – general information

**Note:** *Refer to the precautions given in 'Safety first!' and in Section 1 before starting work. The following tests relate to testing of the main electrical circuits, and should not be used to test delicate electronic circuits (such as the anti-lock braking system or fuel injection system), particularly where an electronic control unit is used.*

### General

**1** A typical electrical circuit consists of an electrical component, any switches, relays, motors, fuses, fusible links or circuit breakers related to that component, and the wiring and connectors which link the component to both the battery and the vehicle body. To help to pinpoint a problem in an electrical circuit, wiring diagrams are shown at the end of this Chapter.

**2** Before attempting to diagnose an electrical fault, first study the appropriate wiring diagram to obtain a complete understanding of the components included in the particular circuit concerned. The possible sources of a fault can be narrowed down by noting if other components related to the circuit are operating properly. If several components or circuits fail at one time, the problem is likely to be related to a shared fuse or earth connection.

**3** Electrical problems usually stem from simple causes, such as loose or corroded connections, a faulty earth connection, a blown fuse, a melted fusible link, or a faulty relay (refer to Section 3 for details of testing relays). Inspect the condition of all fuses, wires and connections in a problem circuit before testing the components. Use the wiring diagrams to determine which terminal connections will need to be checked in order to pinpoint the trouble spot.

**4** The basic tools required for electrical fault finding include a circuit tester or voltmeter (a 12 volt bulb with a set of test leads can also be used for certain tests); a self-powered test light (sometimes known as a continuity tester); an ohmmeter (to measure resistance); a battery and set of test leads; and a jumper wire, preferably with a circuit breaker or fuse incorporated, which can be used to bypass suspect wires or electrical components. Before attempting to locate a problem with test instruments, use the wiring diagram to determine where to make the connections.

**5** To find the source of an intermittent wiring fault (usually due to a poor or dirty connection, or damaged wiring insulation), a 'wiggle' test can be performed on the wiring. This involves wiggling the wiring by hand to see if the fault occurs as the wiring is moved. It should be possible to narrow down the source of the fault to a particular section of wiring. This method of testing can be used in conjunction with any of the tests described in the following sub-Sections.

**6** Apart from problems due to poor connections, two basic types of fault can occur in an electrical circuit – open-circuit, or short-circuit.

**7** Open-circuit faults are caused by a break somewhere in the circuit, which prevents current from flowing. An open-circuit fault will prevent a component from working, but will not cause the relevant circuit fuse to blow.

**8** Short-circuit faults are caused by a 'short' somewhere in the circuit, which allows the current flowing in the circuit to 'escape' along an alternative route, usually to earth. Short-circuit faults are normally caused by a breakdown in wiring insulation, which allows a feed wire to touch either another wire, or an earthed component such as the bodyshell. A short-circuit fault will normally cause the relevant circuit fuse to blow.

### Finding an open-circuit

**9** To check for an open-circuit, connect one lead of a circuit tester or voltmeter to either the negative battery terminal or a known good earth.

**10** Connect the other lead to a connector in the circuit being tested, preferably nearest to the battery or fuse.

**11** Switch on the circuit, bearing in mind that some circuits are live only when the ignition switch is turned to a particular position.

**12** If voltage is present (indicated either by the tester bulb lighting or a voltmeter reading, as applicable), this means that the section of the circuit between the relevant connector and the battery is problem-free.

**13** Continue to check the remainder of the circuit in the same fashion.

**14** When a point is reached at which no voltage is present, the problem must lie between that point and the previous test point with voltage. Most problems can be traced to a broken, corroded or loose connection.

### Finding a short-circuit

**15** To check for a short-circuit, first disconnect the load(s) from the circuit (loads are the components which draw current from a circuit, such as bulbs, motors, heating elements, etc).

**16** Remove the relevant fuse from the circuit, and connect a circuit tester or voltmeter to the fuse connections.

**17** Switch on the circuit, bearing in mind that some circuits are live only when the ignition switch is turned to a particular position.

**18** If voltage is present (indicated either by the tester bulb lighting or a voltmeter reading, as applicable), this means that there is a short-circuit.

**19** If no voltage is present, but the fuse still blows with the load(s) connected, this indicates an internal fault in the load(s).

### Finding an earth fault

**20** The battery negative terminal is connected to 'earth' – the metal of the engine/transmission unit and the car body – and most systems are wired so that they only receive a positive feed, the current returning via the metal of the car body. This means that the component mounting and the body form part of that circuit. Loose or corroded mountings can therefore cause a range of electrical faults, ranging from total failure of a circuit, to a puzzling partial fault. In particular, lights may shine dimly (especially when another circuit sharing the same earth point is in operation), motors (eg, wiper motors or the radiator cooling fan motor) may run slowly, and the operation of one circuit may have an apparently-unrelated effect on another. Note that on many vehicles, earth straps are used between certain components, such as the engine/transmission and the body, usually where there is no metal-to-metal contact between components, due to flexible rubber mountings, etc.

**21** To check whether a component is properly earthed, disconnect the battery, and connect one lead of an ohmmeter to a known good earth point. Connect the other lead to the wire or earth connection being tested. The resistance reading should be zero; if not, check the connection as follows.

**22** If an earth connection is thought to be faulty, dismantle the connection, and clean back to bare metal both the bodyshell and the wire terminal or the component earth connection mating surface. Be careful to remove all traces of dirt and corrosion, then use a knife to trim away any paint, so that a clean metal-to-metal joint is made. On reassembly, tighten the joint fasteners securely; if a wire terminal is being refitted, use serrated washers between the terminal and the bodyshell, to ensure a clean and secure connection. When the connection is remade, prevent the onset of corrosion in the future by applying a coat of petroleum jelly or

**3.1 Fuses and relays are located in the engine compartment on the left-hand side**

**3.2 Unclip the lid to gain access to the fuses and relays**

**3.3 Removing a fuse from the fuse/relay box**

silicone-based grease. Alternatively, at regular intervals, spray on a proprietary ignition sealer or a water-dispersant lubricant.

### 3 Fuses and relays – general information

#### Fuses

1 Most of the fuses are located in the fuse/relay box in the engine compartment **(see illustration)**. The fuse/relay box is located next to the coolant expansion tank on the left-hand side inner wing panel.

2 To gain access to the fuses, unclip the fuse/relay box lid **(see illustration)**.

3 To remove a fuse, first switch off the circuit concerned (or the ignition), then pull the fuse out of its terminals **(see illustration)**. The wire within the fuse is clearly visible; if the fuse is blown, it will be broken or melted.

4 Always renew a fuse with one of an identical rating; never use a fuse with a different rating from the original, nor substitute anything else. Never renew a fuse more than once without tracing the source of the trouble. The fuse rating is stamped on top of the fuse; note that the fuses are also colour-coded for easy recognition.

5 If a new fuse blows immediately, find the cause before renewing it again; a short to earth as a result of faulty insulation is most likely. Where a fuse protects more than one circuit, try to isolate the defect by switching on each circuit in turn (if possible) until the fuse blows again. Always carry a supply of spare fuses of each relevant rating on the vehicle, a spare of each rating should be clipped into the base of the fuse/relay box.

#### Relays

6 Most of the relays are located in the fuse/relay box in the engine compartment **(see illustration 3.1)**. On diesel engine models, additional relays are located in a second relay box attached to the ABS hydraulic modulator at the front of the engine compartment.

7 If a circuit or system controlled by a relay develops a fault and the relay is suspect, operate the system; if the relay is functioning, it should be possible to hear it click as it is energised. If this is the case, the fault lies

with the components or wiring of the system. If the relay is not being energised, then either the relay is not receiving a main supply or a switching voltage, or the relay itself is faulty. Testing is by the substitution of a known good unit, but be careful; while some relays are identical in appearance and in operation, others look similar but perform different functions.

8 To renew a relay, first ensure that the ignition switch is off. The relay can then simply be pulled out from the socket and the new relay pressed in.

### 4 Switches – removal and refitting

**Note:** *Disconnect the battery negative terminal (refer to 'Disconnecting the battery' in the Reference Chapter) before removing*

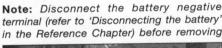

*any switch, and reconnect the terminal after refitting.*

#### Ignition switch/ steering column lock

1 Refer to Chapter 10.

#### Steering column switch

2 With the steering wheel in the straight-ahead position, turn the wheel 90° to the left, then prise the clip to release one side of the upper shroud. Turn the wheel 180° to the right, then release the clip to release the other side of the upper shroud **(see illustrations)**. Withdraw the upper shroud from the steering column.

3 Undo the lower retaining screw and the upper retaining screws, then remove the lower steering column shroud **(see illustrations)**. On models with steering adjustment handle, undo the retaining bolt and remove the handle from the steering column.

**4.2a Release the two retaining clips (arrowed) . . .**

**4.2b . . . and unclip the upper shroud – steering wheel removed for clarity**

**4.3a Unscrew the lower shroud retaining screw . . .**

**4.3b . . . and upper screws (arrowed) and remove shroud from the column**

**4.4a  Depress the retaining clips (arrowed) and slide out the switch . . .**

**4.4b  . . . then release the securing clip (arrowed) and disconnect its wiring connector**

**4.5  Make sure the securing clip is locked (arrowed)**

**4.6  Pull off the lighting switch knob**

**4.7a  Release the retaining clips . . .**

**4.7b  . . . and withdraw the lighting switch from the facia**

**4** Depress the retaining clips, and release the relevant switch assembly from the column bracket. Disconnect the wiring connector, and remove the switch assembly from the vehicle **(see illustrations)**. If necessary, remove the opposite switch assembly in the same way.

**5** Refitting is a reversal of the removal procedure, making sure the wiring connector is fitted correctly **(see illustration)**.

### Lighting switch assembly

**6** Turn the knob to the headlight 'on' position, and pull the knob out **(see illustration)**.

**7** Insert two small screwdrivers through the holes in each side of the turn knob recess to release the retaining clips, then slide the switch assembly out from the facia **(see illustrations)**.

**8** Note that the switch assembly cannot be dismantled; if any of its functions are faulty, the complete assembly must be renewed.

**9** Refitting is a reversal of the removal procedure.

### Hazard warning switch

**10** Unclip the front cover from the hazard switch **(see illustration)**.

**11** Release the upper and lower retaining clips and withdraw the hazard switch out of facia **(see illustration)**.

**12** On refitting, refit the front cover to the switch first **(see illustration)**, then push the complete switch back into position until it clicks into the facia.

### Heated rear window/ blower motor switch

**13** Remove the heater control panel as described in Chapter 3. Carefully unclip the heated rear window and blower motor switch assembly from the heater control housing **(see illustrations)**.

**4.10  Removing the hazard warning light switch cover**

**4.11  Release the retaining clips (arrowed) and withdraw the switch**

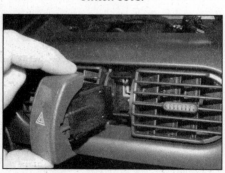

**4.12  Refit the switch as a complete assembly**

**4.13a  Release the retaining clips . . .**

4.13b  . . . and withdraw the switch assembly

14.14  Unclip the cover from around the handbrake lever

4.15  Undo the retaining bolt (arrowed) and remove the handbrake warning light switch from the lever

### Handbrake warning light switch

14 Unclip the cover from around the handbrake lever **(see illustration)**.
15 Disconnect the wiring connector, then undo the retaining bolt and remove the switch from the handbrake lever mounting bracket **(see illustration)**.
16 Install the new switch, securely tightening its retaining bolt and refit the wiring connector. Refit the cover around the handbrake lever.

### Stop-light switch

17 Refer to Chapter 9.

### Courtesy light switch

18 Open the door, then undo the switch retaining screw. Withdraw the switch from the pillar, disconnecting its wiring connector as it becomes accessible **(see illustrations)**. Tie a piece of string to the wiring, to prevent it falling back into the door pillar.
19 Refitting is a reverse of the removal procedure.

### Luggage area light switch

20 The luggage area light switch is fitted to the bottom of the tailgate.
21 Undo the retaining screw, then withdraw the switch and disconnect it from its wiring connector **(see illustration)**. Tie a piece of string to the wiring, to prevent it falling back into the tailgate.

22 Refitting is a reverse of the removal procedure.

### Electric window switches

#### Driver's door

23 Release the retaining clips, taking care not to damage the door trim panel and remove the switch assembly. Disconnect the wiring block connector **(see illustrations)**.
24 Refitting is the reverse of removal, ensuring that the wiring is correctly routed inside the door pocket.

#### Passenger's door

25 Carefully release the retaining clips and remove the switch from the panel, then disconnect the switch wiring connector and remove the switch from the vehicle.
26 Refitting is the reverse of removal.

4.18a  Undo the retaining screw (arrowed) . . .

### Electric mirror switch

27 Carefully unclip the switch from the door trim panel, then disconnect the switch wiring connector, and remove the switch from the vehicle.
28 Refitting is the reverse of removal.

### Electric sunroof switch

29 Carefully prise the sunroof switch out of position, and disconnect it from its wiring connector.
30 When refitting, connect the wiring connector, and clip the switch back into position.

### Air conditioning system switch

31 The air conditioning system control switch is an integral part of the heating/ventilation control unit, and cannot be removed. Should the switch become faulty, the complete control unit assembly must be renewed (see Chapter 3).

4.18b  . . . and withdraw the switch from the door pillar, then disconnect its wiring connector

4.21  Undo the retaining screw (arrowed) and withdraw the switch

4.23a  Release the retaining clips . . .

4.23b  . . . and remove the switch assembly, then disconnect its wiring connector

**4.33 Unclip the horn switch cover from the steering wheel**

**4.34a Withdraw the horn switch . . .**

**4.34b . . . then disconnect its wiring connector**

### Horn switch

**32** Remove the driver's airbag as described in Section 23.

**33** Using a small screwdriver, carefully release the relevant switch cover from the switch in the steering wheel **(see illustration)**.

**34** Unclip the switch from the steering wheel, disconnect the wiring connector and remove the switch **(see illustrations)**.

**35** Refit the wiring connector and switch and the switch cover, then refit the airbag as described in Section 23.

### 5 Bulbs (exterior lights) – renewal

### General

**1** Whenever a bulb is renewed, note the following points:

a) *Make sure the switch is in the 'off' position for the bulb you are working on.*

b) *Remember that if the light has just been in use, the bulb may be extremely hot.*

c) *Always check the bulb contacts and holder, ensuring that there is clean metal-to-metal contact between the bulb and its live(s) and earth. Clean off any corrosion or dirt before fitting a new bulb.*

d) *Wherever bayonet-type bulbs are fitted, ensure that the live contact(s) bear firmly against the bulb contact.*

e) *Always ensure that the new bulb is of the correct rating, and that it is completely clean before fitting it; this applies particularly to headlight/foglight bulbs.*

### Halogen type headlight unit

**Note 1:** *If working on the left-hand headlight unit it will be necessary to lift off the fuse/relay box cover for access to the rear of the headlight unit. On diesel models, it will also be necessary to unclip the additional relay box attached to the ABS hydraulic modulator. If working on the right-hand headlight unit, it will be necessary to unclip the intake duct from the air cleaner housing.*

**Note 2:** *On the halogen type headlight unit, the outer bulb is the dipped beam bulb and the inner bulb is the main beam bulb.*

### Dipped beam

**2** Rotate the plastic cover anti-clockwise and remove it from the rear of the headlight unit.

**3** Push the wiring connector and bulb downward, tip it back at the top and withdraw it from the headlight unit. Hold the bulb by its base and disconnect the wiring connector. When handling the new bulb, use a tissue or clean cloth to avoid touching the glass with the fingers; moisture and grease from the skin can cause blackening and rapid failure of this type of bulb. If the glass is accidentally touched, wipe it clean using methylated spirit.

**4** Fit the wiring connector to the new bulb, then refit the bulb to the headlight unit. Ensure that the lug on the bulb engages with the recess in the headlight unit.

**5** Refit the plastic cover to the rear of the headlight unit, then refit any components removed for access.

### Main beam

**6** Rotate the plastic cover anti-clockwise and remove it from the rear of the headlight unit **(see illustration)**.

**7** Disconnect the wiring connector from the bulb **(see illustration)**.

**8** Push the retaining spring clip forward then swivel it to one side to disengage the retaining lugs. Withdraw the bulb from the rear of the headlight unit **(see illustration)**.

**9** When handling the new bulb, use a tissue or clean cloth to avoid touching the glass with the fingers; moisture and grease from the skin can cause blackening and rapid failure of this type of bulb. If the glass is accidentally touched, wipe it clean using methylated spirit.

**10** Install the new bulb, ensuring that its locating tabs are correctly located in the headlight unit cut-outs. Secure the bulb with the spring clip and reconnect the wiring connector.

**11** Refit the plastic cover to the rear of the unit, then refit any components removed for access.

### Front sidelight

**12** Rotate the plastic cover behind the headlight main beam bulb anti-clockwise and remove it from the rear of the headlight unit **(see illustration 5.6)**.

**13** Withdraw the sidelight bulbholder from the

**5.6 Remove the plastic cover from the rear of the headlight . . .**

**5.7 . . . disconnect the wiring connector . . .**

**5.8 . . . release the retaining clip and withdraw the headlight bulb**

5.13a Remove the sidelight bulbholder from the headlight unit . . .

5.13b . . . and withdraw the capless bulb

5.15 Release the front indicator bulbholder from the headlight unit . . .

5.16 . . . and remove the bayonet fit bulb from the bulbholder

5.19 Depress the retaining tabs and lift off the plastic cover at the rear of the headlight

5.20 Disconnect the wiring connector from the bulb

rear of the headlight unit. The bulb is of the capless (push-fit) type, and can be removed by simply pulling it out of the bulbholder **(see illustrations)**.

**14** Refitting is the reverse of the removal procedure, ensuring that the bulbholder is fully engaged. On completion, refit any components removed for access.

### Front indicator

**15** Twist the indicator bulbholder anti-clockwise, and remove it from the rear of the headlight unit **(see illustration)**.

**16** The bulb is a bayonet fit in the holder, and can be removed by pressing it and twisting in an anti-clockwise direction **(see illustration)**.

**17** Refitting is a reverse of the removal procedure. On completion, refit any components removed for access.

### *Ellipsoidal type headlight unit*

**Note:** *On the ellipsoidal type headlight unit, the inner bulb is the dipped beam bulb and the outer bulb is the main beam bulb.*

#### Dipped beam

**18** Remove the headlight unit as described in Section 7.

**19** Depress the retaining tabs and lift off the plastic cover at the rear of the headlight unit **(see illustration)**.

**20** Disconnect the wiring connector from the bulb **(see illustration)**.

**21** Using pliers, disengage the retaining spring clip by pushing each leg forward then moving it sideways. Withdraw the bulb from the rear of the headlight unit **(see illustrations)**.

**22** When handling the new bulb, use a tissue or clean cloth to avoid touching the glass with

the fingers; moisture and grease from the skin can cause blackening and rapid failure of this type of bulb. If the glass is accidentally touched, wipe it clean using methylated spirit.

**23** Install the new bulb, ensuring that its locating tabs are correctly located in the headlight unit cut-outs. Secure the bulb with the spring clip and reconnect the wiring connector.

**24** Refit the plastic cover to the rear of the unit, then refit the headlight unit as described in Section 7.

#### Main beam

**25** Remove the headlight unit as described in Section 7.

**26** Rotate the plastic cover anti-clockwise and remove it from the rear of the headlight unit **(see illustration)**.

5.21a Disengage the retaining spring clip by pushing each leg forward then moving it sideways. . .

5.21b . . . then withdraw the headlight bulb

5.26 Remove the cover from the rear of the headlight

**5.27 Disconnect the wiring connector from the bulb**

**5.28a Disengage the retaining spring clip by pushing each leg forward then moving it outwards . . .**

**5.28b . . . then withdraw the headlight bulb**

**5.34a Remove the sidelight bulbholder from the headlight unit . . .**

**5.34b . . . and withdraw the capless bulb**

**27** Disconnect the wiring connector from the bulb **(see illustration)**.

**28** Using pliers, disengage the retaining spring clip by pushing each leg forward then moving it outwards, away from the bulb. Withdraw the bulb from the rear of the headlight unit **(see illustrations)**.

**29** When handling the new bulb, use a tissue or clean cloth to avoid touching the glass with the fingers; moisture and grease from the skin can cause blackening and rapid failure of this type of bulb. If the glass is accidentally touched, wipe it clean using methylated spirit.

**30** Install the new bulb, ensuring that its locating tabs are correctly located in the headlight unit cut-outs. Secure the bulb with the spring clip and reconnect the wiring connector.

**31** Refit the plastic cover to the rear of the unit, then refit the headlight unit as described in Section 7.

### Front sidelight

**32** Remove the headlight unit as described in Section 7.

**33** Rotate the plastic cover behind the headlight main beam bulb anti-clockwise and remove it from the rear of the headlight unit **(see illustration 5.26)**.

**34** Withdraw the sidelight bulbholder from the rear of the headlight unit. The bulb is of the capless (push-fit) type, and can be removed by simply pulling it out of the bulbholder **(see illustrations)**.

**35** Refitting is the reverse of the removal procedure, ensuring that the bulbholder is fully engaged. On completion, refit the headlight unit as described in Section 7.

### Front indicator

**Note:** If working on the left-hand headlight unit it will be necessary to lift off the fuse/relay box cover for access to the rear of the headlight

unit. On diesel models, it will also be necessary to unclip the additional relay box attached to the ABS modulator. If working on the right-hand headlight unit, it will be necessary to unclip the intake duct from the air cleaner housing.

**36** Twist the bulbholder anti-clockwise, and remove it from the rear of the headlight unit **(see illustration)**.

**37** The bulb is a bayonet fit in the holder, and can be removed by pressing it and twisting in an anti-clockwise direction **(see illustration)**.

**38** Refitting is a reverse of the removal procedure. On completion, refit any components removed for access.

### Xenon type headlight unit

⚠️ *Warning: Xenon dipped beam headlights operate at very high voltage. Do not touch the associated wiring when the headlights are switched on.*

**Note:** On the Xenon type headlight unit, the inner bulb is the dipped beam bulb and the outer bulb is the main beam bulb.

#### Dipped beam

**39** Remove the headlight unit as described in Section 7.

**40** Depress the retaining tabs and lift off the plastic cover at the rear of the headlight unit **(see illustration 5.19)**.

**41** Disconnect the wiring connector from the bulb by turning it anti-clockwise.

**42** Undo the three screws and lift off the bulb retaining ring. Withdraw the bulb from the rear of the headlight unit.

**43** When handling the new bulb, use a tissue or clean cloth to avoid touching the glass with the fingers; moisture and grease from the skin can cause blackening and rapid failure of this type of bulb. If the glass is accidentally touched, wipe it clean using methylated spirit.

**44** Install the new bulb, ensuring that its locating tabs are correctly located in the headlight unit cut-outs. Secure the bulb with the retaining ring and reconnect the wiring connector.

**45** Refit the plastic cover to the rear of the unit, then refit the headlight unit as described in Section 7.

#### Main beam

**46** Remove the headlight unit as described in Section 7.

**5.36 Release the front indicator bulbholder from the headlight unit . . .**

**5.37 . . . and remove the bayonet fit bulb from the bulbholder**

**47** Rotate the plastic cover anti-clockwise and remove it from the rear of the headlight unit **(see illustration 5.26)**.

**48** Disconnect the wiring connector from the bulb.

**49** Using pliers, disengage the retaining spring clip by pushing each leg forward then moving it outwards, away from the bulb. Withdraw the bulb from the rear of the headlight unit.

**50** When handling the new bulb, use a tissue or clean cloth to avoid touching the glass with the fingers; moisture and grease from the skin can cause blackening and rapid failure of this type of bulb. If the glass is accidentally touched, wipe it clean using methylated spirit.

**51** Install the new bulb, ensuring that its locating tabs are correctly located in the headlight unit cut-outs. Secure the bulb with the spring clip and reconnect the wiring connector.

**52** Refit the plastic cover to the rear of the unit, then refit the headlight unit as described in Section 7.

### Front sidelight

**53** Remove the headlight unit as described in Section 7.

**54** Rotate the plastic cover behind the headlight main beam bulb anti-clockwise and remove it from the rear of the headlight unit **(see illustration 5.26)**.

**55** Withdraw the sidelight bulbholder from the rear of the headlight unit. The bulb is of the capless (push-fit) type, and can be removed by simply pulling it out of the bulbholder **(see illustrations 5.34a and 5.34b)**.

**56** Refitting is the reverse of the removal procedure, ensuring that the bulbholder is fully engaged. On completion, refit the headlight unit as described in Section 7.

### Front indicator

**Note:** *If working on the left-hand headlight unit it will be necessary to lift off the fuse/relay box cover for access to the rear of the headlight unit. On diesel models, it will also be necessary to unclip the additional relay box attached to the ABS modulator. If working on the right-hand headlight unit, it will be necessary to unclip the intake duct from the air cleaner housing.*

**57** Twist the bulbholder anti-clockwise, and remove it from the rear of the headlight unit **(see illustration 5.36)**.

**5.70 Remove the two retaining screws (arrowed) . . .**

**58** The bulb is a bayonet fit in the holder, and can be removed by pressing it and twisting in an anti-clockwise direction **(see illustration 5.37)**.

**59** Refitting is a reverse of the removal procedure. On completion, refit any components removed for access.

### Indicator side repeater

**60** Carefully prise the rear edge of the indicator side repeater light out from the wing, if necessary using a suitable plastic wedge, taking great care not damage the painted finish of the wing.

**61** Withdraw the light unit from the wing, and pull the bulbholder out of the light unit. The bulb is of the capless (push-fit) type, and can be removed by simply pulling it out of the bulbholder.

**62** Refitting is a reverse of the removal procedure.

### Front foglight

**63** Remove the front bumper as described in Chapter 11.

**64** Undo the three foglight unit retaining bolts, withdraw the light unit from the front bumper and disconnect the wiring connector.

**65** Twist the cover and free it from the foglight, disconnect the wiring connector from the foglight bulb.

**66** Release the spring clip and withdraw the foglight bulb from the light unit.

**67** When handling the new bulb, use a tissue or clean cloth to avoid touching the glass with the fingers; moisture and grease from the skin can cause blackening and rapid failure of

**5.71 . . . disconnect the wiring block connector . . .**

this type of bulb. If the glass is accidentally touched, wipe it clean using methylated spirit.

**68** Insert the new bulb, making sure it is correctly located, and secure it in position with the spring clip.

**69** Connect the bulb wire to the terminal, then refit the cover to the rear of the unit. Refit the foglight unit to the bumper, then refit the bumper as described in Chapter 11.

### Rear light cluster

#### Corsa and Corsavan models

**70** Open the tailgate and remove the two retaining screws from the rear light unit **(see illustration)**.

**71** Disconnect the wiring block connector from the rear of the light unit **(see illustration)**.

**72** Undo the four retaining screws and remove the bulbholder from the rear of the light unit **(see illustration)**.

**73** The relevant bulb can then be renewed; all bulbs have a bayonet fitting **(see illustration)**. Note that the stop/tail-light bulb has offset locating pins, to prevent it being installed incorrectly.

**74** Refitting is the reverse of the removal sequence, ensuring that the light unit locates securely into position.

#### Combo Van models

**75** From inside the vehicle luggage compartment, depress the retaining catches, and open the trim panel flap to gain access to the rear of the light unit **(see illustration)**.

**76** Undo the two rear light cluster retaining nuts, disconnect the wiring connector and

**5.72 . . . undo the four retaining screws and remove the bulbholder . . .**

**5.73 . . . then withdraw the relevant bulb**

**5.75 Open the trim panel flap . . .**

**5.76a** . . . disconnect the wiring block connector . . .

**5.76b** . . . undo the two retaining nuts . . .

**5.76c** . . . and withdraw the light unit from the vehicle

**5.77a** Press the clips together to release the bulbholder from the light unit . . .

**5.77b** . . . then withdraw the relevant bulb

**5.79a** Undo the upper plastic nut (arrowed) . . .

free the rear light unit from the vehicle **(see illustrations)**.

**77** Release the bulbholder from the rear of the light unit, then the relevant bulb can then

be renewed; all bulbs have a bayonet fitting **(see illustrations)**. Note that the stop/tail-light bulb has offset locating pins, to prevent it being installed incorrectly.

**78** Refitting is the reverse of the removal sequence, ensuring that the bulbholder is securely clipped into position.

### Rear foglight

**79** From under the wheel arch, undo the upper plastic nut, and lower retaining screw and withdraw the foglight cover panel **(see illustrations)**.

**80** Disconnect the wiring connector from the foglight bulbholder **(see illustration)**.

**81** Twist the bulbholder anti-clockwise, and remove it from the foglight unit **(see illustration)**.

**82** The bulb is a bayonet fit in the holder, and can be removed by pressing it and twisting in an anti-clockwise direction.

**83** Refitting is a reverse of the removal procedure.

### Number plate light

#### Corsa and Corsavan models

**84** Using a small flat-bladed screwdriver, care-fully prise the light out from the rear bumper.

**85** Twist the bulbholder to remove it from the light unit, and remove the bulb.

**86** Refitting is a reverse of the removal procedure.

#### Combo Van models

**87** Undo the two retaining screws, then

**5.79b** . . . and lower retaining screw (arrowed) . . .

**5.79c** . . . then withdraw the foglight cover panel

**5.80** Disconnect the wiring connector from the foglight bulbholder

**5.81** Twist the bulbholder anti-clockwise, and remove it from the foglight unit

**5.87  Undo the two retaining screws . . .**

**5.88a  . . . withdraw the light unit . . .**

**5.88b  . . . and release the festoon bulb**

unclip the light unit from the rear trim panel **(see illustration)**.

**88**  The bulb is a festoon type which can be removed by unclipping it from the contact springs **(see illustrations)**.

**89**  Refitting is a reverse of the removal procedure.

### High-level stop-light

**90**  The high-level stop-light bulbs are of the LED (light emitting diode) type and cannot be individually renewed. Remove the complete light unit as described in Section 7.

### 6  Bulbs (interior lights) – renewal

### General

**1**  Refer to Section 5, paragraph 1.

### Front courtesy light

**2**  Using a suitable screwdriver, carefully prise the light unit out of position, and release the bulb from the light unit contacts **(see illustrations)**.

**3**  Install the new bulb, ensuring that it is securely held in position by the contacts, and clip the light unit back into position.

### Courtesy light with map reading lights

**4**  Using a small flat-bladed screwdriver, carefully prise the light unit out from its surround. Disconnect the wiring connector, and remove the light **(see illustration)**.

**5**  Unclip the lens from the light unit, and release the bulb from its contacts **(see illustrations)**.

**6**  Install the new bulb, ensuring that it is securely held in position by the contacts, and clip the lens back into position.

**7**  Connect the wiring connector, and clip the light back into position in the surround.

### Luggage compartment light

**8**  Using a suitable screwdriver, carefully prise the light unit out of position, and release the bulb from the light unit contacts **(see illustrations)**.

**6.2a  Carefully prise the courtesy light unit out of position . . .**

**6.2b  . . . and release the festoon bulb from its wiring contacts**

**6.4  Release the interior light unit from the surround trim**

**6.5a  Unclip the lens from the light unit . . .**

**6.5b  . . . and remove the capless bulb**

**6.8a  Unclip the luggage compartment light unit . . .**

**6.8b  . . . and remove the festoon bulb**

**6.11 Removing an instrument panel illumination/warning light bulb**

**6.15a Use a screwdriver to twist the bulbholder . . .**

**6.15b . . . and remove the clock/multifunction display illumination bulb**

**6.17 Unclip the cigarette lighter/switch panel from the centre console**

9 Install the new bulb, ensuring that it is securely held in position by the contacts, and clip the light unit back into position.

### Instrument illumination/ warning lights

10 Remove the instrument panel as described in Section 9.
11 Twist the relevant bulbholder anti-clockwise, and withdraw it from the rear of the panel **(see illustration)**.
12 All bulbs are integral with their holders. Be very careful to ensure that the new bulbs are of the correct rating, the same as those removed; this is especially important in the case of the ignition/no-charge warning light.
13 Refit the bulbholder to the rear of the instrument panel, then refit the instrument panel as described in Section 9.

### Clock/multifunction display illumination

14 Remove the clock/multifunction display unit as described in Section 10.
15 Twist the bulbholder anti-clockwise, and withdraw it from the rear of the clock **(see illustrations)**. The bulb is integral with its holder.
16 Refit the bulbholder to the rear of the unit, then refit the unit as described in Section 10.

### Cigarette lighter/ ashtray illumination

17 Unclip the cigarette lighter surround from the centre console **(see illustration)**.
18 Slide the illumination bulbholder out of the panel, and renew the bulb. The bulbs is of the capless (push-fit) type; pull the old bulb

out of the holder, and press the new one into position.
19 Slide the illumination bulbholder back into position, and refit the trim by reversing the removal procedure.

### Heater control panel illumination

20 Withdraw the heater control panel as described in Chapter 3, so that access to the rear of the panel can be gained. Note there is no need to remove the panel completely; the control cables can be left attached.
21 Carefully unclip the heated rear window and blower motor switch assembly from the heater control housing as described in Section 4, paragraph 13.
22 Unclip the bulbholder cover. The bulbs are of the capless (push-fit) type; pull the relevant bulb out of the holder, and press the new one into position **(see illustrations)**.
23 Refit the bulbholder, and install the control panel as described in Chapter 3.

### Glovebox light

24 Open the glovebox. Using a small flat-bladed screwdriver, carefully prise the light unit out of position, then release the bulb from its contacts. Install the new bulb, ensuring it is securely held in position by the contacts, and clip the light unit back into position.

### Switch illumination

25 All the switches are fitted with illumination bulbs; some are also fitted with a bulb to show when the circuit concerned is operating. These bulbs are an integral part of the switch assembly, and cannot be obtained separately.

### Automatic transmission selector illumination

26 Remove the centre console as described in Chapter 11.
27 Unclip the selector lever cover from the selector housing and lift it upwards.
28 Withdraw the relevant bulbholder from the underside of the selector lever cover and release the bulb from the bulbholder.
29 Install the new bulb, refit the bulbholder and clip the selector lever cover back into position.
30 Refit the centre console as described in Chapter 11.

**6.22a Unclip the cover from the switch assembly . . .**

**6.22b . . . and remove the illumination bulbs**

## 7 Exterior light units – removal and refitting

**Note:** *Disconnect the battery negative terminal (refer to 'Disconnecting the battery' in the Reference Chapter) before removing any light unit, and reconnect the terminal after refitting.*

**7.2a  Undo the two upper retaining bolts (arrowed) . . .**

**7.2b  . . . and the lower retaining bolt (arrowed) . . .**

**7.2c  . . . then disconnect the wiring connectors from the headlight unit as it is withdrawn**

**7.3a  Unclip the cover from the rear of the light unit . . .**

**7.3b  . . . then rotate the adjustment motor clockwise and unclip the balljoint (arrowed) . . .**

**7.3c  . . . and disconnect the wiring connector**

## Headlight

⚠️ **Warning: Xenon dipped beam headlights operate at very high voltage. Do not touch the associated wiring when the headlights are switched on.**

**1** Remove the front bumper as described in Chapter 11.

**2** Undo the three retaining bolts and withdraw the headlight unit from the vehicle. Disconnect the wiring connectors from rear of the headlight unit as it is withdrawn **(see illustrations)**.

**3** On models fitted with halogen type headlight units, the headlight beam adjustment motor can be removed and refitted as follows. On all other headlight types the motor is an integral part of the light unit. Unclip the cover then rotate the adjustment motor clockwise to free the motor from the rear of the headlight unit. Unclip the balljoint from the rear of the light reflector and disconnect the wiring connector **(see illustrations)**.

**4** On refitting, align the motor balljoint with the light unit socket, and clip it into position. Engage the motor assembly with the light, and twist it anti-clockwise to secure it in position.

**5** Refitting is a reverse of the removal procedure. On completion, check the headlight beam alignment using the information given in Section 8.

## Front indicator light

**6** The front direction indicator lights are integral with the headlight units. Removal and refitting is as described above.

## Indicator side repeater light

**7** Carefully prise the rear edge of the indicator side repeater light out from the wing, if necessary using a suitable plastic wedge, taking great care not damage the painted finish of the wing.

**8** Withdraw the light unit from the wing, and disconnect its wiring connector. Tie a piece of string to the wiring, to prevent it falling back into the wing.

**9** On refitting, connect the wiring connector, and clip the light unit back into position.

## Front foglight

**10** Remove the front bumper as described in Chapter 11.

**11** Disconnect the wiring connector, then undo the three foglight retaining screws and remove the light unit from the bumper.

**12** Refit the light unit to the bumper, and securely tighten its retaining screws.

**13** Secure the front bumper in position, then adjust the foglight aim through the hole in the bumper to the side of the foglight.

## Rear light cluster

### Corsa and Corsavan models

**14** Open the tailgate and remove the two retaining screws from the rear light unit **(see illustration 5.70)**.

**15** Disconnect the wiring block connector from the rear of the light unit **(see illustration 5.71)**.

**16** Refitting is the reverse of the removal sequence, ensuring that the light unit locates securely into position.

### Combo Van models

**17** From inside the vehicle luggage compartment, depress the retaining catches, and open the trim panel flap to gain access to the rear of the light unit **(see illustration 5.75)**.

**18** Undo the two rear light cluster retaining nuts, disconnect the wiring connector and free the rear light unit from the vehicle **(see illustrations 5.76a, 5.76b and 5.76c)**.

**19** Refitting is the reverse of the removal sequence, ensuring that the light unit locates securely into position.

## Number plate light

### Corsa and Corsavan models

**20** Using a small flat-bladed screwdriver, carefully prise the light out from the rear bumper and disconnect it from the wiring connectors.

**21** Refitting is a reversal of removal.

### Combo Van models

**22** Undo the two retaining screws, then unclip the light unit from the rear trim panel **(see illustration 5.88a)**.

**23** Refitting is a reversal of removal.

## High-level stop-light

**24** Open the tailgate.

**25** Unclip the light unit from the tailgate door

**7.25 Unclip and withdraw the light unit from the tailgate . . .**

**7.26 . . . then disconnect the wiring connector**

**7.30 Undo the retaining bolt (arrowed) and remove the foglight from the rear bumper**

panel and withdraw it from its location (see illustration).

26 Release the wiring harness, disconnect the wiring connector and remove the light unit (see illustration).

27 Refitting is a reversal of removal.

### Rear foglight

28 From under the wheel arch, undo the upper plastic nut, and lower retaining screw and withdraw the foglight cover panel (see illustrations 5.75a, 5.75b and 5.75c).

29 Disconnect the wiring connector from the foglight bulbholder (see illustration 5.76).

30 Undo the retaining bolt and remove the foglight from the rear bumper (see illustration).

### 8 Headlight beam alignment – general information

1 Accurate adjustment of the headlight beam is only possible using optical beam-setting equipment, and this work should therefore be carried out by a Vauxhall dealer or suitably-equipped workshop.

2 For reference, the headlights can be adjusted using the adjuster assemblies fitted to the top of each light unit. The inner adjuster, alters the horizontal position of the beam. The outer adjuster alters the vertical aim of the beam.

3 Some models have an electrically-operated headlight beam adjustment system, controlled via a switch in the facia. The recommended settings are as follows. **Note:** *When adjusting the headlight aim, ensure that the switch is set to position 0.*

### Corsa and Corsavan with rear seats

0 Front seat(s) occupied

1 All seats occupied

2 All seats occupied, and load in luggage compartment

3 Driver's seat occupied and load in the luggage compartment

### Corsavan and Combo Van without rear seats

0 Seat(s) occupied

1 Seats occupied and load compartment approximately half-loaded

2 Seats occupied and luggage compartment fully-loaded

3 Driver's seat only occupied and luggage compartment fully-loaded

### 9 Instrument panel – removal and refitting

**Note:** *The instrument panel is a complete assembly, and no dismantling of the instrument panel is possible. The only additional work possible is the renewal of a bulb (see Section 6).*

### Removal

1 Disconnect the battery negative terminal (refer to *Disconnecting the battery* in the Reference Chapter).

2 Unclip the driver's side lower storage tray,

**9.2 Undo the retaining screws and remove the driver's side lower trim panels**

**9.5a Unscrew the shroud lower retaining screws (arrowed) . . .**

then undo the retaining screws and remove the driver's side lower trim panels (see illustration)

3 With the steering wheel in the straight-ahead position, turn the wheel 90° to the left, then prise the clip to release one side of the upper shroud. Turn the wheel 180° to the right, then release the clip to release the other side of the upper shroud (see illustration). Withdraw the upper shroud from the steering column.

4 Undo the lower retaining screw and the upper retaining screws, then remove the lower steering column shroud. On models with steering adjustment handle, undo the retaining bolt and remove the handle from the steering column.

5 Undo the three retaining screws, and remove the instrument panel shroud from the facia (see illustrations).

**9.3 Release the two retaining clips (arrowed) and unclip the upper shroud – steering wheel removed for clarity**

**9.5b . . . and the upper retaining screw (arrowed)**

**9.6  Unscrew the instrument panel lower retaining screws (arrowed)**

**9.7  Release the upper securing clip (arrowed) and remove the instrument panel**

**6** Unscrew the two retaining screws from the base of the instrument panel **(see illustration).**
**7** Depress the panel upper retaining clip, and withdraw the instrument panel from the facia. The wiring connector disconnects automatically as the panel is removed **(see illustration).**

### Refitting

**8** Clip the instrument panel back into position, aligning it with its wiring connector, and secure it in position with the two retaining screws.
**9** Refit the instrument panel shroud, and securely tighten its retaining screws.
**10** Install the upper and lower steering column shrouds, and securely tighten all the retaining screws. Fit the rubber seal to the ignition switch/lock and the trim caps to the upper screws.

**11** Refit the driver's side lower trim panels and storage tray.
**12** Reconnect the battery, and check the operation of the panel warning lights to ensure that they are functioning correctly.

## 10  Clock/multifunction display components – removal and refitting

### Removal

**1** Disconnect the battery negative terminal (refer to *Disconnecting the battery* in the Reference Chapter).
**2** Remove the central air vents as described in Chapter 3.
**3** Undo the two retaining screws located in

the vent apertures, then withdraw the clock/multifunction display from the facia **(see illustrations).**
**4** Release the securing clip and disconnect the wiring connector, then remove the unit from the vehicle **(see illustration).**

### Refitting

**5** Reconnect the wiring connector, then manoeuvre the unit back into position.
**6** Securely tighten the screws, and install the vents as described in Chapter 3.
**7** Reconnect the battery negative terminal, then reset the clock and enter the radio security code.

## 11  Cigarette lighter – removal and refitting

### Removal

**1** Unclip the cigarette lighter surround from the centre console.
**2** Disconnect the wiring connector from the rear of the cigarette lighter **(see illustration).**
**3** Release the retaining tangs and push out the metal insert, then remove the plastic outer section of the lighter.

### Refitting

**4** Refitting is a reversal of the removal procedure.

## 12  Horn – removal and refitting

### Removal

**1** Undo the retaining screws and remove the inner wheel arch liner from the right-hand front wing.
**2** Undo the retaining nut/bolt and remove the horn, disconnecting its wiring connectors as they become accessible **(see illustration).**

### Refitting

**3** Refitting is the reverse of removal.

**10.3a  Undo the retaining screws (arrowed) . . .**

**10.3b  . . . and remove the multifunction display unit**

**10.4  Release the securing clip (arrowed), then disconnect the wiring connector**

**11.2  Disconnecting the wiring connector from the cigarette lighter**

**12.2  Undo the retaining nut (arrowed) and remove the horn**

13.2 Unclip the cover and remove the spindle nut (arrowed)

14.3a Peel the seal off the engine compartment bulkhead . . .

14.3b . . . then unclip the cover from the battery cables

## 13 Wiper arm –
removed and refitting

### Removal

1 Operate the wiper motor, then switch it off so that the wiper arm returns to the at-rest (parked) position.

 **HAYNES HINT** *Stick a piece of masking tape along the edge of the wiper blade, to use as an alignment aid on refitting.*

2 Unclip the wiper arm spindle nut cover, then slacken and remove the spindle nut **(see illustration)**.
3 Lift the blade off the glass, and pull the wiper arm off its spindle. If necessary, the arm can be levered off the spindle using a suitable flat-bladed screwdriver. **Note:** *If both windscreen wiper arms are to be removed at the same time, mark them for identification. The arms are not interchangeable; the passenger-side wiper arm is longer than the driver's-side arm, and its shaft is also cranked slightly.*

### Refitting

4 Ensure that the wiper arm and spindle splines are clean and dry, then refit the arm to

14.4 Unclipping the battery cables from the water deflector

the spindle, aligning the wiper blade with the tape fitted on removal. Refit the spindle nut, tightening it securely, and clip the nut cover back in position.

## 14 Windscreen wiper motor and linkage –
removal and refitting

### Removal

1 Disconnect the battery negative terminal (refer to *Disconnecting the battery* in the Reference Chapter).
2 Remove the wiper arms as described in the previous Section.
3 Peel the bonnet seal off the engine

compartment bulkhead, then unclip the cover from the battery cables **(see illustrations)**.
4 Unclip the battery cables from the water deflector, and move them to one side **(see illustration)**.
5 Undo the three retaining screws – one at each end and one in the middle **(see illustrations)**. Remove both halves of the water deflector trim, release the trim from the engine compartment bulkhead and wiper spindles. Disconnect the washer pipe for the washer jets as the trim is removed from the vehicle.
6 Remove the large rubber grommets from each wiper spindle **(see illustration)**.
7 Disconnect the wiring connector from the wiper motor. Undo the two retaining bolts, and remove the wiper motor and linkage assembly out from the vehicle **(see illustrations)**.

14.5b . . . and the right-hand end (arrowed) . . .

14.5c . . . then the centre of the deflector

14.6 Removing the large rubber grommet from the wiper spindle

14.5a Undo the retaining screw (arrowed) from the left-hand end . . .

**8** If necessary, mark the relative positions of the motor shaft and linkage arm, then unscrew the retaining nut from the motor spindle. Free the wiper linkage from the spindle, then remove the three motor retaining bolts, and separate the motor and linkage **(see illustrations)**. **Note:** *It is not necessary to remove the linkage assembly from the vehicle to remove the motor.*

### Refitting

**9** Where necessary, assemble the motor and linkage, and securely tighten the motor retaining bolts. Locate the linkage arm on the motor spindle, aligning the marks made prior to removal, and securely tighten its retaining nut.
**10** Manoeuvre the motor assembly back into position in the vehicle. Refit the retaining bolts, and tighten them securely.
**11** Reconnect the wiper motor wiring connector and refit the large rubber grommets to the wiper spindles.
**12** Refit the water deflector, making sure it is correctly located on the bulkhead and wiper spindles, install both halves of the trim, and securely tighten the retaining screws.
**13** Refit the battery cables and cover into position then refit the bonnet seal to the engine compartment bulkhead.
**14** Install both the wiper arms as described in Section 13, and reconnect the battery negative terminal.

---

### 15  Tailgate wiper motor – removal and refitting

### Removal

**1** Remove the wiper arm as described in Section 13. It may be necessary to use a puller on the wiper arm if it is tight on the wiper motor spindle **(see illustration)**.
**2** Open the tailgate, undo the four retaining screws then unclip the inner trim panel from the tailgate **(see illustration)**.
**3** Disconnect the wiper motor wiring connector, and release the wiring from any relevant retaining clips **(see illustration)**.
**4** Slacken and remove the wiper motor mounting bolts and remove the wiper motor. Where applicable, recover any spacers from the motor mounting bracket, and slide the inner mounting rubber off the motor spindle **(see illustration)**.
**5** Examine the motor mounting rubbers for signs of damage or deterioration, and renew as necessary.

### Refitting

**6** Where applicable, slide the inner mounting rubber onto the motor spindle, and ensure

**14.7a  Disconnect the wiring connector . . .**

**14.8a  Undo the retaining nut and free the wiper linkage . . .**

that any rubbers are correctly fitted to the motor mountings.
**7** Refit the wiper motor mounting bolts and tighten them securely.
**8** Reconnect the wiper motor wiring connector.

**15.1  Using a puller on the wiper arm to release it from the spindle**

**15.3  Disconnect the wiper motor wiring . . .**

**14.7b  . . . undo the two retaining bolts (arrowed) and remove the wiper assembly**

**14.8b  . . . then remove the three motor retaining bolts (arrowed)**

**9** Refit the trim panel to the tailgate, ensuring that it is securely retained by all of its screws and clips.
**10** Refit the wiper arm as described in Section 13.

**15.2  Undo the retaining screws and unclip the trim panel**

**15.4  . . . and undo the retaining bolts (arrowed)**

16.1 Slide the fluid reservoir upwards to release from its retaining bracket

16.2a Disconnect the wiring connector . . .

16.2b . . . and washer hoses (arrowed)

16.8a Use a screwdriver to release the retaining clip . . .

16.8b . . . then withdraw the washer jet

16.11 Prise the washer jet from the tailgate

## 16 Windscreen/tailgate washer system components – removal and refitting

### Washer system reservoir

1 Slide the fluid reservoir upwards to release it from its retaining bracket **(see illustration)**.
2 Disconnect the wiring connector from the washer pump, then disconnect the hose(s) from the base of the pump and remove the reservoir from the vehicle **(see illustrations)**. Wash off any spilt fluid with cold water.
3 Refitting is the reverse of removal, ensuring that the washer hose(s) are securely connected.

### Washer pump

4 Remove the washer reservoir as described above.
5 Tip out the contents of the reservoir, then carefully ease the pump out from the reservoir and recover its sealing grommet.
6 Refitting is the reverse of removal, using a new sealing grommet if the original one shows signs of damage or deterioration.

### Windscreen washer jets

7 Remove the water deflector trim panels as described in paragraphs 3 to 5 of Section 14.
8 Release the retaining clip, then carefully prise the nozzle from the rear of the trim panel,

taking great care not to damage the trim **(see illustrations)**.
9 Disconnect the nozzle from its fluid hose, and remove it from the vehicle.
10 On refitting, securely connect the nozzle to the hose, and clip it into position in the trim panel. Check the operation of the jet. If necessary, adjust the nozzle using a pin, aiming the spray to a point slightly above the centre of the swept area.

### Tailgate washer jet

11 Carefully prise the washer jet out of the top of the tailgate/spoiler **(see illustration)**, and disconnect it from its supply pipe. Whilst the jet is removed, tie a piece of string to the supply pipe, to ensure that it does not fall back into the tailgate.
12 When refitting, ensure that the jet is clipped securely in position. Check the operation of the jet. If necessary, adjust the nozzle using a pin, aiming the spray to a point slightly above the centre of the swept area.

## 17 Radio/cassette/CD player – removal and refitting

**Note:** The following removal and refitting procedure is for the range of radio/cassette/CD units which Vauxhall fit as standard equipment. Removal and refitting

procedures of non-standard units may differ slightly.

### Removal

1 All the radio/cassette/CD players fitted by Vauxhall have DIN standard fixings. Two special tools, obtainable from most car accessory shops, are required for removal. Alternatively, suitable tools can be fabricated from 3 mm diameter wire, such as welding rod.
2 Disconnect the battery negative terminal (refer to *Disconnecting the battery* in the Reference Chapter).
3 Unscrew the four grub screws from the corners of the radio/cassette/CD player, using a suitable Allen key **(see illustration)**.
4 Insert the tools into the holes exposed by removal of the grub screws, and push them

17.3 Unscrew the four grub screws . . .

**17.4 ... insert the tools and withdraw the radio/cassette/CD player out of the facia**

**18.1 Unclipping the exterior mirror inner trim panel from the door**

**18.2 Disconnect the wiring connector(s)**

**18.5a Undo the retaining screws (arrowed) ...**

**18.5b ... remove the speaker and disconnect the wiring connector**

**18.10 Undo the retaining screws (arrowed) and remove the speaker**

until they snap into place. The radio/cassette/CD player can then be slid out of the facia **(see illustration)**.

### Refitting

**5** To refit the radio/cassette player/CD, simply push the unit into the facia until the retaining lugs snap into place, then refit the grub screws. On completion, reconnect the battery and enter the radio security code, where applicable.

## 18 Speakers – removal and refitting

### Front small (treble) speaker

**1** Carefully unclip the exterior mirror inner trim panel from the door. On models with manually-operated mirrors, it will be necessary to pull the knob off the adjusting lever in order to remove the panel **(see illustration)**.
**2** Unclip the speaker from the handle, disconnecting its wiring connectors as they become accessible **(see illustration)**.
**3** Refitting is the reverse of removal.

### Front large (bass) speaker

**4** Remove the front door inner trim panel as described in Chapter 11.
**5** Undo the retaining screws, then free the speaker from the door. Disconnect the wiring connectors and remove the speaker **(see illustrations)**.
**6** Refitting is the reverse of removal.

### Rear speaker

**7** Remove the rear parcel shelf. If the left speaker is to be removed, remove the interior light unit from the trim panel as described in Section 6.
**8** Remove the rear trim panels as described in Chapter 11.
**9** Turn the panel around to gain access to the speaker and disconnect the speaker wiring connector. Note that it is not necessary to detach the seat belt completely unless the trim panel is to be removed.
**10** Undo the three retaining screws, and remove the speaker from the trim panel **(see illustration)**.
**11** Refitting is a reverse of the removal procedure. Make sure that the trim panel is securely retained by all the relevant clips

and screws. If the left trim panel is being installed, do not forget to feed the interior light wiring through the trim panel aperture before fastening the panel in position.

## 19 Radio aerial – removal and refitting

### Corsa and Corsavan

**1** Open the tailgate, then prise out the trim clips and release the rear of the headlining from the roof. Carefully peel the headlining back until access is gained to the aerial retaining nut and wiring connectors **(see illustrations)**.
**2** Disconnect wiring connector, then undo the

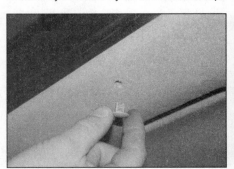

**19.1a Prise out the trim clips ...**

**19.1b ... and release the headlining**

**19.2a Disconnect the wiring connector (arrowed) . . .**

**19.2b . . . and undo the retaining nut (arrowed)**

**19.4 Unclip the interior light from the surround**

**19.5 Disconnect the wiring connector and undo the retaining nut (arrowed)**

retaining nut and remove the aerial from the roof **(see illustrations)**.
3 Locate the aerial in roof hole and refit its retaining nut, tightening it securely. Reconnect the wiring connectors, then clip the headlining back into position.

### Combo Van

4 Unclip and remove the front interior light from the headlining trim surround **(see illustration)**.
5 Trace the wiring from the aerial then dis-connect wiring connector. Undo the retaining nut and remove the aerial from the roof **(see illustration)**.
6 Locate the aerial in roof hole and refit its retaining nut, tightening it securely. Reconnect the wiring connectors, then clip the interior light back into position.

### 20 Anti-theft alarm system – general information

**Note:** *This information is applicable only to the anti-theft alarm system fitted by Vauxhall as standard equipment.*
1 Most models in the range are fitted with an anti-theft alarm system as standard equipment. The alarm is automatically armed and disarmed when the deadlocks are operated using the driver's door lock or remote control key. The alarm has switches on all the doors (including the tailgate), the bonnet, the radio/cassette/CD player and the ignition and starter circuits. If the tailgate, bonnet or any of the doors are opened whilst the alarm is set, the alarm

horn will sound and the hazard warning lights will flash. The alarm also has an immobiliser function which makes the ignition and starter circuits inoperable whilst the alarm is triggered.
2 The alarm system performs a self-test every time it is switched on; this test takes approximately 10 seconds. During the self-test, the LED (light emitting diode) in the hazard warning light switch will come on. If the LED flashes, then either the tailgate, bonnet or one of the doors is open, or there is a fault in the circuit. After the initial 10 second period, the LED will flash to indicate that the alarm is switched on. On unlocking the driver's door lock, the LED will illuminate for approximately 1 second, then go out, indicating that the alarm has been switched off.
3 With the alarm set, if the tailgate is unlocked, the tailgate switch sensing will automatically be switched off, but the door and bonnet switches will still be active. Once the tailgate is shut and locked again, the tailgate switch sensing will be switched back on after approximately 10 seconds.
4 Should the alarm system develop a fault, the vehicle should be taken to a Vauxhall dealer for examination.

### 21 Heated front seat components – general information

On models with heated front seats, a heater mat is fitted to both the seat back and seat cushion. Renewal of either heater mat involves peeling back the upholstery, removing the old

mat, sticking the new mat in position and then refitting the upholstery. Note that upholstery removal and refitting requires considerable skill and experience if it is to be carried out successfully, and is therefore best entrusted to your Vauxhall dealer. In practice, it will be very difficult for the home mechanic to carry out the job without ruining the upholstery.

### 22 Airbag system – general information and precautions

#### General information

A driver's airbag is fitted as standard equip-ment on all models. The airbag is fitted in the steering wheel centre pad. Additionally, a passenger's airbag located in the facia, side airbags located in the front seats, and curtain airbags located in the headlining are optionally available.

The system is armed only when the ignition is switched on, however, a reserve power source maintains a power supply to the system in the event of a break in the main electrical supply. The steering wheel and facia airbags are activated by a 'g' sensor (deceleration sensor), and controlled by an electronic control unit located under the centre console. The side airbags and curtain airbags are activated by severe side impact and operate independently of the main system. A separate electrical supply, control unit and sensor is provided for the side/curtain airbags on each side of the car.

The airbags are inflated by a gas generator, which forces the bag out from its location in the steering wheel, facia, seat back frame, or headlining.

#### Precautions

⚠️ *Warning: The following precautions must be observed when working on vehicles equipped with an airbag system, to prevent the possibility of personal injury.*

#### General precautions

The following precautions must be observed when carrying out work on a vehicle equipped with an airbag:
a) *Do not disconnect the battery with the engine running.*
b) *Before carrying out any work in the vicinity of the airbag, removal of any of the airbag components, or any welding work on the vehicle, de-activate the system as described in the following sub-Section.*
c) *Do not attempt to test any of the airbag system circuits using test meters or any other test equipment.*
d) *If the airbag warning light comes on, or any fault in the system is suspected, consult a Vauxhall dealer without delay.* **Do not** *attempt to carry out fault diagnosis, or any dismantling of the components.*

## Precautions when handling an airbag

a) Transport the airbag by itself, bag upward.
b) Do not put your arms around the airbag.
c) Carry the airbag close to the body, bag outward.
d) Do not drop the airbag or expose it to impacts.
e) Do not attempt to dismantle the airbag unit.
f) Do not connect any form of electrical equipment to any part of the airbag circuit.

## Precautions when storing an airbag

a) Store the unit in a cupboard with the airbag upward.
b) Do not expose the airbag to temperatures above 80°C.
c) Do not expose the airbag to flames.
d) Do not attempt to dispose of the airbag – consult a Vauxhall dealer.
e) Never refit an airbag which is known to be faulty or damaged.

## De-activation of airbag system

The system must be de-activated before carrying out any work on the airbag components or surrounding area:

a) Switch on the ignition and check the operation of the airbag warning light on the instrument panel. The light should illuminate when the ignition is switched on, then extinguish.
b) Switch off the ignition.
c) Remove the ignition key.
d) Switch off all electrical equipment.
e) Disconnect the battery negative terminal (refer to 'Disconnecting the battery' in the Reference Chapter).
f) Insulate the battery negative terminal and the end of the battery negative lead to prevent any possibility of contact.
g) Wait for at least two minutes before carrying out any further work. Wait at least ten minutes if the airbag warning light did not operate correctly.

## Activation of airbag system

To activate the system on completion of any work, proceed as follows:

a) Ensure that there are no occupants in the vehicle, and that there are no loose objects around the vicinity of the steering wheel. Close the vehicle doors and windows.
b) Ensure that the ignition is switched off then reconnect the battery negative terminal.
c) Open the driver's door and switch on the ignition, without reaching in front of the steering wheel. Check that the airbag warning light illuminates briefly then extinguishes.
d) Switch off the ignition.
e) If the airbag warning light does not operate as described in paragraph c), consult a Vauxhall dealer before driving the vehicle.

### 23  Airbag system components – removal and refitting

⚠ **Warning: Refer to the precautions given in Section 22 before attempting to carry out work on any of the airbag components.**

1 De-activate the airbag system as described in the previous Section, then proceed as described under the relevant heading.

### Driver's airbag

2 With the steering wheel in the straight-ahead position, undo the two retaining screws from the rear of the steering wheel **(see illustration)**.
3 Carefully lift the airbag assembly away from the steering wheel, release the locking pin and disconnect the wiring connector from the rear of the unit **(see illustrations)**. Note that the airbag must not be knocked or dropped, and should be stored the correct way up, with its padded surface uppermost.
4 Refitting is a reversal of the removal procedure. Make sure the locking pin is secure in the wiring block connector **(see illustration)**, then tighten the airbag retaining screws to the specified torque setting.

### Passenger's airbag

5 Disconnect the battery negative terminal (refer to *Disconnecting the battery* in the Reference Chapter).

6 Remove the glovebox as described in Chapter 11.
7 Release the locking pin and disconnect the airbag wiring plug from the side of the unit.
8 Undo the screws securing the airbag to the mounting brackets, and withdraw the airbag out through the glovebox aperture. Note that the airbag must not be knocked or dropped, and should be stored the correct way up (as mounted in the vehicle).
9 Refitting is a reversal of the removal procedure. Make sure the locking pin is secure in the wiring block connector, then tighten the airbag retaining screws to the specified torque setting.

### Side airbags

10 The side airbags are located internally within the front seat back and no attempt should be made to remove them. Any suspected problems with the side airbag system should be referred to a Vauxhall dealer.

### Curtain airbags

11 The curtain airbags are located behind the headlining above the doors on each side and no attempt should be made to remove them. Any suspected problems with the curtain airbag system should be referred to a Vauxhall dealer.

### Airbag control unit

12 Remove the centre console as described in Chapter 11.
13 Disconnect the control unit wiring connector, then undo the retaining nuts and

**23.2  Undo the two retaining screws (one side arrowed)**

**23.3a  Lift the airbag assembly away from the steering wheel . . .**

**23.3b  . . . release the locking pin (arrowed) and disconnect the wiring connector**

**23.4  Make sure the locking pin (arrowed) is secure**

**23.13a Release the locking clip (arrowed) and disconnect the wiring connector . . .**

**23.13b . . . then undo the retaining nuts (arrowed)**

**23.18a Release the two retaining clips (arrowed) and unclip the upper shroud**

**23.18b Undo the lower shroud upper screws (arrowed) . . .**

**23.18c . . . and the lower retaining screw then unclip the shroud**

**23.19 Depress the retaining clips (arrowed) and slide out the switch**

remove the control unit from the vehicle **(see illustrations)**. Note the fitted position of the control unit – the arrow on the top of the unit is facing forwards.

**14** Refitting is the reverse of removal. If a new control unit is being installed, the vehicle must be taken to a Vauxhall dealer for the control unit to be reprogrammed at the earliest possible opportunity. **Note:** *The airbag system will not be operational until the new control unit is reprogrammed; this will be indicated by the warning light in the instrument panel being illuminated.*

### Airbag wiring contact unit

**15** Disconnect the battery negative terminal (refer to *Disconnecting the battery* in the

Reference Chapter) and wait for 2 minutes.
**16** Remove the steering wheel as described in Chapter 10.
**17** Where necessary, undo the retaining screw and release the steering column adjustment handle from under the steering column.
**18** Unclip the upper steering column shroud from the lower shroud, then undo the retaining screws and remove the lower steering column shrouds **(see illustrations)**.
**19** Depress the retaining clips, and release the left- and right-hand combination switches from the column. Release the securing clips and disconnect the wiring connectors, then remove the switches from the vehicle **(see illustration)**.

**20** Release the retaining clip and disconnect the wiring connector from the contact unit **(see illustration)**.
**21** Unclip the four securing lugs and slide the contact unit from the top of the steering column. DO NOT turn the contact unit centre, as it is set in the vehicle straight-ahead position for refitting **(see illustrations)**.
**22** Refitting is the reverse of removal noting the following points:
a) If a new contact unit is being installed, remove the transport lock (sticker) before refitting, this locks the contact unit in the centre position ready for refitting.
b) Press the contact unit on squarely, taking care not to damage the securing lugs

**23.20 Disconnect the wiring connector from the back of the contact unit**

**23.21a Release the securing lugs (one arrowed) . . .**

**23.21b . . . and withdraw the contact unit from the steering column**

## Vauxhall Corsa wiring diagrams

Diagram 1

### Key to symbols

 Fusible link, link number and rating

 Fuse, fuse number and rating

 Bulb

 Heating element with indicated current rating

 Electric motor

 Dotted outline indicates the item (bulb) is part of a larger assembly

 Solid outline and drop shadow indicates the item (bulb) is an individual part and not part of a larger assembly

 Interface connector pins

 Number indicates pin number

 Shape indicates the pin is grouped to one particular connector on the item

 Ganged switch with multiple contacts

 Single switch with multiple contacts

 Momentary switch

 Relay

 Graphical representation of a component for which no additional detail is provided

 Link to another circuit; where appropriate the interfacing pin numbers are shown

 Item reference; refering to key at top of diagram page

Connecting wires

 Wire splice or soldered joint

 Alternative layout depending on model / year

 Wire colour (Green with blue tracer)

Continuation point (follow arrow) used to improve diagram readability

 Wire enclosed in a screen (bonded both ends)

 Diode

 Chain dashed box indicates item specific to a paricular variant

 Earth point

 Earth point with reference (see earth locations on this page)

### Key to circuits

| | |
|---|---|
| Diagram 1 | Information on wiring diagrams. |
| Diagram 2 | Power supply distribution. |
| Diagram 3 | Starting and charging systems, radiator fan (petrol)(diesel). |
| Diagram 4 | Headlights, side and tail lights, headlight levelling (xenon/non-xenon). |
| Diagram 5 | Directional indicators, front and rear fog lights, licence plate lights. |
| Diagram 6 | Reversing lights, brake lights, switch illumination, horn. |
| Diagram 7 | Windscreen wipers, rear screen wiper, headlight wiper, washers. |
| Diagram 8 | Central locking, cigar lighter, sunroof, power steering. |
| Diagram 9 | Anti-lock brake system, motorised door mirrors, motorised window lifts. |
| Diagram 10 | Heating system, seat heaters, interior lighting. |
| Diagram 11 | Diagnostic connector, trailer connector, speed sensor. |
| Diagram 12 | Radio installation, instruments. |
| Diagram 13 | Engine fusebox details. |

### Earth locations

| | |
|---|---|
| E2 | Battery negative lead chassis connection |
| E3 | Left hand side of engine bay inner wing |
| E5 | Tunnel connection forward of gear shift |
| E4 | Left hand side inner body panel |
| E7 | Behind trim panel adjacent to wiper motor |

| | |
|---|---|
| E1 | Right hand side rear engine bay on inner wing |
| E8 | Base of door pilar behind trim panel |
| E6 | Tunnel connection forward of handbrake |

H33535

**Wire colours**

| | | | |
|---|---|---|---|
| **B** | Black | **P** | Purple |
| **G** | Green | **R** | Red |
| **K** | Pink | **S** | Grey |
| **Lg** | Light green | **U** | Blue |
| **N** | Brown | **W** | White |
| **O** | Orange | **Y** | Yellow |

**Key to items**

1  Battery
2  Engine bay fuse box
3  Inline fuse FB1
4  Ignition switch
5  Ignition circuit (15) relay (K50)
6  Circuit 15a relay (K72)
7  Power train main relay (K26)

**Diagram 2**

H33536

**Power supply distribution, ignition switch and primary circuit relays**

2003 fuse values
[1] 5A
[2] 10A
[3] 15A
[4] 20A

## Wire colours

| | | | |
|---|---|---|---|
| B | Black | P | Purple |
| G | Green | R | Red |
| K | Pink | S | Grey |
| Lg | Light green | U | Blue |
| N | Brown | W | White |
| O | Orange | Y | Yellow |

## Key to items

8  Starter relay (K61)
9  Starter motor
10  Automatic transmission selector switch
11  Alternator
12  Radiator coolng fan motor
13  Relay, fan speed control (K30A)
14  Relay, fan speed control (K30B)

15  Relay, fan speed control (K30C)
16  Relay, fan speed control (K30D)

**Diagram 3**

H33537

### Power supply outline

See diagram 2 for enhanced
power distribution information

### Starting system

### Charging system

### Engine cooling (petrol)
Typical petrol with a/c and 3 level fan speed and
(boxed) 2003 no a/c and with single speed fan

### Engine cooling (diesel)
Typical diesel with a/c and 4 level fan speed

## Wire colours

| | | | |
|---|---|---|---|
| B | Black | P | Purple |
| G | Green | R | Red |
| K | Pink | S | Grey |
| Lg | Light green | U | Blue |
| N | Brown | W | White |
| O | Orange | Y | Yellow |

## Key to items

18  Left headlight cluster
  a  dip beam unit
  b  main beam unit
  c  dip beam unit (xenon)
  d  side light
19  Right headlight cluster
  a  dip beam unit
  b  main beam unit
  c  dip beam unit (xenon)
  d  side light

20  Dip beam relay (K43)
21  Main beam relay (K45)
22  Light switch
  a  side/headlights
  b  headlight levelling
  c  switch illumination
23  Left tail light cluster
  a  tail light
24  Right tail light cluster
  a  tail light

**Diagram 4**

25  Main/dip/flash column switch
26  Sidelight relay
  a  Sidelight relay (K76) [all models]
     annotated K76R 2003 only
  b  Sidelight relay (K76L) [2003 only]
27  Headlight levelling control unit
28  Left hand headlight levelling motor
29  Right hand headlight levelling motor

H33538

### Power supply outline
See diagram 2 for enhanced power distribution information

### Headlights
Xenon and Non-xenon varients shown

### Side and tail lamps
XX = 2003 pin numbers

### Headlight levelling
Xenon headlight varient

### Headlight levelling
Non-xenon headlight varient

## Wire colours

| | | | |
|---|---|---|---|
| B | Black | P | Purple |
| G | Green | R | Red |
| K | Pink | S | Grey |
| Lg | Light green | U | Blue |
| N | Brown | W | White |
| O | Orange | Y | Yellow |

## Key to items

22 Light switch
  d  front fog lights
  e  rear fog lights
30 Left turn signal
  a  left front
  b  left side repeater
  c  left rear
31 Right turn signal
  a  right front
  b  right side repeater
  c  right rear

32 Turn signal relay
  a  combined R/LH 2004 on (K66)
  b  RH relay 2003 only (K66R)
  c  LH relay 2003 only (K66L)
33 Turn signal column switch
34 Licence plate lights relay (K54)
35 Licence plate light RH
36 Licence plate light LH
37 Front foglights relay (K39)
38 Rear foglights relay (K58)

39 Front fog lights
  a  RH side
  b  LH side
40 Rear fog lights
  a  RH side
  b  LH side
41 Hazard warning switch with LED
42 Alarm LED

**Diagram 5**

H33539

**Power supply outline**

See diagram 2 for enhanced
power distribution information

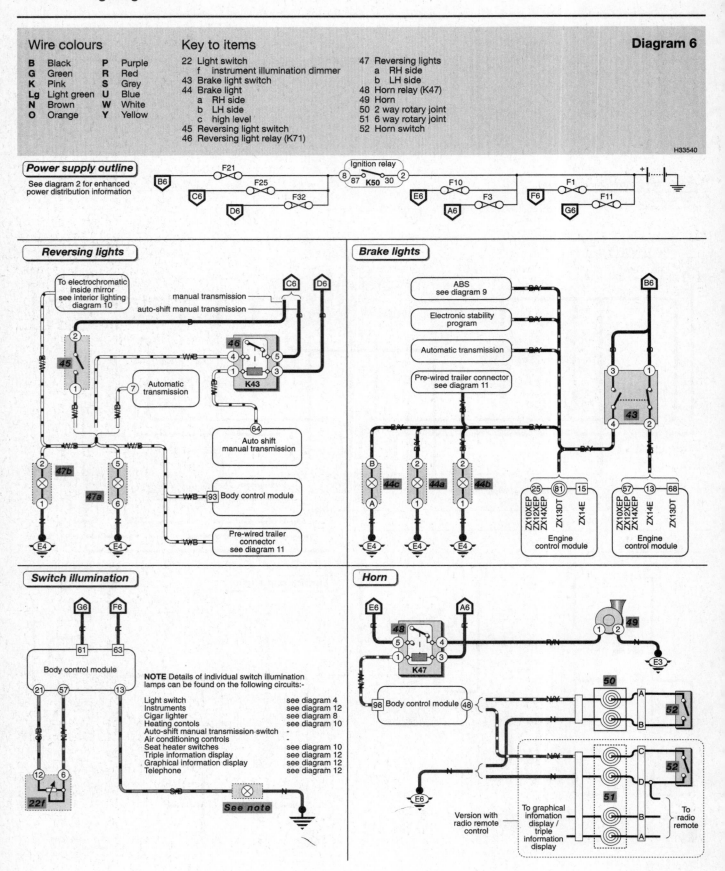

## Wire colours

| | | | |
|---|---|---|---|
| B | Black | P | Purple |
| G | Green | R | Red |
| K | Pink | S | Grey |
| Lg | Light green | U | Blue |
| N | Brown | W | White |
| O | Orange | Y | Yellow |

## Key to items

22 Light switch
  f instrument illumination dimmer
43 Brake light switch
44 Brake light
  a RH side
  b LH side
  c high level
45 Reversing light switch
46 Reversing light relay (K71)

47 Reversing lights
  a RH side
  b LH side
48 Horn relay (K47)
49 Horn
50 2 way rotary joint
51 6 way rotary joint
52 Horn switch

**Diagram 6**

H33540

### Power supply outline

See diagram 2 for enhanced power distribution information

### Reversing lights

To electrochromatic inside mirror see interior lighting diagram 10

manual transmission
auto-shift manual transmission

Automatic transmission

Auto shift manual transmission

Body control module

Pre-wired trailer connector see diagram 11

### Brake lights

ABS see diagram 9

Electronic stability program

Automatic transmission

Pre-wired trailer connector see diagram 11

Engine control module

Engine control module

### Switch illumination

Body control module

**NOTE** Details of individual switch illumination lamps can be found on the following circuits:-

| | |
|---|---|
| Light switch | see diagram 4 |
| Instruments | see diagram 12 |
| Cigar lighter | see diagram 8 |
| Heating contols | see diagram 10 |
| Auto-shift manual transmission switch | - |
| Air conditioning controls | - |
| Seat heater switches | see diagram 10 |
| Triple information display | see diagram 12 |
| Graphical information display | see diagram 12 |
| Telephone | see diagram 12 |

See note

### Horn

Version with radio remote control

To graphical infomation display / triple information display

To radio remote

## Wire colours

| | | | |
|---|---|---|---|
| **B** | Black | **P** | Purple |
| **G** | Green | **R** | Red |
| **K** | Pink | **S** | Grey |
| **Lg** | Light green | **U** | Blue |
| **N** | Brown | **W** | White |
| **O** | Orange | **Y** | Yellow |

## Key to items

53  Wiper relay stage I (K69A)
54  Wiper relat stage 2 (K69B)
55  Windscreen wiper motor
56  Screen wash pump relay (K74)
57  Screen wash pump relay (K70)
58  Screen wash pump
59  Headlight wash relay (K46)
60  Headlight wash pump
61  Washer and wiper column switch
   a  front/rear wash and rear wipe switch
   b  windscreen wiper switch

**Diagram 7**

H33541

### Power supply outline

See diagram 2 for enhanced power distribution information

### Windscreen wipers

### Rear screen wiper

### Front / rear screen washer

### Wash/wiper switch

### Headlight washer

## Wire colours

| | | | |
|---|---|---|---|
| B | Black | P | Purple |
| G | Green | R | Red |
| K | Pink | S | Grey |
| Lg | Light green | U | Blue |
| N | Brown | W | White |
| O | Orange | Y | Yellow |

## Key to items

53 Wiper relay stage I (K69A)
54 Wiper relat stage 2 (K69B)
55 Windscreen wiper motor
56 Screen wash pump relay (K74)
57 Screen wash pump relay (K70)
58 Screen wash pump
59 Headlight wash relay (K46)
60 Headlight wash pump
61 Washer and wiper column switch
   a  front/rear wash and rear wipe switch
   b  windscreen wiper switch

62 Drivers door lock relay (K24A)
63 Unlock relay (K24C)
64 Deadlock relay (K24D)
65 Lock relay (K24B)
66 Drivers door lock motor
67 Drivers door deadlock motor
68 Passenger door lock motor
69 Passenger door deadlock motor
70 Rear RH door lock motor
71 Rear RH door deadlock motor
72 Rear LH door lock motor

73 Rear LH door deadlock motor
74 Fuel flap lock release motor
75 Hatchback lock release motor
76 Hatchback key switch
77 Drivers door central locking switch
78 Cigar lighter
79 Sun roof switch
80 Sun roof motor
81 Power steering motor
82 Steering position sensor
83 Power steering control unit

## Diagram 8

H33542

### Power supply outline

See diagram 2 for enhanced power distribution information

### Central locking

### Cigar lighter

### Sun roof

### Power steering

## Wire colours

| B | Black | P | Purple |
|---|---|---|---|
| G | Green | R | Red |
| K | Pink | S | Grey |
| Lg | Light green | U | Blue |
| N | Brown | W | White |
| O | Orange | Y | Yellow |

## Key to items

84 Drivers door switch panel
  a  drivers door window switch
  b  passenger door window switch
85 Passenger door switch panel
  a  passenger door window switch
86 Drivers door window motor
87 Passenger door window motor
88 Door mirror switch
  a  axis 1 adjustment
  b  axis 2 adjustment

89 Door mirror selector switch
90 Drivers door mirror
  a  position adjustment motors
  b  mirror heater
91 Passenger door mirror
  a  position adjustment motor
  b  mirror heater
92 ABS control unit
93 Front left wheel speed sensor
94 Front right wheel speed senso

95 Rear left wheel speed sensor
96 Rear right wheel speed sensor97
Steering angle sensor
98 Steering rate sensor

**Diagram 9**

H33543

### Power supply outline

See diagram 2 for enhanced power distribution information

### Typical anti-lock brake system

Vehicle speed signal to:
Engine control module
Manual transmission
auto shift
Xenon headlights — Diagram 4
Power steering — Diagram 8
Information display
Carphone / radio — Diagram 12
Navigation system

Steering angle sensor
Contact unit
Steering wheel rotation rate sensor
Contact unit

Auto shift manual transmission
Engine control module
Body control module
Manual transmission models

ABS
**92**

Manual transmission models

To diagnostic socket
see diagram 11

To brake lights
see diagram 6

### Motorised door mirrors

To heated rear window
see diagram 10

### Motorised Window lifts

Reversed for LHD

To sunroof
see diagram 8

Body control module

## Wire colours

| | | | |
|---|---|---|---|
| **B** | Black | **P** | Purple |
| **G** | Green | **R** | Red |
| **K** | Pink | **S** | Grey |
| **Lg** | Light green | **U** | Blue |
| **N** | Brown | **W** | White |
| **O** | Orange | **Y** | Yellow |

## Key to items

99 Heated rear screen relay (R49)
100 Heating unit
101 Heating controls
  a 4 speed fan
  b panel illumination
  c rear screen heater switch
102 Resistor pack (fan speed)
103 Fan motor
104 Heating element (rear screen)
105 Passenger compartment light

106 Luggage compartment light
107 Rear reading light
108 Passenger compartment light
  a interior lights
  b front reading lights
109 Drivers door contact
110 Passengers door contact
111 Rear RH door contact
112 Rear LH door contact
113 Boot lid contact

114 LH seat heater switch
115 RH seat heater switch
116 LH seat heater
117 RH seat heater

**Diagram 10**

H33544

Power supply outline

See diagram 2 for enhanced
power distribution information

Heating system

Seat heating

Interior lighting

## Wire colours

| | | | |
|---|---|---|---|
| B | Black | P | Purple |
| G | Green | R | Red |
| K | Pink | S | Grey |
| Lg | Light green | U | Blue |
| N | Brown | W | White |
| O | Orange | Y | Yellow |

## Key to items

118  Diagnostic connector
119  Rear fog light switch (trailer connector)
120  Trailer connector
121  Signal converter
122  Signal converter (auto-shift models)
123  LH front wheel speed sensor
124  RH front wheel speed sensor

**Diagram 11**

H33545

### Power supply outline

See diagram 2 for enhanced power distribution information

C11   F32   Ignition relay  8  87  K50  30  2   F4   +   F3   B11   A11

### Diagnostic connector

A11

| Graphic infomation display | Triple infomation display | Immobiliser | Electric power steering see diagram 8 | Add on fuel heater | Airbag control unit | Xenon headlight levelling control unit see diagran 4 | Body control module | ABS see diagram 9 | Electronic climate control | Instruments see diagram 12 |
|---|---|---|---|---|---|---|---|---|---|---|
| 22 23 | 22 23 | 6 | 2 | F | 30 | 5 | 44 | 11 | 31 | 12 |

N/W
W
G
R
N/W
N/G
N

2005-06 version  118   16 3 11 7 8 12 4 5   E5

A11

| Graphic infomation display | ABS see diagram 9 | Immobiliser | Electric power steering see diagram 8 | Add on fuel heater | Airbag control unit | Telematics control unit | Body control module | Triple infomation display | Electronic climate control | Instruments see diagram 12 |
|---|---|---|---|---|---|---|---|---|---|---|
| 27 | 11 | 6 | 2 | F | 30 | 26 | 44 | 8 | 31 | 12 |

N/W
G
R
N/W
N/G
N

2003-04 version  118   16 3 7 8 12 4 5   E5

| Graphic info display | Radio | GPS | Multi info display |
|---|---|---|---|
| 14 | 27 | 15 | 14 |

### Trailer connector

B11

119
1
3

120
2 9 1 4 5 6 7 8 3 13

B/U } To fog light circuit see diagram 5
B/U
B/W  To turn signal circuit see diagram 5
B/G  To turn signal circuit see diagram 5
S/R  To tail light circuit see diagram 4
B/Y  To brake light circuit see diagram 6
To tail light circuit see diagram 4
To reversing light circuit see diagram 6

G/B  W/B  N   E4

### Speed sensor (non ABS models)

C11

| Engine control unit | Radio | Power steering | Triple info display | Graphic info display |
|---|---|---|---|---|
| | 5 | 6 | 9 | 12 |

U/R

6  121  4  B  B  4  122  6  U/R  79  Auto shift manual transmission control unit
2 8 5               2 8 5

E1  123   1 2        E1  124   1 2

Additional sensor (auto shift manual transmission models)

## Wire colours

| | | | |
|---|---|---|---|
| B | Black | P | Purple |
| G | Green | R | Red |
| K | Pink | S | Grey |
| Lg | Light green | U | Blue |
| N | Brown | W | White |
| O | Orange | Y | Yellow |

## Key to items

125 Radio unit
126 Front speakers
  a RH loudspeaker
  b LH loudspeaker
  c RH tweeter
  d LH tweeter
127 Side panel speakers
  a RH loudspeaker
  b LH loudspeaker

128 Remote control (radio)
129 Microphone (carphone)
130 Aerial/head amplifier
  (radio, phone, DAB)
131 Phone connector
132 Instruments
  a display, gauges, status lamps etc
  b airbag warning lamp
  c engine warning lamp

133 Handbrake switch
134 Brake fluid level switch

**Diagram 12**

H33546

### Power supply outline

See diagram 2 for enhanced power distribution information

### Typical radio installation

includes phone connector and DAB reciever

### Instruments

**Diagram 13**

## Engine compartment fuse box

| Fuse | Rating | Function |
|------|--------|----------|
| F1 | 7.5A | Body control module |
| F2 | 7.5A | Engine control module |
| F3 | 7.5A | Turn signals, horn, wipers, anti-theft system, rear wiper, screen washers, headlamp washer, heated rear screen(ECC), light switch, hazard warning switch, diagnostic connector, instruments, ECC, immobiliser, relay K72, (2006/05/04 electronic stability program), (Z13DT engine cooling fan) (2004/03 above + licence plate light relay, triple info display) |
| F4 | 20A | Trailer connector |
|  | 5A | (2003 Licence plate lamps) |
| F5 | 20A | Window lifts (2005 not used) |
| F6 | 10A | Automatic transmission (A/T), (05/06 above + trailer connector) |
| F7 | 30A | Headlamp washer |
| F8 | 10A | Ignition switch |
| F9 | 20A | Fuel pump, add on heater |
| F10 | 10A | Horn |
| F11 | 15A | Body control module |
| F12 | 10A | (Z13DT) |
|  | 20A | (Petrol)(2003) } Graphic info display, radio |
| F13 | 7.5A |  |
|  | 10A | (2004/03) } Anti-theft system |
| F14 | 7.5A | Electric mirrors |
| F15 | 15A | Screen washers |
| F16 | 7.5A | } Anti-theft system (sensor), |
|  | 5A | (2004/03) } interior lights |
| F17 | 20A | Central locking |
| F18 | 20A | Sunroof |
| F19 | 20A | Window lifts |
|  | 5A | (2003 Anti-theft system [powered sounder]) |
| F20 | 5A | Xenon lights |
|  | 20A | (2003) Window lifts |
| F21 | 5A | Xenon lights (2003 not used) |
| F22 | 5A | Instruments, immobiliser |
| F23 | 30A | Windscreen wiper |
| F24 | 5A | Interior lamp, wiper (rain sensor module), light switch, triple info display, electric power steering, graphic info display, (2005/04/03 above + multi info display), (2006 phone) |
| F25 | 20A | Reversing lamps, A/T, add on heater, cigar lighter (04 above + trailer connector) |
|  | 10A | (2003) Stop light switch |

| Fuse | Rating | Function |
|------|--------|----------|
| F26 | 15A | Seat heater RHS |
|  | 20A | (2003) Reversing lamps, A/T, add-on heater, cigar heater |
| F27 | 15A | Seat heater LHS (2003 seat heated RHS) |
| F28 | 25A | ABS (2003 seat heater LHS) |
| F29 | 20A | Rear screen wiper |
| F30 | 15A | Engine control module, ignition coil, [Diesel engine control unit] |
| F31 | 15A | Air conditioning |
| F32 | 5A | Reversing lamp relay, anti-theft system powered sounder, vehicle speed sensor, ABS, A/T switch, A/T control unit, manual transmission, auto shift control unit, airbag, (2003 above + traction control), (2006/05/04 above + steering angle sensor, rate sensor), (2006/05 above +start-up assistance switch) (Z13DT 2006/05 glow plug control unit, fuel filter water level sensor), air mass meter |
| F33 | 15A | Engine electrics |
| F34 | 30A | (Z13DT Fuel filter heater) |
| F35 | 5A | Sun roof, window lifts, (2006/05 above + triple info display, graphic info display) (2004/03 above + radio) |
| F36 | 10A | (15A Xenon) Low beam left |
| F37 | 10A | (15A Xenon) Low beam right, (headlamp levelling non Xenon only) |
| F38 | 5A | Parking lamp left, tail lamp left |
| F39 | 5A | Parking lamp right, tail lamp right |
| F40 | 10A | Stop lamp switch (2003 not used) |
| F41 | 15A | Front fog lamps |
| F42 | 10A | Rear fog lamps |
| F43 | 10A | Hi beam left |
| F44 | 10A | Hi beam right |
| F45 | 30A | (ECC ) Blower regulator, (Non ECC) Heating controls, air conditioning |
| F46 | 20A | Engine control unit relay |
| F47 | 30A | Heated rear window |
| F48 | 30A | Starter relay |
| F49 | 50A | Electric power steering |
| F50 | 40A | ABS & traction control |
| F51 | 60A | Manual transmission auto shift |
|  | 80A | (Z13DT Glow plug control unit) |
| F52 | 20A | (Z10XE, Z12XE, Z13DT no AC) |
|  | 30A | (Petrol models with AC) |
|  | 40A | (Z14XE, ZX12EP no AC) } Engine cooling |
|  | 40A | (Z13DT with AC) |
| F53 | 30A | (2005/03 Petrol with AC) } Engine cooling |
|  | 40A | (Z13DT) |
| F54 | 60A | (2003 not used), (Z13DT) Manual transmission auto shift |
| FB1 | 20A | (Z13DT) Radio, carphone, navigation (located behind car battery in engine compartment) |

Z13DT Fuse panel

Petrol model fuse panel

Location: Front RHS of engine compartment adjacent to coolant expansion tank

H33557

# Notes

# Dimensions and weights

**Note:** *All figures are approximate and may vary according to model. Refer to manufacturer's data for exact figures.*

## Dimensions

Overall length:
  All models except Combo Van . . . . . . . . . . . . . . . . . . . . . . . . . . . . 3817 to 3839 mm
  Combo Van models . . . . . . . . . . . . . . . . . . . . . . . . . . . . . . . . . . . 4322 mm
Overall width:
  All models except Combo Van:
    Excluding door mirrors . . . . . . . . . . . . . . . . . . . . . . . . . . . . . . . . 1646 mm
    Including door mirrors. . . . . . . . . . . . . . . . . . . . . . . . . . . . . . . . . 1955 mm
  Combo Van models:
    Excluding door mirrors . . . . . . . . . . . . . . . . . . . . . . . . . . . . . . . . 1684 mm
    Including door mirrors. . . . . . . . . . . . . . . . . . . . . . . . . . . . . . . . . 1892 mm
Overall height (unladen):
  All models except Combo Van . . . . . . . . . . . . . . . . . . . . . . . . . . . . 1440 mm
  Combo Van models . . . . . . . . . . . . . . . . . . . . . . . . . . . . . . . . . . . 1801 mm
Wheelbase:
  All models except Combo Van . . . . . . . . . . . . . . . . . . . . . . . . . . . . 2491 mm
  Combo Van models . . . . . . . . . . . . . . . . . . . . . . . . . . . . . . . . . . . 2716 mm
Turning circle diameter (wall to wall):
  All models except Combo Van . . . . . . . . . . . . . . . . . . . . . . . . . . . . 10.45 metres
  Combo Van models . . . . . . . . . . . . . . . . . . . . . . . . . . . . . . . . . . . 11.25 metres
Front track . . . . . . . . . . . . . . . . . . . . . . . . . . . . . . . . . . . . . . . . . . . 1429 mm
Rear track. . . . . . . . . . . . . . . . . . . . . . . . . . . . . . . . . . . . . . . . . . . . 1420 mm
Ground clearance. . . . . . . . . . . . . . . . . . . . . . . . . . . . . . . . . . . . . . 122 mm

## Weights

**Kerb weight**

3-door Hatchback:
  1.0 litre petrol models. . . . . . . . . . . . . . . . . . . . . . . . . . . . . . . . . . 913 kg to 1045 kg
  1.2 litre petrol models. . . . . . . . . . . . . . . . . . . . . . . . . . . . . . . . . . 935 kg to 1095 kg
  1.4 litre petrol models. . . . . . . . . . . . . . . . . . . . . . . . . . . . . . . . . . 998 kg to 1110 kg
  1.3 litre diesel models. . . . . . . . . . . . . . . . . . . . . . . . . . . . . . . . . . 1110 to 1185 kg
  1.7 litre diesel models. . . . . . . . . . . . . . . . . . . . . . . . . . . . . . . . . . 1020 kg to 1117 kg
5-door Hatchback:
  1.0 litre petrol models. . . . . . . . . . . . . . . . . . . . . . . . . . . . . . . . . . 940 kg to 1080 kg
  1.2 litre petrol models. . . . . . . . . . . . . . . . . . . . . . . . . . . . . . . . . . 960 kg to 1120 kg
  1.4 litre petrol models. . . . . . . . . . . . . . . . . . . . . . . . . . . . . . . . . . 1023 kg to 1073 kg
  1.3 litre diesel models. . . . . . . . . . . . . . . . . . . . . . . . . . . . . . . . . . 1135 to 1210 kg
  1.7 litre diesel models. . . . . . . . . . . . . . . . . . . . . . . . . . . . . . . . . . 1045 kg to 1175 kg
Corsavan models:
  1.2 litre petrol models. . . . . . . . . . . . . . . . . . . . . . . . . . . . . . . . . . 965 kg to 1065 kg
  1.4 litre petrol models. . . . . . . . . . . . . . . . . . . . . . . . . . . . . . . . . . 1055 to 1080 kg
  1.3 litre diesel models. . . . . . . . . . . . . . . . . . . . . . . . . . . . . . . . . . 1130 to 1155 kg
  1.7 litre diesel models: . . . . . . . . . . . . . . . . . . . . . . . . . . . . . . . . . 1050 kg to 1085 kg
Combo Van models . . . . . . . . . . . . . . . . . . . . . . . . . . . . . . . . . . . . 1210 kg
Gross vehicle weight . . . . . . . . . . . . . . . . . . . . . . . . . . . . . . . . . . . Refer to information contained on the vehicle identification plate
Maximum roof load (including weight of rack) . . . . . . . . . . . . . . . . . 100 kg

# Conversion factors

## Length (distance)

| | | | | | |
|---|---|---|---|---|---|
| Inches (in) | x 25.4 | = Millimetres (mm) | x 0.0394 | = Inches (in) |
| Feet (ft) | x 0.305 | = Metres (m) | x 3.281 | = Feet (ft) |
| Miles | x 1.609 | = Kilometres (km) | x 0.621 | = Miles |

## Volume (capacity)

| | | | | | |
|---|---|---|---|---|---|
| Cubic inches (cu in; in³) | x 16.387 | = Cubic centimetres (cc; cm³) | x 0.061 | = Cubic inches (cu in; in³) |
| Imperial pints (Imp pt) | x 0.568 | = Litres (l) | x 1.76 | = Imperial pints (Imp pt) |
| Imperial quarts (Imp qt) | x 1.137 | = Litres (l) | x 0.88 | = Imperial quarts (Imp qt) |
| Imperial quarts (Imp qt) | x 1.201 | = US quarts (US qt) | x 0.833 | = Imperial quarts (Imp qt) |
| US quarts (US qt) | x 0.946 | = Litres (l) | x 1.057 | = US quarts (US qt) |
| Imperial gallons (Imp gal) | x 4.546 | = Litres (l) | x 0.22 | = Imperial gallons (Imp gal) |
| Imperial gallons (Imp gal) | x 1.201 | = US gallons (US gal) | x 0.833 | = Imperial gallons (Imp gal) |
| US gallons (US gal) | x 3.785 | = Litres (l) | x 0.264 | = US gallons (US gal) |

## Mass (weight)

| | | | | | |
|---|---|---|---|---|---|
| Ounces (oz) | x 28.35 | = Grams (g) | x 0.035 | = Ounces (oz) |
| Pounds (lb) | x 0.454 | = Kilograms (kg) | x 2.205 | = Pounds (lb) |

## Force

| | | | | | |
|---|---|---|---|---|---|
| Ounces-force (ozf; oz) | x 0.278 | = Newtons (N) | x 3.6 | = Ounces-force (ozf; oz) |
| Pounds-force (lbf; lb) | x 4.448 | = Newtons (N) | x 0.225 | = Pounds-force (lbf; lb) |
| Newtons (N) | x 0.1 | = Kilograms-force (kgf; kg) | x 9.81 | = Newtons (N) |

## Pressure

| | | | | | |
|---|---|---|---|---|---|
| Pounds-force per square inch (psi; lbf/in²; lb/in²) | x 0.070 | = Kilograms-force per square centimetre (kgf/cm²; kg/cm²) | x 14.223 | = Pounds-force per square inch (psi; lbf/in²; lb/in²) |
| Pounds-force per square inch (psi; lbf/in²; lb/in²) | x 0.068 | = Atmospheres (atm) | x 14.696 | = Pounds-force per square inch (psi; lbf/in²; lb/in²) |
| Pounds-force per square inch (psi; lbf/in²; lb/in²) | x 0.069 | = Bars | x 14.5 | = Pounds-force per square inch (psi; lbf/in²; lb/in²) |
| Pounds-force per square inch (psi; lbf/in²; lb/in²) | x 6.895 | = Kilopascals (kPa) | x 0.145 | = Pounds-force per square inch (psi; lbf/in²; lb/in²) |
| Kilopascals (kPa) | x 0.01 | = Kilograms-force per square centimetre (kgf/cm²; kg/cm²) | x 98.1 | = Kilopascals (kPa) |
| Millibar (mbar) | x 100 | = Pascals (Pa) | x 0.01 | = Millibar (mbar) |
| Millibar (mbar) | x 0.0145 | = Pounds-force per square inch (psi; lbf/in²; lb/in²) | x 68.947 | = Millibar (mbar) |
| Millibar (mbar) | x 0.75 | = Millimetres of mercury (mmHg) | x 1.333 | = Millibar (mbar) |
| Millibar (mbar) | x 0.401 | = Inches of water (inH₂O) | x 2.491 | = Millibar (mbar) |
| Millimetres of mercury (mmHg) | x 0.535 | = Inches of water (inH₂O) | x 1.868 | = Millimetres of mercury (mmHg) |
| Inches of water (inH₂O) | x 0.036 | = Pounds-force per square inch (psi; lbf/in²; lb/in²) | x 27.68 | = Inches of water (inH₂O) |

## Torque (moment of force)

| | | | | | |
|---|---|---|---|---|---|
| Pounds-force inches (lbf in; lb in) | x 1.152 | = Kilograms-force centimetre (kgf cm; kg cm) | x 0.868 | = Pounds-force inches (lbf in; lb in) |
| Pounds-force inches (lbf in; lb in) | x 0.113 | = Newton metres (Nm) | x 8.85 | = Pounds-force inches (lbf in; lb in) |
| Pounds-force inches (lbf in; lb in) | x 0.083 | = Pounds-force feet (lbf ft; lb ft) | x 12 | = Pounds-force inches (lbf in; lb in) |
| Pounds-force feet (lbf ft; lb ft) | x 0.138 | = Kilograms-force metres (kgf m; kg m) | x 7.233 | = Pounds-force feet (lbf ft; lb ft) |
| Pounds-force feet (lbf ft; lb ft) | x 1.356 | = Newton metres (Nm) | x 0.738 | = Pounds-force feet (lbf ft; lb ft) |
| Newton metres (Nm) | x 0.102 | = Kilograms-force metres (kgf m; kg m) | x 9.804 | = Newton metres (Nm) |

## Power

| | | | | | |
|---|---|---|---|---|---|
| Horsepower (hp) | x 745.7 | = Watts (W) | x 0.0013 | = Horsepower (hp) |

## Velocity (speed)

| | | | | | |
|---|---|---|---|---|---|
| Miles per hour (miles/hr; mph) | x 1.609 | = Kilometres per hour (km/hr; kph) | x 0.621 | = Miles per hour (miles/hr; mph) |

## Fuel consumption*

| | | | | | |
|---|---|---|---|---|---|
| Miles per gallon, Imperial (mpg) | x 0.354 | = Kilometres per litre (km/l) | x 2.825 | = Miles per gallon, Imperial (mpg) |
| Miles per gallon, US (mpg) | x 0.425 | = Kilometres per litre (km/l) | x 2.352 | = Miles per gallon, US (mpg) |

## Temperature

Degrees Fahrenheit = (°C x 1.8) + 32          Degrees Celsius (Degrees Centigrade; °C) = (°F - 32) x 0.56

*It is common practice to convert from miles per gallon (mpg) to litres/100 kilometres (l/100km), where mpg x l/100 km = 282*

Spare parts are available from many sources, including maker's appointed garages, accessory shops, and motor factors. To be sure of obtaining the correct parts, it will sometimes be necessary to quote the vehicle identification number. If possible, it can also be useful to take the old parts along for positive identification. Items such as starter motors and alternators may be available under a service exchange scheme – any parts returned should be clean.

Our advice regarding spare parts is as follows.

## Officially appointed garages

This is the best source of parts which are peculiar to your car, and which are not otherwise generally available (eg, badges, interior trim, certain body panels, etc). It is also the only place at which you should buy parts if the vehicle is still under warranty.

## Accessory shops

These are very good places to buy materials and components needed for the maintenance of your car (oil, air and fuel filters, light bulbs, drivebelts, greases, brake pads, touch-up paint, etc). Components of this nature sold by a reputable shop are of the same standard as those used by the car manufacturer.

Besides components, these shops also sell tools and general accessories, usually have convenient opening hours, charge lower prices, and can often be found close to home. Some accessory shops have parts counters where components needed for almost any repair job can be purchased or ordered.

## Motor factors

Good factors will stock all the more important components which wear out comparatively quickly, and can sometimes supply individual components needed for the overhaul of a larger assembly (eg, brake seals and hydraulic parts, bearing shells, pistons, valves). They may also handle work such as cylinder block reboring, crankshaft regrinding, etc.

## Tyre and exhaust specialists

These outlets may be independent, or members of a local or national chain. They frequently offer competitive prices when compared with a main dealer or local garage, but it will pay to obtain several quotes before making a decision. When researching prices, also ask what 'extras' may be added – for instance fitting a new valve and balancing the wheel are both commonly charged on top of the price of a new tyre.

## Other sources

Beware of parts or materials obtained from market stalls, car boot sales or similar outlets. Such items are not invariably sub-standard, but there is little chance of compensation if they do prove unsatisfactory. In the case of safety-critical components such as brake pads, there is the risk not only of financial loss, but also of an accident causing injury or death.

Second-hand components or assemblies obtained from a car breaker can be a good buy in some circumstances, but his sort of purchase is best made by the experienced DIY mechanic.

# Vehicle identification

Modifications are a continuing and unpublished process in vehicle manufacture, quite apart from major model changes. Spare parts manuals and lists are compiled upon a numerical basis, the individual vehicle numbers being essential to correct identification of the component required.

When ordering spare parts, always give as much information as possible. Quote the car model, year of manufacture and vehicle identification and/or engine numbers as appropriate.

The *vehicle identification plate* is riveted to the engine compartment front crossmember (see illustration) and includes the Vehicle Identification Number (VIN), vehicle weight information and paint and trim colour codes. This information also appears on the right-hand front door B-pillar or on the right-hand front suspension tower in the engine compartment (see illustration).

The *Vehicle Identification Number (VIN)* is given on the vehicle identification plate and is also stamped into the body floor panel between the right-hand front seat and the door sill panel (see illustration); lift the flap in the carpet to see it. The number is also fixed to the left-hand end of the instrument panel, and can be viewed through the windscreen (see illustration).

The *engine number* is stamped on a horizontal flat located on the front of the cylinder block, at the transmission end. The first part of the engine number gives the engine code – eg Z12XEP (see illustration).

Engine codes are as follows:

*1.0 litre petrol engine: Z10XE, Z10XEP and Z10XE-ECO*
*1.2 litre petrol engine: Z12XE and Z12XEP*
*1.4 litre petrol engine: Z14XE and Z14XEP*
*1.3 litre diesel engine: Y13DT and Z13DT*
*1.7 litre diesel engine: Y17DT and Y17DTL*

Vauxhall/Opel use a 'Car pass' scheme for vehicle identification. This is a card which is issued to the customer when the car is first purchased. It contains important information, eg, VIN number, key number and radio code. It also includes a special code for diagnostic equipment, therefore it must be kept in a secure place and not in the vehicle.

**Vehicle Identification Number (VIN) plate on the front crossmember**

**The VIN plate also appears on the right-hand front suspension tower**

**The VIN number is stamped into the body floor next to the right-hand front seat**

**The VIN number can also be viewed through the left-hand side of the windscreen**

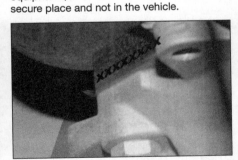

**The engine number is stamped on the front of the cylinder block**

Whenever servicing, repair or overhaul work is carried out on the car or its components, observe the following procedures and instructions. This will assist in carrying out the operation efficiently and to a professional standard of workmanship.

### Joint mating faces and gaskets

When separating components at their mating faces, never insert screwdrivers or similar implements into the joint between the faces in order to prise them apart. This can cause severe damage which results in oil leaks, coolant leaks, etc upon reassembly. Separation is usually achieved by tapping along the joint with a soft-faced hammer in order to break the seal. However, note that this method may not be suitable where dowels are used for component location.

Where a gasket is used between the mating faces of two components, a new one must be fitted on reassembly; fit it dry unless otherwise stated in the repair procedure. Make sure that the mating faces are clean and dry, with all traces of old gasket removed. When cleaning a joint face, use a tool which is unlikely to score or damage the face, and remove any burrs or nicks with an oilstone or fine file.

Make sure that tapped holes are cleaned with a pipe cleaner, and keep them free of jointing compound, if this is being used, unless specifically instructed otherwise.

Ensure that all orifices, channels or pipes are clear, and blow through them, preferably using compressed air.

### Oil seals

Oil seals can be removed by levering them out with a wide flat-bladed screwdriver or similar implement. Alternatively, a number of self-tapping screws may be screwed into the seal, and these used as a purchase for pliers or some similar device in order to pull the seal free.

Whenever an oil seal is removed from its working location, either individually or as part of an assembly, it should be renewed.

The very fine sealing lip of the seal is easily damaged, and will not seal if the surface it contacts is not completely clean and free from scratches, nicks or grooves. If the original sealing surface of the component cannot be restored, and the manufacturer has not made provision for slight relocation of the seal relative to the sealing surface, the component should be renewed.

Protect the lips of the seal from any surface which may damage them in the course of fitting. Use tape or a conical sleeve where possible. Where indicated, lubricate the seal lips with oil before fitting and, on dual-lipped seals, fill the space between the lips with grease.

Unless otherwise stated, oil seals must be fitted with their sealing lips toward the lubricant to be sealed.

Use a tubular drift or block of wood of the appropriate size to install the seal and, if the seal housing is shouldered, drive the seal down to the shoulder. If the seal housing is unshouldered, the seal should be fitted with its face flush with the housing top face (unless otherwise instructed).

### Screw threads and fastenings

Seized nuts, bolts and screws are quite a common occurrence where corrosion has set in, and the use of penetrating oil or releasing fluid will often overcome this problem if the offending item is soaked for a while before attempting to release it. The use of an impact driver may also provide a means of releasing such stubborn fastening devices, when used in conjunction with the appropriate screwdriver bit or socket. If none of these methods works, it may be necessary to resort to the careful application of heat, or the use of a hacksaw or nut splitter device. Before resorting to extreme methods, check that you are not dealing with a left-hand thread!

Studs are usually removed by locking two nuts together on the threaded part, and then using a spanner on the lower nut to unscrew the stud. Studs or bolts which have broken off below the surface of the component in which they are mounted can sometimes be removed using a stud extractor.

Always ensure that a blind tapped hole is completely free from oil, grease, water or other fluid before installing the bolt or stud. Failure to do this could cause the housing to crack due to the hydraulic action of the bolt or stud as it is screwed in.

For some screw fastenings, notably cylinder head bolts or nuts, torque wrench settings are no longer specified for the latter stages of tightening, "angle-tightening" being called up instead. Typically, a fairly low torque wrench setting will be applied to the bolts/nuts in the correct sequence, followed by one or more stages of tightening through specified angles.

When checking or retightening a nut or bolt to a specified torque setting, slacken the nut or bolt by a quarter of a turn, and then retighten to the specified setting. However, this should not be attempted where angular tightening has been used.

### Locknuts, locktabs and washers

Any fastening which will rotate against a component or housing during tightening should always have a washer between it and the relevant component or housing.

Spring or split washers should always be renewed when they are used to lock a critical component such as a big-end bearing retaining bolt or nut. Locktabs which are folded over to retain a nut or bolt should always be renewed.

Self-locking nuts can be re-used in non-critical areas, providing resistance can be felt when the locking portion passes over the bolt or stud thread. However, it should be noted that self-locking stiffnuts tend to lose their effectiveness after long periods of use, and should then be renewed as a matter of course.

Split pins must always be replaced with new ones of the correct size for the hole.

When thread-locking compound is found on the threads of a fastener which is to be re-used, it should be cleaned off with a wire brush and solvent, and fresh compound applied on reassembly.

### Special tools

Some repair procedures in this manual entail the use of special tools such as a press, two or three-legged pullers, spring compressors, etc. Wherever possible, suitable readily-available alternatives to the manufacturer's special tools are described, and are shown in use. In some instances, where no alternative is possible, it has been necessary to resort to the use of a manufacturer's tool, and this has been done for reasons of safety as well as the efficient completion of the repair operation. Unless you are highly-skilled and have a thorough understanding of the procedures described, never attempt to bypass the use of any special tool when the procedure described specifies its use. Not only is there a very great risk of personal injury, but expensive damage could be caused to the components involved.

### Environmental considerations

When disposing of used engine oil, brake fluid, antifreeze, etc, give due consideration to any detrimental environmental effects. Do not, for instance, pour any of the above liquids down drains into the general sewage system, or onto the ground to soak away. Many local council refuse tips provide a facility for waste oil disposal, as do some garages. You can find your nearest disposal point by calling the Environment Agency on 08708 506 506 or by visiting www.oilbankline.org.uk.

*Note: It is illegal and anti-social to dump oil down the drain. To find the location of your local oil recycling bank, call 08708 506 506 or visit www.oilbankline.org.uk.*

The jack supplied with the vehicle tool kit should only be used for changing roadwheels – see Wheel changing at the front of this manual. Ensure the jack head is correctly engaged before attempting to raise the vehicle. When carrying out any other kind of work, raise the vehicle using a hydraulic jack, and always supplement the jack with axle stands positioned under the vehicle jacking points.

When jacking up the vehicle with a trolley jack, position the jack head under one of the relevant jacking points (note that the jacking points for use with a hydraulic jack are different to those for use with the vehicle jack). Use a block of wood between the jack or axle stand and the sill – the block of wood should have a groove cut into it , in which the welded flange of the sill will locate. **Do not** jack the

vehicle under the sump or any of the steering or suspension components. Supplement the jack using axle stands **(see illustrations)**.

 *Warning: Never work under, around, or near a raised vehicle, unless it is adequately supported in at least two places.*

**Front jacking point for hydraulic jack or axle stands**

**Rear jacking point for hydraulic jack or axle stands**

**Axle stands should be placed under, or adjacent to, the jacking point (arrowed)**

# Disconnecting the battery

Numerous systems fitted to the vehicle require battery power to be available at all times, either to ensure their continued operation (such as the clock) or to maintain control unit memories which would be erased if the battery were to be disconnected. Whenever the battery is to be disconnected therefore, first note the following, to ensure that there are no unforeseen consequences of this action:

a) *First, on any vehicle with central locking, it is a wise precaution to remove the key from the ignition, and to keep it with you, so that it does not get locked in, if the central locking should engage accidentally when the battery is reconnected.*

b) *Depending on model and specification, the Vauxhall anti-theft alarm system may be of the type which is automatically activated when the vehicle battery is disconnected and/or reconnected. To prevent the alarm sounding on models so equipped, switch the ignition on, then off, and disconnect the battery within15 seconds. If the alarm is activated when the battery is reconnected, switch the ignition on then off to deactivate the alarm.*

c) *If a security-coded audio unit is fitted, and the unit and/or the battery is disconnected, the unit will not function again on reconnection until the correct*

*security code is entered. Details of this procedure, which varies according to the unit fitted, are given in the vehicle audio system operating instructions. Ensure you have the correct code before you disconnect the battery. If you do not have the code or details of the correct procedure, but can supply proof of ownership and a legitimate reason for wanting this information, a Vauxhall dealer may be able to help.*

d) *The engine management electronic control unit is of the 'self-learning' type, meaning that as it operates, it also monitors and stores the settings which give optimum engine performance under all operating conditions. When the battery is disconnected, these settings are lost and the ECU reverts to the base settings programmed into its memory at the factory. On restarting, this may lead to the engine running/idling roughly for a short while, until the ECU has re-learned the optimum settings. This process is best accomplished by taking the vehicle on a road test (for approximately 15 minutes), covering all engine speeds and loads, concentrating mainly in the 2500 to 3500 rpm region.*

e) *On models equipped with automatic transmission, the transmission selector lever assembly incorporates an*

*electrically-operated selector lever lock mechanism that prevents the lever being moved out of the P position unless the ignition is switched on and the brake pedal is depressed. If the selector lever is in the P position and the battery is disconnected, it will not be possible to move the selector lever out of position P by the normal means. Although it is possible to manually override the system (see Chapter 7B), it is sensible to move the selector lever to the N position before disconnecting the battery.*

f) *On models with electric windows, it will be necessary to reprogramme the motors to restore the one-touch function of the buttons, after reconnection of the battery. To do this, fully close both front windows. With the windows closed, depress the up button of the driver's side window for approximately 5 seconds, then release it and depress the passenger side window up button for approximately 5 seconds.*

g) *On models with an electric sliding sunroof, it will be necessary to fully open and fully close the sunroof after battery reconnection, to recalibrate the sensors.*

h) *On all models, when reconnecting the battery after disconnection, switch on the ignition and wait 10 seconds to allow the electronic vehicle systems to stabilise and re-initialise.*

## Introduction

A selection of good tools is a fundamental requirement for anyone contemplating the maintenance and repair of a motor vehicle. For the owner who does not possess any, their purchase will prove a considerable expense, offsetting some of the savings made by doing-it-yourself. However, provided that the tools purchased meet the relevant national safety standards and are of good quality, they will last for many years and prove an extremely worthwhile investment.

To help the average owner to decide which tools are needed to carry out the various tasks detailed in this manual, we have compiled three lists of tools under the following headings: *Maintenance and minor repair*, *Repair and overhaul*, and *Special*. Newcomers to practical mechanics should start off with the *Maintenance and minor repair* tool kit, and confine themselves to the simpler jobs around the vehicle. Then, as confidence and experience grow, more difficult tasks can be undertaken, with extra tools being purchased as, and when, they are needed. In this way, a *Maintenance and minor repair* tool kit can be built up into a *Repair and overhaul* tool kit over a considerable period of time, without any major cash outlays. The experienced do-it-yourselfer will have a tool kit good enough for most repair and overhaul procedures, and will add tools from the *Special* category when it is felt that the expense is justified by the amount of use to which these tools will be put.

## Maintenance and minor repair tool kit

The tools given in this list should be considered as a minimum requirement if routine maintenance, servicing and minor repair operations are to be undertaken. We recommend the purchase of combination spanners (ring one end, open-ended the other); although more expensive than open-ended ones, they do give the advantages of both types of spanner.

☐ *Combination spanners:*
 *Metric - 8 to 19 mm inclusive*
☐ *Adjustable spanner - 35 mm jaw (approx.)*
☐ *Spark plug spanner (with rubber insert) - petrol models*
☐ *Spark plug gap adjustment tool - petrol models*
☐ *Set of feeler gauges*
☐ *Brake bleed nipple spanner*
☐ *Screwdrivers:*
 *Flat blade - 100 mm long x 6 mm dia*
 *Cross blade - 100 mm long x 6 mm dia*
 *Torx - various sizes (not all vehicles)*
☐ *Combination pliers*
☐ *Hacksaw (junior)*
☐ *Tyre pump*
☐ *Tyre pressure gauge*
☐ *Oil can*
☐ *Oil filter removal tool (if applicable)*
☐ *Fine emery cloth*
☐ *Wire brush (small)*
☐ *Funnel (medium size)*
☐ *Sump drain plug key (not all vehicles)*

## Repair and overhaul tool kit

These tools are virtually essential for anyone undertaking any major repairs to a motor vehicle, and are additional to those given in the *Maintenance and minor repair* list. Included in this list is a comprehensive set of sockets. Although these are expensive, they will be found invaluable as they are so versatile - particularly if various drives are included in the set. We recommend the half-inch square-drive type, as this can be used with most proprietary torque wrenches.

The tools in this list will sometimes need to be supplemented by tools from the *Special* list:

☐ *Sockets to cover range in previous list (including Torx sockets)*
☐ *Reversible ratchet drive (for use with sockets)*
☐ *Extension piece, 250 mm (for use with sockets)*
☐ *Universal joint (for use with sockets)*
☐ *Flexible handle or sliding T "breaker bar" (for use with sockets)*
☐ *Torque wrench (for use with sockets)*
☐ *Self-locking grips*
☐ *Ball pein hammer*
☐ *Soft-faced mallet (plastic or rubber)*
☐ *Screwdrivers:*
 *Flat blade - long & sturdy, short (chubby), and narrow (electrician's) types*
 *Cross blade – long & sturdy, and short (chubby) types*
☐ *Pliers:*
 *Long-nosed*
 *Side cutters (electrician's)*
 *Circlip (internal and external)*
☐ *Cold chisel - 25 mm*
☐ *Scriber*
☐ *Scraper*
☐ *Centre-punch*
☐ *Pin punch*
☐ *Hacksaw*
☐ *Brake hose clamp*
☐ *Brake/clutch bleeding kit*
☐ *Selection of twist drills*
☐ *Steel rule/straight-edge*
☐ *Allen keys (inc. splined/Torx type)*
☐ *Selection of files*
☐ *Wire brush*
☐ *Axle stands*
☐ *Jack (strong trolley or hydraulic type)*
☐ *Light with extension lead*
☐ *Universal electrical multi-meter*

**Sockets and reversible ratchet drive**

**Brake bleeding kit**

**Torx key, socket and bit**

**Hose clamp**

**Angular-tightening gauge**

## Special tools

The tools in this list are those which are not used regularly, are expensive to buy, or which need to be used in accordance with their manufacturers' instructions. Unless relatively difficult mechanical jobs are undertaken frequently, it will not be economic to buy many of these tools. Where this is the case, you could consider clubbing together with friends (or joining a motorists' club) to make a joint purchase, or borrowing the tools against a deposit from a local garage or tool hire specialist.

The following list contains only those tools and instruments freely available to the public, and not those special tools produced by the vehicle manufacturer specifically for its dealer network. You will find occasional references to these manufacturers' special tools in the text of this manual. Generally, an alternative method of doing the job without the vehicle manufacturers' special tool is given. However, sometimes there is no alternative to using them. Where this is the case and the relevant tool cannot be bought or borrowed, you will have to entrust the work to a dealer.

- [ ] Angular-tightening gauge
- [ ] Valve spring compressor
- [ ] Valve grinding tool
- [ ] Piston ring compressor
- [ ] Piston ring removal/installation tool
- [ ] Cylinder bore hone
- [ ] Balljoint separator
- [ ] Coil spring compressors (where applicable)
- [ ] Two/three-legged hub and bearing puller
- [ ] Impact screwdriver
- [ ] Micrometer and/or vernier calipers
- [ ] Dial gauge
- [ ] Tachometer
- [ ] Fault code reader
- [ ] Cylinder compression gauge
- [ ] Hand-operated vacuum pump and gauge
- [ ] Clutch plate alignment set
- [ ] Brake shoe steady spring cup removal tool
- [ ] Bush and bearing removal/installation set
- [ ] Stud extractors
- [ ] Tap and die set
- [ ] Lifting tackle

## Buying tools

Reputable motor accessory shops and superstores often offer excellent quality tools at discount prices, so it pays to shop around.

Remember, you don't have to buy the most expensive items on the shelf, but it is always advisable to steer clear of the very cheap tools. Beware of 'bargains' offered on market stalls, on-line or at car boot sales. There are plenty of good tools around at reasonable prices, but always aim to purchase items which meet the relevant national safety standards. If in doubt, ask the proprietor or manager of the shop for advice before making a purchase.

## Care and maintenance of tools

Having purchased a reasonable tool kit, it is necessary to keep the tools in a clean and serviceable condition. After use, always wipe off any dirt, grease and metal particles using a clean, dry cloth, before putting the tools away. Never leave them lying around after they have been used. A simple tool rack on the garage or workshop wall for items such as screwdrivers and pliers is a good idea. Store all normal spanners and sockets in a metal box. Any measuring instruments, gauges, meters, etc, must be carefully stored where they cannot be damaged or become rusty.

Take a little care when tools are used. Hammer heads inevitably become marked, and screwdrivers lose the keen edge on their blades from time to time. A little timely attention with emery cloth or a file will soon restore items like this to a good finish.

## Working facilities

Not to be forgotten when discussing tools is the workshop itself. If anything more than routine maintenance is to be carried out, a suitable working area becomes essential.

It is appreciated that many an owner-mechanic is forced by circumstances to remove an engine or similar item without the benefit of a garage or workshop. Having done this, any repairs should always be done under the cover of a roof.

Wherever possible, any dismantling should be done on a clean, flat workbench or table at a suitable working height.

Any workbench needs a vice; one with a jaw opening of 100 mm is suitable for most jobs. As mentioned previously, some clean dry storage space is also required for tools, as well as for any lubricants, cleaning fluids, touch-up paints etc, which become necessary.

Another item which may be required, and which has a much more general usage, is an electric drill with a chuck capacity of at least 8 mm. This, together with a good range of twist drills, is virtually essential for fitting accessories.

Last, but not least, always keep a supply of old newspapers and clean, lint-free rags available, and try to keep any working area as clean as possible.

**Micrometers**

**Dial test indicator ("dial gauge")**

**Oil filter removal tool (strap wrench type)**

**Compression tester**

**Bearing puller**

This is a guide to getting your vehicle through the MOT test. Obviously it will not be possible to examine the vehicle to the same standard as the professional MOT tester. However, working through the following checks will enable you to identify any problem areas before submitting the vehicle for the test.

It has only been possible to summarise the test requirements here, based on the regulations in force at the time of printing. Test standards are becoming increasingly stringent, although there are some exemptions for older vehicles.

An assistant will be needed to help carry out some of these checks.

*The checks have been sub-divided into four categories, as follows:*

**1** Checks carried out **FROM THE DRIVER'S SEAT**

**2** Checks carried out **WITH THE VEHICLE ON THE GROUND**

**3** Checks carried out **WITH THE VEHICLE RAISED AND THE WHEELS FREE TO TURN**

**4** Checks carried out on **YOUR VEHICLE'S EXHAUST EMISSION SYSTEM**

---

**1** Checks carried out **FROM THE DRIVER'S SEAT**

### Handbrake (parking brake)

☐ Test the operation of the handbrake. Excessive travel (too many clicks) indicates incorrect brake or cable adjustment.

☐ Check that the handbrake cannot be released by tapping the lever sideways. Check the security of the lever mountings.

☐ If the parking brake is foot-operated, check that the pedal is secure and without excessive travel, and that the release mechanism operates correctly.

☐ Where applicable, test the operation of the electronic handbrake. The brake should engage and disengage without excessive delay. If the warning light does not extinguish when the brake is disengaged, this could indicate a fault which will need further investigation.

### Footbrake

☐ Depress the brake pedal and check that it does not creep down to the floor, indicating a master cylinder fault. Release the pedal,

wait a few seconds, then depress it again. If the pedal travels nearly to the floor before firm resistance is felt, brake adjustment or repair is necessary. If the pedal feels spongy, there is air in the hydraulic system which must be removed by bleeding.

☐ Check that the brake pedal is secure and in good condition. Check also for signs of fluid leaks on the pedal, floor or carpets, which would indicate failed seals in the brake master cylinder.

☐ Check the servo unit (when applicable) by operating the brake pedal several times, then keeping the pedal depressed and starting the engine. As the engine starts, the pedal will move down slightly. If not, the vacuum hose or the servo itself may be faulty.

### Steering wheel and column

☐ Examine the steering wheel for fractures or looseness of the hub, spokes or rim.

☐ Move the steering wheel from side to side and then up and down. Check that the steering wheel is not loose on the column, indicating wear or a loose retaining nut. Continue moving the steering wheel as before, but also turn it slightly from left to right.

☐ Check that the steering wheel is not loose on the column, and that there is no abnormal movement of the steering wheel, indicating wear in the column support bearings or couplings.

☐ Check that the ignition lock (where fitted) engages and disengages correctly.

☐ Steering column adjustment mechanisms (where fitted) must be able to lock the column securely in place with no play evident.

### Windscreen, mirrors and sunvisor

☐ The windscreen must be free of cracks or other significant damage within the driver's field of view. (Small stone chips are acceptable.) Rear view mirrors must be secure, intact, and capable of being adjusted.

☐ The driver's sunvisor must be capable of being stored in the "up" position.

## Seat belts and seats

**Note:** *The following checks are applicable to all seat belts, front and rear.*

☐ Examine the webbing of all the belts (including rear belts if fitted) for cuts, serious fraying or deterioration. Fasten and unfasten each belt to check the buckles. If applicable, check the retracting mechanism. Check the security of all seat belt mountings accessible from inside the vehicle, ensuring any height adjustable mountings lock securely in place.

☐ Seat belts with pre-tensioners, once activated, have a "flag" or similar showing on the seat belt stalk. This, in itself, is not a reason for test failure.

☐ The front seats themselves must be securely attached and the backrests must lock in the upright position.

## Doors

☐ Both front doors must be able to be opened and closed from outside and inside, and must latch securely when closed.

## Bonnet and boot/tailgate

☐ The bonnet and boot/tailgate must latch securely when closed.

## 2 Checks carried out WITH THE VEHICLE ON THE GROUND

## Vehicle identification

☐ Number plates must be in good condition, secure and legible, with letters and numbers correctly spaced – spacing at (A) should be 33 mm and at (B) 11 mm. At the front, digits must be black on a white background and at the rear black on a yellow background. Other background designs (such as honeycomb) are not permitted.

☐ The VIN plate and/or homologation plate must be permanently displayed and legible.

## Electrical equipment

☐ Switch on the ignition and check the operation of the horn.

☐ Check the windscreen washers and wipers, examining the wiper blades; renew damaged or perished blades. Also check the operation of the stop-lights.

☐ Check the operation of the sidelights and number plate lights. The lenses and reflectors must be secure, clean and undamaged.

☐ Check the operation and alignment of the headlights. The headlight reflectors must not be tarnished and the lenses must be undamaged.

☐ Switch on the ignition and check the operation of the direction indicators (including the instrument panel tell-tale) and the hazard warning lights. Operation of the sidelights and stop-lights must not affect the indicators - if it does, the cause is usually a bad earth at the rear light cluster. Indicators should flash at a rate of between 60 and 120 times per minute – faster or slower than this could indicate a fault with the flasher unit or a bad earth at one of the light units.

☐ Check the operation of the rear foglight(s), including the warning light on the instrument panel or in the switch.

☐ The warning lights must illuminate in accordance with the manufacturer's design. For most vehicles, the ABS and other warning lights should illuminate when the ignition is switched on, and (if the system is operating properly) extinguish after a few seconds. Refer to the owner's handbook.

## Footbrake

☐ Examine the master cylinder, brake pipes and servo unit for leaks, loose mountings, corrosion or other damage. If ABS is fitted, this unit should also be examined for signs of leaks or corrosion.

☐ The fluid reservoir must be secure and the fluid level must be between the upper (A) and lower (B) markings.

☐ Inspect both front brake flexible hoses for cracks or deterioration of the rubber. Turn the steering from lock to lock, and ensure that the hoses do not contact the wheel, tyre, or any part of the steering or suspension mechanism. With the brake pedal firmly depressed, check the hoses for bulges or leaks under pressure.

## Steering and suspension

☐ Have your assistant turn the steering wheel from side to side slightly, up to the point where the steering gear just begins to transmit this movement to the roadwheels. Check for excessive free play between the steering wheel and the steering gear, indicating wear or insecurity of the steering column joints, the column-to-steering gear coupling, or the steering gear itself.

☐ Have your assistant turn the steering wheel more vigorously in each direction, so that the roadwheels just begin to turn. As this is done, examine all the steering joints, linkages, fittings and attachments. Renew any component that shows signs of wear or damage. On vehicles with power steering, check the security and condition of the steering pump, drivebelt and hoses.

☐ Check that the vehicle is standing level, and at approximately the correct ride height.

## Shock absorbers

☐ Depress each corner of the vehicle in turn, then release it. The vehicle should rise and then settle in its normal position. If the vehicle continues to rise and fall, the shock absorber is defective. A shock absorber which has seized will also cause the vehicle to fail.

## Exhaust system

☐ Start the engine. With your assistant holding a rag over the tailpipe, check the entire system for leaks. Repair or renew leaking sections.

**3** Checks carried out **WITH THE VEHICLE RAISED AND THE WHEELS FREE TO TURN**

*Jack up the front and rear of the vehicle, and securely support it on axle stands. Position the stands clear of the suspension assemblies. Ensure that the wheels are clear of the ground and that the steering can be turned from lock to lock.*

## Steering mechanism

☐ Have your assistant turn the steering from lock to lock. Check that the steering turns smoothly, and that no part of the steering mechanism, including a wheel or tyre, fouls any brake hose or pipe or any part of the body structure.

☐ Examine the steering rack rubber gaiters for damage or insecurity of the retaining clips. If power steering is fitted, check for signs of damage or leakage of the fluid hoses, pipes or connections. Also check for excessive stiffness or binding of the steering, a missing split pin or locking device, or severe corrosion of the body structure within 30 cm of any steering component attachment point.

## Front and rear suspension and wheel bearings

☐ Starting at the front right-hand side, grasp the roadwheel at the 3 o'clock and 9 o'clock positions and rock gently but firmly. Check for free play or insecurity at the wheel bearings, suspension balljoints, or suspension mount-ings, pivots and attachments.

☐ Now grasp the wheel at the 12 o'clock and 6 o'clock positions and repeat the previous inspection. Spin the wheel, and check for roughness or tightness of the front wheel bearing.

☐ If excess free play is suspected at a component pivot point, this can be confirmed by using a large screwdriver or similar tool and levering between the mounting and the component attachment. This will confirm whether the wear is in the pivot bush, its retaining bolt, or in the mounting itself (the bolt holes can often become elongated).

☐ Carry out all the above checks at the other front wheel, and then at both rear wheels.

## Springs and shock absorbers

☐ Examine the suspension struts (when applicable) for serious fluid leakage, corrosion, or damage to the casing. Also check the security of the mounting points.

☐ If coil springs are fitted, check that the spring ends locate in their seats, and that the spring is not corroded, cracked or broken.

☐ If leaf springs are fitted, check that all leaves are intact, that the axle is securely attached to each spring, and that there is no deterioration of the spring eye mountings, bushes, and shackles.

☐ The same general checks apply to vehicles fitted with other suspension types, such as torsion bars, hydraulic displacer units, etc. Ensure that all mountings and attachments are secure, that there are no signs of excessive wear, corrosion or damage, and (on hydraulic types) that there are no fluid leaks or damaged pipes.

☐ Inspect the shock absorbers for signs of serious fluid leakage. Check for wear of the mounting bushes or attachments, or damage to the body of the unit.

## Driveshafts (fwd vehicles only)

☐ Rotate each front wheel in turn and inspect the constant velocity joint gaiters for splits or damage. Also check that each driveshaft is straight and undamaged.

## Braking system

☐ If possible without dismantling, check brake pad wear and disc condition. Ensure that the friction lining material has not worn excessively, (A) and that the discs are not fractured, pitted, scored or badly worn (B).

☐ Examine all the rigid brake pipes underneath the vehicle, and the flexible hose(s) at the rear. Look for corrosion, chafing or insecurity of the pipes, and for signs of bulging under pressure, chafing, splits or deterioration of the flexible hoses.

☐ Look for signs of fluid leaks at the brake calipers or on the brake backplates. Repair or renew leaking components.

☐ Slowly spin each wheel, while your assistant depresses and releases the footbrake. Ensure that each brake is operating and does not bind when the pedal is released.

□ Examine the handbrake mechanism, checking for frayed or broken cables, excessive corrosion, or wear or insecurity of the linkage. Check that the mechanism works on each relevant wheel, and releases fully, without binding.

□ It is not possible to test brake efficiency without special equipment, but a road test can be carried out later to check that the vehicle pulls up in a straight line.

## Fuel and exhaust systems

□ Inspect the fuel tank (including the filler cap), fuel pipes, hoses and unions. All components must be secure and free from leaks. Locking fuel caps must lock securely and the key must be provided for the MOT test.

□ Examine the exhaust system over its entire length, checking for any damaged, broken or missing mountings, security of the retaining clamps and rust or corrosion.

## Wheels and tyres

□ Examine the sidewalls and tread area of each tyre in turn. Check for cuts, tears, lumps, bulges, separation of the tread, and exposure of the ply or cord due to wear or damage. Check that the tyre bead is correctly seated on the wheel rim, that the valve is sound and properly seated, and that the wheel is not distorted or damaged.

□ Check that the tyres are of the correct size for the vehicle, that they are of the same size and type on each axle, and that the pressures are correct.

□ Check the tyre tread depth. The legal minimum at the time of writing is 1.6 mm over the central three-quarters of the tread width. Abnormal tread wear may indicate incorrect front wheel alignment or wear in steering or suspension components.

□ If the spare wheel is fitted externally or in a separate carrier beneath the vehicle, check that mountings are secure and free of excessive corrosion.

## Body corrosion

□ Check the condition of the entire vehicle structure for signs of corrosion in load-bearing areas. (These include chassis box sections, side sills, cross-members, pillars, and all suspension, steering, braking system and seat belt mountings and anchorages.) Any corrosion which has seriously reduced the thickness of a load-bearing area (or is within 30 cm of safety-related components such as steering or suspension) is likely to cause the vehicle to fail. In this case professional repairs are likely to be needed.

□ Damage or corrosion which causes sharp or otherwise dangerous edges to be exposed will also cause the vehicle to fail.

## Towbars

□ Check the condition of mounting points (both beneath the vehicle and within boot/hatchback areas) for signs of corrosion, ensuring that all fixings are secure and not worn or damaged. There must be no excessive play in detachable tow ball arms or quick-release mechanisms.

**4** Checks carried out on **YOUR VEHICLE'S EXHAUST EMISSION SYSTEM**

## Petrol models

□ The engine should be warmed up, and running well (ignition system in good order, air filter element clean, etc).

□ Before testing, run the engine at around 2500 rpm for 20 seconds. Let the engine drop to idle, and watch for smoke from the exhaust. If the idle speed is too high, or if dense blue or black smoke emerges for more than 5 seconds, the vehicle will fail. Typically, blue smoke signifies oil burning (engine wear);

black smoke means unburnt fuel (dirty air cleaner element, or other fuel system fault).

□ An exhaust gas analyser for measuring carbon monoxide (CO) and hydrocarbons (HC) is now needed. If one cannot be hired or borrowed, have a local garage perform the check.

### CO emissions (mixture)

□ The MOT tester has access to the CO limits for all vehicles. The CO level is measured at idle speed, and at 'fast idle' (2500 to 3000 rpm). The following limits are given as a general guide:

*At idle speed* – Less than 0.5% CO
*At 'fast idle'* – Less than 0.3% CO
*Lambda reading* – 0.97 to 1.03

□ If the CO level is too high, this may point to poor maintenance, a fuel injection system problem, faulty lambda (oxygen) sensor or catalytic converter. Try an injector cleaning treatment, and check the vehicle's ECU for fault codes.

### HC emissions

□ The MOT tester has access to HC limits for all vehicles. The HC level is measured at 'fast idle' (2500 to 3000 rpm). The following limits are given as a general guide:

*At 'fast idle'* – Less then 200 ppm

□ Excessive HC emissions are typically caused by oil being burnt (worn engine), or by a blocked crankcase ventilation system ('breather'). If the engine oil is old and thin, an oil change may help. If the engine is running badly, check the vehicle's ECU for fault codes.

### Diesel models

□ The only emission test for diesel engines is measuring exhaust smoke density, using a calibrated smoke meter. The test involves accelerating the engine at least 3 times to its maximum unloaded speed.

**Note:** *On engines with a timing belt, it is VITAL that the belt is in good condition before the test is carried out.*

□ With the engine warmed up, it is first purged by running at around 2500 rpm for 20 seconds. A governor check is then carried out, by slowly accelerating the engine to its maximum speed. After this, the smoke meter is connected, and the engine is accelerated quickly to maximum speed three times. If the smoke density is less than the limits given below, the vehicle will pass:

*Non-turbo vehicles*: 2.5m-1
*Turbocharged vehicles*: 3.0m-1

□ If excess smoke is produced, try fitting a new air cleaner element, or using an injector cleaning treatment. If the engine is running badly, where applicable, check the vehicle's ECU for fault codes. Also check the vehicle's EGR system, where applicable. At high mileages, the injectors may require professional attention.

## Engine

- [ ] Engine fails to rotate when attempting to start
- [ ] Engine rotates, but will not start
- [ ] Engine difficult to start when cold
- [ ] Engine difficult to start when hot
- [ ] Starter motor noisy or excessively-rough in engagement
- [ ] Engine starts, but stops immediately
- [ ] Engine idles erratically
- [ ] Engine misfires at idle speed
- [ ] Engine misfires throughout the driving speed range
- [ ] Engine hesitates on acceleration
- [ ] Engine stalls
- [ ] Engine lacks power
- [ ] Engine backfires
- [ ] Oil pressure warning light illuminated with engine running
- [ ] Engine runs-on after switching off
- [ ] Engine noises

## Cooling system

- [ ] Overheating
- [ ] Overcooling
- [ ] External coolant leakage
- [ ] Internal coolant leakage
- [ ] Corrosion

## Fuel and exhaust systems

- [ ] Excessive fuel consumption
- [ ] Fuel leakage and/or fuel odour
- [ ] Excessive noise or fumes from exhaust system

## Clutch

- [ ] Pedal travels to floor – no pressure or very little resistance
- [ ] Clutch fails to disengage (unable to select gears)
- [ ] Clutch slips (engine speed increases, with no increase in vehicle speed)
- [ ] Judder as clutch is engaged
- [ ] Noise when depressing or releasing clutch pedal

## Driveshafts

- [ ] Vibration when accelerating or decelerating
- [ ] Clicking or knocking noise on turns (at slow speed on full-lock)

## Manual transmission

- [ ] Noisy in neutral with engine running
- [ ] Noisy in one particular gear
- [ ] Difficulty engaging gears
- [ ] Jumps out of gear
- [ ] Vibration
- [ ] Lubricant leaks

## Automatic transmission

- [ ] Fluid leakage
- [ ] Transmission fluid brown, or has burned smell
- [ ] General gear selection problems
- [ ] Transmission will not downshift (kickdown) with accelerator pedal fully depressed
- [ ] Engine will not start in any gear, or starts in gears other than Park or Neutral
- [ ] Transmission slips, shifts roughly, is noisy, or has no drive in forward or reverse gears

## Braking system

- [ ] Vehicle pulls to one side under braking
- [ ] Noise (grinding or high-pitched squeal) when brakes applied
- [ ] Excessive brake pedal travel
- [ ] Brake pedal feels spongy when depressed
- [ ] Excessive brake pedal effort required to stop vehicle
- [ ] Judder felt through brake pedal or steering wheel when braking
- [ ] Brakes binding
- [ ] Rear wheels locking under normal braking

## Suspension and steering

- [ ] Vehicle pulls to one side
- [ ] Wheel wobble and vibration
- [ ] Excessive pitching and/or rolling around corners, or during braking
- [ ] Wandering or general instability
- [ ] Excessively-stiff steering
- [ ] Excessive play in steering
- [ ] Lack of power assistance
- [ ] Tyre wear excessive

## Electrical system

- [ ] Battery will not hold a charge for more than a few days
- [ ] Ignition/no-charge warning light remains illuminated with engine running
- [ ] Ignition/no-charge warning light fails to come on
- [ ] Lights inoperative
- [ ] Instrument readings inaccurate or erratic
- [ ] Horn inoperative, or unsatisfactory in operation
- [ ] Windscreen wipers inoperative, or unsatisfactory in operation
- [ ] Windscreen washers inoperative, or unsatisfactory in operation
- [ ] Electric windows inoperative, or unsatisfactory in operation
- [ ] Central locking system inoperative, or unsatisfactory in operation

# Introduction

The vehicle owner who does his or her own maintenance according to the recommended service schedules should not have to use this section of the manual very often. Modern component reliability is such that, provided those items subject to wear or deterioration are inspected or renewed at the specified intervals, sudden failure is comparatively rare. Faults do not usually just happen as a result of sudden failure, but develop over a period of time. Major mechanical failures in particular are usually preceded by characteristic symptoms over hundreds or even thousands of miles. Those components which do occasionally fail without warning are often small and easily carried in the vehicle.

With any fault-finding, the first step is to decide where to begin investigations. Sometimes this is obvious, but on other occasions, a little detective work will be necessary. The owner who makes half a dozen haphazard adjustments or replacements may be successful in curing a fault (or its symptoms), but will be none the wiser if the fault recurs, and ultimately may have spent more time and money than was necessary. A calm and logical approach will be found to be more satisfactory in the long run. Always take into account any warning signs or abnormalities that may have been noticed in the period preceding the fault – power loss, high or low gauge readings, unusual smells, etc – and remember that failure

of components such as fuses or spark plugs may only be pointers to some underlying fault.

The pages which follow provide an easy-reference guide to the more common problems which may occur during the operation of the vehicle. These problems and their possible causes are grouped under headings denoting various components or systems, such as Engine, Cooling system, etc. The general Chapter which deals with the problem is also shown in brackets; refer to the relevant part of that Chapter for system-specific information. Whatever the fault, certain basic principles apply. These are as follows:

*Verify the fault*. This is simply a matter of being sure that you know what the symptoms are before starting work. This is particularly important if you are investigating a fault for someone else, who may not have described it very accurately.

*Don't overlook the obvious.* For example, if the vehicle won't start, is there fuel in the tank? (Don't take anyone else's word on this particular point, and don't trust the fuel gauge either!) If an electrical fault is indicated, look for loose or broken wires before digging out the test gear.

*Cure the disease, not the symptom.* Substituting a flat battery with a fully-charged one will get you off the hard shoulder, but if the underlying cause is not attended to, the new battery will go the same way. Similarly, changing oil-fouled spark plugs for a new set will get you moving again, but remember that the reason for the fouling (if it wasn't simply an incorrect grade of plug) will have to be established and corrected.

*Don't take anything for granted.* Particularly, don't forget that a 'new' component may itself be defective (especially if it's been rattling around in the boot for months), and don't leave components out of a fault diagnosis sequence just because they are new or recently-fitted. When you do finally diagnose a difficult fault, you'll probably realise that all the evidence was there from the start.

*Consider what work, if any, has recently been carried out.* Many faults arise through careless or hurried work. For instance, if any work has been performed under the bonnet, could some of the wiring have been dislodged or incorrectly routed, or a hose trapped? Have all the fasteners been properly tightened? Were new, genuine parts and new gaskets used? There is often a certain amount of detective work to be done in this case, as an apparently-unrelated task can have far-reaching consequences.

## Diesel fault diagnosis

The majority of starting problems on small diesel engines are electrical in origin. The mechanic who is familiar with petrol engines but less so with diesel may be inclined to view the diesel's injectors and pump in the same light as the spark plugs and distributor, but this is generally a mistake.

When investigating complaints of difficult starting for someone else, make sure that the correct starting procedure is understood and is being followed. Some drivers are unaware of the significance of the preheating warning light – many modern engines are sufficiently forgiving for this not to matter in mild weather, but with the onset of winter, problems begin.

As a rule of thumb, if the engine is difficult to start but runs well when it has finally got going, the problem is electrical (battery, starter motor or preheating system). If poor performance is combined with difficult starting, the problem is likely to be in the fuel system. The low-pressure (supply) side of the fuel system should be checked before suspecting the injectors and high-pressure pump. The most common fuel supply problem is air getting into the system, and any pipe from the fuel tank forwards must be scrutinised if air leakage is suspected. Normally the pump is the last item to suspect, since unless it has been tampered with, there is no reason for it to be at fault.

# Engine

## Engine fails to rotate when attempting to start

- [ ] Battery terminal connections loose or corroded (see *Weekly checks*)
- [ ] Battery discharged or faulty (Chapter 5A)
- [ ] Broken, loose or disconnected wiring in the starting circuit (Chapter 5A)
- [ ] Defective starter solenoid or ignition switch (Chapter 5A or 12)
- [ ] Defective starter motor (Chapter 5A)
- [ ] Starter pinion or flywheel ring gear teeth loose or broken (Chapter 2 or 5A)
- [ ] Engine earth strap broken or disconnected (Chapter 5A)
- [ ] Engine suffering 'hydraulic lock' (eg from water drawn into the engine after traversing flooded roads, or from a serious internal coolant leak) – consult a main dealer for advice
- [ ] Automatic transmission not in position P or N (Chapter 7B)

## Engine rotates, but will not start

- [ ] Fuel tank empty
- [ ] Battery discharged (engine rotates slowly) (Chapter 5A)
- [ ] Battery terminal connections loose or corroded (see *Weekly checks*)
- [ ] Ignition components damp or damaged – petrol models (Chapter 1A or 5B)
- [ ] Immobiliser fault, or 'uncoded' ignition key being used (Chapter 12 or Roadside repairs)
- [ ] Broken, loose or disconnected wiring in the ignition circuit – petrol models (Chapter 1A or 5B)
- [ ] Worn, faulty or incorrectly-gapped spark plugs – petrol models (Chapter 1A)
- [ ] Preheating system faulty – diesel models (Chapter 5C)
- [ ] Fuel injection/engine management system fault (Chapter 4)
- [ ] Air in fuel system – diesel models (Chapter 4)
- [ ] Major mechanical failure (eg timing chain snapped) (Chapter 2)

## Engine difficult to start when cold

- [ ] Battery discharged (Chapter 5A)
- [ ] Battery terminal connections loose or corroded (see *Weekly checks*)

- [ ] Worn, faulty or incorrectly-gapped spark plugs – petrol models (Chapter 1A)
- [ ] Other ignition system fault – petrol models (Chapter 1A or 5B)
- [ ] Preheating system faulty – diesel models (Chapter 5C)
- [ ] Fuel injection/engine management system fault (Chapter 4)
- [ ] Wrong grade of engine oil used (*Weekly checks*, Chapter 1A or 1B)
- [ ] Low cylinder compression (Chapter 2)

## Engine difficult to start when hot

- [ ] Air filter element dirty or clogged (Chapter 1A or 1B)
- [ ] Fuel injection/engine management system fault (Chapter 4)
- [ ] Low cylinder compression (Chapter 2)

## Starter motor noisy or excessively-rough in engagement

- [ ] Starter pinion or flywheel ring gear teeth loose or broken (Chapter 2 or 5A)
- [ ] Starter motor mounting bolts loose or missing (Chapter 5A)
- [ ] Starter motor internal components worn or damaged (Chapter 5A)

## Engine starts, but stops immediately

- [ ] Loose or faulty electrical connections in the ignition circuit – petrol models (Chapter 1A or 5B)
- [ ] Vacuum leak at the throttle body or inlet manifold – petrol models (Chapter 4A or 4B)
- [ ] Blocked injectors/fuel injection system fault (Chapter 4A or 4B)

## Engine idles erratically

- [ ] Air filter element clogged (Chapter 1A or 1B)
- [ ] Vacuum leak at the throttle body, inlet manifold or associated hoses – petrol models (Chapter 4A or 4B)
- [ ] Worn, faulty or incorrectly-gapped spark plugs – petrol models (Chapter 1A)
- [ ] Uneven or low cylinder compression (Chapter 2)
- [ ] Camshaft lobes worn (Chapter 2)
- [ ] Blocked injectors/fuel injection system fault (Chapter 4)

# Engine (continued)

### Engine misfires at idle speed

- ☐ Worn, faulty or incorrectly-gapped spark plugs – petrol models (Chapter 1A)
- ☐ Vacuum leak at the throttle body, inlet manifold or associated hoses – petrol models (Chapter 4A or 4B)
- ☐ Blocked injectors/fuel injection system fault (Chapter 4)
- ☐ Faulty injector(s) – diesel models (Chapter 4)
- ☐ Uneven or low cylinder compression (Chapter 2)
- ☐ Disconnected, leaking, or perished crankcase ventilation hoses (Chapter 4E)

### Engine misfires throughout the driving speed range

- ☐ Fuel filter choked (Chapter 1A or 1B)
- ☐ Fuel pump faulty, or delivery pressure low – petrol models (Chapter 4A or 4B)
- ☐ Fuel tank vent blocked, or fuel pipes restricted (Chapter 4C)
- ☐ Vacuum leak at the throttle body, inlet manifold or associated hoses – petrol models (Chapter 4A or 4B)
- ☐ Worn, faulty or incorrectly-gapped spark plugs – petrol models (Chapter 1A)
- ☐ Faulty injector(s) – diesel models (Chapter 4)
- ☐ Faulty ignition module – petrol models (Chapter 5B)
- ☐ Uneven or low cylinder compression (Chapter 2)
- ☐ Blocked injector/fuel injection system fault (Chapter 4)
- ☐ Blocked catalytic converter (Chapter 4)
- ☐ Engine overheating (Chapter 3)

### Engine hesitates on acceleration

- ☐ Worn, faulty or incorrectly-gapped spark plugs – petrol models (Chapter 1A)
- ☐ Vacuum leak at the throttle body, inlet manifold or associated hoses – petrol models (Chapter 4A or 4B)
- ☐ Blocked injectors/fuel injection system fault (Chapter 4)
- ☐ Faulty injector(s) – diesel models (Chapter 4)

### Engine stalls

- ☐ Vacuum leak at the throttle body, inlet manifold or associated hoses – petrol models (Chapter 4A or 4B)
- ☐ Fuel filter choked (Chapter 1A or 1B)
- ☐ Fuel pump faulty, or delivery pressure low – petrol models (Chapter 4A or 4B)
- ☐ Fuel tank vent blocked, or fuel pipes restricted (Chapter 4)
- ☐ Blocked injectors/fuel injection system fault (Chapter 4)
- ☐ Faulty injector(s) – diesel models (Chapter 4)

### Engine lacks power

- ☐ Air filter element blocked (Chapter 1A or 1B)
- ☐ Fuel filter choked (Chapter 1A or 1B)
- ☐ Fuel pipes blocked or restricted (Chapter 4)
- ☐ Worn, faulty or incorrectly-gapped spark plugs – petrol models (Chapter 1A)
- ☐ Engine overheating (Chapter 3)
- ☐ Fuel tank level low – diesel models (Chapter 4)
- ☐ Accelerator pedal position sensor faulty (Chapter 4)
- ☐ Vacuum leak at the throttle body, inlet manifold or associated hoses – petrol models (Chapter 4A or 4B)
- ☐ Blocked injectors/fuel injection system fault (Chapter 4)
- ☐ Faulty injector(s) – diesel models (Chapter 4)
- ☐ Fuel pump faulty, or delivery pressure low – petrol models (Chapter 4A or 4B)
- ☐ Uneven or low cylinder compression (Chapter 2)
- ☐ Blocked catalytic converter (Chapter 4)
- ☐ Brakes binding (Chapter 1A, 1B or 9)
- ☐ Clutch slipping (Chapter 6)

### Engine backfires

- ☐ Vacuum leak at the throttle body, inlet manifold or associated hoses – petrol models (Chapter 4A or 4B)
- ☐ Blocked injectors/fuel injection system fault (Chapter 4)
- ☐ Blocked catalytic converter (Chapter 4)
- ☐ Faulty ignition module – petrol models (Chapter 5B)

### Oil pressure warning light illuminated with engine running

- ☐ Low oil level, or incorrect oil grade (see Weekly checks)
- ☐ Faulty oil pressure sensor, or wiring damaged (Chapter 2)
- ☐ Worn engine bearings and/or oil pump (Chapter 2)
- ☐ High engine operating temperature (Chapter 3)
- ☐ Oil pump pressure relief valve defective (Chapter 2)
- ☐ Oil pump pick-up strainer clogged (Chapter 2)

### Engine runs-on after switching off

- ☐ Excessive carbon build-up in engine (Chapter 2)
- ☐ High engine operating temperature (Chapter 3)
- ☐ Fuel injection/engine management system fault (Chapter 4)

### Engine noises

#### Pre-ignition (pinking) or knocking during acceleration or under load

- ☐ Ignition timing incorrect/ignition system fault – petrol models (Chapter 1A or 5B)
- ☐ Incorrect grade of spark plug – petrol models (Chapter 1A)
- ☐ Incorrect grade of fuel (Chapter 4)
- ☐ Knock sensor faulty – petrol models (Chapter 4A or 4B)
- ☐ Vacuum leak at the throttle body, inlet manifold or associated hoses – petrol models (Chapter 4A or 4B)
- ☐ Excessive carbon build-up in engine (Chapter 2)
- ☐ Fuel injection/engine management system fault (Chapter 4)
- ☐ Faulty injector(s) – diesel models (Chapter 4)

#### Whistling or wheezing noises

- ☐ Leaking inlet manifold or throttle body gasket – petrol models (Chapter 4A or 4B)
- ☐ Leaking exhaust manifold gasket or pipe-to-manifold joint (Chapter 4)
- ☐ Leaking vacuum hose (Chapter 4, 5 or 9)
- ☐ Blowing cylinder head gasket (Chapter 2)
- ☐ Partially blocked or leaking crankcase ventilation system (Chapter 4E)

#### Tapping or rattling noises

- ☐ Worn valve gear or camshaft (Chapter 2)
- ☐ Ancillary component fault (coolant pump, alternator, etc) (Chapter 3, 5A, etc)

#### Knocking or thumping noises

- ☐ Worn big-end bearings (regular heavy knocking, perhaps less under load) (Chapter 2E)
- ☐ Worn main bearings (rumbling and knocking, perhaps worsening under load) (Chapter 2E)
- ☐ Piston slap – most noticeable when cold, caused by piston/bore wear (Chapter 2E)
- ☐ Ancillary component fault (coolant pump, alternator, etc) (Chapter 3, 5A, etc)
- ☐ Engine mountings worn or defective (Chapter 2)
- ☐ Front suspension or steering components worn (Chapter 10)

# Cooling system

### Overheating

- [ ] Insufficient coolant in system (see *Weekly checks*)
- [ ] Thermostat faulty (Chapter 3)
- [ ] Radiator core blocked, or grille restricted (Chapter 3)
- [ ] Cooling fan faulty, or resistor pack fault on models with twin fans (Chapter 3)
- [ ] Inaccurate coolant temperature sensor (Chapter 3)
- [ ] Airlock in cooling system (Chapter 1A, 1B or 3)
- [ ] Expansion tank pressure cap faulty (Chapter 3)
- [ ] Engine management system fault (Chapter 4)

### Overcooling

- [ ] Thermostat faulty (Chapter 3)
- [ ] Inaccurate coolant temperature sensor (Chapter 3)
- [ ] Cooling fan faulty (Chapter 3)
- [ ] Engine management system fault (Chapter 4)

### External coolant leakage

- [ ] Deteriorated or damaged hoses or hose clips (Chapter 1A or 1B)
- [ ] Radiator core or heater matrix leaking (Chapter 3)
- [ ] Expansion tank pressure cap faulty (Chapter 1A or 1B)
- [ ] Coolant pump internal seal leaking (Chapter 3)
- [ ] Coolant pump gasket leaking (Chapter 3)
- [ ] Boiling due to overheating (Chapter 3)
- [ ] Cylinder block core plug leaking (Chapter 2E)

### Internal coolant leakage

- [ ] Leaking cylinder head gasket (Chapter 2)
- [ ] Cracked cylinder head or cylinder block (Chapter 2)

### Corrosion

- [ ] Infrequent draining and flushing (Chapter 1A or 1B)
- [ ] Incorrect coolant mixture or inappropriate coolant type (see *Weekly checks*)

# Fuel and exhaust systems

### Excessive fuel consumption

- [ ] Air filter element dirty or clogged (Chapter 1A or 1B)
- [ ] Fuel injection system fault (Chapter 4)
- [ ] Engine management system fault (Chapter 4)
- [ ] Crankcase ventilation system blocked (Chapter 4E)
- [ ] Tyres under-inflated (see *Weekly checks*)
- [ ] Brakes binding (Chapter 1A, 1B or 9)
- [ ] Fuel leak, causing apparent high consumption (Chapter 1 or 4)

### Fuel leakage and/or fuel odour

- [ ] Damaged or corroded fuel tank, pipes or connections (Chapter 4)
- [ ] Evaporative emissions system fault – petrol models (Chapter 4E)

### Excessive noise or fumes from exhaust system

- [ ] Leaking exhaust system or manifold joints (Chapter 1, or 4)
- [ ] Leaking, corroded or damaged silencers or pipe (Chapter 1 or 4)
- [ ] Broken mountings causing body or suspension contact (Chapter 1A or 1B)

# Clutch

**Note:** *Fault finding for the Easytronic semi-automatic clutch should be entrusted to a Vauxhall dealer.*

### Pedal travels to floor – no pressure or very little resistance

- [ ] Air in hydraulic system/faulty master or slave cylinder (Chapter 6)
- [ ] Faulty hydraulic release system (Chapter 6)
- [ ] Clutch pedal return spring detached or broken (Chapter 6)
- [ ] Broken clutch release bearing or fork (Chapter 6)
- [ ] Broken diaphragm spring in clutch pressure plate (Chapter 6)

### Clutch fails to disengage (unable to select gears)

- [ ] Air in hydraulic system/faulty master or slave cylinder (Chapter 6)
- [ ] Faulty hydraulic release system (Chapter 6)
- [ ] Clutch disc sticking on transmission input shaft splines (Chapter 6)
- [ ] Clutch disc sticking to flywheel or pressure plate (Chapter 6)
- [ ] Faulty pressure plate assembly (Chapter 6)
- [ ] Clutch release mechanism worn or incorrectly assembled (Chapter 6)

### Clutch slips (engine speed increases, with no increase in vehicle speed)

- [ ] Faulty hydraulic release system (Chapter 6)
- [ ] Clutch disc linings excessively worn (Chapter 6)
- [ ] Clutch disc linings contaminated with oil or grease (Chapter 6)
- [ ] Faulty pressure plate or weak diaphragm spring (Chapter 6)

### Judder as clutch is engaged

- [ ] Clutch disc linings contaminated with oil or grease (Chapter 6)
- [ ] Clutch disc linings excessively worn (Chapter 6)
- [ ] Faulty or distorted pressure plate or diaphragm spring (Chapter 6).
- [ ] Worn or loose engine or transmission mountings (Chapter 2)
- [ ] Clutch disc hub or transmission input shaft splines worn (Chapter 6)

### Noise when depressing or releasing clutch pedal

- [ ] Worn clutch release bearing (Chapter 6)
- [ ] Worn or dry clutch pedal bushes (Chapter 6)
- [ ] Worn or dry clutch master cylinder piston (Chapter 6)
- [ ] Faulty pressure plate assembly (Chapter 6)
- [ ] Pressure plate diaphragm spring broken (Chapter 6)
- [ ] Broken clutch disc cushioning springs (Chapter 6)

# Driveshafts

### Vibration when accelerating or decelerating

- [ ] Worn inner constant velocity joint (Chapter 8)
- [ ] Bent or distorted driveshaft (Chapter 8)
- [ ] Worn intermediate bearing (Chapter 8)

### Clicking or knocking noise on turns (at slow speed on full-lock)

- [ ] Worn outer constant velocity joint (Chapter 8)
- [ ] Lack of constant velocity joint lubricant, possibly due to damaged gaiter (Chapter 8)

# Manual transmission

**Note:** *Fault finding for the Easytronic transmission should be entrusted to a Vauxhall dealer.*

## Noisy in neutral with engine running

☐ Lack of oil (Chapter 7A or 7C)
☐ Input shaft bearings worn (noise apparent with clutch pedal released, but not when depressed) (Chapter 7A)*
☐ Clutch release bearing worn (noise apparent with clutch pedal depressed, possibly less when released) (Chapter 6)

## Noisy in one particular gear

☐ Worn, damaged or chipped gear teeth (Chapter 7A)*

## Difficulty engaging gears

☐ Clutch fault (Chapter 6)
☐ Worn, damaged, or poorly-adjusted gearchange (Chapter 7A)
☐ Lack of oil (Chapter 7A or 7C)
☐ Worn synchroniser units (Chapter 7A)*

## Jumps out of gear

☐ Worn, damaged, or poorly-adjusted gearchange (Chapter 7A)
☐ Worn synchroniser units (Chapter 7A)*
☐ Worn selector forks (Chapter 7A)*

## Vibration

☐ Lack of oil (Chapter 7A or 7C)
☐ Worn bearings (Chapter 7A)*

## Lubricant leaks

☐ Leaking driveshaft or selector shaft oil seal (Chapter 7A)
☐ Leaking housing joint (Chapter 7A)*
☐ Leaking input shaft oil seal (Chapter 7A)*

* *Although the corrective action necessary to remedy the symptoms described is beyond the scope of the home mechanic, the above information should be helpful in isolating the cause of the condition, so that the owner can communicate clearly with a professional mechanic.*

# Automatic transmission

**Note:** *Due to the complexity of the automatic transmission, it is difficult for the home mechanic to properly diagnose and service this unit. For problems other than the following, the vehicle should be taken to a dealer service department or automatic transmission specialist. Do not be too hasty in removing the transmission if a fault is suspected, as most of the testing is carried out with the unit still fitted. Remember that, besides the sensors specific to the transmission, many of the engine management system sensors described in Chapter 4 are essential to the correct operation of the transmission.*

## Fluid leakage

☐ Automatic transmission fluid is usually dark red in colour. Fluid leaks should not be confused with engine oil, which can easily be blown onto the transmission by airflow.
☐ To determine the source of a leak, first remove all built-up dirt and grime from the transmission housing and surrounding areas using a degreasing agent, or by steam-cleaning. Drive the vehicle at low speed, so airflow will not blow the leak far from its source. Raise and support the vehicle, and determine where the leak is coming from. The following are common areas of leakage:
a) *Fluid pan*
b) *Dipstick tube (Chapter 1A)*
c) *Transmission-to-fluid cooler unions (Chapter 7B)*

## Transmission fluid brown, or has burned smell

☐ Transmission fluid level low (Chapter 1A)

## General gear selection problems

☐ Chapter 7B deals with checking the selector cable on automatic transmissions. The following are common problems which may be caused by a faulty cable or sensor:

a) *Engine starting in gears other than Park or Neutral.*
b) *Indicator panel indicating a gear other than the one actually being used.*
c) *Vehicle moves when in Park or Neutral.*
d) *Poor gear shift quality or erratic gear changes.*

## Transmission will not downshift (kickdown) with accelerator pedal fully depressed

☐ Low transmission fluid level (Chapter 1A)
☐ Engine management system fault (Chapter 4A)
☐ Faulty transmission sensor or wiring (Chapter 7B)
☐ Incorrect selector cable adjustment (Chapter 7B)

## Engine will not start in any gear, or starts in gears other than Park or Neutral

☐ Faulty transmission sensor or wiring (Chapter 7B)
☐ Engine management system fault (Chapter 4)
☐ Incorrect selector cable adjustment (Chapter 7B)

## Transmission slips, shifts roughly, is noisy, or has no drive in forward or reverse gears

☐ Transmission fluid level low (Chapter 1A)
☐ Faulty transmission sensor or wiring (Chapter 7B)
☐ Engine management system fault (Chapter 4)

**Note:** *There are many probable causes for the above problems, but diagnosing and correcting them is considered beyond the scope of this manual. Having checked the fluid level and all the wiring as far as possible, a dealer or transmission specialist should be consulted if the problem persists.*

# Braking system

**Note:** *Before assuming that a brake problem exists, make sure that the tyres are in good condition and correctly inflated, that the front wheel alignment is correct, and that the vehicle is not loaded with weight in an unequal manner. Apart from checking the condition of all pipe and hose connections, any faults occurring on the anti-lock braking system should be referred to a Vauxhall dealer for diagnosis.*

## Vehicle pulls to one side under braking

☐ Worn, defective, damaged or contaminated brake pads/shoes on one side (Chapter 1A, 1B or 9)
☐ Seized or partially-seized brake caliper piston/wheel cylinder (Chapter 1A, 1B or 9)
☐ A mixture of brake pad/shoe lining materials fitted between sides (Chapter 1A, 1B or 9)

☐ Brake caliper/backplate mounting bolts loose (Chapter 9)
☐ Worn or damaged steering or suspension components (Chapter 1A, 1B or 10)

## Noise (grinding or high-pitched squeal) when brakes applied

☐ Brake pad/shoe friction lining material worn down to metal backing (Chapter 1A, 1B or 9)
☐ Excessive corrosion of brake disc/drum (may be apparent after the vehicle has been standing for some time (Chapter 1A, 1B or 9)
☐ Foreign object (stone chipping, etc) trapped between brake disc and shield (Chapter 1A, 1B or 9)

# Braking system (continued)

### Excessive brake pedal travel

☐ Faulty master cylinder (Chapter 9)
☐ Air in hydraulic system (Chapter 1A, 1B, 6 or 9)
☐ Faulty vacuum servo unit (Chapter 9)

### Brake pedal feels spongy when depressed

☐ Air in hydraulic system (Chapter 1A, 1B, 6 or 9)
☐ Deteriorated flexible rubber brake hoses (Chapter 1A, 1B or 9)
☐ Master cylinder mounting nuts loose (Chapter 9)
☐ Faulty master cylinder (Chapter 9)

### Excessive brake pedal effort required to stop vehicle

☐ Faulty vacuum servo unit (Chapter 9)
☐ Faulty vacuum pump – diesel models (Chapter 9)
☐ Disconnected, damaged or insecure brake servo vacuum hose (Chapter 9)
☐ Primary or secondary hydraulic circuit failure (Chapter 9)
☐ Seized brake caliper/wheel cylinder piston (Chapter 9)
☐ Brake pads/shoes incorrectly fitted (Chapter 9)
☐ Incorrect grade of brake pads/shoes fitted (Chapter 9)
☐ Brake pad/shoe linings contaminated (Chapter 1A, 1B or 9)

### Judder felt through brake pedal or steering wheel when braking

**Note:** *Under heavy braking on models equipped with ABS, vibration may be felt through the brake pedal. This is a normal feature of ABS operation, and does not constitute a fault*

☐ Excessive run-out or distortion of discs/drums (Chapter 1A, 1B or 9)
☐ Brake pad/shoe linings worn (Chapter 1A, 1B or 9)
☐ Brake caliper/backplate mounting bolts loose (Chapter 9)
☐ Wear in suspension or steering components or mountings (Chapter 1A, 1B or 10)
☐ Front wheels out of balance (see *Weekly checks*)

### Brakes binding

☐ Seized brake caliper/wheel cylinder piston (Chapter 9)
☐ Incorrectly-adjusted handbrake mechanism (Chapter 9)
☐ Faulty master cylinder (Chapter 9)

### Rear wheels locking under normal braking

☐ Rear brake pad/shoe linings contaminated or damaged (Chapter 1 or 9)
☐ Rear brake discs/drums warped (Chapter 1 or 9)
☐ Rear brake pressure regulating valve faulty – where fitted (Chapter 9)

# Suspension and steering

**Note:** *Before diagnosing suspension or steering faults, be sure that the trouble is not due to incorrect tyre pressures, mixtures of tyre types, or binding brakes.*

### Vehicle pulls to one side

☐ Defective tyre (see *Weekly checks*)
☐ Excessive wear in suspension or steering components (Chapter 1A, 1B or 10)
☐ Incorrect front wheel alignment (Chapter 10)
☐ Accident damage to steering or suspension components (Chapter 1A or 1B)

### Wheel wobble and vibration

☐ Front wheels out of balance (vibration felt mainly through the steering wheel) (see *Weekly checks*)
☐ Rear wheels out of balance (vibration felt throughout the vehicle) (see *Weekly checks*)
☐ Roadwheels damaged or distorted (see *Weekly checks*)
☐ Faulty or damaged tyre (see *Weekly checks*)
☐ Worn steering or suspension joints, bushes or components (Chapter 1A, 1B or 10)
☐ Wheel bolts loose (Chapter 1A or 1B)

### Excessive pitching and/or rolling around corners, or during braking

☐ Defective shock absorbers (Chapter 1A, 1B or 10)
☐ Broken or weak spring and/or suspension component (Chapter 1A, 1B or 10)
☐ Worn or damaged anti-roll bar or mountings (Chapter 1A, 1B or 10)

### Wandering or general instability

☐ Incorrect front wheel alignment (Chapter 10)
☐ Worn steering or suspension joints, bushes or components (Chapter 1A, 1B or 10)
☐ Roadwheels out of balance (see *Weekly checks*)
☐ Faulty or damaged tyre (see *Weekly checks*)
☐ Wheel bolts loose (Chapter 1A or 1B)
☐ Defective shock absorbers (Chapter 1A, 1B or 10)
☐ Electric power steering system fault (Chapter 10)

### Excessively-stiff steering

☐ Seized steering linkage balljoint or suspension balljoint (Chapter 1A, 1B or 10)
☐ Incorrect front wheel alignment (Chapter 10)
☐ Steering rack damaged (Chapter 10)
☐ Electric power steering system fault (Chapter 10)

### Excessive play in steering

☐ Worn steering column/intermediate shaft joints (Chapter 10)
☐ Worn track rod balljoints (Chapter 1A, 1B or 10)
☐ Worn steering rack (Chapter 10)
☐ Worn steering or suspension joints, bushes or components (Chapter 1A, 1B or 10)

### Lack of power assistance

☐ Electric power steering system fault (Chapter 10)
☐ Faulty steering rack (Chapter 10)

### Tyre wear excessive

#### Tyres worn on inside or outside edges

☐ Tyres under-inflated (wear on both edges) (see *Weekly checks*)
☐ Incorrect camber or castor angles (wear on one edge only) (Chapter 10)
☐ Worn steering or suspension joints, bushes or components (Chapter 1A, 1B or 10)
☐ Excessively-hard cornering or braking
☐ Accident damage

#### Tyre treads exhibit feathered edges

☐ Incorrect toe-setting (Chapter 10)

#### Tyres worn in centre of tread

☐ Tyres over-inflated (see *Weekly checks*)

#### Tyres worn on inside and outside edges

☐ Tyres under-inflated (see *Weekly checks*)

#### Tyres worn unevenly

☐ Tyres/wheels out of balance (see *Weekly checks*)
☐ Excessive wheel or tyre run-out
☐ Worn shock absorbers (Chapter 1A, 1B or 10)
☐ Faulty tyre (see *Weekly checks*)

# Electrical system

**Note:** *For problems associated with the starting system, refer to the faults listed under 'Engine' earlier in this Section.*

## Battery will not hold a charge for more than a few days

- ☐ Battery defective internally (Chapter 5A)
- ☐ Battery terminal connections loose or corroded (see *Weekly checks*)
- ☐ Auxiliary drivebelt worn or incorrectly adjusted (Chapter 1A or 1B)
- ☐ Alternator not charging at correct output (Chapter 5A)
- ☐ Alternator or voltage regulator faulty (Chapter 5A)
- ☐ Short-circuit causing continual battery drain (Chapter 5A or 12)

## Ignition/no-charge warning light remains illuminated with engine running

- ☐ Auxiliary drivebelt broken, worn, or incorrectly adjusted (Chapter 1A or 1B)
- ☐ Internal fault in alternator or voltage regulator (Chapter 5A)
- ☐ Broken, disconnected, or loose wiring in charging circuit (Chapter 5A or 12)

## Ignition/no-charge warning light fails to come on

- ☐ Warning light bulb blown (Chapter 12)
- ☐ Broken, disconnected, or loose wiring in warning light circuit (Chapter 5A or 12)
- ☐ Alternator faulty (Chapter 5A)

## Lights inoperative

- ☐ Bulb blown (Chapter 12)
- ☐ Corrosion of bulb or bulbholder contacts (Chapter 12)
- ☐ Blown fuse (Chapter 12)
- ☐ Faulty relay (Chapter 12)
- ☐ Broken, loose, or disconnected wiring (Chapter 12)
- ☐ Faulty switch (Chapter 12)

## Instrument readings inaccurate or erratic

### Fuel or temperature gauges give no reading

- ☐ Faulty gauge sender unit (Chapter 3 or 4)
- ☐ Wiring open-circuit (Chapter 12)
- ☐ Faulty gauge (Chapter 12)

## Fuel or temperature gauges give continuous maximum reading

- ☐ Faulty gauge sender unit (Chapter 3 or 4)
- ☐ Wiring short-circuit (Chapter 12)
- ☐ Faulty gauge (Chapter 12)

## Horn inoperative, or unsatisfactory in operation

### Horn operates all the time

- ☐ Horn push either earthed or stuck down (Chapter 12)
- ☐ Horn cable-to-horn push earthed (Chapter 12)

### Horn fails to operate

- ☐ Blown fuse (Chapter 12)
- ☐ Cable or connections loose, broken or disconnected (Chapter 12)
- ☐ Faulty horn (Chapter 12)

### Horn emits intermittent or unsatisfactory sound

- ☐ Cable connections loose (Chapter 12)
- ☐ Horn mountings loose (Chapter 12)
- ☐ Faulty horn (Chapter 12)

## Windscreen wipers inoperative, or unsatisfactory in operation

### Wipers fail to operate, or operate very slowly

- ☐ Wiper blades stuck to screen, or linkage seized or binding (Chapter 12)
- ☐ Blown fuse (Chapter 12)
- ☐ Battery discharged (Chapter 5A)
- ☐ Cable or connections loose, broken or disconnected (Chapter 12)
- ☐ Faulty relay (Chapter 12)
- ☐ Faulty wiper motor (Chapter 12)

## Wiper blades sweep over too large or too small an area

- ☐ Wiper blades incorrectly fitted, or wrong size used (see *Weekly checks*)
- ☐ Wiper arms incorrectly positioned on spindles (Chapter 12)
- ☐ Excessive wear of wiper linkage (Chapter 12)
- ☐ Wiper motor or linkage mountings loose or insecure (Chapter 12)

## Wiper blades fail to clean the glass effectively

- ☐ Wiper blade rubbers dirty, worn or perished (see *Weekly checks*)
- ☐ Wiper blades incorrectly fitted, or wrong size used (see *Weekly checks*)
- ☐ Wiper arm tension springs broken, or arm pivots seized (Chapter 12)
- ☐ Insufficient windscreen washer additive to adequately remove road film (see *Weekly checks*)

## Windscreen washers inoperative, or unsatisfactory in operation

### One or more washer jets inoperative

- ☐ Blocked washer jet
- ☐ Disconnected, kinked or restricted fluid hose (Chapter 12)
- ☐ Insufficient fluid in washer reservoir (see *Weekly checks*)

### Washer pump fails to operate

- ☐ Broken or disconnected wiring or connections (Chapter 12)
- ☐ Blown fuse (Chapter 12)
- ☐ Faulty washer switch (Chapter 12)
- ☐ Faulty washer pump (Chapter 12)

### Washer pump runs for some time before fluid is emitted

- ☐ Faulty one-way valve in fluid supply hose (Chapter 12)

## Electric windows inoperative, or unsatisfactory in operation

### Window glass will only move in one direction

- ☐ Faulty switch (Chapter 12)

### Window glass slow to move

- ☐ Battery discharged (Chapter 5A)
- ☐ Regulator seized or damaged, or in need of lubrication (Chapter 11)
- ☐ Door internal components or trim fouling regulator (Chapter 11)
- ☐ Faulty motor (Chapter 11)

### Window glass fails to move

- ☐ Blown fuse (Chapter 12)
- ☐ Faulty relay (Chapter 12)
- ☐ Broken or disconnected wiring or connections (Chapter 12)
- ☐ Faulty motor (Chapter 11)

## Central locking system inoperative, or unsatisfactory in operation

### Complete system failure

- ☐ Remote handset battery discharged, if applicable (Chapter 1A or 1B)
- ☐ Blown fuse (Chapter 12)
- ☐ Faulty relay (Chapter 12)
- ☐ Broken or disconnected wiring or connections (Chapter 12)
- ☐ Faulty motor (Chapter 11)

### Latch locks but will not unlock, or unlocks but will not lock

- ☐ Remote handset battery discharged, if applicable (Chapter 1A or 1B)
- ☐ Faulty master switch (Chapter 12)
- ☐ Broken or disconnected latch operating rods or levers (Chapter 11)
- ☐ Faulty relay (Chapter 12)
- ☐ Faulty motor (Chapter 11)

### One solenoid/motor fails to operate

- ☐ Broken or disconnected wiring or connections (Chapter 12)
- ☐ Faulty operating assembly (Chapter 11)
- ☐ Broken, binding or disconnected latch operating rods or levers (Chapter 11)
- ☐ Fault in door latch (Chapter 11)

**Note:** *References throughout this index are in the form* "**Chapter number**" • "**Page number**". *So, for example, 2C•15 refers to page 15 of Chapter 2C.*

*Note: References throughout this index are in the form "**Chapter number**" • "**Page number**". So, for example, 2C•15 refers to page 15 of Chapter 2C.*

**Note:** *References throughout this index are in the form* "**Chapter number**" • "**Page number**". *So, for example, 2C•15 refers to page 15 of Chapter 2C.*

# Haynes Manuals – The Complete UK Car List

| Title | Book No. |
|---|---|
| **ALFA ROMEO** Alfasud/Sprint (74 - 88) up to F * | 0292 |
| Alfa Romeo Alfetta (73 - 87) up to E * | 0531 |
| **AUDI** 80, 90 & Coupe Petrol (79 - Nov 88) up to F | 0605 |
| Audi 80, 90 & Coupe Petrol (Oct 86 - 90) D to H | 1491 |
| Audi 100 & 200 Petrol (Oct 82 - 90) up to H | 0907 |
| Audi 100 & A6 Petrol & Diesel (May 91 - May 97) H to P | 3504 |
| Audi A3 Petrol & Diesel (96 - May 03) P to 03 | 4253 |
| Audi A4 Petrol & Diesel (95 - 00) M to X | 3575 |
| Audi A4 Petrol & Diesel (01 - 04) X to 54 | 4609 |
| **AUSTIN** A35 & A40 (56 - 67) up to F * | 0118 |
| Austin/MG/Rover Maestro 1.3 & 1.6 Petrol (83 - 95) up to M | 0922 |
| Austin/MG Metro (80 - May 90) up to G | 0718 |
| Austin/Rover Montego 1.3 & 1.6 Petrol (84 - 94) A to L | 1066 |
| Austin/MG/Rover Montego 2.0 Petrol (84 - 95) A to M | 1067 |
| Mini (59 - 69) up to H * | 0527 |
| Mini (69 - 01) up to X | 0646 |
| Austin/Rover 2.0 litre Diesel Engine (86 - 93) C to L | 1857 |
| Austin Healey 100/6 & 3000 (56 - 68) up to G * | 0049 |
| **BEDFORD** CF Petrol (69 - 87) up to E | 0163 |
| Bedford/Vauxhall Rascal & Suzuki Supercarry (86 - Oct 94) C to M | 3015 |
| **BMW** 316, 320 & 320i (4-cyl) (75 - Feb 83) up to Y * | 0276 |
| BMW 320, 320i, 323i & 325i (6-cyl) (Oct 77 - Sept 87) up to E | 0815 |
| BMW 3- & 5-Series Petrol (81 - 91) up to J | 1948 |
| BMW 3-Series Petrol (Apr 91 - 99) H to V | 3210 |
| BMW 3-Series Petrol (Sept 98 - 03) S to 53 | 4067 |
| BMW 520i & 525e (Oct 81 - June 88) up to E | 1560 |
| BMW 525, 528 & 528i (73 - Sept 81) up to X * | 0632 |
| BMW 5-Series 6-cyl Petrol (April 96 - Aug 03) N to 03 | 4151 |
| BMW 1500, 1502, 1600, 1602, 2000 & 2002 (59 - 77) up to S * | 0240 |
| **CHRYSLER** PT Cruiser Petrol (00 - 03) W to 53 | 4058 |
| **CITROËN** 2CV, Ami & Dyane (67 - 90) up to H | 0196 |
| Citroën AX Petrol & Diesel (87 - 97) D to P | 3014 |
| Citroën Berlingo & Peugeot Partner Petrol & Diesel (96 - 05) P to 55 | 4281 |
| Citroën BX Petrol (83 - 94) A to L | 0908 |
| Citroën C15 Van Petrol & Diesel (89 - Oct 98) F to S | 3509 |
| Citroën C3 Petrol & Diesel (02 - 05) 51 to 05 | 4197 |
| Citroen C5 Petrol & Diesel (01-08) Y to 08 | 4745 |
| Citroën CX Petrol (75 - 88) up to F | 0528 |
| Citroën Saxo Petrol & Diesel (96 - 04) N to 54 | 3506 |
| Citroën Visa Petrol (79 - 88) up to F | 0620 |
| Citroën Xantia Petrol & Diesel (93 - 01) K to Y | 3082 |
| Citroën XM Petrol & Diesel (89 - 00) G to X | 3451 |
| Citroën Xsara Petrol & Diesel (97 - Sept 00) R to W | 3751 |
| Citroen Xsara Picasso (03-08) | 4784 |
| Citroën Xsara Picasso Petrol & Diesel (00 - 02) W to 52 | 3944 |
| Citroën ZX Diesel (91 - 98) J to S | 1922 |
| Citroën ZX Petrol (91 - 98) H to S | 1881 |
| Citroën 1.7 & 1.9 litre Diesel Engine (84 - 96) A to N | 1379 |
| **FIAT** 126 (73 - 87) up to E * | 0305 |
| Fiat 500 (57 - 73) up to M * | 0090 |
| Fiat Bravo & Brava Petrol (95 - 00) N to W | 3572 |
| Fiat Cinquecento (93 - 98) K to R | 3501 |
| Fiat Panda (81 - 95) up to M | 0793 |
| Fiat Punto Petrol & Diesel (94 - Oct 99) L to V | 3251 |
| Fiat Punto Petrol (Oct 99 - July 03) V to 03 | 4066 |
| Fiat Punto Petrol (03-07) 03 to 07 | 4746 |
| Fiat Regata Petrol (84 - 88) A to F | 1167 |
| Fiat Tipo Petrol (88 - 91) E to J | 1625 |
| Fiat Uno Petrol (83 - 95) up to M | 0923 |
| Fiat X1/9 (74 - 89) up to G * | 0273 |
| **FORD** Anglia (59 - 68) up to G * | 0001 |

| Title | Book No. |
|---|---|
| Ford Capri II (& III) 1.6 & 2.0 (74 - 87) up to E * | 0283 |
| Ford Capri II (& III) 2.8 & 3.0 V6 (74 - 87) up to E | 1309 |
| Ford Cortina Mk I & Corsair 1500 ('62 - '66) up to D* | 0214 |
| Ford Cortina Mk III 1300 & 1600 (70 - 76) up to P * | 0070 |
| Ford Escort Mk I 1100 & 1300 (68 - 74) up to N * | 0171 |
| Ford Escort Mk I Mexico, RS 1600 & RS 2000 (70 - 74) up to N * | 0139 |
| Ford Escort Mk II Mexico, RS 1800 & RS 2000 (75 - 80) up to W * | 0735 |
| Ford Escort (75 - Aug 80) up to V * | 0280 |
| Ford Escort Petrol (Sept 80 - Sept 90) up to H | 0686 |
| Ford Escort & Orion Petrol (Sept 90 - 00) H to X | 1737 |
| Ford Escort & Orion Diesel (Sept 90 - 00) H to X | 4081 |
| Ford Fiesta (76 - Aug 83) up to Y | 0334 |
| Ford Fiesta Petrol (Aug 83 - Feb 89) A to F | 1030 |
| Ford Fiesta Petrol (Feb 89 - Oct 95) F to N | 1595 |
| Ford Fiesta Petrol & Diesel (Oct 95 - Mar 02) N to 02 | 3397 |
| Ford Fiesta Petrol & Diesel (Apr 02 - 07) 02 to 57 | 4170 |
| Ford Focus Petrol & Diesel (98 - 01) S to Y | 3759 |
| Ford Focus Petrol & Diesel (Oct 01 - 05) 51 to 05 | 4167 |
| Ford Galaxy Petrol & Diesel (95 - Aug 00) M to W | 3984 |
| Ford Granada Petrol (Sept 77 - Feb 85) up to B * | 0481 |
| Ford Granada & Scorpio Petrol (Mar 85 - 94) B to M | 1245 |
| Ford Ka (96 - 02) P to 52 | 3570 |
| Ford Mondeo Petrol (93 - Sept 00) K to X | 1923 |
| Ford Mondeo Petrol & Diesel (Oct 00 - Jul 03) X to 03 | 3990 |
| Ford Mondeo Petrol & Diesel (July 03 - 07) 03 to 56 | 4619 |
| Ford Mondeo Diesel (93 - 96) L to N | 3465 |
| Ford Orion Petrol (83 - Sept 90) up to H | 1009 |
| Ford Sierra 4-cyl Petrol (82 - 93) up to K | 0903 |
| Ford Sierra V6 Petrol (82 - 91) up to J | 0904 |
| Ford Transit Petrol (Mk 2) (78 - Jan 86) up to C | 0719 |
| Ford Transit Petrol (Mk 3) (Feb 86 - 89) C to G | 1468 |
| Ford Transit Diesel (Feb 86 - 99) C to T | 3019 |
| Ford Transit Diesel (00-06) | 4775 |
| Ford 1.6 & 1.8 litre Diesel Engine (84 - 96) A to N | 1172 |
| Ford 2.1, 2.3 & 2.5 litre Diesel Engine (77 - 90) up to H | 1606 |
| **FREIGHT ROVER** Sherpa Petrol (74 - 87) up to E | 0463 |
| **HILLMAN** Avenger (70 - 82) up to Y | 0037 |
| Hillman Imp (63 - 76) up to R * | 0022 |
| **HONDA** Civic (Feb 84 - Oct 87) A to E | 1226 |
| Honda Civic (Nov 91 - 96) J to N | 3199 |
| Honda Civic Petrol (Mar 95 - 00) M to X | 4050 |
| Honda Civic Petrol & Diesel (01 - 05) X to 55 | 4611 |
| Honda CR-V Petrol & Diesel (01-06) | 4747 |
| Honda Jazz (01 - Feb 08) 51 - 57 | 4735 |
| **HYUNDAI** Pony (85 - 94) C to M | 3398 |
| **JAGUAR** E Type (61 - 72) up to L * | 0140 |
| Jaguar MkI & II, 240 & 340 (55 - 69) up to H * | 0098 |
| Jaguar XJ6, XJ & Sovereign; Daimler Sovereign (68 - Oct 86) up to D | 0242 |
| Jaguar XJ6 & Sovereign (Oct 86 - Sept 94) D to M | 3261 |
| Jaguar XJ12, XJS & Sovereign; Daimler Double Six (72 - 88) up to F | 0478 |
| **JEEP** Cherokee Petrol (93 - 96) K to N | 1943 |
| **LADA** 1200, 1300, 1500 & 1600 (74 - 91) up to J | 0413 |
| Lada Samara (87 - 91) D to J | 1610 |
| **LAND ROVER** 90, 110 & Defender Diesel (83 - 07) up to 56 | 3017 |
| Land Rover Discovery Petrol & Diesel (89 - 98) G to S | 3016 |
| Land Rover Discovery Diesel (Nov 98 - Jul 04) S to 04 | 4606 |
| Land Rover Freelander Petrol & Diesel (97 - Sept 03) R to 53 | 3929 |
| Land Rover Freelander Petrol & Diesel (Oct 03 - Oct 06) 53 to 56 | 4623 |

| Title | Book No. |
|---|---|
| Land Rover Series IIA & III Diesel (58 - 85) up to C | 0529 |
| Land Rover Series II, IIA & III 4-cyl Petrol (58 - 85) up to C | 0314 |
| **MAZDA** 323 (Mar 81 - Oct 89) up to G | 1608 |
| Mazda 323 (Oct 89 - 98) G to R | 3455 |
| Mazda 626 (May 83 - Sept 87) up to E | 0929 |
| Mazda B1600, B1800 & B2000 Pick-up Petrol (72 - 88) up to F | 0267 |
| Mazda RX-7 (79 - 85) up to C * | 0460 |
| **MERCEDES-BENZ** 190, 190E & 190D Petrol & Diesel (83 - 93) A to L | 3450 |
| Mercedes-Benz 200D, 240D, 240TD, 300D & 300TD 123 Series Diesel (Oct 76 - 85) | 1114 |
| Mercedes-Benz 250 & 280 (68 - 72) up to L * | 0346 |
| Mercedes-Benz 250 & 280 123 Series Petrol (Oct 76 - 84) up to B * | 0677 |
| Mercedes-Benz 124 Series Petrol & Diesel (85 - Aug 93) C to K | 3253 |
| Mercedes-Benz A-Class Petrol & Diesel (98-04) S to 54) | 4748 |
| Mercedes-Benz C-Class Petrol & Diesel (93 - Aug 00) L to W | 3511 |
| Mercedes-Benz C-Class (00-06) | 4780 |
| **MGA** (55 - 62) * | 0475 |
| MGB (62 - 80) up to W | 0111 |
| MG Midget & Austin-Healey Sprite (58 - 80) up to W * | 0265 |
| **MINI** Petrol (July 01 - 05) Y to 05 | 4273 |
| **MITSUBISHI** Shogun & L200 Pick-Ups Petrol (83 - 94) up to M | 1944 |
| **MORRIS** Ital 1.3 (80 - 84) up to B | 0705 |
| Morris Minor 1000 (56 - 71) up to K | 0024 |
| **NISSAN** Almera Petrol (95 - Feb 00) N to V | 4053 |
| Nissan Almera & Tino Petrol (Feb 00 - 07) V to 56 | 4612 |
| Nissan Bluebird (May 84 - Mar 86) A to C | 1223 |
| Nissan Bluebird Petrol (Mar 86 - 90) C to H | 1473 |
| Nissan Cherry (Sept 82 - 86) up to D | 1031 |
| Nissan Micra (83 - Jan 93) up to K | 0931 |
| Nissan Micra (93 - 02) K to 52 | 3254 |
| Nissan Micra Petrol (03-07) 52 to 57 | 4734 |
| Nissan Primera Petrol (90 - Aug 99) H to T | 1851 |
| Nissan Stanza (82 - 86) up to D | 0824 |
| Nissan Sunny Petrol (May 82 - Oct 86) up to D | 0895 |
| Nissan Sunny Petrol (Oct 86 - Mar 91) D to H | 1378 |
| Nissan Sunny Petrol (Apr 91 - 95) H to N | 3219 |
| **OPEL** Ascona & Manta (B Series) (Sept 75 - 88) up to F * | 0316 |
| Opel Ascona Petrol (81 - 88) | 3215 |
| Opel Astra Petrol (Oct 91 - Feb 98) | 3156 |
| Opel Corsa Petrol (83 - Mar 93) | 3160 |
| Opel Corsa Petrol (Mar 93 - 97) | 3159 |
| Opel Kadett Petrol (Nov 79 - Oct 84) up to B | 0634 |
| Opel Kadett Petrol (Oct 84 - Oct 91) | 3196 |
| Opel Omega & Senator Petrol (Nov 86 - 94) | 3157 |
| Opel Rekord Petrol (Feb 78 - Oct 86) up to D | 0543 |
| Opel Vectra Petrol (Oct 88 - Oct 95) | 3158 |
| **PEUGEOT** 106 Petrol & Diesel (91 - 04) J to 53 | 1882 |
| Peugeot 205 Petrol (83 - 97) A to P | 0932 |
| Peugeot 206 Petrol & Diesel (98 - 01) S to X | 3757 |
| Peugeot 206 Petrol & Diesel (02 - 06) 51 to 06 | 4613 |
| Peugeot 306 Petrol & Diesel (93 - 02) K to 02 | 3073 |
| Peugeot 307 Petrol & Diesel (01 - 04) Y to 54 | 4147 |
| Peugeot 309 Petrol (86 - 93) C to K | 1266 |
| Peugeot 405 Petrol (88 - 97) E to P | 1559 |
| Peugeot 405 Diesel (88 - 97) E to P | 3198 |
| Peugeot 406 Petrol & Diesel (96 - Mar 99) N to T | 3394 |
| Peugeot 406 Petrol & Diesel (Mar 99 - 02) T to 52 | 3982 |

* Classic reprint

| Title | Book No. | Title | Book No. | Title | Book No. |
|---|---|---|---|---|---|
| Peugeot 505 Petrol (79 - 89) up to G | 0762 | SUNBEAM Alpine, Rapier & H120 (67 - 74) up to N * | 0051 | VW 1302 & 1302S (70 - 72) up to L * | 0110 |
| Peugeot 1.7/1.8 & 1.9 litre Diesel Engine (82 - 96) up to N | 0950 | SUZUKI SJ Series, Samurai & Vitara (4-cyl) Petrol (82 - 97) up to P | 1942 | VW Beetle 1303, 1303S & GT (72 - 75) up to P | 0159 |
| Peugeot 2.0, 2.1, 2.3 & 2.5 litre Diesel Engines (74 - 90) up to H | 1607 | Suzuki Supercarry & Bedford/Vauxhall Rascal (86 - Oct 94) C to M | 3015 | VW Beetle Petrol & Diesel (Apr 99 - 07) T to 57 | 3798 |
| PORSCHE 911 (65 - 85) up to C | 0264 | TALBOT Alpine, Solara, Minx & Rapier (75 - 86) up to D | 0337 | VW Golf & Jetta Mk 1 Petrol 1.1 & 1.3 (74 - 84) up to A | 0716 |
| Porsche 924 & 924 Turbo (76 - 85) up to C | 0397 | Talbot Horizon Petrol (78 - 86) up to D | 0473 | VW Golf, Jetta & Scirocco Mk 1 Petrol 1.5, 1.6 & 1.8 (74 - 84) up to A | 0726 |
| PROTON (89 - 97) F to P | 3255 | Talbot Samba (82 - 86) up to D | 0823 | VW Golf & Jetta Mk 1 Diesel (78 - 84) up to A | 0451 |
| RANGE ROVER V8 Petrol (70 - Oct 92) up to K | 0606 | TOYOTA Avensis Petrol (98 - Jan 03) R to 52 | 4264 | VW Golf & Jetta Mk 2 Petrol (Mar 84 - Feb 92) A to J | 1081 |
| RELIANT Robin & Kitten (73 - 83) up to A * | 0436 | Toyota Carina E Petrol (May 92 - 97) J to P | 3256 | VW Golf & Vento Petrol & Diesel (Feb 92 - Mar 98) J to R | 3097 |
| RENAULT 4 (61 - 86) up to D * | 0072 | Toyota Corolla (80 - 85) up to C | 0683 | VW Golf & Bora Petrol & Diesel (April 98 - 00) R to X | 3727 |
| Renault 5 Petrol (Feb 85 - 96) B to N | 1219 | Toyota Corolla (Sept 83 - Sept 87) A to E | 1024 | VW Golf & Bora 4-cyl Petrol & Diesel (01 - 03) X to 53 | 4169 |
| Renault 9 & 11 Petrol (82 - 89) up to F | 0822 | Toyota Corolla (Sept 87 - Aug 92) E to K | 1683 | VW Golf & Jetta Petrol & Diesel (04 - 07) 53 to 07 | 4610 |
| Renault 18 Petrol (79 - 86) up to D | 0598 | Toyota Corolla Petrol (Aug 92 - 97) K to P | 3259 | VW LT Petrol Vans & Light Trucks (76 - 87) up to E | 0637 |
| Renault 19 Petrol (89 - 96) F to N | 1646 | Toyota Corolla Petrol (July 97 - Feb 02) P to 51 | 4286 | VW Passat & Santana Petrol (Sept 81 - May 88) up to E | 0814 |
| Renault 19 Diesel (89 - 96) F to N | 1946 | Toyota Hi-Ace & Hi-Lux Petrol (69 - Oct 83) up to A | 0304 | VW Passat 4-cyl Petrol & Diesel (May 88 - 96) E to P | 3498 |
| Renault 21 Petrol (86 - 94) C to M | 1397 | Toyota RAV4 Petrol & Diesel (94-06) L to 55 | 4750 | VW Passat 4-cyl Petrol & Diesel (Dec 96 - Nov 00) P to X | 3917 |
| Renault 25 Petrol & Diesel (84 - 92) B to K | 1228 | Toyota Yaris Petrol (99 - 05) T to 05 | 4265 | VW Passat Petrol & Diesel (Dec 00 - May 05) X to 05 | 4279 |
| Renault Clio Petrol (91 - May 98) H to R | 1853 | TRIUMPH GT6 & Vitesse (62 - 74 ) up to N * | 0112 | VW Polo & Derby (76 - Jan 82) up to X | 0335 |
| Renault Clio Diesel (91 - June 96) H to N | 3031 | Triumph Herald (59 - 71) up to K * | 0010 | VW Polo (82 - Oct 90) up to H | 0813 |
| Renault Clio Petrol & Diesel (May 98 - May 01) R to Y | 3906 | Triumph Spitfire (62 - 81) up to X | 0113 | VW Polo Petrol (Nov 90 - Aug 94) H to L | 3245 |
| Renault Clio Petrol & Diesel (June '01 - '05) Y to 55 | 4168 | Triumph Stag (70 - 78) up to T * | 0441 | VW Polo Hatchback Petrol & Diesel (94 - 99) M to S | 3500 |
| Renault Espace Petrol & Diesel (85 - 96) C to N | 3197 | Triumph TR2, TR3, TR3A, TR4 & TR4A (52 - 67) up to F * | 0028 | VW Polo Hatchback Petrol (00 - Jan 02) V to 51 | 4150 |
| Renault Laguna Petrol & Diesel (94 - 00) L to W | 3252 | Triumph TR5 & 6 (67 - 75) up to P * | 0031 | VW Polo Petrol & Diesel (02 - May 05) 51 to 05 | 4608 |
| Renault Laguna Petrol & Diesel (Feb 01 - Feb 05) X to 54 | 4283 | Triumph TR7 (75 - 82) up to Y * | 0322 | VW Scirocco (82 - 90) up to H * | 1224 |
| Renault Mégane & Scénic Petrol & Diesel (96 - 99) N to T | 3395 | VAUXHALL Astra Petrol (80 - Oct 84) up to B | 0635 | VW Transporter 1600 (68 - 79) up to V | 0082 |
| Renault Mégane & Scénic Petrol & Diesel (Apr 99 - 02) T to 52 | 3916 | Vauxhall Astra & Belmont Petrol (Oct 84 - Oct 91) B to J | 1136 | VW Transporter 1700, 1800 & 2000 (72 - 79) up to V * | 0226 |
| Renault Megane Petrol & Diesel (Oct 02 - 05) 52 to 55 | 4284 | Vauxhall Astra Petrol (Oct 91 - Feb 98) J to R | 1832 | VW Transporter (air-cooled) Petrol (79 - 82) up to Y * | 0638 |
| Renault Scenic Petrol & Diesel (Sept 03 - 06) 53 to 06 | 4297 | Vauxhall/Opel Astra & Zafira Petrol (Feb 98 - Apr 04) R to 04 | 3758 | VW Transporter (water-cooled) Petrol (82 - 90) up to H | 3452 |
| ROVER 213 & 216 (84 - 89) A to G | 1116 | Vauxhall/Opel Astra & Zafira Diesel (Feb 98 - Apr 04) R to 04 | 3797 | VW Type 3 (63 - 73) up to M * | 0084 |
| Rover 214 & 414 Petrol (89 - 96) G to N | 1689 | Vauxhall/Opel Astra Petrol (04 - 08) | 4732 | VOLVO 120 & 130 Series (& P1800) (61 - 73) up to M * | 0203 |
| Rover 216 & 416 Petrol (89 - 96) G to N | 1830 | Vauxhall/Opel Astra Diesel (04 - 08) | 4733 | Volvo 142, 144 & 145 (66 - 74) up to N * | 0129 |
| Rover 211, 214, 216, 218 & 220 Petrol & Diesel (Dec 95 - 99) N to V | 3399 | Vauxhall/Opel Calibra (90 - 98) G to S | 3502 | Volvo 240 Series Petrol (74 - 93) up to K | 0270 |
| Rover 25 & MG ZR Petrol & Diesel (Oct 99 - 04) V to 54 | 4145 | Vauxhall Carlton Petrol (Oct 78 - Oct 86) up to D | 0480 | Volvo 262, 264 & 260/265 (75 - 85) up to C * | 0400 |
| Rover 414, 416 & 420 Petrol & Diesel (May 95 - 98) M to R | 3453 | Vauxhall Carlton & Senator Petrol (Nov 86 - 94) D to L | 1469 | Volvo 340, 343, 345 & 360 (76 - 91) up to J | 0715 |
| Rover 45 / MG ZS Petrol & Diesel (99 - 05) V to 55 | 4384 | Vauxhall Cavalier Petrol (81 - Oct 88) up to F | 0812 | Volvo 440, 460 & 480 Petrol (87 - 97) D to P | 1691 |
| Rover 618, 620 & 623 Petrol (93 - 97) K to P | 3257 | Vauxhall Cavalier Petrol (Oct 88 - 95) F to N | 1570 | Volvo 740 & 760 Petrol (82 - 91) up to J | 1258 |
| Rover 75 / MG ZT Petrol & Diesel (99 - 06) S to 06 | 4292 | Vauxhall Chevette (75 - 84) up to B | 0285 | Volvo 850 Petrol (92 - 96) J to P | 3260 |
| Rover 820, 825 & 827 Petrol (86 - 95) D to N | 1380 | Vauxhall/Opel Corsa Diesel (Mar 93 - Oct 00) K to X | 4087 | Volvo 940 petrol (90 - 98) H to R | 3249 |
| Rover 3500 (76 - 87) up to E * | 0365 | Vauxhall Corsa Petrol (Mar 93 - 97) K to R | 1985 | Volvo S40 & V40 Petrol (96 - Mar 04) N to 04 | 3569 |
| Rover Metro, 111 & 114 Petrol (May 90 - 98) G to S | 1711 | Vauxhall/Opel Corsa Petrol (Apr 97 - Oct 00) P to X | 3921 | Volvo S40 & V50 Petrol & Diesel (Mar 04 - Jun 07) 04 to 07 | 4731 |
| SAAB 95 & 96 (66 - 76) up to R * | 0198 | Vauxhall/Opel Corsa Petrol & Diesel (Oct 00 - Sept 03) X to 53 | 4079 | Volvo S60 Petrol & Diesel (01-08) | 4793 |
| Saab 90, 99 & 900 (79 - Oct 93) up to L | 0765 | Vauxhall/Opel Corsa Petrol & Diesel (Oct 03 - Aug 06) 53 to 06 | 4617 | Volvo S70, V70 & C70 Petrol (96 - 99) P to V | 3573 |
| Saab 900 (Oct 93 - 98) L to R | 3512 | Vauxhall/Opel Frontera Petrol & Diesel (91 - Sept 98) J to S | 3454 | Volvo V70 / S80 Petrol & Diesel (98 - 05) S to 55 | 4263 |
| Saab 9000 (4-cyl) (85 - 98) C to S | 1686 | Vauxhall Nova Petrol (83 - 93) up to K | 0909 | | |
| Saab 9-3 Petrol & Diesel (98 - Aug 02) R to 02 | 4614 | Vauxhall/Opel Omega Petrol (94 - 99) L to T | 3510 | **DIY MANUAL SERIES** | |
| Saab 9-3 Petrol & Diesel (02-07) 52 to 57 | 4749 | Vauxhall/Opel Vectra Petrol & Diesel (95 - Feb 99) N to S | 3396 | The Haynes Air Conditioning Manual | 4192 |
| Saab 9-5 4-cyl Petrol (97 - 04) R to 54 | 4156 | Vauxhall/Opel Vectra Petrol & Diesel (Mar 99 - May 02) T to 02 | 3930 | The Haynes Car Electrical Systems Manual | 4251 |
| SEAT Ibiza & Cordoba Petrol & Diesel (Oct 93 - Oct 99) L to V | 3571 | Vauxhall/Opel Vectra Petrol & Diesel (June 02 - Sept 05) 02 to 55 | 4618 | The Haynes Manual on Bodywork | 4198 |
| Seat Ibiza & Malaga Petrol (85 - 92) B to K | 1609 | Vauxhall/Opel 1.5, 1.6 & 1.7 litre Diesel Engine (82 - 96) up to N | 1222 | The Haynes Manual on Brakes | 4178 |
| SKODA Estelle (77 - 89) up to G | 0604 | VW 411 & 412 (68 - 75) up to P * | 0091 | The Haynes Manual on Carburettors | 4177 |
| Skoda Fabia Petrol & Diesel (00 - 06) W to 06 | 4376 | VW Beetle 1200 (54 - 77) up to S | 0036 | The Haynes Manual on Diesel Engines | 4174 |
| Skoda Favorit (89 - 96) F to N | 1801 | VW Beetle 1300 & 1500 (65 - 75) up to P | 0039 | The Haynes Manual on Engine Management | 4199 |
| Skoda Felicia Petrol & Diesel (95 - 01) M to X | 3505 | | | The Haynes Manual on Fault Codes | 4175 |
| Skoda Octavia Petrol & Diesel (98 - Apr 04) R to 04 | 4285 | | | The Haynes Manual on Practical Electrical Systems | 4267 |
| SUBARU 1600 & 1800 (Nov 79 - 90) up to H * | 0995 | | | The Haynes Manual on Small Engines | 4250 |
| | | | | The Haynes Manual on Welding | 4176 |

* Classic reprint

CL24.08/09

# Preserving Our Motoring Heritage

< The Model J Duesenberg Derham Tourster. Only eight of these magnificent cars were ever built – this is the only example to be found outside the United States of America

Almost every car you've ever loved, loathed or desired is gathered under one roof at the Haynes Motor Museum. Over 300 immaculately presented cars and motorbikes represent every aspect of our motoring heritage, from elegant reminders of bygone days, such as the superb Model J Duesenberg to curiosities like the bug-eyed BMW Isetta. There are also many old friends and flames. Perhaps you remember the 1959 Ford Popular that you did your courting in? The magnificent 'Red Collection' is a spectacle of classic sports cars including AC, Alfa Romeo, Austin Healey, Ferrari, Lamborghini, Maserati, MG, Riley, Porsche and Triumph.

## A Perfect Day Out

Each and every vehicle at the Haynes Motor Museum has played its part in the history and culture of Motoring. Today, they make a wonderful spectacle and a great day out for all the family. Bring the kids, bring Mum and Dad, but above all bring your camera to capture those golden memories for ever. You will also find an impressive array of motoring memorabilia, a comfortable 70 seat video cinema and one of the most extensive transport book shops in Britain. The Pit Stop Cafe serves everything from a cup of tea to wholesome, home-made meals or, if you prefer, you can enjoy the large picnic area nestled in the beautiful rural surroundings of Somerset.

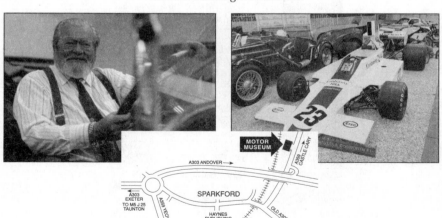

John Haynes O.B.E., Founder and Chairman of the museum at the wheel of a Haynes Light 12.

< Graham Hill's Lola Cosworth Formula 1 car next to a 1934 Riley Sports.

The Museum is situated on the A359 Yeovil to Frome road at Sparkford, just off the A303 in Somerset. It is about 40 miles south of Bristol, and 25 minutes drive from the M5 intersection at Taunton.
Open 9.30am - 5.30pm (10.00am - 4.00pm Winter) 7 days a week, *except Christmas Day, Boxing Day and New Years Day*
Special rates available for schools, coach parties and outings  Charitable Trust No. 292048